Legal and Ethical Issues in Human Reproduction

To my sister Mimi

The International Library of Medicine, Ethics and Law
Series Editor: Michael D. Freeman

Legal and Ethical Issues in Human Reproduction

Edited by

Bonnie Steinbock

University at Albany, State University of New York, USA

Routledge
Taylor & Francis Group

LONDON AND NEW YORK

First published 2002 by Ashgate Publishing

Published 2016 by Routledge
2 Park Square, Milton Park, Abingdon, Oxon OX14 4RN
711 Third Avenue, New York, NY 10017, USA

Routledge is an imprint of the Taylor & Francis Group, an informa business

British Library Cataloguing in Publication Data
Legal and ethical issues in human reproduction. – (The
   international library of medicine, ethics and law)
   1. Human reproduction – Moral and ethical aspects 2. Human
   reproduction – Law and legislation 3. Human reproductive
   technology – Moral and ethical aspects 4. Human reproductive
   technology – Law and legislation
   I. Steinbock, Bonnie
   176

Library of Congress Cataloging-in-Publication Data
Legal and ethical issues in human reproduction / editor, Bonnie Steinbock.
      p. cm. — (The international library of medicine, ethics, and law)
   Includes bibliographical references.

      1. Human reproduction—Law and legislation. 2. Human reproduction—Moral and
ethical aspects. I. Steinbock, Bonnie. II. Series.

K3611.A77 L44 2001
176—dc21   00-050270

ISBN 9780754620495 (hbk)

Contents

Acknowledgements

The editor and publishers wish to thank the following for permission to use copyright material.

American Society of Law, Medicine & Ethics for the essays: Bonnie Steinbock (1988), 'Surrogate Motherhood as Prenatal Adoption', *Law, Medicine & Health Care*, **16**, pp. 44-50. Copyright © 1988. Reprinted with permission of the American Society of Law Medicine & Ethics. All rights reserved; Abby Lippman (1991), 'Prenatal Genetic Testing and Screening: Constructing Needs and Reinforcing Inequities', *American Journal of Law & Medicine*, **XVII**, pp. 15–50. Copyright © 1991. Reprinted with permission of the American Society of Law Medicine & Ethics. All rights reserved; Jeffrey R. Botkin (1998), 'Ethical Issues and Practical Problems in Preimplantation Genetic Diagnosis', *Journal of Law, Medicine & Ethics*, **26**, pp. 17–28. Copyright © 1998. Reprinted with permission of the American Society of Law Medicine & Ethics. All rights reserved.

Blackwell Publishers for the essay: Derek Morgan and Robert G. Lee (1997), 'In the Name of the Father? *Ex parte Blood*: Dealing with Novelty and Anomaly', *The Modern Law Review*, **60**, pp. 840–56. Copyright © 1997. The Modern Law Review Ltd.

Duke University School of Law for the essay: Elizabeth S. Scott (1986), 'Sterilization of Mentally Retarded Persons: Reproductive Rights and Family Privacy', *Duke Law Journal*, pp. 806–65.

Hofstra Law Review for the essay: John A. Robertson (1999), 'Two Models of Human Cloning', *Hofstra Law Review*, **27**, pp. 609–38.

Princeton University Press for the essay: Debra Satz (1992), 'Markets in Women's Reproductive Labor', *Philosophy & Public Affairs*, **21**, pp. 107–31. Copyright © 1992. Reprinted by permission of Princeton University Press

Southern California Interdisciplinary Law Journal for the essay: Philip G. Peters (1999), 'Harming Future Persons: Obligations to the Children of Reproductive Technology', *Southern California Interdisciplinary Law Journal*, **8**, pp. 375–400. Copyright © 1999 by the University of Southern California. Reprinted with permission of the *Southern California Interdisciplinary Law Journal*.

John A. Robertson (1986), 'Embryos, Families, and Procreative Liberty: The Legal Structure of the New Reproduction', *Southern California Law Review*, **59**, pp. 939–1041. Copyright © 1986 John A. Robertson.

Series Preface

Few academic disciplines have developed with such pace in recent years as bioethics. And because the subject crosses so many disciplines important writing is to be found in a range of books and journals, access to the whole of which is likely to elude all but the most committed of scholars. The International Library of Medicine, Ethics and Law is designed to assist the scholarly endeavour by providing in accessible volumes a compendium of basic materials drawn from the most significant periodical literature. Each volume contains essays of central theoretical importance in its subject area, and each throws light on important bioethical questions in the world today. The series as a whole – there will be fifteen volumes – makes available an extensive range of valuable material (the standard 'classics' and the not-so-standard) and should prove of inestimable value to those involved in the research, teaching and study of medicine, ethics and law. The fifteen volumes together – each with introductions and bibliographies – are a library in themselves – an indispensable resource in a world in which even the best-stocked library is unlikely to cover the range of materials contained within these volumes.

It remains for me to thank the editors who have pursued their task with commitment, insight and enthusiasm, to thank also the hard-working staff at Ashgate – theirs is a mammoth enterprise – and to thank my secretary, Anita Garfoot for the enormous assistance she has given me in bringing the series from idea to reality.

MICHAEL FREEMAN
Series Editor
Faculty of Laws
University College London

Introduction

With the birth of Louise Brown on 25 July 1978, the era of assisted reproductive technologies (ART) began. Since Brown's birth, IVF and other ART procedures, such as gamete intrafallopian transfer (GIFT) and zygote intrafallopian transfer (ZIFT), have become an important part of infertility treatment. While such advances in reproductive medicine have enabled thousands of couples worldwide to achieve their deepest desire – to have children – they raise a plethora of ethical, philosophical and legal questions. This collection is an attempt to address some of those issues.

Procreative Liberty and Assisted Reproduction

Part I concerns questions about the nature and scope of the right to reproduce. In a statement issued through the UN Secretary-General in the late 1960s, 30 world leaders asserted that 'the opportunity to decide the number and spacing of their children is a basic human right' of all persons. This has most often been interpreted as a right *not* to reproduce – a right to prevent pregnancy through contraception and abortion. Such a right is usually based on the physical, emotional and economic harms to individuals that come from unwanted pregnancy and child-rearing.[1] However, the inability to reproduce can impose equally severe emotional and even physical (if not economic) harms. In addition, the right to make one's own choices about reproduction is central to self-definition, as the decision to become, or not to become, a parent is among the most intensely personal and meaningful decisions a person can make. For this reason, John Robertson argues, in his classic essay, 'Embryos, Families, and Procreative Liberty: The Legal Structure of the New Reproduction' (Chapter 1), that decisions about procreation should be left up to individuals and that the moral case for a legal right *to* reproduce is as compelling as the right to *avoid* reproduction.

Robertson provides an analysis of the right to reproduce, based on US constitutional law. Although the Supreme Court admittedly has not directly addressed the right to reproduce, again and again in *dicta* it has recognized a married couple's right to have and raise children. This suggests that the right of married people at least to reproduce is a fundamental constitutional right or, as it is usually termed today, a 'protected liberty interest'. Laws that limit fundamental rights are subject to the 'strict scrutiny' test which requires the state to establish that it has a 'compelling' interest justifying the law (*Black's Law Dictionary*, 1990, p. 1422). Clearly, Robertson says, laws imposing involuntary or mandatory sterilization, contraception or abortion fall into this category, and would be struck down by the Supreme Court (except in the unlikely event that the state could prove a compelling state interest). However, Robertson finds a constitutional justification for a broader interpretation of the right to reproduce. In particular, he argues that the same reasons for protecting coital reproduction from government interference extend to non-coital reproduction, or medically assisted conception, because the motivations, interests and values are the same. It follows that laws that limit ART violate the basic right of infertile people to reproduce, unless a compelling state interest justifying the laws can be found.

Robertson then canvasses the reasons usually advanced in favour of limiting IVF and collaborative arrangements, such as surrogacy and egg donation, and concludes that, while some regulation to protect the autonomy of the parties might be justified, none is sufficiently compelling to justify a complete ban.

One of Robertson's most provocative claims concerns the potential for harm to offspring. This ground for limiting ART might seem obvious. If the state can protect consumers against unsafe food, medicine, workplaces, automobiles and so on, surely it has the right and the responsibility to ensure that medically assisted conception is safe both for progenitors and offspring. However, Robertson argues that the issue is more complicated than it first appears. A key distinction he makes is between avoidable and unavoidable damage to offspring. If the child could have been born healthy, the harm is avoidable. It is legitimate to restrict people's liberty to prevent avoidable harms; it is wrong to use reproductive techniques that cause children to be born damaged when they could have been born 'healthy and whole'. However, if the harm is unavoidable – that is, if the child could not have been born healthy – then no wrong to the offspring has been done, even though it is foreseeable that the child will be born in a damaged condition. Robertson says, 'From the child's perspective, the risk-creating activity is welcome, since there is no alternative way for this child to be born' (p. 52). And if the child is glad that his or her parents acted as they did, how can anyone else claim that the child has been wronged or harmed, on balance? Robertson acknowledges that if the child will have a life *worse than non-existence*, then the child's life can be characterized as 'wrongful'. Such a child has been wronged by those who knowingly brought him or her into existence under these conditions. However, Robertson thinks that few, if any, children will have lives so dreadful that they would prefer never to have been born. They may well wish they had been born without the harmful condition, but the point is that this is not an option for them. It's life with the harmful condition or no life at all. So long as life is worth living, children whose very existence is made possible by risky technologies have not been harmed by them. Therefore, protection of offspring rarely, if ever, justifies limits on ART.

Another key distinction for Robertson is between 'tangible' and 'symbolic' harms. Only tangible harms, those that directly thwart or set back the interests of the people affected, can justify limiting constitutional rights. 'Merely symbolic' harms, those that express moral or religious values, cannot justify infringing the fundamental rights of those who have different views. This is not to say that moral or religious qualms about ART are unimportant, but rather that they cannot justify state intervention into procreative liberty: 'As a result, a regime of private discretion in efforts to procreate, with minimal regulation, must legally prevail' (p. 1040).

In Chapter 2 Ann MacLean Massie begins her critique of Robertson's provocative analysis of procreative liberty by pointing out some of its unacceptable implications. For example, a publicly supported IVF clinic would have no choice but to serve an HIV-infected woman.

> Her fundamental right 'to bear or beget a child' would override any interest that the state might assert in restricting her access to IVF because the resulting child – whether HIV-positive or not, whether its mother would live very long or not, and whether there were another available loving adult to raise the child or not – would be better off to have been born than not to have been born. (pp. 112–13)

Massie also rejects Robertson's constitutional analysis which she thinks focuses solely on the value of self-fulfilment or self-definition, ignoring the other values which were implicated in the contraception and abortion cases, such as respect for an individual's bodily integrity. Clearly, mandated contraception, sterilization and abortion violate bodily integrity. More controversially, laws that prohibit contraception and abortion also infringe on bodily integrity, since if women cannot prevent pregnancy, they are condemned to being unwilling life-support systems for foetuses.[2] However, bodily integrity is not at stake in laws restricting ART. Furthermore, she cites *Bowers* v. *Hardwick* (upholding the right of states to prohibit sodomy) as evidence that personal meaningfulness alone does not implicate a constitutional right: 'Heightened protection is not triggered simply by the fact that any particular conduct represents a search for meaning in life or because the persons involved are seeking self-fulfillment central to their self-definition' (p. 134). Because the constitutional right not to reproduce is based as much on respect for an individual's bodily integrity as it is on the central value to individuals of making their own reproductive decisions, Massie concludes that it does not imply a broad-based right to reproduce, which includes access to medically assisted conception.

The success of Massie's critique depends in part on whether one conceives of constitutional analysis as descriptive or normative. From a descriptive perspective, constitutional rights are determined by what the Supreme Court has in fact decided. The Court did in fact decide in *Bowers* that there is no fundamental constitutional right of consenting adults to engage in sexual acts in private, despite the personal significance such acts have for many people. However, many have argued that *Bowers* was wrongly decided because the best interpretation of the constitutional right of privacy protects sexual acts in private between consenting adults.[3] Reliance on *Bowers* seems a weak basis for dismissing personal fulfilment or meaningfulness as a rationale for a constitutional right. In any event, Robertson's claim is not that self-fulfilment *per se* deserves protection, but a particular kind of self-fulfilment – namely, the kind that results from having children. Infertile couples, he writes, '... seek the same experiences of marital intimacy and family integrity that are involved in coital reproduction. If coital reproduction qualifies for constitutional protection, then noncoital reproduction should as well' (Robertson, 1995, p. 247).

Massie also objects to Robertson's dismissal of arguments based on the welfare of offspring, suggesting that it favours the procreative liberty of would-be parents over the interests of the children. However, Robertson would say that she has misunderstood his argument. He is not giving greater weight to the interests of would-be parents as opposed to the interests of offspring. Rather, he is pointing out that the children's interests are best served by enabling them to come into existence, even under adverse conditions, so long as they find their lives worth living and better than non-existence. This vexing issue is addressed again in Part V 'Limits to Procreative Liberty'.

Assisted Reproduction and the Family

The discussion of a right to reproduce based on United States constitutional law may seem of interest only to Americans. However, Europeans are finding themselves addressing the same issues in slightly different forms. European human rights legislation protects 'the right to marry and found a family'. Exactly the questions debated by Robertson and Massie arise here: how should the right to marry and found a family be interpreted? Is the right restricted to those who can reproduce coitally or does it protect non-coital reproduction? Is it limited to heterosexual couples, or do gays and lesbians, or single people, also have a right to have children? What are the implications for older, postmenopausal women? Or for widows who want to reproduce with their dead husbands' sperm? In an interview with *The Guardian*, Ruth Deech, chairwoman of the Human Fertilisation and Embryology Authority (HFEA), predicted that the Human Rights Act of 1998, now in force in the UK as of October 2000, will result in a spate of test cases:

> I think people will come forward and say, 'I want this; I have a right to private and family life, I have a right to marry and found a family.' ... If a single woman were rejected for treatment by a clinic, she might say, 'I demand my human rights'. If a lesbian couple, perhaps, had a baby abroad or were rejected by a clinic here, they would challenge any refusal to treat them like a heterosexual couple, because there is a clause which says that rights and liberties in this act must be extended to people without discrimination as to status. I'm not saying that all the careful protection we have will crumble, but it seems to be likely that some very deep questions will be posed to the courts. (Bosely *et al.*, 2000)

This brings us to a second set of questions which concern the meaning of parenthood and family. Ordinarily, children are born to parents to whom they are genetically related and who will rear them. ART not only severs rearing from biological parenthood (as do artificial insemination and adoption), but also divides biology into its genetic and gestational components. Gamete (egg and sperm) donors are genetically related to the resulting offspring, while the woman who gestates the foetus and gives birth is biologically, though not genetically, related to the child. A further refinement is theoretically possible. Using a technique called *in vitro* ovum nuclear transfer (IVONT), the nucleus (which contains the DNA) of an egg from one woman could be transplanted into another's woman egg, from which the nucleus has been removed, leaving the surrounding cytoplasm which contains the mitochondria (Bonnicksen, 1998). Such a procedure might be used to enable a woman with mitochondrial disease to have a child to whom she was genetically related, without fear of passing on a possibly lethal disease.

The possibility of multiple parents from ART is not merely speculative. In a California case, *In re Buzzanca*,[4] the intended rearing parents used a sperm donor and an egg donor to create an embryo, which they then had implanted in a surrogate. The resulting child, Jaycee, had five individuals who could be viewed as her parents: the intended rearing parents (who had no biological connection to her), the biological father (the sperm donor), the genetic mother (the egg donor) and the gestational mother (the surrogate). Unlike other well-known disputes,[5] the case was not a fight between competing parties for parental rights, but rather concerned Mr Buzzanca's attempt to avoid parental responsibilities. Before Jaycee was born, Luanne and John Buzzanca split up. Mr Buzzanca refused to pay child support, arguing that the resulting child was not a child of the marriage. The trial court agreed. Indeed, it held that Jaycee Buzzanca had no legal parents, and that Luanne, who had cared for Jaycee since birth, would have to adopt her. The appeal court overturned the decision, holding that the intent to parent made John and Luanne the lawful parents of Jaycee.

The appeal court's decision is foreshadowed in John L. Hill's essay, 'What Does It Mean To Be a "Parent"?' (Chapter 3). Hill writes: 'What is essential to parenthood is not the biological tie between parent and child but the preconception intention to have a child, accompanied by undertaking whatever action is necessary to bring a child into the world' (p. 414). Hill gives three arguments for the moral priority of the intended parents. First, they are the originators of the child's birth; but for their orchestration of procreation, the child would never have been born. The *Buzzanca* court concurred, saying, 'Let us get right to the point: Jaycee never would have been born had not Luanne and John both agreed to have a fertilized egg implanted in a surrogate.'

Second, the gestational host and genetic donors agreed to waive their claims to parental rights and responsibilities. They should not now be able to go back on their promise, not only because promise-breaking is generally wrong, but also because it was in virtue of their commitment that the intended rearing parents involved them in their procreative project: '... where the gestational host, or the genetic progenitor, for that matter, has gained access to the procreative relationship initiated by another, she should not be permitted the double injustice of reneging and, more importantly, retaining custody of the child' (p. 416). The third argument in favour of giving priority to the intended rearing parents is the social utility of establishing with certainty the legal parents of the child at conception. All parties engaging in collaborative reproduction must understand in advance what their rearing rights and responsibilities will be.

Clearly, parenthood is not based on biology alone. The desire and ability to take care of a child is as much a part of being a parent as genetic connection. But is Hill right to maintain that the intention to parent should invariably trump the claims of genetic or gestational parents? In part, his argument seems based on the assumption, long unchallenged in the law, that there can be only two people who have parental rights and responsibilities, and therefore when there are competing claims, courts must decide who are the 'real' parents. It is precisely this assumption that Alta Charo questions in 'And Baby Makes Three – or Four, or Five, or Six: Redefining the Family after the Reprotech Revolution' (Chapter 4). Charo suggests that courts should recognize that children can have more than two parents, and they need not necessarily be of different genders. 'While courts and legislatures may see the need to determine who has a primary role in raising the child, there may well be no need to cut these other people out entirely. Indeed, from the child's point of view, it may simply be wrong to do so' (p. 237).

Contractual Reproduction: Gamete Donation and Surrogacy Arrangements

Part III examines issues, aside from custody, that are raised by gamete donation and surrogacy. In 'Bioethics and Fatherhood' (Chapter 5) Dan Callahan argues that biological connection creates inescapable moral obligations. Artificial insemination by donor (AID) is 'fundamentally wrong', according to Callahan, because a sperm donor is a *father*, who has all the duties of any other biological father. The puzzling thing to Callahan is the widespread social acceptance of AID. He attributes this in part to its having been introduced under medical auspices, despite there being nothing particularly 'medical' about the procedure, and in part to a lessening of respect for the traditional family which manifests itself in tolerating male irresponsibility. The charge of irresponsibility, however, bears a closer look. Callahan thinks that sperm donation is irresponsible because he thinks it is analogous to abandoning a woman when she becomes pregnant. He says:

> The only difference between the male who impregnates a woman in the course of sexual liaison and then disappears, and the man who is asked to disappear voluntarily after providing sperm, is that the latter kind of irresponsibility is, so to speak, licensed and legitimated. Indeed, it is treated as a kindly,

beneficent action. The effect on the child is of course absolutely identical – an unknown, absent father. (p. 248)

It may be objected that most children born as a result of sperm donation are not in the same situation as children whose fathers abandoned their mothers. They *do* have fathers: the men who arranged their births in order to raise them. Why should the title 'father' be limited to men who have a biological connection to their children? Instead of viewing the sperm donor as evading his parental rights and responsibilities, he can be seen as enabling a man who wants to parent a child to be a father. Why is that irresponsible?

Besides questions of custody, and who will have parental rights and responsibilities, collaborative reproduction raises a plethora of legal, ethical, and social issues, addressed in Part III. As John Robertson points out in 'Legal Issues in Human Egg Donation and Gestational Surrogacy' (Chapter 6), egg donation is one of the fastest growing areas of assisted reproduction. Introduced just over a decade ago, the majority of IVF programmes now offer this option (New York State Task Force, 1998, p. 236). As of 1995 (the latest data available for the United States), 189 programmes reported using donor eggs, approximately 73 per cent of the ART programmes reporting to the CDC (Center for Disease Control and Prevention, 1997, cited in ibid., p. 237). Despite its widespread use, many legal and ethical issues have not yet been resolved.

One area of lack of clarity concerns rearing rights and duties in offspring. Whereas most states recognize the consenting husband as the legal father in a sperm donation arrangement, very few states have adopted such legislation as regards egg donation.[6] In theory, an egg donor could attempt to gain rearing rights, although it is most likely that a court faced with a dispute over rearing rights and duties would follow the sperm donation model. By the same token, it is possible, though highly unlikely, that an egg donor could face liability for child support or other rearing duties.

The largest pool of donors consists of healthy young women who are recruited as egg donors for payment. Although the complication rate is low, donors face significant health risks, including ovarian hyperstimulation syndrome, damage to the ovary, and possibly an increased risk of ovarian cancer. Who will be responsible for the medical and other costs of such injuries? Many donors simply assume (wrongly) that all costs will be covered by the infertility programme that recruited them. Another issue is the ethics and legality of payment to egg donors. At one end of the spectrum is the position taken by the Canadian Royal Commission on New Reproductive Technologies. Maintaining that it is 'unethical to allow people to risk their health to sell parts of their bodies', the Commission recommended against any payment for egg donation (Royal Commission, 1993, cited in Bonnicksen, 1996, p. 160). By contrast, the New York State Task Force on Life and the Law did not recommend prohibition of egg donation as a matter of state law, since '[i]n our society, individuals are generally free to take risks with their own bodies, provided they do so with a full understanding of the nature and extent of the risks involved' (New York State Task Force, 1998, p. 234). Robertson agrees; indeed, he thinks that it would be discriminatory to ban payment to egg donors, since they suffer greater burdens than sperm donors who are paid. Robertson also concurs with the recommendation of the Task Force that while gametes and embryos should not be bought and sold, donors should be offered compensation for the time and inconvenience associated with donation: 'Thus payment should depend on the number and kind of procedures undergone and not be calibrated to the production of eggs or of any number of eggs' (p. 258). However, it may be difficult to prevent recipient couples from attempting to get 'high quality' eggs by advertising large sums of money to donors with particular traits. Although the usual rate of compensation to egg donors is between $1000 and $5000 a cycle in the United States, advertisements have been placed in college newspapers offering as much as $80 000 for donors over 5'6", with SAT scores over 1400, who have mathematical or musical ability. Since the time and inconvenience of egg donation remains the same, regardless of the donor's attributes, it is hard to see such large sums as anything but payment for eggs. This raises issues not only of commodification, but also of eugenics, visited again in Part IV, 'Reprogenetics'.

Even more controversial than egg donation is surrogate motherhood. One of the most famous cases, that of 'Baby M', is discussed by Bonnie Steinbock in 'Surrogate Motherhood as Prenatal Adoption' (Chapter 7). Steinbock is sceptical of the claims that commercial surrogacy is necessarily exploitive, inconsistent with human dignity or harmful to the children born of such arrangements. As to whether surrogacy amounts to baby-selling, Steinbock takes the same approach outlined above for egg donation: that payment be viewed as compensation for the risk, sacrifices, loss of income and discomfort the surrogate undergoes during pregnancy and delivery. A very contentious issue is whether the infant should be taken from the surrogate by force, if she finds herself unable to relinquish the child after birth, as happened in the Baby M case. To avoid such heart-rending (if rare) scenarios, Steinbock advocates building into surrogacy statutes a 'change of mind' period, analogous to those provided in many adoption statutes. In the United Kingdom a surrogate cannot waive her rights prior to the birth of the child. The birth mother and her partner/husband are the legal parents of a child born through a surrogacy arrangement until legal parentage is transferred to the commissioning couple. Moreover, the surrogate parents may not consent to an order transferring parentage earlier than six weeks after the birth of the child.[7] In the United States, several states adopted a change of mind period in the wake of the Baby M case but, as Robertson points out, most of those statutes do not make clear whether they also extend to gestational surrogacy, in which there is no genetic relation between the surrogate and the child she bears. He predicts that most courts faced with a claim from a gestational surrogate would follow the California Supreme Court in *Johnson* v. *Calvert*, and give the child to the genetic parents. However, it is not clear that it is genetic connection that is crucial, as opposed to the intention to rear. The court's subsequent ruling in *Buzzanca* suggests that the Calverts would have prevailed over Anna Johnson, even if they had not been the genetic parents but only the intended rearing parents.

In 'Markets in Women's Reproductive Labor' (Chapter 8), Debra Satz examines in greater detail the commodification argument, giving a feminist analysis of what is wrong with contract pregnancy. Rejecting the view put forth by Margaret Radin and others that reproductive labour is *essentially* something that should not be bought and sold, Satz argues that the real problem is gender inequality: 'Markets in women's reproductive labor are especially troubling because they reinforce gender hierarchies in a way that other accepted labor markets do not' (p. 110). Under conditions of genuine equality between the sexes, such contracts would be less objectionable.

Reprogenetics

'Reprogenetics', the combination of reproductive and genetic technologies, is the topic of

Part IV. Examples of reprogenetics include manipulations of egg cells, such as IVONT and somatic cell nuclear cloning, as well as technologies for discovering genetic disease such as preimplantation genetic diagnosis (PGD). The union of genetics and reproduction offers new possibilities for the conception of children, as well as unprecedented possibilities for selecting offspring characteristics. Although gene therapy has had only limited success so far, in future it may be possible to replace defective genes with normal ones, to prevent genetic disease in offspring. At present, prevention of disorders like Down's syndrome, spina bifida and many genetic diseases is primarily accomplished through prenatal testing, which has become a routine part of prenatal care, at least for women over 35 (in the USA) or 40 (in the UK). Pro-life organizations generally oppose prenatal testing, since if a disease in the foetus is detected, abortion is usually the result. Opposition to prenatal testing has also been voiced by some pro-choice feminists and disability rights advocates. Both positions are represented in this volume by Abby Lippman (Chapter 9). Lippman is unconvinced that prenatal testing and selective abortion benefit either women or their children. Such testing is often based on the assumption that people with disabilities are doomed to live miserable lives, and that they would be better off unborn. While this is undoubtedly true for the most dire conditions (Tay-Sachs disease, for example), it is not the case for some of the most common conditions for which prenatal diagnosis is performed, such as Down's syndrome, spina bifida or cystic fibrosis. Lippman also notes the social pressures on women both to be tested and to abort, both because such testing has become routinized and because society does not truly accept children with disabilities or provide for their nurturance: 'Thus, a woman may see no realistic alternative to diagnosing and aborting a fetus likely to be affected' (p. 32). This is not, in Lippman's view, genuinely 'voluntary testing' or a real 'choice to abort'.

Even those who take a more favourable attitude toward prenatal testing will acknowledge that the termination of an otherwise wanted pregnancy is a choice most women would prefer not to make. A recent form of prenatal diagnosis is preimplantation genetic diagnosis (PGD) which has the advantage of avoiding abortion because the diagnosis is made on extracorporeal embryos created through IVF. Embryos discovered to have a genetic defect can be discarded and only healthy embryos implanted to begin a pregnancy. However, for reasons given by Jeffrey Botkin (Chapter 10), PGD is not a good substitute for ordinary prenatal diagnosis for most people because it requires IVF, which imposes physical burdens on the woman, is expensive, and is less likely to result in pregnancy than sexual intercourse. Those at risk of genetic disease who wish to avoid abortion at any cost might prefer PGD (at least, if they are not opposed to embryo discard). However, at this stage, PGD requires prenatal diagnosis as a back-up, so that abortion may not be avoidable after all.

One of the newest and most controversial technologies is somatic cell nuclear transfer (SCNT) cloning, which could in theory produce a human baby just as it has produced sheep, cows, and mice.[8] If it were feasible, should cloning be used as a treatment for infertility? There appears to be widespread agreement that cloning should not be done for reproductive purposes. In a joint communique, the leaders of Canada, France, Germany, Italy, Japan, Russia, the United Kingdom, and the United States agreed to 'the need for appropriate domestic measures and close international cooperation to prohibit the use of somatic cell nuclear transfer to create a child' (Wadman, 1997 cited in New York State Task Force, 1998, p. 393). The following reasons are usually given against cloning human beings. It would be 'playing God'. It would threaten the cloned child's independent identity, individuality or free will. It would make possible the creation of a 'race' of inferior beings who would be exploited or alternatively, it would make possible the creation of 'super-children' who would be desired not for themselves but for their superior traits, endangering the parent–child relationship and leading to eugenics. It would enable women to have children without men or (if an artificial womb is developed) men to have children without women, threatening the family and society as we know it. The very idea of cloning children is repugnant.

John Robertson argues in Chapter 11 that a distinction should be made between what he calls 'Model 1' and 'Model 2' reproductive cloning. Model 1 cloning would be used as a treatment for infertility, to enable infertile couples to have and rear a child with whom they have a biological connection. Consider the following example. A couple cannot have a child due to male factor infertility. Even intracytoplasmic sperm injection (ICSI), a technique whereby a single sperm is injected directly into the egg, fails to result in fertilization. They are offered the usual remedy, sperm donation, but they prefer not to bring a third party into their marriage and attempt to have a child. SCNT cloning could be the solution. A somatic cell would be taken from the husband to obtain his DNA which would then be put into an enucleated egg cell from the wife. The resulting embryo would be replaced in the wife's uterus for gestation. The baby would be biologically related to both parents: genetically related to the husband and gestationally related to the wife. Since the intentions and motives are the same as in ART, Robertson argues that Model 1 cloning should be treated like any other reproductive technology. By contrast, Model 2 cloning is not used because of infertility, but rather is chosen in order to have a child with a particular genome. Robertson says, '... it is hard to empathize with and therefore respect a couple's desire to clone one of themselves when they could reproduce sexually ...'. What makes Model 2 cloning morally problematic, in a way that Model 1 cloning is not, is that Model 2 cloning provokes fears about the use of the technology for enhancement and eugenics. Robertson concludes that Model 2 cloning does not fall within our current understanding of procreative freedom, although he acknowledges that this may change in the future.

Limits to Procreative Liberty

Finally, Part V examines possible justifications for limiting procreative freedom. In Chapter 12 Elizabeth S. Scott argues that current law, out of concern to protect the rights of mentally disabled individuals, often prohibits sterilization, even where this would be in the individual's best interests. The development of the law is understandable in light of increasing awareness of the rights of mentally retarded people, combined with awareness of sterilizations performed in the name of eugenics during the first part of the twentieth century. 'However,' Scott maintains, 'in its singleminded effort to prevent erroneous sterilizations, the law departs from what would be its underlying objectives: to protect where possible the individual's right to make her own reproductive decisions and to ensure that any decision made by others will best protect her interests' (p. 807). Scott argues persuasively that the interest in reproduction is not simply an interest in having genetic progeny, but rather an interest in having and rearing a child. Where there is no ability to assume the role of parent, there is no legal right to reproduce.

One of the knottiest philosophical problems to arise in connection with ART is how to think about the potential for harm to offspring. We began to examine this issue in Part I with Robertson's distinction between avoidable and unavoidable harms. If a harm is unavoidable, that is, the child has no other way of being born except with the harmful condition, then, according to Robertson, the child is not harmed or wronged by being born, nor have his parents or others who facilitated his birth acted irresponsibly, unless the child's existence is so awful that non-existence would be preferable. In 'Harming Future Persons: Obligations to Children of Reproductive Technology' (Chapter 13), Philip G. Peters argues that this approach (which he calls 'the wrongful life approach'), while well-suited to tort law, is inappropriate from a public health perspective: 'Because public health regulation is concerned with community welfare, it can and should take into account the unnecessary harm that reproductive choices can inflict on future children as a class' (p. 399). Peters' analysis is unquestionably more in tune with the moral intuitions of most people than Robertson's. It can explain why sperm banks should screen for genetic disease, why doctors should restrict the number of embryos implanted, even when the prospective parents are willing to risk a multiple birth, and why doctors should be reluctant to clone a child for a fertile couple (Model 2 cloning). Nevertheless, some will find odd the notion of harming a class of children none of whose members is actually made worse off than he or she would or could have been.

The last essay, by Derek Morgan and Robert G. Lee, concerns the case of Diane Blood and post mortem insemination. Diane and Stephen Blood had planned to start a family when Stephen suddenly contracted bacterial meningitis. After he went into a coma, Diane asked his doctors to retrieve sperm from his body. The sperm was removed by electro-ejaculation, frozen, and stored. When Stephen died shortly thereafter, Diane began her efforts to be artificially inseminated with her husband's sperm. The main difficulty was that he had not given written consent, as required by the Human Fertilisation and Embryology Act of 1990, and therefore the HFEA said that the recovery and storage of the sperm was unlawful, and Diane could not be artificially inseminated with her husband's frozen sperm.

According to Diane, the Bloods had intended to have children. Diane further maintained that she and her husband had discussed what he would want to happen should he die before she became pregnant, and that he had said that he would want her to be artificially inseminated with his sperm after his death. One may be sceptical that this conversation actually took place; it is difficult to imagine a healthy, newly married couple discussing the prospect of the husband's death before their reproductive plans could be completed. Nevertheless, Diane may have felt, based on her knowledge of her husband, that Stephen would have approved of her plan. In seeking to be artificially inseminated, she was doing what he would have consented to, if there had been time to get his consent before his death. This distinguishes this case of post-mortem insemination from others where there is no evidence about what the man would have wanted, and no reason to think that he would have consented. Perhaps the most bizarre case involved a 38-year-old Nevada woman, Pamela Reno, who persuaded doctors to remove sperm from her 19-year-old son, after he killed himself while playing Russian roulette. ' "I told them I have to get my son's sperm. It's the only way I can be a grandma," said Reno, who is single.' (Associated Press, 1998, p. 172). Reno allegedly planned either to use a surrogate or to be artificially inseminated herself.

Foiled by the HFEA, Diane Blood went to the Court of Appeal, which got round the requirement of written consent for post-mortem insemination by finding that the provision of infertility treatment is an economic activity provided for remuneration, and hence a 'service' under the Treaty of Rome. The Court concluded that, under European Union (EU) law, Diane had a right to export her husband's sperm. She was artificially inseminated in Belgium, and gave birth to a son, Liam, on 11 December 1998 in the Jessop Hospital for Women in Sheffield.

According to Morgan and Lee, the Court's 'most obvious sleight of hand' is that:

> ... in treating rights to access services as though they are unrestricted, pretending that it raises no issues of morality or public policy, the Court effectively constructs a European by pass round the route which the Member State has signposted as carrying its fundamental ethical judgments; the vehicle which transports its national determination of the public policy issues is blocked. (p. 473)

They write:

> Originally seen as a response to the emergent evidence that involuntary childlessness caused by reproductive inability might seriously harm or compromise a woman's physical and mental health, *Blood* illustrates how quickly we are moving along a direction which runs from desire and longing to demands and litigation. The careful, albeit controversial scheme put in place by the Human Fertilisation & Embryology Act less than a decade ago has been shaken to its foundations by someone who has only limited need of the techniques of reproductive medicine. (p. 480)

Presumably, Diane Blood's 'limited need of the techniques of reproductive medicine' stems from the fact that she was not infertile. However, the relevance of this is unclear, since the Act would have permitted her to be artificially inseminated with her husband's sperm if he had provided written consent, which is unrelated to her fertility or 'need' for assisted reproduction.

The rationale for requiring written consent for post-mortem insemination is to ensure that gametes should not be used for reproduction without the individual's permission. Without written consent it is difficult to know if the man would have wanted to have a child after his death, since the evidence usually consists in private conversations between husband and wife, offered in testimony by the one who wishes to reproduce. However, there could be a case in which there was other evidence, making it clear that the husband would have wanted his wife to be artificially inseminated after his death, and would have given written consent, but died before he could do so. In such a case, the requirement of written consent might seem excessively stringent and legalistic.

On the other hand, the mere fact that someone has given written consent for post-mortem insemination does not settle the question of whether it would be ethically or legally permissible. Another British case concerns a couple determined to have a grandchild, using their dead son's sperm and a surrogate (Hall, 1999, p. 4). Natasha and Barry Smith's son, Lance, was killed in a car crash in November 1998. They had his sperm removed within 24 hours of the accident so that they could attempt to create a child with the help of a surrogate mother. Unlike Stephen Blood, Lance Smith had left written consent in the form of two documents. The first gave permission to take his sperm, in the event of his death, to enable his girlfriend of ten years to bear his child. However, she decided against the treatment. At that point, his parents produced a second document which was more general and did not restrict the use of his sperm to a particular woman. However, the fertility centre at the Priory Hospital in Birmingham, which took the specimen, has refused to release the sperm, unless there is a declaration from the high court that the consent form is legally valid. It is not known if the consent form was properly ratified, or if Mr. Smith had been offered counselling or received relevant information before making his decision, as required by the 1990 Human Embryology Act. However, even if the consent form is determined to be legally valid, the clinic would have to decide whether using the sperm would be in the best interests of the child who would be created. Many people would be troubled by creation of a child who would lack both father and mother, and find this scenario quite different from Diane Blood's attempt to have her husband's baby. Others, like John Robertson, would argue that the child's life, while not ideal, would be better than no life, and therefore that the grandparents should prevail. While post-mortem insemination is an unusual use of ART, it is a fitting way to end the volume as it provides a test case for our understanding of the nature and scope of procreative liberty, the significance of procreation without the possibility of rearing, and assessment of the welfare of the child.

Notes

1   In the United States, *Griswold* v. *Connecticut*, 381 US 479 (1965) established the constitutional right of married people to use contraceptives. *Eisenstadt* v. *Baird*, 405 US 438 (1972) extended this right to unmarried people. *Roe* v. *Wade*, 410 US 113 (1973), gave women the right to terminate a pregnancy up to the foetus's viability.
2   The classic statement of the right to abortion as a right to bodily self-determination is Thomson (1971).
3   Perhaps the most powerful statement of the normative approach to interpreting the Constitution is given by Ronald Dworkin. See, for example, Dworkin (1996), especially the 'Introduction', 'The Moral Reading' and the 'Majoritarian Premise', pp. 1–38.
4   *In re Buzzanca*, 61 Cal. App. 4th 1410; 1998 Cal. App. LEXIS 180; 72 Cal. Rptr. 2d 280; 98 Cal. Daily Op. Service 1782.
5   *Matter of Baby M.*, 109 NJ 396, 537 A.2d 1227 (1988); *Johnson* v. *Calvert*, 5 Cal.4th 84, 851 P.2d 776, *cert. denied*, 510 US 874 (1993).
6   In New York, the Committee on Biotechnology and the Law, a committee of the New York State Bar Association, has recommended that New York's Domestic Relations Law, section 73, which provides that a child born to a married woman by means of artificial insemination is the legitimate child of that woman and her husband, be amended to cover egg and embryo donation. See *New York State Bar Association*, Fall (1999).
7   Human Fertilisation and Embryology Authority, *Code of Practice*, Fourth Edition, July 1998, p. 65.
8   John Robertson says that the techniques used to clone sheep, cows, and mice 'could easily be adapted to human beings'. Others are not so sure. For an article about the difficulties posed by cloning generally and human cloning in particular, see Pennise and Vogel (2000).

References

Associated Press (1998), 'Woman has Dead Son's Sperm Frozen', *Albany Times Union*, 2 October, p. A2.
Black's Law Dictionary (6th edn), St Paul, MN: West Publishing Co., 1990.
Bonnicksen, Andrea L. (1996), 'Private and Public Policy Alternatives in Oocyte Donation', in Cynthia B. Cohen (ed.), *New Ways of Making Babies: The Case of Egg Donation*, Bloomington and Indianapolis: Indiana University Press.
Bonnicksen, Andrea L. (1998), 'Transplanting Nuclei between Human Eggs: Implications for Germ-Line Genetics', *Politics and the Life Sciences*, March, pp. 3–10.
Boseley, Sarah, Ward, Lucy and Brewer, Julia H. (2000), 'Human Rights Test for Fertility Rules', *The Guardian*, 14 February.
Center for Disease Control and Prevention *et al.* (1997), *Assisted Reproductive Technology Success Rates*, Atlanta: Center for Disease Control and Prevention.
Dworkin, Ronald (1996), *Freedom's Law*, Cambridge, MA: Harvard University Press.

Hall, Sarah (1999), 'Couple Fight for Child from Dead Son's Sperm', *The Guardian*, 29 December, Home Pages, p. 4.

New York State Bar Association Health Law Journal, **4**(3), Summer/Fall 1999, pp. 29–30.

New York State Task Force on Life and the Law (1998), *Assisted Reproductive Technologies: Analysis and Recommendations for Public Policy*, New York: New York State Task Force on Life and the Law.

Pennise, Elizabeth and Vogel, Gretchen (2000), 'Clones: A Hard Act to Follow', *Science*, **288** (5472) pp. 1722–27.

Robertson, John A. (1995), 'Liberalism and the Limits of Procreative Liberty: A Response to my Critics', *Washington and Lee Law Review*, **52**(1), pp. 233–67.

Royal Commission on New Reproductive Technologies (1993), *Proceed with Care: Final Report of the Royal Commission on New Reproductive Technologies*, Ottawa: Minister of Government Services, Canada.

Thomson, Judith J. (1971), 'A Defense of Abortion', *Philosophy & Public Affairs*, **1**(1).

Wadman, M. (1997), 'Cloning Research Should be Allowed', *Nature*, **388**.

Further Reading

Anderson, E.S. (1990), 'Is Women's Labor a Commodity?', *Philosophy & Public Affairs*, **19** (1), pp. 71–92.

Andrews, L. (1999), *The Clone Age: Adventures in the New World of Reproductive Technology*, New York: Henry Holt.

Arneson, R. (1992), 'Commodification and Commercial Surrogacy', *Philosophy & Public Affairs*, **21** (2), pp. 132–64.

Asch, A. (1995), 'Parenthood and Embodiment: Reflections on Biology, Intentionality, and Autonomy', *Graven Images*, **2**, pp. 229–36.

Benatar, D. (1999), 'The Unbearable Lightness of Bringing into Being', *Journal of Applied Philosophy*, **16** (2), pp. 173–80.

Bayles, M.D. (1979), 'Limits to a Right to Procreate', in Onora O'Neill and William Ruddick (eds), *Having Children: Philosophical and Legal Reflections on Parenthood*, New York: Oxford University Press.

Buchanan, A., Brock, D.W., Daniels, N. and Wikler, D. (2000), *From Chance to Choice: Genetics and Justice*, Cambridge: Cambridge University Press.

Cohen, C.B. (ed.) (1996), *New Ways of Making Babies: The Case of Egg Donation*, Bloomington and Indianapolis: Indiana University Press.

Cohen, S. and Taub, N. (eds) (1989), *Reproductive Laws for the 1990s*, Clifton, NJ: Humana Press.

'Developments in the Law: Medical Technology and Law', *Harvard Law Review*, **103**, 1990, p. 1519.

Field, M.A. (1988), *Surrogate Motherhood*, Cambridge, MA: Harvard University Press.

Glover, Jonathan *et al.* (1989), *Ethics of New Reproductive Technologies: The Glover Report to the European Commission*, DeKalb, Ill.: Northern Illinois University Press.

Gostin, L.O. (ed.) (1990), *Surrogate Motherhood: The Legal and Human Issues*, Bloomington: Indiana University Press.

Harris, J. and Holm, S. (eds) (1998), *The Future of Human Reproduction: Ethics, Choice, and Regulation*, Oxford: Clarendon Press.

Lauritzen, P. (1993), *Pursuing Parenthood: Ethical Issues in Assisted Reproduction*, Bloomington: Indiana University Press.

Macklin, R. (1991), 'Artificial Means of Reproduction and Our Understanding of the Family', *Hastings Center Report*, **21** (1), pp. 5–11.

Moomnjy, M., Cholst, I., Davis, O.K., Applegarth, L.D. and Rosenwaks, Z. (1995), 'Donor Oocytes in Assisted Reproduction', *Seminars in Reproductive Endocrinology*, **13** (3), pp. 173–86.

Murray, T. (1996), *The Worth of a Child*, Berkeley: University of California Press.

Note (1986), 'Rumpelstiltskin Revisited: The Inalienable Rights of Surrogate Mothers', *Harvard Law Review*, **99**, p. 36.

O'Neill, O. (1979), 'Begetting, Bearing, and Rearing', in Onora O'Neill and William Ruddick (eds), *Having Children: Philosophical and Legal Reflections on Parenthood*, New York: Oxford University Press.

Paulson, R.J. (1995), 'Ethical Considerations Involving Donation and Gestational Surrogacy', *Seminars in Reproductive Endocrinology*, **13** (3), August, pp. 225–30.

Peters, P.G. (1989), 'Protecting the Unconceived: Nonexistence, Avoidability, and Reproductive Technology', *Arizona Law Review*, **31**, p. 487.

Purdy, L.M. (1995), *'Children of Choice*: Whose Children? At What Cost?', *Washington and Lee Law Review*, **52**, p. 197.

Purdy, L.M. (1996), *Reproducing Persons: Issues in Feminist Bioethics*, Ithaca, NY: Cornell University Press.

Radin, M.J. (1987), 'Market-Inalienability', *Harvard Law Review*, **100**, pp. 1839–947.

Rao, R. (1995), 'Law and Equality: Constitutional Misconceptions', *Michigan Law Review*, **93**, p. 1473.

Roberts, M. (1993), 'Good Intentions and a Great Divide: Having Babies by Intending Them', *Law and Philosophy*, **12**, pp. 287–317.

Roberts, M. (1996), 'Parent and Child in Conflict: Between Liberty and Responsibility', *Notre Dame Journal of Law, Ethics & Public Policy*, **10** (2), pp. 485–542.

Roberts, M. (1998), *Child vs. Childmaker: Future Persons and Present Duties in Ethics and the Law*, New York: Rowman & Littlefield.

Robertson, J.A. (1983), 'Procreative Liberty and the Control of Conception, Pregnancy, and Childbirth', *Virginia Law Review*, **69**, April.

Robertson, J.A. (1989), 'Resolving Disputes Over Frozen Embryos', *Hastings Center Report*, November–December.

Robertson, J.A. (1990), 'In the Beginning: The Legal Status of Early Embryos', *Virginia Law Review*, **76**, p. 437.

Robertson, J.A. (1994), *Children of Choice: Freedom and the New Reproductive Technologies*, Princeton, NJ: Princeton University Press.

Robertson, J.A. (1994), 'Posthumous Reproduction', *Indiana Law Journal*, **69** (4), pp. 1027–65.

Robertson, J.A. (1996), 'Assisted Reproductive Technology and the Family', *Hastings Law Journal*, **47**, April, pp. 911–33.

Robertson, J.A. (1998), 'Liberty, Identity, and Human Cloning', *Texas Law Review*, **76**, May, p. 1371.

Rothman, B.K. (1989), *Recreating Motherhood: Ideology and Technology in a Patriarchal Society*, New York: W.W. Norton & Company, Inc.

Sauer, M.V. (1995), 'Oocyte Donation to Women of Advanced Reproductive Age', *Seminars in Reproductive Endocrinology*, **13** (3), August, pp. 231–36.

Shultz, M.M. (1990), 'Reproductive Technology and Intent-Based Parenthood: An Opportunity for Gender Neutrality', *Wisconsin Law Review*, **2**, pp. 297–398.

Singer, P. and Wells, D. (1985), *Making Babies: The New Science and Ethics of Conception*, New York: Charles Scribner's Sons.

Steinbock, B. (1994), 'The Moral Status of Extracorporeal Embryos: Preborn Children, Property or Something Else?', in Anthony Dyson and John Harris (eds), *Ethics and Biotechnology*, London and New York: Routledge, pp. 79–92.

Steinbock, B. (1995), 'Sperm as Property', *Stanford Law & Policy Review*, **6** (2), pp. 57–71.

Steinbock, B. (1996), 'Procreative Liberty: Robertson's *Children of Choice*', *Criminal Justice Ethics*, Winter/Spring.

Steinbock, B. (2000), 'Human Cloning: Sorting through the Ethical Issues', in Barbara Mackinnon (ed.), *Human Cloning: Science, Ethics, and Public Policy*, Urbana and Chicago: University of Illinois Press, pp. 68–84.

Steinbock, B. (2000), 'The Ethics of Human Cloning', in Michael Freeman and Andrew Lewis (eds), *Law and Medicine, Current Legal Issues*, **3**, Oxford: Oxford University Press, pp. 177–88.

Steinbock, B. (2000), 'What Does "Respect for Embryos" Mean in the Context of Stem Cell Research?', *Women's Health Issues*, **10** (3), (May/June), pp. 127–30.

Steinbock, B. (2000), 'Reproduction, Ethics, Moral status of the fetus' entry', in Thomas Murray and Maxwell Mehlman (eds), *The Encyclopedia of Ethical, Legal & Policy Issues in Biotechnology*, New York: John Wiley & Sons, Inc, pp. 947–56.

Steinbock, B. (2001), 'Preimplantation Genetic Diagnosis and Embryo Selection', in Justine Burley and John Harris (eds), *A Companion to Genetics: Philosophy and the Genetic Revolution*, Oxford: Blackwell Publishers.

Steinbock, B. (2001), 'Respect for Human Embryos', in Paul Lauritzen (ed.), *Cloning and the Future of Human Embryo Research*, Oxford: Oxford University Press, pp. 21–33.

Steinbock, B. (2001), 'Disability, Prenatal Testing, and Selective Abortion', in Erik Parens and Adrienne Asch (eds), *Prenatal Testing and Disability Rights*, Washington, D.C.: Georgetown University Press, pp. 108–23.

Strong, Carson (1997), *Ethics in Reproductive and Perinatal Medicine*, New Haven: Yale University Press.

Warnock, Mary (1985), *A Question of Life: The Warnock Report on Human Fertilisation and Embryology*, Oxford: Basil Blackwell.

Warren, Mary Anne (1988), 'IVF and Women's Interests: An Analysis of Feminist Concerns', *Bioethics*, **2** (1), pp. 37–57.

Part I
Procreative Liberty and Assisted Reproduction

[1]

EMBRYOS, FAMILIES, AND PROCREATIVE LIBERTY: THE LEGAL STRUCTURE OF THE NEW REPRODUCTION

JOHN A. ROBERTSON

942   *SOUTHERN CALIFORNIA LAW REVIEW*   [Vol. 59:939

EMBRYOS, FAMILIES, AND PROCREATIVE LIBERTY: THE LEGAL STRUCTURE OF THE NEW REPRODUCTION†

JOHN A. ROBERTSON*

Infertility, a perennial human problem, is increasing in the United States. Several noncoital reproductive technologies now exist to treat infertility. Central among them is extracorporeal fertilization of human eggs, a development that has far-reaching ramifications. What are the interests and values at stake? How should conflicts among them be resolved? The legal structure of the new reproduction is the subject of this Article.

I. THE NEW REPRODUCTION: INFERTILITY, TECHNOLOGY, NORMATIVE ISSUES

While noncoital conception by artificial insemination has been widely practiced since 1950, the explosion of interest in the "new" reproduction has resulted from the development of extracorporeal or in vitro fertilization (IVF) of human eggs.[1] The first child resulting from extracorporeal fertilization of a human egg was born in England on July 25,

†   © 1986 John A. Robertson.
*   Baker and Botts Professor of Law, University of Texas at Austin. A.B. 1964, Dartmouth College; J.D. 1968, Harvard University. I am grateful to the University Research Institute of the University of Texas at Austin for financial support, and to Lori Andrews, Patricia Cain, Bernard Dickens, Rebecca Dresser, and Thomas Vaughn for helpful comments on an earlier draft. I wish also to thank George Annas, John Busten, Clifford Grobstein, Ruby Fisher, Richard Marrs, Dudley Posten, Terri Sullivan, Leroy Walters, Norma Wikler, William Yee and The St. David's Community Hospital IVF Program for kindly sharing with me their knowledge of the subjects discussed in this Article.

1. For an account of the early use of artificial insemination by donor and the initial legal questions, see Smith, *Through a Test Tube Darkly: Artificial Insemination and the Law*, 67 MICH. L. REV. 127, 128-29 (1968).

The "new" reproduction umbrellas many different activities related to reproduction. While most demand for the new reproduction stems from infertility, some demand comes from fertile single women whose life-style choices have not made impregnation by a male partner possible. Thus, while most of the new reproduction occurs in a medical setting under the aegis of physicians, some of it occurs without the help of medical professionals. The common link among all examples of the new reproduction seems to be that conception is noncoital. Noncoital conception may involve artificial insemination or external or in vitro fertilization, and may or may not involve donor assistance. It is

1978.[2] After many years of frustrating research, Drs. Edwards and Steptoe had succeeded in removing an egg from an ovarian follicle, fertilizing it in a dish, and transferring the developing zygote to a uterus where it implanted and was brought to term.

In the seven years since that birth, IVF has improved greatly and diffused widely. With more than two thousand children born worldwide, the technique is now recognized as "an acceptable treatment for achieving pregnancy for couples in which the wife has absent or irreparably damaged fallopian tubes."[3] IVF programs vary widely in their success rates. However, the best programs report a 90 percent success rate for egg recovery, fertilization, and early embryonic cleavage,[4] and a 20 to 25 percent rate per treatment cycle of achieving pregnancy. Two-thirds of the pregnancies result in live birth. Even a 10 to 15 percent chance of taking a baby home is a great boon for infertile couples who are otherwise unable to have children.

IVF has rapidly caught on and spread throughout the United States, Canada, Europe, and Australia. In the United States over 130 IVF programs already exist, bringing the technique within easy geographic reach of most couples.[5] The rapidity of the spread is remarkable because the procedure is expensive,[6] stressful (it requires laparoscopic surgery under

the latter developments that have propelled the new reproduction into public awareness and are the main focus of this Article.

2. Louise Brown, the first baby born as a result of IVF, became a worldwide celebrity. For accounts of her birth from the doctors' perspective, see R.G. EDWARDS & P. STEPTOE, A MATTER OF LIFE (1980). The parents' perspective is described in L. BROWN & J. BROWN, OUR MIRACLE CHILD CALLED LOUISE, A PARENT'S STORY (1979).

3. American Fertility Society, 16 FERTIL. NEWS insert (1982).

4. Grobstein, Flower & Mendelhoff, *External Human Fertilization: An Evaluation of Policy*, 222 SCI. 127, 128 (1983).

5. Blakeslee, *Some Caveats for Childless Couples*, N.Y. Times, May 4, 1986, § 4, at 8, col. 3. Small cities with major medical centers, such as Rochester, Minnesota and Madison, Wisconsin have IVF programs, as do cities such as Austin, Texas, that do not have medical schools or major medical centers. Dallas, Houston, Los Angeles, and several other major cities have more than one IVF program serving the same geographical area. The success rate of these programs varies widely, with many programs not yet reporting a pregnancy. *See infra* text accompanying note 330.

6. Grobstein, Flower, and Mendeloff report a typical total cost to the patient for an initial treatment (screening, laparoscopy, and embryo transfer) to be about $7500, with each subsequent attempt (omitting screening) costing about $5000. At current levels of efficacy, estimated at roughly 10% for a given laparoscopy, about $38,000 would be required to ensure a roughly 50% chance of a live birth for a particular patient. Grobstein, Flower & Mendeloff, *supra* note 4, at 130.

While health insurance may cover some of the charges, such as the diagnostic screening and laparoscopy, the remaining out-of-pocket costs make IVF and fertility treatment a consumption item reserved for the upper and middle classes. As these costs are factored into the total costs of having a child, they may deter some people from seeking IVF. Belkin, *Parents Weigh Costs of Children*, N.Y. Times, May 5, 1985, at 19, col. 1. Important policy issues are whether insurance should cover IVF treatment and whether the state should subsidize such treatment for people unable to afford it. *See*

general anesthesia), and does not guarantee a baby.[7]

A.   INFERTILITY AND DEMAND FOR THE NEW REPRODUCTION

The desire of infertile couples to achieve pregnancy has fueled the rapid growth of IVF and may lead to demand for the many options that control and manipulation of the extracorporeal embryo will present. In 1983 more than one in eight American married couples had failed to conceive after one year of trying.[8] While 40 percent of these couples can be helped by conventional medical treatment, in many cases the infertility is due to blocked fallopian tubes, usually the result of pelvic inflammatory disease.[9] IVF holds special hope for these women, because it bypasses the fallopian tubes and allows a fertilized egg to reach the uterus. IVF is also indicated for women with infertility of unknown origin and for men with oligospermia.[10]

Although there is a demographically significant trend in the United States toward voluntary childlessness,[11] cultural norms supporting

---

Dresser, *Social Justice in New Reproductive Techniques*, in GENETICS AND THE LAW III 159 (1985). Maryland now requires private health insurance policies to cover IVF services. MD. ANN. CODE art. 48A, § 35400 (Supp. 1985).

7.   While IVF will enable some women to have children, its success rate is still low. The 90% success rate for egg recovery, fertilization, and cleavage and 20 to 25% rate per laparoscopy for pregnancy in the best programs is not matched by many programs. Patients in the first years of an IVF program may have even a lesser chance of success, a fact that physicians might gloss over with glowing reports of high success rates.

8.   Centers for Disease Control, *Infertility—United States, 1983*, 34 MORBIDITY & MORTALITY WEEKLY REP. 197 (1985).

9.   Grobstein, Flower, and Mendeloff estimate that over one million women have tube damage that makes pregnancy difficult, if not impossible. Grobstein, Flower & Mendeloff, *supra* note 4, at 130. The conventional treatment for tube blockage is tuboplasty, or tubal reconstruction. It involves delicate microsurgery under general anesthesia, and probably can help at most forty percent of women with severe tubal damage. Grobstein, Flower, and Mendeloff estimate that some 70,000 women per year might desire IVF. *Id.*

10.   Marrs, Vargyas, & Berger, *Human In Vitro Fertilization: An Answer to Male Infertility*, in SEMINARS IN UROLOGY (1984). Although the woman bears the main physical burdens of infertility treatment and workups, the man also is subject to scrutiny. He must produce sperm for analysis and then for insemination attempts. His sperm will be counted and tested for motility and compatibility with cervical mucous. Its penetrability will be measured by its ability to penetrate hamster eggs in the Zona-Free hamster egg test. Yanagimachi, *Zona-Free Hamster Eggs: Their Use in Assessing Fertilizing Capacity and Examining Chromosomes of Human Spermatozoa*, 10 GAMETE RESEARCH 187 (1984). A low sperm count (oligospermia) or low motility is an indication for IVF, since sperm will not have to travel as far nor through cervical mucous if brought together with the egg in a dish. For further discussion of the male role, see *infra* note 270.

11.   The trend toward voluntary childlessness that has existed since the 1960's in the United States is linked with broader changes regarding fertility control, contraceptive technology, sexual and family norms, and female work patterns. Posten & Kramer, *Voluntary and Involuntary Childlessness in the United States, 1955-1973*, 30 SOC. BIOLOGY 290, 304 (1983).

reproduction remain very powerful. The inability to beget, bear, and rear children is a great loss for many infertile men and women.[12] Infertility often implicates the most fundamental feelings about self and one's relation to the natural order, and may leave persons feeling handicapped or defective in an area central to personal identity and fulfillment. Infertile couples often experience, and may suffer enormously from, isolation, guilt, marital strife, and intense assaults on feelings of self-worth.[13] Not surprisingly, they are ready to seek medical assistance and use techniques such as IVF that offer the hope of fertility.

The alacrity to seek IVF and other noncoital solutions to infertility is due also in part to the changing demographics of infertility and changing patterns of medical practice. The infertile have traditionally been concentrated among older, poorer, black, uneducated persons, with high exposure to sexually transmitted diseases, poor nutrition, and low access to health care.[14] They have not had ready access to the infertility treatments that were available. But infertility is now appearing with greater frequency among large numbers of white, educated, middle and upper income women in their twenties and thirties. The rise has been most significant for white women between twenty and twenty-four, a prime age for childbearing.[15] When members of this age cohort who have deferred childrearing attempt to conceive, a corresponding rise in infertility in older age groups is likely.

The rising rate of infertility can be explained by changes in sexual behavior, work roles, and postponement of marriage and childbearing.[16] Changing work roles and the availability of contraception have led many women to postpone childbearing. Deferring childbirth allows age-related endogenous biologic factors to reduce the ability to conceive. It also gives infectious, occupational, and environmental factors a longer time to exert their cumulative effect on infertility.[17] Changing sexual practices

---

12. Indeed, infertility is even more devastating for third world women, who are at greater risk for infertility and are more likely to suffer social consequences if they are not fecund. G. GREER, SEX AND DESTINY 59-74 (1984).

13. Manning, *The Emotional Needs of Infertile Couples*, 34 FERTILITY & STERILITY 313 (1980). Men and women may experience infertility in different ways, but Manning emphasizes that it is a problem of the couple and not simply one member.

14. Aral & Cates, *The Increasing Concern with Infertility*, 250 J. A.M.A. 2327 (1983).

15. Centers for Disease Control, *supra* note 8, at 198.

16. Aral & Cates, *supra* note 14, at 2328-29. Indeed, these changes reflect larger social and cultural changes that explain the willingness to resort to novel reproductive interventions in the first place.

17. *Id.* at 2329.

among the middle class is also a key factor. A trend to earlier first intercourse and multiple sexual partners has increased the frequency of sexually transmitted disease, which in turn leads to the pelvic inflammatory disease that often causes infertility. Widespread use of the intrauterine device by nulliparous women has also increased pelvic inflammatory disease.[18]

A growing number of middle class women suffering from infertility have the means and the disposition to seek medical services for their problem. As members of the baby boom generation, they are the first generation to have complete control of fertility during their reproductive years and appear willing to use whatever medical means are available to achieve fecundity. Unlike the poor, they usually have the health insurance or private means to cover the costs of infertility treatment, though cost remains a barrier for some. In 1983 there were over two million visits for infertility, making it a $200 million industry.[19] Widespread publicity about the latest fertility treatment, the absence of easily adoptable children,[20] and a growing number of physicians entering this field,[21] also contribute to the interest in IVF.

The baby boom generation's inability to reproduce has thus increased professional interest in the field, and spawned technical advances that are likely to increase demand for IVF and its donor-assisted variations. A strong demand for infertility treatments is likely to continue. Thus, demographic change and the continued evolution of sexual, work, and family roles converge to place noncoital, external conception and its collaborative variations on the public agenda.

---

18. Cramer, Schiff, Schoenbaum, Gibson, Belisle, Albrecht, Stillman, Berger, Wilson, Stadel & Seibel, *Tubal Infertility and the Intrauterine Device*, 312 NEW ENG. J. MED. 941 (1985).

19. The estimated number of visits to private physicians' offices for infertility-related consultation increased from approximately 600,000 in 1968 to 900,000 in 1972. The number has more than doubled to 2,000,000 visits in 1983, a trend that is continuing. *See* Centers for Disease Control, *supra* note 8, at 197.

20. The difficulty in obtaining healthy, white infants for adoption has increased tremendously, both because of increased abortion and the willingness of unwed mothers to keep their babies. Plumez, *Adoption: Where Have All The Babies Gone?*, N.Y. Times, Apr. 13, 1980, § 6 (Magazine), at 34, col. 1.

21. The increasing demand for infertility treatment has led more physicians to enter into the subspecialty of reproductive endocrinology (particularly as there are fewer babies for obstetricians to deliver). Aral and Cates report that the number of board-certified subspecialists has more than doubled since 1978, as has membership in the American Fertility Society, the professional organization of infertility specialists. Aral & Cates, *supra* note 14, at 2330. Growing professional interest has stimulated further scientific research and patient consultations, which has reinforced the growth and public visibility of the infertility field.

B. IVF TECHNOLOGY AND ITS POSSIBILITIES

IVF, like all infertility treatments, objectifies the physical processes of human reproduction, diagnoses the cause of infertility, and then intervenes to correct it. While there is a vast array of infertility treatments, ranging from fertility drugs to tubal reconstruction by microsurgery and artificial insemination, all of these treatments aim to bring about fertilization of the egg within the woman's body and successful completion of a term pregnancy.[22] IVF is unique in that fertilization occurs outside the body, with the fertilized egg then placed in the uterus to initiate the pregnancy. IVF thus brings the formerly invisible process of fertilization and early embryonic development into view, greatly extending the potential for control of the reproductive process.

Women are selected for IVF treatment after a diagnostic workup to determine the cause of infertility.[23] The ovulatory cycle is closely monitored to assure that ovulation is occuring. Because male factor infertility is a common problem, the male partner's sperm is analyzed. A hysterosalpingogram, the injection of radio-opaque dye to allow the uterus and the fallopian tubes to be observed, shows whether the tubes are patent and the uterus structurally sound. If fallopian tube damage not reparable by other methods is present, if the male partner is severely oligospermic, or if infertility of unknown origin persists, the couple is a candidate for IVF.

---

22. Consider, for example, the Gametic Intrafallopian Transfer (GIFT) program which is not a treatment for tube blockage, since it depends on fertilization occurring in the fallopian tube. In this procedure, a woman's ovaries are stimulated and a laparoscopy performed to retrieve eggs. Rather than fertilize the eggs in vitro, however, the egg and sperm are placed in the fallopian tube during the laparoscopy that retrieves the eggs. The aim is to allow egg and sperm to meet in the fallopian tube where conception and early embryonic development normally occur. Asch, Ellsworth, Balmaceda & Wong, *Pregnancy After Translaparoscopic Gamete Intrafallopian Transfer*, 1984 LANCET 1034 (letter to editor). Although only a few pregnancies by this technique have been reported, the logic of relying on the natural site is favorably viewed by many infertility specialists. Personal communication with Dr. Thomas Vaughn (August 15, 1985).

23. The rigors of infertility workups and treatments should not be underestimated. Barbara Eck Menning, founder of Resolve, Inc., a national support group for infertile persons, describes her experience:

There was a year of testing on me—biopsies, dyerotubograms [sic], postcoitals; as well as repeated tests of my husband. We had a programmed sex life keyed to a basal temperature chart. At the end of that year an acute abdominal episode, improperly handled, cost me the ovary and tube on the right side. After recovery from surgery, on to a new doctor—more tests, more programmed sex life—everything was just fine, 'relax.' Relaxing did no good. On to a new doctor. Discovery of a cyst on the left ovary—resection by surgery. Six months later, success. Pregnancy—followed by miscarriage at 13 weeks. On to another doctor—an activist. "We'll have you pregnant in no time!" Emergency admission to the hospital after an acute reaction to the fertility pills he prescribed. My cycles ceased. The best efforts of men and medicine could not coax another cycle forth.

G. COREA, THE MOTHER MACHINE 175 (1985) (quoting Barbara Eck Menning).

The standard IVF treatment regime requires that the ovaries be stimulated to produce several eggs, because the chance of pregnancy is very small if only one fertilized egg is transferred to the uterus.[24] Beginning on days three to seven of the woman's menstrual cycle, drugs that stimulate ovarian follicular development are given for several days.[25] Blood estrogen levels are measured (a sign of ovarian action) and follicular development is monitored by ultrasound. Usually one or more follicles containing eggs will develop. Shortly before the surge of luteinizing hormone that indicates that the egg has been shed from the follicle (ovulation), another drug to assure egg maturation is given. Several eggs are then aspirated from the follicles by laparoscopy, which is performed under general anesthesia.[26]

The eggs are examined for maturity,[27] and if immature, may be incubated in special solution. Mature eggs are mixed in a dish with sperm that has been examined and prepared for insemination. After about twenty-four hours, the eggs are examined for signs of fertilization, and after forty-eight hours for evidence of division or cleavage. If the fertilized egg, or zygote, is dividing normally, it will have reached four cells. At this point, or soon thereafter, the zygote will be transferred by a catheter transcervically to the uterus.[28] Since transfer of multiple fertilized eggs increases the risk of multiple gestation, the optimal number to be transferred is three to four eggs. However, most programs will transfer

---

24. Edwards and Steptoe had not stimulated ovaries to produce the birth of Louise Brown. *See* R.G. EDWARDS & P. STEPTOE, *supra* note 2. Dr. Alan Trounson at Melbourne, Australia developed the superovulation technique that has become standard practice in IVF programs. While increasing efficacy, the technique also makes excess embryos and embryo selection possible, and thus is the source of many of the ethical issues that arise in this area. *See infra* text accompanying notes 127-29.

25. IVF programs differ in the stimulatory drugs they use and the exact time of administration. Vargyas, Morente, Shangold & Marrs, *The Effect of Different Methods of Ovarian Stimulation for Human In Vitro Fertilization and Embryo Replacement*, 42 FERTILITY & STERILITY 745 (1984).

26. The number of eggs retrieved will depend upon the number of follicles visible and accessible. In order to limit the number of eggs to be fertilized, and hence transferred to the uterus, not all follicles may be aspirated.

Some programs in Europe and at least one in the U.S. retrieve eggs by ultrasound-guided transvaginal aspiration without general anesthesia. While this avoids laparoscopy and general anesthesia, it is less effective in retrieving eggs since the follicles cannot be seen directly as they can during laparoscopy. Improvement in efficacy would make it the preferable procedure.

27. Egg maturity is determined by observation of the egg, and measurement of its size and the size of the corona. An important feature is whether the first polar body has extruded. See Marrs, Saito, Yee, Sato & Brown, *Effect of Variation of In Vitro Culture Techniques upon Oocyte Fertilization and Embryo Development in Human In Vitro Fertilization Procedures*, 41 FERTILITY & STERILITY 519 (1984).

28. Polyspermic eggs—eggs fertilized by two spermatozoa—are associated with miscarriage and early neonatal death, and thus usually will not be transferred to the uterus. *See infra* note 125.

as many eggs as have been fertilized, though they may aspirate or fertilize fewer eggs than are available to avoid not transferring all fertilized eggs.[29] The implantation of the embryo should occur in the next two to three days; detection of pregnancy will be possible at about ten to fourteen days following replacement.

The rapid progress that has characterized the field since 1978 is likely to continue. Success rates for many patient groups will improve at the same time that the burdens and costs of the treatment are reduced.[30] A major development in efficacy and cost reduction will be the ability to store fertilized eggs for significant periods by cryopreservation. By preserving excess embryos for later use, cryopreservation avoids the dilemma of embryo destruction or risk of multiple births when more than four eggs have been fertilized. Storage will also lessen the cost and rigors of subsequent cycles of treatment, since ovarian stimulation and laparoscopy on subsequent cycles will be unnecessary.[31] Embryo transfer after storage may also improve the chances of achieving pregnancy, since the body will be free of the drugs that are used in the ordinary IVF treatment cycle.[32]

The cryopreservation of embryos obtained by in vivo conception and retrieval by lavage is now well established in the cattle industry.[33] Research into cryopreservation of human embryos is increasing, with

---

29. To avoid the issue of embryo destruction, which it is feared will bring adverse publicity and controversy with right-to-life groups, many programs have agreed to transfer all embryos to the uterus of the woman who has provided the egg, even though there is a high risk of multiple gestation if more than three or four fertilized eggs are transferred. *See infra* text accompanying note 125. Of course, a woman could refuse to accept transfer.

30. IVF treatment is stressful and invasive, involving the administration of powerful ovarian stimulatory drugs, frequent monitoring, and general anesthesia for egg recovery. Infertile couples bent on reproducing undergo these burdens willingly, but they should not overestimate the chance of success. Physicians should honestly disclose these burdens and the rate of success. *See infra* text accompanying note 330. Gena Corea, a feminist polemicist, describes the psychological roller coaster experienced by women in an IVF program:

> Of the thousands of women hoping to get a baby through the 2000-odd IVF programs across the globe, the vast majority have been disappointed. The cycle of hopes raised (she's accepted into the program) and dashed (doctor could not get an egg), raised (got an egg) and dashed (egg was abnormal), raised (got a normal egg) and dashed (embryo did not implant), raised (embryo implanted) and dashed (miscarried) harms women in ways pharmacrats have not acknowledged.

G. COREA, THE MOTHER MACHINE 180 (1985).

31. Treatment during subsequent cycles will involve monitoring the cycle to know when ovulation occurs and hence when the uterus may be ready to accept the embryo, with embryo transfer done transcervically by catheter. The stress on the woman and her partner during the subsequent treatment cycle would be greatly reduced.

32. The ovarian stimulation drugs and anesthesia used during an IVF treatment cycle could render the uterus less likely to accept a transferred embryo.

33. Seidel, *Superovulation and Embryo Transfer in Cattle*, 211 SCI. 351 (1981).

successful births after freezing and thawing embryos reported in Austra-lia, Holland, and the United States.[34] It would not be surprising to see freezing of human embryos widely adopted once further research shows that freezing and thawing of human embryos is safe for the resulting offspring.

The ability to preserve embryos for later use by freezing will enable several other reproductive maneuvers to be carried out. For example, IVF will make egg and embryo donations and the use of surrogate wombs practical. Women without ovaries, anovulatory women, and wo-men who are carriers of a genetic defect could now bear children by ob-taining donor eggs, which would be fertilized in vitro with their partners' sperm and then transferred for gestation.[35] In some cases, egg and sperm donation could occur together, either as two separate gamete gifts or as the donation of an embryo.

Infertility due to uterine dysfunction, as in the case of hysterectomy, diethylstibesterol, or medical risk to the mother may also be amenable to treatment through IVF. A woman may have sufficient ovarian function to provide an egg, but be physically unable (or unwilling for career or other reasons) to undergo pregnancy. Eggs retrieved from her and fertil-ized by her partner's sperm could be transferred to a woman who is will-ing to gestate the embryo and, at birth, present the genetic mother with an infant to rear.[36]

Embryo transfer and donation may even occur without external fer-tilization. Applying to humans embryo transfer techniques now widely used in cattle breeding,[37] the treating physician artificially inseminates a woman with the sperm of the husband of an infertile woman. Five days later, the doctor flushes out her uterus and retrieves the fertilized egg, which may have grown to the blastocyst stage of one hundred cells. The

---

34. *See* Mohr, Trounson & Freemann, *Deep-Freezing and Transfer of Human Embryos*, 2 J. IN VITRO FERTILIZATION & EMBRYO TRANSFER 1 (1985). Research into freezing of human embryos is now occurring on an experimental basis in several programs in the United States. The first birth of a child from a cryopreserved embryo in the United States was reported on June 5, 1986 in Los Angeles. *U.S. Markes Frozen-Embryo Birth*, Austin American Statesman, June 5, 1986, at 1, col. 4.

35. Reports of egg donation are now appearing in the literature. Navot, Laufer, Koplovic, Rabinowitz, Birkenfeld, Lewin, Granat, Margalioth & Schenker, *Artificially Induced Endometrial Cycles and Establishment of Pregnancies in the Absence of Ovaries*, 314 NEW ENG. J. MED. 806 (1986).

36. The first birth by such a procedure occurred in the United States in Cleveland, Ohio. N.Y. Times, Apr. 17, 1986, at 10, col. 4. For an analysis of the legal issues involved, see *infra* text accom-panying notes 245-55.

37. Bustillo, Buster, Cohen, Thorney, Croft, Simon, Boyers, Marshall, Seed, Louw & Seed, *Nonsurgical Ovum Transfer as a Treatment in Infertile Women*, 251 J. A.M.A. 1171 (1984).

blastocyst is transferred to the uterus of the wife, whose menstrual cycle is synchronized with that of the donor. The wife then gestates and rears the child.[38] Although still in the developmental stage, a technique that removes an embryo conceived in vivo and transfers it to another woman is a major reproductive development.[39]

In the long run, the greatest significance of external conception may be the window of opportunity it provides for examination and alteration of the embryo.[40] By excising one cell of a four, six, or eight cell zygote and examining its chromosomes, it will be possible to identify the sex and genetic makeup of the embryo before transfer of the remaining cells.[41] Identifying a chromosomal defect at this stage can avoid the need for amniocentesis and abortion later. Eventually, it will be possible to identify and insert or excise a defective gene.[42] Twinning, cloning and other maneuvers involving the embryo may also become possible.[43]

C. Normative Issues

The new reproduction — in particular IVF — has been greeted with both huzzas and homilies. Relieving infertility is praiseworthy, but extracorporeal fertilization is potentially troubling. The most extreme fears fantasize a Huxleyian world[44] where all babies are genetically programmed and decanted from bottles. More immediate concerns focus on the extracorporeal embryo, harm to offspring, the blurring of kinship relations, and alienation from the natural order.

---

38. Unlike IVF, this technique involves no drugs or surgery and may have a higher success rate than IVF because the blastocysts are transferred at a more advanced stage of development than the four or eight cell embryo transferred in IVF. Personal communication with Dr. Richard Marrs (May 10, 1985). Having overcome earlier barriers that many fertilized eggs do not, they may be healthier and more likely to survive. The necessity of embryo donation after uterine lavage, however, makes this technique more complex medically, ethically, and legally.

39. Another noncoital technique involving in vivo rather than in vitro conception is the current practice of surrogate mothering, in which the surrogate provides both egg and gestation. The surrogate agrees to conceive a child by artificial insemination, carry it to term, and then relinquish it to the couple providing the sperm. *See infra* text accompanying notes 242-55.

40. Clifford Grobstein articulated the concept of a window on the embryo. *See* C. GROBSTEIN, FROM CHANCE TO PURPOSE (1981).

41. P. SINGER & D. WELLS, THE REPRODUCTION REVOLUTION: NEW WAYS OF MAKING BABIES 168 (1984). The remaining cells have the capacity to divide, implant, and come to term.

42. For the possibilities of gene therapy, see C. GROBSTEIN, *supra* note 40; OFFICE OF TECHNOLOGY ASSESSMENT, U.S. CONGRESS, HUMAN GENE THERAPY (1984).

43. *See generally* C. GROBSTEIN, *supra* note 40; P. SINGER & D. WELLS, *supra* note 41, at 150-66.

44. *See* A. HUXLEY, BRAVE NEW WORLD (1946).

It is too early to know precisely what the effects and consequences of the new birth technology will be, or how many of its variations will be accepted. Indeed, we are still searching for a language to describe the entity created by extracorporeal fertilization and the activities then done to it.[45] We are also searching for a set of norms or rules for guiding use of the new technology. While governmental bodies in the United States, Canada, Great Britain, and Australia have addressed some aspects of IVF,[46] all the issues and problems presented have not been fully adumbrated, much less closely analyzed. Nor have the legal relations of reproductive collaborators to each other, to the embryo, and to offspring been adequately clarified.[47] The situation is marked by a fair degree of normative uncertainty.[48]

---

45. Whether to call the developing fertilized egg a conceptus, embryo, pre-embryo, or zygote is still unsettled. The term "pre-embryo" is medically accurate, since the embryo proper does not develop until after implantation, but it seems cumbersome. Transfer of the fertilized egg to the uterus has been termed "replacement," even though no fertilized egg had been removed. There are also differences in referring to nontransfer of embryos as discard or destruction. *See infra* note 129. Another linguistic anomaly is that paid providers of sperm are usually referred to as "donors." *See infra* text accompanying notes 270-74. Confusion also exists over "embryo adoption" versus "embryo donation." *See infra* text accompanying notes 239-40. Thus, language uncertainties convey the normative ambiguity currently surrounding IVF and extracorporeal developments.

46. The Ethical Advisory Board in the United States, U.S. Dept. of Health, Education & Welfare, Ethics Advisory Board, *HEW Support of Research Involving Human In Vitro Fertilization and Embryo Transfer*, 44 Fed. Reg. 35,033 (1979) [hereinafter Report of Ethics Advisory Board], the WARNOCK COMMITTEE REPORT IN GREAT BRITAIN, UNITED KINGDOM, DEPT. OF HEALTH & SOCIAL SECURITY, REPORT OF THE COMMITTEE OF INQUIRING INTO HUMAN FERTILISATION AND EMBRYOLOGY (1984), [hereinafter WARNOCK COMMITTE REPORT], VICTORIAN COMMITTEE TO CONSIDER THE SOCIAL, ETHICAL & LEGAL ISSUES ARISING FROM IN VITRO FERTILIZATION, REPORT ON DONOR GAMETES IN IVF (1983) (the Waller Committee reports in Australia) [hereinafter WALLER COMMITTEE], REPORT ON THE DISPOSITION OF EMBRYOS PRODUCED BY IVF (1984), and the ONTARIO LAW REFORM COMMISSION, REPORT ON HUMAN ARTIFICIAL REPRODUCTION AND RELATED MATTERS (1985) have done useful work in clarifying some of the issues and articulating widely shared assumptions. However, their reports leave many important issues untouched, beg important questions, and do not withstand close scrutiny. For example, see Kennedy, *The Moral Status of the Embryo*, 34 KING'S COUNSEL 21 (1985), for a critique of the Warnock Committee Report. Much normative analysis remains to be done.

47. *See infra* text accompanying notes 339-45.

48. The legal environment is marked by an absence of direct regulation and uncertainty about the extent to which laws devised for other purposes will apply. This may be unduly laissez-faire. If existing laws have no application, doctors and their clients are legally free to develop and use the new birth technology without regard to social consequences, using surrogates, donors, and other techniques as they wish. There may be interests of offspring, collaborators, or society at stake which justify concern or even regulation.

On the other hand, the uncertain legal situation might instill excessive caution in clinicians, detouring research into less fruitful avenues and preventing infertile couples from using techniques that could meet their reproductive needs. Programs may, for example, refuse to combine IVF with egg donation or surrogacy, or accept single women, thus denying access to many persons whose interest in reproduction seems worthy of respect. Legislation to clarify the legality of these procedures would, from both a social and consumer perspective, be desirable.

Correct policies regarding IVF and the manipulation of the extracorporeal embryo to relieve infertility are neither obvious nor easy to formulate. The practices involved are ethically complex and require careful attention to several related issues, including the meaning of procreation and procreative liberty, the respect due embryos and offspring, the nature of the family, and the relation of women and men to the natural order of reproduction. The legal structure of the new reproduction is especially important. While it reflects these conflicting concerns, it also creates the framework that shapes its use and further development.

A brief word about each of the main issues discussed below is in order. First is the meaning of reproduction for individuals when conception is externalized and the genetic, gestational, and rearing aspects of reproduction are isolated or recombined in new ways. A major issue is the extent to which the procreative liberty of individuals and couples establishes the right to acquire children noncoitally, including the right to separate and recombine the various factors of reproduction as necessary to produce a child.

A second set of issues concerns the respect due the embryo prior to implantation. What is at stake in creating and manipulating embryos? Do embryos have independent moral status? What value can reasonably be assigned to fertilized eggs and pre-implantation embryos? Can they be discarded, stored, or used in research?

A third issue concerns the welfare of children born as a result of IVF. What physical or psychosocial harms might occur? Are children born of donated gametes and embryos, or of surrogates, harmed by such collaborative reproduction? Do parents have the right to select offspring characteristics? When do the interests of resulting offspring or society justify regulation of reproductive decisions?

Closely related to these issues is a fourth issue concerning the nature of the family. Noncoital collaborative reproduction involves third parties providing eggs, sperm, embryos, or even gestation. Their relation to the resulting child and to the rearing parents affects kinship relations and the meaning of "family." At a time when demographic, social, and cultural forces are drastically changing the makeup of the family, does noncoital collaborative reproduction threaten further change that justifies regulation?

A final set of issues concerns the impact of noncoital birth technology on the role of women and the relation of both men and women to the natural order. Reproduction without sex and the separation of genetic and gestational parentage in women may alter the reproductive roles of women. These possiblities could free women from their age-old identification with gestation and rearing, or reify them as baby-making machines. In any case, they raise the specter of technologizing reproduction in ways that risk alienating children from their parents and both women and men from the natural order.

This Article analyzes the legal structure of the new reproduction by focusing on the normative issues that arise in noncoital and extracorporeal fertilization of human eggs. It begins by examining the question of the procreative liberty of persons who wish to acquire a child through IVF or its collaborative variations. It then examines the interests of extracorporeal embryos, resulting offspring, reproductive collaborators and families, and concerns about reification and commercialism as justifications for restricting that liberty. A final section addresses regulatory needs.

II. NONCOITAL REPRODUCTION AND PROCREATIVE LIBERTY

Normative analysis of the legal structure of the new reproduction begins with a discussion of procreative liberty. IVF is now widely accepted, though a few years ago there were strong objections to it. Today, however, many people would support a ban on certain IVF activities, such as gamete and embryo donation and surrogacy.[49] Since legal restrictions on use of noncoital reproductive techniques might preclude persons from the only reproduction possible for them, their procreative liberty would be limited significantly. Yet all liberty can be limited when its exercise substantially burdens others. Accordingly, we begin with a discussion of the scope of procreative liberty and the extent of constitutional protection for noncoital conception and its collaborative variations.

---

49. Some people, for example, would ban IVF for single women, surrogacy, and destruction of, or research on, unwanted embryos. Others would ban the payment of fees for transfer of embryos or for surrogacy. The federal government still refuses to fund embryo research. While controversy over IVF has only sporadically heated up in the political arena, the first IVF program in the United States was opposed by right-to-life groups when it sought a certificate of need to open up in Norfolk, Virginia. Marsh & Self, *In Vitro Fertilization: Moving from Theory to Theory*, 10 HASTINGS CENTER REP., June 1980, at 5. Since then, right-to-life groups have been silent about IVF but there are many issues that are likely to mobilize activity, such as embryo research, embryo donation, and destruction or freezing of fertilized eggs. Future right-to-life agitation and legal controversy over IVF is likely.

A. The Nature and Scope of Procreative Liberty

"Procreative liberty" denotes freedom in activities and choices related to procreation, but the term does not tell us which activities fall within its scope. A crucial distinction is between actions designed to *avoid* procreation and those designed to *cause* procreation. In many societies cultural duties to procreate exist. In the United States, however, individuals and couples have no legal duty to procreate. The burdens of unwanted pregnancy and childrearing are deemed so substantial that any competent person—married, single, adult, minor—may choose to abort up to the fetus' viability[50] and use contraceptives to avoid pregnancy.[51]

The right to procreate—to do those things that will lead to biological descendants—is equally or even more significant to persons, yet has not received the explicit legal recognition that the avoidance of procreation has. The absence of explicit law is significant, for it shows how widespread and deep is the social understanding of the right to reproduce through sexual intercourse. While sterilization, fornication, and marriage laws have prevented some persons from reproducing, no law has prohibited or penalized married couples from having children, as often as they like and can.[52]

Extracorporeal conception and manipulation of the fertilized egg forces us to consider several new questions about the scope of the right to reproduce when that right, lodged as it is in the community's background assumptions, has itself received little critical scrutiny. Do persons with the right to reproduce coitally also have a right to do so noncoitally, if coital reproduction is not possible? May they enlist gamete donors and surrogate gestators to overcome their infertility? May they choose to limit their participation to discrete, unconnected reproductive roles, such as gamete or embryo donor or surrogate? Questions of posthumous procreation, embryo storage, and selection of offspring characteristics also arise.

---

50. City of Akron v. Akron Center for Reproductive Health, 462 U.S. 416 (1983); Bellotti v. Baird, 443 U.S. 622 (1979); Planned Parenthood v. Danforth, 428 U.S. 52 (1976); Roe v. Wade, 410 U.S. 113 (1973). The right to avoid reproduction recognized in those cases should be distinguished from a right to engage in consensual heterosexual or homosexual sexual activities, which some persons have argued those cases establish. Although the two are closely related, the burdens of the prohibitions differ, and thus can legally be distinguished.

51. Carey v. Population Services Int'l, 431 U.S. 678 (1977); Eisenstadt v. Baird, 405 U.S. 438 (1972); Griswold v. Connecticut, 381 U.S. 479 (1965).

52. *See generally* Dandridge v. Williams, 397 U.S. 471 (1970) (failure to increase welfare benefits when additional children are born is not a penalty on the right to reproduce, but a failure of the state to provide welfare benefits, which it is under no obligation to provide).

Determining the scope of the right to procreate—and hence of reproductive liberty involving extracorporeal human embryos—depends on exploration of two issues that have never been isolated in this way. The first is the extent to which the basis for valuing reproduction applies when conception occurs noncoitally or collaboratively. The second concerns the meaning and scope of responsibility in reproduction, and thus the circumstances in which reproduction can justifiably be limited.

The first question requires us to examine the moral or value basis for according reproduction such high value. Reproduction is the creation of biological descendants through gametic fusion with a partner, gestation by the female, and usually rearing by one or both of the procreators. Creating and rearing biological descendants is immensely meaningful for individuals and for society. The case for according persons a large degree of liberty in creating and rearing biological descendants is plausible and appealing, and, at least within marriage, has been widely accepted.

It would seem, then, that freedom to procreate noncoitally should also be recognized, since it may be the only way for the person to reproduce. By the same token, the use of sperm, egg, embryo, or uterus donors may also be necessary for the person to have or rear biological descendants. While the possibility of harms unique to IVF procreation should be explored, a plausible argument to extend procreative liberty to transactions involving the extracorporeal embryo can be made.

This understanding of procreative liberty, however, can be distinguished from reproductive roles played by persons who are not themselves attempting to acquire offspring of their own. For the donor or surrogate, participation in partial reproductive roles, such as gamete or embryo donor, or gestator, may have less of the meaning that gives reproduction its significance, and therefore need not be as fully protected.[53] Similarly, the liberty to have one's heirs conceived or transferred to a uterus posthumously, which gamete and embryo storage makes possible, seems less compelling than the liberty to have heirs during one's life. Extension of the scope of procreative liberty thus raises questions about life, death, and one's continuity with the natural order. Analogies and similarities to current practices abound, but none is identical. Whether the dissimilarities are morally significant must await further experience

---

53. The recipient of the donation, however, may have the full procreative interest, even if the donor does not. Thus, persons desiring to reproduce may have a right to receive gametes and gestation from others, even if the others have no independent right to provide those services. *See infra* text accompanying notes 68-70.

and the evolution of shared understandings about the personal and social importance of the procreative interests at stake.

There is also normative uncertainty about the scope of reproductive responsibility—a second issue in need of clarification. May a person's freedom to acquire children for rearing or to engage in other activities with reproductive significance be limited to protect offspring and others? Reproductive decisions affect offspring and may lead directly to burdens for others. Yet there have been few efforts to assure reproductive responsibility, and the idea of reproductive responsibility is seldom addressed in countries without a population problem. In developed countries most people are free, if they have a partner, to reproduce when and as often as they like.

IVF will force elucidation of the concept of reproductive responsibility, for actions done to create or manipulate fertilized eggs may directly hurt offspring or others. In assessing reproductive responsibility in use of noncoital technologies, concerns about overpopulation, producing handicapped children, imposing rearing costs on others, maternal behavior during pregnancy, and the ability to parent competently must be distinguished. The limits of acceptable behavior will depend on the burdens and benefits of particular techniques and on the emerging meaning of reproduction as these techniques filter into common use.

B. Constitutional Recognition of a Right to Procreate

The legal structure of noncoital reproduction will reflect these questions concerning the meaning and scope of procreative liberty. The current legal situation is marked by an absence of direct regulation and uncertainty about the extent to which fetal research, adoption, and artificial insemination by donor (AID) laws apply to embryo manipulation and to donor and surrogate transactions.[54] Future regulation limiting IVF and noncoital options is certainly a possibility. Discussion of the

---

54. With the exception of Pennsylvania, PA. STAT. ANN., tit. 18, § 3213(e) (Supp. 1985), no state expressly prohibits or even regulates IVF and its variations, yet the possibility that laws designed for other purposes would be applied to IVF injects uncertainty into physician and patient planning. State laws against fetal research may apply because of loose use of the terms embryo and fetus. *See* Quigley & Andrews, *infra* note 124, at 349. State adoption and AID laws may also be relevant in cases of noncoital conception that involve the donation of gametes and embryos or surrogate gestators. Neither set of laws, however, is presently an adequate source of guidance.

The AID laws address the rights and duties of husband and donor in the offspring when AID occurs in a marriage with husband consent. While they recognize a contractual model for allocating rearing rights and duties, in this situation, it is unclear whether the contract model will be applied to unmarried persons and to egg and embryo donations and surrogacy. *See infra* text accompanying notes 217-33. In cases where the surrogate is married, these laws may be a barrier since they state

constitutional right to procreate will illuminate the underlying normative problems, indicate the scope of possible state intrusion, and thus define the freedom to make noncoital and collaborative reproductive decisions.[55]

1. *The Right To Noncoital and Donor-Assisted Reproduction*

The starting point of analysis is the recognition that married persons (and possibly unmarried persons as well) have a right to reproduce by sexual intercourse. Although laws regulating fornication, cohabitation, and adultery have limited the freedom of unmarried persons to reproduce,[56] laws limiting coital reproduction by a married couple have been notably absent. As a result, there are no cases that directly involve a married couple's right to coital reproduction.

In dicta, however, the Supreme Court on numerous occasions has recognized a married couple's right to procreate in language broad enough to encompass coital, and most noncoital, forms of reproduction. In *Meyer v. Nebraska*, for example, the Court stated that constitutional liberty included the right of an individual "to marry, establish a home and bring up children."[57] In striking down a mandatory sterilization law for habitual criminals in *Skinner v. Oklahoma*, the Court noted that the law interfered with marriage and procreation, which were among "the basic civil rights of man."[58] In *Stanley v. Illinois* the Court observed that "[t]he rights to conceive and raise one's children have been deemed 'essential,' 'basic civil rights of man,' and '[r]ights far more precious . . . than property rights.' "[59] The Court has noted that "freedom of personal choice in matters of marriage and family life is one of the liberties protected by the Due Process Clause of the Fourteenth Amendment."[60] An

---

that the husband of the woman who is artificially inseminated is the legal father of offspring. *See, e.g.*, CAL. CIV. CODE § 7005(b) (West 1983).

55. Whatever the constitutional posture of procreative liberty, persons in the private sector will remain free to make decisions concerning IVF and their participation in it. *See infra* text accompanying note 83.

56. It is difficult to show that these laws actually have prevented people from reproducing as they wish, yet their continued presence on the books in some twenty states expresses the view of many people that reproduction should not occur outside marriage. For a recent analysis of cohabitation laws, see Fineman, *Law and Changing Patterns of Behavior: Sanctions on Non-Marital Cohabitation*, 1981 WIS. L. REV. 275.

57. 262 U.S. 390, 399 (1923).

58. 316 U.S. 535, 541 (1942). San Antonio Indep. School Dist. v. Rodriquez states that "[i]mplicit in the Court's opinion is the recognition that the right of procreation is among the rights of personal privacy protected under the Constitution." 411 U.S. 1, 34 n.76 (1973).

59. 405 U.S. 645, 651 (1972) (citations omitted) (brackets in original).

60. Cleveland Bd. of Educ. v. LaFleur, 414 U.S. 632, 639-40 (1973) (citations omitted).

especially explicit statement of the right to procreate appeared in Justice Brennan's opinion in *Eisenstadt v. Baird*: "If the right of privacy means anything, it is the right of the individual, married or single, to be free of unwarranted governmental intrusion into matters so fundamentally affecting a person as the decision whether to bear or beget a child."[61]

The Court's statements have not distinguished carefully between conceiving and rearing a child, analyzed the interests behind this protection, nor taken account of new reproductive technologies. Moreover, these statements arise in a context where government control over entrance to, and exit from, marriage is not in question,[62] and where public policy may mandate government interference with the reproduction of mentally incompetent persons.[63] Yet it seems indisputable that even a conservative Supreme Court would find that married couples have a fundamental constitutional right to reproduce by coitus.[64]

One need only imagine the result if a state passed a law that limited a married couple's freedom to reproduce by sexual intercourse. Involuntary sterilization, mandatory contraception and abortion laws, laws limiting the number of children, or other laws restricting coital reproduction

---

61. 405 U.S. 438, 453 (1972) (emphasis omitted). Only four members of the Court concurred in Justice Brennan's opinion. *See also* Bowers v. Hardwick, 106 S. Ct. 2841, 2851 (1986) (Blackmun, J., dissenting) ("We protect the decision whether to have a child because parenthood alters so dramatically an individual's self-definition, not because of demographic considerations or the Bible's command to be fruitful and multiply.").

62. Although the right to marry is deemed a fundamental right, Zablocki v. Redhail, 434 U.S. 374, 383 (1977); Loving v. Virginia, 388 U.S. 1, 12 (1967), it is clear that the state may place age, gender, and quantity restrictions on marriage. *See, e.g.*, U.S. v. Reynolds, 98 U.S. 145, 161-67 (1878) (Congress may prohibit polygamy).

63. *See* Buck v. Bell, 274 U.S. 200, 207 (1927); *see also In re* Grady, 85 N.J. 235, 251-52, 426 A.2d 467, 475 (1981) (courts can order sterilization under parens patriae jurisdiction). Recognition of the state's right to sterilize mentally incompetent persons implicitly supports the notion of the married couple's right to reproduce. These cases assume that persons have a procreative right not to be sterilized and they examine whether mental retardation allows the right to be overridden. Although the grounds or source of the person's right is never examined, it could be justified as necessary to protect against unwanted physical intrusion and to protect the ability to reproduce if one later marries.

64. The claim of a married couple's right to reproduce coitally is a claim of substantive due process—a claim that unwritten rights exist and are appropriately identified by the Supreme Court within the confines of the fourteenth amendment. Although the fortunes of substantive due process have waxed and waned since Lochner v. New York, 198 U.S. 45 (1905), and considerable dispute exists over the scope of unwritten rights, even conservative members of the Court recognize some irreducible substratum of unwritten rights. For example, Justices Rehnquist, O'Connor, and Burger accept a right to travel, a right to vote, and presumably a right of bodily integrity. *See, e.g.*, Lee v. Winston, 104 S. Ct. 1924 (1984). I think that they would also recognize a right of married couples to have children, at least by coital means, even though the Constitution does not explicitly mention it, if a state law limiting the right came before the Court. *See* Flannery, Weisman, Lipsett & Braverman, *Test Tube Babies: Legal Issues Raised by In Vitro Fertilization*, 67 GEO. L.J. 1295, 1300-11 (1979).

doubtlessly would be subjected to the same strict scrutiny that laws restricting abortion and contraception now receive. Such laws would be struck down unless some compelling ground for such a drastic restriction of marital freedom could be shown.[65]

If the Supreme Court would recognize a married couple's right to coital reproduction, it should recognize a couple's right to reproduce noncoitally as well. The couple's interest in reproducing is the same, no matter how conception occurs, for the values and interests underlying coital reproduction are equally present. Both coital and noncoital conception enable the couple to unite egg and sperm and thus acquire a child of their genes and gestation for rearing. Aside from religious views that see coitus and reproduction as inextricably linked,[66] the particular technique used to bring egg and sperm together is less important than the resulting offspring. The use of noncoital techniques such as IVF or artificial insemination to unite egg and husband's sperm, made necessary by the couple's infertility, should then also be protected.

The need for a third party donor or surrogate to provide the sperm, egg, or uterus necessary for the couple to beget, bear, or otherwise acquire a child should, under these principles of procreative liberty, also fall within the married couple's procreative rights. Although not as directly entailed as noncoital conception, the assistance of a third party collaborator should be treated similarly. The donor assists the couple in reproducing by contributing a factor of conception or gestation that the couple lacks. The donor is essential if the couple is to rear a child that has a gametic or gestational connection with the couple.[67] Since they are otherwise qualified to be parents, and would be free, if fertile, to

---

65. The point is that state restriction of coital reproduction would be tested by a standard more rigorous than a rational basis test. Extraordinary situations like the need to reduce population because of severe over-population or food shortages might meet such a standard, Comment, *Legal Analysis and Population Control: The Problem of Coercion*, 84 HARV. L. REV. 1856 (1971), but a moral dislike of the way people are choosing to reproduce would not. Another conceivable ground for limitation might be when a person knowingly and avoidably conceives and brings to term a severely handicapped child and passes the costs and burdens of rearing that child to others. *See infra* text accompanying notes 166-76.

66. A traditional Catholic view is that the unitive and the procreative should be combined in one act, thus making the separation of sex and reproduction, either to procure pleasure or to procure offspring, wrong. For a description of this view, see R. MCCORMICK, How BRAVE A NEW WORLD 311-12 (1981).

67. With donor egg or sperm, the wife will be bearing and the couple rearing, the genetic child of one partner. Where they contribute an embryo to another couple, they are reproducing by providing the genes for another's child. If they receive an embryo donation, they are reproducing in the sense of gestating and raising children, the usual result of coital reproduction. In the case of surrogates, the couple will be rearing a child that has genes of one, if not of both, partners. A full gestational surrogate would be providing gestation only and no genes, while a partial surrogate

reproduce as often as they wished, they should be free to procreate with the help of gamete or womb donors.

Unpacking the meaning of procreation by sexual intercourse, as IVF and noncoital conception require us to do, we see that the reasons and values that support a right to reproduce coitally apply equally to noncoital activities involving external conception and collaborators. While the case is strongest for a couple's right to noncoital and external conception, a strong argument for their right to enlist the aid of gamete and womb donors can also be made. Both enable a couple to rear a child that is the biological descendant of, or has been gestated by, one of them.

If the couple's right to reproduce were fully recognized, married persons would have the right to engage in a wide range of noncoital activities involving embryos, donors and surrogates in their attempt to reproduce. They would have the right to determine the use of their gametes and the disposition of embryos created with those gametes.[68] They would also have the right to contract with others for the provision of gametes or embryos, or gestation, with the contract settling the parties rearing rights and duties in resulting offspring. While the state could regulate the circumstances under which parties enter into reproductive contracts, it could not ban or refuse to enforce such transactions altogether without compelling reason.[69] In short, the interests and values

would provide genes as well, thus leading to a genetic link with only one partner. *See infra* text accompanying notes 242-55.

68. Thus, existing fetal research, adoption and AID laws that limit noncoital reproductive options are of doubtful constitutionality, and may be struck down if challenged. Similarly, legal presumptions about who is the rearing father and mother in situations involving donor gametes and surrogates may also fall, once the full implications of procreative liberty are recognized. For a discussion of the gamete source's right to discard embryos, see *infra* text accompanying notes 130-43.

69. Refusal to enforce reproductive contracts and prohibitions on money payments would amount to an interference with procreative liberty, since it would prevent couples from obtaining the donor assistance that they need to acquire a child genetically or gestationally related to them. For more on this issue, see *infra* text accompanying notes 270-91.

The right to contract for reproductive assistance asserted here may be compared with the right of persons contemplating marriage to regulate by contract the relation between them and a future divorce settlement. Both reproductive and prenuptial contracts illustrate the social movement from status to contract in family and reproductive relations. *See generally* Shultz, *Contractual Ordering of Marriage: A New Model for State Policy*, 70 CALIF. L. REV. 204 (1982) (discussing contract as a legal alternative for resolving marital disputes); Note, *For Better or For Worse . . . but Just in Case, Are Antenuptial Agreements Enforceable?*, 1982 U. ILL. L. REV. 531 (discussing trend toward validating antenuptial agreements and parallel trend in societal attitudes toward divorce).

Recognition of such a contract right also raises the question of why contracts to adopt children made before or after conception but before birth would not be valid, nor why parties should not be free after birth to make private contracts for adoption directly with women who want to relinquish their children. The logic of my argument is that persons, at least if married, have a right to acquire a child for rearing purposes, and may resort to the medical or social means necessary to do so.

supporting the right to reproduce by sexual intercourse extend to external conception and the need to contract with donors, surrogates, and physicians for the creation, gestation, and rearing of children. While the state is not obligated to facilitate or provide the means to reproduce, it would need a compelling justification to interfere with noncoital reproductive choices made by freely consenting persons in the private sector.

2. *Unmarried Persons*

Although no law prohibits reproduction by unmarried persons, fornication, cohabitation and paternity laws that penalize nonmarital coitus still exist in many states. Of more immediate concern is the reluctance of physicians and hospitals to make donor insemination and other reproductive options available to single persons. Access for unmarried persons takes on greater significance as single women and same sex couples seek to beget and rear children.

The argument for the right to reproduce coitally is clearest in the case of married persons, but can also be made for unmarried persons. If their right to reproduce by sexual intercourse were recognized, then they too would have a right to noncoital and donor-assisted reproduction.

A strong argument that unmarried persons should have a right to reproduce coitally can be made.[70] Unmarried persons also have needs or desires to have and rear biological descendants, and may be as competent parents as married couples. They may not be able or willing to marry to satisfy this desire.[71] Given the personal significance of reproduction, it

Although IVF and its variations preserve a genetic or gestational link with one of the rearing parents, the right at issue may not be so easily confined. It may be that the law of adoption needs to be rethought in light of the right to contract for noncoital reproductive assistance.

70.   The argument for a single person's right to procreate sexually must be distinguished from the argument for the right of a single person to have sex with consenting others and the right to avoid reproduction. Recognition of the unmarried person's right to avoid procreation through access to birth control and abortion does not necessarily imply either a right to procreate or a right to have sex with consenting others. Sexual liberty would not necessarily entail reproduction (merely sex with contraception), and a right to reproduce would not necessarily entail sexual freedom beyond the sexual or other acts required for reproduction.

71.   Legal claims for an unmarried person's right to reproduce have arisen as women have entered the workforce in large numbers, postponed marriage, and chosen female lovers. Indeed, a growing number of women now are choosing to follow in the footsteps of John Irving's Jenny Fields and reproduce without a man to assist in rearing. As the character, Jenny Fields, wrote in her biography: "I wanted a job and I wanted to live alone. That made me a sexual suspect. Then I wanted a baby, but I didn't want to share my body or my life to have one. That made me a sexual suspect, too." J. IRVING, THE WORLD ACCORDING TO GARP 13 (1976).

While some single women desiring to reproduce will choose coital conception, others prefer artificial insemination. Yet only 10% of physicians doing AID will inseminate single women. *See* Curie-Cohen, Luttrell & Shapiro, *Current Practice of Artificial Insemination by Donor in the United*

would seem to deserve protection for unmarried as well as married persons.[72] Indeed, banning coital or noncoital conception by single persons seems absurd when unmarried sexual relations are common and when single women cannot be forced to use contraception or to abort after pregnancy has occurred.[73] Surely capable rearers should not be denied the opportunity just because they are unmarried.

While the argument for the right of single persons to reproduce coitally persuades many persons, it is not clear that it would be accepted by the Supreme Court. The single person's right to use contraception and to continue a pregnancy once begun does not necessarily entail a right to conceive in the first place. Preventing conception and pregnancy by requiring contraception and abortion interferes with bodily integrity in a way that preventing conception in the first place—by preventing access to the needed means—does not.[74] Like the distinction between reading pornography in the home and purchasing it to bring home,[75] these

---

States, 300 NEW ENG. J. MED. 585, 585 (1979). Some of the reluctance of physicians to inseminate single women may be their fear that single women, particularly lesbians, will not be good parents. *But see* McGuire & Alexander, *Artificial Insemination of Single Women*, 43 FERTILITY & STERILITY 182 (1985) (research indicates that children in single head of household families are not psychologically damaged by the absence of a father); Strong & Schinfeld, *The Single Woman and Artificial Insemination by Donor*, 29 J. REPRODUCTIVE MED. 293 (1984) (artificial insemination requests by single women should be honored in some cases).

As a result, a practice of "amateur insemination" has grown up. M. FABE & N. WIKLER, UP AGAINST THE CLOCK 163 (1979); Stern, *Amateur Insemination*, in THE NEXT WHOLE EARTH CATALOGUE 345 (1980). Sperm is obtained from male friends or go-betweens, and the woman inseminates herself. The sperm donor relinquishes all rearing rights and duties, which devolve solely upon the mother. However, there are legal uncertainties and medical risk in such a practice. *See infra* text accompanying notes 217-18.

72. While poor, young, single mothers who are unemployed or lack skills arguably may not be well-situated to raise families, unmarried persons with means clearly could be. Indeed, many poor, single women are capable mothers, and more single parents than ever now raise children. Since unmarried status or single parenthood is not in itself grounds for termination of parental rights, unmarried status is, arguably, a poor reason to prevent conception or the means to achieve it.

73. A single person may have a right to go to term once she has conceived, i.e., a woman cannot be forced to have an abortion even if she is single. But this right may be based on a right of bodily integrity, rather than on a right to reproduce. Similarly, a single woman who has given birth cannot be forced to relinquish a child just because she is single. But in this case it would be a heavy intrusion to separate mother and child on the basis of unmarried status when her parenting capacity is clear. Also, a single person is constitutionally guaranteed the right to access to contraceptives in order to avoid the burdens of reproduction. But these cases do not demonstrate that a single person cannot be penalized for fornication. If so, the state could deny IVF and other noncoital reproductive services to single persons.

74. The distinction is admittedly strained. In the one case, the state is forcing one type of burden on the woman, and in the second, another type of burden altogether. But difference in type of burden seems less important than the significance or magnitude of the burden. On this score there appears to be no morally cognizable difference between the two.

75. *Compare* Stanley v. Georgia, 394 U.S. 557 (1969) (state power to regulate obscenity does not extend to mere possession of pornography by an individual in the privacy of the home) *with* U.S.

distinctions might be appealing to a Supreme Court not disposed to extend the list of fundamental rights. While traditions of family[76] and of reproduction within marriage make it difficult for the Court to deny the procreative liberty of married persons, it may be less willing to recognize the right of single persons to reproduce. For example, the Supreme Court has not yet held that fornication and marriage laws violate an unmarried person's right of privacy. In any event, if the right of single persons to reproduce coitally is recognized, then they too should have the right to reproduce through IVF and other forms of noncoital reproduction.

3. *Limits on the Right to Noncoital Reproduction*

If the foregoing analysis seems startling, it may be because we are unpacking the implications of a right that never, because of technology, had to be unpacked. If procreative liberty protects a wider swath of reproductive activities than one might have thought, limits on reproductive choice may nevertheless exist, either because the values behind reproduction are not significantly implicated or because valid state interests justify limiting the right.

Recognition of a right to reproduce noncoitally and to contract with donors and surrogates to that end leaves unanswered many questions raised by noncoital conception. Even if there is a right to use IVF to have and rear biological descendants, it may be that IVF activities not aimed at acquiring a child for rearing are not protected. For example, a married or single person's desire to play a partial reproductive role, such as providing gametes or gestation *tout court*, may not involve the underlying values that support a right to reproduce to such an extent as to deserve protection in its own right.[77] Similarly, the values underlying a

---

v. Reidel, 402 U.S. 351 (1971) (first amendment does not protect the right to do business in pornography and distribute it through the mail).

76.   The importance of family tradition is evident in Justice Powell's opinion in Moore v. City of East Cleveland, 431 U.S. 494 (1977), in which a zoning ordinance preventing a grandmother from living with grandchildren was struck down on the basis of a substantive due process right to live with one's lineal descendants. Surely the right of a married couple to have children is as strong a candidate for fundamental right status.

77.   This example focuses attention on the interests that make reproduction so highly valued and on whether they are present when gestation and rearing without a gene link occur. Indeed, it is not clear that we would say that such persons have reproduced. In the reverse case, a gene link without gestation and rearing, we might accurately say that reproduction has occurred. For example, an anonymous sperm donor has reproduced himself when a child is born from his donation even if there is never any contact between them. It would not follow, however, that the choice to give or withhold the sperm is part of protected liberty, for some additional interest could be required before a reproductive incident is constitutionally protected. The case of rearing or gestating without the

right to reproduce may be too attenuated to deserve protection when posthumous disposition of stored gametes or embryos is at issue.[78] Nor may reproductive values be strongly implicated in a person's wish to manipulate the genes of extracorporeal embryos in order to select or control offspring characteristics.[79] Whether such reproductive choices deserve constitutional protection will depend upon the evolving social and individual meanings attached to reproduction and its disaggregated components.[80]

A second important limit on IVF and noncoital activities would be prevention of harm to other persons or to important state interests. The main concerns with IVF have centered around harm to extracorporeal embryos, offspring, family, and the human dignity of reproduction. While some of the debate concerns the meaning of harm in a reproductive context, this Article concludes that most noncoital maneuvers pose a

---

hereditary link may have those other incidents and thus merit constitutional protection even though the avoidance or creation of an hereditary link alone does not. For further discussion of these issues, see *infra* text accompanying notes 130-43.

78. This issue involves an assessment of the importance to people of the knowledge that a biological descendant will come into being and live after one has died. The importance of reproduction to people is based partly on the continuity with nature and feelings of immortality that genetic transmission or reproduction involves. *See* R. LIFTON, THE LIFE OF THE SELF 29-33 (1976). Distinctions between having biological heirs during one's life and having them after one dies may have to be made to accommodate the possibilities of gamete and embryo storage and implantation after death of the gamete provider.

The right to transmit property to embryos and children born posthumously of stored gametes is a separate matter. If the usual presumption in favor of clearly expressed testator intent controls, a person would be able to devise property to the children born of stored gametes and embryos, who are not born until long after the testator's death. If the state chose to limit testator intent in such cases to foster the efficient administration of probate, its constitutionality would depend on whether the testator was exercising procreative liberty. This in turn depends on whether the satisfaction that comes from knowing that one's genetic heirs, some of whom are never born while the testator is alive deserve protection. It is too early to tell whether this interest falls within the scope of the right to reproduce.

79. The argument would be that banning selection of offspring characteristics interferes with the right to procreate, since the child's characteristics may influence the person's decision to reproduce. *See* Robertson, *Procreative Liberty and the Control of Conception, Pregnancy and Childbirth*, 69 VA. L. REV. 405, 431 (1983). Alternatively, an independent right to select the characteristics of children that one has produced, perhaps as an incident of the freedom to rear as one chooses, could be made. However, the interest in producing a child with specific characteristics could be found to lie outside of the interests and values that warrant protection under the rubric of the right to procreate.

80. Questions about the rights of persons to transfer their full bundle of rights to another, and the scope of the transferee's rights, also arise. *See infra* text accompanying notes 210-41. In addition, the right of the individual or couple to dispose of gametes and embryos, including discard, raises issues about the scope of the right not to procreate. *See infra* text accompanying notes 130-43.

low risk of the kinds of harm that might justify prohibition of their use.[81] Thus, regulation to assure free, informed entry into donor and surrogate transactions might be justified to protect the autonomy of the parties, but a complete ban on collaborative arrangements would ordinarily not be justified.

Noncoital reproduction, however, does raise the possibility of symbolic harm. Its main impact may be on moral or religious notions about sexuality, reproduction, family, female roles, and similar value-laden concerns. Such concerns are of immense importance to individuals and society. In choosing values, persons and societies understand themselves as beings and groups with particular ethical or moral beliefs. Because these choices are so fundamental, individuals may vary widely in their choice of and commitment to such values. It is no surprise that activities that carry such symbolic weight are controversial and lead to efforts to enlist legal institutions to enforce one's views of the matter.

Constitutional protection for noncoital reproduction thus has enormous importance, for symbolic concerns without direct, tangible harm to others are usually insufficient to justify infringing the fundamental rights of persons with different views.[82] Views of the rightness or wrongness of particular means of conception might properly animate individual choices to avoid, seek or provide such services. They also permit the state to refrain from funding or subsidizing the activity.[83] But they generally do not justify public action that interferes with the exercise of the right.

---

81. However, prohibition in particular instances might be justified. For example, the offspring's interest in knowing her genetic roots may justify a ban on collaborative reproduction that does not maintain records concerning the gamete source.

82. There is no way to understand cases such as Roe v. Wade, 410 U.S. 113 (1973), Eisenstadt v. Baird, 405 U.S. 438 (1972), Griswold v. Connecticut, 381 U.S. 479 (1965), and a host of others other than as standing for the proposition that symbolic or moral evaluation of protected conduct without more does not justify state interference with the conduct. The community's power to enforce or impose morality stops at the threshold of another person's fundamental rights.

83. Since procreative liberty is (like most constitutional rights) a negative—not a positive—right, it obligates the state to refrain from interference with reproductive arrangements among consenting adults and physicians. It does not obligate the state to fund these activities or allow the activities in state institutions, any more than the state is obligated to fund abortions or contraception. *See* Harris v. McCrae, 448 U.S. 297 (1980) (states participating in the Medicaid program are not obligated to fund medically necessary abortions); Maher v. Roe, 432 U.S. 464 (1977) (the equal protection clause does not require a state participating in Medicaid to fund nontherapeutic abortions for indigent women simply because it has made a policy choice to pay the expenses incident to childbirth.); Poelker v. Doe, 432 U.S. 519 (1977) (city does not violate Constitution by electing, as a policy choice, to provide publicly financed hospital services for childbirth but not for nontherapeutic abortions). Nor is the private sector obligated to offer IVF services. Hospitals may refuse to allow

In short, IVF and noncoital reproduction illustrate the recurring dilemma of rights in a society of limited governmental powers. Recognition of fundamental rights is essential in the constitutional scheme, yet it permits activities that may run counter to the values that a majority holds and may even lead to changes in those values. Yet the community through law may not stop the exercise of those rights, even though an impact on its value structure may occur.[84] Noncoital reproduction is thus left to the moral discretion of patients, physicians and other actors in the private sector.

The remainder of this Article examines many of the legal and normative issues that arise in noncoital reproduction, in light of the constitutional presumption accorded procreative liberty.

III. STATUS OF EXTRACORPOREAL EMBRYOS

A major source of normative conflict in the new reproduction concerns the status of the extracorporeal embryos produced by IVF. Formerly hidden in the fallopian tube and uterus, the earliest stages of human development are now visible and open to manipulation, raising policy questions about the treatment of embryos.

In most IVF programs the opportunity for control is now quite brief, for embryos will be transferred at the two-, four-, six-, or eight-cell stage, which usually occurs two to three days after fertilization. But the potential power to manipulate is significant. The embryos created by IVF can be observed, tested, frozen, thawed, altered, transferred, or discarded. Attempts to maintain the embryo externally for longer periods no doubt will also occur. Do these actions harm embryos? Who should exercise dispositional authority over embryos? Are substantive limits on actions with embryos ethically desirable and legally available?

Answers to these questions depend to a large extent on the moral and legal status of embryos. I first examine the biological status of pre-

---

IVF or may restrict the reproductive transactions that it allows. Doctors and institutions conducting IVF may set their own limits on what they will permit. The power of the private sector suggests that patient-physician relations may be as important as constitutional limitations in determining the development and impact of the new reproduction. *See infra* text accompanying notes 329-38.

84. This issue occupied H.L.A. Hart and Lord Devlin in their famous debate on the propriety of the state enforcing a moral view about sexual relations in order to maintain the moral fabric of society. *See* P. DEVLIN, THE ENFORCEMENT OF MORALS 9-23 (1965); H.L.A. HART, LAW, LIBERTY AND MORALITY 69-77 (1962). Similar issues would arise if the state attempted to ban noncoital reproduction in order to preserve a particular deontological moral view about how reproduction should occur.

implantation embryos and then analyze their moral and legal status, and consider questions of decisionmaking authority, discard, and research.

A. BIOLOGICAL STATUS OF THE EXTRACORPOREAL EMBRYO

IVF produces a preimplantation embryo by inseminating a human egg in a glass dish. Fertilization, which is marked by the emergence of pronuclei in the inseminated egg and subsequent cleavage, is not instantaneous but occurs gradually over several hours after insemination.[85] In the forty-eight to seventy-two hours between insemination and transfer to a uterus (typical of most IVF programs), the fertilized egg or zygote divides several times, into two, four, six, or eight cells. At this point the zygote is an undifferentiated aggregate of cells called blastomeres.

When sixteen or more cells result from cleavage, the cells hang together in a loosely packed configuration, similar to that of a blackberry, called a morula.[86] At some point in the morula stage a fluid-filled space begins to form within the substance of the morula. Successive cleavages and further accumulation of fluid lead to the blastocyst stage.[87]

At the blastocyst stage the cellular aggregate shows a central cavity surrounded by a peripheral cellular layer with some distinguishable inner cells.[88] The outer cells develop into a trophoblastic or feeding layer that becomes the extra-embryonic placenta rather than the embryo proper. Only cells of the inner mass can give rise to an embryo proper, which in turn can give rise to a fetus.[89]

The blastocyst stage marks the development of the capability to interact with maternal cells of the uterine lining, which is essential for implantation and later development to occur. At six to nine days, the developing cellular mass having acquired the ability to implant or embed in the uterine wall as the placenta, jointly derived from embryonic and

---

85. Grobstein, *The Early Development of Human Embryos*, 10 J. MED. & PHIL. 213, 214 (1985). Much of the ensuing account of embryonic development is a summary of Grobstein's excellent survey of early human and mammalian development.

86. The morula is the spheroidal mass of cells or blastomeres (one of the cells that the egg divides into after fertilization) resulting from the early cleavage or divisions of the zygote. STEDMAN'S MEDICAL DICTIONARY 160, 796 (22d ed. 1972); *see also* WARNOCK COMMITTEE REPORT, *supra* note 46, at 58-59.

87. WARNOCK COMMITTEE REPORT, *supra* note 46, at 59.

88. Grobstein, *supra* note 85, at 216-17.

89. *Id.* at 219.

maternal cells, begins to form.[90] The embedding process, or implantation, marks the beginning of pregnancy as a maternal state. At this stage the embryonic mass has a clearly distinguishable outer cellular layer which plays the major role in the implantation process. It is the as yet undeveloped inner cell mass, however, that is the source of the embryo proper.[91]

When the blastocyst is well established in the uterine wall (late in the second postfertilization week) the inner cell mass reorganizes into two layers that make up the embryonic disc. The first true rudiment of the embryo is the site of the formation of the embryonic axis, along which the major organs and structures of the body will be differentiated.[92] By the end of the fourth postconception week the major organs are more fully formed and cardiovascular circulation has begun.[93] By the eighth week an anatomically recognizable human miniature exists, displaying very primitive neuromuscular function, but still extremely immature by all structural and functional criteria.[94] The higher parts of the brain do not show any electrical activity or nerve cell connections until twelve weeks after conception.[95] If abortion does not occur, birth will complete the gestational process.

Biological experts agree on three points about early embryonic development. First, the earliest events in development "relate more to the formation of extra-embryonic rather than embryonic structures and functions. In consequence, the first developmental steps do not establish an embryo, but a feeding layer or trophoblast. The trophoblast has already begun to function before an embryonic rudiment is demonstrable."[96] Accordingly, the zygote, morula, and early blastocyst stages may be regarded as pre-embryonic stages (sometimes referred to as the conceptus or pre-embryo), with the term "embryo" reserved by some persons for the rudiments of the whole individual that appear at the end of

---

90. *Id.* at 219, 232. As Grobstein has noted in an unpublished draft, "the first cellular differentiation of the new generation is to assure physiologic interaction between offspring and mother."

91. Grobstein, *supra* note 85, at 219.

92. *Id.* at 220-21. Grobstein also argues that biologic individuality emerges only after implantation and the emergence of the embryonic axis. Prior to that time, several or no embryos might emerge from the developing fertilized egg. *See infra* text accompanying note 98.

93. Grobstein, *supra* note 85, at 221-23.

94. *Id.* at 217.

95. I intend no definitive stand on when the fetus actually feels pain, since for my purposes it suffices to show that before and shortly after implantation the embryo does not feel pain.

96. American Fertility Society, *Ethical Considerations In the Use of New Reproductive Technologies,* 46 FERTILITY & STERILITY (1986) (spec. supp.).

the second week after fertilization.[97]

Second, the preimplantation embryo or pre-embryo is not yet individual. Developmental individuality "in the sense of singleness is not established until an embryonic axis is formed, an event which roughly corresponds to the time of implantation and to the initiation of physiological changes of pregnancy in the mother."[98] Prior to this point, the pre-embryo is not individual since twinning, which produces two individuals, or mosaicism, which produces less than one, could still occur.

Third, the preimplantation embryo is substantially different in physiology and development from an implanted embryo and later fetus. The embryonic disc, axis, and primitive streak, which begin to emerge at or after implantation, are the precursors of embryonic and fetal nervous structures. Until they emerge there is no possibility of feeling or experience of any sort. It is considerably later in gestation—roughly six to eight weeks—that a spinal column and nervous system develop. Biologists may disagree over whether sentience occurs before the twelfth week, but there is unanimity that the preimplantation embryo has not yet developed the rudimentary structures of a nervous system, and thus lacks the capacity to experience or suffer.[99]

In sum, although the likelihood that a transferred embryo will implant in the uterus and come to term is quite low,[100] the embryo has the potential, if certain other conditions and events occur, to develop sentience and eventually personhood. Before implantation, however, the embryo is not yet individual, lacks a differentiated nervous system, and is not sentient.

---

97. The term "embryo" is used throughout this Article to refer both to preimplantation and postimplantation embryos. However, in most cases the embryo under discussion will be the preimplantation embryo.

98. American Fertility Society, *supra* note 96, at 5.

99. Although Grobstein does not directly discuss the capacity to feel, the clear implication of his survey is that the embryo lacks this capacity. *See* Grobstein, *supra* note 85, at 232-35. Establishing the precise point at which brain waves or sentience occurs in fetuses is not necessary to support my argument about preimplantation embryos, if it is granted that a nervous system of considerable complexity, far beyond that of preimplantation and recently implanted embryos, is necessary to experience pain.

100. The chance that any single transferred embryo will implant is said to be one in ten, which means an even lower chance that it will come to term, since there is usually a 25 to 35% wastage or spontaneous abortion of implanted embryos. *See* Grobstein, Flower & Mendeloff, *supra* note 4, at 128-29.

B. THE MORAL AND LEGAL STATUS OF THE PREIMPLANTATION EMBRYO

What moral and legal status should be assigned to the preimplantation embryo? Until IVF and the technological ability to isolate the human embryo, the question of embryo status did not have to be directly addressed. The tendency has been to apply one's views about the fetus and abortion almost automatically to the preimplantation embryo.[101] However, views for or against abortion should not automatically determine the status of pre-embryos, because they differ so significantly from fetuses in terms of physiological development and location. The questions of value and meaning that preimplantation embryos present require independent treatment and analysis.

The embryo that is intended to be transferred to a uterus may have moral significance because it has the potential to come into existence as a person. Thus, embryo research or other maneuvers on embryos followed by placement in a uterus may create duties not to hurt or injure the potential offspring.[102] More contested is the question of whether there is a duty to transfer all embryos to a uterus, so that they have a chance to realize their biological potential. Controversy also arises over use of embryos in research or as a source for tissue and organs.

Three major positions have been articulated in considering these questions. At one extreme is the embryo-as-person position, which views the embryo as a human subject after fertilization and requires that it be accorded the rights of persons. This position entails an obligation to provide an opportunity for implantation to occur and bans any action before transfer that might harm the embryo, such as freezing and most kinds of embryo research. This position has been held by right to life groups and the Catholic Church.[103]

---

101. Both pro-choice and pro-life groups tend to confuse the two, and assign equivalent value or disvalue to all stages of prenatal, postconception human life. *See* Robertson, *Extracorporeal Embryos and the Abortion Debate*, 2 J. CONTEMPORARY HEALTH L. & POL'Y 53, 53-58 (1986).

102. Robertson, *supra* note 79, at 437-42. Similar issues arise with fetal therapy and the question of maternal duties to assure the well-being of the child that the woman has decided to bring into the world. *Id.* In such cases the fetus is said to possess rights not to be harmed, but its rights exist by virtue of the fact that the fetus will be brought to term. Hence, the right is not that of the fetus so much as the right of the child that the fetus will become. Similarly, the preimplantation embryo may be said to have rights by virtue of the fact that it may be transferred to a uterus and eventually become a person. Strictly speaking, it is the potential offspring, and not the embryo itself, that has the right not to be harmed by prenatal or preconception action.

103. The Catholic position is typified by Rev. Donald McCarthy's testimony before Rep. Albert Gore, Jr. in subcommittee hearings on human embryo transfer. *See Hearings Before the Subcomm. on Investigations and Oversight of the House Comm. on Science and Technology*, 98th Cong., 2d Sess.

At the opposite extreme is the view that the embryo has no status different from that of any other extracorporeal human tissue. Holders of this view maintain that as long as those with decisionmaking authority over the embryo consent, no limits should be imposed on actions regarding embryos.[104]

A third view takes an intermediate position between these two. It holds that the preimplantation embryo deserves respect greater than that accorded human tissue, but not the respect accorded persons. According to this view, greater respect is due embryos than is accorded other human tissue because of their potential to become persons, and because of the symbolic meaning embryos may elicit. Yet, this view holds, the embryo should not be treated as a person because it has not yet developed the biological structures of personhood and is not yet developmentally individual. Even so the embryo can to some extent be respected as a symbol of human life.

This third view is reflected in official and professional reports, in law, and in ethical and philosophical discussion. For example, such a position was articulated by the Ethics Advisory Board in 1979, the first and most authoritative examination of the issues arising out of IVF in the United States. The Board found that "the human embryo is entitled to profound respect; but this respect does not necessarily encompass the full legal and moral rights attributed to persons."[105] This view has been enunciated by the Warnock Committee,[106] the Ontario Law Reform Commission[107] and other expert bodies that have examined the

---

350-59 (1984) (statement of Rev. Donald McCarthy) [hereinafter *Gore Hearings*]. This view holds that IVF is wrong because sperm must be obtained by masturbation or because embryos will be placed at risk in some way. A more moderate Catholic position is held by Richard McCormick, who finds IVF to be morally acceptable as long as the participants are a married couple. *See* R. McCor-MICK, *supra* note 66, at 321-33.

104. The position is not openly espoused as such, but clearly some people hold it, for it is reflected in their willingness to allow discard and research on embryos without limitation.

105. Report of Ethics Advisory Board, *supra* note 46, at 35-56.

106. WARNOCK COMMITTEE REPORT, *supra* note 46, at 63 states: "the human embryo . . . is not under the present law of the UK accorded the same status as a living child or an adult, nor do we necessarily wish it to be accorded the same status. Nevertheless, we were agreed that the embryo of the human species ought to have a special status."

107. ONTARIO LAW REFORM COMMISSION, *supra* note 46, at 209. The Ontario Law Reform Commission concludes, after stating the human subject view of the embryo, that "it is neither necessary nor desirable to impose a total prohibition on research on fertilized ova outside the body." *Id.* Such a position could not be taken if the Commission viewed the embryo as a person or rights-bearing entity in its own right.

matter.[108]

With the exception of former laws that prohibited abortion, the law has never regarded fetuses as rights-bearing entities.[109] Thus the preimplantation embryo is not a legal subject in its own right and is not protected by laws against homicide or wrongful death.[110] It has legal cognizance only if the interests of an actual person are at stake, such as when transfer will occur or when someone wrongfully interferes with the authority of another person to determine disposition of the embryo.[111]

Outside of the Catholic Church, few philosophers or ethicists argue that mere biological potential contained in a living but nonsentient entity creates obligations to that entity. Even philosophers who find that abortion is wrong usually require that implantation and some development of nervous system structures occur before granting the fetus a right to life.[112] Persons concerned about animal rights, for example, limit their concern to animals that can suffer and feel and thus have interests.[113] Similarly, most philosophers would agree that transplantable organs are

---

108. For the position taken by other professional and advisory bodies that have considered the matter, see the excellent survey in Walters, *Ethical Issues in Human In Vitro Fertilization and Embryo Transfer*, in GENETICS AND THE LAW III 215 (1985).

109. Legal personhood requires that the fetus be born alive—separated from the mother and existing independently, albeit with support. *See, e.g.*, People v. Chavez, 77 Cal. App. 2d 621, 176 P.2d 92 (1947) (legal personhood for homicide purposes).

The extracorporeal embryo is not likely to be included in this definition of person because of its rudimentary biological status, and because it must be transferred to a uterus for development, and eventually birth, to occur. However, ectogenesis, the complete ability to gestate outside of the body, might challenge this definition of legal personhood and force a rethinking of legal personhood, in terms of functional ability and developmental status rather than relation to a gestating uterus. This evaluation would involve specifying the aspects of "late gestation" that lead Nancy Rhoden to find a cut-off in abortions at around 22 weeks in her insightful article *Trimesters and Technology: Revamping* Roe v. Wade, 95 YALE L.J. 639, 669-73 (1986).

Such a moral concept of personhood would focus on functional abilities and capacities. Although the precise line can be debated, a person must have some minimal brain capacity for consciousness, reflection, thinking, feeling, etc. Whether fetuses and infants qualify under this standard, preimplantation embryos clearly do not. *See* T. ENGLEHARDT, THE FOUNDATIONS OF BIOETHICS 104-13 (1986); Tooley, *Abortion and Infanticide*, 2 Phil. & Pub. Aff. 37 (1971).

110. A review of applicable laws in the United States is contained in Westfall, *Beyond Abortion: The Potential Reach of a Human Life Amendment*, in DEFINING HUMAN LIFE 174 (1983).

111. *See infra* text accompanying notes 121-23.

112. For example, see the position against abortion outlined in Glover, *Matters of Life and Death*, N.Y. REV. BOOKS, MAY 30, 1985, at 19, 22-23.

113. Philosophers debate vigorously whether nonhuman sentient creatures, such as animals, have sufficient capacity to qualify for independent moral status. *See* T. REGAN, THE CASE FOR ANIMAL RIGHTS 243-48 (1983); Feinberg, *The Rights of Animals and Unborn Generations*, in RIGHTS, JUSTICE AND THE BOUNDS OF LIBERTY 159, 168-69 (1980). But there is wide consensus that collections of cells do not have independent moral status. Thus animal rights theorists such as Tom Regan, who believe that sentience confers moral status and rights on all sentient animals, would not argue that animal embryos also deserve respect. The debates over whether there is a

objects of value because of the life they can provide to other persons, and not because the organ itself is a rights-bearing entity.[114]

The biology of early embryo development strongly supports the view that the preimplantation embryo is not a person or a rights-bearing entity in its own right. As we have just seen, the embryo does not have differentiated organs, much less a developed brain and nervous system which persons and sentient animals ordinarily have.[115] Since it is not sentient, it cannot feel pain. It is not yet individual, since twinning or mosaicism could still occur. Even if one takes a very cautious position on when a nervous system begins, the earliest possible time of arguable relevance is the formation of the primitive streak, the precursor to the nervous system. Yet this first structure of the embryo proper does not develop until implantation has occurred, some ten to fourteen days after fertilization. Prior to that stage and for some time thereafter, preimplantation embryos would not qualify for protection on the basis of duties owed the embryo itself.[116]

The embryo may, however, be accorded respect on grounds other than what it is owed by virtue of its present biological status. Although neither a person nor an entity possessing interests, it may be the subject of duties created to demonstrate a commitment to human life and persons generally. Justice may not require that we grant the embryo rights, but we may choose to treat the embryo differently than other human tissue as a sign of respect for human life generally.[117] Since the embryo is

---

sufficient degree of sentience to qualify for moral status thus do not apply to the preimplantation embryo, which is so rudimentary in development that it cannot in itself claim moral status.

114. Thus, organs and tissues removed during surgery, or from cadavers, are never regarded as having moral status in themselves nor thought of as the objects of duties. However, we may still show respect for human tissue in order to symbolize respect for human life and personhood generally, a respect shown in the limits placed on disposition of tissue, organs, and cadavers. A major difference between donated organs and embryos is that the former will enable an existing person to continue to live, while the latter, if transferred to a uterus and brought to term, will enable a new person to live. As a result, intentional destruction of a donated organ necessary to enable another person to live, could amount to homicide, while intentional destruction of a preimplantation embryo could not be homicide under existing laws.

115. *See supra* text accompanying notes 89-94.

116. *Id.*

117. *See* 2 J. FEINBERG, THE MORAL LIMITS OF THE CRIMINAL LAW: OFFENSE TO OTHERS 56-57 (1985). The desire to demonstrate such protection will depend on social, economic, medical, political, and other developments. At a time of growing willingness to terminate treatment for comatose, terminally ill, and severely handicapped persons, and to abort fetuses that are sentient or at advanced ages, many people might find it useful or reassuring to take a firm stance on such potent symbols of human life as embryos, in order to demonstrate that society still values human life highly, despite other actions that appear to denigrate it. David Ozar makes such an argument in Ozar, *The Case Against Thawing Unused Frozen Embryos*, 15 HASTINGS CENTER REP., Aug. 1985, at 7, 10-12.

living, human, and has the potential to become a person if transfer occurs, it activates sentiments in much the same way that dead persons and cadavers do.[118] Thus, as long as the basis for valuation is clear and embryos are not given the full respect accorded persons, it may be desirable to assign embryos a higher value than accorded to other extracorporeal human tissue in order to symbolize respect for human life. Such symbolizing is an essential part of any human community, and helps constitute and identify the community's values.[119]

But this process of symbolic valuation is optional and thus must be balanced against interests in procreative liberty. The benefits of symbolizing respect by restricting activities with preimplantation embryos need to be weighed against the costs of doing so, and a policy judgment thus made on that basis.[120] The following discussion of decisionmaking authority over embryos and the issues surrounding discard of, and research on, embryos illustrates this balancing process with respect to embryo status.

C. DECISIONMAKING AUTHORITY OVER EMBRYOS

The question of embryo status is clearly at issue in questions of decisionmaking authority over embryos. Decisionmaking authority involves questions of what can be done with embryos and who has the authority to make the choices that are available.

---

118. For a discussion of the symbolic meanings that can attach to cadavers and the dangers of excess symbolization or sentimentality, see Feinberg, *The Mistreatment of Dead Bodies*, 15 HASTINGS CENTER REP., Feb. 1985, at 31; May, *Religious Justifications for Donating Body Parts*, 15 HASTINGS CENTER REP., Feb. 1985, at 38. The controversy over whether the Elgin marbles in the British Museum should be returned to Greece also illustrates the importance of symbolic meaning—in this case the symbolic meaning of place in connection with an important cultural artifact. Merryman, *Thinking About the Elgin Marbles*, 83 MICH L. REV. 1881 (1985).

119. Although embryos do not have interests and therefore are not owed respect in their own right, a community may choose to hold the embryo "deserving of profound respect" in order to symbolize its regard for human life and persons generally. *See* Report of Ethics Advisory Board, *supra* note 46, at 35-56. Such symbolic lawmaking, however, may not be a sufficient ground to override fundamental constitutional rights, though it clearly provides a rational basis for legislation. *See supra* text accompanying notes 82-86.

120. Some living, human, genetically unique biological entities are better equipped or more likely to serve as effective symbols of respect for human life than are others. Gametes, on this view, are not as promising as embryos. It is difficult to envisage a society that would mourn the loss of an egg in menstruation or the loss of sperm in a nocturnal emission, or that would punish onanism as homicide. On the other hand, cadavers and brain-dead persons are well-equipped to serve symbolic functions, since they so starkly remind us of the life that has just passed.

Thus, the limits of acceptable activity with embryos will vary with the situation in which the question arises and public perceptions of the costs and benefits of embryo protection policies. Symbolic concerns might overwhelm a rational assessment, but it is likely that high costs will be taken into account in the policymaking process.

Within the limits of decisional discretion set by the state, it is reasonable to assume that the gamete providers have primary decisionmaking authority and that they are free to transfer their control to others. Between the person providing the body part and other parties, the courts are likely to recognize the person from whom the body part has come as the owner, or decisionmaking authority. Thus in disputes concerning control or disposition of embryos, the persons providing the gametes, rather than physicians or third parties, would have presumptive decisionmaking authority.[121] The gamete providers would have the right to consent to, or object to, activities with embryos formed by their gametes until they cede this control to others.

The more controversial question is whether there are substantive limits to the decisions that the gamete providers or their transferees may make about embryos. Although the gamete providers are the "owners" of the embryos as against others seeking to exercise control, are there limits on their ownership?[122] Clearly, policies concerning the options of transfer, donation, embryo research, storage, and discard can be made by the individual physicians, programs, and institutions offering IVF service, thus limiting the options actually available to gamete providers.[123] The question of the state's power to limit the authority of gamete providers on questions of discard and research is discussed in the next sections.

---

121. *See* N.Y. Times, July 20, 1978, at B12, col. 1. Just as one "owns" their own body and its parts vis-a-vis other persons, so gametes are owned by the parties providing them or their transferees. It follows that the embryo resulting from the fusion of gametes from two persons is owned by the persons providing the gametes. The gamete providers' wishes should control over the wishes of other parties, at least until they transfer that authority to other persons. The procreative significance of embryos to the gamete source also supports the law's likely assignment of primary decision-making authority over embryos to the gamete providers. No doubt wrongful interference with the gamete providers' disposition of embryos will lead to damage awards in appropriate cases.

It does not follow that transferees would have the same dispositional control that the original holder has. This will depend on whether the transferee's interest in the donated embryos is procreative, as it might be if donated so that a recipient might achieve pregnancy. Restrictions aimed at the transferee, however, might violate the procreative liberty either of the original grantor or of potential transferees. It is unclear, however, whether the grantor has a protected procreative interest in assigning full dispositional authority to another person, since the grantor's procreative interest might not include having another person exercise the same control. *See supra* text accompanying notes 77-81.

State restrictions on the transferee, however, might interfere with the procreative rights of persons who seek to acquire those embryos from the transferee for their own reproduction, thus giving the first transferee a derivative right to dispose of embryos and gametes.

122. *See infra* text accompanying notes 256-69.
123. *See infra* text accompanying notes 329-38.

D. Discard: Mandatory Embryo Donation and the Meaning of the Gene Link

Discard of unwanted embryos raises the question of embryo status and the substantive limits on the gamete providers' dispositional authority. No law now requires that all fertilized eggs and preimplantation embryos be transferred to a uterus.[124] However, a de facto policy against discarding embryos currently exists. To avoid controversy with right-to-life groups and gain hospital approval, most American IVF programs claim to transfer all fertilized eggs to a uterus.[125]

However, many occasions will arise in which the gamete providers or others with decisionmaking authority over embryos will want to discard embryos.[126] Most common is the situation in which transfer of several embryos to a woman's uterus runs the risk of multiple births.[127] Other occasions for discard will arise when embryos are frozen. Couples may die before the embryos are thawed or couples may want the unused embryos discarded rather than donated to others, in order to avoid the social and psychological complications of biological offspring. Discard of some embryos will also occur to avoid the birth of a handicapped child once the genetic makeup of the embryo can be identified.[128]

---

124. Some states have fetal research laws that could be interpreted to require transfer, though no enforcement seems to have occurred. *See* Quigley & Andrews, *Human In Vitro Fertilization and the Law*, 42 Fertility & Sterility 348, 349-50 (1984). These laws might not withstand the constitutional strict scrutiny suggested in this Article.

125. A typical IVF program will base acceptance into the program upon agreement that all embryos be transferred to the woman regardless of the embryos' condition. *See, e.g.*, Ethical Statement of St. David's Community Hospital In Vitro Fertilization Program. To avoid the dilemma described here, many programs will not aspirate more than five or six eggs, or will not fertilize more eggs than they plan to place in the uterus. The only acknowledged exception is for polyspermic eggs, which are certain to miscarry or lead to early neonatal death. Fertilization by more than one sperm gives the fertilized egg a third set of chromosomes, making it triploid rather than diploid, as is normal and essential for development. A triploid egg may develop, but most triploids abort spontaneously in early pregnancy and those that proceed to a live birth do not survive the neonatal period. Uchida & Freeman, *Triploidy and Chromosomes*, 151 Am. J. Obstetrics & Gynecology Jan. 1985, at 65.

126. For example, patients may change their minds, have accidents, or get sick during the 48 to 72 hours between egg retrieval and embryo transfer.

127. The risks of multiple gestation are to the mother and to the offspring. The mother may have to have a cesarean section, and may experience more complications during pregnancy. Multiple gestation leads to prematurity and a high neonatal mortality rate. The recent birth in California of septuplets after treatment with pergonal, an ovarian stimulation drug often used in IVF, illustrates these risks. *See* Lyons, *Father Says Multiple Births Were Not Aim of Treatment*, N.Y. Times, May 24, 1985, at A12, col. 4.

128. Pretransfer genetic screening techniques, in which one cell of a cleaving embryo is removed and examined, are likely to be developed, which will lead to more instances where a couple will refuse transfer of an embryo on genetic grounds.

The standard IVF regimen stimulates the ovaries to produce multiple eggs, which commonly leads to retrieval of seven or more eggs. Since recovered eggs vary in maturity, they may not all fertilize or cleave, but it is common to have five or more embryos to place. If storage or donation to another woman is not possible, it may be in the interest of the IVF patient to discard the excess embryos rather than have them placed in her uterus.[129]

Would a policy preventing the gamete providers from discarding embryos, when a willing recipient is available and hence no rearing duties would be imposed on them, violate the gamete providers' procreative rights?[130] At issue is their right to avoid biological procreation, rather than their right to procreate. Mandatory donation does not infringe the couple's right to procreate because it does not interfere with any actions designed to relieve infertility. It is their desire to destroy the embryo, not to create, store, and transfer it in order to reproduce, which is at issue here.[131]

Mandatory embryo donation does interfere with the gamete source's desire not to have lineal descendants, and thus raises the question of whether the fourteenth amendment protects against unwanted, anonymous, biological descendants.[132] The Supreme Court's birth control and

---

129. Discard or destruction are possible ways of describing the death of the embryo from nontransfer. The egg could be destroyed before it is finished dividing by flushing it down a drain. Or it could be said to be allowed to die, by not taking steps to save it by transfer, which suggests passive euthanasia by nontreatment, the equivalent of a "Do not resuscitate" order.

It is unclear how couples and doctors will react to discarding embryos. Will they grieve for their loss? Will bonding have occurred? Should embryo discard be marked by some ritual or ceremony? These questions have not yet been explored with regard to transferred embryos which do not implant. Couples may be extremely disappointed by the failure to achieve pregnancy, but it is not clear that they regard it as the death of an expected child to the extent that they do with miscarriage. *See supra* note 30. Attitudes on these issues may depend on whether other embryos are transferred, whether pregnancy occurs, and whether childrearing plans are completed. They will also depend upon moral views and attitudes toward human life and the embryo, attitudes which to a large extent are in the process of formation as society adapts to IVF technology.

130. Such a policy would not interfere with the woman's right to avoid gestation, because it does not force her to accept the embryo into her body. Rather, the issue is whether she can prevent someone else from accepting the embryo.

131. Such a law would burden the right to relieve infertility only in those cases where persons would be unwilling to try IVF because they would not have the option, once eggs were fertilized, to discard them. The knowledge that a child of one's genes could later result without the person's consent is unlikely to deter many people from use of IVF. The theoretic chance that some persons would be deterred probably does not amount to an infringement of the right to relieve infertility through IVF. *See* Whalen v. Roe, 429 U.S. 589 (1977) (prescription drug reporting requirement does not infringe fundamental right because it is not found to deter people from seeking medical advice).

132. This question forces us to consider the meaning of reproduction when its genetic, gestational, and rearing components are disaggregated and a particular component of reproduction is

abortion precedents are not directly on point, since the procreation sought to be avoided in those cases involved unwanted gestation or rearing, and not the possibility of an anonymous hereditary tie *tout court*.[133]

Mandatory embryo donation, however, does not impose unwanted gestation or rearing. The embryo is outside the body. It cannot be forcibly placed in the woman who provides the egg.[134] Nor will rearing duties be imposed. The couple will presumably never see, hear from nor indeed, even know whether a biological descendant was ever born.[135]

The claim of a right to avoid having an unknown descendant would have to be grounded in the importance of avoiding an unwanted biological link with offspring. Although the biological link at issue involves procreation, something more than the procreative label is necessary to establish a right. Whether an unwanted but unidentified biological link is sufficient to ground a right will depend upon the social and psychological significance which individuals and society place on the existence of lineal descendants when anonymity and no rearing obligations exist.

Persons may differ in their perception of the burdens entailed by such a link. Some persons might be exceedingly troubled by the knowledge that a person of their blood is "out there" raised by another and might experience guilt or an intense desire for contact that leaves them frustrated and angry.[136] Others might fear unwanted contact with genetic offspring. Although intended to be an anonymous link, offspring

---

isolated from the others. In this case it is the genetic tie, without more, that is at issue, the significance of which must now be considered in developing embryo discard policies.

133. *See, e.g.,* Roe v. Wade, 410 U.S. 113 (1973). Since Commonwealth v. Edelin, 371 Mass. 497, 359 N.E.2d 159 (1976), it has been well-established that doctors doing a lawful abortion that could cause the death of a fetus have a duty to rescue viable fetuses that are born alive in the abortion procedure. The woman's right to remove the fetus from her body does not give her the right to control disposition, if it emerges alive, even if its survival will lead to an unwanted genetic link that causes the mother suffering and psychological discomfort. The discomfort in such a case may be considerably greater than would occur with the existence of a child born from an unwanted but mandatory embryo donation. Morever, the situation is different because the live-born abortus may independently have rights that arise from its more advanced development thus justifying overriding the mother's wish to avoid a genetic tie.

134. If a woman may remove an implanted embryo by abortion, it would follow that she could refuse transfer of the embryo to her in the first place.

135. Of course, the system may not work perfectly, and information about biologic parenthood may become available to the genetic parents or offspring.

136. A powerful example of the emotional meaning and attachment of the genetic link is captured in John Updike's *Rabbit is Rich*, when he describes Rabbit Angstrom's sneaking onto property of a former lover to see if he can find signs of a daughter that he thinks he might have fathered. J. UPDIKE, RABBIT IS RICH (1981). A comic treatment of the same issue appears in the 1984 French film, *Les Comperes*. A woman concerned about her runaway teenage son and frustrated by her

may discover the identity of their genetic parents and wish to make contact, form a relationship, or seek financial support.[137] Any of these events could set off powerful psychological tremors of obligation and guilt. For other persons, however, the genetic link alone may have little or no negative impact and may even be a source of satisfaction once established.[138]

In assessing a claim of a right to avoid having unknown descendants, the Supreme Court would have to weigh the importance of avoiding a genetic link *tout court* against the symbolic benefits of attempting to rescue and transfer every embryo. It is possible that the Supreme Court would find it within the state's power to implement laws reflecting such a policy. The Court has been willing to construe narrowly the rearing rights of absent illegitimate fathers, despite the biologic tie.[139] If no gestational or rearing obligations are imposed, the Court may find that there is no fundamental right to prevent unknown lineal descendants.[140]

However the Supreme Court decides this question, the state would have the power to prevent the discard of embryos when the protected procreative interest is not directly at stake, such as where the gamete sources are unknown or dead.[141] It might also prevent discard when the

---

husband's complacency enlists the help of two lovers of 17 years previous. She tells them that unbeknownst to them at the time, they had impregnated her and she now needs their help in finding the son. Each man finds the sudden revelation of the existence of a son to be quite powerful and leaps to her assistance. When they learn that the other is a competitor for being the father, they compete with each other to establish paternity by the zeal of their rescue efforts.

137. *See infra* text accompanying notes 256-69.

138. Some persons might be proud, or find it satisfying, that they have genetic heirs about in the world. After all, they have replicated more of their genes than have others. Some such motivation may operate with sperm donors, who may find the ability to transfer their genes to be as powerful an incentive as payment for sperm donation. *See* Annas, *Fathers Anonymous: Beyond the Best Interest of the Sperm Donor*, 14 FAM. L. Q. 1 (1980).

139. *See* Lehr v. Robertson, 463 U.S. 248 (1983); Parham v. Hughes, 441 U.S. 347 (1979).

140. A parallel though not exactly analogous situation would be mandatory or presumed consent organ donation laws. A family that is not asked or that opposes donation of a deceased member's organs may feel aggrieved by use of body parts without their consent. However, in that case no ongoing, unwanted genetic link is imposed.

141. The relation between reproductive liberty and posthumous embryo donations is discussed *infra* text accompanying notes 194-97. The right to control by will the disposition of embryos and gametes depends upon the extent to which reproductive meaning and satisfactions that underlie the right to procreate are present in testamentary disposition of gametes and embryos.

An example of rescue of "orphan" embryos arose in the case of Mario and Elsa Rios, deceased "parents" of two frozen embryos widely reported in the press and media. The situation raised the issue of whether frozen embryos should be discarded or donated when the gamete providers had died without leaving instructions and a substantial inheritance was at stake. Embryo Destruction Blocked in Australia, Austin American Statesman, Oct. 24, 1984, at 1, col. 1; Australia Dispute Arises on Embryos, N.Y. Times, June 22, 1984, at A30, col. 4; New Issue in Embryo Case Raised Over Use of Donor, N.Y. Times, June 21, 1984, at A16, col. 1.

two gamete providers disagree about disposition. As long as the unwilling partner is not forced into gestational or rearing burdens, the partner wishing to procreate might be given priority over the partner wishing to avoid biological offspring.[142]

Even if the state or IVF programs have the constitutional authority to insist on transfer or donation of all embryos, the wisdom and desirability of mandatory embryo donation policies can be questioned. Given the powerful meanings aroused by biological offspring, creating biological offspring against a person's wishes should require a very strong justification. Since the rights of embryos are not violated by discard, imposing unwanted biological offspring on a person seems a heavy price to pay for a symbolic statement of commitment to human life generally. It seems more desirable to leave the question of disposition of excess embryos to the gamete providers, just as disposition of cadavers is left to next of kin.[143]

E. RESEARCH WITH EMBRYOS

Embryo research also raises questions of embryo status. Research with embryos is essential to further progress in IVF and other forms of infertility treatment. It could also provide useful knowledge about birth defects, contraception, cancer, and a wide range of other important topics.[144] Yet many people object to embryo research as wrong or undesirable. The controversy over embryo research illustrates the need to be clear about one's reasons for valuing embryos and limiting activities with them.

Concerns about embryo research depend upon whether the embryo will then be destroyed or transferred to a uterus. If transferred, the question of embryo research raises a question of prenatal rights of offspring, for the research could directly affect the well-being of offspring. The right of a couple to risk harm to offspring by prenatal manipulation is

---

142. It is not certain that the Court would give priority to the partner wanting genes transferred. However, it would not be unreasonable for the Court to find that this interest was more worthy of protection than the interest in avoiding gene transfer. Since unwanted gestation and rearing are not imposed, cases denying the father or spouse a veto over a woman's wish for an abortion would not control. *See, e.g.,* Planned Parenthood v. Danforth, 482 U.S. 52 (1976).

143. The situations are not exactly parallel. However, the case for mandatory embryo donation seems weaker than the case for mandatory treatment of a live-born abortus when the aborting mother wishes the abortus not to be treated, *see supra* note 133, or than the case for mandatory organ donation, where the life or death of another person may be directly at stake.

144. Robertson, *Embryo Research*, 24 W. ONTARIO L. REV. 15, 17 (1986).

discussed in the next section.[145]

If no transfer will occur, we again confront the issue of the respect due a nontransferred preimplantation embryo. As we have seen, the fertilized egg is insufficiently developed to be owed respect in its own right. It is not sentient, lacks a brain, and does not yet have even the rudiments of a nervous system. Limits on embryo research can no more be based on the independent interests of the embryo than can mandatory embryo donation be justified on this ground.

Research limits, however, can be justified as a symbolic statement about society's attitude toward human life. Although embryos may not have rights as such, our treatment of them may demonstrate respect for human dignity or human life generally. Certain manipulations may seem unacceptably instrumental or offensive precisely because they are done to living human cells that have the potential, if transferred to a uterus, to become a person. Limiting research maneuvers, even when implantation is not intended, may be a meaningful way of demonstrating respect for human life.

Legislative restrictions on embryo research, intended to demonstrate respect for human life, would easily satisfy the rational basis test.[146] It is unclear, however, whether stricter scrutiny would be required. Research limits would arguably interfere with a fundamental right to procreate if the banned research sought knowledge essential to reproductive decisions. Since embryo research would be most useful in improving the efficacy of IVF, developing contraceptives, and preventing handicapped births, a close link with reproductive choice might be established.[147] In that case, a symbolic demonstration of respect by limiting research on nontransferred embryos might be invalid.

---

145. Of course, if the embryo would not be transferred unless the research had occurred, banning transfer after research does not help the embryo, for it would never come into being at all. Banning transfer after research, however, would not violate the embryo's right to be born, because it has none. By the same token, such a ban would not violate the couple's right, since they have no right to bring the embryo into the world damaged, when a healthy birth is possible, even if a ban on transfer after research would deter them from reproducing at all. *See supra* note 102.

146. *See* Maher v. Roe, 432 U.S. 464, 478 (1976) (state's interest in prenatal, postconception life during first two trimesters of pregnancy provides rational basis for state action).

147. The constitutionality of laws limiting embryo research directed at improving the treatment of infertility, reducing birth defects, or developing better contraception would depend upon the extent to which they interfere with procreative choice. Banning such research might deprive persons of information essential for their reproductive decisionmaking. Prohibiting embryo research thus might be found to interfere with the fundamental right to procreate or to avoid procreation. *See* Robertson, *The Scientist's Right to Research: A Constitutional Analysis*, 51 S. CAL. L. REV. 1203, 1212-14 (1978). If so, some interest other than a moral or symbolic concern with showing respect for human life would be necessary to justify the interference.

If restrictions on embryo research are not found to interfere with procreative liberty, their desirability is a policy question to be settled by the political process. Observation and manipulation of nontransferred embryos could produce important knowledge about infertility and its treatment, the origin and prevention of birth defects, improvements in contraceptives, and the replacement of adult tissue and organs.[148]

Given the gains from embryo research, the case for banning all embryo research is not compelling. The Ethical Advisory Board in 1979, in the first systematic look at the ethical issues of IVF, concluded that research with embryos for valid scientific purposes, after appropriate review, was consistent with respect for the embryo.[149] A majority of the Warnock Committee also found embryo research to be morally acceptable,[150] as have most of the other advisory bodies that have examined the issue.[151] Since embryos do not have the moral status of persons, using them as a means to further knowledge does not violate norms against research on persons without their consent.[152] The judgment is reasonably made that the expected benefits of research outweigh the symbolic gain in respect for human life that a ban on all embryo research seeks.

The advisory committees in the United States, Great Britain, and Australia that have examined embryo research, however, have consistently agreed that certain limits on research procedures are justified.[153] A brief discussion of two issues—the length of extracorporeal gestation and the source of embryos used in research—illustrates again how judgments of embryo status and symbolic meaning animate the embryo research debate.

The advisory committees, for example, consistently agree that embryos should not be maintained in culture for more than fourteen days, a conservative estimate of when implantation begins and the embryonic axis, along which the neuromuscular structure of the body will evolve, first appears.[154] This line is intended to avoid the possibility of doing research on an embryo that possesses a rudimentary nervous system and

---

148. Editorial, *Embryo Research*, LANCET, Feb. 2, 1985, at 255-56; Timmins, *Five Reasons for Embryo Research*, The Times (London), Feb. 13, 1985, at 13, col. 2.

149. Report of Ethics Advisory Board, *supra* note 46, at 35-57.

150. WARNOCK COMMITTEE REPORT, *supra* note 46, at 64-67.

151. *See* WALTERS, *supra* note 108, at 215-27.

152. *See* G. ANNAS, L. GLANTZ & B. KATZ, INFORMED CONSENT TO HUMAN EXPERIMENTATION: THE SUBJECT'S DILEMMA 75-93, 139-83 (1977) (discussion of issues surrounding consent to experimentation on minors and mentally infirm).

153. *See* Robertson, *supra* note 144, at 28-30, 33-35.

154. *Id.* at 33-35.

thus might be injured, as well as to symbolize respect for the embryo and potential persons generally.

Drawing the line at fourteen days, however, may be unnecessarily conservative. The emergence of the embryonic axis does not mean that the brain has formed or that the capacity for feeling or experience exists. Rather, it marks the beginning of the developmental structure that several weeks later will result in the brain and feeling capacity. Formation of the embryonic axis is still so distant from formation of a functioning nervous system that extending the line to twenty or even twenty-five days would prevent harm to embryos and honor symbolic concerns while allowing additional, useful research to occur.[155]

The ethical controversy over the source of embryos used for research also illustrates the symbolic nature of the embryo research debate. One appropriate source of research embryos may be spare embryos left over from an IVF treatment cycle.[156] However, few spares may be available, since most embryos will be used by the source or donated to others to achieve pregnancy. In addition, spare embryos may be less healthy than those which are transferred, thus making them an unsuitable research vehicle. Moreover, this position would ban all research on gametes and fertilization methods that end in the creation of an embryo.[157] An alternative source would be embryos created solely for research purposes from donated sperm and from eggs donated by women undergoing IVF treatment or other abdominal surgery or recruited solely for donative purposes.

A controversy over creating embryos solely for research purposes has developed in Great Britain and Australia. A majority of the Waller Committee[158] and a minority of the Warnock Commission found "it

---

155. Since so little embryo research is now being conducted, it is difficult to be more than tentative about this argument. Much will depend upon the benefits of research beyond 14 days and also upon more accurate and precise information about the state of embryo development in the period beyond 14 days. The point is that the first appearance of the primitive streak should not be sacred, if a strong need to conduct research beyond that point can be shown.

156. Since ovarian stimulation will usually produce more eggs than can be safely transferred, embryos that would otherwise be discarded or not transferred could be used for research, either immediately or after a period of storage shows that the source no longer wants them transferred. Since embryo research is permissible, it is appropriate to use them, with the consent of the source and in accordance with other research restrictions.

157. *See* Robertson, *supra* note 144, at 35-36.

158. WALLER COMMITTEE, *supra* note 46, at 18.

would be morally wrong to bring human embryos into being for the purpose of research."[159]

Like other issues of embryo research, this controversy concerns a conflict between the need to acquire useful knowledge and the need to demonstrate respect for human dignity. Given the wide consensus that the embryo itself has no right to be transferred and no right not to be used in research (except when transfer will occur), conflict over the source of research embryos quite clearly implicates judgments of embryo status and the symbolic meanings that attach to embryos. Resolution of the issue entails a policy judgment that compares the need for, and benefits of, such a symbol against the loss in knowledge that a ban on deliberate creation of embryos for research would entail.[160]

The Warnock Committee's approval of deliberately creating embryos for research is a sound position for a national body defining research standards, and is likely to be followed elsewhere. Given the scientific benefits and the symbolic costs, it seems best to leave persons and physicians discretion to create research embryos with gametes over which they have lawful control.[161] Persons are free to refuse to donate egg and sperm to create research embryos, and are free not to participate in such research themselves. But personal beliefs about the appropriate uses of donated gametes should not prevent other persons from giving gametes to create embryos for research purposes. The symbolic gain from such a position is too small, and the cost to science too great.

F. Embryos as Organ Sources

A brief word about the use of embryos as a source for tissue and organs for transplant is also in order. Certain anatomical structures, such as the insulin-producing islets of the pancreas and the blood-producing cells of the liver, develop very early in embryos and could provide a much needed source of transplantable tissue and organs.[162] Transplant

---

159. WARNOCK COMMITTEE REPORT, *supra* note 46, at 67. Deliberate creation for some people symbolizes a disregard or denigration of human life, for a potential person is created to be then used and discarded. Others object because they hold the widely rejected human subject view of embryo status.

160. Persons who find that deliberate creation of embryos for research purposes is unacceptable cannot hold this view on the basis of actual harm to the embryos involved, since they are willing to permit research with spare, nontransferred embryos. If spare embryos are not harmed by research, it would be inconsistent to hold that deliberately created embryos are harmed.

161. *See supra* text accompanying notes 121-23.

162. For an example of the use of fetal tissue for transplants in connection with the Chernobyl nuclear disaster, see Schmeck, *Fetal Tissue Is Alternative to Marrow Transplants*, N.Y. Times, May 15, 1986, at 8, col. 1 (Midwest edition).

of embryonic tissue is especially attractive, because rejection by the recipient is less likely to occur.

Could the state ban creating or growing embryos for transplant purposes? The issues are similar to the ones discussed under embryo research, and initially would arise as a question of research, as the safety and efficacy of such transplants are established. Since procreative liberty is not implicated, the question is one of policy and the weight that one attaches to the burdens and benefits of such a ban.

A key issue is whether such use would injure or harm the the embryo in its own right. The answer depends upon the embryo's stage of development. To yield usable tissue, extracorporeal gestation beyond fourteen days will probably have to occur, with full development of the embryonic axis and early neurostructures. However, as long as the neurological development essential for sentience has not been achieved, harvesting embryonic tissue would not harm embryos, since they are still too rudimentary to have interests. As the embryo becomes a fetus and approaches the minimal conditions for sentience, harm to the embryo fetus in its own right becomes a serious concern. At some point removing tissue and organs would harm an entity that itself deserves respect.[163]

If the embryo itself is not at risk, the question is whether "farming" embryos for tissue symbolizes a disregard or denigration of human dignity, a similarly troubling feature of embryo research. The willingness to use a living human entity that ordinarily has the potential to become a person for instrumental ends may be perceived as degrading to human dignity, even though the entity is not itself harmed and would not otherwise be transferred. The more developed the embryonic entity, the greater the symbolic harm from using it. Farming very early embryos, say up to twenty days of development, might cause insufficient symbolic harm to outweigh the benefits that accrue to persons from embryonic transplants. It is possible, however, that the symbolic harm from using embryos at later stages short of sentience would outweigh the benefits sought and appropriately, would be banned.

---

163. The issue relates to use of nonviable aborted fetuses for research or as sources for transplantable organs. The stage of development of the human entity from which the organ or tissue is retrieved will be determinative. Some persons may also object to the deliberate creation of an embryo or fetus for this purpose. *See generally Can the Fetus Be an Organ Farm?*, 8 HASTINGS CENTER REP., Oct. 1978, at 23 (commentaries by M. Warren, D. Maguire and C. Levine debating the propriety of transplant of kidneys from purposefully conceived and aborted fetuses).

IV. PROTECTION OF OFFSPRING

Some of the concern about noncoital reproduction arises from fears of its potential for harm to offspring. It is commonly assumed that noncoital reproduction could and should be restricted if offspring were to suffer significant physical or psychosocial damage from their mode of conception. This section examines some normative and legal issues that arise in assessing the impact of noncoital reproduction on offspring.

A. REPRODUCTIVE RESPONSIBILITY AND HARM TO OFFSPRING

The assumption that reproductive techniques that produce damaged or unhappy children are unethical and should be banned has intuitive appeal. But the bounds of reproductive responsibility have never been clearly defined, and there are complications lurking beneath the surface.[164] Before we assess the need to limit noncoital procreation on this basis, we must be clear about how noncoital procreative choices could harm offspring.

1. *Avoidable and Unavoidable Damage*

A key distinction is the avoidability of the harm to the offspring. If the child can be born healthy, then clearly it is a wrong to use techniques that cause the child to be born damaged.[165] Just as parents must refrain from harming children after birth, they have a responsibility—arising from their choice to reproduce—to avoid causing harm by prenatal, preimplantation, or even preconception actions.[166]

---

164. Reproductive responsibility has been most closely considered with regard to population control. *See supra* note 53. However, the question of obligation to avoid having handicapped children has recently drawn attention, because of advances in genetic screening, prenatal diagnosis, and fetal therapy. The ability to detect severe handicaps before birth thus raises questions of obligation to undergo such testing, to obtain available treatments or even to terminate such pregnancies. *See supra* text accompanying note 102; Johnsen, *The Creation of Fetal Rights: Conflicts with Women's Constitutional Rights to Liberty, Privacy and Equal Protection,* 95 YALE L.J. 599, 614-15 (1986) (discussing state regulation of pregnant women's actions as threat to the "right to be left alone").

165. Children who are going to be born have prenatal, preimplantation, and even preconceptual rights not to be subjected to avoidable harm. *See supra* text accompanying note 102; *see also* Feinberg, *Wrongful Conception and the Right Not to Be Harmed,* 1 HARV. J. L. & PUB. POL'Y 57 (1985); Robertson, *Toward Rational Boundaries of Tort Liability for Injury to the Unborn: Prenatal Injuries, Preconception Injuries and Wrongful Life,* 1978 DUKE L.J. 1401.

166. A person who has a right not to be injured by prenatal or preconception actions of another also has this right against parents. The demise of intrafamilial immunity makes possible suits by children against parents, including mothers, for prenatal negligence. Grodin v. Grodin, 102 Mich. App. 396, 301 N.W.2d 869 (1980). For a discussion of this case and its implications, see Robertson, *supra* note 79, at 437-42. However, the theoretic possibility of tort liability does not justify the wide range of state restrictions on behavior during pregnancy that some have proposed. *Id.*

Risking damage to offspring would not seem to wrong the offspring if it were not possible for them to be conceived or born without undergoing the risk of damage. If the only possible means of conception or implantation also risks damaging offspring, no wrong to offspring occurs with use of that means.[167] Avoiding the damage means avoiding the birth of the child. From the child's perspective, the risk-creating activity is welcome, since there is no alternative way for this child to be born.

This is not to deny the theoretic possibility of a wrongful life claim by offspring against parents and physicians in a very extreme case. If the damage that is inextricably linked to conception or birth is so severe, so fraught with pain and suffering, that the child might find death preferable, then it might wrong the child to allow birth to occur at all. Such cases are theoretically possible, for we recognize the reasonableness of adult decisions to forego living and also recognize that medical treatments, even feeding, can be withheld from severely ill infants and adults.[168] If life is so burdensome that sustaining it wrongs the child, the remedy—indeed, the obligation—would be to cease all sustaining efforts once such a birth occurs.

While the concept of wrongful life may be valid and coherent (although the courts remain confused on the issue),[169] it will have limited reach in assessing the impact of noncoital reproduction. In most instances the damage at issue is unavoidable if conception or birth is to occur at all, since it is inextricably linked with the mode of conception. From the perspective of the offspring, alienation, genetic bewilderment, even a physical handicap, is preferable to no existence when the damage

---

167. This statement is qualified by the discussion of wrongful life in the following paragraph.

168. J. ROBERTSON, THE RIGHTS OF THE CRITICALLY ILL (1984); *see also* Child Abuse Amendments of 1984, Pub. L. No. 98-457, 42 U.S.C. §§ 5101-03 (Supp. 1985). As these sources make clear, a choice that further life is not in the person's interest can be inferred or imputed to incompetent persons, as well as honored when made by competent adults.

169. *See* Robertson, *In Vitro Conception and Harm to the Unborn*, 8 HASTINGS CENTER REP., Oct 1978, at 13. While the courts have allowed parents to recover damages, they have invariably rejected wrongful life suits by handicapped children. However, recently the California, Washington, and New Jersey Supreme Courts allowed children to recover special but not general damages on a claim of wrongful life in situations in which their parents were able to recover both special and general damages for the child's birth. *See* Turpin v. Sortini, 31 Cal. 3d 220, 643 P.2d 954, 182 Cal. Rptr. 337 (1982); Procanik v. Cillo, 97 N.J. 339, 478 A.2d 755 (1984); Harbeson v. Parke-Davis, 98 Wash. 2d 460, 656 P.2d 483 (1983). Perhaps the results in these cases are defensible as a means to assure that the tortfeasor internalizes the full cost of the tort. However, the cases are confused about the meaning of wrongful life and inconsistent within their own terms, because they do not allow the child recovery for general damages. If the child has been wronged by being born, then such damages also should be awarded. However, they should cover only the period before the decision to withhold sustaining care, which, if life is truly "wrongful," should be made as soon as possible. Generally, these distinctions have escaped the courts and the critical commentary on wrongful life.

and birth of the child is unavoidable. Unavoidable prenatal injury so severe as to constitute, from the child's perspective, "wrongful life" is highly unlikely with noncoital conception.[170] If it did occur, the remedy and obligation would be to limit further damage by immediately ceasing all sustaining efforts.

2. *Unavoidable Damage: Burdens on Others*

In addition to harming the child, producing a damaged child when a healthy one is not possible could harm other persons, if the parents are unable or unwilling to rear the child. The burdens could be financial— the need for taxpayers to subsidize medical and educational costs. Or rearing burdens could be directly imposed, when the parents are unwilling to care for offspring. If reproduction without damage is not possible and other persons will be left with the costs or burdens of rearing, should one still be free to reproduce?

One could argue that persons should not, in order to satisfy their procreative desires, be free to risk imposing rearing burdens on others.[171] Even if the child is not harmed, the harm to other people deserves consideration. At the present time the state has no legal obligation to provide infertility services to indigents (e.g., Medicaid need not pay for infertility treatment).[172] Therefore, the state would have no obligation to subsidize reproduction indirectly by allowing procreative behavior that imposes substantial costs on others.

Indeed, the argument for either a direct or indirect subsidy would be strongest only where the person is willing to rear the desired offspring.

---

170. Further evidence of judicial confusion in the wrongful life cases is the tendency to deem relatively mild (in comparison to what could occur) handicaps sufficient to constitute wrongful life. *See Turpin*, 31 Cal. 3d at 220, 643 P.2d at 954, 182 Cal. Rptr. at 337; *Procanik*, 97 N.J. at 339, 478 A.2d at 755. The congenital deafness in *Turpin* and Down's Syndrome in *Procanik*, while serious for the parents and children involved, hardly seem of a severity to render the child's life not worth living. Similarly, even if noncoital reproduction leads to a higher rate of congenital anomalies or psychosocial difficulties, the defects may fall far short of what would be necessary to establish a truly wrongful life.

171. Of course, a qualifying term such as "unduly" or "unreasonably" should be inserted here. Some risks are acceptable, if they are small and the chances of reproducing a healthy child are great. As the risk rises, however, it may reach a point where it is unreasonable to seek a healthy child, given that the risk of a handicap, and hence burdens on others, is so great.

172. One could argue that such subsidies should be given, on the theory that reproduction is so central to personal fulfillment that everyone should be provided with the means to enjoy it. Even though infertility patients are now lobbying for health insurance coverage for IVF with some success, it is unlikely that state coverage of infertility services for indigents will be required by the fourteenth amendment. *See* Dresser, *supra* note 6, at 168-69.

At the present time, few persons would find creating a biological descendant or gestating a child without rearing to be so important to individual identity to warrant state subsidization of this partial reproductive experience.[173]

However, willingness to rear damaged offspring would not necessarily create an obligation on the part of the state or others to provide the needed subsidy by permitting access to the damage-engendering techniques. The risk of bias or overbroad applications makes any direct state prohibition on procreative choice undesirable on policy grounds.[174] Yet a ban on access by persons unable to cover rearing costs in the event of damage to offspring might be constitutional, since they have no right to impose such costs on others.[175]

Analytically, then, the concern about protecting offspring is considerably more problematic than first apparent. The risks of noncoital reproduction to offspring would seldom rise to the level of wrongful life, because the likely damage rarely approaches such severity. In any event, there is no way for the offspring to be born undamaged when the damage is linked to the noncoital technique itself.

As a result, it may not be possible to ban noncoital techniques completely because of harm to offspring. Regulation to reduce the risk of avoidable harm is proper and desirable, but a total ban on the technique would interfere with procreative choice without benefit to offspring who would not be conceived at all if the ban existed. However, banning noncoital techniques to prevent financial or rearing burdens to others

---

173. The value of reproduction in such circumstances is one of the questions of the scope of procreative liberty that has not yet had to be confronted. Of course, most people would not be interested in having a handicapped child that they will not rear, solely for the pleasure of gene transfer or gestation. However, they might be willing to run such a risk in order to obtain a healthy child.

174. The danger is that less powerful and stigmatized groups will have their reproductive freedom limited. The history of eugenic sterilization of the mentally ill is illustrative. *See* Buck v. Bell, 274 U.S. 200 (1927); North Carolina Ass'n for Retarded Children v. North Carolina, 420 F. Supp. 451 (M.D.N.C. 1976); *In re* Cavitt, 182 Neb. 712, 157 N.W.2d 171 (1968); *In re* Grady, 85 N.J. 235, 426 A.2d 467 (1981). A further danger is that ill-considered and unnecessary measures will be enacted, reflecting prejudice or misguided good will. The plea for state-imposed behavioral restrictions on maternal behavior during pregnancy illustrates this. *See supra* note 164.

175. Such a position would make wealth the criteria for access to unavoidably risky reproductive technologies. If the couple were willing to pay the full costs of rearing the handicapped child, they would injure no one in undertaking the unavoidable risk of damage. Infertile persons without the means to cover the cost of a handicapped birth would not have the same option to use unavoidably risky techniques to relieve infertility. Of course, wealth discrimination in access to infertility treatments such as IVF already exists. But discrimination that results from state action prohibiting use of noncoital techniques, as opposed to failure to fund them, may be less acceptable in a society ostensibly committed to equal protection of the law.

could be justified.[176]

B. The Risks to Offspring of Noncoital Conception

Noncoital reproduction may pose both physical and psychosocial risks to offspring. IVF, embryo transfer, freezing, and other embryo manipulations may induce physical damage in offspring. The risk of infectious or genetic disease exists with donor insemination. Noncoital techniques may also pose psychosocial risks, such as might occur from lengthy storage of embryos or the use of gamete donors and surrogates. When analyzed in terms of harm, however, the protection of offspring does not appear to be a sufficient ground for state prohibitions on private sector use of these techniques.

1. *Physical Risks: Handicapped or Damaged Offspring*

The question of physical damage to offspring must be distinguished from the question of damage to gametes and embryos. External manipulation, freezing and thawing, embryo biopsy, and the like may damage the embryo, destroying cells and rendering the embryo less likely to develop, implant, and successfully complete pregnancy.[177] While these maneuvers may make pregnancy less likely, efficiency of reproduction is not an issue of offspring protection.

The concern for offspring assumes that noncoital techniques will be efficient enough to initiate pregnancy and produce offspring, but fears that the resulting offspring will be physically handicapped or damaged have not proven accurate. IVF, as presently practiced, has shown no higher rate of congenital deformity than occurs with coital reproduction.[178] Nor has psychological harm in the offspring caused by the site of fertilization been uncovered.[179]

---

176. The point is one about constitutional law and the limits of state power when procreative choice imposes costs on others. As a practical matter, the issue will not arise as long as the current wealth-based system of providing infertility services exists. However, even if the state-funded infertility services for indigents, it might not choose to fund services that had a high risk of producing damaged offspring, because of the additional rearing costs involved.

177. Freezing embryos, for example, often destroys some of the blastomeres, though this does not necessarily mean that further development and implantation after thawing is not possible. *See* Mohr, Trounson & Freemann, *supra* note 34, at 3-7.

178. *See* Grobstein, Flower & Mendeloff, *supra* note 4, at 130.

179. The evidence for serious psychological harm is speculative, for no studies of psychological effects have yet been done. One feared harm is the psychological effect of knowing that one was conceived in a test tube and not a fallopian tube. The first births by IVF in a community may well have celebrity status, though not the status of Louise Brown, the first IVF baby, who made it to the cover of *Time*. Later births will be routine and hardly of interest. If one's site of conception were

However, the question of physical risk with IVF variations, such as freezing and thawing of sperm, eggs, and embryos, embryo biopsy, and other manipulations cannot yet be ruled out. Although the natural inefficiency of human reproduction suggests that those embryos hardy enough to survive manipulation and implant and go to term will not be handicapped, the possibility remains until more experience establishes a low risk of teratogenic effects. Is it ethical and legal to transfer manipulated embryos to a uterus when little data exists as to potential outcome?

The problem is similar to that faced by the first physicians attempting IVF. They could not be sure that developmental malformations would not occur. Indeed, noted ethicists had argued that IVF was unethical because of the risk that the resulting children might be born damaged.[180] They condemned the selfishness of couples who were so bent on having children that they were willing to risk the birth of handicapped children.[181] No doubt the same charges could be levelled at persons willing to extend IVF techniques, such as the cryopreservation of eggs and embryos, and the wider use of donor eggs, embryos and surrogates.

Yet transferring embryos and thus risking damaged offspring in such cases cannot be condemned on grounds of protection of offspring, because transferred embryos have no alternative way to be born without risk of damage. The offspring have no grounds for wrongful life suits against their parents or the physicians involved, because the damage was

---

known and stigma attached to IVF, the child might suffer the ridicule of peers. P. SINGER & D. WELLS, *supra* note 41, at 49-51. However, it does not appear that IVF conception is, or will be, stigmatizing. Moreover, the site of one's conception is normally a private matter, possibly not even known by the child. Even if the child knew, and the knowledge complicated parent-child relations, from the child's perspective the harm would not make the alternative of foregoing IVF conception altogether preferable, for the harm is inextricably bound up with the child's conception.

180.   *See* R. MCCORMICK, *supra* note 66, at 330-33; P. RAMSEY, FABRICATED MAN 22-52, 112-51 (1970); Kass, *Making Babies — The New Biology and the "Old" Morality*, 26 PUB. INTEREST 18, 19-30, 48-49, 55-56 (1972); Kass, *"Making Babies" Revisited*, 54 PUB. INTEREST 32, 34-48 (1979); Ramsey, *Manufacturing Our Offspring: Weighing the Risks*, 8 HASTINGS CENTER REP., Oct. 1978, at 7; Tiefel, *Human In Vitro Fertilization: A Conservative View*, 247 J. A.M.A. 3235, 3237-39 (1982).

181.   The selfishness of couples willing to use methods that risk harm to children or others is a recurring theme in the literature of IVF. *See* Kass, *Making Babies — The New Biology and the "Old" Morality, supra* note 180, at 48-49, 55-56; Kass, *"Making Babies" Revisited, supra* note 180, at 45-46. This argument overlooks the absence of harm to offspring when a healthy birth is not possible, and the fact that few people will be willing to use noncoital techniques if there is a high risk of damaged offspring, particularly if they must cover the costs of rearing. A further variation of the selfishness argument is the claim that it is wrong to use expensive medical techniques to reproduce when there are plenty of minority and handicapped children waiting for adoption. Yet, this argument would apply to any infertility treatment, indeed, to any couple choosing to conceive coitally rather than adopt those children.

unavoidable.[182]

Yet asking the parties to bear the cost of harm they incur is also reasonable, and could be a sufficient ground for restricting use of the technique. If the risk is not taken, the offspring will never be born. But if the risk is taken, other persons might be harmed by the necessity to care for resulting offspring. If couples are willing to risk a handicapped birth with a new technique in order to procreate, they could be required to cover the costs that might be entailed. Their procreative liberty would not extend to imposing rearing costs on others, even if the offspring were not wronged as a result.[183] This analysis may be illustrated by two situations involving IVF that present the possibility of some physical risk to offspring.

a. *Embryo transfer after research*: Attempts to improve IVF or treat genetic defects will eventually require experimental transfers of manipulated embryos to a uterus. Yet frequently, statements are made to the effect that it is unethical to transfer an embryo after experimentation.[184]

The strongest case for a charge of unethical or irresponsible conduct would be where the research manipulations appear likely to harm potential offspring. As we have seen, however, if the embryo used in the research would otherwise have been destroyed or not transferred, transfer would not necessarily wrong the offspring. It is not injured if it could not otherwise be born undamaged. Transfer in such a case could injure the persons who end up bearing the costs of caring for the handicapped offspring, and might appear unduly callous. Since procreative liberty probably would not include the right to harm others in this way, such transfers would be unethical and could be prohibited.[185]

---

182. One cannot predict how the courts that have found a limited wrongful life recovery would handle such cases. If the point of the suit is to assure that those responsible bear the full costs of rearing, then a suit against parents who are trying to shift rearing burdens to others might be successful. However, it does not appear that courts would award offspring general damages for having been born damaged as a result of noncoital reproduction. *See supra* note 169.

183. *See supra* text accompanying notes 146-55.

184. Most of the authoritative bodies that have made recommendations on embryo research have opposed embryo transfer after research, perhaps because they have had in mind embryo transfer after nontherapeutic research. *See* Robertson, *Embryo Research, supra* note 144, at 28-30.

185. If the researchers or other persons making decisions were willing to bear the rearing costs entailed, this problem would be eliminated. Presumably, however, the researchers do not intend to rear the child and thus have no clearly protected procreative interest in bringing a damaged child into the world.

In many cases, however, transfer after research would be ethical and, indeed, required by procreative liberty, since it enhances the possibility of a healthy birth and imposes no costs on others. The ethics of embryo transfer depend upon an assessment of the risks and benefits of the transfer to offspring (and hence others). If there is a reasonable basis for thinking that the research maneuver will enable offspring to be born healthy (e.g., if it were treatment for a genetic defect or if it made implantation and successful pregnancy more likely), the transfer should be permitted.[186] Of course, prior review to assure that these judgments are reasonably made would be desirable.[187]

      b.   *Embryo transfer after freezing and thawing*: The ethics of embryo transfer after freezing and thawing may be analyzed similarly. The first attempts at transfer after thawing are necessarily experimental. Until the practice occurs, there is no way to tell whether it is safe and effective, although animal studies suggest that it is.[188] The first cases thus run the risk of producing damaged children, just as the first embryo transfers after IVF did.

Since offspring would have had no alternative route to a healthy birth, embryo transfer after freezing and thawing would not harm offspring, and therefore, could not be banned on that basis.[189] Indeed, a ban on embryo transfer after thawing might interfere with the procreative liberty of the couple storing the embryo who now wish it transferred to the woman's uterus. It would also burden the woman who prefers to freeze excess embryos and thus avoid ovarian stimulation and laparoscopy in subsequent attempts to achieve pregnancy.

The physician and couple desiring to transfer thawed embryos would not have wronged a child who was damaged as a result of their experimental procedure. Unless the freezing and thawing had occurred, the child would never have been born. From the child's perspective, he

---

     186.   Effective therapy for gene defects may require insertion of genes before implantation, by manipulations of fertilized eggs. But until transfers after gene insertion occur, there is a risk that the offspring will be damaged by the attempt to cure their defect and make their birth possible. Similarly, transfer after freezing may give embryos that would have been destroyed a chance to achieve personhood.

     187.   The Ethics Advisory Board provided prior review on a national scale before human IVF and embryo transfer occurred in the United States in 1979. *See* Report of Ethics Advisory Board, *supra* note 46; *see also* Robertson, *supra* note 144, at 30.

     188.   The animal data is based on the extensive experience with frozen embryos in the cattle industry. *See* Seidel, *supra* note 33, at 353-54.

     189.   While transfer before freezing in theory could have enabled this offspring to be born without the damage from freezing, usually this option will not be available, so as a practical matter there is no alternative route to birth that avoids the risks of freezing.

or she is better off alive, although handicapped. If the parents are able to pay the full costs of treating the handicap and caring for the child, they will not have wronged anyone with their choice of reproductive technique.

If they cannot cover those costs, the parents, in effect, are demanding that their need to reproduce be subsidized by imposing rearing costs on others. If society does not fund infertility services for indigents, presumably they would have no right to have these rearing costs subsidized. A direct prohibition on freezing embryos for persons unable to bear the costs of rearing offspring may thus fit with the concept of reproductive responsibility. However, if the decision to freeze and then thaw is clinically reasonable, the social costs of a wealth-based prohibition on use of this procreative technique will be troubling for a society committed to a high degree of procreative liberty.[190]

2. Psychological Damage

In addition to physical damage, noncoital reproduction also presents several novel possibilities for psychosocial harm in offspring. An obligation to avoid such harm may be imposed where the harm is in fact avoidable. In most cases, however, the psychosocial threat is intimately linked with the reproductive technique that enables offspring to be born. Therefore, concern with this harm will not justify a state ban on use of these techniques.

IVF itself is no more likely to produce psychological harm in offspring than is coital conception, since the gamete providers will gestate and rear the offspring. Only the site of conception and early cleavage differ. However, cryopreservation of embryos for long periods, posthumous conception and implantation, and the use of donor gametes, donor embryos, and surrogates raise the possibility of psychosocial harm. The following discussion shows that these potential sources of psychosocial harm to offspring are not a sufficient basis for interfering with private use of these techniques.

a. *Psychological damage from storage or posthumous implantation*: Reservations about cryopreservation of gametes and embryos include the possibility of psychosocial harm because of a long gap between conception and implantation and the possibility of conception, implantation, or

---

190. This issue would arise only if the couple has access to IVF and freezing but could not pay the costs of rearing any damaged offspring that result. Since access to IVF is dependent on wealth, as a practical matter, this further wealth discrimination is unlikely to arise.

birth after the death of one or both of the gamete providers. Professional and official advisory groups have recommended that cryopreservation of embryos should be limited to a finite period such as five or ten years, and in any case not beyond the reproductive life of the mother.[191] They also oppose posthumous IVF conception and embryo transfer.[192]

Assuming the physical safety and efficacy of gamete and embryo storage, presumably the fear is that offspring will be traumatized or psychologically harmed once they learn that they were conceived or implanted after a long period of gamete or embryo storage, or after one or both of their genetic parents have died.[193]

Could long storage or posthumous conception or implantation harm offspring? The trauma of learning that one's genetic parents have been long dead is a rare but occasional experience that is unfortunate but not ordinarily considered a fate worse than death. Fathers die after conception and mothers die in childbirth. Children are orphaned at tender ages. As long as adequate childrearers are substituted, the death of genetic parents before or shortly after birth does not ordinarily make the child's life not worth living. Thus, it is not clear why the death of genetic parents before conception, as would occur with the posthumous use of stored gametes, or long before one's earlier embryonic form found a safe harbor in a womb, as might occur with embryo freezing, is so undesirable as to justify policies against posthumous conception or implantation of stored gametes and embryos. Once the genetic parent has died, there is no alternative to posthumous conception or implantation, if this child is to be born.

Even an extreme case, such as transfer to a uterus fifty or one hundred years after the genetic source's death, would not necessarily subject offspring to a life worse than death. As newsworthy as their life may be, the offspring are not likely to prefer the alternative of never being born.

Less extreme cases would involve a period of storage, but transfer or conception while the gamete provider is still alive, but older. This could lead to the rearing parent being older than ordinary, especially if a gestational surrogate is used. Even if there are unique psychosocial problems

---

191. *See, e.g.* WARNOCK COMMITTEE REPORT, *supra* note 46, at 55; American Fertility Society, *Ethical Statement on In Vitro Fertilization*, 41 FERTILITY AND STERILITY 12 (1984).

192. *Id.*

193. One can only speculate about how long embryos will be stored, since the practice is so new. It is likely that most couples would maintain embryos in storage only for the period of time that they are interested in reproducing, but this could vary greatly. On the other hand, gametes stored before undertaking hazardous employment or undergoing radiation for cancer could be stored for long periods before use.

posed, it is difficult to see how the child's interests are hurt, since its alternative is no birth at all.[194]

Thus, it is doubtful that the interests of offspring are served by a policy limiting the length of storage. Since they will not otherwise be born without lengthy storage, the delay would have to be so long as to make nonstorage and nonexistence the preferable alternative. Nor is there the same likelihood of imposing rearing costs on others that could arise with the risk of physical damage from storage.

The conclusion that offspring are better off from long storage does not fully dispel the discomfort felt at the idea of posthumous conception and implantation, or embryo transfer after long periods of cryopreservation. The idea of postponing conception or implantation until long after the gene source's death is new and strange. Even if no harm to offspring is shown, our concept of birth and parentage is severely tested. The technology thus presents a novel situation that tests our understanding of reproductive responsibility and the welfare of offspring.

Discomfort at the use of such novel techniques may well animate the actions which persons and physicians in the private sector are willing to entertain. However, state restrictions on posthumous conception, implantation, and length of storage could interfere with the procreative liberty of persons desiring to procreate in this way. Banning posthumous use of stored gametes and embryos would interfere with the procreative liberty of the spouse who wishes to have and rear the deceased spouse's child.[195] It might also interfere with the procreative liberty of the deceased person, who contemplated posthumous reproduction.[196]

A state law prohibiting embryo storage beyond menopause would clearly interfere with the procreative liberty of women undergoing premature menopause, but who retain uterine function. It would also prevent stored embryos from being donated or gestated by a surrogate after a twenty-eight year old woman had a hysterectomy because of severe

---

194. Unknown is the effect on offspring of a gap between the time of conception and implantation. It is not clear why suspending early embryonic development until a later point, particularly when the suspension enables the later implantation to occur, hurts offspring. *See* Grobstein, Flower & Mendelhoff, *Frozen Embryos: Policy Issues*, 312 NEW ENG. J. MED. 1584, 1586 (1985).

195. Dionne, *Widow Wins Paris Case for Husband's Sperm*, N.Y. Times, Aug. 2, 1984, at A96, col. 1.

196. This interest may or may not be included in the bundle of rights protected by procreative liberty. *See supra* text accompanying notes 54-84.

endometriosis or cancer.[197] Since the child will never be born at all if a ban on posthumous or post-sterility conception or implantation is in effect, concern for offspring cannot justify such restrictions.

This brief analysis shows that a concern for the welfare of offspring does not adequately explain or justify restrictions on length of storage or posthumous use of stored gametes and embryos. Like other issues in the new reproduction, symbolic concerns about how conception and reproduction should occur seem to lay behind policy limits on the length of gamete and embryo storage. Such concerns may animate private choice, and lead to private and professional restrictions, but they would not justify state restriction of procreative choice in most cases.

b. *Psychological harm from donor-assisted reproduction*: Special concern for offspring is often voiced when the use of donor gametes and embryos and surrogates is discussed. A common fear is that psychosocial damage to offspring is likely because of the novelty of the relations and the genetic or kinship confusion which the child will experience from the recombination of genetic, gestational, and social parentage.

Two concerns in particular have been voiced. One fear is that the need to resort to a donor will foster conflict between partners and lead to marital instability or lingering resentment, with resulting psychosocial difficulties for offspring.[198] Just as adopted children have a greater risk of psychosocial difficulties, so it is thought that the children of noncoital, collaborative reproduction will be less happy and less well-adjusted than are the offspring of coital reproduction.

The effects of various donor and surrogate arrangements on offspring and family stability need study and monitoring. Studies of families and offspring of donor insemination reveal occasional problems, but on the whole reveal positive experiences for all participants.[199] There is no reason to think that other collaborative arrangements, such as egg and embryo donation and surrogates, will be more likely than donor insemination to produce family instability. Indeed, there are reasons to expect less pathology. For egg and embryo recipients will gestate, and thus have

---

197. Many other illnesses could require a hysterectomy at such an age. In addition, oophorectomy (removal of the ovaries) might also be taken to end a woman's reproductive life under these guidelines, thus increasing the number of conditions that would limit the length of storage.

198. The fear is that the asymmetry in the genetic relationship to the child will create resentment or lessen the feeling of rearing responsibility in the nongenetic parent. This concern and other possible effects on offspring are analyzed in greater detail in the next part of the Article.

199. R. Snowden, G. Mitchell & E. Snowden, Artificial Reproduction: A Social Investigation 50-54, 71-82, 97-104 (1983).

a gestational tie that does not exist in adoption. Even children born of surrogacy arrangements will have a genetic tie with one or both rearing parents.[200] The risk of family instability appears tolerable, even if single and same sex parenting raise novel problems.

A second psychosocial concern is that offspring will suffer genetic bewilderment or confusion from a multiplicity of parents. The relation of collaborating donors to the offspring or recipient, although ordinarily anonymous, is sufficiently undefined and unstructured that sticky situations can easily be imagined. For example, the child may wish contact with the genetic or gestational contributor. Or the donors and surrogates may wish to get to know "their" child. Perhaps the rearing parents are family innovators and will welcome donors, surrogates, and their siblings and parents into one big extended family.[201] These possibilities generate fears that the offspring will be so confused about their identity and relation to kin and rearers that such reproduction should be discouraged.

The likelihood of adverse impact on offspring does not appear so great that donor assistance should be prohibited. The separation of genetic, gestational, and social parentage has long occurred through adoption, death, divorce, and remarriage, with the result that the rearing parent is not always the gestational or genetic parent.[202] Family conflict,

---

200. The use of surrogates, however, may pose special problems for the surrogate and her family, even if there is no more strain imposed on the rearing family. *See infra* text accompanying notes 242-55.

201. This situation, with the child having a genetic, gestational, or rearing relation with at least five persons, is the extreme case of family confusion that is often cited as a potential harm from IVF. *See* Andrews, *The Stork Market: The Law of the New Reproduction Technologies*, 70 A.B.A. J. 50 (1984); Capron, *The New Reproductive Possibilities: Seeking a Moral Basis for Concerted Action in a Pluralistic Society*, 12 L. MED. & HEALTH CARE 192 (1984).

Such results from IVF are likely to be rare. Couples employing donors or surrogates will usually want no contact with them at all, and donors and surrogates will want protection against responsibilities beyond the service they agreed to. In a few cases, however, all the parties might agree to have an ongoing relation with each other and the offspring. For example, the surrogate gestator or gamete donor might wish to maintain relations with the child and rearing couple and include them as part of an extended family that includes the siblings, spouse, and other children of the surrogate or donor. The couple may find such an enlarged family appealing and, in fact, think it beneficial for the child. Now that the 1960's are past, such arrangements are likely only when siblings, cousins, or friends provide gestation or gametes, or when reproduction is part of a political or religious program.

IVF is not likely to increase the incidence of such variations on the blended or extended family, since most uses of IVF will not involve donors. Moreover, IVF is not essential to implement philosophies of the ideal family, since coitus and artificial insemination are largely adequate for that purpose. The relative rarity of such experimental extended families suggests that they are likely to be rare with IVF as well.

202. Examples abound. John McPhee's account of how two Scottish chiefs exchanged sons, each rearing the son of the other, reminds us of the prevalence of such practices throughout history. J. McPhee, The Crofter and the Laird 11-13 (1969).

identity confusion and other disruption may result, but such arrangements may also be productive and satisfying for all parties. The mere fact that genetic, gestational, and social parentage is divided is not itself a cause for concern.

The use of donors and surrogates, however, can be distinguished by the deliberateness of the choice involved. Those other collaborative arrangements result from tragic accident, divorce, illegitimacy, or inability to rear. They are not often deliberately chosen, as is donor-assisted reproduction. Yet it is not clear why that should make a difference, since absent these arrangements the offspring would not exist. Even if there is a higher degree of confusion, unhappiness, or maladjustment in donor-assisted reproduction, a child would seem better off under this collaborative structure than not to exist at all.

Indeed, there are reasons to think that the potential kinship confusion from collaborative reproduction may be even less disruptive than some other blended family arrangements. IVF does allow egg and embryo donation to occur, but unlike adoption, the child's rearing mother will also have gestated. Similarly, donor sperm gives offspring a genetic and gestational tie with the mother that does not exist in adoption or stepparenthood. Gestational surrogacy does permit a genetic tie with the offspring, even though not a gestational one. Handled sensitively, offspring should not be at such a risk of genetic confusion that their chance to be born at all should be eliminated.[203]

Of course, collaborative reproductive transactions should be structured and conducted in ways to minimize any psychological burdens and problems that may result.[204] Yet the risk of harm is not enough to justify a total ban, since the donor or surrogate is essential to the offspring's existence.

---

203. Many of the problems that arise with surrogacy arrangements grow out of secrecy and nondisclosure to offspring and the difficulty offspring have in learning about or meeting their missing genetic or gestational parent. *See infra* text accompanying notes 256-69.

204. Some of the harm feared here may, in fact, be avoidable. For example, collaborators need not maintain relations with each other and offspring, and ordinarily will not. Offspring may be informed of the use of donors and surrogates and given information about them or even the chance to meet. An open, honest approach to the situation may help immensely in reducing psychosocial costs to offspring.

V. COLLABORATIVE REPRODUCTION AND PROTECTION OF FAMILY RELATIONS

A major concern about noncoital reproduction is its potential impact on the traditional family. Some noncoital techniques (IVF or artificial insemination with husband sperm) are clearly supportive of family since they enable a married couple to achieve pregnancy and rear their own children.[205]

Collaborative reproduction[206]—the use of donors or surrogates to provide the gametes or gestation needed by the couple—introduces a third party into the traditional husband-wife parenting situation. The degree to which the parties will interact and the extent of conflict and problems for the collaborators and offspring are uncertain. Depending on the resulting relationship among donor, offspring, and couple, potentially serious effects could occur. But it is also possible that reproductive collaboration will be positive for all parties. Uncertainty about the scope and impact of these effects has made collaborative reproduction a controversial area of the new reproduction.

No doubt other pressures on traditional family structure contribute to the malaise felt about collaborative reproduction. A high divorce rate, an increase in single person households, and a growing number of children raised by single parents have led some people to fear that the traditional nuclear family is a fast-ebbing ideal of the past.[207] Donor-assisted

---

205. Embryo freezing and other manipulations may affect the family's reproduction, but in most cases these effects will occur within the context of a traditional nuclear family rearing arrangement.

206. All reproduction is collaborative, since no human reproduces alone. The term "collaborative" is used here to refer to the situation of another person providing the genes or gestation or rearing that a person or couple wishing to reproduce lacks.

207. *One-Parent Families Increasing, Study Says,* N.Y. Times, May 16, 1985, at A52, col. 6; Rosenbaum, *Moynihan Reassessing Problems of Families,* N.Y. Times, Apr. 7, 1985, at A1, col. 2. The increasing number of families in which single women rear children, often with state assistance, is of particular concern because it perpetuates a cycle of poverty and social disarray, which has grown "so pronounced . . . that it should provide common ground for concern among liberals and conservatives." *Id.* Senator Patrick Moynihan predicts that one-third of all children born in 1980 will be dependent on welfare at some time before they become adults, thus making children, at a time when poverty among the elderly is decreasing, the largest group of the poor. *Id.*

The high divorce rate is also of concern. In part a cause of the growth of single parent households, it also leads to remarriage and the creation of blended families, in which children of previous marriages live in a household with one genetic parent and the children of his or her new spouse. In either case we have moved far from the traditional notion that a nongenetically related couple rears genetically related children.

Finally, the trend toward single parent families has a counterpart in the large growth of single person households from deferred childbearing by women in the workforce and the emergence of gay lifestyles.

deviations from the nuclear family are perceived by some as a further sign of the family's demise.

The possibility of egg and embryo donors and gestational surrogates is indeed new and startling, but many forms of collaborative reproduction of offspring have existed throughout history. Children have often been reared by nongenetically related stepparents, wetnurses, nannies, babysitters, and other surrogates. Donor insemination has been available for forty years as an accepted treatment for male infertility.

What is new is the possibility of separating the female genetic and gestational role, so that separate genetic, gestational, and rearing mothers are now possible. The egg fertilized in vitro can be transferred to a physiologically receptive womb other than that of the egg source. Either woman, or a third party, might then rear the child. Parental variations based on the source of the sperm are also possible.[208]

Attitudes toward these developments are intimately tied up with attitudes and practices regarding donor insemination. Although established as a treatment for male infertility, it remains problematic for many people, as is evident in the secrecy that usually attends it. The problems of donor sperm are also highlighted by its use by single women and same sex couples as a way to reproduce.[209] While these users are not treatments of medical infertility, they are an important component of the new reproduction and also raise issues of family integrity.

While most noncoital reproduction involves a traditional couple seeking to rear a child of their genes and gestation, the demand for gamete donation and surrogacy cannot be ignored. The conflict between particular views of family integrity and collaborative reproduction is addressed in this section.

A. PROCREATIVE LIBERTY AND COLLABORATIVE REPRODUCTION

The use of donors and surrogates involves the assistance of collaborators to provide the gametes or gestation essential for reproduction to occur. I have argued earlier that the procreative liberty of married persons protects their rights to use the assistance of others to reproduce

---

208. The sperm can be provided by the husband of the egg source, the husband of the gestator, or by a person unrelated to any of the parties. Such variations allow the multiplicity of paternal-offspring relations discussed *supra* note 201.

209. *See supra* note 71. Even if the number of single women choosing to bear children increases, and access to IVF is provided, IVF will not be a major contributor to single motherhood since only a small portion of single women desiring to reproduce will need IVF treatment to achieve their goal.

when they are infertile.[210] This right would include the right to contract with donors and surrogates for the gestation or gametes necessary for the couple to acquire offspring of their genes or gestation for rearing. Procreative liberty thus requires that the contract among the parties for the disposition of gametes, embryo, and uterus and the assignment of rearing rights and duties in offspring control, unless harm to offspring or other important state interests can be established. The couple seeking to reproduce will have discretion to select donors (and donors discretion to select recipients) and the right to pay them for their assistance.[211] The state may regulate entry into collaborative contracts, but it will have limited power to prohibit or ignore such contracts.

Unmarried persons will also have rights to enter into collaborative contracts for gametes, embryos, and surrogacy if their right to coital reproduction is recognized. Followed to the limits of its logic, the contractual model may encourage new procreative roles and relations and even cause a reevaluation of the regulatory apparatus that surrounds the present law of adoption.[212]

The following section discusses the role of contract in settling rearing responsibilities in offspring born of gamete and embryo donation and surrogacy, with special attention paid to the question of anonymity of donors and money payment for their services. The discussion will show how concerns for the integrity of the traditional family may affect legal relations among reproductive collaborators.

---

210. *See supra* text accompanying notes 67-69.

211. The issue of payment is discussed at greater length *infra* text accompanying notes 270-91. The rights of recipients to select donors and of donors to select recipients raise similar but distinguishable issues. The recipient would seem to have the right to select the donor or surrogate, just as a person has the right to select a partner for coital reproduction. Selection on eugenic grounds is thus within a person's discretion, since one can now select spouses or decide whether to reproduce on that basis. A limitation on the right to choose collaborators might arise when the desired donor is a biological relation or a friend. *See infra* note 222.

The donor or surrogate would have a right to refuse donation or surrogacy, except perhaps in the case of embryo donation, if discard is prohibited. However, it may be that the donor's right to make a donation is derivative of the recipient's right to procreate, and does not exist independently. The partial reproductive role of donor or surrogate, when no rearing is sought, might not be protected as part of procreative liberty to the same extent as the desire to acquire and rear offspring of one's genes or gestation or that of one's spouse.

212. This argument may lead to greater claims for independent or privately arranged adoptions when they are viewed as an aspect of the procreative liberty of the couple seeking to adopt.

B. DONOR GAMETES

The role of contract is evident in the relationship between gamete donors and recipients in determining rearing rights and duties in resulting offspring. Since the experience with donor sperm and donor eggs is so different, they are treated separately.

1. *Donor Sperm*

It is estimated that, as a treatment for male infertility, AID produces some 10,000 to 15,000 children a year in the United States.[213] Donor insemination usually occurs in a physician's office, often with frozen sperm procured from commercial sperm banks.[214] It may also be used in conjunction with IVF treatment for oligospermia, either directly or as a back-up system to assure that retrieved eggs are fertilized, or to avoid the transmission of genetic diseases.[215] While some religious groups condemn any form of gametic donation, and while the need for standards of selection, screening, and recordkeeping exists,[216] donor sperm has secured an important niche in the treatment of male infertility.

Donor insemination is also sought by unmarried women without male partners, who plan to rear offspring alone or in a same sex family. Since most physicians have been unwilling to inseminate single women, a practice of amateur or self-insemination has arisen outside of medical

---

213. There are no exact figures on the number of AID births, since records often are not kept. Annas estimates six to ten thousand births a year but gives no source. Annas, *supra* note 138.

214. Frozen sperm may be safer because it allows testing for acquired immune deficiency syndrome and other infectious diseases before use.

215. Oligospermia is a very low sperm count, while azoospermia is the absence of sperm altogether. IVF has proven to be an effective treatment for oligospermic couples, since it allows the egg to be exposed to a washed concentrate of sperm, which could enhance the chance of fertilization. However, it may require that a woman without tube damage undergo ovary stimulation and laparoscopy in order to enable the male partner to rear a lineal descendant. If IVF fails, noninvasive AID is still an option.

The use of IVF to treat oligospermic couples may lead to donor sperm being used as a back-up in case the husband's sperm does not fertilize the eggs after laparoscopy. This option may make for some hard choices. A couple expecting the husband's sperm to fertilize must decide, when fertilization does not occur, to try with donor sperm. Because they have had the hope that the husband's sperm would work, they may not be fully prepared to use donor sperm, yet feel pressed to use it, because the egg is now available. To avoid later recriminations, special care should be taken in obtaining consent to this use of donor sperm.

216. Some Catholic commentators accept IVF with a married couple, but find donor sperm morally unacceptable because of the third party introduced into the marital relation. *See* American Fertility Society, *supra*, note 96, spec. supp. (dissenting statement by Richard McCormick). For a discussion of other problems with donor sperm, see generally Annas, *supra* note 138.

settings.[217] The woman procures semen from friends, contacts, or intermediaries, and inseminates herself without screening for disease or genetic factors and often without attention to the legal implications.

The legal status of donor insemination has been partially clarified, but a number of uncertainties remain. The law is clearest in the case of a married couple who, through a physician, obtain sperm from an anonymous donor who relinquishes rearing rights and duties in offspring. The consenting husband then acquires the rearing rights and duties that attend biological paternity, with the offspring his legitimate heir. Statutes in twenty-eight states give effect to this contractual understanding between donor, the brokering sperm bank or physician, and recipient.[218] In the absence of statute, the same result is likely.[219] Indeed, a failure to honor the agreement of the parties for assigning rearing rights and duties in offspring would arguably violate the procreative liberty of the couple, and possibly the donor. Neither the interests of the donor in knowing or parenting his offspring, the interests of the husband in avoiding rearing duties toward nonbiological offspring, nor the interests of the offspring, would justify a different result.[220]

Less clear would be the effect of an agreement for the sperm donor to have some rearing rights and duties in the offspring. While such agreements have been recognized where the recipient is unmarried, perhaps in order to assure a male rearing parent for offspring, these agreements might be overridden to prevent a multiplicity of male rearers and the attendant confusion and conflict when a consenting husband is present. However, refusal to honor this type of contract would interfere with the procreative liberty of the couple. Legislative or judicial refusal to

---

217. One survey revealed that only 10% of physicians providing donor inseminations are willing to inseminate single women. *See* Curie-Cohen, Luttrell & Shapiro, *supra* note 71, at 585. One commentator estimates that at least 1500 single women are inseminated annually. *See* Donovan, *The Uniform Parentage Act and Nonmarital Motherhood-by-Choice*, 11 N.Y.U. REV. L. & SOC. CHANGE 193, 195 (1983) (citing Fleming, *New Frontiers in Conception*, N.Y. Times, July 20, 1980, § 6 (Magazine), at 14, col. 1).

218. For citations to state AID laws, see American Fertility Society, *supra* note 3, at 2; Kritchevsky, *The Unmarried Woman's Right to Artificial Insemination: A Call for an Expanded Definition of Family*, 4 HARV. WOMEN L.J. 1, 10 n.51, 11 n.52 (1981).

219. *See* People v. Sorenson, which imposed rearing duties on a consenting husband who later sought to avoid paying support for the donor sperm offspring. 68 Cal. 2d 280, 437 P.2d 495, 66 Cal. Rptr. 7 (1968). It is likely that this case would be followed in states without legislation.

220. A donor's genetic tie, alone, would probably not justify overriding the collaborative contract to allow the donor to rear, given Lehr v. Robertson, 463 U.S. 248 (1983), and other cases that terminate the rearing rights of coital parents. Nor is the husband's interest in avoiding the burden a weighty one if he has consented to the transaction. Nor would the interest of offspring justify such a result, since they might not be born at all if the donor is later able to assert rearing rights over the wishes of the couple.

enforce such contracts, or requirements that the donation be anonymous to prevent new forms of family relations from emerging, would conflict with couples' desires to create a family, and thus would require strict scrutiny.[221] Distaste for such an innovative family structure alone would probably not suffice. Similar questions would arise if the sought-for donor is biologically related to the recipient or the recipient's husband.[222]

The legal situation of unmarried women accepting donor sperm is more uncertain. While a few states outlaw self-insemination, requiring that only physicians perform the artificial insemination procedure, no state prohibits physicians from performing the procedure on unmarried women.[223] Less clear is the resulting relationship of the donor to offspring. A few states, such as California, permit the parties to relieve the sperm donor of all rearing rights and duties, if a physician has done the insemination.[224] However, most state donor insemination laws do not address the issue, leaving open the question of whether the sperm donor will escape rearing rights and duties.[225]

If the right of unmarried persons to procreate coitally and noncoitally were recognized, then a strong argument for a right of the donor and recipient to exclude the donor from rearing responsibilities would exist. The contract should then prevent the mother from seeking financial support from the donor. However, the contract would not necessarily exclude the state from seeking child support from the donor, if the recipient cannot provide for the child and goes on welfare.[226] The

---

221. In such a situation the couple is asserting a right to obtain gametes so that they might have a child of the wife's genes and gestation for rearing, which they will share with the sperm donor. They are clearly exercising procreative choice, and arguably a right to form a family. Given the biologic and marital ties among the parties, this choice is likely to be protected, and thus limited only by the need to avoid some tangible, nonsymbolic harm.

222. The question of intrafamilial donations arises occasionally with sperm donations, and is likely to arise more often with egg, embryo and surrogate transactions. *See infra* note 284. While procreative liberty and family autonomy appear to protect such choices, it may be that the state's control of families through marriage and incest laws would allow it to restrict intrafamilial gamete donations. However, a showing of actual harm to offspring or the parties would probably have to be established, rather than mere disapproval of biologically intermingled families.

223. Artificial insemination of single women is not per se illegal, though a few states require that only physicians inseminate. *See, e.g.,* GA. CODE ANN. § 43-34-42 (1982). The chief legal barrier is the uncertainty of the donor's rearing rights and duties. Few of the 28 state artificial insemination laws foresaw this possiblity, addressing instead the relations between the sperm donor and the consenting husband. *See* Kritchevsky, *supra* note 218, at 10-12.

224. Cal. Civ. Code § 7005 (West 1983); *see also* Jhordan C. v. Mary K., No. AO27810 (Cal. Ct. of App. Apr. 25, 1986) (holding that semen donor's status as father is preserved where semen is not obtained by recipient through a licensed physician).

225. *See supra* note 223.

226. Jhordan C. v. Mary K. involved a situation where the inseminated woman eventually sought welfare for herself and the child. The state then sought a support order against the donor.

state's interest in assuring that the parties, and not taxpayers, pay the costs of their procreative activity might justify imposing support obligations on the donor in such a case.[227] Such a result would pose special problems if the source of the sperm is a commercial sperm bank.

Ironically, the contract among unmarried parties has been recognized where it was found to contemplate the donor having a rearing relation with offspring. Men providing sperm for artificial insemination to unmarried women have been awarded access to offspring (and support obligations as well) when they have been able to convince a court that the sperm was provided as part of an agreement for access to resulting offspring.[228] The outcome of such claims by donors depends on establishing the existence of an agreement to rear. It has made unmarried women seeking sperm donors outside of a medical setting uneasy, since the donor may be able to obtain a rearing role by claiming an agreement to that effect.[229]

The experience with donor sperm suggests that the contract among the parties will play an important role in determining rearing rights and duties in offspring. This is clearest in the case of a married couple and donor seeking to relinquish all rearing rights and duties. It also seems to be the case with an unmarried recipient and donor who provides the

---

No. A027810 (Cal. Ct. of App.) For the imposition of child support obligations on men who had been assured by the woman that pregnancy could not result from their act of intercourse, see Hughes v. Hutt, 500 Pa. 209, 455 A.2d 623 (1982); Stephen K. v. Roni L., 105 Cal. App. 3d 604, 164 Cal. Rptr. 618 (1980); In re Pamela P., 443 N.Y.S.2d 343, 110 Misc. 2d 978 (1981).

227. See supra text accompanying notes 171-76.

228. C. M. v. C. C., 152 N.J. Super. 160, 377 A.2d 821 (Cumberland County Ct. 1977); Jhordan C. v. Mary K., No. A027810 (Cal. Ct. of App.). At least one trial court has awarded visitation rights to the lesbian lover of a woman who had been artificially inseminated with the lover's brother's sperm, in part to implement the agreement of the mother and lover to jointly raise the offspring. Lesbians' Argument Over Child Custody Presents New Issues, N.Y. Times, Sept. 9, 1984, at A44, col. 1. While this case does not involve the rearing rights of the donor, it does show that an agreement to share parenting with another person, in this case a same sex, nonbiologically related person, will be recognized, at least where the agreement has led to that party becoming a de facto parent.

229. This is a particular fear of lesbians undergoing AID, who want to guarantee that the sperm donor will not be able to have access to the child. Cases such as C. M. v. C. C., 152 N.J. Super. 160, 377 A.2d 821 (Cumberland County Ct. 1977), have been criticized because of the ease with which the claim of an agreement to share rearing with the donor can be made and the bias of courts toward assuring that each child has a father. See Kritchevsky, supra note 218, at 12-16. It has led to elaborate go-between systems to make sure that the sperm source will never learn who received his sperm. Davies, Artificial Insemination in WOMEN AND THE LAW 8-1, 8-21-8-22 (C. H. Lefcourt ed. 1984).

sperm on the condition that he will have rearing rights and duties. Depending on the scope of procreative liberty granted married and unmarried persons, it should be recognized in the two other situations discussed as well.

2. Donor Eggs

The use of donor eggs allows women with ovarian failure or premature menopause to gestate and rear children. Egg donation was not possible until the development of IVF and the ability to transfer the extracorporeal embryo to a physiologically receptive uterus other than that of the egg source. IVF thus makes donor eggs an attractive treatment for women unable to produce adequate eggs of their own.

Donor eggs can be acquired from women undergoing ovarian stimulation as part of an IVF cycle, or from women undergoing other abdominal surgery who agree to superovulation in order to donate eggs. As egg donation is more widely practiced, women, who themselves are not facing any medical procedure, may be recruited as donors.[230]

The acceptability of donor sperm and IVF suggests that there is no principled objection to the use of donor eggs. If sperm donation is permitted, egg donation should be as well. The absence of a genetic link to the rearing female is no more ominous for the offspring than is the absence of a genetic link to the rearing male. In fact, donor eggs permit a gestational link with offspring by the partner lacking gametes which is not possible with donor sperm. This link may reduce the chance of conflict between parents, or between parent and child, that could occur with adoption and donor sperm.[231]

The legal relations between egg donors, recipients, and offspring should parallel that of sperm donation. Donor sperm statutes do not by their terms apply to donor eggs (egg donation was not possible when they were enacted), but they could be reasonably interpreted to apply to both

---

230. Seeking egg donations from women not themselves undergoing intrusive medical procedures can be questioned on ethical grounds if other egg sources are available, since the risk of superovulation and retrieval are not trivial, even with ultrasound-guided transvaginal aspiration of eggs rather than laparoscopy. However, the need for paternalistic protection of egg donors, beyond assuring informed consent and compensating for injuries suffered in the process of retrieval, can also be questioned.

231. The possibility of lingering resentment or unresolved conflict between the partners because of gametic inadequacy and the resulting genetic asymmetry of rearing partners toward offspring cannot be discounted, even though it does not justify banning gamete donations. But, collaborative transactions that more closely approach the traditional coital situation are less likely to pose the same risk of conflict as those less similar, such as adoption, do.

male and female gametes.[232] In any case, different legal treatment of donor eggs and donor sperm is not justified. Just as the husband consenting to donor sperm assumes the donor's rearing rights and duties, so the consenting wife (who is also the gestational mother) should take on rearing rights and duties, terminating those of the egg donor. Indeed, given the law's tendency to view the birthing woman as the rearing mother, the contractual assignment of rearing rights and duties to the couple would probably be given legal effect without new legislation.[233] Agreements to allow the egg donor to play some rearing role should be respected to the same extent that they are with donor sperm.

Since egg donation also requires IVF, an underground or nonmedical movement similar to the self-insemination practices with donor sperm is unlikely to arise. However, single or unmarried women will occasionally be candidates for donor eggs due to ovarian failure. Once again, the legal agreement among the parties should control as to rearing rights and duties, to the same extent as with donor sperm. Indeed, it is less likely that the egg donor would be given rearing rights and duties in the absence of a contract to that effect, since a rearing mother will be present, which distinguishes the situation of sperm donors.

C. EMBRYO DONATION

IVF treatment also permits the donation of preimplantation embryos to occur. The donated embryo is transferred to the uterus of a physiologically receptive woman who gestates and then rears the resulting child.[234] The gestating mother (who presumably will also rear) has no genetic link with the child.

Indeed, the embryo need not even be conceived externally for donation to occur. Buster and his colleagues, adapting techniques used in cattle breeding, succeeded in flushing an embryo fertilized in vivo by artificial insemination from a woman's uterus before implantation and transferring it to the uterus of another woman, who then carried the donated

---

232. A creative judge could read the term "sperm" or "insemination" to refer to the transfer of all gametes, and not merely male gametes, in order to avoid an attack on grounds of gender discrimination. A stricter constructionist might await legislation, but take the artificial insemination statute to indicate that the legislature intends the agreement of the parties to control until it says otherwise.

233. Indeed, a contrary result would appear to be unconstitutional under the analysis presented in this Article. Legislation, however, would reduce uncertainty so that parties may plan accordingly, and prevent ill-considered judicial decisions. *See infra* text accompanying notes 343-45.

234. Trounson, Leeton, Besanko, Wood & Conti, *Pregnancy Established in an Infertile Patient after Transfer of a Donated Embryo Fertilised In Vitro*, 286 BRIT. MED. J. 835 (1983).

embryo to term.[235] While not yet widely practiced, this technique presents a novel twist on embryo donation, since insemination with the sperm of the recipient's husband can occur.

Embryo donation is not likely to occur on a large scale until the freezing and thawing of embryos is established, given the logistical problems that coordination of donor and recipient menstrual cycles entails. The supply of embryos for donation would increase with the enactment of mandatory embryo donation laws or IVF clinic policies designed to prevent embryo discard.[236] Some couples may also choose to donate excess embryos rather than discard them. In some instances donation might occur after one or both of the gamete sources is dead.

It is not clear that the demand for donor embryos will be equal to the supply. Donor embryos would be indicated to relieve infertility only where both the male and female are unable to provide gametes, since donor sperm or donor eggs will take care of gametic failure of one party alone. However, the unavailability of donor eggs, or an altruistic willingness to "rescue" abandoned embryos, might add to the demand for embryo donations.

The case for prohibiting embryo donations is no stronger than is the case for prohibiting separate gamete donations. As with donor gametes, offspring are not harmed, for they would not exist at all but for the donation. Unlike some forms of collaborative reproduction, embryo donation has the advantage that the rearing couple will have gestated the child.[237] The child born of embryo donation will thus have a closer tie with the rearing mother than will adopted children, even if a genetic tie to either partner is lacking.

Similarly, there is no good reason not to enforce the parties' assignment of rearing rights and duties, as would occur with separate gamete donations.[238] Indeed, at the present time, it would be surprising if the law did not honor the terms of the donation and treat the recipient who gestates and gives birth as the rearing mother, regardless of the method

235. *See supra* note 37. In this case, however, there will ordinarily be a genetic link with the husband, whose sperm has artificially inseminated the embryo donor.

236. *See supra* text accompanying notes 121-43. Whatever the state's power or inclination to act, physicians and institutions providing IVF would be free to set their own conditions on provision of services. They could, for example, require that parties storing embryos agree to donate them to others, if they refuse placement themselves. The issue of physician-patient allocation of dispositional authority over the extracorporeal embryo is treated *infra* text accompanying notes 329-38.

237. The woman will have a biologic tie, and thus the situation may be more favorably inclined to family stability than is the case with adoption.

238. *See supra* text accompanying notes 67-70, 213-29.

of producing the embryo and the source of the sperm, and her consenting partner or spouse as the rearing father.[239]

The tendency of some persons to refer to embryo donations as embryo "adoptions" should not alter the role of the agreement between donor and recipient in regulating the transaction. The term "adoption" is misleading if it is meant to suggest that the same procedures for adoption of children should be followed. Since a donated embryo must undergo the arduous course of implantation and pregnancy to be born, the situation is more akin to gamete donation than to adoption of an actual child.[240] While fused gametes or embryos might have a symbolic meaning that gametes alone do not, existing laws would not require that the parenting abilities of the recipient couple be scrutinized before the donation any more than they require the parental fitness of donor sperm recipients to be reviewed. Requiring the recipients of donor embryos and gametes to undergo prior review of their parental fitness would raise serious questions of infringement of procreative liberty.[241]

D. Gestational Surrogates

If an embryo can be transferred to the physiologically receptive uterus of another woman for gestation, that woman need not rear the resulting child. She could give the child to its genetic parents or others

---

239. The question "Who is the mother?" is misleading because "motherhood" can be genetic, gestational, or social. A more precise formulation is "Who is the rearing mother?" With embryo donation, there is no reason not to treat the gestating woman as the rearing mother, other than a claim of the egg source to rear. Yet given the egg source's voluntary relinquishment of the embryo, and the gestation undertaken by the recipient for the purpose of rearing, the agreement of the egg source to relinquish rearing rights and duties should be observed. Indeed, to give her rearing rights and duties when the agreement stated otherwise would unconstitutionally interfere with the procreative liberty of the recipient couple.

240. Calling embryo donations "adoptions" appears to smuggle in a value premise about the moral status of the embryo by those who view the embryo itself as a person.

241. Given the absence of parental fitness tests for coital reproduction, requiring married couples to pass parental competency tests before receiving gamete or embryo donations would raise serious constitutional questions. An argument in favor of such tests might exist if there were a body of reliable data showing an increased risk to offspring in certain situations.

The possibility of tort liability against the physician for negligent selection of the recipient of donor gametes or donor embryos should also be considered. If it were reasonably foreseeable that a recipient would engage in prenatal or postnatal actions likely to cause serious injury to offspring, offspring would in theory have a cause of action against the person selecting the recipient of an embryo donation. *See supra* text accompanying notes 165-71. However, the suit would have to establish that an alternative recipient existed who could have successfully brought the child into the world without the damage complained of, since negligently selecting a recipient would not be a harm to offspring if no nondamaging alternative recipient existed. Such a suit would not lie for negligent selection of the recipient of egg or sperm donations, since an alternative recipient would have produced different offspring with the gametes in question.

for rearing. The possibility of embryo donation thus opens the door to surrogate gestators—women who gestate a couple's embryo and return it to them for rearing.[242]

Although not yet widely available, gestational surrogacy may be essential for some couples to reproduce or otherwise acquire a child for rearing. Consider the situation of a woman who, for medical resons, is unable to bear and birth her own offspring. A surrogate gestator may be the only way for a woman with ovaries who has undergone a hysterectomy, or who has a variety of other medical problems, to beget and rear a child of her genes.[243] Eventually, some fertile women might engage surrogate gestators for career, leisure, or lifestyle reasons.[244]

Not surprisingly, the prospect of surrogate gestators is controversial, and the legality and efficacy of surrogate contracts unclear. While not illegal per se, statutes against paying money beyond medical expenses for adoption might make paying surrogate fees a crime.[245] In addition, there is doubt about the enforceability of surrogate contracts. The surrogate gestator would probably have to terminate her parental rights and the genetic mother adopt the child for the transaction currently to be legally effectuated.[246] If the surrogate refused to relinquish custody of offspring,

---

242. Such a transaction differs from embryo donation in that the gestating woman does not rear the child. It also differs from both ordinary adoption and the current practice of "surrogate mothering" in that the gestating woman provides gestation only and not an egg as well. While this latter practice of "partial" surrogacy, in which the surrogate provides the egg and gestation, currently receives considerable attention in the media, and to some extent in the law journals, surrogacy in this Article is used to refer primarily to a surrogate who gestates the embryo provided by another, and who thus does not give birth to a child who is a lineal descendant.

243. Other medical indications would be if she has cancer of the uterus and needs to undergo radiation treatment, or is severely diabetic and hypertensive, or has phenylketonuria and will not be able to stay on the special diet necessary to prevent damage to a fetus.

244. This possiblity is presently theoretic, but one can expect that some women will prefer to avoid pregnancy for such reasons, if another woman is available to carry her child. It could lead to the development of an idea of "social infertility," and thus fit within the rubric of infertility treatment. *See infra* note 322.

245. Doe v. Kelley, 100 Mich. App. 169, 307 N.W.2d 438 (1981) held that the Michigan "baby-selling" statute could constitutionally be applied to a surrogate transaction in which a married couple paid a surrogate to be inseminated, carry the child to term and relinquish it to the couple at birth. However, the Kentucky Supreme Court has held that a similar surrogate arrangement does not violate the Kentucky statute against "baby selling." Surrogate Parenting, Inc. v. Kentucky, 704 S.W.2d 209 (Ky. 1986). For an argument against paying surrogates, see Annas, *The Baby Broker Boom*, 16 HASTINGS CENTER REP., June 1986, at 30, 31; H. Krause, *Artificial Conception: Legal Approaches*, 19 FAM. L.Q. 185, 199-204 (1985).

246. The presumption in favor of the birthing mother as the rearing mother would control, because until the development of IVF, the possibility of conflict with the genetic mother could not have arisen. However, greater recognition of surrogate contracts may be emerging. In the first reported birth of a child by a gestational surrogate in the United States, a trial court in Cleveland, Ohio permitted the couple to bring a "maternity" action to have the egg source, rather than the

many people assume that the courts would not specifically enforce the surrogate's agreement to relinquish the child at birth.[247]

A prohibition on surrogate contracts, however, can be questioned on constitutional grounds. Restrictions on paying surrogate fees and on enforcing surrogate contracts would infringe the procreative liberty of the couple providing the embryo. Unless the couple can hire a surrogate to bring the embryo to term, the couple will never be able to rear a child of their blood.[248] The couple's reproductive experience will be limited to gene transfer without rearing (through gamete or embryo donation), or rearing without gene transfer (through adoption).[249]

Such an interference with procreative liberty requires a justification beyond the prevention of symbolic harm or elevation of a particular morality of reproduction. Since the transfer of an embryo to a woman not providing the ovum does not physically damage the child, the main concerns with surrogacy are the psychosocial impact on offspring of rearing by a nongestating couple, the effect on the surrogate, and the symbolic meaning of hiring wombs for gestation.

Once again, the possibility of harm to offspring must be evaluated in light of the alternative. In most cases of gestational surrogacy there is no alternative way for the offspring to be born. If surrogate contracts are not enforced, couples will be hesitant to enter into them, and offspring will never be born by surrogacy.[250] Moreover, the lack of gestational bonding in rearing parents is widely accepted in adoption and step-parenting and is not ordinarily deemed so harmful to the child as to make death or nonexistence the preferable alternative. Indeed, in this respect surrogate gestation may be more desirable than existing adoption,

---

gestational surrogate, listed as the mother on the birth certificate. *See* Smith v. Jones, No. 85-53201402 (Mich. Cir. Ct.). Presumably she will be the rearing mother as well. Syrkowski v. Appleyard also allows the father of a child conceived through a partial surrogacy arrangement to use the state paternity act to establish his paternity, as part of the process by which the contracting couple acquires custody of the child borne by the surrogate. 420 Mich. 367, 375, 362 N.W.2d 211, 214 (1985).

247. *See, e.g.,* Annas, *Contracts to Bear A Child,* 11 HASTINGS CENTER REP., Apr. 1981, at 23-24. *But see In Court Battle for Baby M., Emotions Are Fierce,* N.Y. Times, Aug. 23, 1986, at 8, col. 1 (family court orders that custody of child born of partial surrogacy contract be awarded to contracting couple).

248. A similar, though probably less persuasive, argument can be made even if the surrogate is engaged for social reasons or convenience, rather than medical inability to bear a child. *See infra* note 322.

249. The surrogate could also argue that she has a right to satisfy her own procreative needs by having a nongenetically related gestational experience. Again, whether partial reproductive experiences will be protected in all cases remains to be seen.

250. *See supra* text accompanying notes 171-76.

foster parent, and stepparent practices, since the rearing couple will also be the genetic parents.[251]

Harm to the surrogate is a real possibility, but it may not be sufficient ground for overriding contractual commitments. Although a surrogate may be able to think of the gestating fetus as the couple's, as pregnancy continues and birth approaches, she is likely to begin regarding it as "hers." Relinquishing the child at birth may be extremely difficult, and could lead to grief, depression and the need for counselling.[252] Yet preventing informed women from playing such partial procreative roles denies them the freedom to decide how best to fulfill their own procreative needs. If they are willing to undergo those risks, it may be unfairly paternalistic to prevent them from doing so.

Beyond the potential harm to offspring and the surrogate, many people find a woman's detached and instrumental attitude toward her gestating capacity distasteful. Site of our gestation and the most intimate bond of all, the womb, is fraught with symbolic significance. Surrogate gestation appears to treat the body as a reproductive machine and the child as an instrument to selfish ends. In doing so, surrogate gestation denigrates a concept of motherhood that posits a sacred, natural bond between biological mother and child. Such meanings run deep and are of great significance. Yet they are symbolic concerns, and symbolic concerns do not generally justify infringement of reproductive liberty.

An analysis finding surrogate contracts to be constitutionally protected suggests that the allocation of rearing rights and duties in surrogate contracts should be given legal effect. Allowing a surrogate gestator to violate the agreement and abort or retain custody of the child at birth overlooks the impact of nonenforcement on the ability of couples to procreate through such contracts. Refusing to enforce a surrogate contract as against public policy would infringe the couple's procreative liberty as

---

251. In ordinary adoption women rear children whom they have not gestated, and women who gestate do not rear. The fact that the agreement to sever gestation and rearing is made before implantation, rather than after birth, may not be significant. Although women rarely conceive in order to bear a child to be reared by another, they sometimes decide soon after conception to carry to term and give up for adoption rather than abort. In this case the rearing couple will have a genetic tie with the offspring, even though another woman has gestated.

252. With surrogates, the complex of motives may include a wish for the attention and meaning of pregnancy without the obligation to rear, and the opportunity to relive and master a previous incident of relinquishing a child. Parker, *Motivation of Surrogate Mothers: Initial Findings*, 140 AM. J. PSYCHIATRY 117, 117 (1983).

much as an outright ban. Without the assurance of an enforceable contract, couples will be leery of entrusting their embryos to surrogates,[253] and will be deprived of this solution to their infertility.

One solution to the contract enforcement problem is to distinguish damages from specific performance as a remedy for the surrogate's breach of contract. Procreative liberty requires that the contract be honored, but it does not require that it be enforced by specific performance. If a surrogate is not enjoined from aborting, she can be ordered to pay damages to the couple for the loss that they have suffered. Similarly, in lieu of specific performance, damages can be awarded when the surrogate refuses to relinquish the child at birth.[254]

However, the case for specific performance of the promise to relinquish the child is strong in the case of a surrogate gestator. The surrogate received the couple's embryo on condition that she relinquish it to them at birth. Assuming all parties are fit parents, it is unclear why her wish to rear should override her promise to honor the genetic bond. The surrogate would never have had the embryo to bear if she had not agreed to return a child nine months later.[255] As "trustee" of the embryo for the couple, she should be obligated to transfer custody at birth.

E. ANONYMITY AND DISCLOSURE TO OFFSPRING

The secrecy of donor and surrogate transactions is a contested issue in collaborative reproduction. The interests of offspring in knowing their genetic and gestational roots conflicts with the desire of donors, surrogates, and recipients for privacy, and their freedom to collaborate anonymously for reproduction.[256]

---

253. It will also deny women wishing to be surrogates the opportunity to have the gestational experience without also having a genetic or rearing tie to offspring, a procreative experience which may be protected independently. *See supra* text accompanying notes 77-79.

254. While a woman cannot be prevented from aborting, it may be that she should be free to waive her right not to abort. If finding surrogates who will provide a surety bond or otherwise assure payment of damages in case of change of mind is difficult, this alternative may not be practical, and may also be constitutionally dubious if it deters couples from entering into surrogate contracts.

255. Of course, there is still a value judgment being made here about the importance of the gestational bond. The point is that its value may depend on how one comes to have that bond. If acquired with the promise to return the fully developed embryo to the hiring couple, the judgment is that the importance of the bond must give way to the promise made and the interest of the couple who provided the embryo.

256. Several different privacy interests are involved. Donors and surrogates may not want their identity known to offspring or to others. Recipients may not want others to know that they resorted to a donor or surrogate. Analysis of the privacy interests must distinguish the precise privacy concerns at stake.

Disclosure practices with donor sperm illustrate the pattern that egg and embryo donations are likely to follow. The donation is arranged by one or more intermediaries, without contact or disclosure of identity between donor and recipient, and little information provided to each about the other.[257] Since infertility itself is often hidden, the use of a donor is generally kept hidden from family and friends.[258]

Egg donations and embryo donations also require a medical intermediary, and thus little occasion for the parties to meet. The same desires for secrecy will operate, and it is unlikely that a different pattern will emerge.

Surrogate practices may involve more contact among the participants, because of the heavier investment of the surrogate and the ongoing nature of the relationship. Indeed, some surrogate programs now allow the parties to meet, and to be involved in the pregnancy in varying degrees throughout gestation. The couple may nevertheless hesitate to disclose the surrogate arrangement to others.[259]

Offspring learning of the existence of a missing genetic or gestational parent may yearn for contact with, or knowledge of, the absent parent. If the experience of adopted children is a guide, many of them will care deeply about this parent and some will be strongly driven to make contact, suffering enormously until they do.[260] Rearing parents willing to discuss the matter with offspring may have no further information to provide, since the transaction was handled anonymously through an intermediary. In many cases the intermediary providing the sperm will have no records of donor identity.[261] If records are available, they are

---

257. Some programs or sperm banks will show the recipients pictures of donors or provide other information, but donor identities are usually kept confidential. In many cases the recipients may have little say in selection of the donor. Similarly, the donor may have little say in selection of the recipient.

258. The obstetrician delivering the child often will not know whether the child was conceived with donor sperm, and will list the husband as the father on the birth certificate.

259. Sam Shepard's play, *Buried Child*, illustrates how deep dark family secrets eventually come out and wreak havoc in the process.

260. A moving account of an adopted person's desire to learn her genetic roots is found in B. LIFTON, TWICE BORN: MEMOIRS OF AN ADOPTED DAUGHTER (1975). The offspring might need to know if there is a family history of genetic defects which could affect her own offspring. Or she might need to locate siblings, to request a bone marrow or kidney transplant for which they may be the best match. *2 Long-Lost Siblings Might Provide Cure for a Cancer Victim*, N.Y. Times, Mar. 20, 1985, at 15, col. 4.

The interests of donors in knowing their offspring should also be considered. They too may want to meet or know their offspring, but have no way of doing so.

261. Many physicians performing donor insemination keep no records of the sperm donors. *See* Curie-Cohen, Luttrell & Shapiro, *supra* note 71, at 588.

likely to be kept confidential out of fear of legal liability.[262]

What should the policy be concerning maintenance of identifying records and disclosure of information to offspring? Resolution of the policy question requires an evaluation of the importance of knowing and avoiding disclosure of one's identity to biological descendants. If knowledge of genetic roots is deemed central to identity, then procreative freedom must give way to the needs of the child. Persons have no right to bring children into the world unless they are willing to do what is necessary, as reasonably decided by the community, for the child's well-being.[263]

Since adopted children have no constitutional right to learn their genetic and gestational roots,[264] it is unlikely that children born of embryo or gametic donation or surrogacy would have a right to learn confidential information about their genetic and gestational parents, even if such information existed. It is doubtful whether laws that allow adopted children to pierce adoption records for good cause would apply to donor and surrogate offspring, unless a formal post-birth adoption also occurred.[265] However, the state could protect future offspring by requiring that records be kept and by providing offspring access to them. Judging from the experience of adopted children, it is essential to have some information available to collaborative offspring who seek it. There are various ways to satisfy the child's need to know without violating the privacy of the parties.[266] If privacy cannot be protected, it would not be unreasonable to conclude that the needs of offspring should control.

Disclosure policies, however, might conflict with the desires of the collaborators to maintain privacy. Laws requiring that identifying records or other information be kept, or that access be provided, would conflict with the collaborators' procreative liberty and their desire for

---

262. Disclosure of this information could lead to legal liability for breach of confidentiality, as has occurred in wrongful disclosure about an adoption. Humphers v. First Interstate Bank of Oregon, 298 Or. 706, 696 P.2d 527 (1985).

263. The point is debatable, but the interest in procreating could be deemed protected only when there is an open or at least identifiable link with offspring. An anonymous gene link, in which the parent is not willing to be identified, might not give enough reproductive meaning to be included within procreative liberty.

264. Alma Society, Inc. v. Mellon, 601 F.2d 1225 (2d Cir.), cert. denied, 444 U.S. 995 (1979).

265. Note, Sealed Adoption Records and the Constitutional Right of Privacy of the Natural Parent, 34 RUTGERS L. REV. 451 (1982); Note, The Adult Adoptee's Constitutional Right to Know His Origins, 48 S. CAL. L. REV. 1196 (1975); Comment, Adoption Records Reform: Impact on Adoptees, 67 MARQ. L. REV. 110 (1983).

266. One alternative would be to keep nonidentifying information that would be available to the offspring at a certain age. Another would be to allow the donor to provide information at the time of donation or at any later time that the donor is willing to be contacted or known.

privacy. Absent a pledge of confidentiality, they might be unwilling to collaborate with others for reproduction. Freedom of reproductive choice would seem to give them the right to order their relations as they choose, including keeping their identity secret from recipients or offspring.

But there is a further complication that shows the tricky nature of reasoning about reproductive choice. If the law allowing genetic disclosure had been on the books, the people now seeking that knowledge never would have been born. The donor and recipient may not have agreed on the transaction if they could not be assured secrecy, preferring no donation to later disclosure.[267] By satisfying the offsprings' need to know their roots, the law might prevent the birth of future children through collaborative arrangements. Without guaranteed anonymity, donors and recipients may not enter into collaborative transactions. However the offspring who would be born only if anonymity were guaranteed might still prefer a deracinated existence where genetic parents are unknown to not being been born at all.

But this is not a sufficient argument for frustrating the need of existing persons to know their genetic roots. There is no obligation to potential persons to bring them into existence. Failure to birth them does them no wrong, for no person exists to be wronged.[268] The state may prefer to satisfy the need of existing persons to know their genetic roots, rather than increase the number of children born of donors and surrogates, even if the latter would find an anomic life preferable to none at all.[269] The welfare of offspring is a sufficient basis for limiting reproductive contracts. The state may enact—and arguably should enact—policies that protect offsprings' need to know their genetic and gestational roots.

F. THE SALE OF GAMETES AND EMBRYOS

In the United States, sperm "donors" sell their sperm to physicians or sperm banks which then sell it to the recipient.[270] The system grew

---

267. The recipients might also want it kept a secret, so that the child will think they are the parents in every sense, or to avoid the potential discomfort of seeing contact made between the gene source and offspring.

268. D. PARFIT, REASONS AND PERSONS 351-59 (1985); Bayles, *Harm to the Unconceived*, 5 PHIL. & PUB. AFF. 292, 294 (1976).

269. That is, if they come to exist at all, they would find it preferable. If they never exist, then their feelings do not matter.

270. There is a question of proper terminology here, since "donors" are not usually thought of as "sellers." Yet fees are paid, and the transaction involves a transfer of gametes to an intermediary

out of the need to compensate the donor for the time, effort, and inconvenience of required abstinence and availability, and generally has not been controversial.[271]

If sperm donors are paid, should egg donors also be paid? They too undergo inconvenience and are, in fact, at greater physical risk than are sperm donors.[272] They too are relinquishing rights in potential offspring. To deny female gamete donors payment while permitting it for males would arbitrarily discriminate on the basis of sex.

A similar case can be made for compensating embryo donors. They will have undergone the same burdens as gamete donors, and might reasonably want to recoup the considerable costs of embryo production and storage. A totally uncompensated transaction might be unfair, given the costs of egg retrieval, fertilization, and storage. We do not, for example, expect organ or tissue donors to pay for the costs of organ removal.[273]

Yet some people object to paying gamete donors, and would object strongly to buying and selling embryos. Some of the concern is instrumental—the fear that money will drive the donor's choice and lead to dishonesty about personal health or family history that, if revealed, might disqualify them as donors:[274] While this might be a factor in the selling of blood and sperm, it appears less likely to operate with egg and embryo donations, though it could operate with surrogates.

A deeper source of concern is a view of the corrupting effects of markets on altruism and the symbolic meaning of buying and selling embryos. As argued in Richard Titmuss's famous work on blood, a market

---

and eventual recipient for consideration. The inseminating physician charges a fee for sperm procurement, and may not think of it as a purchase from the donor or sperm bank and a sale to the recipient. A small voluntary system does exist with semen. In some cases gifts, or noncompensated transfers, of sperm occur between friends or family members.

271. Perhaps because the system has not been closely examined. Some countries, such as Australia, find payment for gametes objectionable, and ban it. P. SINGER & D. WELLS, *supra* note 41, at 80-81.

272. *See supra* text accompanying note 230.

273. The organ donor is donating the organ, not the costs of the organ retrieval and transplant operations. Of course, a very generous person would make that gift as well, though ordinarily we ask organ donors only to provide the organ and not the other costs associated with the transplant.

274. Little is known about physician selection of sperm donors and characteristics and motivations of donors. *See generally* Annas, *supra* note 138. It may be that physicians are not asking questions about medical and family history that would lead some potential donors, perhaps motivated by a desire to reproduce, to lie if they thought that truthful answers would disqualify them.

tends to drive out the possibility of altruism, and increase costs for everyone.[275] Just as money payment to organ donors is deemed unethical and illegal,[276] payment to reproductive collaborators for gametes and embryos could be viewed as unethical and also be prohibited in order to give the community an opportunity to show social solidarity through voluntary donations.

Objections to the sale of embryos is closely tied to the symbolic meaning that attaches to human embryos. Since the embryo is a genetically unique, potential person, payment seems to signify the buying and selling of potential persons, and conjures up dehumanizing images of slavery or trading of embryos like commodities in the marketplace.[277] A fee to give up the embryo—to relinquish the right to discard, transfer, or otherwise control the potential person—is deemed unacceptable because of the attitude it conveys or symbolizes about human life generally. However, it should be noted that paying for an embryo would not give unlimited power over the embryo or the person it might become. The recipient who "owns" the embryo, in the sense of having primary decision-making authority over it, does not have unlimited power to control it, much less injure any offspring that resulted from the transaction.[278]

Such concerns are important symbolic, constitutive concerns, just as are other concerns about embryo disposition.[279] They may well motivate private sector actors, and should be respected. A different question is whether they are sufficient to justify a state ban on embryo sales. This would depend on whether payment is necessary for a couple to obtain embryos to reproduce. It may be that mandatory embryo donation policies and the willingness of people to donate will engender a supply of

---

275. R. TITMUSS, THE GIFT RELATIONSHIP (1971); Arrow, *Gifts and Exchanges*, 1 PHIL. & PUB. AFF. 343 (1972); *cf.* P. HAGEN, BLOOD: GIFT OR MERCHANDISE (1982); Singer, *Altrusim and Commerce: A Defense of Titmuss Against Arrow*, 2 PHIL. & PUB. AFF. 312 (1973).

276. Paying consideration for organs beyond the costs of retrieval is a federal crime. Title III, 98 Stat. 2339, 2346 (1984). The exploitation possible in the sale of organs for transplants is not present with gamete or embryo donors. Their acquisition does not threaten the life or health of the donor in the way that buying organs from live donors would. However, the symbolic taint that arises with the sale of cadaver organs and tissue might exist with buying and selling gametes and embryos. However, the federal law does not address paying consideration for gamete and embryos.

277. Annas thinks that permitting the sale of embryos will lead to application of the Uniform Commercial Code warranty provisions to embryo sales. Annas, *Redefining Parenthood and Protecting Embryos*, 14 HASTINGS CENTER REP., Oct. 1984, at 50-52. However, the UCC treatment of sales of human tissue as sales of services, and hence exempt from implied warranties of merchantability and fitness, might also apply to embryos. UCC § 2-316(S). If not, the statute could be amended to reach the same result.

278. *See supra* text accompanying notes 120-23.

279. *See supra* text accompanying notes 115-20.

embryos sufficient to the demand, and thus obviate the need for payment.[280]

However, if payment is necessary to obtain embryos, a state ban on payment would interfere with a couple's ability to obtain the embryo or gametes they need to gestate and rear children. Since a person's right to procreate includes contracting with gamete donors, the state could not rely on symbolic distate alone to justify a ban on paid embryo donations.[281] The perceived indignity in transferring embryos for money does not appear sufficient to justify interference with procreative liberty.[282]

G. PAYING SURROGATES

A similar analysis applies to paying surrogates for their services, a prospect that has raised considerable controversy. Payment is thought to exploit the surrogate's financial need and to be illegal under laws prohibiting "baby-selling."[283]

A ban on paying surrogates would interfere with the procreative liberty of the person engaging the surrogate and possibly the surrogate as well. The burdens of gestation are so great that few unrelated women will choose to gestate the embryo of another for altruism alone.[284] A woman in need will thus not be able to reproduce unless she can pay a gestator to bear "her" child and return it to her for rearing.

---

280. As noted previously, demand for embryo donations as an infertility treatment is likely to be small. *See supra* text accompanying notes 236-37. Physicians will have a great influence in determining whether altruistic donations will meet the need, since they can encourage people to donate and can influence whether donors will request reimbursement of embryo production and storage charges.

281. *See supra* text accompanying notes 82-84.

282. A ban on sale of embryos for research purposes is a different matter, since the ban would not appear to interfere with procreative liberty. Payment to embryo holders is probably not necessary to induce a sufficient supply for reseach purposes, since separate egg and sperm donations may meet the need. Thus, a ban on sale of embryos for research purposes would be a policy question similar to other questions of embryo research policy, and would not directly implicate procreative rights. *See supra* text accompanying notes 144-61.

283. *See* Doe v. Kelley, 106 Mich. App. 169, 307 N.W.2d 438, (1981), *cert. denied*, 459 U.S. 1183 (1983); Holder, *Surrogate Motherhood: Babies for Fun and Profit*, CASE & COMMENT, Mar.-Apr. 1985, at 3-5. The Warnock Committee recommended that commercial surrogacy arrangements be criminalized and that surrogate contracts not be enforced. WARNOCK, COMMITTEE REPORT, *supra* note 46, at 46-47. The Kentucky Supreme Court has held that state"baby-selling" laws do not prohibit paid surrogacy. Surrogate Parenting, Inc. v. Kentucky, 704 S.W.2d 209 (Ky. 1986).

284. The practice of intrafamilial surrogacy (and gamete and embryo donation) may also occur to some extent. *Surrogate Mother Gives Birth to Niece*, Austin American Statesman, Nov. 8, 1985, at 6, col. 1. Indeed, it was a woman's willingness to bear the child of her sister's husband which led Noel Keane, the Detroit lawyer who started the American practice of surrogacy, into the field. N. KEANE & D. BREO, THE SURROGATE MOTHER (1981). It is unclear what the social and psychological effects of intrafamilial surrogacy will be.

Assuming that altruistic surrogacy is permitted, are there additional harms, when surrogates are paid, that would justify this interference with a couple's procreative choice? "Baby-selling" laws prohibit fees for adoption in order to protect the child from unfit parents and the mother from exploitation and coercion.[285] But these concerns do not apply to surrogate gestators who freely choose this reproductive role before pregnancy occurs, uninfluenced by the stigma of illegitimacy or the financial burdens of single parenthood. An acceptable system of paid surrogacy must assure that the surrogate is fully informed, has independent legal counsel, and has made a deliberative choice.[286]

There is also a fear that surrogates will be drawn primarily from poorer groups, who will serve the rich with their bodies as well as their housekeeping and childrearing services. Indeed, money is likely to be a prime motive in the decision of women to serve as surrogates, but other factors are reported to play a role.[287] It is not apparent that only poor women will select that occupation, much less that the operation of a labor market in this area is more unjust than labor markets in other areas.

A more basic concern is the acceptability of women freely choosing to "rent" their uteri to others as a source of income. The idea of paying women to gestate for nine months, with all the attendant physical and psychological complications of pregnancy and birth, followed by transfer of the child to another, is discomforting. Part of the discomfort arises from witnessing another person risking life and limb for money, just as witnessing the backbreaking labor of manual workers' discomforts.[288]

Discomfort also arises from the symbolic devaluation of the maternal bond that payment signifies. A widespread and perhaps dominant moral sensibility recoils at transforming the mystery of birth into a commercial transaction.[289] The surrogate is literally renting her womb to

---

285. *See supra* text accompanying note 283.

286. The surrogate has sometimes been represented by the lawyer hired by the couple to contract with the surrogate. While this conflict of interest is not unethical if disclosed to the surrogate, it would be more desirable for the surrogate to have independent legal counsel.

287. *See supra* note 252.

288. The role of money in leading people to engage in physical labors, including highly risky ones, is accepted in numerous ways. In fact, many occupations can be characterized as the slow sale of one's body, health, and vitality over time. Consider the slow erosion of the bodies of miners, petrochemical workers, and professional athletes in the course of their work. Indeed, the Internal Revenue Code gives professional sports team owners the right to depreciate the players, a recognition of the way that their bodies are used in their work. Pregnancy is a unique physical experience, but many kinds of work also involve strenous, physical labor.

289. George Annas has articulated this idea in several contexts. *See, e.g.,* Annas, *Redefining Parenthood and Protecting Embryos: Why We Need New Laws,* 14 HASTINGS CENTER REP., Oct. 1984, at 50, 50-62.

another couple. She is willing to alienate "her" child and forsake the sacred maternal bond for money. Banning the practice is a way to show that the community supports the importance of the mother-child bond.[290]

The goal is a laudable one. However, the surrogate and couple engaging her are likely to see matters differently. They would probably rate their desire to procreate or to assist others to do so to be more important than the need to maintain this symbol of the maternal-child bond. If the contract implications of procreative liberty are recognized and the interests of the parties or offspring are not tangibly harmed, gestator salaries should remain a matter of individual choice, and should not be prohibited by state law.[291]

VI. THE REIFICATION OF REPRODUCTION

Beyond fears of harm to embryo, offspring, family or collaborators is a more generalized concern that technologizing conception demeans human dignity and exploits women, and may lead down a slippery slope to complete genetic and technical control of humans.

A powerful image of these fears is Huxley's description in *Brave New World* of state hatcheries where babies with predetermined characteristics are decanted from bottles with pre-assigned social roles.[292] Such images influence perceptions of IVF and the public policy that should control its use.

IVF may be the first step toward such a world, but a host of factors independent of noncoital conception would have to coalesce to bring about that dystopia. Such a hypothetical possibility does not justify denying married couples safe and effective infertility treatments now. Generalized fears about technology often reflect symbolic, moral, or religious concerns and thus are not constitutional grounds for government action in the public sphere. But they do caution us to use noncoital technology safely and reasonably, taking steps to avert the most likely kinds of harm.

---

290. Surely no one expects the unrelated surrogate's contribution to include the payment of medical and legal expenses incurred in the surrogacy. Nor would people probably object to paying any lost wages, and even something to cover the stresses of pregnancy and relinquishment, which could be considerable. The problem concerns the symbolic meaning of renting the womb and the transfer of rearing rights and duties in an actual child for money. However, the payment can also be characterized as a payment for services that lead to the child to be transferred.

291. Regulation to assure informed consent and free choice in making such contracts would be constitutional. *See supra* text accompanying notes 67-70, *infra* text accompanying notes 339-45.

292. A. HUXLEY, *supra* note 44.

A privately-derived ethic is necessary, even if a public one is not constitutionally available.

To explore these issues, this section discusses concerns with objectifying nature and the impact on women of the new reproduction.

A. OBJECTIFYING THE NATURAL ORDER AND SLIPPERY SLOPES

At the most general level is an anxiety or fear that IVF goes too far in objectifying and manipulating the intimacies of procreation. Undermining the integrity of the procreative process, it is thought, will ultimately undermine human dignity and pave the way to more nefarious uses.

For example, some persons may accept noncoital separation of sex and reproduction, but recoil at the coldly instrumental reductionism of IVF.[293] They see the mystery of conception and reproduction reduced to a series of technical maneuvers intended to implant an embryo in a uterus and coax a child out. The ovaries are bombarded with powerful drugs and the ripening follicles punctured to remove the eggs. Fertilization occurs in a dish, rather than in the dark recesses of the fallopian tubes. After further manipulations, the extracorporeal embryo is transported to the uterus, with the hope that it will there find a home. Further extensions, such as freezing, thawing, splitting embryos, cloning, and surrogacy, compound the felony of treating the body as manipulatable matter.

Yet the attitude toward body and reproduction decried here is no different than that which underlays standard infertility treatment, indeed, obstetrics and medical science generally. Science objectifies the natural order, so that it may be understood and manipulated for human ends. Medical science objectifies the natural order to combat disease and illness. Extracorporeal conception is unique, but not because it objectifies the body more than ordinary obstetrics and gynecology do.[294]

---

293. This theme is not always directly stated, but it lurks in the background of much commentary on IVF. It stems from a romantic, Luddite view of the relation of technology to the natural order, as represented in such works as T. ROSZAK, THE MAKING OF A COUNTER CULTURE (1969). *See* R. MCCORMICK, *supra* note 66, at 312-21 (1981).

294. One need only recall standard maneuvers in infertility treatment and obstetrics. Infertility workups include stimulated cycles, hysterosalpinograms, and other tests that objectify the mystery of conception. Microsurgical tubal reconstruction or reanastomosis after tubal ligation is the competing alternative to IVF. *See supra* text accompanying notes 22-24. Modern obstetrical practice relies on electronic fetal monitors, labor induction and postponement drugs, and cesarean section. Robertson, *supra* note 79, at 452-58. None of these procedures are distinguishable from the invasive and objectifying techniques used in other areas of medicine.

The potential for dehumanization sensed in IVF may also stem from the attitude toward offspring that some people think it signifies. Couples resorting to IVF, at a time of overpopulation and disabled and minority children awaiting adoption, are sometimes viewed as selfish consumers who view children as commodities whose sole value is in providing parental satisfaction. Such an attitude conflicts with a pervasive reproductive ideology, which holds that children should be brought into the world out of love for themselves and not to serve parental needs.

Such a charge could, however, be levelled at any couple investing in medical treatment of infertility.[295] Parental motivations for infertility treatment and consequences for offspring are no doubt more complicated than this charge acknowledges. Parents usually love their children, but ends and means intertwine. Children are instruments for parental meaning and satisfaction, at the same time that they are loved for themselves. We use them and are used by them; we love them for themselves, and hope that we are loved in return.

IVF does not appear to hold any greater risk of commodification than other currently accepted modes of conception and acquisition of children.[296] Like other infertility treatments, IVF does view the body as an object to be prodded into satisfying parental desires for offspring. But extracorporeal conception should not lessen parental regard for offspring well-being. Indeed, having gone through so much, they may value children and nature more highly.[297]

Finally, one must contend with the slippery slope fear captured so well in Huxley's dystopic image of babies being decanted from bottles in state hatcheries. People fear that IVF crosses a significant threshold toward such practices. Indeed, access to the embryo appears to be an essential precondition for genetic manipulation of offspring. Access to the embryo will facilitate pre-transfer genetic screening and selection, and eventually enable gene therapy for serious disease to occur. Perhaps some of the more exotic work occurring in animal husbandry, such as splitting embryos, co-culture, and worldwide transportation of frozen

---

295. The same charge could be levelled at any couple that reproduces coitally before the supply of disabled and minority children awaiting adoption is exhausted, since they are "selfishly" pursuing their desire for genetically related children.

296. Persons making this charge usually overlook how traditional reproductive practices could also be condemned on this basis. Robertson, *Surrogate Mothers: Not so Novel After All*, 13 HASTINGS CENTER REP., Oct. 1983, at 28 (replying to Krimmel, *The Case Against Surrogate Parenting*, 13 HASTINGS CENTER REP., Oct. 1983, at 35).

297. They have seen the mystery of fertilization up close, and may come away awed by the sight—humbled by their crude efforts to replicate nature.

embryos may one day also occur.[298] Yet taking the first small steps does not mean the intermediate steps will also be taken in the near future, much less the grander, apocalyptic ones.[299] Given the difficulties in getting fertilized eggs to implant, making the freezing and thawing of eggs or embryos clinically available alone will be a major achievement. The possibility of engineering multifactorial genetic traits sometime in the next several generations is more easily imagined than accomplished. It should not prevent treatment of infertility problems now.[300]

B. IMPACT ON WOMEN

The reification-dehumanization argument may also be examined through its impact on women and their reproductive roles. Sexual inequality can be traced to women's gestational role in human reproduction and the early nurturing role which that entails.[301] A technology that alters the site of conception and allows female genetic and gestational parentage to be separated is potentially significant for women. This technology should expand freedom by increasing the range of reproductive choice, and may contribute to new reproductive and social roles for women. This section discusses whether the new reproduction is good for women.

---

298. Foote, *In Vitro Fertilization and Embryo Transfer in Domestic Animals: Applications in Animals and Implications for Humans* (1986) (unpublished manuscript) (available from the *Southern California Law Review*).

299. *See* PRESIDENT'S COMMISSION FOR THE STUDY OF ETHICAL PROBLEMS IN MEDICINE AND BIOMEDICAL AND BEHAVIORAL RESEARCH, SPLICING LIFE 62-64 (1982) (fears that genetic engineering will lead to attempts to control or interfere with the "wisdom of evolution" are unfounded) [hereinafter PRESIDENT'S COMMISSION]; Schauer, *Slippery Slope*, 99 HARV. L. REV. 361 (1985) (explaining the slippery slope argument as the perceived inability of future decisionmakers to recognize, comprehend, or defend doctrinal lines drawn by their predecessors).

300. PRESIDENT'S COMMISSION, *supra* note 299, at 62-64. Nor should technical possibilities in future societies be harshly condemned from our present vantage point, since societies with such visionary techniques available may well have undergone social and normative change that makes such uses perfectly acceptable to them. Professor Lawrence Tribe is quite perceptive on this point. *See* Tribe, *Technology Assessment and the Fourth Discontinuity: The Limits of Instrumental Rationality*, 46 S. CAL. L. REV. 617 (1973); Tribe, *Ways Not to Think About Plastic Trees: New Foundations for Environmental Law*, 83 YALE L.J. 1315 (1974).

301. S. FIRESTONE, THE DIALECTICS OF SEX (1970) and D. DINNERSTEIN, THE MERMAID AND THE MINOTAUR (1976) are important works tying sexual inequality to gender differences in early nurturing, a situation that results from the female role in gestation. Full sexual equality is then possible only if gestation and early nurturance is shared with men or performed in an artificial womb.

1. *The Dark Side: Reinforcing the Mother Machine*

Most feminist writing on the new reproduction has been critical, condemning it as an extension of patriarchy into the reproductive affairs of women.[302] Having wrested control of birthing with anesthesia, cesarean section, and fetal monitoring, male-dominated obstetrics is viewed as using IVF to extend patriarchal control to conception itself, thus providing a further opportunity to exploit women.[303]

While this critique makes no attempt to assess the benefits of IVF, it does recall past gynecological abuses. The experience with hysterectomy, radical mastectomy, and cesarean section suggests caution in the face of offers by male doctors to cut into women's bodies for women's supposed benefit.[304] Since women may feel obligated to use IVF to satisfy male demands for lineal offspring or their own internalized concept of self as mother,[305] women rather than men should have primary control over this technology.

Feminists have also been concerned that women serving as egg and embryo donors and surrogates will be objectified or exploited as reproductive machines. The feminist critics are suspicious of "free" exchange of reproductive services through contract, for the neutral forms of contract may mask substantive inequality in bargaining power and needs. They fear that third world and poor women will be exploited to meet the reproductive needs of the middle and upper classes, adding the gestation

---

302. Feminist concern with reproductive autonomy generally has focused on abortion and contraception, and has paid less attention to the treatment of infertility. The attention it has paid has usually been hostile. *See, e.g.*, R. ARDITTI, R. KLEIN & S. MINDEN, TEST-TUBE WOMEN (1984); G. COREA, *supra* note 30; H. HOLMES, B. HOSKINS & M. GROSS, THE CUSTOM-MADE CHILD (1981); B. ROTHMAN, THE TENTATIVE PREGNANCY 235-43 (1986).

303. *See* A. RICH, OF WOMAN BORN: MOTHERHOOD AS EXPERIENCE AND INSTITUTION 117-48 (1976); Leavitt, *Birthing and Anesthesia: The Debate Over Twilight Sleep*, 6 SIGNS 147 (1980). A hidden premise here is that women are powerless to resist a technology once it is available, and thus that doctors will be able to use it on women with ease. *See* Rothman, *The Products of Conception: The Social Context of Reproductive Choices*, 11 J. MED. ETHICS 188, 192 (1985).

304. BOSTON WOMEN'S HEALTH BOOK COLLECTIVE, THE NEW OUR BODIES, OURSELVES: A BOOK BY AND FOR WOMEN (1984); G. COREA, THE HIDDEN MALPRACTICE: HOW AMERICAN MEDICINE TREATS WOMEN AS PATIENTS AND PROFESSIONALS (1977) (tracing effects of male domination of medical profession on health care received by women); B. EHRENREICH & D. ENGLISH, COMPLAINTS AND DISORDERS: THE SEXUAL POLITICS OF SICKNESS (1973) (tracing history of institutional sexism in health care). IVF is thus perceived as another opportunity for male gynecologists and obstetricians to profit from women's reproduction.

305. The internalized image of oneself as mother may be seen alternatively as an expression of freedom happily accepted by the woman, or as a male engendered plot to keep women shackled to biological functions, "barefoot and pregnant," so to speak. Indeed, some women undergoing IVF would be happy to adopt or conceive with donor sperm, but feel pressured to give their spouse a lineal descendant.

of babies to the housekeeping and childrearing services which disadvantaged women now provide.

The notion of gestational surrogates is especially offensive to feminists, since it views women as wombs to be rented and then discarded for the greater glory of middle and upper class couples. While surrogacy frees some women of gestational burdens and thus places them on a reproductive par with men, it transfers the burden to women who cannot resist the offer to bear the children of the rich. Feminists are also offended at a system which, for money, callously denies the maternal bond to offspring.[306]

Even egg and embryo donation may exploit and objectify women as cogs in mother machines. For example, flushing embryos after in vivo conception for transfer to other women literally treats the donors like the breeding cows that inspired the technique.[307] Even egg donation can be exploitive if women are not otherwise undergoing medical procedures, for it requires superovulatory drugs and surgery to harvest a sufficient number of eggs.[308]

An overarching concern is that separation of women into discrete reproductive roles denies the maternal bond and treats them as less than full persons. The fear is that technology will reify donors and surrogates as components of a reproductive process with baby as product. Like subcontractors in a business enterprise, participating women will relate to a broker or contractor and have no contact with each other or the resulting child. As the parties negotiate at arm's length over the terms of gamete and uterine exchange, the human essence of reproduction is replaced by the male model of competitive, arms length marketplace transactions.

---

306. Women have long been paid to do housekeeping and childrearing for other women, and in the past have functioned as wetnurses. Yet creating a class of gestators is more offensive, because of the risks to the surrogate and the devaluation of the maternal gestational bond. The underlying value issue concerns the importance of the genetic or gestational tie *tout court* in women, an issue that, prior to IVF technology, has not had to be faced.

307. This is the Buster program described *supra* note 37. The procedure has now become standard practice in the cattle industry. Seidel, *supra* note 33, at 54. This program has been controversial because it has been funded by private venture capital, induced in part by the application for a patent on the procedures and instruments used in the lavage and embryo transfer process. Since medical process patents have been rare, the patent application has stirred debate, particularly because of its connection with reproduction. Leroy Walters and George Annas have opposed issuance of such a patent. *See Gore Hearings, supra* note 103, at 319-20 (statement of Leroy Walters). They have not, however, considered the role of patents in inducing investment in research that could prove beneficial to infertile persons.

308. *See* Murphy, *Egg Farming and Women's Future,* in TEST-TUBE WOMEN, *supra* note 302, at 68-76.

Feminists are also not sanguine about technical developments that aim to improve the efficacy of IVF. For example, an important step in the further development of IVF will be the ability to select out the best embryos for transfer, with the rest discarded or used in research. Embryo selection will also allow genetic screening and even gene therapy to occur. Yet this power carries the ability to deselect embryos on the basis of gender. Given societal preferences for firstborn males, feminists fear that preimplantation sex selection will merely reflect, and hence perpetuate, patriarchy.[309]

In sum, initial feminist writing on the new reproduction is skeptical, mistrustful, and in some cases outraged by the notion of superovulation, egg retrieval, embryo freezing and transfer, and the use of egg donors and surrogates. Some writers come close to recommending a total ban on IVF.[310] While such a position risks inconsistency with claims of freedom to control reproduction, it does remind us of the need to proceed cautiously with noncoital reproduction.

2. *The Bright Side: Increasing Reproductive Choice*

A more rounded view would consider how IVF and noncoital reproduction enhances choice for women. In decrying potential abuses, the feminist critics lose sight of the freedom it gives women, for noncoital reproduction expands women's choices over when and how to reproduce, thus increasing freedom. Control of the timing of reproduction is usually liberating for women.

Despite dangers of misuse, noncoital reproduction has many positive features for women. The widest use of IVF will be by infertile couples, enabling them to conceive, bear, and rear a child of their genes and gestation. This will be a major achievement, relieving these couples of guilt and conflict and giving meaning to their lives. Further experience should reduce the costs and increase the efficacy of IVF. The development of professional standards and certification will help assure that women get competent services for their fee. Indeed, given its costs, a major problem will be to assure access to IVF services for all women who could benefit from them.[311]

---

309. *See* B. ROTHMAN, *supra* note 302, at 116-39.

310. Corea's polemical *The Mother Machine*, so harshly condemns IVF that one is left with the impression that the author would ban IVF totally. *See* G.. COREA, *supra* note 30.

311. *See* Dresser, *supra* note 6, at 160-65, for consideration of justice arguments for the provision of infertility services to indigent persons.

A remedy for infertility is implicitly supportive of the behaviors that cause infertility. By reducing the risks of infertility from postponed childbearing, women will be free to start careers before families, thus overcoming some of the biological differences that prevent women and men from having equal access to work roles. Control over the timing of pregnancy is central to a woman's reproductive freedom, and IVF promotes such control.[312]

The ability to separate the maternal genetic and gestational parent through IVF further enhances reproductive choice in several important ways. It gives women without ovarian or uterine function the ability to be genetic or gestational, as well as rearing, parents.[313] There is no reason why their particular biological need should go unfullfilled when others' procreative needs are satisfied.

The donors may also find satisfaction in the discrete or partial reproductive roles decried by the feminist critics. They may find reproductive meaning in contributing eggs or embryos to others while avoiding the burdens of gestation and childrearing.[314] Even gestational surrogacy may be satisfying for particular women, despite the disappointment and

---

312.   The point is that IVF indirectly supports such behavior by reducing the risks. It is no guarantee that pregnancy will occur when desired. (IVF thus should not encourage disregard of measures to prevent venereal disease, merely because the resulting tubal damage from pelvic inflammatory disease might be alleviated by IVF.) Further control over the timing of pregnancy will come with advances in embryo freezing and selection. For example, genetic screening of embryos might allow healthy embryos created when the woman is young to be stored until education, career, or relationship goals are worked out. They can then be transferred to the woman when there is a lower risk of a handicapped birth than if fertilization occurred shortly before implantation. IVF thus provides a hedge against maternal age-related offspring handicaps.

313.   It would also allow surrogacy for fertile women who want to rear their genetic children without undergoing the physical experiences of childbearing. The question of surrogacy for convenience, decried by almost everyone, may turn out to be more acceptable if it proves to be an effective way for women to combine work and reproduction. Since men have and rear offspring without gestation, should not women also, if only to compete more equally with men in the workplace? As long as surrogate interests are protected, an optimal situation for all might result from surrogacy for convenience, if one accepts the change in the concept of mother that it would appear to entail.

314.   Some sperm donors seem to derive reproductive meaning from anonymous donation, so some egg and in vivo conceived embryo donors probably will as well. An embryo donor in Dr. Buster's program emphasized this motivation in testimony before Congress. When interviewed about her reasons for wishing to become a donor, she said:

> All I did was hold up a picture of my son, and I figured that if I can help another woman have a child that is as healthy as my child and be as happy having a child and being a mother, then why not help her since I just have these glorious eggs, and I should donate them.

> I come from an extremely healthy background. I have two 90-year-old grandmothers. I have no cancer, no diabetes, disfigurements, or any type of catastrophic diseases, and I figured that I should just have someone else use these genes since I wouldn't be using them.

Gore Hearings, supra note 103, at 255 (statement of Ms. Cynthia Imhot).

guilt experienced in handing over the fruit of one's womb to the contracting couple.

If collaborative reproduction is viewed positively, reproduction contracts become the instruments of reproductive freedom. Contract facilitates the exercise of procreative liberty by giving certainty of the performance bargained for, thus encouraging people to make collaborative reproductive arrangements.[315] In fact, the fear that cold contract will override the personal aspects of human reproduction may be undercut when women are primary participants. The relational instincts of women might lead to cooperation rather than conflict in postbirth relations among reproductive collaborators, extending, rather than closing, the net of family.[316]

Noncoital reproduction also will be helpful to lesbian and single women who wish to reproduce without having to resort to a male partner. Although they will demand donor sperm more frequently than IVF, they stand to benefit from social recognition of the general freedom to control procreation by noncoital means. While some doctors may continue to shun such patients, the medical marketplace is now commodious enough to meet their needs. Indeed, medical supervision of donor insemination is desirable, since it can assure proper screening and timing and thus avoid the medical and legal risks of "amateur" insemination.[317]

IVF is also promising for those women at risk for offspring with genetic disease. By making the embryo accessible, IVF may lead to the ability to identify the sex and genes of the extracorporeal embryo. Genetic screening of embryos will avoid the need for later prenatal testing and abortion of genetically handicapped fetuses.[318] While the ability to

---

315. Which is why failure to enforce the surrogate's contract constitutes an interference with procreative liberty, and thus requires the state to honor surrogate contracts in accordance with existing principles of contract law. *See supra* text accompanying notes 247-51.

316. C. GILLIGAN, IN A DIFFERENT VOICE (1980); Held, *Feminism and Epistemology: Recent Work on the Connection Between Gender and Knowledge,* 14 PHIL. & PUB. AFF. 296, 300-01 (1985). It is not unduly idealistic to think that a substantial number of collaborative transactions might have wholesome outcomes. Rituals and norms to regulate these relations are still to be determined, and may lead genetic and gestational mothers to share rearing, or choose the extent of interaction with each other that they wish, rather than be blotted from each other's lives as the contract mode coldly permits.

317. The risks of infection and legal uncertainty have been described *supra* text accompanying notes 223-29. A male factor is necessary for women to reproduce, but not necessarily a male partner. Cloning and other techniques may eventually relieve women of the need for a male factor altogether. J. CHERFAS & J. GRIBBEN, THE REDUNDANT MALE (1985).

318. This is an advantage only for persons at high risk, since for purposes of embryo selection, fetal screening techniques such as amniocentesis, ultrasonography, and chorion villi biopsy can be done much more easily than an IVF procedure.

sex embryos is troubling because of the likely preference for male first children, it is women who will be choosing and participating in preferences for offspring of particular gender.[319]

The claim that noncoital technology enhances freedom should not be exaggerated. The technology does not always work and has considerable expense and stress associated with it.[320] Moreover, noncoital technology is liberating and freedom-enhancing only in a context in which personal meaning for women is closely tied to their gestational functions in reproduction. IVF does not liberate from gestation, and hence from the intimate and unequal tie with childrearing that gestation entails. While IVF will eventually enable some women to rear their genetic offspring without gestation and others to gestate or have genetic offspring without rearing, it does not free women entirely from their biological role in human gestation.

A more revolutionary, though far distant, development would be the complete extracorporeal gestation of human beings. Perhaps ectogenesis is necessary to cut the female tie with childrearing, and thus provide full, substantive equality with men.[321] Yet ectogenesis, when uterine gestation is possible, entails another loss, for it deprives offspring of the gestational bond.[322]

---

319. At the very least it would help women who would abort because of the sex of the fetus and save marriages where partners strongly desire offspring of a particular sex. Since this mode of sex selection also requires the woman to undergo the rigors of IVF, it may be used only where there is a very strong desire for sex selection.

320. *See supra* note 7 and *infra* text accompanying notes 339-41. Thus a major problem is the traditional health care problem of assuring access and competent care.

321. *See supra* note 301. Another alternative that might effect sexual equality would be male pregnancy, now said to be a biological possibility. Mansfield, *A Womb of His Own*, Washington Post, May 9, 1986, at D1, col. 4. Yet much more than biological possibility would be necessary for male pregnancy to end female identification with gestation and early nurturing. Many women do not share the radical feminist view that men also should bear children, and would want to retain their gestational functions. Nor would men necessarily leap at the opportunity to gestate offspring. One needs to go to literature to find the appropriate image for nongender-specific gestation. The state of "kemmer" described in U. Le Guin, The Left Hand of Darkness 89-97 (1969) permits both men and women to be either father or mother to offspring, without advance knowledge of which reproductive role they will play, which thus removes the gestational role from personal control. Ectogenesis goes one step further and removes the need for human gestation altogether.

322. Ectogenesis allows both men and women to have and rear genetic offspring without anyone providing gestation. It breaks the female biological tie to early nurturance and childrearing by removing the need for human gestation altogether, rather than by shifting it to men or other women. One can question whether sexual equality achieved at the price of removing human gestation is desirable. This will depend in part on the importance to offspring and parents of a human gestational bond. If there is no chance for a healthy birth, ectogenesis may be an acceptable alternative, despite its violence to the notion of mother.

3. *Conclusion: It's Not What You Do But How You Do It*

In the immediate future, the benefits of noncoital technology are likely to outweigh the risks for women, since the technologies will be used mainly by couples desiring to have biological offspring. More problematic donor-assisted practices are likely to be a small part of the foreseeable uses of IVF reproduction. In any event, properly managed donor assistance can be satisfying for all the parties. A still smaller percentage of cases will involve surrogacy, and may require special attention to avoid exploitation and conflict. Other troubling practices, such as embryo donation after lavage, may never be widely used.[323]

If the relief of infertility is a good, there is a reasonable basis for thinking that the bright, liberating side of the new reproduction will outshine darker uses. In the final analysis, the impact of noncoital technology on women depends on how it is used more than on what it is. While opportunity for misuse exists, there is a reasonable basis for thinking that people on the whole will use it well. Indeed, steps should be explored to assure that noncoital technology is used wisely, while respecting the preserve of procreative liberty. If laws cannot prohibit some of the most ethically troubling uses of IVF, they can still regulate to minimize harm to donors, recipients, offspring, and other parties. Regulatory alternatives to minimize damage from noncoital technology are discussed in the final section.

VII. REGULATORY ISSUES AND ALTERNATIVES: THE NEED FOR A PUBLIC POLICY

As the use of noncoital technology increases, the need for more explicit public policy in several areas must be addressed. Since few laws explicitly address the new reproduction, and professional norms and codes remain inchoate, the current public policy is implicitly laissez faire. Implicit policies, however, create uncertainty for doctors and patients about proper conduct with embryos and collaborators. The result may leave too much room for private reproductive agendas, causing preventable injury to collaborators, offspring, or society.

---

323. While initially promising, Buster's program has not taken off the way originally envisaged. Research has stopped while venture capital funds have been sought. Ethical concern has been expressed about the risks of ectopic pregnancy and abortion for donors. Buster's vision of an efficient, widely diffused program, with a large pool of donors to simplify the problem of synchronizing recipient cycles, with insemination, lavage, and transfer performed by non-physicians at shopping centers or banks, is not likely to be realized in the near future.

Implicit policies may also deter people from satisfying procreative goals because of legal uncertainty and suspected social or moral illegitimacy. For example, uncertainty chills the use of frozen embryos, donor eggs, and gestational surrogates by infertile couples and may deter much needed embryo research.[324] Explicit policies could remove doubts and clarify norms, thus facilitating the safe and effective use of noncoital techniques

While private sector actors have wide discretion to use noncoital technology to meet their reproductive goals, they have no right to be free of reasonable regulation designed to enhance autonomy and protect the welfare of offspring.[325] We can identify several aspects of noncoital reproduction which need more explicit public or professional policy development. This section discusses regulatory issues concerning embryos, the medical profession, and reproductive collaborators.

A. EMBRYOS

The future development of IVF would probably benefit from more explicit clarification of embryo status and thus the limits of conduct with embryos. The implicit consensus on embryo status should be clarified so that parties may act in accordance with it.[326]

Clifford Grobstein and others have suggested a national deliberative body as a mechanism for clarifying embryo status and specifying norms of conduct.[327] It may not be possible to constitute a national deliberative body on embryo status free of the politics of the right-to-life and abortion debate. However, a deliberative body that focused on discrete problems such as conditions for embryo research, for freezing and storage of embryos, and for embryo discard might usefully define currently acceptable standards of conduct with embryos. The role of institutional review boards or a national licensing authority to implement embryo policies

---

324. Uncertainty about embryo status is directly responsible for the lack of federal funding of embryo research. Although the Department of Health and Human Services' Ethics Advisory Board recommended guidelines for conducting embryo research, the Board was disbanded and never reconstituted to provide the review essential for federal funding of embryo research. There is thus a de facto moratorium on federal funding of embryo research that also deters privately funded research. *See* 45 C.F.R. § 46.304(e) (1985); Fletcher & Schulman, *Fetal Research: The State of the Question*, 15 HASTINGS CENTER REP., Apr. 1985, at 6, 10-11.

325. *See supra* text accompanying notes 67-69.

326. The analysis in this Article suggests that an implicit consensus on embryo status exists that could be made manifest. *See supra* text accompanying notes 89-98.

327. *See* Grobstein, Flower & Mendelhoff, *supra* note 194.

should also be addressed.[328]

B. THE MEDICAL PROFESSION

Regulation of the medical profession's role in noncoital reproduction is desirable in several areas. Most important is the need to assure that competent infertility services are provided. The profession itself, and to a lesser extent law, has an important role to play in assuring quality care.

Infertility patients, though not threatened by disability or death as are other patients, are vulnerable and are at emotional, physical, and financial risk in their encounters with the medical profession.[329] The rapid expansion of IVF has improved patient access, but also has exposed patients to suboptimal care from physicians unskilled in IVF procedures. For example, most IVF programs have not reported an actual pregnancy, yet patients may enter these programs thinking that they have the same possibility of success (roughly 20 to 25 percent) that the best programs report.[330]

Professional efforts at quality assurance are particularly necessary to assure adequate training and operation of IVF programs. For example, professional standards for handling eggs, embryos, donors, and surrogates would be helpful in improving the level of practice. Professional standards for reporting success rates at every stage are also desirable. With adequate peer involvement, more explicit legal controls, such as the national licensing authority suggested in the Warnock Report, need not

---

328. The Warnock Committee proposed a national licensing body to oversee embryo manipulation. WARNOCK COMMITTEE REPORT, *supra* note 46, at 75-79. In the United States, institutional review boards will play a major oversight and review role.

329. Talcott Parsons' classic description of the sick role informs us that doctor-patient relations are usually asymmetrical in knowledge, power, and detachment. The technically competent and affectively neutral physician faces the vulnerable and technically ignorant patient. T. PARSONS, THE SOCIAL SYSTEM 439-47 (1951). Although infertility patients are not as vulnerable as patients confronting serious illness, death, or even childbirth, and may become quite knowledgeable, they have a very strong need, in some cases a desperate need, to achieve pregnancy and thus are vulnerable to medical exploitation. *See supra* text accompanying notes 12-13.

330. A successful IVF program requires skilled physician and laboratory work, and requires experience in developing stimulatory regimes, egg retrieval, and fertilization before achieving success. In May, 1984 it was reported that 1209 pregnancies resulted from 9641 IVF treatment cycles, giving a 13% viable pregnancy rate. Another way to state the rate is per number of embryos transferred, which ranges from 10% viable pregnancies per single embryo transfer, to 19% per three embryos transferred. However, only a minority of programs achieve this rate, and some programs have never had a pregnancy—facts which should be conveyed to patients. Soules, *The In Vitro Fertilization Pregnancy Rate: Let's Be Honest With One Another*, 43 FERTILITY & STERILITY 511-12 (1985).

take root in American soil.[331]

Infertility patients themselves can play an important role in disciplining physicians if they are provided relevant information.[332] It is therefore essential that information about program safety and efficacy be routinely gathered and disseminated. All programs should make data available to patients on attempts at egg retrieval, fertilization rates, transfer rates, pregnancy rates, and take-home baby rates. Program policies concerning embryo discard, storage, research, donation, and price should also be available. The medical profession can play an important role in providing this information.[333]

The law can help assure quality by adapting tort remedies to an infertility context involving embryos and collaborators. Negligent delivery of infertility services can do great damage to patients, offspring, and donors, and therefore should be cognizable by the tort system. For example, patients can invest much time, money, and emotion in treatments that are physically intrusive and ultimately unsuccessful, and which deny them the pregnancy they might have achieved in another program. Failure to screen donors and surrogates for sexually transmitted disease can lead to infectious disease in patients and offspring. Negligence in handling or storing embryos may lead to the loss of reproductive opportunities. Failure to keep records might cause collaborative offspring intense anguish.[334]

Some injuries caused by negligent physician handling of noncoital technology might not be covered by existing malpractice doctrines. For example, establishing damages for negligent failure to relieve infertility may be difficult because of problems in showing that proper care would have produced a pregnancy. Similarly, negligent destruction of embryos may not be actionable,[335] or it may not generate sufficient damages to

---

331. The American Fertility Society has issued guidelines for IVF programs, and together with the American Association of Tissue Banks, recommended guidelines for donor sperm. *Ethical Statement on In Vitro Fertilization, supra* note 191.

332. After some experience, they might become quite knowledgeable about treatments, and with the help of patient support groups and networks at both the national and local level, will exercise informed judgment.

333. The American Fertility Society, for example, has created an In Vitro Fertilization Special Interest Group. Acceptance as a member requires keeping and providing such information on an annual basis, with publication planned in *Fertility & Sterility*, the journal of the American Fertility Society.

334. Other harms are possible, such as wrongful disclosure of confidential information pertaining to donors, recipients, or offspring.

335. Negligent handling of embryos leading to an avoidable handicapped birth is not the issue, since the duty to act with reasonable care prior to birth or even conception is well established. Since

support a suit, since it may be difficult to show that the embryo in question would have implanted and gone to term. Injuries arising from unwanted imposition or prevention of a genetic tie *tout court* may also be difficult to remedy, because such injuries are entirely psychological. Yet patients have legitimate reproductive interests at stake, which adaptation of traditional tort remedies can help protect.

A final area of regulatory concern is transfer of authority over embryos and gametes from patients to IVF programs and physicians. Doctors are free to ask patients to donate eggs and embryos, and patients are free to donate.[336] However, it does not follow that physicians should be able to require, as a condition of treatment, that excess embryos or eggs accrue to the program.[337] Given the reproductive significance of transfer to patients, and physicians' potentially greater bargaining power, a more desirable policy is to retain dispositional authority in gamete providers, who have a significant procreative interest in how spare gametes and embryos are used. As long as dispositional authority is clear, physicians have no need to gain control of spare embryos at the outset.[338]

C. COLLABORATIVE REPRODUCTION

Clarification of the legal relations among donors, surrogates, recipients, and offspring is also needed. Donor sperm is increasingly popular, and the demand for donor eggs, embryos, and surrogates is likely to

---

many state wrongful death statutes do not cover previable fetuses that are not born alive, it is doubtful that they will apply to embryos that are negligently stored or handled. *See* Robertson, *supra* note 165.

While damages could be awarded on other grounds, assigning value to the couple's loss of a single embryo will be difficult, since the chances of one embryo implanting are less than 10%. However, a trial court in New York awarded $50,000 damages for intentional infliction of emotional distress when a physician intentionally destroyed the embryo of another physician's patient. *See* Fanta, *Legal Issues Raised By In Vitro Fertilization and Embryo Transfer in the United States*, 2 IN VITRO FERTILIZATION & EMBRYO TRANSFER 65, 80-81 (1985); *see also* Cohen, *The Brave New Baby and the Law: Fashioning Remedies for the Victims of In Vitro Fertilization*, 4 AM. J. L. & MED. 319 (1978) (proposing a new tort, "wrongful destruction," in such cases).

336. *See supra* text accompanying notes 121-23.

337. The question of disposition will be especially acute when embryos are frozen. WARNOCK COMMITTEE REPORT, *supra* note 46, at 55, suggested that the storage facility gain dispositional control if parties storing embryos had died without leaving instructions or were otherwise unavailable to direct disposition. Annas thinks that this will lead to embryos being viewed as leftover luggage, to be auctioned off to the highest bidder. *See* Annas, *supra* note 277, at 51.

338. Thus, persons storing embryos or gametes should leave instructions concerning disposition in case they are not available when a further decision is necessary. They could, of course, agree to then transfer control to others, including the program. It should be noted, however, that the extent of dispositional control in the transferee may not be as great as in the transferor, because the transferee ordinarily will lack the transferor's reproductive interest in the embryo or gametes at issue.

grow. Although the state cannot prohibit or ignore collaborative contracts, it can regulate them to protect the autonomy of the parties and the well-being of offspring. Several kinds of regulation should be considered.

Since the collaborative contract has great legal significance, the circumstances of contract formation may need specification to assure that free, knowing bargains are struck, with the parties fully aware of the reproductive significance of their agreement. Rules that specify required contract provisions, that address responsibility for handicapped births, and that require separate legal representation for surrogates are desirable and constitutionally permissible, since they provide a structure for the autonomous exercise of rights.[339] Registration and witnessing of collaborative contracts to solemnize the exchange of reproductive factors should also be considered.[340]

Legislation to assure the well-being of offspring in collaborative transactions could take many forms. Most important is to establish certainty about who the rearing parents are, by clearly defining the rearing rights and duties of donors, surrogates, and recipients. Recording information about donors and surrogates will be essential if information about these persons is to be provided to offspring desiring to know. Other regulations will help insure that resulting offspring have a reasonable level of welfare as a class. For example, limitations on number of offspring per donor may prevent unwitting incest. Legislation requiring donor screening to avoid neonatal infection may also be desirable for the class of offspring generally, as well as for their parents and society.[341] It is less clear, however, that a review of parental fitness prior to collaboration is needed.[342]

---

339. The need for such rules is evident in light of the practice of some surrogate programs to have the surrogate agree to be represented by the same lawyer who represents the couple, a clearly undesirable arrangement, even if the surrogate's consent makes it legally acceptable. Rules prohibiting such conflicts and requiring other measures to assure free, informed consent do not impinge on liberty enough to constitute an interference requiring a compelling interest justification. *See* Planned Parenthood of Missouri v. Danforth, 428 U.S. 52 (1976). *Compare* Akron v. Akron Reproductive Center, 103 S.Ct. 2481 (1983) (slanting information against one option may interfere with, rather than foster the exercise of, reproductive autonomy).

340. Marking collaborative transactions with ceremony may serve symbolic purposes as well as make enforcement of agreements more practical and certain.

341. The offspring born infected by failure to screen donors for infection is not harmed, since screening would have prevented birth altogether, and the effects will not usually amount to wrongful life. However, the offspring that do exist as a class will be better off, even if no right of individual offspring would be violated by a failure to screen. The parents are also better off in having healthy rather than ill or handicapped offspring.

342. *See supra* note 241.

A major need for legislation to clarify relations among gamete and embryo donors, surrogates and the persons who engage their services exists, so that the role of the collaborative contract in fixing rights and duties among the parties is clearly defined. It is essential for all parties that the resulting legal relations toward each other are well-defined. This includes specification of rearing rights and duties, including responsibility for handicapped offspring and tests to establish maternity or paternity.[343] Questions of inheritance and health and safety measures like testing donor sperm for infectious disease should also be considered.[344]

Legislation to achieve these goals does present something of a dilemma, since a symbolic dimension inevitably arises. The passage of legislation would seem to legitimate and thus encourage practices that some persons view as morally and socially questionable. Yet failure to legislate may prevent access to legitimate infertility treatments and fail to prevent untoward effects that will otherwise occur. A complicating factor is insufficient data to inform legislation in some areas. Yet enough is known to justify legislative clarification of the basic relations among the parties and rearing rights and duties toward offspring. The benefits of legal certainty far outweigh the costs of symbolically legitimizing collaborative practices.[345]

CONCLUSION

Examination of procreative liberty and noncoital technology shows the normative fault lines along which future developments and conflicts will occur. Most striking is how IVF forces consideration of both new and old normative issues. It forces us to confront respect for persons in a new way in assessing the moral status of the preimplantation embryo and collaborative reproduction. It also forces us to think about the meaning of family and genetic and gestational ties, as well as the reproductive roles of women and our relation to the natural order and technology generally.

---

343. Such testing is essential, because a surrogate or embryo donor-by-lavage's claim that she had refrained from sexual relations might not be reliable, and responsibility for rearing handicapped children might be at stake. Legislation may also address the question of monitoring surrogate behavior during pregnancy to minimize health risks.

344. The role of testator intent in questions of inheritance in particular needs resolution. *See supra* note 78.

345. Comprehensive donor and surrogate legislation has been considered in several states, including Michigan, Mich. H. Bill 4554, 4555, April 16, 1985, and California, Cal. Assembly Bill 1707, 1985-86 Regular Sess. Both bills are workable models for clarifying the questions to be settled, though the California bill does not deal with embryo donation, storage, or surrogates who gestate the embryo of another.

The analysis in this Article has tried to show how a constitutionally coherent concept of procreative liberty protects a wide range of decisions affecting human embryos and reproductive collaborators. Procreative liberty protects the freedom to contract for the provision, receipt, transfer, and storage of embryos and gametes, when necessary to achieve protected reproductive goals. It also protects collaborative reproductive transactions with donors and surrogates. In most instances, the interests of embryos, offspring, the family, and others do not justify interference with these choices. Some judge these practices as morally problematic and wish them stopped. But the tangible harm necessary for state intervention is often difficult to show. As a result, a regime of private discretion in efforts to procreate, with minimal regulation, must legally prevail.

This result is not surprising when we recall the role of constitutional rights and the importance of reproduction in the life-plan of individuals. The very notion of fundamental rights means that individuals are free to pursue their conception of the good, without constraint by government. Reproductive choice is so intimate and so central to a person's life-plan that personal, subjective determination of reproductive meaning deserves a privileged position vis-a-vis majority opinion. Without evidence of tangible harm to others, moral distaste alone will not support state interference with choices to procreate any more than moral judgment justifies interference with the avoidance of reproduction through abortion and contraception. The right to engage in IVF conception and to contract for gamete, embryo, and womb donations thus follows.

Viewed as a stark formalism, the full reach of procreative liberty seems frightening. Legal liberty allows persons to treat each other as means to reproductive ends, with their negotiating ability and other resources determining the fate of future offspring. The extracorporeal embryo, that potent symbol of human life, becomes subject to the vagaries of a market that drives people to buy or sell reproductive factors and services. Yet such freedom also allows people to determine and satisfy their welfare more efficaciously than by government prescription. In liberal society, the invisible hand of procreative preference must be allowed to flourish, despite the qualms of those who think it debases our humanity.

Such a jaundiced view of procreative liberty arises when procreative decisions are viewed abstractly, detached from their relationship to people desiring to reproduce. Choices about the the disposition of gametes, embryos, and reproductive capacity arise in a matrix of traditions, attitudes, values, relations, and feelings, that more than constitutional status will determine the impact of the new reproductive technologies on society. This matrix, with its respect for personal autonomy in matters generative, will shape the assimilation of noncoital technology into our lives. The options made available may subtly alter values, but only in combination with other social changes.

Noncoital reproductive technology raises important issues. Yet it is less a threat to existing procreative values than an opportunity to realize them, thereby helping women and men to connect with new generations, or not, as they choose.

[2]

Regulating Choice: A Constitutional Law Response to Professor John A. Robertson's *Children of Choice*

Ann MacLean Massie[*]

I. Introduction

To begin, I would like to add my applause to others' for Professor John A. Robertson's splendid new book, *Children of Choice: Freedom and the New Reproductive Technologies*.[1] Professor Robertson sets forth a comprehensive and coherent theory for the formation of social policy respecting the use of artificial insemination, *in vitro* fertilization (IVF), and surrogacy contracts as means for achieving parenthood. Along the way, he

[*] Associate Professor of Law, Washington and Lee University School of Law. A.B., Duke University; M.A., University of Michigan; J.D., University of Virginia. I owe a tremendous debt of gratitude to the Frances Lewis Law Center, Washington and Lee University School of Law, and the Law Center Committee for their financial and personal support in the execution of a symposium in an area of particular interest to me, bioethics. Most especially, I would like to thank Professor Brian C. Murchison of the Washington and Lee University School of Law, then Director of the Frances Lewis Law Center, for his warm friendship and tireless efforts in planning the symposium, coordinating the work of the participants, arranging the countless minute details, and seeing the project through to its successful conclusion, even after his tenure in office had officially expired. The new Director of the Frances Lewis Law Center, Professor David K. Millon of the Washington and Lee University School of Law, provided support and assistance with last-minute details. The editors of the *Washington and Lee Law Review* played an integral role at every stage. I am grateful to Professor Randall P. Bezanson, at that time Dean of the Washington and Lee University School of Law, for his valuable comments and advice, both before and after completion of a prior draft. I am also grateful to Professors Joan M. Shaughnessy and Allan Ides of the Washington and Lee University School of Law for their helpful critiques of an earlier version of this manuscript. Finally, I would like to thank my patient and extremely capable research assistant, Lindsay B. King, without whose help this project would not have materialized.

1. *See* JOHN A. ROBERTSON, CHILDREN OF CHOICE: FREEDOM AND THE NEW REPRODUCTIVE TECHNOLOGIES back jacket cover (1994) (quoting five prominent ethicists in philosophy, law, and medicine who praise Robertson's book and note its importance).

applies the same framework of values to an examination of collateral issues raised by the new reproductive technologies — the development and use of Norplant and RU486, embryo research, cryopreservation and discard, and techniques and uses of genetic screening and manipulation. The whole is a prodigious accomplishment, presenting a cohesive and unified philosophy that will enlighten policymakers and enliven the public debate on technological advances that are already changing dramatically the landscape of reproductive possibilities open to infertile couples who are so diligently, and often desperately, seeking assistance in order to have their own biologically related children.[2] This Symposium promises to be only one sample of the wide-ranging response that *Children of Choice* is certain to receive.

Professor Robertson's central thesis is the primacy of "procreative liberty — the freedom to decide whether or not to have offspring and to control the use of one's reproductive capacity."[3] Noting that "this value is widely acknowledged when reproduction occurs *au naturel*,"[4] the author states that "it should be equally honored when reproduction requires technological assistance."[5] In Robertson's view, "procreative liberty deserves presumptive respect because of its central importance to individual meaning, dignity, and identity";[6] hence, his succinctly stated proposition: "I propose that procreative liberty be given presumptive priority in all conflicts,

---

2. Although the actual incidence of infertility has not significantly increased in recent years, except in the group of married couples with wives 20 to 24 years old, the number of office visits to private physicians for treatments for infertility has risen from about 600,000 in 1968 to about 1.6 million in 1984, with a particularly sharp increase between 1980 and 1983. OFFICE OF TECHNOLOGY ASSESSMENT, U.S. CONGRESS, INFERTILITY: MEDICAL AND SOCIAL CHOICES 55 (1988) [hereinafter OTA, INFERTILITY]. This increase is due in part to both the increasing number of physicians providing infertility services and the new reproductive technologies used to treat infertility. *See id.* at 56. A survey by the Office of Technology Assessment (OTA) estimated that "172,000 women underwent artificial insemination in 1986-87, at an average cost of $953, resulting in 35,000 births from artificial insemination by husband (AIH), and 30,000 births from artificial insemination by donor (AID)." OFFICE OF TECHNOLOGY ASSESSMENT, U.S. CONGRESS, ARTIFICIAL INSEMINATION: PRACTICE IN THE UNITED STATES 3 (1988) [hereinafter OTA, ARTIFICIAL INSEMINATION]. The OTA also estimated that nearly 600 babies had been born through surrogacy arrangements by 1988. OTA, INFERTILITY, *supra*, at 267. *Time* estimated that over 2000 births resulted from surrogacy arrangements between 1987 and 1990. *And Baby Makes Four*, TIME, Aug. 27, 1990, at 53; *see also* ROBERTSON, *supra* note 1, at 98 (citing recent statistical increases in usage of reproductive technologies).

3. ROBERTSON, *supra* note 1, at 16.

4. *Id.* at 4.

5. *Id.*

6. *Id.* at 16.

REGULATING CHOICE   137

with the burden on opponents of any particular technique to show that
harmful effects from its use justify limiting procreative choice."[7]

Given this hypothesis, "[a] central question in this enterprise is to
determine whether effects on embryos, families, women, and other
participants rise to the level of severity necessary to justify infringing a basic
right."[8] Professor Robertson concedes that "what counts as the 'substantial
harm' that justifies interference with procreative choice may often be
contested,"[9] but he devotes substantial portions of the book to arguments that
almost no conceivable counterinterest actually sustains the burden of proving
the sufficiency of its importance. In Robertson's words, "it is difficult to
show that the alleged harms of noncoital reproduction are sufficient to justify
overriding procreative liberty."[10]

The evaluation of any alleged harm rests initially, in Robertson's view,
on a distinction "between harms to individuals and harms to personal
conceptions of morality, right order, or offense."[11] Professor Robertson
dismisses the latter concerns in almost every instance, for in a pluralistic
society, "[a] majoritarian view of 'right' reproduction or 'right' valuation of
prenatal life, family, or the role of women should not suffice to restrict
actions based on differing individual views of such preeminently personal
issues."[12] Thus, the "presumptive priority" of procreative liberty "will give
persons directly involved the final say about use of a particular technology,
unless tangible harm to the interests of others can be shown."[13]

One might think, as do a number of commentators, that the well-being
of the children resulting from assisted conception would constitute precisely
the sort of weighty counterinterest that could justify restrictions on the
procreative liberty of adult would-be parents whenever there were grounds
to think that the use of reproductive technologies might threaten or

---

7. *Id.*

8. *Id.* at 17.

9. *Id.* at 24.

10. *Id.* at 40.

11. *Id.* at 41.

12. *Id.* Robertson does, however, concede that "[a]t a certain point, . . . a practice such
as cloning, enhancement, or intentional diminishment of offspring may be so far removed
from even pluralistic notions of reproductive meaning that they leave the realm of protected
reproductive choice." *Id.*; *see also id.* at 149-72 (addressing these extreme situations). *But
see* John A. Robertson, *The Question of Human Cloning*, HASTINGS CENTER REP., Mar.-Apr.
1994, at 6, 9-14 (defending cloning on grounds similar to arguments generally used in
Children of Choice).

13. ROBERTSON, *supra* note 1, at 41-42.

jeopardize the welfare of resulting offspring.[14] Professor Robertson readily admits that impact on offspring is an important consideration,[15] but he

---

14.　*See, e.g.,* ELIZABETH BARTHOLET, FAMILY BONDS: ADOPTION AND THE POLITICS OF PARENTING 229 (1993) ("If we really care about children, we should question why there is so much talk of the adult's right to procreate, right to control his or her body, and right to parent, but so little talk of the child's right to anything."); OTA, INFERTILITY, *supra* note 2, at 226-28; *id.* at 234 ("Whether or not future children can be seen as having rights, society has an obligation to protect them in reasonable ways from foreseeable harms, and States and the Federal Government have some constitutional authority to do so."); George J. Annas, *Regulating the New Reproductive Technologies, in* REPRODUCTIVE LAWS FOR THE 1990'S 411, 418 (Sherrill Cohen & Nadine Taub eds., 1989) [hereinafter Annas, *Regulating*] (arguing that government may have large role in regulating new reproductive technologies — "not only protecting interests of the adults in quality services and informed consent, but also taking reasonable steps to protect the interests of future children that are 'created' by these methods"); Philip G. Peters, Jr., *Protecting the Unconceived: Nonexistence, Avoidability, and Reproductive Technology,* 31 ARIZ. L. REV. 487, 548 (1989) ("[I]njuries which are likely to deny a child a reasonable opportunity for minimal health and happiness may harm the child, even if that life is not worse than death. If so, intervention to prevent the implementation of technologies likely to cause these injuries finds support in the interests of the would-be children."); Maura A. Ryan, *The Argument for Unlimited Procreative Liberty: A Feminist Critique,* HASTINGS CENTER REP., July-Aug. 1990, at 6, 8 (arguing that unlimited procreative liberty protects parental desires and affords too little protection to offspring's "essential autonomy," which is necessary for development of full personhood). For examples of arguments against constitutional protection of surrogacy arrangements specifically, see MARTHA FIELD, SURROGATE MOTHERHOOD 69-74 (expanded ed. 1990); CHRISTINE OVERALL, ETHICS AND HUMAN REPRODUCTION: A FEMINIST ANALYSIS 185-90 (1987); George J. Annas, *Fairy Tales Surrogate Mothers Tell,* 16 LAW, MED. & HEALTH CARE 27, 29-30 (1988); A.M. Capron & M.J. Radin, *Choosing Family Law over Contract Law as a Paradigm for Surrogate Motherhood,* 16 LAW, MED. & HEALTH CARE 34, 38-41 (1988); Angela R. Holder, *Surrogate Motherhood and the Best Interests of Children,* 16 LAW, MED. & HEALTH CARE 51, 53-54 (1988); Ann M. Massie, *Restricting Surrogacy to Married Couples: A Constitutional Problem?,* 18 HASTINGS CONST. L.Q. 487, 506-15 (1991); Shari O'Brien, *Commercial Conceptions: A Breeding Ground for Surrogacy,* 65 N.C. L. REV. 127, 143-47 (1986); Margaret J. Radin, *Market-Inalienability,* 100 HARV. L. REV. 1849, 1932-36 (1987); Barbara L. Keller, Comment, *Surrogate Motherhood Contracts in Louisiana: To Ban or to Regulate?,* 49 LA. L. REV. 143, 186-89 (1988). *See also* UNIF. STATUS OF CHILDREN OF ASSISTED CONCEPTION ACT prefatory note, 9B U.L.A. 153-54 (Supp. 1994) [hereinafter UNIF. CONCEPTION ACT] (explaining that purpose of Act is to serve best interests of children created by assisted conception).

15.　*See* ROBERTSON, *supra* note 1, at 13 (recognizing welfare of offspring as one of six ethical considerations that must be taken into account in connection with use of reproductive technologies); *id.* at 75-76 (discussing impact on offspring of irresponsible reproduction); *id.* at 121-22 (discussing potential psychological harms to children of collaborative reproduction — i.e., those born as result of donor or surrogacy arrangements); *id.* at 217 ("The important question is not what brought about conception and delivery, but what happens to these children afterwards."); *see also* John A. Robertson, *Embryos, Families, and Procreative*

invariably trumps its potential to restrict adult procreative interests by noting that, with respect to any given child born with the use of assisted conception, its only choice would be either existence under the limitations imposed by the parental behavior or total nonexistence.[16] Citing "wrongful life" cases to support his views,[17] Robertson is unable to conjure up conditions under which it would have been better for the child not to have been born at all. For example, a child born with the help of IVF to a mother who tests positive for the human immunodeficiency virus (HIV) may well turn out to be HIV-positive itself and therefore destined to end a short life with an agonizing death.[18] Even if the child escapes this fate, its mother will likely

---

Liberty: The Legal Structure of the New Reproduction, 59 S. CAL. L. REV. 939, 1034 (1986) [hereinafter Robertson, *Embryos*]. (noting legitimacy of reasonable regulation of noncoital technology, which enhances autonomy and protects welfare of offspring); John A. Robertson, *Procreative Liberty and the Control of Conception, Pregnancy, and Childbirth*, 69 VA. L. REV. 405, 434 (1983) [hereinafter Robertson, *Procreative Liberty*] ("The state's concern with the well-being of offspring may also justify regulation.").

16.   *See* ROBERTSON, *supra* note 1, at 117 (discussing unmarried persons, persons who have tested positive for human immunodeficiency virus (HIV), and couples and individuals who are unstable or unfit to be parents); *id.* at 253 n.40 (discussing older mothers). Indeed, Robertson allows the presumptive primacy of procreative liberty to override interests of the created children with respect to virtually all reproductive technologies that implicate procreative liberty interests. *See id.* at 111 (posthumous reproduction); *id.* at 153 (positive selection of offspring traits); *id.* at 162 (germline intervention); *id.* at 169 (cloning).

17.   *See id.* at 247 n.18 (citing Smith v. Cote, 513 A.2d 341 (N.H. 1986); Becker v. Schwartz, 386 N.E.2d 807 (N.Y. 1978); Nelson v. Krusen, 678 S.W.2d 918 (Tex. 1984)); *see also id.* at 75-76 (noting that children born with genetic handicaps or HIV and children born into illegitimacy, poverty, or abusive situations might experience life as net benefit even though it would involve some degree of suffering); *id.* at 85 & n.43 (noting that Tay-Sachs disease might present strongest case for wrongful life claim); Robertson, *Embryos*, *supra* note 15, at 988-89 (explaining that wrongful life claims cannot prevail in instances of noncoital reproduction because there is no way for individual claimant to exist except in condition about which he complains).

18.   The estimated rate of perinatal transmission of HIV varies in the medical literature from 13% to 60%. *See* Clara Gabiano et al., *Mother-to-Child Transmission of Human Immunodeficiency Virus Type 1: Risk of Infection and Correlates of Transmission*, 90 PEDIATRICS 369, 369 (1992). A 1992 study indicates a mother-to-offspring transmission rate of 23.9%. *See id.* at 370-71. That study notes that when a first-born child was infected, 40% of second-born children were also infected, as compared with only 8.3% of second-born children infected when the first-born was uninfected. *See id.* at 372. In a 1989 study, the rate of perinatal HIV infection was found to be approximately 30%. *See* Stephane Blanche et al., *A Prospective Study of Infants Born to Women Seropositive for Human Immunodeficiency Virus Type 1*, 320 NEW ENG. J. MED. 1643, 1646 (1989). According to that study, about 20% of the HIV-infected infants will die by the age of 18 months. *See id.* at 1643. In some cases, infants infected with HIV may later become seronegative, but continue to suffer from severe

be alive for only a short period of the child's life, and we cannot be sure of the presence of another loving adult to bring up the child. Nonetheless, Robertson maintains that IVF services in this situation "would not harm children who have no other way to be born, and thus may ethically be provided if [an IVF] program is so inclined."[19]

Of course, Robertson is speaking here of private clinics, which, he notes, commonly screen out HIV-positive applicants.[20] But what happens if the clinic is a state actor, as so many of them are?[21] If Professor Robertson's theory of the primacy of procreative liberty were to be not simply an ethical framework setting the stage for public debate, but rather were to become an established principle of constitutional law — if, in other words, procreative liberty (defined to include the right to use reproductive technologies to achieve biological parenthood) were to be construed as a constitutionally protected "fundamental right," subject to restriction only in the service of a "compelling state interest," and then only by "narrowly tailored means"[22] — then, according to Professor Robertson's analysis, a publicly supported IVF clinic would have no choice but to serve the HIV-positive applicant. Her fundamental right "to bear or beget a child"[23] would

---

immune deficiency. *See id.* at 1646. In at least one case, an infant who became seronegative, though completely symptom-free, carried the HIV genome. *See id.* The children who become perinatally infected with HIV have a very poor prognosis, and, although asymptomatic at birth, most develop symptoms before age one. *See* Gwendolyn B. Scott et al., *Survival in Children with Perinatally Acquired Human Immunodeficiency Virus Type 1 Infection*, 321 NEW ENG. J. MED. 1791, 1791, 1795 (1989). The median survival age for these children is 77 months. *See id.* at 1793.

19.   ROBERTSON, *supra* note 1, at 117.

20.   *See id.*

21.   Out of the 169 U.S. facilities that offered IVF or gamete intrafallopian transfer as of March 1988, the OTA listed at least 39 facilities that appeared to be related to state-run institutions. *See* OTA, INFERTILITY, *supra* note 2, at 311-20.

22.   This is the traditional language of "strict scrutiny," or independent judicial review, that describes the criteria for measuring the validity of restrictions upon constitutionally protected rights. *See* JOHN E. NOWAK & RONALD D. ROTUNDA, CONSTITUTIONAL LAW § 14.3, at 575 (4th ed. 1991) (discussing strict scrutiny test); *id.* §§ 14.26-.30(a) (discussing right of privacy); LAURENCE H. TRIBE, AMERICAN CONSTITUTIONAL LAW §§ 11-1 to -4 (2d ed. 1988) (discussing constitutional protections for certain "preferred rights"); *id.* §§ 15-9 to -11 (discussing right of privacy); *id.* §§ 16-6 to -7 (discussing strict scrutiny in equal protection/fundamental rights context).

23.   Eisenstadt v. Baird, 405 U.S. 438, 453 (1972) (invalidating restrictions on access to contraceptive devices by single persons). Dictum in Justice Brennan's majority opinion in *Eisenstadt* states: "If the right of privacy means anything, it is the right of the *individual*, married or single, to be free from unwarranted governmental intrusion into matters so

override any interest that the state might assert in restricting her access to IVF because the resulting child — whether HIV-positive or not, whether its mother would live very long or not, and whether there were another available loving adult to raise the child or not — would be better off to have been born than not to have been born. This is precisely the approach that Professor Robertson advocates *as a matter of constitutional law.*

Before I probe this notion, let me offer some other examples of issues that might seem ripe for public debate, but that would be virtually foreclosed to discussion if Professor Robertson's views of constitutional analysis prevailed. Throughout *Children of Choice*, Robertson writes from the basic assumption that reproductive technologies would be used by infertile individuals or, more specifically, infertile couples. Elsewhere, however, he has stated more explicitly that the effect of his interpretation of the substantive liberty interest protected by the Constitution would be to prohibit government regulation of the reasons for resort to assisted reproduction,[24] just as the government is barred from regulating the reasons for a woman's choice to have an abortion.[25] Thus, mere convenience — a woman's desire

---

fundamentally affecting a person as the decision whether to bear or beget a child." *Id.* This characterization has become the banner reference describing the concept of procreative liberty. *See, e.g.*, Cleveland Bd. of Educ. v. LaFleur, 414 U.S. 632, 640 (1974) (invalidating school boards' mandatory unpaid maternity leave policies); *see also* TRIBE, *supra* note 22, § 15-10, (citing cases); *cf.* ROBERTSON, *supra* note 1, at 36-37 (referring to *Eisenstadt* language as "[t]he most ringing endorsement of this right").

24. *See* Robertson, *Procreative Liberty, supra* note 15, at 430 ("The right of married persons to use noncoital and collaborative means of conception to overcome infertility must extend to any purpose, including selecting the gender or genetic characteristics of the child or transferring the burden of gestation to another. Restricting the right of noncoital or collaborative reproduction to one purpose, such as relief of infertility, contradicts the meaning of a right of autonomy in procreation and also raises insuperable problems of definition and monitoring.").

25. *See* Roe v. Wade, 410 U.S. 113, 163 (1973) (establishing that for previability abortions, "the attending physician, in consultation with his patient, is free to determine, without regulation by the State, that, in his medical judgment, the patient's pregnancy should be terminated. If that decision is reached, the judgment may be effectuated by an abortion free of interference by the State"); ROBERTSON, *supra* note 1, at 46 ("No limits on the reasons for abortion can be imposed prior to viability, nor can third parties be given veto power over the woman's choice."); *id.* at 63 ("*Roe-Casey* does prohibit any inquiry into motives or reasons for abortion, and thus probably protects conceptions and abortions designed to produce embryos or fetal tissue for research or transplant, and even abortion on gender grounds."); *id.* at 159 ("[U]nder *Roe v. Wade* the reason or indication for the abortion is irrelevant — abortions may occur for strong or weak reasons, for major or for trivial genetic defects."); *id.* at 213 ("Under *Roe v. Wade*, there is no limit on the reasons or motivations for previability abortion — the pregnant woman is the sole judge of the need.").

to remain slim, to avoid the physical burdens of pregnancy and childbirth, or to pursue an uninterrupted career — would support a decision to hire a gestational surrogate, for example. By contrast, the Uniform Status of Children of Assisted Conception Act, in its proposal for legalized surrogacy contracts, requires the precondition of functional infertility — that is, a finding that the intended mother is unable to bear a child or unable to do so without unreasonable risk to the child or to herself.[26] The Uniform Act also requires that the intended parents in a surrogacy arrangement be "a man and woman, married to each other."[27] In *Children of Choice* and other writings, Professor Robertson acknowledges that the procreative liberty that he advances inheres primarily in the marital relationship;[28] however, he advocates a constitutional reading that would protect access to reproductive technologies by single persons and by gay or lesbian couples, as well as by married or cohabiting heterosexual couples.[29]

Again, consider the controversial situation of a postmenopausal woman who desires the implantation of a fertilized egg into her womb so that she may become pregnant, deliver the baby, and, most likely, rear the child.[30]

---

26. *See* UNIF. CONCEPTION ACT, *supra* note 14, § 6(b)(2), 9B U.L.A. 159 (Supp. 1994).

27. *Id.* § 1(3), 9B U.L.A. 155 (Supp. 1994).

28. *See* ROBERTSON, *supra* note 1, at 35-40; Robertson, *Embryos, supra* note 15, at 956-62; Robertson, *Procreative Liberty, supra* note 15, at 415-18, 427-32, 459.

29. *See* ROBERTSON, *supra* note 1, at 128 (unmarried women who are either single or cohabitating with male or female partners); Robertson, *Embryos, supra* note 15, at 962-64, 1003 (unmarried persons); *id.* at 1031 (lesbian and single women); Robertson, *Procreative Liberty, supra* note 15, at 418, 433, 459-60 (unmarried persons).

30. On July 18, 1994, a 62-year-old Italian woman, Rosanna Della Corte, gave birth to a boy whom she named after her dead teenage son. *See Italian Woman Gives Birth at 62*, WASH. POST, July 19, 1994, at A14. Dr. Severino Antinori arranged Della Corte's pregnancy through IVF with a donor's egg and sperm from Della Corte's husband. *See id.* She is the oldest known woman ever to have given birth. *See id.* Dr. Antinori was also responsible for the pregnancy of a 59-year-old British woman who gave birth to twins in December 1993. *See* Bill Hewitt et al., *Turning Back the Clock*, PEOPLE WKLY., Jan. 24, 1994, at 37, 37. Antinori has helped 54 women over the age of 50 become pregnant and give birth. *See id.* However, he considers age 63 or age 64 to be "the outer limit" for this technique. *Id.* at 41. Another Italian fertility specialist, Professor Carlo Flamigni, helped Liliana Cantadori, a 61-year-old woman, become pregnant and give birth to a healthy baby boy. *See id.* at 39. Cantadori lied to Flamigni about her age by telling him that she was only 47. *See id.* Rumors in the Italian press say that she may be trying to get pregnant again. *See id.* The United States has also had its share of postmenopausal pregnancies and births. Elke Archangel, a 52-year-old postmenopausal woman, bore twins in March 1993 as a result of IVF with a 34-year-old donor's egg. *See* Denise Fortino, *Never Say Never*, GOOD HOUSEKEEPING, June 1994, at 70,

REGULATING CHOICE   143

In January 1994, a bill passed the French Senate that would prohibit the use of reproductive options in such cases,[31] and reproductive clinics in this country commonly use age as a screening device.[32] Robertson's constitutional analysis would invalidate governmental regulation on this issue and bar a publicly funded clinic from using age as a criterion, although presumably individualized assessment of any woman's health to ensure her reasonable welfare during pregnancy and childbirth would be permissible prior to the provision of assisted reproductive services.

73-74 [hereinafter Fortino, *Never*]. The process was conducted by Dr. Mark Sauer of the University of Southern California (USC) IVF program in Los Angeles. *See id.* at 74. One of the twins has Down's Syndrome. *See id.* Since 1990, 13 out of 29 women over the age of 50 have given birth through the IVF program at USC. *See* Denise Fortino, *Menopause and Motherhood*, GOOD HOUSEKEEPING, June 1994, at 74, 74. Seven of them are grandparents as well as new parents; five are first-time mothers. *See id.* Dr. Sauer predicts that the improvements taking place in the IVF field will increase the success rate in women over age 50 from the current 30% to about 50%. *See id.*; *see also* FIELD, *supra* note 14, at 36-37 (discussing surrogate in South Africa, Pat Anthony, who gave birth to her own triplet grandchildren by gestating ova supplied by her daughter and fertilized by sperm of her daughter's husband).

31. *See* Alexander M. Capron, *Grandma? No, I'm the Mother!*, 24 HASTINGS CENTER REP., Mar.-Apr. 1994, at 24, 25. In January 1994, France considered introducing a new package of bills that entail some of the world's toughest restrictions on access to artificial reproductive techniques. *See* Scott Kraft, *France May Limit Artificial Pregnancies*, L.A. TIMES, Jan. 6, 1994, at A7. If approved, the bills "would allow 'medically assisted procreation' only to remedy sterility or to avoid the transmission of disease to the child. It could not be used for women without partners, homosexuals or women past menopause." *Id.* The laws would also provide barriers to artificial insemination and embryo implantation in cases in which the couple intending to rear the child thereby created would have no biological connection to the child. *See id.*

32. A 1987 survey of 1,473 private physicians who perform artificial insemination revealed that 9% of the physicians had rejected applicants over 40 years old, 26% were likely to reject such applicants, and 62% were not likely to reject such applicants. *See* OTA, ARTIFICIAL INSEMINATION, *supra* note 2, at 29; *see also* LORI B. ANDREWS, NEW CONCEPTIONS: A CONSUMER'S GUIDE TO THE NEWEST INFERTILITY TREATMENTS, INCLUDING *IN VITRO* FERTILIZATION, ARTIFICIAL INSEMINATION, AND SURROGATE MOTHERHOOD 123 (1984) (noting that American clinics offering IVF in 1984 set age limit of 35 to 39 years for woman of couple); BARTHOLET, *supra* note 14, at 192 (noting her discovery that only three out of about 20 IVF clinics in her personal search were willing to accept woman over 40 years old); Capron, *supra* note 31, at 25 (citing, as example, Dr. Mark V. Sauer, obstetrics and gynecology professor at University of Southern California, who pioneered use of egg donation for postmenopausal pregnancies in this country, but has chosen 55 as cutoff age); Fortino, *Never*, *supra* note 30, at 73 (citing, as example, Genetic and IVF Institute in Fairfax, Virginia, which will not accept couples over age 41).

All of these instances of persons desiring access to reproductive technologies — HIV-positive women, single persons, gay or lesbian couples, individuals or couples who do not need the service for reasons of infertility, and women well above natural childbearing age — present situations in which reasonable persons might well differ on issues of whether such access ought to be permitted and in which many might consider society's stake in the outcomes to be high. Specifically, it might well be argued that a due regard for the welfare of the resulting children would militate in favor of particular kinds of regulations, or at least in favor of proceeding cautiously during the next few years as we make our way through the thorny social considerations raised by advancing reproductive technologies.

Yet Professor Robertson's analysis would, as a matter of constitutional law, decide for us that in each of the situations posed the would-be parent's procreative liberty overrides competing considerations and prevents any regulations other than those designed purely to ensure safe medical practices. The effect of his constitutional interpretation is to foreclose debate and remove the issues from the public forum, for, in this view, the "rights" of adults preclude the possibility of regulation that public consensus might deem desirable. The conversation is over before it has had a chance to begin.[33]

A primary objection to Professor Robertson's global approach is that it ignores both the manner in which constitutional interpretation comes about and the underlying reasons for the way in which the Supreme Court approaches constitutional questions. It is axiomatic that the Supreme Court will address a question of constitutional interpretation only in the context of a case or controversy, and then only when the case cannot be decided on any other basis. The Court refuses to anticipate future (though related) constitutional questions; instead, it insists upon deciding any constitutional issue upon the narrowest possible grounds.[34] At least part of the reason for the Court's adherence to this set of principles is its belief that wise and workable constitutional doctrine can develop only through an evolutionary, case-by-case process in which issues are sharply focused and "pressed before

---

33. *See* MARY ANN GLENDON, RIGHTS TALK: THE IMPOVERISHMENT OF POLITICAL DISCOURSE 14 (1991) (arguing that assertion of rights fails to take account of social responsibility by cutting off discussion that would potentially aid in "the process of self-correcting learning"). As Glendon so aptly observes, "[I]n its simple American form, the language of rights is the language of no compromise. The winner takes all and the loser has to get out of town. The conversation is over." *Id.* at 9.

34. *See* Ashwander v. Tennessee Valley Auth., 297 U.S. 288, 346-47 (1936) (Brandeis, J., concurring) (summarizing rules that Supreme Court has developed "for its own governance in the cases confessedly within its jursidiction").

the Court with that clear concreteness provided when a question emerges precisely framed and necessary for decision from a clash of adversary argument exploring every aspect of a multi-faced situation embracing conflicting and demanding interests."[35]

The body of doctrine that emerges from a line of case law can certainly serve a predictive purpose for evaluating the validity of some instances of proposed future action. Obviously, it can also serve as a useful springboard for framing social policy perspectives. However, the process of extrapolating from a body of Supreme Court cases a full-blown theory of broad-based social policy, applying that theory to a number of issues whose very form is changing shape almost daily with the development of increasingly sophisticated technology, and then insisting that all behavior within the theoretical umbrella must be the subject of heightened constitutional protection seems to me to be dubious at best. As the Supreme Court's jurisprudential approach suggests, current attempts to resolve questions that are not yet fully defined, or whose implications we cannot yet entirely appreciate, run the danger of leading to socially undesirable consequences if our current resolution does not retain the flexibility to adapt to each new situation as it comes up. Setting an entire realm of social policy into constitutional concrete poses this danger.

I submit, therefore, that Professor Robertson's definition of "procreative liberty" paints with too broad a brush insofar as constitutional interpretation is concerned. By foreclosing discussion and the possibility of social control over issues important to the future of us all, he reaches results that are unnecessary for the protection of constitutional values and undesirable from the standpoint of public policy. His glib recitation of the rubric that, from the perspective of any individual, it is invariably better to have been born than not to have been born makes too short a shrift of a concern central to the reproductive technologies debate — namely, what we should do to ensure the physical, mental, and psychological well-being of the children whom we are deliberately bringing into existence.

Please do not misunderstand me. As a mother who would have been devastated by infertility, I have only the strongest sympathies for those who desperately desire to become parents and whose fondest wish is for children with a genetic tie to at least one of the rearing parents. I am not even saying that, as a matter of social policy, I would vote with those who would restrict access to assisted reproduction by single persons, gay or lesbian couples, or,

---

35. United States v. Fruehauf, 365 U.S. 146, 157 (1961); *see also* TRIBE, *supra* note 22, §§ 3-9 to -10 (discussing ban on advisory opinions and doctrine of ripeness).

146 *52 WASH. & LEE L. REV. 135 (1995)*

for that matter, any of the parties that I mentioned earlier in my chronicle of controversial situations.

What I am saying, quite simply, is that the development of new reproductive technologies raises issues too numerous and complex for us to deal with — or even to foresee — all at one time. In the final chapter of *Children of Choice*, Professor Robertson addresses "critiques of procreative liberty," several of which are represented in this Symposium.[36] In characterizing those who might disagree with him, he states that some "may simply be more cautious."[37] I would place myself in that camp. However, there is no room for caution, or for addressing the issues piecemeal in the public forum, if Professor Robertson is correct that "procreative liberty," *as he defines it*, is a fundamental right protected by standards of strict scrutiny under the United States Constitution. It is to that contention that I now turn.

II. The Constitutional Argument

A. Robertson's Thesis

Much of the discussion in *Children of Choice* of the primacy of procreative liberty as an overriding value is couched in terms of social policy arguments, not necessarily constitutional ones. From a purely social policy perspective, I do not disagree with Professor Robertson that the procreative interests of would-be parents is *a* primary value, worthy of a great deal of respect and accommodation as we consider the increasing sophistication and usage of reproductive technologies. Indeed, his "lens of procreative liberty,"[38] as he characterizes it, does provide us with "a useful framework"[39] for evaluating both current issues and future developments in this rapidly evolving area. As a matter of social policy, my disagreement with Professor Robertson is more one of emphasis than of kind. I would endow the procreative interests of would-be parents with a less thoroughgoing primacy and would place more weight on the interests of the children resulting from the use of these technologies.

---

36. *See* ROBERTSON, *supra* note 1, at 220-35 (answering critiques that his rights-based approach to procreative liberty is overly individualistic, ignores social responsibility and community needs, fails to account for economic and class effects, and risks exploiting and oppressing women).

37. *Id.* at 222.

38. *Id.* at 220.

39. *Id.* at 222.

Where I differ from Professor Robertson is with his insistence that procreative liberty as a constitutionally protected fundamental right should be broadly construed in a manner that protects from all but minimal regulation virtually any means of achieving biological parenthood for virtually any would-be parent. Although the constitutional argument per se is not as prominent in *Children of Choice* as in some of Professor Robertson's other writings,[40] he does advance it in Chapter 2,[41] and his basic phraseology throughout the book mirrors the constitutional parlance of fundamental rights language.[42]

His examination of both Supreme Court holdings and dicta in a number of cases leads Professor Robertson to the conclusion that "[i]n the United States laws restricting coital reproduction by a married couple would have to withstand the strict scrutiny applied to interference with fundamental constitutional rights."[43] From there, he invokes equal protection reasoning and notes that the desire of infertile couples "to have a family — to beget, bear, and rear offspring — is as strong as in fertile couples."[44] This proposition then follows:

> [I]f bearing, begetting, or parenting children is protected as part of personal privacy or liberty, those experiences should be protected whether they are achieved coitally or noncoitally. In either case they satisfy the basic biologic, social, and psychological drive to have a biologically

---

40. *See* Robertson, *Embryos, supra* note 15, at 954-67; Robertson, *Procreative Liberty, supra* note 15, at 414-20, 427-36.

41. ROBERTSON, *supra* note 1, at 22-42. For especially relevant sections, see *id.* at 28-29, 35-40.

42. There is very little difference between a declaration that any restriction upon procreative liberty (broadly defined to include the use of assisted reproduction) must be subjected to strict scrutiny and can be upheld only if it is narrowly tailored to support a compelling state interest, *see supra* note 22 and accompanying text, and Professor Robertson's statement that "procreative liberty [should] be given presumptive priority in all conflicts, with the burden on opponents of any particular technique to show that harmful effects from its use justify limiting procreative choice," ROBERTSON, *supra* note 1, at 16. *Cf. id.* at 40-41 ("If procreative liberty is taken seriously, a strong presumption in favor of using technologies that centrally implicate reproductive interests should be recognized. Although procreative rights are not absolute, those who would limit procreative choice should have the burden of establishing substantial harm. This is the standard used in ethical and legal analyses of restrictions on traditional reproductive decisions. Because the same procreative goals are involved, the same standard of scrutiny should be used for assessing moral or governmental restrictions on novel reproductive techniques.").

43. ROBERTSON, *supra* note 1, at 36.

44. *Id.* at 39.

related family. Although full genetic reproduction might not exist in each case, the interest of the couple in rearing children who are biologically related to one or both rearing partners is so close to the coital model that it should be treated equivalently. Noncoital reproduction should thus be constitutionally protected to the same extent as coital reproduction, with the state having the burden of showing severe harm if the practice is unrestricted.[45]

B. *The Current Constitutional Status of Procreative Liberty*

1. *Supreme Court Decisions*

To assess Professor Robertson's arguments, it is first necessary to determine as precisely as possible what interests the Supreme Court has held to be subject to heightened protection under the Constitution. Identifying the core values at stake in defined liberty interests should then lead to logical conclusions about the potential scope of procreative liberty as an element of the right of privacy.

Professor Robertson and other commentators have accurately noted that the Supreme Court's clearest jurisprudence in this area concerns the right *not* to procreate — i.e., not to bear unwanted children.[46] In 1965, *Griswold v. Connecticut*[47] first identified a right of access to contraceptive devices as part of a "right of privacy"[48] inherent in the marital relation-

---

45.   *Id.* For the viewpoint that collaborative reproductive techniques (i.e., AID, surrogacy, or IVF with a donor embryo) are more similar to adoption than to coital reproduction, see BARTHOLET, *supra* note 14, at 218-29.

46.   *See, e.g.*, OTA, INFERTILITY, *supra* note 2, at 219-20; ROBERTSON, *supra* note 1, at 28-29, 45-48; Annas, *Regulating, supra* note 14, at 416; Massie, *supra* note 14, at 502-04; O'Brien, *supra* note 14, at 139-40; Robertson, *Embryos, supra* note 15, at 955 n.50; Robertson, *Procreative Liberty, supra* note 15, at 405 n.3, 415-16; Ryan, *supra* note 14, at 7; Keller, *supra* note 14, at 172-73.

47.   381 U.S. 479 (1965).

48.   *See* Griswold v. Connecticut, 381 U.S. 479, 486 (1965) ("We deal with a right of privacy older than the Bill of Rights — older than our political parties, older than our school system. Marriage is a coming together for better or for worse, hopefully enduring, and intimate to the degree of being sacred."). In his opinion for the Court, Justice Douglas found the privacy right in "penumbras, formed by emanations" from specific guarantees in the Bill of Rights, including the First Amendment's freedom of association, the Fourth Amendment's protection of the home from unreasonable searches and seizures, and the Fifth Amendment's self-incrimination clause, as well as the Ninth Amendment's provision concerning the retention of unenumerated rights by the people. *Id.* at 484.

ship.[49] *Eisenstadt·v. Baird*[50] extended the same right of privacy to single persons in 1972.[51] In 1977, *Carey v. Population Services International*[52] held that minors could not be barred from purchasing contraceptives.[53] Meanwhile, the 1973 decision of *Roe v. Wade*[54] found that the right of privacy "is broad enough to encompass a woman's decision whether or not to terminate her pregnancy,"[55] at least during the first trimester.[56] Mature minors possess the same right;[57] other minors may obtain an abortion with parental consent or through a judicial proceeding.[58] *Planned Parenthood v. Casey*[59] recently reaffirmed a woman's previability abortion right,[60] although the Court softened its prior trimester framework to an undue burden standard for evaluating government regulation.[61]

It is clear that the government must respect an individual's right to prevent procreation by the use of contraception or by previability abortion, but what is the picture when we look to the positive side of procreative liberty — the right *to* procreate? As long ago as 1942, in *Skinner v.*

---

49. *See id.* at 485-86.

50. 405 U.S. 438 (1972). Justice Brennan characterized the right of privacy expansively: "If the right of privacy means anything, it is the right of the *individual*, married or single, to be free from unwarranted governmental intrusion into matters so fundamentally affecting a person as the decision whether to bear or beget a child." Eisenstadt v. Baird, 405 U.S. 438, 453 (1972).

51. *See id.*

52. 431 U.S. 678 (1977).

53. Carey v. Population Servs. Int'l, 431 U.S. 678, 693 (1977) (opinion of Brennan, J.).

54. 410 U.S. 113 (1973).

55. Roe v. Wade, 410 U.S. 113, 153 (1973). Justice Blackmun's opinion for the Court grounded the privacy right in the "Fourteenth Amendment's concept of personal liberty and restrictions upon state action." *Id.*

56. *See id.* at 163.

57. *See* Planned Parenthood v. Danforth, 428 U.S. 52, 74 (1976) (invalidating statute giving parent veto power over minor's abortion decision).

58. *See* Bellotti v. Baird, 443 U.S. 622, 643-44 (1979) (holding that state may require parental notification or consent, but only if it establishes judicial bypass procedure, which must permit mature minor to make decision herself or — if she is not mature — must allow court to decide whether abortion is in her best interest). *See generally* Hodgson v. Minnesota, 497 U.S. 417 (1990) (involving judicial bypass procedure); Ohio v. Akron Ctr. for Reprod. Health, 497 U.S. 502 (1990) (same).

59. 112 S. Ct. 2791 (1992).

60. *See* Planned Parenthood v. Casey, 112 S. Ct. 2791, 2816 (1992) (joint opinion of O'Connor, Kennedy, and Souter, JJ.).

61. *See id.* at 2818-20.

Oklahoma,[62] the Court in dictum referred to procreation as "one of the basic civil rights of man"[63] and noted that "marriage and procreation are fundamental to the very existence and survival of the race."[64] *Skinner*, however, was an equal protection case concerning the state's power to render someone permanently sterile, and its reference was to natural procreative *capacity*, not to procreative acts.[65]

Since *Skinner*, in construing the liberty interest protected by the Due Process Clause of the Fourteenth Amendment, the Court has delineated, in Justice Powell's words, "[a] host of cases . . . [that] have consistently acknowledged a 'private realm of family life which the state cannot enter.'"[66] This realm includes personal decisions "relating to marriage, procreation, contraception, family relationships, and child rearing and education."[67] Accordingly, the Court has struck down policies restricting an individual's choice of whom[68] and when to marry,[69] zoning regulations burdening rights of blood relatives to live together in a single household,[70] and laws deemed to interfere with parental rights to raise and educate children as one sees fit.[71] Although no case attempts to define a positive right to procreate as such, recognition of such a right is certainly implicit

---

62.   316 U.S. 535 (1942).

63.   Skinner v. Oklahoma, 316 U.S. 535, 541 (1942).

64.   *Id.*

65.   *See id.* at 536-37.

66.   Moore v. City of E. Cleveland, 431 U.S. 494, 499 (1977) (opinion of Powell, J.) (quoting Prince v. Massachusetts, 321 U.S. 158, 166 (1944)). Justice Powell actually traces the lineage of these cases to two decisions preceding *Skinner. See* Pierce v. Society of Sisters, 268 U.S. 510, 534-35 (1925) (holding that parents have right to educate their children in private schools); Meyer v. Nebraska, 262 U.S. 390, 403 (1923) (holding that state law prohibiting foreign language instruction violates Fourteenth Amendment).

67.   Carey v. Population Servs. Int'l, 431 U.S. 678, 685 (1977) (citations omitted).

68.   *See* Loving v. Virginia, 388 U.S. 1, 11-12 (1967) (invalidating Virginia's antimiscegenation statute).

69.   *See* Zablocki v. Redhail, 434 U.S. 374, 388 (1978) (invalidating statute requiring court's approval of marriage of resident having minor children who are not in his custody and whom he is under legal duty to support).

70.   *See Moore*, 431 U.S. at 499-500 (opinion of Powell, J.) (invalidating single-family residential ordinance that defined "family" so narrowly as to prevent grandmother from living in same house with her son and two grandsons who were cousins, not brothers).

71.   *See* Pierce v. Society of Sisters, 268 U.S. 510, 534-35 (1925) (holding that parents have right to educate their children in private schools); Meyer v. Nebraska, 262 U.S. 390, 403 (1923) (holding that state law prohibiting foreign language instruction violates Fourteenth Amendment).

in *Cleveland Board of Education v. LaFleur*,[72] in which the requirements of two school boards for extensive maternity leave were held to constitute impermissible burdens on a protected area of "freedom of personal choice in matters affecting marriage and family life."[73] In his opinion for the court, Justice Stewart specifically linked the pregnancy choice of the teachers with Justice Brennan's characterization in *Eisenstadt v. Baird* of the right "to be free from unwarranted governmental intrusion into matters so fundamentally affecting a person as the decision whether to bear or beget a child."[74] Justice Stewart's reference was arguably significant for the fact that he cited contraception cases (dealing with the right *not* to procreate) to imply support for an expansive *positive* constitutional concept of procreative liberty.

Yet we must also keep in mind some sharp cutoff points that the Court has earmarked in its delineation of the constitutionally protected right of privacy. In *Bowers v. Hardwick*,[75] the Court refused to characterize homosexual behavior as an aspect of the freedom of intimate association.[76] Instead, the Court upheld a state prohibition against homosexual sodomy on the grounds that the practice had long constituted a criminal offense and hence did not fit within the "fundamental liberties . . . 'deeply rooted in this Nation's history and tradition.'"[77]

Again, in *Michael H. v. Gerald D.*,[78] the Court upheld a statutory presumption of a child's legitimacy, irrebuttable by all but the marital couple, and, in so doing, brushed aside a natural father's claim of rights both to prove his paternity and to maintain a relationship with his daughter under circumstances in which the mother had been married and living with her husband at the time of the birth.[79] Claims of parental rights by natural fathers of illegitimate children are given constitutional respect when those fathers have participated in the child's maintenance and care.[80] In *Michael*

---

72. 414 U.S. 632 (1974).

73. Cleveland Bd. of Educ. v. LaFleur, 414 U.S. 632, 639 (1974).

74. *Id.* at 640 (quoting Eisenstadt v. Baird, 405 U.S. 438, 453 (1972)).

75. 478 U.S. 186 (1986).

76. *See* Bowers v. Hardwick, 478 U.S. 186, 191-92 (1986).

77. *Id.* at 192 (quoting Moore v. City of E. Cleveland, 431 U.S. 494, 503 (1977) (opinion of Powell, J.)).

78. 491 U.S. 110 (1989).

79. *See* Michael H. v. Gerald D., 491 U.S. 110, 119-30 (1989) (opinion of Scalia, J.).

80. *See, e.g.*, Stanley v. Illinois, 405 U.S. 645, 658 (1972) (holding that denial to

H., however, the Court found that the state policy favoring (1) the child's interests in a status of legitimacy and (2) the preservation of the integrity of the family unit overrode any interests that either the natural father or the child herself might otherwise assert.[81]

Given the parameters of the Supreme Court's right of privacy decisions, how are we to interpret the scope of the enunciated "right to decide whether to bear or beget a child"?[82] I suggest that the answer to this question lies in an examination of the underlying *values* at stake in the decided cases. The second question is how broadly *should* that right extend as questions involving the new reproductive technologies make their way into our legal system? Although full exploration of that question is beyond the scope of this Article, I submit that formulating the answer calls for social policy considerations that give weight and value to concerns beyond simply, or even primarily, the procreative liberty interests of the affected adults.

2. Values Underlying the Decisions

Professor Robertson's reading of the privacy cases leads him to conclude that coital reproduction within marriage is a fundamental right subject to the highest degree of constitutional protection.[83] Because the underlying motivations and desires are the same, he argues that noncoital

---

unmarried father of parental fitness hearing afforded other parents whose custody is challenged by state violates Equal Protection Clause); *see also* Lehr v. Robertson, 463 U.S. 248, 267-68 (1983) (holding that Equal Protection Clause does not require state to afford mothers and fathers similar legal rights with respect to their children when father has failed to attempt to establish relationship with child); Caban v. Mohammed, 441 U.S. 380, 392-93 (1979) (holding that New York statute prohibiting adoption of child without natural mother's consent, but allowing adoption of child without natural father's consent unless father can prove adoption not to be in child's best interests, violates Equal Protection Clause when natural father has established substantial relationship with child).

81. *See Michael H.*, 491 U.S. at 119-20 (opinion of Scalia, J.); *see also id.* at 125 (citing common-law presumption of legitimacy of any child born during marriage and stating that "[t]he primary policy rationale underlying the common law's severe restrictions on rebuttal of the presumption appears to have been an aversion to declaring children illegitimate . . . . A secondary policy concern was the interest in promoting the 'peace and tranquillity of States and families'").

82. Eisenstadt v. Baird, 405 U.S. 438, 453 (1972); *see also supra* notes 50-51, 74 and accompanying text.

83. *See* ROBERTSON, *supra* note 1, at 36; *see also supra* note 43 and accompanying text.

reproduction should receive the same degree of constitutional deference.[84] Are these conclusions justified? I submit that the first one is, but the second one is not. The distinction becomes apparent upon an examination of the values underlying the cases involving procreative choice.

Professor Robertson argues that the primary value at stake here is the "central importance [of procreative liberty] to individual meaning, dignity, and identity"[85] for both fertile and infertile couples. In other words, what matters is the shared wish of both fertile and infertile couples "to replicate themselves, transmit genes, gestate, and rear children biologically related to them."[86] The desire is the same, the motivations are the same, and the goal is the same. Therefore, he reasons, infertile couples should have the same protected right to noncoital reproduction that fertile couples have to coital reproduction.[87] This syllogism has an appealing ring to it and, as a social policy proposition, deserves respect if not wholesale accommodation. In the realm of constitutional law, however, there are many instances in which there is a sharp distinction between the degree of protection specifically provided to a belief or motivation and the degree of protection provided to the conduct arising from that belief or motivation.

3. The Belief/Conduct Distinction

Professor Robertson is surely correct in identifying self-fulfillment as a major concern of the privacy cases and a key rationale underlying the protection given to procreative choice.[88] Citing those decisions, the *Casey* Court declared:

> These matters, involving the most intimate and personal choices a person may make in a lifetime, choices central to personal dignity and autonomy, are central to the liberty protected by the Fourteenth Amendment. At the heart of liberty is the right to define one's own concept of existence, of meaning, of the universe, and of the mystery of human life. Beliefs about these matters could not define the attributes of personhood were they formed under compulsion of the State.[89]

---

84. *See* ROBERTSON, *supra* note 1, at 39; *see also supra* note 45 and accompanying text.
85. ROBERTSON, *supra* note 1, at 16.
86. *Id.* at 32.
87. *See id.* at 39.
88. *See id.* at 24-25.
89. Planned Parenthood v. Casey, 112 S. Ct. 2791, 2807 (1992).

The primacy of beliefs to any person's self-definition, and the centrality of freedom of self-definition to the concept of liberty generally, cannot be gainsaid. Nor can it be denied that liberty must entail, at the very least, the right to make certain choices about how to live one's life in a manner that will give meaning and value to the existence of the person making the choices. In other words, liberty must involve not only freedom of belief, but also a meaningful opportunity to act upon the beliefs central to self-definition.

Nonetheless, it is also true that our system of constitutional government, for all its emphasis upon individual liberties as particularly recognized in the Bill of Rights, has always insisted upon the importance of the distinction between beliefs, on the one hand, and conduct stemming from those beliefs, on the other. Beliefs often possess, for the believer, the quality of the absolute; certainly, from the standpoint of government, they possess the quality of the unregulable. The government may attempt to influence beliefs, but it ultimately lacks the power either to instill or to expunge them from the minds of those who hold them. Conduct, on the other hand, is the stuff with which regulation is concerned. Given that beliefs are both central to self-definition and essentially ungovernable, while conduct is both the natural outgrowth of beliefs and the arena of regulation, the important question becomes: To what extent must government accommodate conduct in order to respect belief and to preserve the right of self-definition, as it simultaneously acts in the best interests of all by promulgating regulations that seem desirable to a majority?

I know of no thoroughgoing answer to this question — at least, not in the developed jurisprudence of constitutional case law — but particularized answers abound, especially in the area of First Amendment interpretation. The Religion Clauses present a striking example of constitutional protection for belief: Government is specifically prohibited from establishing any religion, but it is also required to respect "the free exercise thereof."[90] "Exercise" is in fact an active word and might seem to connote a component of protected conduct, as well as belief. Yet time and again, the Supreme Court has stated that although the Free Exercise Clause protects belief absolutely, religiously motivated conduct "remains subject to regulation for the protection of society."[91] Thus, child labor

---

90. U.S. CONST. amend. I. The First Amendment states: "Congress shall make no law respecting an establishment of religion, or prohibiting the free exercise thereof . . . ." *Id.*

91. *Cantwell v. Connecticut*, 310 U.S. 296, 303-04 (1940); *see also Sherbert v. Verner*, 374 U.S. 398, 402-03 (1963) (stating that, although "[t]he door of the Free Exercise Clause

laws,[92] universal immunization requirements,[93] and antipolygamy laws[94] have all been upheld against religious objections to compliance. In each case, the Court favored larger social values perceived to be at stake — for example, in the polygamy cases, common notions of morality and an ordered society, and in the immunization cases, concerns related to both the general public health and the individual welfare of the children most directly affected. Furthermore, challenged regulations have not necessarily been held to a "strict scrutiny" standard of review; at least, criminal laws of general applicability need not accommodate religiously based conduct and need not rest upon a compelling state interest.[95]   Although the Religious Freedom

---

stands tightly closed against any governmental regulation of religious *beliefs* as such," resulting conduct may be circumscribed when it poses "some substantial threat to public safety, peace or order"); Braunfeld v. Brown, 366 U.S. 599, 603-04 (1961) ("[L]egislative power over mere opinion is forbidden but it may reach people's actions when they are found to be in violation of important social duties or subversive of good order, even when the actions are demanded by one's religion."); Reynolds v. United States, 98 U.S. 145, 166 (1878) ("Laws are made for the government of actions, and while they cannot interfere with mere religious belief and opinions, they may with practices.").

92. *See* Prince v. Massachusetts, 321 U.S. 158, 167 (1944) ("[T]he state has a wide range of power for limiting parental freedom and authority in things affecting the child's welfare; and . . . this includes, to some extent, matters of conscience and religious conviction.").

93. *See generally* Cude v. State, 377 S.W.2d 816 (Ark. 1964); Mosier v. Barren County Bd. of Health, 215 S.W.2d 967 (Ky. 1948); Sadlock v. Board of Educ., 58 A.2d 218 (N.J. 1948); Board of Educ. v. Maas, 152 A.2d 394 (N.J. Super. Ct. App. Div. 1959), *aff'd*, 158 A.2d 330 (N.J.), *cert. denied*, 363 U.S. 843 (1960); City of New Braunfels v. Waldschmidt, 207 S.W. 303 (Tex. 1918). These cases all cited Jacobson v. Massachusetts, 197 U.S. 11 (1905), as authority for defending compulsory immunization requirements against religious objections. The *Jacobson* Court specifically stated, "According to settled principles the police power of a State must be held to embrace, at least, such reasonable regulations established directly by legislative enactment as will protect the public health and the public safety." *Id.* at 25. Further, the Court stated, "Whatever may be thought of [the mandatory vaccination] statute, it cannot be affirmed to be, beyond question, in palpable conflict with the Constitution." *Id.* at 31; *accord Prince*, 321 U.S. at 166-67 ("[One] cannot claim freedom from compulsory vaccination for the child more than for himself on religious grounds. The right to practice religion freely does not include liberty to expose the community or the child to communicable disease or the latter to ill health or death.").

94. *See Reynolds*, 98 U.S. at 165-66 (arguing that marriage, as foundation of society, creates social obligations and duties that must be subject to governmental regulation lest social order be destroyed).

95. *See* Employment Div. v. Smith, 494 U.S. 872, 888 (1990) ("[P]recisely because we value and protect . . . religious divergence, we cannot afford the luxury of deeming *presumptively invalid*, as applied to the religious objector, every regulation of conduct that does not protect an interest of the highest order.").

156   *52 WASH. & LEE L. REV. 135 (1995)*

Restoration Act of 1993[96] attempts to impose such a requirement, its constitutional validity remains to be tested. In any event, the positive protection afforded by the Free Exercise Clause arguably justifies stronger protections for conduct stemming from religious beliefs than for conduct that has other motivational roots.[97]

Again, consider the freedom of expression. Pure expression — the simple statement of a thought, belief, idea, or factual piece of knowledge — is surely the closest thing to the holding of that thought, belief, idea, or knowledge, and hence deserves a degree of protection almost as absolute, as reflected in the strong requirement that government remain viewpoint neutral in its regulatory policies.[98] Even so, simple statements can be constrained or punished based upon their content in the service of

---

96.   Pub. L. No. 103-141, 107 Stat. 1488 (1993).

97.   *See, e.g., Employment Div.*, 494 U.S. at 891-907 (O'Connor, J., concurring in judgment) (taking strong issue with Court's rationale on ground that Free Exercise Clause provides positive protection for areas of religiously motivated behavior); *id.* at 907-21 (Blackmun, J., dissenting) (dissenting on similar grounds). Several commentators have made this argument. *See generally* Douglas Laycock, *Formal, Substantive, and Disaggregated Neutrality Toward Religion*, 39 DEPAUL L. REV. 993 (1990); Douglas Laycock, *The Remnants of Free Exercise*, 1990 SUP. CT. REV. 1 (arguing generally that Free Exercise Clause requires some accommodations for religiously motivated conduct and permits others that legislatures might decide to grant); Ira C. Lupu, *Reconstructing the Establishment Clause: The Case Against Discretionary Accommodation of Religion*, 140 U. PA. L. REV. 555 (1991); Ira C. Lupu, *The Trouble with Accommodation*, 60 GEO. WASH. L. REV. 743 (1992) (arguing against legislative accommodations for religiously motivated conduct, but also maintaining that Free Exercise Clause requires some accommodations); Michael W. McConnell, *Accommodation of Religion*, 1985 SUP. CT. REV. 1; Michael W. McConnell, *Accommodation of Religion: An Update and a Response to the Critics*, 60 GEO. WASH. L. REV. 685 (1992) (arguing generally that Free Exercise Clause requires some accommodations for religiously motivated conduct and permits others that legislatures might decide to grant).

98.   *See, e.g.*, Texas v. Johnson, 491 U.S. 397, 414 (1989) ("If there is a bedrock principle underlying the First Amendment, it is that the government may not prohibit the expression of an idea simply because society finds the idea itself offensive or disagreeable."); Perry Educ. Ass'n v. Perry Local Educators' Ass'n, 460 U.S. 37, 60-61 (1983) (Brennan, J., dissenting) (noting that case law "provide[s] some support for the notion that the government is permitted to exclude certain subjects from discussion in nonpublic forums," but "[o]nce the government permits discussion of certain subject matter, it may not impose restrictions that discriminate among viewpoints on those subjects whether a nonpublic forum is involved or not"); City of Madison Joint Sch. Dist. No. 8 v. Wisconsin Employment Relations Comm'n, 429 U.S. 167, 175-76 (1976) ("[T]he participation in public discussion of public business cannot be confined to one category of interested individuals. To permit one side of a debatable public question to have a monopoly in expressing its views to the government is the antithesis of constitutional guarantees.").

REGULATING CHOICE 157

a compelling state interest, such as the national security at stake in antiespionage statutes[99] or the public order preserved by prohibitions against incitement to riot.[100]

Beyond these quite specific and rare circumstances of potentially permissible content regulation, however, speech is actually subject to a relatively high degree of circumscription in the guise of reasonable time, place, and manner regulations.[101] Any speaker is entitled to express her beliefs, thoughts, ideas, or knowledge, but certainly not anywhere, at any time, or in any manner of her choosing. Although time, place, and manner regulations trigger a heightened standard of review, their validity does not require a compelling state interest, and the government's burden is not difficult to sustain, so long as the rules are applied evenhandedly.[102] Even

---

99. *See, e.g.*, Near v. Minnesota, 283 U.S. 697, 716 (1931) (stating, in dictum, that prior restraint on speech might be permissible in "exceptional cases" and citing as examples "actual obstruction to [a government's] recruiting service or the publication of the sailing dates of transports or the number and location of troops" during wartime, obscenity laws, and "incitements to acts of violence and the overthrow by force of orderly government"); *see also* New York Times Co. v. United States, 403 U.S. 713, 723 (1971) (Douglas, J., concurring) (invalidating injunctions prohibiting publication by two newspapers of so-called "Pentagon Papers" on ground, *inter alia*, that *Near* test was not met). Some Justices in *New York Times*, however, pointed to the possibility of appropriate criminal laws supporting postpublication penal action. *See id.* at 730 (Stewart, J., concurring); *id.* at 733-40 (White, J., concurring); *cf.* Snepp v. United States, 444 U.S. 507, 509 n.3, 515-16 (1980) (per curiam) (noting that Central Intelligence Agency may act to protect substantial government interests in national security secrets by imposing restrictions on employee activities and holding that when employee breached agreement to submit manuscript for prepublication review, judgment imposing constructive trust on book's profits was appropriate).

100. *See* Brandenburg v. Ohio, 395 U.S. 444, 447-48 (1969) (invalidating Ohio's criminal syndicalism statute and holding that statute prohibiting advocacy of illegal conduct is valid only if prohibited conduct is "directed to inciting or producing imminent lawless action" and is "likely to produce such action"). The *Brandenburg* test was reaffirmed in Hess v. Indiana, 414 U.S. 105 (1973) (per curiam), in which the Court held that the test was not met as applied to an alleged incitement to riot during a street protest. *See id.* at 108-09; *see also* TRIBE, *supra* note 22, § 12-9.

101. *See, e.g.*, Clark v. Community for Creative Non-Violence, 468 U.S. 288, 294 (1984) ("[R]easonable time, place, or manner regulations normally have the purpose and direct effect of limiting expression but are nevertheless valid.").

102. *See, e.g., id.* at 293 ("Expression, whether oral or written or symbolized by conduct, is subject to reasonable time, place, or manner restrictions. We have often noted that restrictions of this kind are valid provided that they are justified without reference to the content of the regulated speech, that they are narrowly tailored to serve a significant governmental interest, and that they leave open ample alternative channels for communication of the information."). The requirement of a "significant governmental interest" (rather

158   *52 WASH. & LEE L. REV. 135 (1995)*

the quintessential public forums need not remain constantly available: Public parks are commonly closed from dusk to dawn to protect the public safety, the need for streets to serve vehicular traffic justifies permit requirements,[103] and the authorities can insist that public sidewalks remain sufficiently clear for pedestrian use.[104] The use of sound enhancement devices is clearly subject to reasonable regulation in the service of the public peace.[105] Notice that the more it is possible to characterize the subject matter of the regulation as "conduct" — even "expressive conduct" — rather than as "pure speech," the more likely it is that a regulation will be upheld;[106] hence, the Court's close attention to the appropriate characterization of such activities as draft card burning,[107] the wearing of

---

than "compelling") is the language of an intermediate standard of judicial review. *See also* Ward v. Rock Against Racism, 491 U.S. 781, 798 (1989) ("Lest any confusion on the point remain, we reaffirm today that a regulation of the time, place, or manner of protected speech must be narrowly tailored to serve the government's legitimate, content-neutral interests but that it need not be the least restrictive or least intrusive means of doing so."); *id.* at 798-99 n.6 ("While time, place, or manner regulations must . . . be 'narrowly tailored' in order to survive First Amendment challenge, we have never applied strict scrutiny in this context.").

103. *See, e.g.*, Shuttlesworth v. City of Birmingham, 394 U.S. 147, 153 (1969) (invalidating ordinance requiring permit for parade or demonstration on overbreadth grounds, but noting permissibility of properly drawn statute); Cox v. New Hampshire, 312 U.S. 569, 575-76 (1941) (upholding license requirement for parade or procession on public street after state supreme court narrowly construed statute to limit discretion of licensing authority to appropriate time, place, and manner considerations).

104. *See, e.g.*, Madsen v. Women's Health Ctr., Inc., 114 S. Ct. 2516, 2526 (1994) ("The State . . . has a strong interest in . . . promoting the free flow of traffic on public streets and sidewalks . . . .").

105. *See generally Ward*, 491 U.S. 781; City Council v. Taxpayers for Vincent, 466 U.S. 789 (1984); Kovacs v. Cooper, 336 U.S. 77 (1949).

106. *See, e.g.*, Texas v. Johnson, 491 U.S. 397, 406 (1989) ("The government generally has a freer hand in restricting expressive conduct than it has in restricting the written or spoken word."); *Shuttlesworth*, 394 U.S. at 152 ("[T]he First and Fourteenth Amendments [do not] afford the same kind of freedom to those who would communicate ideas by conduct such as patrolling, marching, and picketing on streets and highways, as these amendments afford to those who communicate ideas by pure speech." (quoting Cox v. Louisiana, 379 U.S. 536, 555 (1965)) (second brackets added by Court)).

107. *See* United States v. O'Brien, 391 U.S. 367, 376 (1968) (upholding congressional prohibition of draft card burning in face of claim that activity was undertaken as form of political protest and noting that "when 'speech' and 'nonspeech' elements are combined in the same course of conduct, a sufficiently important governmental interest in regulating the nonspeech element can justify incidental limitations on First Amendment freedoms").

black armbands,[108] and flag burning.[109]

The privacy cases themselves also leave broad scope for the regulation of conduct. Although the cases most directly related to procreative liberty speak in terms of the "right to decide whether to bear or beget a child"[110] (a mental process), the holdings fall far short of protecting all possible behaviors related to that choice. Instead, the cases defining constitutionally protected *conduct* invariably implicate not only the value of self-fulfillment or self-definition, but one or more other values as well. Generally, these values are characterizable either as respect for an individual's bodily integrity or as social concerns related to the privacy of marital intimacy and the integrity of the family unit.

Bodily integrity is one of the chief values particularly identified for protection in the contraception and abortion cases. Both *Eisenstadt* and *Carey* struck down contraception restrictions partly on the basis that the state had no right to punish concededly illicit sexual conduct by imposing on the miscreant the physical burdens of pregnancy and the birth of an unwanted child.[111] *Roe v. Wade* and other abortion cases expressed similar concerns.[112] These decisions comport with others in which the Court has

---

108. *See* Tinker v. Des Moines Indep. Community Sch. Dist., 393 U.S. 503, 505-06 (1979) (holding that wearing of black armbands by school students could not be prohibited or punished because activity was "akin to 'pure speech'" and neither students nor teachers "shed their constitutional rights to freedom of speech or expression at the schoolhouse gate").

109. *See* United States v. Eichman, 496 U.S. 310, 317-18 (1990) (holding Flag Protection Act of 1989 unconstitutional as content-based regulation of expressive conduct). The *Eichman* Court specifically based its holding upon *Texas v. Johnson*, in which the Court determined that, unlike the statute in *O'Brien*, a Texas anti-flag-burning law was "related to the suppression of free expression" and therefore was outside the more lenient *O'Brien* test. *See Johnson*, 491 U.S. at 407.

110. Eisenstadt v. Baird, 405 U.S. 438, 453 (1972).

111. *See* Carey v. Population Servs. Int'l, 431 U.S. 678, 694-95 (1977) (citing *Eisenstadt*, 405 U.S. at 448, and referring generally to cases supporting abortion rights of minor women as protective of bodily integrity). *See generally* Planned Parenthood v. Danforth, 428 U.S. 52 (1976) (supporting abortion rights of minor women as protective of bodily integrity).

112. *See, e.g.*, Roe v. Wade, 410 U.S. 113, 153 (1973) (detailing aspects of "[t]he detriment that the State would impose upon the pregnant woman by denying this choice altogether"); *see also* TRIBE, *supra* note 22, § 15-10, at 1340 (stating that "it is difficult to imagine a clearer sense of bodily intrusion" than requiring woman to carry child to term); *cf.* Planned Parenthood v. Casey, 112 S. Ct. 2791, 2807 (1992) ("Her suffering is too intimate and personal for the State to insist, without more, upon its own vision of the woman's role . . . .").

protected persons against unwanted surgery or other procedures invasive of bodily integrity.[113] Taken as a whole, this body of law would surely severely restrict or prohibit altogether such practices as state-mandated sterilization, contraception, or abortion — freedom from which constitutes another aspect of procreative liberty[114] — as well as protect access to those procedures performed consensually.

Values related to protecting the intimacy of the marriage relationship and the integrity of the family unit form another central concern of the privacy cases. They are the entire focus of *Griswold v. Connecticut*[115] and of decisions already cited relating to the "private realm of family life."[116] Interestingly, the value of marital integrity provides a key rationale for the major restriction on parenting rights in *Michael H. v. Gerald D.*[117] In that case, the Court permitted California to protect an ongoing marriage against the assault represented by the natural father's assertion of paternal rights to a child born during the marriage.[118]

---

113. *See, e.g.*, Winston v. Lee, 470 U.S. 753, 766 (1985) (holding that surgical intrusion into defendant's body to retrieve bullet fired by victim was unreasonable under Fourth Amendment when medical risks were disputable); Rochin v. California, 342 U.S. 165, 172-73 (1952) (holding that use of morphine capsules as evidence against defendant violated Due Process Clause when capsules were obtained by force and against defendant's will through stomach pump).

114. *See* ROBERTSON, *supra* note 1, at 36-38; *see also id.* at 69-93 (concluding that forced use of Norplant to curb irresponsible reproduction violates procreative liberty and bodily integrity and may only be justified in case of severe mental retardation). Buck v. Bell, 274 U.S. 200 (1927), upheld the validity of a Virginia statute that authorized forced sterilization of people with hereditary forms of mental illness when such sterilization was deemed to be in the best interests of the mentally defective person and society. *See id.* at 207. Although *Buck* has never been overruled, it is generally conceded that in light of the dictum in Skinner v. Oklahoma, 316 U.S. 535 (1942); *see supra* notes 62-65 and accompanying text, and the other right to privacy cases, *see supra* notes 47-81 and accompanying text, the *Buck* decision would be unlikely to be upheld today. *See, e.g.*, NOWAK & ROTUNDA, *supra* note 22, § 14.27, at 759 ("[I]t is doubtful that the Supreme Court would follow *Buck v. Bell* today. If the justices can find no compelling interest to justify the prohibition of abortions, any state interest in sterilization should be held insufficient to impair this fundamental right."); TRIBE, *supra* note 22, § 15-10, at 1340 ("[I]t is hard to square the basic philosophy of *Skinner v. Oklahoma* with the proposition that the state may usurp the individual's procreative choices in an irreversible way — whether by sterilization or by compulsory breeding." (footnote omitted)).

115. 381 U.S. 479 (1965); *see supra* notes 47-49 and accompanying text.

116. Moore v. City of E. Cleveland, 431 U.S. 494, 499 (1977) (quoting Prince v. Massachusetts, 321 U.S. 158, 166 (1944)); *see supra* notes 66-74 and accompanying text.

117. 491 U.S. 110 (1989); *see supra* notes 78-81 and accompanying text.

118. *See* Michael H. v. Gerald D., 491 U.S. 110, 129-30 (1989) (opinion of Scalia, J.).

The marriage relationship, with its concomitant intimacy, thus lies at the heart of the constitutionally protected right of privacy. Within the context of marriage, consensual behavior that might normally be expected to result in procreation — in other words, coital reproduction — certainly comes within the ambit of this protection.

Notice, however, that with respect to other so-called "procreative liberty" decisions, this syllogism does not apply. The Court has made very clear, for example, that outside the context of the marriage relationship, protection of the right of access to contraception does not mean protection of the right to engage in the behavior that makes contraception necessary or desirable,[119] particularly in the case of minors.[120] Thus, laws against fornication and adultery and those prohibiting sexual activities with or on the part of minors are perfectly valid. Similarly, the abortion cases, although protecting the rights of a woman to bodily integrity against the burden of an unwanted pregnancy, have specifically refused to hold that "one has an unlimited right to do with one's body as one pleases."[121]

---

119. *See* Eisenstadt v. Baird, 405 U.S. 438, 448 (1972) (stating that state can constitutionally regulate extramarital and premarital sexual relations); *id.* at 449 (noting that legislature has "a full measure of discretion in fashioning means to prevent fornication"); Griswold v. Connecticut, 381 U.S. 479, 498 (1965) (Goldberg, J., concurring) ("The State of Connecticut does have statutes, the constitutionality of which is beyond doubt, which prohibit adultery and fornication."); *id.* at 505 (White, J., concurring) ("[T]he statute is said to serve the State's policy against all forms of promiscuous or illicit sexual relationships, be they premarital or extramarital, concededly a permissible and legitimate legislative goal."); Poe v. Ullman, 367 U.S. 497, 546 (1961) (Harlan, J., dissenting) ("The laws regarding marriage . . . forbidding adultery, fornication and homosexual practices . . . confining sexuality to lawful marriage, form a pattern so deeply pressed into the substance of our social life that any Constitutional doctrine in this area must build upon that basis."); *id.* at 552-53 ("The right of privacy most manifestly is not an absolute. Thus, I would not suggest that adultery, homosexuality, fornication and incest are immune from criminal enquiry, however privately practiced. So much has been explicitly recognized in acknowledging the State's rightful concern for its people's moral welfare.").

120. *See* Carey v. Population Servs. Int'l, 431 U.S. 678, 707 (1977) (Powell, J., concurring) ("[T]he relevant question in any case where state laws impinge on the freedom of action of young people in sexual matters is whether the restriction rationally serves valid state interests."); *id.* at 713 (Stevens, J., concurring) ("I would describe as 'frivolous' appellees' argument that a minor has the constitutional right to put contraceptives to their intended use, notwithstanding the combined objection of both parents and the State."); *id.* at 719 (Rehnquist, J., dissenting) (arguing that Court's action amounted to denial of state's power to deter sexual conduct among unmarried minors and declaring it "departure from a wise and heretofore settled course of adjudication to the contrary").

121. Roe v. Wade, 410 U.S. 113, 154 (1973).

The clear message is that not all procreative behavior is subject to the heightened protection of the constitutional right of privacy. The next question is whether the special privacy right that inheres in the marriage relationship nonetheless encompasses all consensual procreative behavior, including use of the means of assisted reproduction.

I submit that the answer is no. Unlike coital reproduction, assisted reproduction does not directly implicate the values — bodily integrity, marital intimacy, or integrity of the family unit — that are central to the privacy cases. Heightened protection is not triggered simply by the fact that any particular conduct represents a search for meaning in life or because the persons involved are seeking self-fulfillment central to their self-definition. When invoked, those values have proven to be an insufficient basis for a claim to constitutional protection of the resulting behavior. In *Bowers v. Hardwick*, Justice Blackmun's dissent vehemently called upon these values to protect, as part of the right of intimate association, the conduct prohibited by Georgia's antisodomy statute.[122] The majority, however, disagreed and noted that "[t]he law . . . is constantly based on notions of morality."[123]

4. Conclusions

The foregoing examination of the values that underlie existing privacy cases, and of the criteria pertinent to the regulation of other constitutionally protected rights involving beliefs central to the individual, leads to several conclusions germane to the current discussion. First, it is clear that within the context of marriage, both the consensual behavior and the choices involved in the natural process of "bearing or begetting" children receive full constitutional protection. Second, absent its compelling interest in a viable fetus, the government may not intervene in the reproductive choices of individuals (married or single) in a manner that intrudes upon their bodily integrity. Finally, the cases suggest that the state may constitutionally regulate reproductive behavior outside the particular context of marital intimacy. Apparently, it may ground that regulation in values that the legislature deems sufficiently significant, including common concepts of morality.

Whether as a question of constitutional interpretation or as a point of public policy, one could easily disagree with the outcome in *Bowers v. Hardwick*, and indeed with the notion of regulating any intimate behavior

---

122.   *See* Bowers v. Hardwick, 478 U.S. 186, 204-06 (1986) (Blackmun, J., dissenting).

123.   *Id.* at 196.

between two consenting adults when there is no danger of direct harm to any third person. That disagreement finds a strong foundation in the values invoked by Justice Blackmun in his *Bowers* dissent and by Professor Robertson in his defense of procreative liberty: namely, the right to seek one's self-fulfillment through choices that will give meaning and value to one's life.[124] However, as important as these values are and as central as they may be to a satisfying definition of liberty, the conduct to which they lead must be subject to appropriate circumscription when the welfare of a third person might be endangered or undermined by the actor's unrestrained choice. A potential detrimental effect of an individual's behavior upon a third person is necessarily of concern from a public policy perspective; in constitutional parlance, it may often rise to the level of a state interest sufficiently significant to justify regulation designed to prevent the perceived harm.

Professor Robertson himself concedes that sufficient harm to a third party's interests is an appropriate limit on procreative liberty;[125] however, he repeatedly discounts the notion of harm to the third parties most directly affected by an individual's or a couple's use of reproductive technologies — namely, the resulting children.[126] I believe that Robertson underplays the

---

124. *See id.* at 204-06 (Blackmun, J., dissenting); ROBERTSON, *supra* note 1, at 24-25.

125. *See* ROBERTSON, *supra* note 1, at 17 ("A central question in this enterprise is to determine whether effects on embryos, families, women, and other participants rise to the level of severity necessary to justify infringing a basic right."); *id.* at 37 ("Restrictions on marital reproduction are theoretically possible only if the state can show great harm to others from the reproduction in question."); *id.* at 41-42 (noting that harm necessary to justify infringing one's procreative liberty by restricting access to reproductive technologies must be both tangible and substantial); *id.* at 58 ("At viability . . . the fetus's advanced development lends itself to a more objective valuation of its interests, and the woman's interest in ending pregnancy can be limited."); *id.* at 72 ("[D]ecisions to reproduce should be viewed as presumptive rights that are subject to limitation only upon the showing of substantial harm to the interests of others."); *id.* at 178 ("Even if determinative of a decision to reproduce . . . neither the core values that underlie procreative liberty nor any other protected liberty includes the right to make offspring less than healthy and normal, when a healthy birth is reasonably possible."); *id.* at 179 ("At a certain point one's right to use one's body as one wishes . . . must take account of the interests of others whose needs those decisions directly impinge."); *id.* at 221 ("Procreative choices that clearly harm the tangible interests of others are subject to regulation or even prohibition."); *id.* at 224 ("If harmful effects are clearly established . . . public concerns may take priority over private choice.").

126. *See id.* at 50 ("[A] high standard of justification should be met to warrant overriding the woman's presumptive right to end pregnancy."); *id.* at 153 ("The *risk* of harmful effects does not undercut the presumptive importance of [genetic trait] selection as part of reproductive choice, even if analysis of particular cases shows sufficient harm to justify

interests of the children deliberately created by assisted reproduction and in so doing neglects a primary value that must be given due weight in any responsible social policy concerning these "children of choice." Because my perception of the scope of constitutional protection for procreative choice is narrower than his, I would like to share a few thoughts on this issue from a public policy perspective.

III. The Welfare of Third Parties: The Interests of "Children of Choice"

Throughout *Children of Choice*, whenever Professor Robertson contemplates any potentially negative effects of adults' reproductive choices on the resulting children, he favors the adults' procreative liberty on the ground that, from the standpoint of the children, the only alternative is nonexistence, and it is always "better to have been born than not to have been born."[127] This rubric decides the issue for him: The adults have a fundamental right "to decide whether to bear or beget a child"; the children have no fundamental right to nonexistence and undoubtedly would not choose it if they could.

It seems to me that this approach is conceptually flawed and morally inadequate. The concept stems from so-called "wrongful life" cases. In these cases, disabled children have sought recovery in damages from physicians or genetic counseling services on the ground that their parents were negligently misinformed about the likelihood of the children's severe disabilities — knowledge that would have caused the parents to decide to abort or never to conceive.[128] Although three jurisdictions have allowed

---

limiting the right to select." (emphasis added)); *id.* at 221 ("With this approach . . . we have seen that there are few instances in which the feared harms of the new technology are compelling enough to justify restrictive legal intervention (though the need for responsible use remains)."); *id.* at 222 ("[M]any of the concerns and fears will, upon closer analysis, turn out to be speculative fears or symbolic perceptions that do not justify infringing core procreative interests.").

127. *See supra* notes 15-19 and accompanying text (describing "wrongful life" argument and citing cases).

128. *See generally* Turpin v. Sortini, 643 P.2d 954 (Cal. 1982) (in bank); Gami v. Mullikin Medical Ctr., 22 Cal. Rptr. 2d 819 (Ct. App. 1993); Curlender v. Bio-Science Lab., 165 Cal. Rptr. 477 (Ct. App. 1980); Smith v. Cote, 513 A.2d 341 (N.H. 1986); Procanik v. Cillo, 478 A.2d 755 (N.J. 1984); Berman v. Allan, 404 A.2d 8 (N.J. 1979); Gleitman v. Cosgrove, 227 A.2d 689 (N.J. 1967); Becker v. Schwartz, 386 N.E.2d 807 (N.Y. 1978); Flanagan v. Williams, 623 N.E.2d 185 (Ohio Ct. App. 1993); Speck v. Finegold, 408 A.2d 496 (Pa. Super. Ct. 1979), *aff'd*, 439 A.2d 110 (Pa. 1981); Nelson v. Krusen, 678 S.W.2d

child plaintiffs to recover the special expenses of their extraordinary care and training,[129] no court has awarded general damages for the alleged "injury" of life itself. The courts reason that life, even under the very limiting conditions in which it may be experienced by the severely disabled, is preferable to nonexistence — in other words, it is "better to have been born than not to have been born."[130] This conclusion is augmented by the mind-boggling nature of the task of assessing general damages. If the function of a tort award is to place the plaintiff in the position in which she would have been absent the injury, how can a jury compare the value of a state of nonexistence with the value of the child's impaired life?[131] The fact that

---

918 (Tex. 1984); Harbeson v. Parke-Davis, Inc., 656 P.2d 483 (Wash. 1983) (en banc).

129.   So far, the state supreme courts in California, New Jersey, and Washington have permitted special damage recoveries in wrongful life suits. *See generally* Turpin v. Sortini, 643 P.2d 954 (Cal. 1982) (in bank) (involving congenital deafness); Gami v. Mullikin Medical Ctr., 22 Cal. Rptr. 2d 819 (Ct. App. 1993) (involving spina bifida and following *Turpin*); Curlender v. Bio-Science Lab., 165 Cal. Rptr. 477 (Ct. App. 1980) (involving Tay-Sachs disease and anticipating *Turpin*); Procanik v. Cillo, 478 A.2d 755 (N.J. 1984) (involving congenital rubella syndrome); Harbeson v. Parke-Davis, Inc., 656 P.2d 483 (Wash. 1983) (en banc) (involving fetal hydantoin syndrome).

130.   *See, e.g.*, Turpin v. Sortini, 643 P.2d 954, 961 (Cal. 1982) (in bank) ("[S]ome courts have concluded that the plaintiff has suffered no legally cognizable injury on the ground that considerations of public policy dictate a conclusion that life — even with the most severe of impairments — is, as a matter of law, always preferable to nonlife."); Berman v. Allan, 404 A.2d 8, 12 (N.J. 1979) ("One of the most deeply held beliefs in our society is that life — whether experienced with or without a major physical handicap — is more precious than non-life."); Timothy J. Dawe, Note, *Wrongful Life: Time for a "Day in Court,"* 51 OHIO ST. L.J. 473, 483 (1990) (discussing Gleitman v. Cosgrove, 227 A.2d 689 (N.J. 1967), and noting that, "[i]n denying the parents' claim for wrongful birth, the court demonstrated an overwhelming preference for life over nonexistence, no matter what the conditions of that life.").

131.   *See, e.g.*, *Turpin*, 643 P.2d at 961 ("Because nothing defendants could have done would have given plaintiff an unimpaired life, it appears inconsistent with basic tort principles to view the injury . . . solely by reference to plaintiff's present condition without taking into consideration the fact that if defendants had not been negligent she would not have been born at all."); Procanik v. Cillo, 478 A.2d 755, 763 (N.J. 1984) ("The crux of the problem is that there is no rational way to measure non-existence or to compare non-existence with the pain and suffering of . . . impaired existence."); *Gleitman*, 227 A.2d at 692 ("By asserting that he should not have been born, the infant plaintiff makes it logically impossible for a court to measure his alleged damages because of the impossibility of making the comparison required by compensatory remedies."); Becker v. Schwartz, 386 N.E.2d 807, 812 (N.Y. 1978) ("[A wrongful life claim] demands a calculation of damages dependent on a comparison between the Hobson's choice of life in an impaired state and nonexistence. This comparison the law is not equipped to make."); Nelson v. Krusen, 678 S.W.2d 918, 925 (Tex. 1984) ("[T]he cause of action unavoidably involves the relative benefits of an impaired life as opposed to no

damages must be mitigated by the value of any benefit conferred, when that benefit is life itself, adds to the complexity of the problem.[132]

As a number of judges and commentators have suggested, however, the tenet in wrongful life cases that existence is always preferable to nonexistence is not offered as a factual conclusion about each individual; rather, it is a statement of public policy based upon respect for the sanctity of human life in general and offered to support a jurisprudential conclusion that "wrongful life" is simply not an injury cognizable in the law.[133] Professor

---

life at all. All courts, even the ones recognizing a cause of action for wrongful life, have admitted that this calculation is impossible."); Harbeson v. Parke-Davis, Inc., 656 P.2d 483, 496 (Wash. 1983) (en banc) ("[M]easuring the value of an impaired life as compared to nonexistence is a task that is beyond mortals.").

132.   *See, e.g.*, *Turpin*, 643 P.2d at 964 ("[I]t must be recognized that as an incident of defendant's negligence the plaintiff has in fact obtained a physical existence with the capacity both to receive and give love and pleasure as well as to experience pain and suffering. Because of the incalculable nature of both elements of this harm-benefit equation . . . a reasoned, nonarbitrary award of general damage is simply not obtainable."); Nelson v. Krusen, 678 S.W.2d 918, 924 (Tex. 1984) ("[B]ecause in awarding damages the court must offset any special benefits to the plaintiff resulting from the negligence, such a cause of action involves a weighing of life against non-life, a calculation that cannot be rationally made." (citation omitted)); Dawe, *supra* note 130, at 479-80 ("In wrongful life claims, then, the child usually asserts as 'general' damages the pain and suffering he will endure during his lifetime as a result of the defect, but presumably less the benefits he will derive from his existence, if any. This 'net burden' is then measured not against the value of a 'normal' life, but against the nullity of nonexistence.").

133.   *See, e.g.*, Curlender v. Bio-Science Lab., 165 Cal. Rptr. 477, 486 (Ct. App. 1980) ("Public policy, as perceived by most courts, has been utilized as the basis for denying recovery; in some fashion, a deeply held belief in the sanctity of life has compelled some courts to deny recovery to those among us who have been born with serious impairment."); Procanik v. Cillo, 478 A.2d 755, 760 (N.J. 1984) ("[P]olicy considerations have led [the Supreme Court of New Jersey] in the past to decline to recognize any cause of action in an infant for his wrongful life."); Flanagan v. Williams, 623 N.E.2d 185, 191 (Ohio Ct. App. 1993) ("The common and statutory law of Ohio places an intrinsic value on life. In the absence of guidance from the Supreme Court or the General Assembly, we are not prepared to say that life, even with severe disabilities, constitutes actionable injury."); *Nelson*, 678 S.W.2d at 924 ("At heart, the reluctance of these courts [to award damages for being alive] is based on the 'high value which the law has placed on human life, rather than its absence.'" (quoting Becker v. Schwartz, 386 N.E.2d 807, 812 (N.Y. 1978)); Alexander M. Capron, *Tort Liability in Genetic Counseling*, 79 COLUM. L. REV. 618, 650 (1979) ("In [denying damages for wrongful life], courts are not announcing purely rational conclusions derived from legal principles but are instead proclaiming their personal views on certain value-laden 'facts.'"); Peters, *supra* note 14, at 506-09 (discussing concern of courts that nonexistence comparison in wrongful life claims would weaken social respect for life); Dawe, *supra* note 130, at 493 ("[M]ost of the rationales used by courts to reject wrongful life claims have been variations or extensions of a basic 'sanctity of life' argument.").

Robertson, however, expresses the statement that "it is better to have been born than not to have been born" as an ultimate existential truth — a fact that must necessarily obtain with respect to each individual child who comes into the world, whether or not, for example, that child might be HIV-positive, otherwise severely diseased or disabled, or born to abusive parents.[134] This transposition of an argument from its public policy origins to a statement offered for its universal truth seems to me to be misplaced. One commentator has expressed it eloquently:

> The sanctity-of-life argument is ambiguous. It may advance the view that every life, no matter how severely defective, no matter how filled with suffering, is necessarily a good to the individual who lives it. This seems simply false. Alternatively, it may express the view that every human life has, or should have, value *for us*; that is, every life is worthy of concern and respect.[135]

Current social policy, which respects autonomous patient choice for end-of-life decision-making, reflects a humane awareness that there are conditions under which life may be intolerable to the individual living it.[136] Surely that can be just as true for infants as for those who have lived much longer.[137]

---

134. *See supra* notes 15-19 and accompanying text.

135. Bonnie Steinbock, *The Logical Case for "Wrongful Life,"* HASTINGS CENTER REP., Apr. 1986, at 15, 17.

136. *See generally* SOCIETY FOR THE RIGHT TO DIE, REFUSAL OF TREATMENT LEGISLATION (1991) (containing more than 70 statutes consisting of state legislation pertaining to several kinds of advance directives — wherein patients while competent can provide for decisions to refuse or withdraw life-sustaining medical treatment under certain conditions — including "living will" documents, in which patients detail conditions under which they wish to refuse or halt medical treatment, and durable powers of attorney and surrogate decision-making statutes, which enable individuals to select persons to make choices for them once they become incompetent); 1 SOCIETY FOR THE RIGHT TO DIE, RIGHT-TO-DIE COURT DECISIONS (1976-1986) (analyzing 26 significant court decisions in this area of law); 2 *id.* (1987-1989) (analyzing 23 significant court decisions in this area of law); 3 *id.* (1990-) (analyzing 13 significant court decisions in this area of law). Some surrogate decision-making statutes name individuals to make end-of-life choices for patients who have failed to commit their wishes to writing. *See generally* UNIF. RIGHTS OF THE TERMINALLY ILL ACT, 9B U.L.A. 127 (Supp. 1994). The Patient Self-Determination Act, part of the Omnibus Budget Reconciliation Act of 1990, requires health care providers receiving federal funds to inform patients about their rights under state law and to document whether or not patients have health care directives. *See* 42 U.S.C. § 1395cc(f) (Supp. V 1993).

137. Several judges have noted the connection that exists between "right-to-die" policy and "wrongful life" cases. *See, e.g.,* Turpin v. Sortini, 643 P.2d 954, 962 (Cal. 1982) (in bank) ("[A]t least in some situations — public policy supports the right of each individual to make his or her own determination as to the relative value of life and death."); Procanik v.

52 WASH. & LEE L. REV. 135 (1995)

Even if one concedes that children who owe their existence to assisted reproduction are virtually certain to find their lives to be net benefits rather than net burdens, a social policy choice that is content to rest upon this minimum threshold as the appropriate criterion for acceptability strikes me as highly questionable. In the section of his book titled "Preventing Prenatal Harm to Offspring,"[138] Professor Robertson offers the proposition that pregnant women who have not decided to abort have a strong responsibility to engage in certain behaviors and to avoid others in order to ensure that their children will be born as healthy as possible.[139] He distinguishes the "unavoidable harm" implicated by the procreative choice to reproduce under circumstances in which the child is bound to be born handicapped in some manner from the "avoidable harm" that might result from a woman's prenatal actions.[140] Conduct during pregnancy (other than the abortion choice itself) is not part of procreative liberty, in his view;[141] the harm principle dictates that a woman's rights of autonomy and bodily integrity may be circumscribed at the point at which her choices might impinge on the interests of another, "the child that the fetus will become."[142] Indeed, Professor Robertson believes that these interests are

---

Cillo, 478 A.2d 755, 771 (N.J. 1984) (Handler, J., concurring in part and dissenting in part) ("[If we accept that] individuals may lawfully determine in a necessitous or exigent setting that nonlife may reasonably be preferred over life [as we do in 'right-to-die' cases,] . . . then we ought to conclude that damages flow from the deprivation of this right and that the infant plaintiff should be reasonably compensated."); Nelson v. Krusen, 678 S.W.2d 918, 933 (Tex. 1984) (citing "right-to-die" cases to note that "[t]he judgment of a parent or guardian may be substituted for that of the child when the child is incompetent and unable to decide whether he prefers nonlife to an impaired existence"). Also consider the following scenario posed by Joel Feinberg:

> Suppose that after the death of your body a deity appears to you and . . . proposes to give you an option. You can be born again after death (reincarnated), but only as a Tay-Sachs baby with a painful life expectancy of four years to be followed by permanent extinction, or you can opt for permanent extinction to begin immediately. I should think you would have to be crazy to select the first option.

Joel Feinberg, *Wrongful Life and the Counterfactual Element in Harming*, 4 SOC. PHIL. & POL'Y 145, 164 (1989).

138. ROBERTSON, *supra* note 1, 173-94.
139. *See id.* at 173.
140. *See id.* at 178.
141. *See id.*
142. *Id.* at 179.

sufficiently strong to justify regulation[143] and, in some instances, criminal sanctions[144] for behavior potentially deleterious to the future child, although "the better policy in most cases will be to rely on information, education, and access to treatment."[145]

Robertson's contentions are highly controversial, to say the least, and discussion of them is clearly beyond the scope of this Article. What I wish to suggest here is that the same consideration — the *optimal* (not minimal) well-being of the future children — is the appropriate basis upon which to shape social policy with regard to the use of assisted reproduction.[146] This assertion is not novel. In the area of family law, generally, issues involving the welfare of children are invariably decided on the ground of serving the children's best interests, even when doing so means infringing upon the rights or interests of adults.[147]

The resolution of issues raised by assisted reproduction need not, in fact, go so far. Determining the "best interests" of children whose existence we are planning is a speculative enterprise. We do not even know the nature or extent of potential harms that might uniquely affect children born of assisted reproduction. Commentators raise such considerations as the effect upon self-identity when one does not know who one or both genetic parents are,[148] the confusion of "too many parents" or the

---

143. *See id.* at 182 (contemplating possible exclusion of women from certain areas of workplace if sufficient connection with harm to fetuses can be demonstrated and regulation is narrowly drafted); *id.* at 186-90 (discussing potential "prenatal seizures," such as incarceration for substance abuse and possible court-mandated cesarian sections).

144. *See id.* at 182-86.

145. *Id.* at 180.

146. *Cf.* sources cited *supra* note 14.

147. *See* HOMER H. CLARK, JR., THE LAW OF DOMESTIC RELATIONS IN THE UNITED STATES § 9.4, at 359 (2d ed. 1988) (noting that child's welfare is "primary concern" in child abuse or neglect proceedings); *id.* § 19.1, at 788 (noting that child's best interest is governing principle in custody disputes); *id.* § 19.4, at 797 nn. 3-4 (citing statutes and case law adopting child's best interest as primary criterion for custody); *id.* § 19.6, at 825 (criticizing doctrine of constitutional "parental right" to child custody as coming "dangerously close to treating the child in some sense as the property of his parent"); *id.* § 20.5, at 891 (noting that, in context of termination-of-parental-rights proceedings, "[m]ost courts concede that the welfare of children is a compelling state interest"); *id.* § 20.6, at 905 (noting that some statutes allow parental rights to be terminated when necessary to serve child's best interests); *id.* § 20.7, at 909 (noting that best interest of child is "ultimate standard for both agencies and courts" in adoption proceedings).

148. *See, e.g.,* ANDREWS, *supra* note 32, at 278-80; BARTHOLET, *supra* note 14, at 228-29; FIELD, *supra* note 14, at 54; OVERALL, *supra* note 14, at 111; R. SNOWDEN ET AL.,

psychological harm perhaps engendered by custody battles when surrogate mothers wish to maintain contact with the babies that they have delivered,[149] and the need for full and accurate family medical profiles.[150] A child born to a postmenopausal woman[151] or a child born as a clone of someone else, especially when that child is named after a deceased sibling, may suffer from a heavy burden of preconceived expectations.[152] Deliberate planning for nontraditional families, such as single-parent situations or households in which both parents are of the same gender, poses other issues. The possibilities raised by increasing sophistication in genetic engineering may present the most far-reaching and unpredictable problems likely to arise.

ARTIFICIAL REPRODUCTION: A SOCIAL INVESTIGATION 118-19, 171-72 (1983); Lori B. Andrews & Lisa Douglass, *Alternative Reproduction*, 65 S. CAL. L. REV. 623, 669 (1991); Ethics Committee of the American Fertility Society, *Ethical Considerations of the New Reproductive Technologies*, FERTILITY & STERILITY, Sept. 1986 (Supp. 1), at 1S, 60S; Ryan, *supra* note 14, at 10; Walter Wadlington, *Artificial Conception: The Challenge for Family Law*, 69 VA. L. REV. 465, 499-500 (1983); Keller, *supra* note 14, at 186.

149. *See, e.g.*, FIELD, *supra* note 14, at 54-55; OTA, INFERTILITY, *supra* note 2, at 227; Martha A. Field, *Surrogacy Contracts — Gestational and Traditional: The Argument for Nonenforcement*, 31 WASHBURN L.J. 1, 12-13 (1992); Keller, *supra* note 14, at 187. *Compare In re* Baby M, 537 A.2d 1227, 1235-37 (N.J. 1988) (involving surrogate mother battling with intended parents for custody of child) *with* Holder, *supra* note 14, at 52 (describing case of handicapped newborns resulting from surrogacy contracts and battles in which both intended parents and surrogate mother deny custody). Both of these types of custody battles may potentially cause psychological damage to the child.

150. *See, e.g.*, ANDREWS, *supra* note 32, at 279-80; OTA, INFERTILITY, *supra* note 2, at 227; SNOWDEN ET AL., *supra* note 148, at 176-77; Andrews & Douglass, *supra* note 148, at 660-62; Annas, *Regulating*, *supra* note 14, at 413; Wadlington, *supra* note 148, at 499-500.

151. *See supra* note 30 and accompanying text.

152. *See* Robertson, *supra* note 12, at 11-12 ("[T]here could be special problems faced by [a later born twin]. Its path through life might be difficult if the later born child is seen merely as a replica of the first and is expected to develop and show skills and traits of the first. This might be a special danger if the later born child is used as a replacement for an earlier born child who has died."); Jerry Adler et al., *Clone Hype*, NEWSWEEK, Nov. 8, 1993, at 60, 61-62 (presenting situations in which couple, deciding that they like characteristics of particular person, might decide to thaw clone of that person to be implanted in woman's uterus); Philip Elmer-Dewitt, *Cloning: Where Do We Draw the Line?*, TIME, Nov. 8, 1993, at 65, 68 ("[W]hat about the couple that sets aside, as a matter of course, a clone of each of their children? If one of them died, the child could be replaced with a genetic equivalent."); *id.* ("All parents know how hard it is to separate what they think a child ought to be from what he or she actually is. That difficulty would be compounded — for both the parent and the child — if an exact template for what the child could become in 10 or 20 years were before them in the form of an older sibling.").

IV. Conclusion

Certainly, society as a whole, as well as the individuals involved in the use of assisted reproduction, has a stake in the welfare of the future citizens that we are deliberately creating — not only their physical health, but their psychological and emotional well-being. We already have some parallels upon which to base our judgments, such as the experiences of adopted children or children from divorced or "blended" families. Careful deliberation and due regard for potential pitfalls should enable us to anticipate and to plan carefully to provide resolutions of social policy that will accommodate not only the procreative desires of would-be parents, but also the optimum conditions of health and nurturance for their "children of choice."

Part II
Assisted Reproduction and the Family

[3]

WHAT DOES IT MEAN TO BE A "PARENT"? THE CLAIMS OF BIOLOGY AS THE BASIS FOR PARENTAL RIGHTS

JOHN LAWRENCE HILL*

Modern technology has wreaked havoc on conventional and legal notions of parenthood. For example, the traditional legal presumption granting parental rights to a child's biological mother seems at least questionable when the biological mother differs from the intended mother. As a result, courts employing traditional constitutional and family law doctrines have not adequately sorted out the claims of biological, gestational, and intended parents. In this Article, Professor Hill argues that the claims of those who first intend to have a child should prevail over those who assert parental rights on the basis of a biological or gestational relation. Such a view, he argues, is consistent with existing case law on the constitutional rights to procreation and privacy and supported by moral theory and modern scientific evidence.

INTRODUCTION

In 1799, the first reported use of artificial insemination took place.[1] With this event, the once-insoluble link between coitus and procreation was severed. However, while sporadic experimentation with artificial insemination continued through the first third of the twentieth century,[2] it was not until the 1930s and 1940s that artificial insemination by donor (AID) began to be recognized and employed on a widescale basis as a response to the problem of male infertility.[3] Within the past two de-

* Assistant Professor of Law, Western State University at Irvine. B.A. (Philosophy), 1982, Northern Illinois University; M.A. (Philosophy), 1985, Northern Illinois University; J.D., 1988, Ph.D. (Philosophy), 1989, Georgetown University. I wish to thank my former colleagues at IIT-Chicago Kent Law School for their support in this project. Special thanks go to Professor Sheldon Nahmod for his kind assistance and guidance.

[1] U.S. Cong. Office of Technology Assessment, Infertility: Medical and Social Choices 36 (1988) [hereinafter OTA, Infertility]. Artificial insemination is a process by which sperm from a donor is injected, usually via syringe, into the vaginal opening. Artificial insemination consists of two varieties: artificial insemination by donor (AID) and by husband (AIH). AID is used where a woman's husband is sterile or where a woman wishes to avoid sexual intercourse. Id. at 126-28. AIH is used where normal coital methods of procreation are, for a variety of reasons, ineffective. Id.

[2] In the 1860s, for example, Dr. J. Marion Sims experimented with AID but later renounced the work as immoral. Note, Legal Recognition of Surrogate Gestation, 7 Women's Rts. L. Rep. 107, 119 n.88 (1982).

[3] It is estimated that anywhere from 6000 to 10,000 births a year result from AID. See Curie-Cohen, Luttrell & Shapiro, Current Practice in Artificial Insemination by Donor in the United States, 300 New Eng. J. Med. 585, 588 (1979). One estimate places the number at 20,000 a year. See Note, supra note 2, at 119. Approximately 250,000 Americans now living were born through the use of AID or AIH. Keane, Legal Problems of Surrogate Motherhood, 1980 S. Ill. U.L. Rev. 147, 148. See generally J. Fletcher, Morals and Medicine 101-16 (1954)

354 *NEW YORK UNIVERSITY LAW REVIEW* [Vol. 66:353]

cades, the process of procreation has been fragmented further by the development of a number of techniques, most notably in-vitro fertilization, which separate the conceptive and gestational phases of reproduction.[4] Thus, the genetic and gestational mothers of a child are no longer necessarily the same individual.[5] In this manner, science has distilled the various phases of procreation—coitus, conception, and gestation—into their component parts, wreaking havoc on our prevailing conceptions of parenthood.

This is not to suggest that parenthood always has been recognized as being coextensive with the biological relationship. While legal adoption is a statutory creation not existing at common law,[6] in practice it undoubtedly has taken place from time immemorial.[7] Thus, a strong social tradition recognizes the purely social and psychological dimensions of parenting, even where these occur in the absence of biological ties. Yet even with adoption, adoptive parents may acquire parental status with respect to a particular child only after termination of the parental rights of the child's biological parents, particularly those of the natural mother.[8] With the new reproductive technologies and arrangements,[9]

(discussing and defending artificial insemination).

[4] In-vitro fertilization (IVF) involves the removal of mature oocytes (female germ cells) through a surgical procedure known as laparoscopy or a nonsurgical procedure such as ultrasound-guided oocyte retrieval. Once removed, the ova are combined with sperm in the laboratory. After fertilization, a number of preembryos, generally at the two to 16 cell stage, are transferred to the uterus of the woman who will bear the child. OTA, Infertility, supra note 1, at 123.

[5] The woman to whose uterus the fertilized preembryo is transferred need not be the original egg donor. The first child born in the U.S. of gestational surrogacy—a surrogate arrangement where the surrogate gestates but does not conceive the child—took place in 1985. Id. at 36.

[6] See Smith v. Org. of Foster Families, 431 U.S. 816, 845-46 (1977).

[7] See I. Sloan, The Law of Adoption and Surrogate Parenting 5-10 (1988).

[8] The "presumption of biology" serves as an irrebuttable legal presumption that the birth mother of the child is its legal mother and that adoption can take place only consequent to a termination of the parental rights of the birth mother. See Andrews, Surrogate Motherhood: Should the Adoption Model Apply?, 7 Children's Legal Rts. J. 13, 14-16 (1986) (discussing adoption laws as applied to surrogacy); notes 74-89 and accompanying text infra (discussing presumption of biology).

[9] I distinguish the reproductive "technologies" from "arrangements" to highlight that, while many of these procedures such as AID and IVF involve some use of technology, surrogate parenting involves a social and legal, rather than a technological, innovation. While surrogacy typically uses AID to impregnate the surrogate with the sperm of the intended father or a third-party donor, the characteristic feature of surrogacy is the social arrangement whereby a woman agrees to conceive (in most, but not all cases), to carry, and to relinquish the child upon birth. See Brophy, A Surrogate Mother Contract to Bear a Child, 20 J. Fam. L. 263, 268-91 (1981-82) (explaining surrogate arrangement); see also Hill, The Case for Enforcement of the Surrogate Contract, 8 Pol. & Life Sci. 147, 150-57 (1990) (discussing policy issues surrounding surrogacy); Suh, Surrogate Motherhood: An Argument for Denial of Specific Performance, 22 Colum. J.L. & Soc. Probs. 357, 362-71 (1989) (arguing that bonding process experienced during pregnancy gives woman inalienable right as parent).

however, a more fundamental question arises: where various parties have made distinct contributions to the procreative process, who should be recognized as the parents of the child?

We now live in an era where a child may have as many as five different "parents." These include a sperm donor, an egg donor, a surrogate or gestational host, and two nonbiologically related individuals who intend to raise the child. Indeed, the process of procreation itself has become so fragmented by the variety and combinations of collaborative-reproductive methods that there are a total of sixteen different reproductive combinations, in addition to traditional conception and childbirth. This total is the product of varying the source of the male gametes (whether by husband or third-party sperm donor), the source of the female gametes (whether by wife or third-party egg donor), the location of fertilization (whether in the wife, the laboratory, or the surrogate host), and the site of gestation (either in the wife or the surrogate).[10]

The importance of parental status, and the accompanying controversy where the identity of the parent is not determined, can be observed in a number of currently debated issues concerning collaborative repro-

---

10   ALTERNATIVE REPRODUCTIVE METHODS

	Source of gametes		Site of fertilization	Site of pregnancy	Notes
	Male	Female			
1	H	W	W	W	Customary, AIH
2	S	W	W	W	AID
3	H	W	L	W	IVF
4	S	W	L	W	IVF with donated sperm
5	H	S	L	W	IVF with donated egg
6	S	S	L	W	IVF with both gametes donated (or donated embryo)
7	H	S	S	W	AIH with donor woman plus uterine lavage (semi-donated embryo)
8	S	S	S	W	AID with donor woman plus uterine lavage (donated embryo)
9	H	W	W	S	
10	S	W	W	S	
11	H	W	L	S	
12	S	W	L	S	Surrogate
13	H	S	L	S	Motherhood
14	S	S	L	S	
15	H	S	S	S	
16*	S	S	S	S	

H = Husband; W = Wife; S = Third-party substitute, or surrogate;
L = Laboratory
* Planned procreation for placement; traditional adoption is not part of the schematic.
Chart developed by William B. Weil, Jr. and LeRoy Walters.

Walters, Editor's Introduction, 10 J. Med. & Phil. 209, 210 (1985) (although in theory 24 permutations are possible, only 16 actually would occur because of various overlaps).

duction. For example, one may question whether surrogate-parenting arrangements constitute a highly contrived form of baby-selling.[11] The answer depends upon which parties to the procreative process are deemed to be the "parents" of the child at birth. If the intended parents[12] are recognized as the parents of the child, then it is difficult to see how they could be guilty of buying their own baby. Similarly, if the surrogate is deemed not to be the mother of the child, she cannot, as a logical matter, be culpable for baby-selling.[13]

Determination of parental status also may have great significance in deciding who possesses the right of procreation. Arguably, only a "parent" can exercise the right of procreation[14] with respect to any particular child. Indeed, it is exactly this proposition that this Article defends.[15] It follows that the application of the constitutional right of procreation depends upon an antecedent definitional conclusion regarding the meaning of parenthood. This determination will have fundamental significance where the genetic progenitors, the gestational host, and the intended parents (where the intended parents are not also the genetic parents) all claim parental status based on their respective roles in the procreative process.[16]

Finally, competing conceptions of the rights of the biological parents, and most particularly the gestational host, animate the stormy debate concerning the enforceability of the surrogate contract. Where the

---

[11] "Baby-selling" laws make it a criminal offense to exchange money or other material consideration for the promise of a parent of the child to relinquish custody and parental rights in the child. See Katz, Surrogate Motherhood and the Baby-Selling Laws, 20 Colum. J. L. & Soc. Probs. 1, 8-9 (1986).

[12] I use the term "intended parents" here to describe the person or couple who initially intended to raise the child. Three conditions must be met for persons to be considered intended parents: (1) the intended parents must plan to have a child before the conception of the child; (2) they must take morally permissible measures, not limited to biological procreation, to bring a child into the world; and (3) they must meet certain minimally adequate conditions to be able to raise and care for the child. This last requirement embodies the condition that parents obtain the "constructive consent of the child." See text accompanying notes 171-72 infra.

[13] This outcome would be a departure from the *Baby M* court, which stated that the egg donor/gestational host was "the natural mother inappropriately called the 'surrogate mother.' " In re Baby M., 109 N.J. 396, 411, 537 A.2d 1227, 1234 (1988). Having decided the issue of motherhood, the court went on to state that the surrogacy contract was "the sale of a child, or, at the very least, the sale of a mother's right to her child." Id. at 437-38, 537 A.2d at 1248.

[14] See Skinner v. Oklahoma, 316 U.S. 535, 541 (1942) (currently viewed as establishing right of procreation by holding involuntary sterilization statute unconstitutional); note 67 and accompanying text infra (discussing decisions of *Baby M* court regarding parenthood and right of procreation); see also text accompanying notes 129-30 infra (biological connection offers unique opportunity for parental relationship).

[15] See notes 61-62 and accompanying text infra.

[16] See Allen, Privacy, Surrogacy and the *Baby M* Case, 76 Geo. L.J. 1759, 1774-81 (1988) (discussing four models for privacy-right attribution).

connotations associated with motherhood invariably are linked with the role of the birth mother, the prospect of compelling her to relinquish the child takes on the proportions of a crime against nature. However, where parental status is deemed to attach to the persons who have sought, by whatever means they could marshal, to cause a child to be born so that they could raise it and care for it—in short, where parental status is viewed as distinct from biological consanguinity—enforcement of the surrogate contract will be viewed as a necessary prerequisite to achieving justice.

This Article attempts to arrive at a conception of parenthood which settles conflicting claims to parental status posed by the genetic parents, the gestational host, and the intended parents of the child. Part I begins by posing the paradigmatic procreative scenario in which such conflicting claims to parental status will arise. This Part then evaluates a number of definitional considerations relating to the use of the term "parent," arguing that appeals to traditional definitions are of little use in answering what is essentially a normative question: who should be considered the parent in collaborative-reproduction arrangements? It also argues that, while we lack a concept of parenthood sufficiently definite to resolve modern controversies about *who* is the parent, we nevertheless have a working legal definition of parental rights that can help reveal what is at stake in the controversy. Thus, this Part examines the rights which attach to persons legally recognized as parents, as demonstrated by the parental-rights doctrine.

Whereas Part I concludes by focusing on what rights parents have, Part II turns to the central question of who, legally, may be a parent. Seemingly uncontroversial claims to parental rights can be made by the procreators of a child. Indeed, the Constitution has long recognized that parental status inures to procreators.[17] A problem arises, however, in attempting to define who counts as a procreator. Under existing legal doctrine, although a biological connection between adult and child is not always a sufficient condition to establish procreator status, it is virtually a necessary condition, at least in the ascription of maternal rights. Yet as the remainder of Part II demonstrates, to link biology and procreation so closely is to confuse the right of procreation with the right of privacy. In fact these rights are distinct, and recognition of this distinction suggests that intended parents[18] have a respectable claim to being procreators. Part II concludes that the legal right to procreation can be read to support parental-rights claims of intended parents over the claims of biologi-

---

[17] See, e.g., *Skinner*, 316 U.S. at 541 (procreation is basic, fundamental civil right); *Baby M*, 109 N.J. at 449-52, 537 A.2d at 1254-55 (considering only procreators when discussing parental rights).

[18] See note 12 supra.

358   *NEW YORK UNIVERSITY LAW REVIEW*   [Vol. 66:353

cal parents, where the two types of claims conflict.

Part III looks beyond the law to determine if empirical evidence and moral arguments favor the right of biological progenitors to be accorded primary legal recognition as the parents of a child. More specifically, Part III assesses the claims that a person possesses a parental right in a child by virtue of the following: the genetic relationship which exists between them, the efforts inherent in the gestational relationship, the "bond" which develops between the birth mother and the child as a result of the gestational relationship, and a variety of predicted psychological harms to mother and child resulting from their separation. This Part also evaluates the general claim that it is in the child's best interests to be placed with its natural parents. In addition, Part III investigates a number of extrinsic social and moral arguments focusing not on the rights of particular parties per se, but on a variety of consequences which may follow the adoption of a definition of parent which would favor one group over another. This Part argues that many of the claims posed in defense of the priority of the genetic progenitors or gestational host carry little moral weight and that the case for the primacy of the rights of biological parents is considerably weaker than it might first appear.

Finally, Part IV sketches three arguments favoring the claims of the intended parents—even where they lack any biological ties with the child born of the procreative relationship. This Part argues that, under an "intentional" view of parenting, the claims of the intended parents outweigh those of the gestational host. Thus, the parental rights of the intended parents should be legally recognized from the time of conception.

I

WHAT DOES IT MEAN TO BE A "PARENT"?

A.   The Problem

Imagine the following scenario. A married couple wishes to have a child. Unfortunately, both spouses are infertile. As the result of testicular cancer, the husband physically is incapable of producing sperm. Similarly, due to a condition known as endometriosis, the wife is incapable of producing ova. The condition also has affected her capacity to bring to term a previously conceived embryo.[19] In essence, the couple lacks the biological ability to produce a child genetically or gestationally.

Nevertheless, after repeated unsuccessful attempts at adoption, the couple decides to "have a child of its own." They proceed by contacting

---

[19] See OTA, Infertility, supra note 1, at 65-66 (discussing endometriosis and its effects on women's capacity both to produce ova and to bring fetus to term); id. at 72-73 (discussing effects of cancer on male and female fertility).

a facility which collects and stores donor sperm for artificial insemination. The couple carefully reviews the records indicating a number of general characteristics of the prospective donor including height, weight, age, race, eye color, hair color, occupation, talents, and hobbies. They choose the sperm of an individual whose general physical appearance and professional biography most closely approximate that of the husband. Next, the couple contacts one of the recently established ova banks. They choose ova contributed by a woman with physical and intellectual attributes strikingly similar to that of the wife.[20]

The couple then selects a suitable woman who has expressed an interest in assisting an infertile couple to bring a child into the world. The surrogate is to be paid $10,000 and, to increase the probability of pregnancy, agrees to have three preembryos surgically implanted, after which she will carry and bear the child, relinquishing the child to the couple upon birth. Through the process of in vitro fertilization, the sperm and ova of the two anonymous donors are united. Three days after conception, the preembryos are transferred to the surrogate who carries one of them to term and bears a healthy baby girl. Shortly after birth, the surrogate turns the child over to the commissioning couple. The new "parents" have "brought a child into the world."

But who are the "parents" in the preceding scenario? Should the answer depend upon whether the surrogate willingly relinquishes her claim to the child? Indeed, who is more like a parent here? Are the husband and wife, who carefully and intentionally orchestrated the procreational act, bringing together all the necessary components with the intention of creating a unique individual whom they intend to raise as their own, the parents? Or is the gestational host, who bore the physical burden of pregnancy and the pain of labor, more properly the "mother" of the child? Or should the genetic parents—the anonymous donors—if they knew of the existence of the child, take legal priority as its parents? Thus we are led to inquire: what relevance do the various intentional, genetic, and gestational components of procreation have for the concept of parenthood? The answer depends upon our definition of "parent."

B. The Limits of Definition

The use of definitions in any empirical area poses a curious dilemma.[21] We seek to define a particular concept so that, among other

---

[20] While the couple would have preferred an in-depth psychological and intellectual sketch of each of the two donors, this is not yet available. Consequently, they construct a general psychological picture of each donor based upon the other information present in the biographies.

[21] I classify definitions into the "analytic" and the "empirical." Analytic definitions are those which are true as a matter of logic. The definition is "contained" within the concept.

reasons, we can accurately distinguish uncertain or borderline examples of that concept from counterexamples or instances falling outside of the scope of that concept. In the process of arriving at a definition, we must make antecedent determinations of the scope of the concept. In other words, if we could be certain when a particular object, X, falls within the operational scope of a concept, F, the need to define F would be eliminated, or at least greatly mitigated. Thus, in arriving at a definition of any concept, we must come to some preliminary conclusions about which particular examples fall within the definitional scope of that concept. In short, we seek definition in order to distinguish instances of a concept from noninstances. But we must make these distinctions prior to the definition, in effect deciding in advance whether certain instances fall within the scope of the concept.

In attempting to define the term "parent," for example, we must make certain assessments about uncertain cases. Is a person who raises a child, but who is not biologically related to the child, truly a "parent"? Is an egg donor who does not carry the child to term the "mother" of the child? In deciding these uncertain cases, we implicitly appeal to some preanalytic concept of parenthood, as if presupposing the definition.[22] Yet the entire reason for seeking a definition in the first place is to permit us to know whether an egg donor, for example, is a "mother." Thus, the entire process is circular.

It might appear that we should surmount this obstacle simply by stipulating a definition of parenthood. Thus, we could provide, almost by fiat, that the term "parent" is to be understood as designating a biological parent of the child, or a party who actually raises the child, or some other party. This would provide order where it formerly was ab-

---

But see D. O'Connor & B. Carr, Introduction to the Theory of Knowledge 145-63 (1982) (questioning existence of separate category of analytic truths). So, for example, according to the analytic definition, a triangle is a three-sided closed-plane polygon. To know what a triangle is, is to know whether or not any particular object is in fact a triangle.

Empirical definitions, by contrast, have uncertain boundaries. The concept "chair," for example, appears to have no necessary and sufficient conditions for application. It is uncertain how many legs a chair must have. Similarly, by analyzing the concept of a chair, we cannot determine at what precise width a chair becomes a sofa. Parenthood is an empirical concept. By analyzing the term we cannot arrive at a set of necessary and sufficient limiting criteria for its application.

[22] Concerns such as these led Plato and his followers to posit a realm of the Forms; a nonspatial, nontemporal domain in which the perfect Forms of every particular object exist. See Plato, Paramenides, in The Dialogues of Plato (B. Jowett trans. 4th ed. 1953). Each concept is, in some sense, a mental representation of this transcendental Form. See id. By remembering these Forms we gain a kind of a priori knowledge. Aristotle modified this thesis to exclude the notion of a transcendental realm in which the Forms exist but retained the notion of universals as a representation of the essence of each concept. See Aristotle, The Metaphysics, in The Works of Aristotle (W. Ross ed. 1949); Woozley, Universals, in 8 The Encyclopedia of Philosophy 194 (P. Edwards ed. 1967).

sent since whichever definition of parenthood is chosen, all parties will have prospective notice of the governing definition and will be aware of their corresponding status in light of the definition.

There is, however, a significant problem with this approach. If the definition which we stipulate does not comport with the way in which the term actually is used, the definition may provide theoretical order, but only at the price of alienating the term from its traditional use. For parenthood to continue to be recognized as perhaps the most fundamental social relationship in our culture, carrying with it the basis for a number of basic human rights with which it has historically been associated,[23] a continuity of core meaning must be maintained. To stipulate a meaning for "parenthood" which is fundamentally distinct from the traditional way in which the term is used is to open the door to a changed, and perhaps diminished, social significance for parenthood as an institution. Moreover, the stipulative definition is, in a significant sense, arbitrary. It thus can be challenged as merely asserting by fiat that which it is supposed to answer.

Rather than providing a stipulative definition, we could seek what Professor Copi calls a "lexical" definition.[24] This is a definition of a term reflecting the way people use it in common parlance. The common use of the term, however, may be ambiguous, lacking clear boundaries, and may be equivocal, having conflicting meanings. Moreover, common usage may manifest certain "gaps" in meaning. In the case of the term "parent," for example, the very fact that common usage is unclear in a number of novel situations has motivated this entire definitional search. Consequently, we need something more than an appeal to the lexical use of the term "parent."

Perhaps what is required is what Copi dubs a "precising" definition.[25] A precising definition is, in effect, a hybrid of the stipulative and lexical definitions. It is used in an effort to remain as faithful as possible to the common usage of the term while simultaneously stipulating its scope.[26] In ambiguous cases, the precising definition sets forth a meaning

---

[23] See notes 44-51 and accompanying text infra (discussing constitutional rights accorded by virtue of parental status).

[24] Professor Copi distinguishes five types of definitions: stipulative, lexical, precising, theoretical, and persuasive. Each has a different function and can result in disparate meanings for the same term. The primary logical distinction between a stipulative definition and a lexical definition is that a truth value can be assigned to the latter, but not to the former. In other words, it either is or is not true that a certain term is used in common parlance in a particular way. Conversely, the stipulative meaning need not conform to common usage at all. See I. Copi, Introduction to Logic 140-47 (7th ed. 1986).

[25] See id. at 144-45.

[26] Thus, there is only a partial truth value with precising definitions. To the extent that the definition departs from clearly established common usage, it is similar to the stipulative definition. See id. at 144.

which is consistent with lexical use, while also providing some stipulation clearly limiting the definitional parameters of the term.[27]

The problem with utilizing the precising definition to define terms such as "parent," "mother," and "father," however, is that these terms are not merely ambiguous terms; they are equivocal as well.[28] The term "parent," for example, is used to denote both biological progenitors who do not raise the child ("natural parent") and persons who are not biologically related but who do care for the child ("adoptive parent"). Indeed, it is precisely in disputes between diverse parties such as these that legal conflicts arise. Therefore, a definition that will distinguish these conflicting claims to parental status is required. The precising definition falters because it does not serve to delineate the better of the inconsistent uses of a term that is used in everyday language.

In our attempt to arrive at a cogent definition for the term "parent," we confront a basic dilemma. On the one hand, if we attempt to remain faithful to the everyday use of the term, we are prevented from arriving at a set of necessary and sufficient conditions for its use because the term commonly is used to describe both the noncustodial biological progenitor and the nonbiologically related custodian of the child. On the other hand, if we depart from these everyday uses of the term, we run the risk of abandoning an important part of its meaning. To the extent that the rights of "parents" and the tradition of parenthood are contingent upon this meaning, abandoning the lexical meaning abjures the very basis for these rights and traditions. Ultimately, the problem with finding a purely formal definition of "parent" is that the formal definition ignores the social, moral, and legal contingencies which have shaped our shared social intuitions about parenthood. Thus, the delineation of an appropriate definition must account for the contingent factors which have shaped this social meaning. In essence, the search for a unifying conception of parenthood cannot be simply an exercise in semantics; instead, it must be a genuinely normative quest that accounts for a great deal of empirical evidence and moral assessment.

---

[27] For example, the term "person" might be defined as a human being after the point of viability. The term reflects common usage but also sets a definite line which delimits the scope of the definition, thereby recognizing that the previable fetus is not a "person" under the definition.

[28] Ambiguity may be distinguished from equivocation as follows. Ambiguity, on the one hand, refers to vague definitional boundaries. At what width does a chair become a sofa? At what stage of development does a fetus become a person? When does facial hair become a beard? These various issues, ranging from the mundane to the profound, are all examples of conceptual ambiguity. Equivocation, on the other hand, is where one term is used in two different and perhaps conflicting ways. Thus, the term "guilty" is used to denote both individuals who have committed a crime, whether or not they are convicted—this is "factual guilt"— and those who are convicted of a crime, even if they did not in fact commit the crime—"legal guilt." See I. Copi, supra note 24, at 113 (discussing ambiguity and equivocation).

C. The Parental-Rights Doctrine

Creating a legal definition of "parent" is problematic because it is virtually impossible to delineate a list of necessary and sufficient conditions with which to define "parent." Given that the problem of parenthood cannot be resolved by definitional fiat, perhaps we would do better to look for a provisional definition that focuses on what we expect parents to do, that is, by examining the legal rights which parents possess and the extent to which these rights are limited by other doctrines. Immediately, however, one faces a new complexity—the fundamental dichotomy underlying our present system of family law between the rights of the parent in the child and the interests of the child. This dichotomy has been played out in modern legal practice as a conflict between the parental-rights doctrine and the best-interests-of-the-child test.[29]

The parental-rights doctrine holds that the fit parent has a right to the custody, care, and companionship of his or her child even if the interests of the child would be better served by being placed with a third party.[30] The best-interests test, by contrast, does not focus on the claims of the competing potential custodians but instead attempts to define the interests of the child in being placed with one or another party.[31] The conflict between these two custody approaches is most poignant when the best interests of the child clearly require the child's removal from the parent or, even more dramatically, the irrevocable termination of parental rights.

Traditionally, the parental-rights doctrine took nearly absolute priority. In early English history, parental rights were remarkably similar to property rights; indeed, as late as the tenth century, parents held life

---

[29] See Russell, Within the Best Interests of the Child: The Factor of Parental Status in Custody Disputes Arising from Surrogacy Contracts, 27 J. Fam. L. 587, 620-27 (1988-1989) (discussing tension between these two doctrines); see also McGough & Shindell, Coming of Age: The Best Interest of the Child Standard in Parent-Third Party Custody Disputes, 27 Emory L.J. 209, 212-14, 230-44 (1978) (examining changing balance between these two doctrines in parent/third-party custody disputes).

[30] In deciding custody between parents, courts consider the child's best interests, but they generally do not when deciding custody between a fit parent and a third party. Professor Russell states:

> Courts have long held that primary custody should be granted to the parent who would best serve the interests of the child, and that when the parent's and child's interests conflict, the child's interests must prevail. Courts and scholars also agree, however, that these principles should not operate to remove a child from a fit parent merely to enhance the child's life chances.

Russell, supra note 29, at 600.

[31] See Mnookin, Child-Custody Adjudication: Judicial Functions in the Face of Indeterminacy, 39 Law & Contemp. Probs. 226, 257-61 (1975) (discussing difficulty of determining child's best interests); see also Ruddick, Parents and Life Prospects, in Having Children: Philosophical and Legal Reflections on Parenthood 124-37 (O. O'Neill & W. Ruddick eds. 1979) (providing philosophical account of nature of parenthood and child's interests).

and death sway over their children, at least while the children were young.[32] Recently, however, the priority of the parental-rights doctrine has been placed in question.[33] In particular, considerations of parental unfitness[34] and the child's best interests have acted as limits on parental rights.[35] Indeed, many states have statutes which provide for awards of custody to nonparents if it is in the best interests of the child.[36]

Still, even the more limited, modern parental-rights approach reflects our basic intuition that the parents of the child should not be deprived of their right to nurture their child.[37] For example, all states apply a presumption that placement of the child with its natural parent is in the best interests of the child.[38] While custody awards to nonparents occasionally are made over the claims of fit parents,[39] the fit parent re-

---

[32] See McGough & Shindell, supra note 29, at 210.

[33] See Mnookin, supra note 31, at 246-49 (arguing that, in some contexts, best-interests test appears to have taken precedence over parental rights); Page, Parental Rights, 1 J. Applied Phil. 187, 188 (1984) (arguing that notion of parental right denigrated by holding that parents possess rights in their children only as long as they do not conflict with other social interests).

[34] See McGough & Shindell, supra note 29, at 226-28 (explaining parental-unfitness doctrine).

[35] See Page, supra note 33, at 188.

[36] See Mnookin, supra note 31, at 237.

[37] See id. Mnookin poses the following hypothetical.

> Suppose there are two couples, the Smiths and the Joneses. The Smiths wish to adopt a child. The Joneses have a four-day-old baby daughter whom they wish to keep
>
> . . . .
>
> Suppose both Smith parents were well educated, wealthy, and healthy; loved children; and appeared to be highly successful parents with two older children. Suppose the Joneses were older; had no experience at child rearing; had severe financial problems; and Mr. Jones was in bad health. There are certainly plausible and perhaps even persuasive reasons to believe the child's "life chances" would be greater if placed with the Smiths. And yet, a decision to remove the daughter from the Joneses for placement with the Smiths would be considered by most in our society to be monstrously unjust.

Id.

[38] See Russell, supra note 29, at 622; see also notes 245-46 and accompanying text infra (discussing this presumption).

[39] See, e.g., Painter v. Bannister, 258 Iowa 1390, 1400, 140 N.W.2d 152, 158 (custody of minor granted to maternal grandparents over father's objection so as not to disrupt child's development), cert. denied, 385 U.S. 949 (1966). Cases where a grant of custody is made to a nonparent usually involve situations where the child has been living with the nonparent and has established a psychological relationship. See Note, Psychological Parents vs. Biological Parents: The Courts' Response to New Directions in Child Custody Dispute Resolution, 17 J. Fam. L. 545, 550 (1979). This is plainly distinguishable from a case where a child is removed from the custody of a fit parent to be placed with a nonparent. Such a decision would likely be unconstitutional. See notes 44-51 and accompanying text infra (discussing constitutional status of parents); cf. In re May, 14 Wash. App. 765, 769, 545 P.2d 25, 27 (1976) (refusing to place child under state guardianship, stating that mother had right to attempt parenting before removal proceedings could be instituted). But see In re East, 32 Ohio Misc. 65, 69, 288 N.E.2d 343, 346-47 (1972) (newborn infant removed from custody of its mother on theory of dependency, without showing of parental neglect).

tains a number of rights independent of custody.[40] A nonparent may be awarded full parental status despite the competing claim of a natural parent where the natural parent of an illegitimate child has failed to establish rights in the child.[41] This placement often occurs where the natural father has failed to establish a relationship with the child, either because of indifference or as a result of not knowing about the existence of the child,[42] and where his parental rights already have been extinguished prior to the award of parental rights to a third party.[43]

The parental-rights doctrine, a creature of common law and more recently statutory law, is reinforced by its constitutional analogue. The Supreme Court has stated that parental rights are " '[r]ights far more precious . . . than property rights.' "[44] More specifically, " 'freedom of personal choice in matters of . . . family life is one of the liberties protected by the Due Process Clause of the Fourteenth Amendment.' "[45] The zone of family privacy and parental authority has been afforded both substantive and procedural protection under the due process clause.[46] This cluster of constitutional protections includes the right of the family to live together,[47] the right of parents to raise their children as they deem fit,[48] and the right of parents to educate their children without state interference.[49] The procedural protections recognized pursuant to the due process clause require that parental rights may not be terminated without notice and a hearing,[50] and without at least clear and convincing evidence of parental unfitness.[51]

---

[40] See Note, The Legal Relationship of a Nonbiological Father to His Child: A Matter of Equity, 66 U. Det. L. Rev. 97, 98 (1988) (examining limits on grants of paternal status to nonbiologically related fathers).

[41] See Quilloin v. Walcott, 434 U.S. 246, 256 (1978), in which a woman's new husband was allowed to adopt her child where the child's biological father had forfeited his parental rights by not marrying the mother or seeking to establish a relationship with the child. Essentially, the Court relied upon the best-interests test to permit the adoption where there was, in effect, no father in existence. See id. at 251.

[42] See, e.g., M.H.B. v. H.T.B., 100 N.J. 567, 579, 498 A.2d 775, 781 (1985) (per curiam) (biological father of child, unaware of child's existence, lacked parental rights).

[43] See notes 90-155 and accompanying text infra (discussing parental rights of unwed father).

[44] Stanley v. Illinois, 405 U.S. 645, 651 (1972) (quoting May v. Anderson, 345 U.S. 528, 533 (1953)).

[45] Smith v. Org. of Foster Families, 431 U.S. 816, 842 (1977) (quoting Cleveland Bd. of Educ. v. LaFleur, 414 U.S. 632, 639-40 (1974)).

[46] See id.

[47] See Moore v. City of E. Cleveland, 431 U.S. 494, 505-06 (1977).

[48] See Wisconsin v. Yoder, 406 U.S. 205, 214 (1972).

[49] See Pierce v. Soc'y of Sisters, 268 U.S. 510, 534-35 (1925); Meyer v. Nebraska, 262 U.S. 390, 400 (1923).

[50] See Stanley v. Illinois, 405 U.S. 645, 655-57 (1972).

[51] See Santosky v. Kramer, 455 U.S. 745, 758-68 (1982) (preponderance-of-evidence standard insufficient to deny parental rights).

366   NEW YORK UNIVERSITY LAW REVIEW   [Vol. 66:353

Parents, in short, retain a significant bundle of rights with respect to their children. These legal rights, while not defining "parent," help identify what is at stake in this debate over parenthood. Nevertheless, before resolving this controversy more vexing questions need to be examined. Who is eligible to be a parent? Does the law currently recognize any necessary or sufficient conditions for ascribing parental status?

II

THE EXISTING LAW OF PARENTHOOD

A consideration of the indicia of parental status should commence with an analysis of the legal issues surrounding procreation. This requires an examination of two fundamental issues. First, what is the right of procreation and to which activities does the right extend? More specifically, does the right of procreation encompass collaborative-reproduction technologies? Second, to whom does the right of procreation apply? These issues are considered in the two sections which follow.

A. The Right of Procreation

In *Skinner v. Oklahoma*,[52] the Supreme Court held unconstitutional an Oklahoma statute providing for the involuntary sterilization of certain classes of offenders whose crimes were characterized by "moral turpitude."[53] While the case was decided on equal protection grounds,[54] it since has been incorporated unofficially into substantive due process analysis as part of the privacy right elaborated years later in *Griswold v. Connecticut*[55] and its progeny.[56] However, despite these subsequent de-

---

[52] 316 U.S. 535 (1942).

[53] Id. at 537.

[54] See id. at 541.

[55] 381 U.S. 479, 485-86 (1965) (law forbidding use of contraceptives intrudes upon right to marital privacy).

[56] See, e.g., Roe v. Wade, 410 U.S. 113 (1973); Eisenstadt v. Baird, 405 U.S. 438 (1972). The Supreme Court has not ruled on the right of procreation since *Skinner*. Thus, the Court has never stated that the procreative right is an aspect of the privacy right. Nonetheless, the right to procreation does have all the indicia of a privacy right. First, analogous pre-*Griswold* privacy rights have been subsumed into modern substantive due process analysis. Thus, early cases such as Meyer v. Nebraska, 262 U.S. 390 (1923), which invalidated a law prohibitting instruction in any language other than English, and Pierce v. Soc'y of Sisters, 268 U.S. 510 (1925), which held unconstitutional a law forbidding education outside of public schools, have been recognized as part of the right to privacy. See, e.g., *Roe*, 410 U.S. at 159 (relying upon *Griswold, Meyer, Pierce*, and *Skinner* in privacy-right analysis).

Second, the right of procreation, at least superficially, involves similar issues as those encountered in other privacy-right cases. The rights to use contraception, to have an abortion, and to live with one's family—are all aspects of the privacy right as it has developed over the past quarter-century. See Allen, supra note 16, at 1786-91 (analyzing right of procreation as traditional privacy right); Note, A Taxonomy of Privacy: Repose, Sanctuary, and Intimate Decision, 64 Calif. L. Rev. 1447, 1466-78 (1976) (privacy right of intimate decisions includes

velopments in the area of privacy rights, *Skinner* remains the only Supreme Court decision explicitly addressing the right of procreation.

Skinner is ambiguous for a number of reasons. First, the right of procreation elaborated in *Skinner* appears as a negative right to make procreational decisions without government interference. This is quite distinct from a positive right requiring government assistance to enforce reproductive-services contracts between commissioning couples and surrogates.[57] Second, it is not clear whether the right of procreation extends beyond the scope of traditional two-party sexual reproduction. Specifically, although some state courts have taken a position on these matters,[58] the Supreme Court has not determined whether the right extends to the use of artificial insemination by donor, in vitro fertilization, or surrogate-parenting arrangements.[59]

Two further ambiguities in *Skinner*'s procreative-rights analysis more directly related to the present discussion likewise remain unresolved. First, the substantive content of the right is unclear: does it protect only the biological act of reproduction, or also the corresponding right to parent the child? Second, even if the right applies in the context of collaborative reproduction, and particularly in surrogate-parenting arrangements, to whom does it apply? Does the right attach only to the biological progenitors—the sperm donor, whether or not he is also the intended father, and the surrogate in genetic surrogacy—or does it also extend to the couple possessing the prebirth intention to raise the child? The answer to each of these questions generally will depend on whether procreation is cast purely in biological terms or, alternatively, whether it encompasses an intentional dimension.

The first of these two issues concerns the extension of the right of procreation beyond biological reproduction to include the right to raise the child born through the procreative act. At least one scholar has argued that the right of procreation is not simply a right to beget and bear

---

rights of procreation, cohabitation, child-rearing, bodily integrity, in-home possession, and private sexual activities between consenting adults). But see Robertson, Procreative Liberty and the Control of Conception, Pregnancy, and Childbirth, 69 Va. L. Rev. 405, 414-20 (1983) (distinguishing freedom to procreate from freedom to control every related activity).

[57] See In re Baby M, 109 N.J. 396, 447-49, 537 A.2d 1227, 1253-54 (1988) (rejecting claim of intended parent that his right of procreation required government enforcement of surrogate contract).

[58] See, e.g., Doe v. Kelley, 106 Mich. App. 169, 173-74, 307 N.W.2d 438, 441 (1981) (right of procreation does not extend to surrogate arrangements); *Baby M*, 109 N.J. at 448, 537 A.2d at 1253 ("[t]he right to procreate very simply is the right to have natural children, whether through sexual intercourse or artificial insemination").

[59] If the right of procreation is deemed to extend to collaborative reproduction, yet is treated as a negative right, the effect would be to limit greatly any government involvement in procreational choices—either to enforce or to criminalize collaborative-reproductive agreements.

a child but includes the right to be a parent.[60] This conclusion comports with the commonsense intuition that the procreative right is virtually empty unless it ensures progenitors the right to acquire parental rights in the child. While the contrary interpretation, which construes that right as nothing more than the right to pass along one's genes without a corresponding right to have custody of or to make decisions affecting the child, seems untenable, a range of intermediate positions entitling procreators to parental rights in certain situations has received support in various courts.[61]

The recent case of *In re Baby M*[62] will help formulate an intermediate approach to the right of procreation. The *Baby M* case is one of the few decisions in which a court faced directly the task of elaborating the substantive content of the right of procreation. In *Baby M*, the Sterns commissioned Mary Beth Whitehead to act as a surrogate for them.[63] Ms. Whitehead was artificially inseminated with the sperm of Mr. Stern and gave birth to a baby girl.[64] Ms. Whitehead then changed her mind and attempted to retain custody of the child.[65] Construing the scope of the right of procreation, the New Jersey Supreme Court stated:

> The right to procreate very simply is the right to have natural children, whether through sexual intercourse or artificial insemination. It is no more than that. Mr. Stern has not been deprived of that right. Through artificial insemination of Mrs. Whitehead, Baby M is his child. The custody, care, companionship, and nurturing that follow birth are not parts of the right to procreation . . . .[66]

Thus, according to the court, the right to procreation protects only the right to reproduce physically and possibly some limited aspects of parental rights. The court's ruling makes clear that the right of procreation does not include the right to raise and nurture the child. If it did, then conflicting claims to the custody of a child, as in divorce or contested surrogate arrangements, could not be resolved.[67] The right, nonetheless, does render its possessor a legally recognized "parent."[68]

---

[60] See O'Neill, Begetting, Bearing, and Rearing, in Having Children: Philosophical and Legal Reflections on Parenthood 25-26 (O. O'Neill & W. Ruddick eds. 1979) (intent to procreate creates right, as well as duty, to raise child).

[61] See *Baby M*, 109 N.J. at 466, 537 A.2d at 1263 (demonstrating intermediate position by granting visitation rights to Mrs. Whitehead, egg donor/gestational host).

[62] 109 N.J. 396, 537 A.2d 1227 (1988).

[63] Id. at 411, 537 A.2d at 1235.

[64] Id. at 412, 414, 537 A.2d at 1235-36.

[65] Id. at 415-16, 537 A.2d at 1237.

[66] Id. at 448, 537 A.2d at 1253.

[67] This is clear because while Mrs. Whitehead ultimately did not receive custody of the child, she was accorded visitation privileges as a parental right. See id. at 466, 537 A.2d at 1263.

[68] The decision to award custody of Baby M to the intended parents, the Sterns, was based

More specifically, the right of procreation elaborated in *Baby M* is analogous to that possessed by noncustodial parents: it includes the minimum rights to take part in certain fundamental child-rearing decisions, to visit the child,[69] to bring an action modifying the custody award,[70] and the duty to provide child support.[71] In short, exercising the right of procreation is sufficient to make one a "parent" in the legal sense. Of course, where no conflicting claims exist by parties who have exercised the right, the right to raise the child will inure to both parents. Thus, the pivotal question now becomes: does the right of procreation extend to biological progenitors or intended parents, and for what reason?[72] The analysis prompted by this question can be distilled into two questions under current legal doctrine. First, is genetic consanguinity a sufficient condition for recognizing the biological progenitor as a parent? Second, is it a necessary condition of parenthood?

B. To Whom Does the Right of Procreation Attach?

The right of procreation attaches to those parties identified by the courts as the mother and father of the child at birth.[73] This section examines common-law doctrines, recent statutory law, and constitutional law to determine which participants courts currently designate as parents. This section considers to what extent current concepts of mother-

---

on the additional determination of the child's best interests, not an absolute right to custody on the part of the Sterns. Thus, Mr. Stern's genetic contribution to the arrangement rendered him a "parent" under the court's analysis. The ultimate decision regarding custody, however, was determined under the best-interests test. See id. at 448-54, 537 A.2d at 1254-57.

[69] See J. Areen, Family Law 462-506 (2d ed. 1985) (discussing visitation rights).

[70] See id. at 536-51 (discussing modification of custody awards).

[71] See id. at 591-675 (discussing child support).

[72] See Allen, supra note 16, at 1760-68, 1771-81, 1786-92 (analyzing parental rights in light of privacy rights and procreative rights of intended parents and surrogate); Jackson, *Baby M* and the Question of Parenthood, 76 Geo. L.J. 1811, 1813-16 (1988) (examining definition of parent and role of intent in determining parental status); Robertson, supra note 56, at 427-36 (discussing right of procreation in context of collaborative reproduction). One commentator has put forth one of the most cogent analyses of the right of procreation and the stages of conception, pregnancy, and childbirth, proposing a scheme for reconciling the rights and interests of diverse parties in reproductive arrangements. She argues for an intentional analysis of the right of procreation limited by the privacy-right concerns of the surrogate. As such, her article is one of the few to draw a conceptual distinction between the right of privacy and the right of procreation. See Note, Redefining Mother: A Legal Matrix for New Reproductive Technologies, 96 Yale L.J. 187, 192-202 (1986).

[73] For example, in the *Baby M* case, the right of procreation attached to Mr. Stern and Mrs. Whitehead, the two parties that would be considered the mother and father of Baby M under traditional legal rules. Because Ms. Stern would not be considered the mother of the child under traditional law, the right of procreation did not extend to her. See In re Baby M, 109 N.J. 396, 447-48, 537 A.2d 1227, 1253 (1988) (concluding that egg donor/gestational host was "natural mother . . . entitled to retain her rights as a mother," then discussing Mr. Stern's right of procreation without any indication that Mrs. Stern also could possess this right).

hood and fatherhood are biological constructs and questions whether biology should act as either a necessary or sufficient condition to parenthood.

1. Who is Mother: The Presumption of Biology and the Role of Gestation

The "presumption of biology" manifests the once monolithic and still pervasive legal principle that the mother of the child is the woman who bears the child.[74] This principle reflects the ancient dictum *mater est quam gestation demonstrat* (by gestation the mother is demonstrated).[75] This phrase, by its use of the word "demonstrated," has always reflected an ambiguity in the meaning of the presumption. It is arguable that, while gestation may demonstrate maternal status, it is not the sine qua non of motherhood. Rather, it is possible that the common law viewed genetic consanguinity as the basis for maternal rights.[76] Under this latter interpretation, gestation simply would be irrefutable evidence of the more fundamental genetic relationship.

The debate and, indeed, the distinction itself were in the past only a matter of academic interest, but today, with the increased use of reproductive technologies, it is a matter of palpable significance. For example, in the context of gestational surrogacy,[77] different women play the genetic and gestational roles. The egg donor, who is not capable of bringing the fetus to term, provides a number of fertilized ova to the surrogate with the intention that, upon the birth of the child, the egg donor will assume parental obligations for the child. However, if the surrogate changes her mind and wishes to retain custody of the child, how should the law respond?

Application of the presumption of biology as it traditionally has been understood would give legal priority as mother to the surrogate. But it is not clear that this application comports with either the deeper meaning of the presumption of biology or modern sensibilities regarding this conflict. Indeed, the term "biology" itself is susceptible to equivocal use, implicating both the genetic and the gestational aspects of procreation.

Commentators who have considered this problem have come to op-

---

[74] See Note, supra note 72, at 190-92 (discussing ineffectiveness of presumption of biology in resolving surrogate-mother issues).

[75] See OTA, Infertility, supra note 1, at 282.

[76] See Johnson v. Calvert, No. X 633190 (Cal. App. Dep't Super. Ct. Oct. 22, 1990) (holding that egg donor/intended mother had parental rights over surrogate and discussing common-law background) (on file at New York University Law Review).

[77] This is a surrogate arrangement accompanied by the use of in vitro fertilization, where the surrogate gestator is not the same woman as the egg donor. See id. at 3.

posite conclusions. A number of scholars argue that the egg donor should take precedence because the hereditary and biological characteristics of the child are derived from her.[78] Others, however, argue that the surrogate's greater physical and emotional involvement in carrying the fetus, along with the advantage of simplicity in identifying the gestational host, gives the surrogate a greater right to be designated the legal mother of the child.[79] The relative merits of these alternatives are evaluated in Part III of this Article.[80] The analysis in the remainder of this subsection focuses on the legal rights that flow from the gestational role.

The courts have confronted explicitly the conflict between the egg donor/intended mother and gestational host only twice.[81] In each case, a decision was rendered favoring the egg donor/intended mother. In the first case, *Smith v. Jones*,[82] the proceeding was a "set-up" to allow the egg donor to adopt the child, and, in accordance with the surrogate agreement, the surrogate did not contest the ruling.[83]

In the second and more recent case, *Johnson v. Calvert*,[84] the parties actively disputed the same issue. In *Calvert*, the surrogate, Anna Johnson, had agreed to act as gestational host for the Calverts, the intended parents and sperm and egg donors.[85] However, near the end of her pregnancy, Ms. Johnson changed her mind and decided that she wanted to retain custody of the child.[86] In a loosely reasoned oral opinion, the court awarded full parental rights to the Calverts, analogizing the role of Ms. Johnson to that of a foster parent.[87] Thus, the *Calvert* court implicitly recognized that in a dispute between the egg donor/intended mother and the gestational host, the former has the superior legal claim. Aside from these two cases, the presumption of biology provides for an irrebut-

---

[78] See, e.g., Brahams, The Hasty British Ban on Surrogacy, 17 Hastings Center Rep. 16, 18-19 (1987); Samuels, Warnock Committee: Human Fertilisation and Embryology, 51 Medico-Legal J. 174, 176 (1983).

[79] See, e.g., Annas, Redefining Parenthood and Protecting the Embryos: Why We Need New Laws, 14 Hasting Center Rep. 50, 50-51 (1984) (presumption favoring surrogate mother provides certainty of identification at time of birth); Note, Rumpelstiltskin Revisited: The Inalienable Rights of Surrogate Mothers, 99 Harv. L. Rev. 1936, 1950-51 (1986) (social and emotional bonds formed in childbirth process favor surrogate mother's rights).

[80] See notes 190-307 and accompanying text infra.

[81] While the two cases represent the only existing law on this issue, numerous legislative proposals have been made to remedy the uncertain state of the law in this respect. See OTA, Infertility, supra note 1, at 284 (discussing some legislative proposals).

[82] No. 85-532014 DZ (Mich. Cir. Ct. Mar. 14, 1986) (on file at New York University Law Review).

[83] Id. at 2.

[84] No. X 633190 (Cal. App. Dep't Super. Ct. Oct. 22, 1990) (on file at New York University Law Review).

[85] Id. at 3.

[86] Id. at 11.

[87] See id. at 5-6.

table presumption of motherhood in favor of the birth mother in all states except Arkansas and perhaps Nevada. In these states, the irrebuttable presumption appears to have been abrogated in the case of surrogate arrangements.[88] Additionally, the status of the birth mother is protected in a variety of other ways including the prohibition in every state against enforcing prebirth agreements to consent to adoption.[89]

While both *Smith* and *Calvert* were decided in favor of the egg donors/intended mothers, in other contexts the birth mother appears to retain various rights. Thus, the legal significance of the gestational role is uncertain. As for the genetic role, its relevance is best developed in the context of a discussion of paternal rights.

2. Who is Father: The Presumption of Legitimacy and the Significance of the Genetic Relationship

We now turn to a consideration of two related issues. First, what are the legal requisites for ascription of parental rights? Second, what rights does a natural parent possess by virtue of the genetic relationship between parent and child? It is significant that these two questions are elaborated separately, because, as it turns out, there is only a loose legal relationship between legally recognized fatherhood and genetic consanguinity. The second question is posed and distinguished from the first so that some general conclusions can be drawn regarding the legal significance of the genetic relationship for the egg donor, as well as the sperm donor.

In general, fatherhood is a status which is predominantly a function of the family relationship. More specifically, it is a status accorded to men who entertain certain kinds of relationships with the mother and the child. Ultimately, there is only a contingent relationship between this relational status and the genetic connection between putative father and child.[90]

At common law, the "presumption of legitimacy" provided that any child born to a woman while she was married would be considered the

---

[88] The Arkansas statute provides in relevant part:
(b) A child born by means of artificial insemination . . . shall be presumed to be the child of the woman giving birth . . . except in the case of a surrogate mother, in which event the child shall be that of: 1) The biological father and the woman intended to be the mother if the biological father is married; or 2) The biological father only if unmarried; or 3) The woman intended to be the mother in cases of a surrogate mother when an anonymous donor's sperm was used for artificial insemination.
Ark. Stat. Ann. § 9-10-201 (1991); see also Nevada Rev. Stat. Ann. § 127.287(5) (Michie & Supp. 1989) (lawful surrogacy contract exception to bar against using money to secure adoption).

[89] See OTA, Infertility, supra note 1, at 281, table 14-2 (containing chart of applicable adoption laws).

[90] See notes 96-105 and accompanying text infra.

child of her husband.[91] Indeed, the husband did not have to be physically present at the time of conception. In the words of one court: "If a husband, not physically incapable, was within the four seas of England during the period of gestation, the court would not listen to evidence casting doubt on his paternity."[92]

Correlatively, at common law, a third party possessed no right to bring an action to establish his paternity; rather, this right is a relatively recent creation of statutory law.[93] The common-law presumption would bar a man who wanted to acknowledge responsibility for a child born to a married woman even if one or both of the spouses testified that the child was that of the third party.[94] Despite its harsh ring to the modern ear, this irrebuttable presumption of legitimacy, enshrined as Lord Mansfield's Rule,[95] was well-motivated. The rule not only protected the integrity of the family but also served to ensure the legitimation of the child in a period when illegitimacy carried with it a terrible social stigma and resulted in severe legal consequences.[96]

Under modern statutory law, paternity still is largely presumed. Indeed, in a number of states the presumption of legitimacy remains irrebuttable.[97] Thus, despite the invention of scientific methods conclusively establishing nonpaternity[98] and positively establishing paternity to within a small fraction of certainty,[99] third parties still are precluded from bringing actions to establish paternity. In the majority of

---

[91] See M. Field, Surrogate Motherhood 118-21 (1988).

[92] In re Findlay, 253 N.Y. 1, 7, 170 N.E. 471, 472 (1930).

[93] See A v. X, 641 P.2d 1222, 1222 (Wyo.) (under Wyo. Stat. § 14-2-104 (1977), child, her mother, or man presumed to be her father may bring paternity action to determine whether there is father-child relationship), cert. denied, 459 U.S. 1021 (1982).

[94] See, e.g., State ex rel. H. v. P., 90 A.D.2d 434, 437, 457 N.Y.S.2d 488, 490-91 (1982) (upholding husband's paternal rights where separated wife claimed to have withdrawn from artificial insemination program and instead conceived baby with unnamed third party).

[95] See Goodright v. Moss, 2 Cowp. 591, 98 Eng. Rep. 1257 (1777).

[96] See Sass, The Defense of Multiple Access (*Exceptio Plurium Concubentium*) in Paternity Suits: A Comparative Analysis, 51 Tul. L. Rev. 468, 498-99 (1977) (discussing historical legal status of illegitimate child). During the early period of the common law, illegitimate children had no rights against their male progenitors: the "bastard" could neither inherit nor claim support and was even deprived of legitimation by the subsequent marriage of its natural parents. See id. at 499. Thus, these children were called *filii nullius* ("children of no one"). Id. at 498. In the sixteenth century, however, the Poor Laws partially ameliorated this situation. See Poor Law Act, 18 Eliz. lc. 3 (1576). Under the Poor Laws, illegitimate children were accorded the right to seek support, although they still were not permitted to inherit. See Sass, supra, at 499.

[97] See M. Field, supra note 91, at 118 n.12 (by Oklahoma statute, wife denied opportunity to establish husband's nonpaternity); id. at 119 n.19 (California and Oregon law apply conclusive presumption that cohabiting husband is father of child).

[98] See The Chi. Daily L. Bull., July 21, 1989, at A5.

[99] See id. (predicting that paternity trials eventually will become unnecessary).

those states in which the presumption of legitimacy is rebuttable,[100] the presumption can be challenged only by the mother of the child or her husband.[101] Thus, third parties attempting to establish paternity require the cooperation of one of the spouses. Only in a minority of states can a third party challenge the presumption on his own.[102]

Under the Uniform Parentage Act (UPA or Act),[103] a third party may bring an action to establish paternity only when there is no presumed father under another section of the Act.[104] Thus, the husband of the mother of the child retains legal rights simply by virtue of his relationship with the mother.[105] The legal nexus between a nonbiologically related father and child also is recognized by permitting consensual artificial insemination by donor.[106] This rule protects the paternal status of

---

[100] See, e.g., Cal. Evid. Code § 621(b)(West Supp. 1991).

[101] See, e.g., Cal. Evid. Code § 621(c)-(d) (West Supp. 1991).

[102] See M. Field, supra note 91, at 118-21 (discussing issues involved in third-party challenges).

[103] Unif. Parentage Act §§ 1-29, 9A U.L.A. 579-622 (1973).

[104] Id. § 6(c), 9A U.L.A. at 594. Section 4 of the Act provides, in part:

(a) A man is presumed to be the natural father of a child if:

  (1) he and the child's natural mother are or have been married to each other and the child is born during the marriage, or within 300 days after the marriage is terminated . . . ;

  (2) before the child's birth, he and the child's natural mother have attempted to marry each other by a marriage solemnized in apparent compliance with law, although the attempted marriage is or could be declared invalid . . . ;

  (3) after the child's birth, he and the child's natural mother have married, or attempted to marry, each other by a marriage solemnized in apparent compliance with law, although the attempted marriage is or could be declared invalid, and

    (i) he has acknowledged his paternity of the child in writing filed with the [appropriate court or Vital Statistics Bureau].

    (ii) with his consent, he is named as the child's father on the child's birth certificate, or

    (iii) he is obligated to support the child under a written voluntary promise or by court order;

  (4) while the child is under the age of majority, he receives the child into his home and openly holds out the child as his natural child; or

  (5) he acknowledges his paternity of the child in a writing filed with the [appropriate court or Vital Statistics Bureau], which shall promptly inform the mother of the filing of the acknowledgment, and she does not dispute the acknowledgment within a reasonable time after being informed thereof, in a writing filed with the [appropriate court or Vital Statistics Bureau]. If another man is presumed under this section to be the child's father, acknowledgment may be effected only with the written consent of the presumed father or after the presumption has been rebutted.

Id. § 4, 9A U.L.A. at 590-91. Section 4(b) provides that the presumptions are rebuttable by clear-and-convincing evidence. Id. § 4, 9 U.L.A. at 303-04.

[105] See, e.g., County of San Diego v. Brown, 80 Cal. App. 3d 297, 303, 145 Cal. Rptr. 483, 486 (1978) (conclusive presumption that defendant was child's father barred defendant from adducing evidence that he did not father child).

[106] Consensual AID requires that the husband's consent to artificial insemination be in writing. See OTA, Infertility, supra note 1, at 244. In addition, under the UPA, the procedure

the surrogate's husband while simultaneously providing that the sperm donor is not to be considered the father of the child.[107] It is worth underscoring that this presumption applies only in marital relationships and does not extend to either heterosexual or homosexual cohabitation.[108]

While recognition of the presumption of legitimacy, in its various manifestations, has been conducive to the development of artificial insemination, it poses a significant obstacle to surrogate arrangements. While the wife of an infertile husband, with the assistance of the sperm donor, may plan to conceive and raise the child born of the AID arrangement, the situation is different where an infertile wife and her fertile husband seek the assistance of a married surrogate. In the latter instance, the presumption of legitimacy prevents the sperm donor/intended father from a claim to paternity of the child. Thus, in at least eighteen states, the husband of the surrogate will be considered the child's father.[109]

Understanding the legal framework for determining paternal rights also requires an examination of the constitutional dimension. Within the last two decades, the Supreme Court increasingly has involved itself in the process of explicating the constitutional rights of the unmarried male in establishing paternity. Two general rules have emerged from this case law. First, where the mother of the child is unmarried, the biological connection does afford the biological father a "foot in the door," permit-

---

must be performed under the supervision of a licensed physician. See Unif. Parentage Act § 5(a), 9 U.L.A. 301.

A number of cases have arisen where women artifically inseminated themselves at home. See, e.g., Jhordan C. v. Mary K., 179 Cal. App. 3d 386, 394, 224 Cal. Rptr. 530, 535 (1986) (provisions of UPA held inapplicable where woman used friend's sperm to inseminate herself, thereby allowing friend to petition to establish paternity). Before the Uniform Parentage Act and relatively early in the period in which AID became popular, the status of AID was uncertain. In one case, an Illinois superior court found that consensual AID failed to legitimize the child and rendered the wife guilty of adultery. Doornbos v. Doornbos, 23 U.S.L.W. 2308 (1954), appeal dismissed, 12 Ill. App. 2d 473, 139 N.E.2d 844 (1956). The first case to recognize that the presumption of legitimacy extended to consensual AID was Strnad v. Strnad, 190 Misc. 786, 787, 78 N.Y.S.2d 390, 392 (1948).

For specific discussions of AID issues, see Andrews, The Stork Market: The Law of the New Reproductive Technologies, 70 A.B.A. J. 50, 53 (1984); Hollinger, From Coitus to Commerce: Legal and Social Consequences of Noncoital Reproduction, 18 U. Mich. J.L. Ref. 865 (1985); Robertson, supra note 56; Wadlington, Artificial Conception: The Challenge for Family Law, 69 Va. L. Rev. 564 (1983); Note, Reproductive Technology and the Procreative Rights of the Unmarried, 98 Harv. L. Rev. 669 (1985); Special Project, Legal Rights and Issues Surrounding Conception, Pregnancy and Birth, 39 Vand. L. Rev. 597 (1986).

[107] See Unif. Parentage Act § 5, 9A U.L.A. 592-93.

[108] See *Jhordan C.*, 179 Cal. App. 3d at 395, 224 Cal. Rptr. at 535 (presumption of legitimacy does not accord parental status to man with whom biological mother lived).

[109] See Andrews, supra note 106, at 53 (discussing history of presumption of legitimacy in AID cases); In re Baby Girl, 9 Fam. L. Rep. (BNA) 2348 (Ky. Cir. Ct. Jefferson City Apr. 5, 1983) (presumption of legitimacy operates to deny paternity even when both surrogate and sperm donor/intended father wished to have parental rights accorded to intended father and his wife).

ting him to establish a relationship with the child and justifying certain procedural safeguards of that relationship.[110] Failure to establish this relationship, however, will result in the eventual extinction of these rights.[111] Second, the biological progenitor of a child does not enjoy a constitutional right to establish paternity or to seek any form of legal recognition of the relationship if the mother of the child is married to another man, even where he has actively sought to establish a relationship with the child.[112]

Stanley v. Illionis,[113] the first of four Supreme Court cases to address the right of an unmarried father to establish or maintain a legally recognized relationship with his child, involved a challenge to the constitutionality of an Illinois statute that conclusively presumed every unwed father unfit to care for his children.[114] Appellant Stanley had lived with his children and their mother for eighteen years without benefit of marriage.[115] Upon the mother's death, the State declared the children its wards and assumed responsibility for their care and custody without affording Stanley a hearing or establishing his unfitness.[116] The effect of the state rule was to deny Stanley status as the legally recognized parent of the children.[117] The Supreme Court rejected this statutory scheme because it violated both procedural due process and equal protection guarantees.[118] Implicit in the Court's decision was the view that Stanley was indeed a "parent" for constitutional purposes, notwithstanding the State's more restrictive legislative definition.[119] According to the Court, therefore, under the Constitution, a state may not make marriage a sine qua non for ascription of paternal rights.

This first elaboration of the paternal rights of unmarried men conceivably could have been interpreted as a constitutional protection of the genetic relationship itself. By this theory, a man achieves constitutional

---

[110] This is apparent as a synthesis of the following cases: Lehr v. Robertson, 463 U.S. 248 (1983); Caban v. Mohammed, 441 U.S. 130 (1979); Quilloin v. Walcott, 434 U.S. 246 (1978); Stanley v. Illinois, 405 U.S. 645 (1972). See notes 111-43 and accompanying text infra.

[111] See *Lehr,* 463 U.S. at 248 (1983); *Quilloin,* 434 U.S. at 246 (1978); notes 119-28, 135-41 and accompanying text infra.

[112] See Michael H. v. Gerald D., 491 U.S. 110, 129-32 (1989); notes 144-149 and accompanying text infra.

[113] 405 U.S. 645 (1972).

[114] See id. at 648.

[115] Id. at 646.

[116] Id.

[117] The statutory definition of "parent" at issue in *Stanley* included "the father and mother of a legitimate child, or the survivor of them, or the natural mother of an illegitimate child." The definition did not include unwed fathers. Id. at 650.

[118] See id. at 657-58.

[119] The Court held that the "state's interest in caring for Stanley's children is de minimis if Stanley is shown to be a fit father." Id. Thus, part of what it means to be a "parent" for constitutional purposes is a presumption of fitness.

protection as parent of his child by virtue of the genetic relationship alone.[120] As we shall see, however, this interpretation later was rejected as unduly broad.

The next step in the almost dialectical development of this uncertain area came six years later in *Quilloin v. Walcott.*[121] *Quilloin* involved a Georgia statute permitting the adoption of a child born out of wedlock over the objection of the male progenitor if he had not taken steps to legitimize the child.[122] Here, the mother had married when the child was three years of age and sought to have her husband adopt the child eight years later.[123] The biological progenitor sought to block the adoption of the child upon the filing of the adoption petition,[124] which occurred eleven years after the birth of the child. Even then, the petitioner-biological progenitor did not seek custody but only objected to the adoption of the child by its mother's husband with whom the child had lived for most of its life.[125]

A unanimous Supreme Court upheld the state court's finding that the adoption petition was granted properly over the petitoner's objection, rejecting petitioner's due process and equal protection claims.[126] Significantly, the Court distinguished *Stanley* by invoking the best-interests-of-the-child standard under which it determined that the adoption was appropriate, because it gave legal recognition to an already established family unit.[127]

As previously noted, however, the best-interests test cannot be the basis for terminating parental rights in the absence of a showing of unfitness.[128] Indeed, the *Quilloin* Court noted this, stating that due process would be offended if the state were to attempt to force the breakup of a natural family in the name of the child's best interests.[129] Therefore, the only plausible interpretation of *Quilloin* consistent with the parental-rights doctrine is that, for constitutional purposes, the petitioner was not a "parent" of the child. By failing to assume any significant responsibility in the eleven years since the child's birth, the petitioner had lost, or had never fully actualized, his status as the parent of the child. While the

---

[120] See Lehr v. Robertson, 463 U.S. 248, 271 (1983) (White, J., dissenting) (father's interest entitled to constitutional protection because biological relationship exists, not because of that relationship's quality).

[121] 434 U.S. 246 (1978).

[122] See id. at 248-49.

[123] Id. at 247.

[124] Id. at 250.

[125] Id. at 247.

[126] See id. at 254-56.

[127] See id. at 255.

[128] See note 30 and accompanying text supra.

[129] See *Quilloin*, 434 U.S. at 255.

Quilloin Court did not adopt this view explicitly, subsequent developments render this the most meaningful interpretation of the Court's reasoning.[130]

Caban v. Mohammed,[131] decided one year later, involved the conflicting claims of two unmarried parents both of whom had maintained joint custody of their children until the mother left to marry another man.[132] In *Caban*, the Court upheld the father's constitutional challenge, on equal protection grounds, to a New York statute permitting an unwed mother, but not an unwed father, to prevent adoption by withholding consent.[133] While the New York statute was similar to the Georgia statute under attack in *Quilloin*,[134] the Court struck down the New York statute as an overbroad gender-based classification.[135] Operative in the Court's decision was its finding that the petitioner's relationship with his children was sufficiently "substantial" to warrant protection.[136]

In *Lehr v. Robertson*,[137] the last of its four cases addressing a biological father's claims of parental rights to a child born out of wedlock, the Court elaborated upon the scope of the constitutional recognition of an unmarried man's parental rights. In *Lehr*, the Court explicitly rejected petitioner's claim that the due process and equal protection clauses of the fourteenth amendment, as interpreted by *Stanley* and *Caban*, gave an unwed father an absolute right to notice and an opportunity to be heard before the child could be adopted by the subsequent husband of the child's mother.[138] Again, the Court's decision turned on the relationship of the genetic father to the child. Rejecting petitioner's due process claim, the majority stated that he had "never supported and rarely seen" the child in the two years between the child's birth and the petition for

---

[130] See Lehr v. Robertson, 463 U.S. 248, 261-62 (1983) (suggesting that parental rights can be extinguished by failure to exercise them); cf. Caban v. Mohammed, 441 U.S. 380, 389 n.7, 393 n.14 (1979) (noting appellant's failure in *Quilloin* to act as father toward his child as important factor).

[131] 441 U.S. 380 (1979).

[132] Id. at 394.

[133] See id. at 382, 394. Under the New York statute, to block an adoption, an unwed father was required to prove that the adoption would not be in the child's best interests. See id. at 386-87. In *Quilloin*, by contrast, the Georgia statute allowed an unwed father to legitimate a child and gain parental rights, including the right to block an adoption. See *Quilloin*, 434 U.S. at 249.

[134] See *Quilloin*, 434 U.S. at 248.

[135] See *Caban*, 441 U.S. at 388 n.7 (noting that Georgia statute in *Quilloin* was similar to New York statute in *Caban*).

[136] See id. at 393-94 & n.14; see also Note, *Caban v. Mohammed*: Extending the Rights of Unwed Fathers, 46 Brooklyn L. Rev. 95, 109-10, 115-16 (1979) (concluding that *Caban*'s recognition of qualitative aspects of parental relationship will provide guidance for legislation).

[137] 463 U.S. 248 (1983).

[138] See id. at 250.

adoption by the mother's subsequent husband.[139] The *Lehr* Court also addressed the relevance of the biological relationship directly:

> The significance of the biological connection is that it offers the natural father an opportunity that no other male possesses to develop a relationship with his offspring. If he grasps that opportunity and accepts some measure of responsibility for the child's future, he may enjoy the blessings of the parent-child relationship and make uniquely valuable contributions to the child's development. If he fails to do so, the Federal Constitution will not automatically compel a State to listen to his opinion of where the child's best interests lie.[140]

Thus, according to the *Lehr* majority, the biological tie provides a foundation upon which the progenitor may build, if he wishes, a parent-child relationship and become a legal "father."[141]

The *Lehr* dissent, which took issue with the majority's characterization of the significance of the biological relationship, noted that a " 'mere biological relationship' is not as unimportant in determining the nature of liberty interests as the majority suggests."[142] Indeed, the dissent appeared to argue that the biological relationship warrants protection of the father's rights regarding the child.[143] The disparity in the respective views of the majority and dissent may be reduced to two varying conceptions of the basis of parental rights—one requiring a psychological component characterized by a measure of emotional and financial commitment to the child, the other strictly biological.

Taken together, *Stanley*, *Quilloin*, *Caban*, and *Lehr* require something more than a biological link between progenitor and child to award

---

[139] Id. at 249. The Court noted:

> As we have already explained, the existence or nonexistence of a substantial relationship between parent and child is a relevant criterion in evaluating . . . the rights of the parent.
> . . . Because appellant, like the father in *Quilloin*, has never established a substantial relationship with his daughter, the New York statutes at issue in this case did not operate to deny appellant equal protection.

Id. at 266-67 (citations omitted). The dissent raised the same inquiry, but read the facts differently, alluding to a pattern of deliberate concealment of the child by the mother, accompanied by persistent attempts on the part of appellant to locate mother and child and to establish a relationship with the child. See id. at 269 (White, J., dissenting).

[140] Id. at 262.

[141] Of course, the progenitor, by himself, may not absolve himself of the *duties* of parenthood, such as the payment of child support. See J. Areen, supra note 69, at 665-76 (examining enforcement of child-support orders). Where, however, another is willing to assume these duties, the Court has appeared to embrace the possibility that the biological progenitor may irrevocably lose the *right* to parental status.

[142] *Lehr*, 463 U.S. at 271 (White, J., dissenting) (citations omitted).

[143] Justice White's dissent stated: "Whether Lehr's interest is entitled to constitutional protection does not entail a searching inquiry into the quality of the relationship but a simple determination of the *fact* that the relationship exists." Id. at 272 (White, J., dissenting) (emphasis in original). But see text accompanying note 137 supra (discussing further *Lehr* dissent).

even noncustodial parental rights to an unwed man. Moreover, it is unlikely that the *Lehr* dissent stands for the bald pronouncement that genetic consanguinity alone is sufficient for ascribing parental rights. After all, *Quilloin*, decided just five years earlier, was a unanimous opinion.[144] Further, it is unlikely that even the *Lehr* dissenters would hold unconstitutional a provision similar to article five of the Uniform Parentage Act, providing that a sperm donor is not to be treated as the legal father of a child conceived through artificial insemination.[145] Thus, it is clear that neither statutory law nor the Federal Constitution protects a man's parental status based solely upon the genetic connection.

The rights of a biological father are even more restricted where the mother of the child is married to another man. In *Michael H. v. Gerald D.*,[146] the Supreme Court held that California's presumption of legitimacy did not violate the due process rights of the biological progenitor of a child by preventing him from establishing his status as the child's father.[147] Although the putative father had established through blood tests a probability greater than 98 percent that he was the natural father of the child,[148] the Court invoked the common-law tradition of placing the integrity of the family unit and the status of the child above the claims of the natural father.[149] The Court reached its holding despite the progenitor's commitment to the child and his active assertion of paternity,[150] in contrast to the appellants in *Quilloin* and *Lehr*.

Michael H. represents a potent endorsement of the common-law limitation of the natural father's paternal rights. More importantly, it clearly reiterates the theme that parental rights are not solely a function of one's status as a genetic progenitor. With this case, the Supreme Court rejected a strictly biological conception of parenthood in favor of broader considerations.

The significance of the decision must not be overstated. Neither *Michael H.* nor its predecessor decisions render the genetic relationship of the father to the child irrelevant. It is very unlikely, for example, that

---

[144] See Quilloin v. Walcott, 434 U.S. 246, 247 (1978).

[145] See Unif. Parentage Act § 5, 9A U.L.A. 593. Thus, the unwed father's relationship with the mother of the child establishes rights that the sperm donor clearly lacks. Indeed, it might not even be necessary that a "father" have had sexual relations with the child's mother. See, e.g., Jhordan C. v. Mary K., 179 Cal. App. 3d 386, 224 Cal. Rptr. 530 (1986) (friend of mother permitted to establish paternal relationship with child born after mother inseminated herself with his sperm, partly because parties' conduct reserved his status as family member).

[146] 491 U.S. 110 (1989).

[147] See id. at 118-20.

[148] Id. at 114.

[149] See id. at 124. The Court concluded by wryly stating that the biological father's claim "is not the stuff of which fundamental rights qualifying as liberty interests are made." Id. at 127.

[150] See id. at 114-15.

the Court would object to state laws that dilute the presumption of legitimacy—and therefore strengthen the claims of the genetic father—by permitting either spouse to rebut it[151] or to state laws that permit a challenge by the putative natural father.[152] Finally, even where the presumption remains conclusive, in actuality most legal fathers are biological fathers. Thus, even if it is true by contingent coincidence that most fathers are genetically related to their children, the fact has achieved recognition and legitimacy in the law.

In sum, fatherhood is a function of the confluence of three factors: the man's biological relationship with the child,[153] his legal or social relationship with the child's mother,[154] and the extent of his social and psychological commitment to the child.[155] While in reality the first factor rarely is isolated from the latter two, the purpose of this exercise has been

---

[151] See text accompanying notes 97-102 supra. However, even where permitted, the ability of the spouse to rebut the presumption of legitimacy has been limited in certain situations. For example, where a man has held himself out as the father of a child born during marriage, only to have his wife inform him, upon divorce, that the child is not his, the wife will be estopped from testifying that the child was not that of her former husband. See, e.g., Atkinson v. Atkinson, 160 Mich. App. 601, 609-12, 408 N.W.2d 516, 519-20 (1987) (relying upon doctrine of "equitable parent" to achieve result); M.H.B. v. H.T.B., 100 N.J. 567, 568, 498 A.2d 775, 775 (1985) (husband equitably estopped from denying paternity after child had come to rely on relationship); New York ex rel. H. v. P., 90 A.D.2d 434, 440-41, 457 N.Y.S.2d 488, 492-93 (1982) (equitable estoppel precluded wife from requiring blood test to establish her husband's nonpaternity); cf. Berrisford v. Berrisford, 322 N.W.2d 742, 745 (Minn. 1982) (equitable estoppel not applied against husband where child was too young to rely upon relationship).

[152] See M. Field, supra note 91, at 120 n.23 (Illinois and Wisconsin statutes construed to let putative father try to establish rights).

[153] Controversy has arisen regarding the due process rights of foster and adoptive parents. While the Supreme Court has not ruled on the constitutional status of adoptive parents, it did address the question as to whether foster parents have the same due process rights as natural parents. In Smith v. Org. of Foster Parents, 431 U.S. 816 (1977), the Court strongly suggested in dicta that foster parents lack due process rights equivalent to those possessed by natural parents. The Court stated, "[n]o one would seriously dispute that a deeply loving and interdependent relationship between an adult and a child in his or her care may exist even in the absence of blood relationship." Id. at 844. Nevertheless, "the usual understanding of 'family' implies biological relationships, and most decisions treating the relation between parent and child have stressed this element." Id. at 843. In the end, the Court appeared to create a distinction based on natural law, arguing that the relationship between foster parent and child is a creation of the state, whereas the biological relationship between parent and child is grounded in a "liberty interest in family privacy [which] has its source, and its contours . . . not in state law, but in intrinsic human rights, as they have been understood in 'this Nation's history and tradition.'" Id. at 845 (quoting Moore v. City of E. Cleveland, 431 U.S. 494, 503 (1977)).

[154] While marriage traditionally has been the most important type of relationship, ascription of paternal rights also may depend upon the type of nonmarital relationship. See, e.g., Jhordan C. v. Mary K., 179 Cal. App. 3d 386, 397-98, 224 Cal. Rptr. 530, 537-38 (1986) (despite statute precluding sperm donors from asserting paternity, friend of mother permitted to establish paternal relationship with child born after mother inseminated herself with his sperm, partly because relationship was between social acquaintances).

[155] See notes 109-10 and accompanying text supra.

to attempt to draw some general conclusions about the way in which the law currently treats this variable in isolation.

3. In Re Baby M:[156] *The Biological Interpretation of the Right to Procreate.*

The arguments above demonstrate that a biological link is not, as a matter of the constitutional right to procreation, sufficient to create parental rights. Not all biological parents are procreators. However, the *Baby M* court clearly suggested that a biological link is a *necessary* condition for procreators. Thus, it held that the right of procreation applied only to Mrs. Whitehead, the surrogate, and Mr. Stern, the sperm donor/intended father, by virtue of their respective biological contributions to Baby M, and not to Mrs. Stern, the intended mother.[157] This biological interpretation of the right to procreate inextricably links the *right* to reproduce with the *biological capacity* to do so.

This approach raises numerous questions. First, one may inquire whether a gestational host, who is not genetically related to the child, is also a procreator. The recent ruling in *Johnson v. Calvert* strongly suggests that this is not the case.[158] Note that if gestation alone is deemed sufficient to give the host a stake in the child,[159] then three conflicting claims founded upon the right of procreation are possible: the claims of the sperm donor, the egg donor, and the gestational host.   Second, interpreting the right of procreation to apply solely to those having made a biological contribution to the child, as opposed to those who may have had some instrumental, though nonbiological, role in creating the child, arguably is both overinclusive and underinclusive in scope. It is overinclusive by allowing those with a relatively insignificant role in the procreative process to acquire a right in the child.[160] For example, a sperm

---

[156] 109 N.J. 396, 537 A.2d 1227 (1988).

[157] See id. at 441-44, 537 A.2d at 1248-50 (contract was held ineffective for granting parental rights to Mrs. Stern, who had no biological connection to child).

[158] See notes 84-89 and accompanying text supra (discussing *Calvert* case). Gestational surrogacy is still relatively infrequent; the first reported instance in the United States took place in 1985. See OTA, Infertility, supra note 1, at 36. The process typically involves the use of in vitro fertilization and embryo transfer to the womb of a woman other than the egg donor. See id. at 255.

[159] See Annas, supra note 79, at 50-51 (arguing that gestation alone should trump claims of other parties to procreative relationship).

[160] The relative insignificance of the biological contribution as a basis for ascribing the right of procreation can be seen by comparing the facts of the *Baby M* case with those of our opening scenario where the intended parents biologically were unrelated to the child. From the intended father's standpoint in each of the two scenarios, the only distinction is that, in the *Baby M* case, the intended father contributed his own sperm while the sperm of an anonymous third party was used in the opening scenario. But surely this factor alone should not be the basis for according full parental rights to the intended father and custodial privileges to the intended mother in the former case, while denying them in the latter.

donor contributing his issue to third parties wishing to have a child would satisfy a necessary condition to acquire parental rights in the child even though he never may have intended to parent the child.[161] Simultaneously, the biological interpretation of the right is underinclusive by precluding those who lack the biological capacity to reproduce from exercising the right in a constitutionally protected manner. This interpretation precludes even the intended parents in the procreative relationship from asserting their right to procreate and their corresponding interest in the child simply because they lack the biological ability to reproduce.[162]

As the law currently exists, the legitimate exercise of the right of procreation includes the right to parent a child.[163] If the rationale in *Baby M* is followed, however, only those who possess the biological capacity to reproduce are deemed to possess the right to procreation.[164] Thus, only those with the capacity to reproduce have a constitutional guarantee to do so. Ironically then, the right protects those who are least likely to need its protection.

C. Questioning the Reliance on Biology: Privacy versus Procreation

The right of procreation typically is construed as one aspect or dimension of the right of privacy.[165] And yet, the rights of privacy and procreation are distinct both in their nature and in the types of activities each protects. As Professor Robertson has maintained:

[C]hoices about who may conceive, bear, or rear a child are distinct from choices about the conduct that occurs in the process of conceiving, bearing and rearing. In other words, the freedom *to* procreate is distinct from freedom *in* procreation. Freedom to control every activ-

---

[161] See notes 100-09 supra (discussing laws limiting right of sperm donors to claim paternity).

[162] Significantly, this is not a situation where a party possesses a right in theory but lacks the capacity to exercise it, as with certain economic or social rights. The distinction is important. If the infertile party possessed a constitutional right to procreate, the state could not prohibit collaborative-reproductive arrangements absent a compelling state interest. Thus, infertile persons with the resources to pay others for their biological contributions to the procreative act, but forbidden to do so by statute, differ from indigent persons who cannot afford an education, for in the latter case, the barrier is economic, while in the former, the barrier is legal. It illustrates the difference between economic and legal barriers to note that, in Roe v. Wade, 410 U.S. 113 (1973), the Court held that women had a constitutional right to abortion in certain circumstances, but in Harris v. McRae, 448 U.S. 297 (1980), the Court held that there was no constitutional mandate for the state to provide abortion services when women could not afford them.

It may turn out that the positive/negative right distinction is philosophically unsound. If so, the distinction between possessing a right without the opportunity to exercise it and not possessing a right at all will fall.

[163] See text accompanying notes 60-61 supra.

[164] See text accompanying notes 156-57 supra.

[165] See notes 56-57 and accompanying text supra.

ity related to procreation—to determine how conception will occur, to manage the pregnancy, to decide how, when, where, and with whom parturition occurs, or how the neonatal period will be managed—may be of great significance to individuals and may also deserve protection. Although these activities may be lumped under the broad rubric of procreative freedom, analytically they involve choices distinct from the decision to procreate, which is the decision to conceive, gestate, or rear another person.[166]

In short, the right of privacy, which encompasses the right to use contraceptives,[167] the right to an abortion,[168] and a variety of other activities associated with a right *not* to procreate,[169] is distinct conceptually from the right to procreate. More specifically, the right of privacy is nonrelational while the right to procreate is relational in character.[170] Thus, while the exercise of the right of privacy is not dependent upon the consent or cooperation of others—for example, a woman need not seek the consent of another, even her husband, to obtain an abortion during the first trimester of her pregnancy[171]—the right of procreation does depend upon the acts of others in at least one respect and, arguably, in a second as well. First, because it takes two to procreate, the exercise of the right is dependent upon the cooperation of another.[172] Second, the procreative right arguably is contingent upon the constructive consent of the resulting child. A parent must meet certain minimal conditions in order to acquire the right to be a parent.[173] While actual consent by an unborn child is an obvious impossibility, the notion of constructive consent is an accurate metaphorical reflection of the general intuition that parents must meet a minimum condition of fitness. While failure to meet this condition cannot undo the physical act of procreation, the rights of the parent in the child may be terminated as a result of the parent's failure to meet this minimal condition of fitness.[174]

---

[166] Robertson, supra note 56, at 410.

[167] See Griswold v. Connecticut, 381 U.S. 479 (1965).

[168] See Roe v. Wade, 410 U.S. 113 (1973).

[169] See note 56 supra (discussing right of procreation as part of privacy right).

[170] Relational rights can be exercised only with the assistance or, at a minimum, the consent of others. Nonrelational rights, by contrast, are individual rights the legitimate exercise of which is not contingent upon the consent or participation of others. See Floyd & Pomerantz, Is There a Natural Right to Have Children?, in Morality and Moral Controversies 135-136 (J. Arthur ed. 1981).

[171] See Planned Parenthood v. Danforth, 428 U.S. 52, 69 (1976).

[172] Thus, the act of rape can never be a legitimate exercise of the procreative right. See text accompanying notes 186-88 infra (discussing relevance of rape).

[173] See notes 34-36 and accompanying text supra (discussing parental unfitness).

[174] The right to family integrity is a fundamental right protected by the fourteenth amendment. See Roe v. Conn, 417 F. Supp. 769, 779 (D. Ala. 1976). Thus, statutes permitting the removal of a child from the home or the termination of parental rights on grounds of neglect or parental unfitness are subject to the compelling state-interest test. Id. But where the state

The rights of privacy and procreation also differ conceptually in the nature of their respective relations to other rights. The right of privacy is derivative of a generalized notion of personal autonomy or bodily integrity,[175] whereas the right of procreation is fundamental, and does not flow from some other, more fundamental right.[176] The right to procreate is the right to bring a child into the world in an effort to have a family.[177] As such, it is more than a right of personal expression.[178]

The distinction being drawn here has important ramifications for determining who should be treated as the parent of a child. Even if the right of privacy is intimately associated with the biological concomitants of procreation, pregnancy, and childbirth, the right of procreation, as a distinct normative claim, need not be associated with the biological *capacity* to reproduce. The right of procreation instead can be viewed simply as a normative safeguard to protect the *intention* to create and raise a

---

can show parental unfitness by clear-and-convincing evidence, the termination of parental rights is constitutionally permissible. See Santosky v. Kramer, 455 U.S. 745, 747-48 (1982).

[175] See Comment, A Taxonomy of Privacy: Repose, Sanctuary, and Intimate Association, 64 Calif. L. Rev. 1447, 1471-73 (1976) (discussing which matters related to bodily integrity receive constitutional protection); id. at 1482 (discussing various interpretations of right of privacy). It is not clear which of these two varying notions, personal autonomy or bodily integrity, more clearly approximates the right of privacy. In Roe v. Wade, 410 U.S. 113 (1973), the Court stated that the right to an abortion is not predicated upon a right to do with one's body as one wishes:

> The privacy right involved, therefore, cannot be said to be absolute. In fact, it is not clear to us that the claim asserted by some *amici* that one has an unlimited right to do with one's body as one pleases bears a close relationship to the right of privacy previously articulated in the Court's decisions. The Court has refused to recognize an unlimited right of this kind in the past.

Id. at 154. The right of privacy also does not approximate a right of personal autonomy similar to John Stuart Mill's harm principle. Mill's principle states:

> [T]he sole end for which mankind are warranted, individually or collectively in interfering with the liberty of action of any of their number, is self-protection. That the only purpose for which power can be rightfully exercised over any member of a civilized community, against his will, is to prevent harm to others. . . . In the part which merely concerns himself, his independence is, of right, absolute. Over himself, over his own body and mind, the individual is sovereign.

J.S. Mill, On Liberty 16 (Promoetheus Books ed. 1986) (n.p. 1859). The right of personal autonomy, encompassing psychological and life-style choices, is broader than a right of bodily integrity, strictly speaking.

[176] See O'Neill, supra note 60, at 26 (discussing distinction between basic and derived rights).

[177] In this respect, the view of the right of procreation put forth here diverges from Robertson. Under my view, the intention to parent the child is necessary for the legitimate exercise of the right of procreation. This intention is not necessary in Robertson's view. See Robertson, supra note 56, at 460-61. It appears that even the desire to pass one's genes along to a succeeding generation is sufficient for the right to be exercised under Robertson's interpretation. See id. at 408-10.

[178] Compare C. Fried, Right and Wrong 151-52 (1978) (parental rights are an extension of personal rights) with Page, supra note 33, at 192 (rejecting this view).

child.[179] Biological capacity, on this view, is neither necessary nor sufficient for ascribing the right to procreate. Thus, while surrogate hosts, such as Mary Beth Whitehead in *Baby M*, are protected by constitutional privacy rights in a wide range of decisions regarding whether and how to continue the pregnancy,[180] it is not correct to ascribe the right to procreate automatically to the gestational host or to the sperm or egg donors as the *Baby M* court did in its recent decision.[181]

Adopting this intentional interpretation of the right of procreation would have fundamental significance for the issue of parental rights. Since the legitimate exercise of the right of procreation would accord parental status to the possessor of the right, those to whom the right of procreation does not apply would not have a cognizable claim to parent the child. Thus, where a conflict develops, as in the *Baby M* case, between claims based upon intentionality and those predicated upon biology, the intentional parents[182] would take legal priority as the parents of the child. In *Baby M*, if Mr. Stern possessed a right to procreate and an interest in the child at all, it should have been based not upon the slender thread of genetic consanguinity, but upon his actions initiating the procreative relationship.[183] By this alternative analysis, Mrs. Stern, the intended mother, would have possessed the same right and interest.

The remainder of this Article is devoted to critiquing the current biology-centered view of the procreative right and defending an "intentionalist" account of the right of procreation outlined above. Before proceeding to these arguments, however, it will be helpful to consider two preliminary objections to an intentionalist justification for parental rights. First, one might be concerned that, if the intentional exercise of the right of procreation is the basis for parental rights, those who have not taken part in the creation of the child would be precluded from being

---

[179] See notes 309-18 and accompanying text infra (discussing arguments predicated upon intentional aspect of parenting).

[180] For example, the surrogate retains the right to an abortion. See Note, supra note 72, at 203 n.61 (discussing implications of this division of rights).

[181] See In re Baby M, 109 N.J. 396, 448-49, 537 A.2d 1227, 1254 (1988). Thus, since a surrogate cannot constitutionally waive her right to an abortion, for example, this could not be the basis for a valid contractual provision. Whether the surrogate could be contractually liable for obtaining an abortion, however, is uncertain. See Simons, Rescinding a Waiver of a Constitutional Right, 68 Geo. L.J. 919, 919-24, 945 (1980) (examining propriety of allowing rescission of waiver of constitutional right). As a practical matter, it is likely that the intended parents would be entitled, at a minimum, to a return of any compensation paid to the surrogate. See Hill, In Defense of Surrogate Parenting Arrangements: An Ethical and Legal Analysis 284-94 (discussing legal issues surrounding surrogate's breach of contract) (dissertation available from UMI, 1990). Whether there also would be a cause of action for the intentional infliction of emotional distress, among other theories, for example, is unclear.

[182] For the definition of intentional (or intended) parents, see note 12 supra.

[183] See notes 309-18 and accompanying text infra (defending intentional view of parental rights).

considered parents. For instance, would this approach exclude adoptive parents from the claim to parental rights? Clearly not. Exercising the right of procreation is *sufficient* as the basis for parental rights, but it is not *necessary*. There are other ways of becoming a parent in addition to procreating. Through death, adoption, or involuntary termination of parental rights, as in the case of a determination of unfitness, third parties may acquire parental rights after the fact. However, it is the procreators—the party or parties responsible for bringing the child into the world with the intention of raising it, the prime movers in the procreative relationship—who are the "parents" of the child at birth.

A second concern is that this reconstruction of the right of procreation will deny the biological progenitors of an unplanned, but ultimately wanted, child the opportunity to be considered the legal parents of that child. Once again, however, the objection is unwarranted. Intentionality acts as a trump for the intended parents when conflicting claims are made by parties who have contributed biologically to the creation of the child. Intentionality, however, is not the only way to acquire parental status.[184] Where no party has intended to create a child, as in the case of the unplanned child, there are no intentional parents. Thus, the claims of the biological parents would take precedence.

To sum up the argument to this point, any coherent theory regarding the right of procreation must resolve first, what parental rights the right of procreation entails; second, whether biological consanguinity is either necessary or sufficient to claim the right of procreation; and third, which conditions limit the parental rights stemming from procreation. As to the first, it was suggested above that the right to procreation plausibly entails the parental rights to make decisions affecting the child and, other things being equal, custody rights.[185] Further, once the right of procreation has been exercised, the person or persons exercising this right should be deemed the parents of the child at birth.

With regard to the second issue, biological consanguinity clearly should not be *sufficient* for application of the right of procreation.[186] The

---

[184] To protect the sanctity of the family, high standards should be established for proof of an intentional relationship. Thus, in the case of surrogate gestation, not only should the parties evince their understanding contractually, but also the contract should be reviewed by a court. This would require both the surrogate and the intentional parents to manifest publicly their intentions regarding the procreational relationship. Aside from the evidentiary benefits of judicial review, such a hearing would have the added psychological advantage of requiring the surrogate to come to terms with, and to declare publicly, her stated intention to relinquish the child. This hearing, which would take place prior to the process of artificial insemination, could be instrumental in weeding out prospective surrogates who are uncertain of their ultimate ability to carry out the agreement.

[185] See text accompanying notes 60-72 supra.

[186] See text accompanying notes 179-83 supra (critiquing *Baby M*'s reliance on biology for ascribing parental rights).

case of pregnancy by rape makes this clear. Though the assailant may be the genetic progenitor of the child, he cannot be deemed to have exercised his right to procreate in the course of the act of rape. Similarly, the Supreme Court's ruling in *Michael H.* [187] suggests that biological consanguinity does not itself guarantee its possessor the right to procreate.[188] Thus, biological consanguinity is not sufficient for application of the right of procreation. But neither should biological consanguinity nor capacity be considered *necessary* for one to possess and exercise the right of procreation. The right of procreation should extend to anyone intending to have a child and capable of producing a child, either biologically or by putting together the necessary biological components with the assistance of others. As to the third issue mentioned above, while others subsequently may acquire parental rights in the child, as in the case of adoptive parents, this acquisition can happen only after the parental rights of the procreative agents have been terminated either voluntarily or in order to protect the child.

III

THE CLAIMS OF BIOLOGY RECONSIDERED

We have a technology that takes Susan's egg and puts it in Mary's body. And so we ask, *who* is the mother? Who is the surrogate? Is Mary substituting for Susan's body, growing Susan's baby for Susan? Or is Susan's egg substituting for Mary's, growing into Mary's baby in Mary's body? Our answer depends on where we stand when we ask the question.[189]

The "presumption of biology" and cases like *Baby M* must be read as endorsing a view of parental rights that gives primacy to those who are related biologically or gestationally to the child. This Part considers and rejects a number of arguments which could be made for the priority of the genetic donors or the gestational host over the claims of the intentional parents.

A. The Genetic Donor's Claims for Priority

A number of commentators addressing the conflicting legal claims to parental status between an egg donor and a gestational host have come

---

[187] Michael H. v. Gerald D., 491 U.S. 110, 129-32 (1989) (rejecting constitutional challenge to state laws extending presumption of legitimacy to child of marriage, holding third party with 98% chance of being child's father has no parental rights).

[188] See id. at 121-23 (rejecting claim that natural father outside marriage has substantive liberty interest in obtaining parental recognition); notes 144-50 and accompanying text supra.

[189] B. Katz-Rothman, Recreating Motherhood: Ideology and Technology in a Patriarchal Society 44 (1989) (emphasis in original).

down squarely on the side of the egg donor.[190] While these commentators have adverted to a number of interrelated and overlapping considerations in their defense of the genetic bond, none has undertaken a systematic explication of these arguments. The following discussion sets forth what appear to be the two most compelling claims that can be made in defense of the genetic donor's priority. The first is predicated upon the unique biological relationship shared by parent and child.[191] The second is a property-oriented argument based upon the person's right to any products of his or her body.[192]

1. The Genetic-Identity Argument

It is beyond dispute that an important aspect of parenthood is the experience of creating another in one's "own likeness." Part of what makes parenthood meaningful is the parent's ability to see the child grow and develop *and see oneself in the process of this growth*. Through this process, the parent views himself or herself as a creative agent in nature. This genetic identity accords the parent a kind of limited, genetic immortality, which one commentator has called "the sense of living on *through* and *in* one's sons and daughters and their sons and daughters."[193]

The significance of the genetic connection between parent and child undoubtedly is part of what makes infertility a painful experience.[194] While adoption may satisfy one's desire to provide nurturance for a child, adoption cannot satisfy the yearning to create the child and to watch as a version of oneself unfolds and develops. It is, without doubt, this desire which impels some to use reproductive technologies and arrangements, including surrogate parenting, to create a child rather than to adopt.[195] The fundamental nature of this generative role may have inspired one commentator to argue that, while gestational surrogacy poses no insurmountable moral problems, genetic surrogacy—where the surrogate conceives the child with the intention of giving it up to another—is morally condemnable.[196]

The blood bond between parent and child has achieved both histori-

---

[190] See, e.g., Brahams, supra note 78, at 18-19; Samuels, supra note 78, at 176.

[191] See notes 193-205 and accompanying text infra.

[192] See notes 206-17 and accompanying text infra.

[193] R. Lifton, The Life of the Self 32 (1983) (emphasis in original).

[194] The harmful symptoms of infertility include depression, avoidance of social occasions celebrating the birth or growth of children, the side effects of drugs used to combat the condition causing infertility, and marital tension. OTA, Infertility, supra note 1, at 37. Divorce is not an uncommon result of infertility where the fertile party wishes to remarry and start a family. Id.

[195] See A. Overvold, Surrogate Parenting 81 (1988) (stating that genetic input is important motive in genetic parenting).

[196] See Krimmel, The Case Against Surrogate Parenting, 13 Hastings Center Rep. 35, 35, 38 (1983).

cal and mythological significance in every culture.[197] This connection is a manifestation of both the act of creating the child and the ongoing similarity between parent and child.[198] The significance of this latter feature is experienced both by parent and child, most noticeably when the natural parent and child meet for the first time.[199] The importance of biological similarity is augmented by scientific developments over the past fifty years which strongly suggest that even variables such as psychological dispositions and personal proclivities in such intimate matters as spousal preference and occupational choice may be determined, at least in part, genetically.[200] In sum, it is only natural that our sublime and complex feelings regarding this issue reflect precisely the sentiment that law should preserve as a family unit that which nature has rendered genetically similar.

While the foregoing manifests our general intuitions for the roles of genetic parents as they have developed historically in our culture, the historic basis for these rights is distinct from the type of situation under consideration in this Article. Here we are considering the genetic link unto itself, distinct from the cultural connotations attending the genetic relationship. Our hypothetical situation poses a sperm or ova donor who has no other involvement in the procreative relationship against a number of parties with competing claims. The genetic relationship itself should not be the basis for evaluating the parental claims of genetic donors above these other claims.

First, the sperm donor, who merely hands over a vial of sperm, typically is denied parental rights.[201] The contribution of the egg donor, of course, requires a greater level of physical involvement and risk.[202] While this factor may give that donor a claim intuitively stronger than

[197] See N. Chodorow, The Reproduction of Mothering: Psychoanalysis of Gender (1978) (discussing masculine and feminine parental roles in different societies).

[198] See J. Bluestein, Parents and Children: The Ethics of the Family 142 (1982) (stating that conception and birth are direct cause of emotional attachment to biological child).

[199] For example, one adoptee, upon locating her biological mother, expressed delight simply at hearing a voice identical to hers emanating from the other end of the telephone line for the first time. A. Sorosky, A. Baran & R. Pannor, The Adoption Triangle 159 (1984).

[200] See E. Wilson, On Human Nature 15-51 (1978) (discussing claim that personal and, ultimately, social practices are predicated upon genetic foundation). I do not take a stand here on the ever-present nature-nurture debate. The point is simply that, just as physical traits are heritable, it is likely that the physical processes which underlie psychological functioning also are heritable. This is not rendered any less plausible by social conditions in the child-rearing environment which may reinforce certain psychological dispositions. Thus, a child with a psychological propensity toward learning may be reinforced in her pursuits by a mother with a similar disposition. See R. Lewontin, S. Rose & L. Kamin, Not in Our Genes 83-130 (1984) (discussing influence of genes versus environment on intelligence).

[201] See note 104 supra.

[202] Ova are removed through a surgical process known as laparoscopy. See OTA, Infertility, supra note 1, at 105-06.

that of the sperm donor, that intuition rests on an argument regarding the greater psychological and physical involvement of the egg donor, rather than the genetic connection per se. The active role of parent as the *creator* of the child is lacking in the contribution of the genetic donors here. The sperm or egg donor plays the passive role of providing the seed from which the child will develop. This contribution, in itself, cannot be the basis for a claim to parental rights.

Second, it should not be relevant that the donor and child share similar physical or even psychological characteristics. As one commentator has pointed out, there is no difference genetically between the relationship of the donor and child and the relationship between full siblings.[203] In either case, there is a fifty percent probability, with regard to any particular gene, that the pair will share that gene.[204] By itself, sharing fifty percent of a child's genetic make-up should give the biological progenitor no greater right to parent than it does a sibling. Indeed, if genetic similarity alone were sufficient for ascribing parental rights, an identical twin would possess a greater claim than the parent.[205] The absurdity of this result demonstrates that genetic similarity alone should not serve as a basis for recognizing parental rights.

2. The Property-Rights Argument

The property-rights argument can be put into simple syllogistic form. The major premise states that persons possess property rights in the products, processes, and organs of their bodies and in any commodities developed from these sources.[206] The minor premise provides that a child is a product of a person's genetic issue. Therefore, the syllogism concludes that the genetic progenitor should have property rights or quasi-property rights in the child.

There are, however, a number of preliminary difficulties with this argument. First, because a child is the genetic expression of two persons, a genetic progenitor would have only a half-interest in the child. Second, most sperm and eggs are sold to commercial sperm banks.[207] Consequently, even under traditional principles of property law, the sperm and ova would belong to the purchaser who would have the right to dispose of them as he or she sees fit, within existing legal constraints, free and

---

[203] See B. Katz-Rothman, supra note 189, at 37.

[204] Id.

[205] Identical twins carry all the same genes. Id.

[206] This proposition must be qualified. Persons do not have an absolute right to dispose of their bodies as they deem fit. For instance, there are significant limitations on the sale of organs. See R. Scott, The Body as Property 179-97 (1981); Andrews, My Body, My Property, 16 Hastings Center Rep. 28, 28 (1986).

[207] See Jansen, Sperm and Ova as Property, 11 J. Med. Ethics 123, 124 (1985) (examining ethical implications of unauthorized use of donated sperm, ova, and embryos).

clear of any claims on the part of the gamete donor.[208] Third, even if the sperm or ova had not been sold but had been appropriated accidentally as part of the reproductive process of another, the doctrine of accession might bar the claims of the genetic progenitors. Where a raw material has been remade so as to completely change its nature or greatly increase its value, accession requires that title in the object vests with the person who has performed the labor—in this case either the intending parents or, more literally, the gestational host.[209] Thus, even if the property-rights metaphor were appropriate in this situation, the sperm and ova donors would have no claim to the child.

Overlooking these objections, however, a more fundamental difficulty with the property-rights argument remains. While people may possess property rights in their genetic issue, they certainly do not possess property rights in the results of their genetic contributions. Put more simply, children are not property. While it is true that at common law parental rights were in many ways strikingly similar to property rights,[210] this similarity no longer exists.[211] Thus, while a sperm or egg donor may have something approximating a property right in his or her gametes, their status with respect to an embryo is less certain.[212] The continuum running between the jurisprudential categories of property and personhood is unclear. For example, the progenitors of a frozen embryo awaiting implantation in the uterus may be treated as property owners in some contexts and as prospective parents in others.[213] But

---

[208] See R. Brown, The Law of Personal Property § 9.2 (3d ed. 1955) (discussing passage of title in sale-of-goods context).

[209] Before a court will apply the doctrine of accession, it must find that the raw material was used accidentally or in good faith. See 1 Am. Jur. 2d Accession and Confusion § 2 (1962). Also, the object must be substantially changed or increased in value. See Wetherbee v. Green, 22 Mich. 311 (1871) (rejecting plaintiff's replevin action for hoops made from wood cut from his land).

[210] See McGough & Shindell, supra note 29, at 209-17 (discussing development of state intervention in parent-child relationships). "As late as the tenth century in England, a parent . . . could sell a child under seven into slavery." Id. at 209. Even as recently as the nineteenth century, a parent had a legal right over the child's property, services, and earnings. See id. at 210.

[211] Parental rights now may be terminated, for example, when a parent is deemed unfit. See notes 33-36 and accompanying text supra.

[212] The Warnock Report in Britain recommended that legislation be passed providing that embryos should not be treated like property. See Jansen, supra note 207, at 125.

[213] For example, while the progenitors of a frozen embryo together share the right to dispose of the embryo as they deem fit, this right may be lost to both parties in the event of divorce or passage of time. See Davis v. Davis, No. 180 (Tenn. App. Sept. 13, 1990) (LEXIS, States library, Tenn. file) (divorcing couple litigated disposition of frozen embryos which had not been implanted prior to divorce), leave to appeal granted sub nom. Stowe v. Davis, No. 180 (Tenn. App. Dec. 3, 1990) (LEXIS, States Library, Tenn. file); see also Andrews, The Legal Status of the Embryo, 32 Loy. L. Rev. 357, 402-03 (1989) (analysis of legal issues surrounding frozen embryos).

certainly, upon birth, the property metaphor is no longer apposite.

Perhaps the property-rights argument could be amended to meet this objection by acknowledging that the parents do not retain property rights in the child but rather that their property rights in their gametes "mature" into parental rights with the growth of the fetus. However, the moral intuition underlying the doctrine of accession[214] undermines the modified version of the property-rights argument. The link between gamete and newborn child is too attenuated to support a claim to parent the child by virtue of the genetic contribution alone. Where the genetic donor solely relinquishes his or her issue for the purpose of another carrying the child to term, with the understanding that the genetic donor will raise the child, the genetic donor has a compelling argument. In the absence of this intention, however, the claim is much weaker; and where there exists a clear intention that another will raise the child, the claims of the genetic progenitors are negligible.

This is not to say that the gamete donor has no interest in the use to which the sperm or ovum is put. For example, it has been suggested, perhaps crassly, that the right of the gamete producer is similar to the right of the manufacturer of a computer chip, or the distributor of some copyrighted material.[215] While a party may sell the right to use, view, or listen to the material, the right to duplicate or alter it is not included.[216] Analogously, the genetic progenitor would possess an interest in restricting the uses of his or her genetic material. The progenitor, for example, might have an interest in preventing the purchaser from using his or her gametes to create a race of genetically engineered automatons or to develop some interspecies hybrid.[217]

That the producers of sperm and ova have a interest in preventing certain uses of their issue, however, does not establish that they should be accorded parental rights. Where the gamete producer has transferred to another the right to use his or her issue for legally permissible forms of collaborative reproduction, he or she has relinquished any rights or interest in the issue as long as it is used as provided for by agreement. The genetic source may retain an interest in seeing that the bodily product is not used improperly, just as the publisher may prevent copyright infringement, but this interest gives the genetic source no right to parent the child, just as a publisher has no right to reclaim a book purchased for a legitimate purpose by another.

Thus, the argument for the priority of the genetic progenitor as parent of the child is not, in itself, compelling. To the extent that the genetic

---

[214] See text accompanying note 209 supra.
[215] See Jansen, supra note 207, at 124.
[216] See id.
[217] See id.

394   *NEW YORK UNIVERSITY LAW REVIEW*   [Vol. 66:353

progenitor does have a colorable claim to parent the child, it must be by virtue of some other form of contribution to the procreational arrangement.

B. The Gestational Host's Claims for Priority

> God gave her the child, and gave her, too, an instinctive knowl-
> edge of its nature and requirements . . . which no other mortal being
> can possess. And, moreover, is there not a quality of awful sacredness
> in the relation between this mother and this child.[218]

The claims for the moral and legal priority of the gestational host are much more compelling than are those of the genetic progenitors. At least five distinct genres of argument can be brought to bear in favor of the primary parental status of the gestational host. These include claims predicated on the prenatal and postnatal bonding between the birth mother and child; the best interests of the child; the harmful psychological effects to the birth mother resulting from compelled relinquishment of the child; the physical involvement of the birth mother in bringing the child into the world; and the extrinsic social and moral considerations which portend harmful consequences predicted to result from permitting the legal separation of birth mother and child. Each of these claims will be considered in turn.

1. The Maternal-Bonding Argument

The claim that a deep attachment or bond develops in the course of the prenatal and postnatal relationship between mother and child is, perhaps, the most popular and most controversial argument favoring the priority of the gestational host.[219] The controversy is due, in part, to the

---

[218] N. Hawthorne, The Scarlet Letter 113 (H. Levin ed. 1960) (n.p. 1850).

[219] The bonding claim lies at the very heart of the attack on the proposed enforcement of surrogate contracts. See Suh, supra note 9, at 362 (bonding is among strongest human ties, profoundly affecting birth mother).

The claim is also the subject of numerous articles. See Belsky & Rovine, Nonmaternal Care in the First Year of Life and the Security of Infant-Parent Attachment, 59 Child Dev. 157 (1988) (child's behavioral responses to others influenced by level of care rendered by primary caretaker); Chess & Thomas, Infant Bonding: Mystique and Reality, 52 Am. J. Orthopsychiatry 213 (1982) (critiquing evidence supporting uniqueness of mother-infant attachment and idea that there is critical period for bonding); Egeland & Farber, Infant-Mother Attachment: Factors Related to Its Development and Changes Over Time, 55 Child Dev. 753 (1984) (studying effect of socioeconomic factors on infant-mother bond); Fein, Men's Entrance to Parenthood, 25 Fam. Coordinator 341 (1976) (discussing parental duties as factor in reducing anxiety in paternal role); Fletcher & Evans, Maternal Bonding in Early Fetal Ultrasound Examinations, 308 New Eng. J. Med. 392 (1983) (discussing how sensory contact with fetus facilitates bonding); Goldberg, Parent-Infant Bonding: Another Look, 54 Child Dev. 1355 (1983) (critical look at whether bonding hypothesis has been proven); Herbert, Sluckin & Sluckin, Mother-To-Infant Bonding, 23 J. Child Psychology & Psychiatry 205 (1982) (arguing that evidence fails to support critical-bonding-period hypothesis, especially in light of socioeco-

fundamental implications that the bonding hypothesis has for our view of human nature and for our conception of the nature of the parent-child relationship.[220]

Accordingly, the bonding hypothesis is susceptible to a variety of interpretations and has taken on a corresponding number of diverse theoretical manifestations. First, an ancient claim, now recast in the parlance of sociobiology, asserts that there is a maternal instinct which biologically predisposes a woman to want to bear and nurture a child.[221] A second view suggests that pregnancy and childbirth precipitate a battery of powerful psychoanalytic forces that facilitate the maternal bond.[222] Third, several competing psychosocial theories view the maternal-child relationship as the result of a matrix of social influences.[223] And, of

---

nomic factors and successful adoptions); Isabella, Belsky & von Eye, Origins of Infant Mother Attachment: An Examination of Interactional Synchrony During the Infant's First Year, 25 Dev. Psychology 12 (1989) (arguing that mother-infant interaction is self-reinforcing: behavior of one influences and reinforces responses of other); Kennell & Klaus, Mother-Infant Bonding: Weighing the Evidence, 4 Dev. Rev. 275 (1984) (arguing for critical-bonding-period hypothesis); Lamb, Early Mother-Neonate Contact and the Mother-Child Relationship, 24 Child Psychology and Psychiatry 487 (1983) (arguing that critical-bonding-period hypothesis is not supported by evidence); Lamb & Hwang, Maternal Attachment and Mother-Neonate Bonding: A Critical Review, 2 Advances in Dev. Psychology 1 (1982) (same); Leifer, Psychological Changes Accompanying Pregnancy and Motherhood, 95 Genetic Psychology Monographs 55 (1977) (discussing change in maternal self-image during first pregnancy and early postpartum period); Lewis & Feiring, Infant-Mother and Mother-Infant Interaction Behavior and Subsequent Attachment, 60 Child Dev. 831 (1989) (examining synchronic aspect of mother-infant interaction); Myers, Mother-Infant Bonding: The Status of the Critical Period Hypothesis, 4 Dev. Rev. 240 (1984) (arguing that, on balance, early sensitivity period for maternal bonding has not been proven) [hereinafter Myers, Status]; Myers, Mother-Infant Bonding: Rejoinder to Kennell and Klaus, 4 Dev. Rev. 283 (1984) (same) [hereinafter Myers, Rejoinder]; Shtarkshall, Motherhood as a Dominant Feature in the Self-Image of Female Adolescents of Low Socioeconomic Status, 22 Adolescence 565 (1987) (arguing that plans for becoming parent and feelings about maternity are affected by socioeconomic status); van Ijzerdoorn & van Vliet-Visser, The Relationship Between Quality of Attachment in Infancy and IQ in Kindergarten, 149 J. Genetic Psychology 23 (1988) (positive correlation found between quality of infant-to-mother attachment and child's IQ).

220 Where the bonding hypothesis is viewed as a claim that parental feelings are the product of biologically preprogrammed factors, the implication is that social factors are less important than usually thought. Therefore, parenting, and the feelings of nurturance that accompany it, cannot be learned. See Shtarkshall, supra note 219, at 568-69 (discussing social and economic factors affecting feelings of adolescent girls concerning their self-image as potential mothers).

221 Kennell and Klaus come close to this position but are not unqualified biological reductionists because they admit that the bonding process may be affected by psychosocial factors. See Kennell & Klaus, supra note 219, at 276-77 (reviewing evidence of biologically produced sensitivity period and arguing for critical-bonding-period hypothesis); see also E. Wilson, supra note 200, at 15-53 (theoretical account of sociobiology and claim that biological mechanisms underlie social behavior).

222 See, e.g., S. Freud, Some Psychological Consequences of the Anatomical Distinction Between the Sexes, in 5 Collected Papers 195 (J. Strachey ed. 1959) (discussing penis envy, its renunciation, and female desire to nurture child).

223 Many commentators, particularly feminists, have attacked the biological conception in favor of a psychosocial or social learning view of motherhood. See, e.g., N. Chodorow, supra

course, there are variations and combinations of these diverse themes which further frustrate any attempt to arrive at a univocal conception of the bonding phenomenon.[224] Thus, the meaning of the term "bond" varies from one theoretical orientation to another. This lack of uniformity has important implications for the claim that bonding is an inevitable concomitant of pregnancy and childbirth.[225]

In addition to these theoretical difficulties, confusion exists as to whether bonding occurs before birth, after birth, or throughout both pregnancy and the neonatal period.[226] The answer to this question appears to depend upon the researcher's theoretical orientation—biological determinists place much greater emphasis on prenatal factors than do those from a social-learning perspective. The question is confused further by conflating the mother-to-infant bond and the infant-to-mother bond.[227]

---

note 197, at 40 (study of psychodynamic considerations advances sociological understanding of women's assumption of maternal role); G. Corea, The Mother Machine 283-99 (1985) (examining significance of social factors in development of gender identity and assumption of maternal role).

[224] For example, bonding has been viewed as a fundamentally biological phenomenon which may be affected by social factors. See Kennell & Klaus, supra note 219, at 276-77 (bonding affected by cultural and socioeconomic background as well as hospital-care practices); R. Lewontin, S. Rose & L. Kamin, supra note 200, at 289 (human development is result of complex array of factors).

[225] Biological theories generally suggest that the bond is immutable and inevitable provided there is contact during the critical period. Similarly, psychoanalytic theories appear to render behavior a function of unconscious motivational processes over which the woman has no conscious control. See, e.g., S. Freud, supra note 222, at 191-92. Social-learning theories, by contrast, suggest that behavior can be changed by altering psychological and social conditions which bring about certain behavior. See, e.g., N. Chodorow, supra note 197, at 205-06. For example, the maternal-infant bond may be simply the product of social influences which condition a woman to behave in certain ways toward her baby. If so, where social expectations toward the gestational host do not compare with those directed toward the biological mother who has intended to keep her child, the surrogate may not bond with the child. In short, the social-learning theories interpret human behavior as flexible and more amenable to social influences. See Myers, Rejoinder, supra note 219. Thus, according to social-learning theory, the implications of the bonding hypothesis are less dramatic, at least where the social influences which affect the birth mother's relationship with the child can be altered. Id.

[226] From the standpoint of mother-infant bonding, there are proponents of both the prenatal bond and the postnatal bond. Compare Fletcher & Evans, supra note 219, at 392 (discussing development of prenatal mother-infant attachment) with Kennel & Klaus, supra note 219, at 277-78 (discussing presence of postnatal mother-infant sensitivity period).

[227] Four distinct types of bonds may be distinguished logically: a prenatal infant-to-mother bond, a prenatal mother-to-infant bond, a postnatal infant-to-mother bond, and a postnatal mother-to-infant bond. It is difficult to see how the first of these could be tested. For a discussion of the prenatal mother-to-infant bond, see Fletcher & Evans, supra note 219, at 392-93 (bonding facilitated by ultrasound and sensory contact). For a consideration of the postnatal infant-to-mother bond, see Belsky & Rovine, supra note 219, at 164-65 (child's behavior influenced by level of care); Egeland & Farber, supra note 219, at 769 (socioeconomic factors affect child's attachment to parent). The postnatal mother-to-infant bond is the focus of the present discussion.

Our knowledge of the emotional impact of pregnancy strongly suggests that there are as many feelings and experiences accompanying pregnancy as there are pregnant women. For some women, pregnancy is a time of significant emotional upheaval, psychological disequilibrium, and profound uncertainty in self-identity as their role changes from wife to mother and, possibly, from working woman to child caretaker.[228] Others experience pregnancy, birth, and childcare with an unparalleled sense of personal wholeness.[229] For still other women, the early phase of parenthood is a time of crisis exceeding even that of pregnancy.[230]

Still, despite these variations, the *prenatal* version of the bonding hypothesis is supported by a great deal of evidence, both scientific and anecdotal. Thus, women often report feelings of loyalty toward the fetus early in pregnancy, sometimes as early as the end of the first trimester.[231] Quickening, the point at which a woman begins to feel the movements of the fetus, is important to the development of maternal feelings of attachment to the fetus.[232] Reactions to quickening appear to be an example of the general correlation between the woman's increasing sensory awareness of the fetus and her feelings of loyalty and attachment to it.[233] While both parents interact greatly with the fetus—touching, rubbing, and talking to it, often in response to fetal movements—women have a greater sense of the fetus as a separate individual, often attributing emotional responses to fetal movements.[234] Finally, there is empirical support for the claim that women mourn after the loss of a baby, even a nonviable fetus.[235]

---

[228] See Leifer, supra note 219, at 57-60 (1977) (analyzing empirical evidence on pregnant women's psychological mutations). These changes are particularly significant with the birth of a woman's first child. See A. Oakley, Women Confined 179-80 (1980).

[229] See Leifer, supra note 219, at 89-90; see also K. Rabuzzi, Motherself 48-59, 109-20 (1988) (discussing changes in roles and self-perception brought about by pregnancy and childcare).

[230] See Leifer, supra note 219, at 89.

[231] See Fletcher & Evans, supra note 219, at 392.

[232] See Leifer, supra note 219, at 76. Quickening takes place some time around the end of the first or the begining of the second trimester, from 12 to 16 weeks of gestation. See Hellegers, Fetal Development, in Contemporary Issues in Bioethics 125, 127 (T. Beauchamp & L. Walters eds. 1989).

[233] Thus, it is suggested that ultrasonography, by which ultrasonic pictures of the fetal form are taken, may facilitate feelings of attachment for the fetus on the part of both parents. See Fletcher & Evans, supra note 219, at 392-93.

[234] See Stainton, The Fetus: A Growing Member of the Family, 34 Fam. Rel. 321, 322-24 (1985) (studying prospective parents' impressions of appearance, communication, gender, temperament, and sleep-wake cycle of their fetus).

[235] See Kennell, Slayter & Klaus, The Mourning Response of Parents to the Death of a Newborn Baby, 283 New Eng. J. Med. 344 (1970) (reporting feelings of attachment before tactile contact between fetus and mother).

There appears to be a high correlation between attachment to the baby and anxiety directed toward the fetus. See Leifer, supra note 219, at 91. Further, high self-concern is corre-

Yet the implications for parental-rights arguments are unclear. First, much hinges on the nature-nurture variations of the bonding hypothesis. Notwithstanding this evidence, there is widespread disagreement concerning the bonding hypothesis—or even whether bonding exists as a discrete phenomenon.[236] As a preliminary matter, there are profound conceptual difficulties in the concept of bonding.[237] It is not clear whether the bonding hypothesis, as conceived by its proponents, must necessarily entail some kind of biological link which transcends social factors and influences. For example, if bonding is simply the result of complex social factors which condition or motivate a woman to feel and behave in certain ways toward the child, then these factors can be mitigated by changing the social contingencies which shape the expectations of the gestational host. Indeed, numerous studies strongly suggest that socioeconomic circumstances affect a woman's emotional predisposition to the child.[238] Even the most ardent proponents of the biological interpretation of the bonding hypothesis have qualified their earlier positions to admit that socioeconomic factors affect the mother-infant relationship.[239] Other research refutes the claim that the prenatal bond is a universal concomitant of pregnancy. In one study, researchers asked ninety-seven new mothers when they first felt love for their babies. Only 41% first felt love during pregnancy.[240] This response suggests that prenatal attachment is not an immutable biological imperative that supports a universal legal commitment to the priority of the gestational host.

Nonetheless, even if the prenatal-bonding hypothesis cannot support a general presumption in favor of the gestational parent, in many cases the gestational host does develop strong feelings toward the fetus before birth, and there is some indication that depriving her of the child will result in serious psychological consequences.[241] These cases warrant serious moral consideration. Legal rights are not created in a vacuum.

---

lated with a low level of attachment to the fetus. See id. Also, there appears to be a correlation between maternal feelings early in pregnancy and the disposition toward the fetus much later in pregnancy. See id. at 91-92. Thus, a woman's attitude toward pregnancy early on may affect her subsequent level of attachment.

[236] See note 219 supra.

[237] See Herbert, Sluckin & Sluckin, supra note 219, at 206 (analyzing difficulties in bonding hypothesis).

[238] See, e.g., Egeland & Farber, supra note 219, at 769; Herbert, Sluckin & Sluckin, supra note 219, at 218-19; Myers, Status, supra note 219, at 256, 268; see also Shtarkshall, supra note 219, at 568 (women of low socioeconomic backgrounds tend to have greater desire to become mothers).

[239] See Kennell & Klaus, supra note 219, at 276.

[240] Id. at 281. Twenty-four percent first felt love for their children at birth, 27% felt love during the first week after birth, and the remaining 8% first felt love at some point after the first week. Id.

[241] See notes 270-87 and accompanying text infra (discussing psychological effects of relinquishment).

Rights must account for tangible human feelings and relationships, particularly in an area such as this, where these feelings and relationships are most vulnerable. The weight that these considerations deserve, however, will depend upon the extent to which these feelings may be vitiated or prevented by changing the social expectations of the surrogate. Correspondingly less weight should be given to these considerations where the surrogate's attachment to the child can be precluded by her knowledge that she will not be recognized as the mother of the child.

As for the notion of a postnatal-bonding process or critical period in which the new mother is particularly susceptible to deep feelings of attachment as she interacts with the child, recent research has cast serious doubt on this hypothesis. Minimally, it is clear that there is no magical point at which the bonding process occurs.[242] Moreover, numerous researchers have stated bluntly that there is no evidence to support the critical-period hypothesis.[243]

Arguments predicated upon the bonding hypothesis simply raise more questions than answers regarding the moral status of the gestational host. In addition to the theoretical problems mentioned thus far, it remains to be proven that the bonding process is *qualitatively* distinct from feelings of attachment for the child developed by others in the procreative process. The birth mother obviously is involved most directly with the physical development of the fetus and is the only one physically to experience tactile contact with the fetus. Nevertheless, there is little evidence for the claim that there is a qualitative difference between the feelings of the birth mother and those of another party to the procreative relationship. If there is no qualitative difference, then the claims of the gestational host predicated upon the prenatal-bonding hypothesis may be reduced to the contention that the birth mother has a superior claim to parent the child by virtue of her greater involvement with, and feelings of attachment for, the child at birth. While this may be an important argument in her favor, it does not carry the absolute moral weight conveyed by the onerous connotations of the term "bonding."

As for the argument predicated upon the postnatal-bonding hypothesis, two responses serve to answer the claims for the superiority of the

---

[242] See Chess & Thomas, supra note 219, at 215.

[243] Professor Lamb noted:

[I]t is clear that claims regarding the effects of early contact on mother-infant bonding are not well-supported by the empirical evidence. Most charitably, one could say that advocates of mother-infant bonding have yet to prove their case. More critically, one could say that early contact has no enduring effects on maternal attachment, but may sometimes have modest short-term effects on *some* mothers in *some* circumstances.

Lamb, supra note 219, at 294 (emphasis in original). For other research, see, e.g., Herbert, Sluckin & Sluckin, supra note 219, at 209-12 (evidence fails to support critical-period hypothesis); Myers, Rejoinder, supra note 219, at 283-84 (sensitivity-period hypothesis not proven).

gestational host. First, the very notion of postnatal bonding as a discrete phenomenon empirically is suspect.[244] Parents typically love and nurture their children whether they are natural or adoptive parents. There appears to be nothing intrinsic to the biological parent-child relationship which does not similarly occur in an adoptive relationship. Moreover, difficulties in operationalizing the concept of bonding, together with the lack of evidence for the postnatal-sensitivity period, render the hypothesis an entity of dubious scientific status.

Second, even if the postnatal-bonding hypothesis is correct and new mothers experience a period of sensitivity shortly after birth which readies them for the task of mothering, this sensitivity would give the gestational host the morally superior claim to be a parent of the child if the process of bonding is experienced only by natural parents. If the process of bonding is experienced by all new parents, natural and adoptive, then the intended parents would possess the same propensity to bond with the child as does the birth mother. However, if the bonding process takes place only between the birth mother and the child, because bonding is brought about not by contact with the child but as a physical consequence of pregnancy itself, what would be the negative consequences of placing the child with someone other than the birth mother? There is little moral significance in the claim that relinquishment of the child precludes a bond that *would have* developed had the birth mother retained custody. The only real claim that can be marshalled on behalf of the birth mother is that breaking or precluding the postnatal bond *ab initio* will result in some psychological harm to her. In essence, this reduces to a claim that compelled relinquishment of the child may have severe consequences for the psychological health of the birth mother. Whether or not this is true—and we shall turn to this question shortly— this issue is conceptually distinct from claims predicated upon the bonding process per se.

2. The Best-Interests-of-the-Child Argument

As noted previously, every state has recognized a presumption that it is in the best interests of the child to be placed with its natural parents.[245] While the legal impetus for this presumption may be the parental-rights doctrine,[246] some empirical evidence has linked several psychological problems among adopted children and adolescents to difficulties in the reproductive and early postnatal history of the child.[247] In

---

[244] See notes 242-43 and accompanying text supra.

[245] See notes 38-43 and accompanying text supra.

[246] See notes 29-51 and accompanying text supra (discussing parental-rights doctrine).

[247] See Isabella, Belskey & von Eye, supra note 219, at 12.

general, it is argued that separating the child from the birth mother may affect the child adversely in two ways. First, the child may incur irrevocable psychological harm because the parent and child fail to develop an emotional "bond."[248] These problems have been linked to the inability of both the mother to develop an attachment to the child and the child to develop a bond with its parents. Second, the child may experience psychological harm due to uncertainty regarding its biological heritage.

Throughout the 1960s and 1970s, researchers began to observe an apparent increase in the number of cases of child abuse suffered by prematurely born children.[249] A developing body of evidence suggested that a bond must develop between parent and child during a critical period early in infancy—according to some, within twelve hours of birth.[250] In considering what possible connection might exist between premature births and subsequent parental behavior toward the child, researchers hypothesized that vital medical treatment given to premature babies, requiring the separation of mother and infant, prevented the mother from bonding with the child. They concluded that the failure to bond resulted in a higher incidence of child abuse later in life. Thus, if a mother were precluded from interacting with her child soon after birth, there would be less likelihood that the mother-infant bond would develop.

A great deal of evidence also suggests that a symbiotic relationship between newborns and mothers develops throughout infancy.[251] In particular, it appears that the level of maternal responsiveness to the behavioral and verbal signals of the child may affect the child's sense of attachment[252] and the child's subsequent level of sociability.[253] Thus, the bonding hypothesis posits that early maternal contact with a child is necessary to foster the mother's feelings for the child and, consequently, that development of the mother-to-infant bond is vital for the child's wellbeing. The crux of this first claim for the rights of the gestational host, then, is that the intended mother, not having experienced the mother-to-infant bond, may lack the nurturing qualities of the birth mother.

Insofar as this best-interests-of-the-child argument relies on the

---

[248] See notes 219-44 and accompanying text supra (discussing bonding).

[249] See T. Verney & J. Kelly, The Secret Life of the Unborn Child 149-50 (1981).

[250] See id.; Kennell & Klaus, supra note 219, at 276-77 (authors, research pioneers who propounded bonding hypothesis, reevaluate evidence for sensitivity period, concluding that early mother-infant contact facilitates bonding but is not irreplaceable). But see Lamb, supra note 219, at 488-92 (arguing that sensitivity-period hypothesis is not well-founded).

[251] See Isabella, Belsky & von Eye, supra note 219, at 18 (study of one, three, and nine-month-old infants concluding that secure attachment is fostered where mothers respond consistently and appropriately to infants' signals); Lewis & Feiring, supra note 219, at 832, 836 (studying relationship between three-month-old infants and mothers and infants' later attachment behavior and sociability).

[252] See Isabella, Belsky & von Eye, supra note 219, at 18.

[253] See Lewis & Fiering, supra note 219, at 836.

mother-to-infant bonding hypothesis, it is susceptible to the empirical and philosophical criticisms raised above.[254] Moreover, studies of attachment between adoptive mothers and children report no difference in the quality of attachment between adoptive and natural parent-child relationships.[255] After reviewing the literature on the bonding issue, one group of researchers noted that early contact between mother and child has no provable long-term psychological consequences for the mother's feelings toward the child and, at best, only marginal short-term advantages.[256] In light of these studies, the postnatal mother-to-infant bond cannot be an adequate basis upon which to ground an argument for the best interests of the child.

Alternatively, one might examine bonding from the standpoint of the child, i.e., the infant-to-mother bond. There is little doubt that the development of secure emotional ties between parent and child has fundamental and long-lasting significance. It is well-established that infants failing to form a bond with any adult are likely to lack the ability to form deep and enduring relationships later in life.[257] One study found a strong correlation between insecurely attached infants and those who experience a higher level of nonmaternal care in the first year of life.[258] Another study maintains that *all* infants who are placed for adoption after nine months of age have difficulties with a variety of "socioemotional" matters, including establishing certain kinds of relationships with others.[259] Still other studies indicate that the quality of attachment in infancy may affect the IQ of the child[260] and the development of the child's sense of self-identity, thereby affecting the child's ability to cope with various environments including schools.[261]

---

[254] See text accompanying notes 221-44 supra.

[255] See, e.g., Singer, Brodzinsky & Ramsay, Mother-Infant Attachment in Adoptive Families, 56 Child Dev. 1543, 1544, 1550 (1985) (claiming that while early mother-neonatal bonding is not necessary, adoption should take place in infancy to facilitate attachment).

[256] See Lamb & Hwang, supra note 219, at 21, 29.

[257] See S. Fruiberg, Early Childhood Birthright: In Defense of Mothering 51-62 (1977); Singer, Brodzinsky & Ramsay, supra note 255, at 1544.

[258] See Belsky & Rovine, supra note 219, at 164-65.

[259] See Yarrow & Goodwin, The Immediate Impact of Separation: Reactions of Infants to a Change in Mother Figures, in The Competent Infant: Research and Commentary 1032, 1036-39 (L. Stone, H. Smith & L. Murphy eds. 1973) (study of infants placed in adoption finds that, prior to three months, few infants react to changes in environment; between three and six months, number affected and severity of effect increased; and after nine months all infants demonstrated some adverse effect). But see Singer, Brodzinsky & Ramsay, supra note 255, at 1549-50 (study of adopted infants finding no correlation between timing of adoption and mother-infant attachment). The latter study did not question the general empirical claim that the child must develop a strong relationship with an adult figure in order to mature properly. See id.

[260] See van Ijzendoorn & van Vliet-Visser, supra note 219, at 27.

[261] See Singer, Brodzinsky & Ramsay, supra note 255, at 1544. This study considered a

These studies clearly indicate the importance to the child of developing a secure relationship with at least one parent figure early in childhood. There is absolutely no evidence, however, that the child must form this relationship with a *biological* parent. What is important is the psychology, not the biology, of the relationship.[262] Thus, if a party, other than the gestational host, can render the same care and devotion as do most natural mothers, considerations of the child's best interests give the gestational host no inherently superior claim to the child. Moreover, it appears that younger children require less time to form ties with a new caretaker.[263] Some have suggested that a very young infant may take as little as an hour to form a new bond with another person.[264] Thus, even where a surrogate mother has formed a preliminary relationship with the child soon after birth, this factor alone fails to trump the claims of other participants in the procreative relationship.

The second genre of arguments favoring the gestational host and focusing upon the best interests of the child is founded not upon the prediction that the child will fail to form a bond with the nonbiologically related parent, but upon the argument that the child will suffer psychological harm as a result of the circumstances of birth. Thus, it is argued that the child will feel a sense of psychological "rootlessness" at not knowing her biological identity,[265] or that a child will be disadvantaged by the "unnatural" procreative process that brought her into the world.[266]

There are a number of responses to the charge that a child will suffer long-term psychological harm as a result of its uncertain biological identity. Insofar as this claim appears to address the uncertainty regarding the child's *genetic* heritage, this concern is unwarranted where the intended parents are the genetic parents of the child, as in gestational sur-

---

number of possible reasons why adopted children experience a much higher percentage of psychological problems. These include: (1) a more problematic prenatal and reproductive history, (2) complications associated with the social stigma surrounding adoption, (3) the nature of the transition from foster care to the adoptive home, (4) the effects of adoption placement beyond infancy, (5) difficulties associated with the adoption-revelation process, and (6) the confusion surrounding the adoptee's search for identity. See id. at 1543-44.

[262] See J. Goldstein, A. Freud & A. Solnitz, Beyond the Best Interests of the Child 105-11 (1973) (arguing that child's interests in psychological relationships with its caretaker parents should be protected in custody determination).

[263] See Note, supra note 39, at 546-47 (discussing time factor in child's ability to break old bonds and form new relationships).

[264] See T. Vernay & J. Kelly, supra note 249, at 148.

[265] See Robertson, Surrogate Mothers: Not So Novel After All, 13 Hastings Center Rep. 28, 30 (1983) (concluding that child may experience rootlessness if unable to contact surrogate, but that similar situation is tolerated with adoptions).

[266] Krimmel, for example, argues that because the surrogate conceives without wanting a child, the child suffers knowing that it was "conceived in order to be given away." See Krimmel, supra note 196, at 35.

rogacy. The claim also does not give the surrogate an advantage where neither she nor the intended parents are the genetic progenitors of the child, as where the sperm and eggs of anonymous donors are used. Moreover, even where the surrogate is the genetic progenitor, the child can receive information regarding her biological legacy precisely because surrogacy, unlike adoption, permits the intended parents to develop a complete medical record of the child's history and development.[267]

Finally, and perhaps most fundamentally, while the child may experience a natural curiosity regarding her parentage and biological legacy, there are problems with the prediction that this might affect the child's basic sense of self-identity throughout life. One commentator, for example, has argued that "[c]larity about [one's] origins is crucial for self-identity, itself important for self-respect."[268] This claim is predicated upon a troublesome view of personal identity, which implies that every adopted child is hopelessly insecure and devoid of self-respect. It appears to confuse the psychological notion of self-identity with the relatively more superficial knowledge of one's biological legacy. As such, this view is not only dubious empirically but also an atavistic throwback to the priority of blood ties over all else as a determinant of one's sense of self.

As for the claim that the child may experience psychological self-doubt or alienation as a result of knowing that it was born through collaborative reproduction, it is not clear that this gives the gestational host any advantage over other participants in the procreative relationship. Indeed, since the surrogate initially has agreed to bear and relinquish the child, the child may feel less comfortable with her than with the intended parents. At any rate, this same charge was made against artificial insemination forty years ago.[269] It is no more compelling now than it was then. In conclusion, notwithstanding the prevailing popular belief and the legal fiction that it is in the child's best interests to be raised by its natural mother, the best-interests argument provides little support for according parental rights in the gestational host above the claims of all others. We must, therefore, turn to another consideration raised by our initial dis-

---

[267] See A. Overvold, supra note 195, at 92 (noting willingness of some couples to allow their children to meet surrogate who bore them). Alternatively, a file could be established containing the biological and medical history of the surrogate. This file could be constructed in a manner that would not identify the surrogate, if this is what the parties to the arrangement prefer. Cf. B. Lifton, Twice Born: Memoirs of an Adopted Daughter (1975) (providing personal account of adopted child's difficulties in finding natural parents).

[268] Kass, *Making Babies* Revisited, 54 Pub. Interest 32, 47 (1979).

[269] See J. Fletcher, supra note 3, at 126-27 (reviewing common arguments against artificial insemination and collaborative-reproductive techniques, including claim that child will experience psychic dislocation from its unusual origins). Fletcher rejects this claim by arguing that this issue is actually more problematic in adoption, where the child's original parents may not have wanted it, than in collaborative reproduction, where both parents consent to love and care for the child and desire to bring it into the world. See id.

cussion of the bonding argument: whether the harm caused to the gestational mother by relinquishment of the child warrants granting her parental rights.

3. The Relinquishment Argument

One of the most poignant arguments favoring the right of the gestational host to be considered the mother of the child concerns the effects upon her of relinquishing the child. The effects of relinquishment on the birth mother in the case of adoption are well-documented.[270] Indeed, there is evidence that new mothers experience a kind of separation anxiety when they are separated from their children even for relatively short periods of time.[271] When the separation is permanent, the experience may take on extreme, even pathological proportions, including a deep sense of loss which pervades daily activities.[272] Depression, anxiety, and a host of other emotional consequences may result.[273] In one study, surrendering mothers reported recurring dreams of loss, fantasies involving rescue and reunion, heightened ecstasy in contemplation of the relationship with future children, and a greater than normal level of protectiveness toward their other children.[274] These experiences were reported even by women who were not permitted to see their babies upon birth.[275]

Additional evidence indicates that the surrender of a child may remain a source of conflict and interpersonal difficulties for many years.[276] In one study, 96% of all surrendering mothers reported that they had considered searching for the child while 65% actually had initiated a search.[277] Moreover, secondary infertility was higher among couples in which the woman previously had relinquished a child.[278] Other reported

---

270 See Deykin, Campbell & Patti, The Post-Adoption Experience of Surrendering Parents, 54 Am. J. Orthopsychiatry 271, 276-78 (1984) (women who surrender child for adoption perceive negative influence on marriage, fertility, and parenting); Millen & Roll, Solomon's Mothers: A Special Case of Pathological Bereavement, 55 Am. J. Orthopsychiatry 411, 418 (1985) (experience of mother relinquishing child is similar to pathological mourning, including feelings of intense loss, panic, anger, and incompleteness); Rynearson, Relinquishment and Its Maternal Complications, 139 Am. J. Psychiatry 338, 340 (1982) (relinquishment of child appears to be disjunctive event for women; subsequent maternal attachment is sought intensely).

271 See Hock, McBride & Gnezda, Maternal Separation Anxiety: Mother-Infant Separation from the Maternal Perspective, 60 Child Dev. 793, 794 (1989) (confirming separation anxiety and finding that many factors, including mother's basic personality, genetically determined biases, and cultural background are relevant).

272 See Millen & Roll, supra note 270, at 411-12 (discussing effects of relinquishment in extreme cases).

273 See id. at 413-17; Rynearson, supra note 270, at 338-39.

274 See Rynearson, supra note 270, at 339-40.

275 See id. at 339.

276 See Deykin, Campbell & Patti, supra note 270, at 272.

277 See id. at 274.

278 Secondary infertility is infertility among couples who already have had children. See

effects include marital disharmony (though the divorce rate among these couples was markedly lower) and both positive and negative child-bearing consequences.[279] Finally, there is an increasing body of anecdotal evidence concerning relinquishment as a result of the experiences of Mary Beth Whitehead and other surrogates.[280]

In contrast to voluntary adoption, studies also suggest that the negative effects of relinquishment actually may be exacerbated by a compelled surrender of the child. One study found that parents were more likely to search for the child when external factors, such as family pressure, were instrumental in their decision to relinquish the child.[281] By analogy, one might infer that the consequences of relinquishment may be even more difficult for surrogates required to surrender the child pursuant to a contractual promise than for those who relinquish the child in the absence of external legal coercion. Yet it may be at least as plausible to suggest that surrendering mothers in the adoption situation are more susceptible to the trauma of relinquishment than gestational hosts in the collaborative-reproductive arrangement precisely because the adoptive mother is under no legal compulsion to surrender a child even where she informally has agreed to do so before birth.[282] Indeed, it is likely that many surrendering mothers vacillate as to their decision for some time up to, and in some cases even after, the birth of the child.[283] This wavering may aggravate feelings of loss once the decision is made to surrender the child. In short, expectations may influence feelings. If the postrelinquishment experience of birth mothers is at all related to their previous feelings regarding the child, then it is possible that women who do not expect to raise the child may be relatively less affected by relinquishment. This possibility is suggested by one poll of surrogate mothers in which only one in five reported that relinquishment was the most difficult aspect of the arrangement.[284]

OTA, Infertility, supra note 1, at 50. It is distinguished from primary infertility, where the couple has had no children. See id. The rate of secondary infertility among the study participants was 16% as compared with 6% of the general population. See id. at 276.

[279] See id.

[280] Mary Beth Whitehead was the surrogate in the *Baby M* case. See In re Baby M, 109 N.J. 396, 537 A.2d 1227 (1988). For a narrative of her experiences immediately precipitated by her surrender of Baby M, see M. Whitehead & L. Schwartz-Nobel, A Mother's Story: The Truth About the Baby M Case 17-37 (1989). For the experiences of another surrogate, see A. Overvold, supra note 195, at 33.

[281] See Deykin, Campbell & Patti, supra note 270, at 274.

[282] Prebirth consent to adoption on the part of the birth mother is unenforceable in all fifty states. See Andrews, supra note 8, at 15-16.

[283] If there were not such vacillation before birth and for some period afterward, there would be little need for laws rendering void prebirth consent to adoption as well as laws permitting the birth mother to revoke her consent for a period of time after relinquishment. See id. at 19 (discussing these statutes).

[284] See A. Overvold, supra note 195, at 130.

The relinquishment argument is a vital component of the case for the priority of the gestational host. Nevertheless, more empirical evidence is necessary to evaluate the weight that should be accorded this claim and, in particular, the nature of postrelinquishment emotional effects upon the birth mother. We must determine whether these effects are intrinsic concomitants of the biological changes that occur during and after pregnancy, or whether they may be ameliorated by social influences and the birth mother's expectations regarding her role in the procreative arrangement.

Even if further research suggests that the harm of relinquishment is tangible, however, it is not clear that this effect should give the surrogate legal priority as the mother of the child. First, whatever harm redounds to the surrogate in the event of relinquishment must be weighed against a similar harm to the intended parents in the event that the surrogate does not turn over the child. Particularly where the intended parents are childless and infertile, the emotional significance of the loss of the child they expected to raise is undoubtedly great.[285] Second, and perhaps most important, the surrogate's claims for legal priority resulting from the harms of relinquishment must be evaluated in the context of her earlier contractual agreement to relinquish the child. Parties to contracts often regret having entered into enforceable agreements. In some cases, they may be disadvantaged greatly by the agreement; but as long as the agreement is entered into voluntarily,[286] the argument that the surrogate now regrets having made this choice lacks the moral force it otherwise might have.[287]

4. The Physical-Involvement Argument

It has been suggested by a number of writers that the physical process of bearing the child in itself, independent of considerations of bonding and the effects of relinquishment, carries significant moral weight in determining who should be considered the parent.[288] As one writer has stated:

> And from the woman's point of view? We can use this man's sperm or that one's to have our children. With this or that man as father, our bellies will swell, life will stir, milk will flow. . . . For a man, what makes the child *his* is his seed. For women, what makes the child ours

---

[285] See Kennell, Slayter & Klaus, supra note 235.

[286] See notes 294-303 and accompanying text infra (discussing exploitation and claim that surrogate's decision to enter into agreement is not voluntary).

[287] See notes 284-85 and accompanying text supra (weighing relinquishment argument against claims of intended parents).

[288] See, e.g., P. Chesler, Sacred Bond: The Legacy of Baby M 53-54 (1988) (comparing contribution of birth mother vis-á-vis that of sperm donor).

is the nurturance, the work of our bodies. Wherever the sperm came
from, it is in our bodies that our babies grow, and our physical presence and nurturance that make our babies ours.[289]

Inextricably intertwined with the notion of the birth mother's physical
contribution are claims predicated upon the bonding hypothesis, the effects on the mother of relinquishment, and other related issues which
have been considered in previous sections. This subsection attempts to
abstract from this nest of issues an argument based simply upon the
physical involvement of the gestational host.

The reality and extent of the physical involvement of the gestational
host in the procreative process is obviously paramount. The birth
mother risks sickness and inconvenience during pregnancy. She faces the
certain prospect of painful labor. She even risks the small but qualitatively infinite possibility of death. Throughout all of this discomfort and
uncertainty, it is her body which remains the cradle for the growing fetus. By comparison, the physical involvement of the sperm donor is de
minimis. While the egg donor physically risks more[290] than the sperm
donor, her level of physical involvement pales in comparison with that of
the gestational host. Consequently, the argument postulates that this
greater involvement should be the basis for recognizing the gestational
host as the mother of the child.

Notwithstanding the obvious fact that the gestational host is the
most important physical link in the procreative process, this argument
encounters difficulties similar to those of the arguments for the priority of
the genetic progenitors.[291] The nature of this claim is that the gestational
host has a kind of property right in the child. But, if so, then where she
has entered a contract to act as gestational host for another, she has
transferred this right.[292] Even assuming she could have property rights
in the child, the surrogate has no more of a claim to the "property" by
virtue of this argument than a builder has in a house constructed for
another.[293]

---

[289] B. Katz-Rothman, supra note 189, at 44 (emphasis in original).

[290] The egg is taken by laparoscopy, a surgical procedure by which ova are removed from
the ovaries of the woman. See OTA, Infertility, supra note 1, at 106.

[291] See notes 206-17 and accompanying text supra (reviewing arguments favoring genetic
progenitors on a "property rights" approach).

[292] See notes 206-17 and accompanying text supra (discussing property-rights argument
and transfer-of-rights argument in context of genetic progenitor). Where no contract exists,
however, the surrogate's greater level of physical involvement should be entitled to great
weight as evidence of the woman's intention to raise the child. See notes 308-20 and accompanying text infra (analyzing relevance of intention in procreative process).

[293] At a presentation which I gave recently at IIT-Chicago Kent Law School, various participants took issue with this metaphor. "Children are not houses," it was stated, "nor are
pregnant women housebuilders." I fully appreciate the relevance of this comment. Indeed, I
am arguing that children are not the subject of property rights, though one's procreational

If the argument of the gestational host's greater physical involvement is not a property claim, to what does it amount? One suspects that it is actually an argument predicated upon bonding, relinquishment, or the best interests of the child, or perhaps a combination of these other arguments. Excluding from the present argument claims based on the mother-infant bond, the effects of relinquishment, considerations of the child's best interests, and any theory predicated upon a kind of property analysis, virtually eliminates the argument of the greater physical involvement of the gestational host. Indeed, the argument appears to be a mere restatement of these other considerations.

5. The Exploitation and Commodification Arguments

Scholarly and legislative proposals defending the moral right of a woman to sell her gestational services have been the object of lively, if not vituperative, responses on the part of numerous writers, both in the legal literature[294] and the academic press.[295] The range and scope of these objections are too numerous and too deep to develop and to address systematically in this discussion.[296]

Despite their sheer number and variation, however, these diverse arguments have two main recurring themes. The first, the "exploitation argument," posits that women who enter into surrogate agreements, as a general matter, somehow are unfree with respect to this decision. This moral assessment typically is predicated upon a matrix of social and economic factors which are held to predispose the prospective surrogate to her decision. In the words of one commentator:

> When money animates the transfer of a human substance, the issue of exploitation arises. The danger is that the transferor is exploiting the

services are. My sole point here is that, *even if* the property metaphor were applicable to the transfer of a child, the gestational host would have no claim where the intended couple had compensated her.

[294] See O'Brien, Commercial Conceptions: A Breeding Ground for Surrogacy, 65 N.C.L. Rev. 127 (1986); Olsen, The Family and the Market: A Study of Ideology and Legal Reform, 96 Harv. L. Rev. 1497 (1983); Radin, Market-Inalienability, 100 Harv. L. Rev. 1849 (1987); Wikler, Society's Response to the New Reproductive Technologies: The Feminist Perspectives, 59 S. Cal. L. Rev. 1043 (1986); Note, supra note 79; Note, Surrogate Mother Agreements: Contemporary Legal Aspects of a Biblical Notion, 16 U. Rich. L. Rev. 467 (1982); Note, supra note 2; Recent Developments, An Incomplete Picture: The Debate About Surrogate Motherhood, 8 Harv. Women's L.J. 231 (1985).

[295] See Annas, Baby M: Babies (and Justice) for Sale, 17 Hastings Center Rep. 13 (1987); Annas, Contracts to Bear a Child: Compassion or Commercialism?, 11 Hastings Center Rep. 23 (1981); Ince, Inside the Surrogate Industry, in Test-Tube Women (R. Arditti ed. 1984); Krimmel, supra note 196; Merrick, Selling Reproductive Rights: Policy Issues in Surrogate Motherhood, 8 Pol. & Life Sci. 161 (1990); Rothman, The Meanings of Choice in Reproductive Technology, in Test-Tube Women (R. Arditti ed. 1984); Woliver, Reproductive Technologies and Surrogacy: Policy Concerns for Women, 8 Pol. & Life Sci. 185 (1990).

[296] For a legal and philosophical defense of surrogacy, see Hill, supra note 181.

desperate need of the transferee and that the transferee is exploiting the
financial need of the transferor. . . . For some of the same reasons that
organ donation is prohibited, commercial surrogacy should be
prohibited.[297]

Unlike the exploitation argument, which focuses upon whether the surrogate's decision was the product of causally determinative influences, the
second general theme, the "commodification argument," focuses upon
the object of the transfer. The commodification argument holds that certain intrinsic capacities or properties of the individual should not be
alienable or commodified on the open market, and that a woman's reproductive ability is one such capacity. Professor Radin, a proponent of this
view, has stated:

> Market-inalienability [of surrogacy] might be grounded in a judgment
> that commodification of women's reproductive capacity is harmful for
> the identity aspect of their personhood and in a judgment that the
> closeness of paid surrogacy to baby-selling harms our self-conception
> too deeply.   There is certainly the danger that women's attributes,
> such as height, eye color, race, intelligence, and athletic ability, will be
> monetized. Surrogates with "better" qualities will command higher
> prices by virtue of those qualities.[298]

The frequent allusions to organ donation,[299] prostitution,[300] and
baby-selling,[301] are tempting and powerful analogues. These allusions
run throughout the exploitation and commodification arguments. While
this Article has undertaken an examination of the philosophical justification for these claims elsewhere,[302] it is worth noting the basic difficulties
with each of these two arguments.

The difficulties come in two forms, internal and external. The external difficulty, which will be discussed at the end of this subsection, is that
these arguments are too powerful—they do not argue in favor of the gestational host. Rather, they militate against the very legitimacy of surrogacy as a legally permissible institution. The internal difficulties, by
contrast, stem from flaws in the internal structure of these arguments.
For example, proponents of the exploitation argument never elaborate a
theory of exploitation. This failure sometimes manifests itself in the con-

---

[297] O'Brien, supra note 294, at 142-43.

[298] Radin, supra note 294, at 1932.

[299] Barbara Katz-Rothman claims that "surrogacy is exactly the same as organ donation."
See Levine, Whose Baby Is It?, Village Voice, Nov. 26, 1986, at 17.

[300] One writer has equated the freedom to sell one's reproductive services with "the freedom
to prostitute oneself." See G. Corea, supra note 223, at 227.

[301] See Radin, supra note 294, at 1932.

[302] See Hill, supra note 181, at 109-34 (examining coercion and exploitation as applied to
surrogate arrangements); id. at 134-46 (examining commodification argument).

flation of the concepts of exploitation and coercion.[303] More fundamentally, however, situations involving exploitation are not adequately distinguished from those which do not. For example, how is the situation of a woman from a lower-middle income family who enters a surrogate arrangement distinguished from the situation of this same woman who instead takes a job cleaning bathrooms in a bus station—assuming that this latter alternative is not itself exploitative? Let us assume that the compensation is at a similar rate and that the woman has similar alternative prospects. What distinguishes these two scenarios? If the answer depends upon morally distinguishing the two activities—that cleaning bathroom floors is a morally permissible use of one's body while becoming a surrogate is not—then the respondent is confronted with a fundamental difficulty. The opponent of surrogacy is arguing that surrogacy is wrong because it is exploitative. She cannot then claim, when asked what makes surrogacy exploitative, that the two situations are distinguishable because surrogacy is wrong. This would constitute a blatantly circular argument. If surrogate arrangements are wrong because they are exploitative, then they cannot be exploitative because they are wrong.

However, if what distinguishes these two situations is that surrogacy involves the use of some intimate personal capacity which should not be the subject of barter, while bathroom cleaning does not, then the exploitation argument collapses into the commodification argument. Once the opponent of surrogacy makes this move, she relinquishes the claim that the decision to become a surrogate is, in some sense, *unfree*. Rather, it is wrong because it alienates a fundamental aspect of one's personhood. This reasoning, however, replaces the claim of exploitation with that of commodification.

The commodification argument similarly encounters a number of fundamental philosophical difficulties. The notion of commodification is functionally dependent upon drawing a distinction between a realm of personal capacities and properties which may be the subject of market alienation and those which may not. In one of the most careful and systematic elaborations of the commodification argument, Professor Radin states:

A better view of personhood should understand many kinds of particu-

---

[303] Coercion could be said to occur whenever one's options are reduced by forces external to oneself. See A. Wertheimer, Coercion 40 (1987). Exploitation does not reduce options. Indeed, the exploitative situation typically occurs where an individual is given an additional choice which she cannot easily refuse. See id. at 39 (discussing exploitation of another's existing dilemma); Feinberg, Noncoercive Exploitation, in Paternalism 201 (R. Sartonius ed. 1983) (distinguishing coercion and exploitation by whether subject's options or interests are affected).

412   NEW YORK UNIVERSITY LAW REVIEW   [Vol. 66:353

lars—one's politics, work, religion, family, love, sexuality, friendships, altruism, experiences, wisdom, moral commitments, character, and personal attributes—as integral to the self. To understand any of these as monetizable or completely detachable from the person . . . is to do violence to our deepest understanding of what it is to be human.[304]

Notwithstanding her painstaking historical and philosophical analysis devoted to distinguishing "integral" or "intrinsic" from "extrinsic" personal attributes, Radin's view suffers from three fundamental flaws. First, no principle is presented by which essentially internal, noncommodifiable attributes may be distinguished from external, commodifiable attributes. There is little reason to believe that the attributes which Radin cites—political action, work, love, sexuality, family, experience, and wisdom—are anything more than an ad hoc assortment of incongruous elements invested with varying degrees of importance in our culture. Moreover, without a principle distinguishing the internal and external, it is impossible to make future determinations as to which elements are basic to our sense of self.

Second, Radin admits that drawing the line between the internal and the external, the inalienable and the alienable, is ultimately a moral judgment.[305] If one's reproductive capacity is an attribute which should not be subject to commodification, reproductive capacity will be deemed an essentially internal attribute. But this logic reverses the role of premise and conclusion. It attempts to determine whether a certain attribute is sufficiently internal to our personal identity so that we can render a moral conclusion about whether the attribute should be commodifiable. But Radin's analysis appears to *begin* with this moral assessment regarding the permissibility of commodifying an attribute.[306] In essence, there would be no need to employ the commodification argument if we knew in advance that a particular capacity or attribute should not be commodified. Yet Radin's argument appears to require exactly this prior determination.

Finally, as a practical matter, we cannot sort neatly between inherently intrinsic and extrinsic attributes on the basis of the attribute itself. For example, while Radin suggests that personal attributes should not be commodifiable,[307] they are routinely the subject of commodification. Indeed, it is difficult to imagine anything other than personal attributes which are commodified any time anyone is hired to do a job. The model uses her face and physique, the construction worker uses her physical

---

[304] Radin, supra note 294, at 1905-06.
[305] See id. at 1908.
[306] See id. at 1859.
[307] See id. at 1905-06.

strength, and the professional utilizes her intelligence, character, and motivation—all attributes which go to the very heart of their personhoods. It is striking that those attributes which typically are denigrated as the more superficial or less intrinsic to the individual, such as physical beauty, eye color, and height, are the same attributes which so trouble the proponent of the commodification argument. Indeed, it would be more logical, on this view, to place attributes such as character, personality, and intelligence, which generally are thought to be central to our innermost being, beyond the reach of the market and to permit the commodification of physical attributes such as eye color and sexual attractiveness. On such a view, prostitution would be permitted while teaching philosophy would be placed outside the realm of the market.

In general, the exploitation and commodification arguments raise profound ethical questions which require careful attention and analysis. Unfortunately, this attention has been lacking, even in scholarly appeals to these arguments.

The arguments surveyed in this subsection take us somewhat far afield from the central focus of this piece. We have examined them briefly, however, because of their purported relevance to the parental status of the gestational host. Nevertheless, these arguments encounter a more fundamental difficulty for purposes of the present Article. Even if the exploitation and commodification arguments have some merit, they ultimately are not arguments favoring the parental priority of the gestational host. While they suggest that collaborative-reproductive arrangements should be regulated, even banned, they do not establish that the gestational host is the real "parent." In short, an argument against the social or ethical permissibility of surrogate arrangements is not necessarily an argument in favor of the moral priority of the surrogate as the mother of the child. If such arrangements are valid, the claim of the gestational host as the true mother of the child will have to depend upon other considerations.

IV

THE CLAIMS OF INTENTIONALITY

The previous section considered the claims for the moral priority of the biological progenitors of the child, both the genetic sources and the gestational host. It is time now to consider briefly the possible claims favoring the priority of the intended parents. In this section, I pose the situation of the couple from the opening scenario.[308] This is the case of the intended parents who have no biological connection with the child,

---

[308] See text accompanying notes 19-20 supra.

414   *NEW YORK UNIVERSITY LAW REVIEW*   [Vol. 66:353

but who have orchestrated the procreative relationship from the outset. They have brought together sperm and egg through in-vitro fertilization, and they have contracted for the services of a surrogate to bear the child they intend to raise. What reasons favor recognizing the intended parents as the procreators and, therefore, as the legal parents of the child?

Three arguments can be made for the moral priority of the intended parents. The first focuses upon the prima-facie importance of the intended parents in the procreative relationship. The second concerns the unfairness of permitting the surrogate to break the promise to relinquish the child. Finally, the third addresses important policy considerations in assuring the identity of the parents of the child from the time of conception. These arguments should trump the relatively weaker claims of either the gestational host[309] or the biological progenitors.[310]

A. The "But For"-Causation Argument

Notwithstanding the competing claims of the various biological progenitors of the child, there is one essential fact favoring the moral and legal priority of the intended parents. The intended parents are, so to speak, the "first cause" of the procreative relationship; they are the ones who have engineered the birth of the child. Their desire and intention set into motion the entire process that begins with securing gamete donors and proceeds through the arrangement to have a woman bear the child.

The importance accorded to the intended parents' role as the first cause in the procreative relationship thus depends on adopting a nonbiologically based view of parenthood. What is essential to parenthood is not the biological tie between parent and child but the preconception *intention* to have a child, accompanied by undertaking whatever action is necessary to bring a child into the world. On this view, biological procreation is one way, albeit the most common one, to proceed in having a child. What is fundamental in rendering a biological progenitor a parent is not the biological tie itself, however, but the preconception intention and the preconception and postconception acts which the biological relation evinces.

It might be argued that this is a peculiar approach to the determination of parental status since it places a mental element, intention, over the tangible, biological tie. But just as mental state is relevant in other

---

[309] See notes 219-44 and accompanying text supra (maternal-bonding argument); notes 245-69 and accompanying text supra (best-interests-of-the-child argument); notes 270-87 and accompanying text supra (relinquishment argument); notes 288-93 and accompanying text supra (physical-involvement argument); notes 294-307 and accompanying text supra (exploitation/commodification argument).

[310] See notes 193-205 and accompanying text supra (genetic-identity argument); notes 206-17 and accompanying text supra (property-rights argument).

areas of the law, including contracts, torts, and criminal law, perhaps it is time that the determination of parental status similarly depend upon the preconception intent of the parties.[311]

Slightly recast, the first argument maintains that, while all of the players in the procreative arrangement are necessary in bringing a child into the world, *the child would not have been born but for the efforts of the intended parents*. The efforts of the biological progenitors are instrumental to the act of procreation, but the status of "parent" should go to the persons who constitute the "but for" cause of the child's birth.

It might be argued in response that the child would not have been born but for the assistance of the gamete donors and the gestational host. Thus, the position of the intended parents is not superior in this respect. Still, the position of the intended parents is distinct from that of the biological progenitors in two ways. First, the intended parents are the first cause, or the prime movers, of the procreative relationship. The others are participants only after the intention and actions of the intended parents to have a child. Second, while *some* gestational host and genetic progenitors are necessary to achieve the intention of the intended parents to have a child, no *particular* biological progenitors are necessary. Where one prospective biological contributor is not available, the couple can always seek the services of others. Thus, no one but the intended parents stands in the relationship with the child of being the *but for* cause of the child's existence. This unique causal relationship with the child should afford the intended parents primary status as the parents of the child.

B.   The Contract Argument

The second argument in defense of the priority of the intended parents focuses upon the preconception commitment of others, most notably, the gestational host, to refrain from claiming parental rights. The argument here is familiar: the gestational host and the genetic progenitors should be held to their original promises not to seek any form of parental rights in the child. There are two aspects to this argument, one deontological or rights-based and the other consequentialist. The deontological strain holds that people generally should be held to their promises simply because promise-keeping is a good in itself. The predicament of the intended parents is poignant precisely because the surrogate's promise is the very basis for her involvement in the procreative relationship in the first place. Absent a commitment on her part, the intended parents could seek the assistance of another. But where the

---

[311] See Note, supra note 72, at 195 (family law traditionally has not relied upon mental elements).

416 *NEW YORK UNIVERSITY LAW REVIEW* [Vol. 66:353

gestational host, or the genetic progenitor, for that matter, has gained access to the procreative relationship initiated by another, she should not be permitted the double injustice of reneging and, more importantly, retaining custody of the child.

The consequentialist strain of this argument emphasizes the reliance of the intended parents upon the promise of the other parties in the procreative relationship. The intended parents rely, both financially and emotionally, to their detriment on the promises of the biological progenitors and gestational host. They rely financially by purchasing the material essentials of child-rearing, including baby furniture, clothes, toys, and other accessories. They may even move or expand their home to accommodate the new arrival. If the promise of the other parties were not enforceable, the intended parents could not make these preparations without the possibility of losing their investment.

More importantly, the intended parents rely emotionally on the promises of the others to refrain from claiming parental rights in the child. They rely by preparing themselves psychologically for parenthood and all that it entails. They also rely emotionally to the extent that they have interacted with the surrogate and anticipated the birth of the child.[312]

It has been argued that the gestational host, in particular, should not be held to her promise because of the unpredictable nature of the development of feelings for the child while she is pregnant.[313] Elsewhere, I have proposed guidelines to mitigate this possibility.[314] At any rate, whether the claims of the gestational host should be honored above the claims of the intended parents depends upon a weighing of the broader issues raised by the bonding hypothesis and the compelled-relinquishment argument.[315]

---

[312] Even here, the intended parents' reliance cannot be absolute. The surrogate retains her constitutional rights to obtain an abortion. See text accompanying notes 165-81 supra (discussing surrogate's right of privacy). Nevertheless, particularly during the last trimester, after the point of viability, the surrogate's commitment to having the child will be clear. Reliance on the part of the intended parents after this point would be justified.

[313] See Suh, supra note 9, at 363.

[314] I have proposed a rule that only women who previously have had children should be permitted to become surrogates. See Hill, supra note 181, at 361. This rule would enable the prospective gestational host to predict more adequately her feelings during pregnancy. Also, the process of psychological screening of applicants should be made more rigid to weed out those who would be expected to have a particularly difficult time with relinquishment. See id. at 362. Finally, surrogate contracts should receive judicial screening and approval. See id. at 366. This judicial oversight would require the surrogate to affirm publicly her promise and intention to relinquish the child. This requirement might reduce further the number of surrogates who are uncertain about relinquishing the child.

[315] See notes 219-44 and accompanying text supra (discussing bonding hypothesis); notes 270-87 and accompanying text supra (discussing compelled-relinquishment argument); conclusion infra (discussing relative weights given to these claims).

C. The Avoidance-of-Uncertainty Argument

Where the identity of the parents is not determined at the time of conception, all parties are affected adversely. If the gestational host or the genetic progenitors of the child legally are permitted to claim parental rights in the child, contrary to their earlier promises, then the identity of the child's parents will remain unanswered as litigation may drag on for years after the birth of the child. The ultimate solution may render all concerned parties—the intended parents, the biological progenitors, and the child—victims of the uncertainty.

If there is any truth to the notion that the feelings of the gestational host toward the child are influenced by her expectation of raising the child, then the surrogate may develop proprietary feelings toward the child because she retains the possibility of challenging the claims of the intended parents. However, if this prospect is not open to her, the gestational host will be less likely to entertain such sentiments toward the child. Of course, this claim is dependent upon the empirical observation that the development of maternal feelings is influenced by social factors such as the expectation of raising the child.

From the standpoint of the intended parents, I have argued already that it is important that they be able to rely on their expected status as parents in making preparations, both financial and emotional, for the arrival of the child.[316] Where the prospect remains open that their claims may be subordinated to those of one of the biological progenitors, the logistic and emotional preparation by expectant parents may be inhibited, rendering the transition to parenthood more difficult.[317]

Finally, the uncertainty regarding the identity of the parents takes its most compelling form from the standpoint of the child. In cases where litigation over parental rights takes years, the child may grow up with uncertainty regarding the identity of her parents. This uncertainty only is aggravated by the likely solution to the conflict—a decision dividing the child's time among joint custodians or, as in *Baby M*, a disposition which grants custody to one couple and visitation privileges to another.[318] Permitting challenges to the parental status of the intended parents virtually ensures that the child will grow up in the functional equivalent of a broken home.[319] For all of these reasons, the identity of

---

[316] See text accompanying notes 312-15 supra.

[317] Studies indicate that paternal anxiety is inversely related to the extent of participation on the part of a new father. See Fein, supra note 219, at 341. In other words, once the role of the father is established, he is more likely to feel a part of the child-rearing process with a concomitant reduction of psychological anxiety. This phenomenon might be analogous to that which the expectant intended parents undergo.

[318] See In re Baby M, 109 N.J. 396, 466, 537 A.2d 1227, 1263 (1988).

[319] Of course, a rule providing that the intended parents will take the child unless the surro-

the parents should be determinate *ab initio* from the time of conception.[320]

CONCLUSION

With the expanding popularity of the various collaborative-reproductive techniques and arrangements, including surrogate parenting, it is increasingly imperative to settle the question of parental status in collaborative-reproduction arrangements. Having considered the arguments in defense of the claims of the genetic progenitors, the gestational host, and the intended parents, it is clear why the intended parents should be considered the "parents" of the child born of the reproductive arrangement in the opening scenario.

This Article has argued that the genetic relationship, in itself, should be accorded very little moral weight in the determination of parental status. Claims based on the biological similarity of genetic progenitor and child and those predicated on a kind of quasi-property right in the child simply do not withstand sustained scrutiny. Thus, though the genetic tie historically has been accorded great significance, the genetic link per se places the genetic progenitor in the least-compelling position of all parties in the procreative relationship.

What can be said of the claims of the gestational host? The genre of arguments which predicates the surrogate's priority as parent upon the best interests of the child are not convincing. Similarly, the claims based upon her greater physical involvement in the procreative process, as well as those based upon a number of social and ethical concerns, are of little moral force. At best, the social and ethical arguments suggest only that certain forms of collaborative reproduction, particularly surrogate arrangements, should be regulated or prohibited altogether. They do not speak to the moral priority of the gestational host.

This leaves the arguments founded upon the bonding hypothesis and the harms predicted to result from compelled relinquishment of the child. As we have seen, empirical support for the postnatal mother-to-

---

gate changes her mind, in which case she will be awarded full parental rights, would eliminate this uncertainty from the standpoint of the child. The difficulty with this rule, however, is that with traditional surrogacy, where the intended father is also the sperm donor, parental rights would be split between him and the surrogate. The child would continue to live a life divided between two families. This outcome would be the case unless the proposed rule not only gave the surrogate full rights as mother, but also cut off all rights possessed by the sperm donor/ intended father.

[320] The gestation host should be permitted to renounce the contract at any time before conception has occurred. Furthermore, because the designation of parental status in the intended parents does *not* entail that the gestational host forfeits her constitutional privacy rights, she will retain the right to have an abortion. See notes 165-81 and accompanying text supra (discussing distinction between right of privacy and right of procreation).

infant bond is equivocal at best. Indeed, a preponderance of the more recent evidence contradicts the hypothesis. Nonetheless, it would be preposterous to argue categorically that the gestational host harbors no feelings for the child at birth. The gestational host interacts intimately and directly with the fetus with increasing frequency from the time of quickening. Thus, in some cases, the surrogate possesses strong attachment to the child by the time of birth. But even if these feelings amount to a prenatal mother-to-infant bond, they fail to trump the claims of others. The bonding hypothesis is significant only to the extent that it suggests that it will be more difficult for the gestational host to relinquish the child than for the intended parents to give up their dream of parenting the child. Thus, it appears that the bulk of the claims for the priority of the gestational host boils down to the deleterious consequences of relinquishment, exacerbated as this may be by the lingering effects of the prenatal bond.

It is not likely that the relinquishment argument itself will be sufficient to accord the gestational host legal recognition as the child's mother. Ultimately, the weight of the relinquishment argument will depend in part upon further empirical assessment of the harms of relinquishment. Minimally, however, the argument for the priority of the gestational host has been overstated. Unexamined assertions predicated upon the best interests of the child, the bonding hypothesis, and the greater physical involvement of the gestational host in bearing the child, among others, have been the result of both a mischaracterization of the empirical evidence and a superficial assessment of the moral weight of this evidence.

This Article concludes that the balance of equities favors the claims of the intended parents over those of the gestational host. The moral significance of the intended parents' role as prime movers in the procreative relationship, the preconception promise of the biological progenitors not to claim rights in the child, and the relative importance of having the identity of the parents determined from conception onward outweigh the potential harm to the gestational host in compelled relinquishment. This conclusion, of course, will not be well-regarded in all quarters. An important reason for this skepticism is that a fundamentally biological conception of parenthood is ingrained deeply in the ethos of our culture. It continues to influence our most profound intuitions concerning the nature of parenthood and parental rights.

Nevertheless, the biological conception does not square with a number of other, equally deep, intuitions. It is not consistent with the modern understanding that parenthood is as much a social, psychological, and intentional status as it is a biological one. It also is inconsistent with the sentiment that persons are not invariably and irrevocably predisposed to a role in life—even that of parenthood—by virtue of the inexorable workings of biology. Finally, and most fundamentally, the biological conception of parenthood cannot be reconciled with the belief that other moral considerations sometimes may override claims predicated upon the biological relationship. In essence, the claims of biology cannot be deemed to trump invariably the moral claims of those who entertain no biological connection with the child.

[4]
Wisconsin Women's Law Journal

VOL. VII   1992-93

AND BABY MAKES THREE — OR FOUR, OR FIVE, OR SIX: REDEFINING THE FAMILY AFTER THE REPROTECH REVOLUTION*

*R. Alta Charo, J.D.***

"After four miscarriages, Adria Blum was ecstatic when her son was born four years ago. The child's father, Barry Chersky, comforted Blum in the delivery room during the many hours of labor.

So did Adria's lover, Marilyn. So did Barry's lover, Michael Baiad. Now the four Oakland residents, all in their 40s, share custody of Ari, a rambunctious 3-year-old conceived through artificial insemination. He feels sorry for other kids because they don't all have a Mommy, a Daddy, a Marilyn and a Michael."[2]

The Ten O'Clock News in New York City used to run a public service announcement in the 1970s that read: "It's ten o'clock. Do you know where your children are?" Perhaps it's time to update the message to read: "It's the 1990s. Do you know who all your parents are?" The 1990s offer a marvelous opportunity to rethink our prejudices concerning the definition of a family. Our emotional attachment to a definition based on blood, our modern tendency toward a definition based on contract, and our legal definitions based on fictional re-creations of the biological nuclear family are all ripe for reform and integration. The result could be an

---

* The author wishes to acknowledge the very helpful comments of the participants at the 1992 A.A.A.S./A.B.A. conference on genetic advances, sponsored by the Department of Energy's human genome project, at which an earlier version of this paper was presented, and the audience participants at the March 1993 TJWL conference. She also thanks Peter Carstensen, Mary Coombs, Norm Fost, Dirk Hartog, Neal Komesar, John Robertson, Walter Wadlington, Alan Weisbard, and Dan Wikler for their thoughtful comments on subsequent drafts. Special thanks are due to Gay W. Seidman, for encouraging the author to address the subject at all. A companion article to this piece will be published in Texas Journal of Women and the Law, 1994.

** J.D., Assistant Professor of Law and Medical Ethics, University of Wisconsin, Madison WI 53706.

2. David Tuller, *Gays and Lesbians Try Co-Parenting: Families With 2 Moms, 2 Dads*, S.F. CHRON., Feb. 4, 1993 at A1.

expansion in the number of adults recognized as having parental ties to a particular child, an end to unthinking opposition to gay and lesbian or group marriage, and a flowering of classical liberal theory, in which the role of government is to facilitate individual choice rather than shape it.

This redefinition of "family" is timely for many reasons. First, the increased frequency of divorce and step-parenting has made traditional allocations of parental rights and responsibilities unworkable in light of the day-to-day experience of children living with "step-parents." Second, the frequency of single persons and gay and lesbian couples seeking to parent has strained the two-person, two-gender model of parenthood. Third, the advent of so-called "gestational surrogacy" has clouded identification of "biological" maternity, thus for the first time opening the door to an examination of just what it is about biological parenthood that entitles it to such extraordinary respect.

Finally, the human genome project promises to usher in an era of genetic exploration and invention.[3] As with nineteenth-century advances, this knowledge may well become the basis for profound shifts in public thinking and public policy, just as Darwinian evolutionary theory became the basis of Spencerian libertarian theory and subsequent eugenic social policy.[4] With increasing understanding of genetic influences on physical and psychological phenotypical expression comes the temptation to identify genetic coding as the ultimate expression of personal identity, and genetic linkages as the fundamental expression of human relationships.[5] But such a development would be overly reductionist and lead to unfortunate public policy.

Indeed, the tragic stories of Baby Jessica, Kimberly Mays, and Baby Pete, which captivated the American public in 1993, demonstrate beyond question that simplistic and reductionist approaches fail to capture the emotional complications and the public attitudes toward parenting. In those three cases, a child ended up with her biological parents (Jessica), rearing parent (Kimberly), and both (Pete).

---

3. *See, e.g., Committee on Mapping and Sequencing the Human Genome*, MAPPING AND SEQUENCING THE HUMAN GENOME 22-24 (1988); DANIEL J. KEVLES & LEROY HOOD, THE CODE OF CODES: SCIENTIFIC AND SOCIAL ISSUES IN THE HUMAN GENOME PROJECT (Daniel J. Kevles & Leroy Hood eds., 1992); JERRY E. BISHOP & MICHAEL WALDHOLZ, GENOME: THE STORY OF THE MOST ASTONISHING SCIENTIFIC ADVENTURE OF OUR TIME — THE ATTEMPTS TO MAP ALL THE GENES IN THE HUMAN BODY 15-27 (1990); LOIS WINGERSON, MAPPING OUR GENES: THE GENOME PROJECT AND THE FUTURE OF MEDICINE (1990); JOEL DAVIS, MAPPING THE CODE: THE HUMAN GENOME PROJECT AND THE CHOICES OF MODERN SCIENCE 3-12 (1991).

4. *See, e.g.,* RICHARD C. LEWONTIN, BIOLOGY AS IDEOLOGY: THE DOCTRINE OF DNA 25-26, 74, 76, 241-3, 42-51 (1991); DOROTHY NELKIN & LAURENCE TANCREDI, DANGEROUS DIAGNOSTICS: THE SOCIAL POWER OF BIOLOGICAL INFORMATION 11-12 (1991); DAVID SUZUKI & PETER KNUDTSON, GENETHICS: THE ETHICS OF ENGINEERING LIFE 20-22, 26-27 (1990); DANIEL J. KEVLES, IN THE NAME OF EUGENICS: GENETICS AND THE USES OF HUMAN HEREDITY (1986).

5. *See, e.g.,* RUTH HUBBARD & ELIJAH WALD, EXPLODING THE GENE MYTH (1993).

Baby Jessica, relinquished at birth by her biological mother and a man incorrectly acting as her biological father, was placed with prospective adoptive parents in another state. Very soon thereafter, the birth mother revoked her consent, and the correctly identified biological father refused his consent. After a tortured two-year legal battle, Baby Jessica was returned to her birth parents, now married to one another, while her rearing parents sobbed. They had been portrayed as having superior parenting skills and offering a better chance for a happy home for the child. But the rapidity with which the birth mother revoked her consent, the absence of consent from a correctly identified biological father, and the indisputable biological linkage to the birth mother and her husband militated against leaving Jessica with the rearing parents. Indeed, many commentators opined that the real tragedy here was that the case was not resolved eighteen months earlier.[6]

Kimberly Mays, on the other hand, successfully halted all contact with her biological parents, despite their never having consented to her relinquishment. Mays was switched at birth with another infant, and her biological parents, the Twiggs, reared the other girl, who died in her childhood from a congenital heart defect. Medical treatment for the girl revealed that she could not be the biological daughter of the Twiggs, and after her death these parents tracked down the Mays family as those who had gone home with their biological daughter. Following a tense period of visitation by Kimberly with her biological family, her rearing father requested a temporary end to contact, the Twiggs sought a recognition of their legal status as Kimberly's parents, and Kimberly sought a court order to sever all ties to the Twiggs. A Florida court granted Kimberly her requested relief.[7]

Baby Pete was relinquished at birth by his birth mother and an incorrectly identified genetic father. When the correctly identified genetic father emerged, separated though still legally married to the birth mother, it appeared that a Baby Jessica-style resolution would require relinquishment of the infant by the rearing parents. Instead, the court, with acquiescence of the parties, declared the genetic father to be the legal father, with visitation rights and support responsibilities. It terminated the parental rights of the birth mother, as per her wishes, and declared the rearing mother to be the adoptive, legal, and custodial mother of the child. Of course, as one father was already in the picture, the rearing father was granted no status other than that of a step-parent.[8]

These three cases tested the sympathies of the American public, which wavered wildly among preferring biology over adoption, intention

6. C. McHugh, *Adoption Contests Not Common - But Risks Are*, CHI. DAILY L. BULL., Aug. 30, 1993, at 3.

7. H. Grezlak, *Family Law Attorneys Split Over Decision In Mays Case*, LEGAL INTELLIGENCER, Aug. 20, 1993, at 1.

8. Judith Gaines, *Unique Adoption Ruling; Both Sides Cheer Settlement That Shares Vt. Boy*, BOSTON GLOBE, Aug. 21, 1993, at 1.

over genetics, and happiness over everything. They demonstrated that the law's attempt to make biology (read: genetics and gestation) and contract (read: adoption and surrogacy) yield to public policy (read: heterosexual, marital families that resemble biological families in the wild) is flawed, because no one of these factors can easily and consistently outweigh all the others.

This paper will review the inconsistencies in European and American legal definitions of the family. Following a description of the competing claims of gestational, genetic, and contractual relationships to preferential treatment in cases of contested parenthood, the paper concludes that each type of relationship has been made to yield to significant nonbiological concerns. Thus, over time, biology and intent to parent have been sacrificed to the need for orderly transmission of property between generations, stability of marital units as the fundamental structure of social organization, and finally, protection of children's perceived best interests.

As it appears that social policy provides an acceptable reason to violate the integrity of parent-child relationships, this paper argues that social policy could similarly be used to maintain that integrity. While eschewing empirical arguments on the administrability or psychological superiority of expanded family definitions as beyond the scope of this paper, the paper does maintain that the compartmentalization, commercialization, and contractualization of reproductive materials and relationships offer an intriguing opportunity to re-examine some of the assumptions of current family law.

Specifically, the paper argues that the preference for heterosexual couples as parents is unwarranted, and that single persons, gay and lesbian couples, and larger groups of adults may serve equally well as parents. Furthermore, expanding the definition of parenthood to permit all genetic, gestational, and contractual parents to be recognized permanently and simultaneously could spare courts the task of identifying which adults to discard from the child's life. This abandonment of legal fictions — which maintain that a child has at most two parents of different gender, regardless of biological and psychological reality — is a recognition that law need not slavishly follow cramped visions of nature but could instead facilitate broad visions of justice.

THE GENETIC MODEL OF THE FAMILY

The blood ties between parent and child have almost mythological significance in every culture.[9] They represent both the act of procreation and the physical reflection of the parent's body in the body of the child.[10] The importance of genetic ties is confirmed by research suggesting that

---

9. *See, e.g.,* NANCY CHODOROW, THE REPRODUCTION OF MOTHERING: PSYCHOANALYSIS OF GENDER 13-30 (1978).

10. *See, e.g., Id.* at 202-203; ARTHUR D. SOROSKY, ANNETTE BARAN & REUBEN PANNOR, THE ADOPTION TRIANGLE 55-72 (1978).

many psychological attributes may also be influenced by genetic heritage,[11] although environmental influences may swamp these effects.[12] "In sum," states one commentator, "it is only natural that our sublime and complex feelings regarding this issue reflect precisely the sentiment that law should preserve as a family unit that which nature has rendered genetically similar."[13]

The emotional significance of that biological link became enshrined in religious traditions that grappled with death and the finiteness of humankind. Many cultures and religious traditions, such as Judaism, hold that there is no formal "afterlife." Rather, we live on through our children, a kind of limited, genetic immortality.[14] Their memories of us continue our existence. And when the memories fail, a small part of ourselves, our genes and our traits, still persist. It is no coincidence, then, that Jewish tradition dictates that a man marry his brother's widow if the brother should die childless.[15] To do less would be to allow the brother's genes to go untransmitted, surely condemning him to true death.[16]"The significance of the genetic connection between parent and child," writes one commentator, "undoubtedly is part of what makes infertility a painful experience. While adoption may satisfy one's desire to nurture a child, adoption cannot satisfy the yearning to create the child and to watch as a version of oneself unfolds and develops."[17] And it is the very fact that many reproductive technologies involve relinquishing access to children who are one's genetic progeny that has led some to condemn the practice as "unnatural" or "immoral."[18]

But it is easy to place too much mystical importance on genetic connections. After all, there is no statistically significant genetic difference between a genetic parent and child and the genetic relationship between full siblings.[19] It is the added psychological aspects of parenting that give the parental genetic connection such an entitlement to legal recognition. Nor should the fact that one's child shares one's genes become the basis for a property rights argument, in which the child is in some sense "owned" by the parent. Not only is this a dangerous doctrine that long led

---

11. EDWARD WILSON, ON HUMAN NATURE 20-25 (1978).

12. RICHARD C. LEWONTIN, STEVEN ROSE & LEON KAMIN, NOT IN OUR GENES: BIOLOGY, IDEOLOGY AND HUMAN NATURE 265-290 (1984).

13. John L. Hill, *What Does it Mean to be a "Parent"? The Claims of Biology as the Basis for Parental Rights*, 66 N.Y.U. L. REV. 353, 390 (1991).

14. ROBERT J. LIFTON, THE LIFE OF THE SELF 32 (1983).

15. *Deuteronomy* 25:3-10.

16. Apparently, the ancient Israelites did not consider that the brother's genes would also be transmitted by his sisters, cousins, and other blood relatives.

17. Hill, *supra* note 13, at 389.

18. Steven M. Recht, *M is For Money: Baby M and the Surrogate Motherhood Controversy*, 37 AM. U.L. REV., 1013, 1021 (1988).

19. Office of Technology Assessment of the Congress of the United States, GENETIC WITNESS: FORENSIC USES OF DNA TECHNOLOGY, 1992.

to child abuse and child labor, it fails to distinguish between owning the raw materials and owning the creation arising from them.[20]

Thus, the emphasis on biological formation of families may overvalue the significance of genetic linkages. Further, it marginalizes some children and adults with a significant involvement in the family. It ignores, for example, the frequent presence in nonadoptive families of children with biological ties to only one of the parents. Such children, when unrelated to the *marital* partner of the mother, were until recently deemed illegitimate, severely disadvantaging them and their mothers. The biological model of the family, with this overlay of insistence upon expressing biological relationships within a socially sanctioned, heterosexual marriage, has resulted in the creation of a grand presumption, to wit, that all "real" families follow this biological model.

But the reality has always been that some families have more than two parents. Some became parents by virtue of biology, a bond that cannot be broken no matter how many legal proceedings are used to push the biological parents out of the child's life. Others became parents by contract, and by virtue of marriage to the child's mother or contract with the state created a psychological, economic, and legal relationship with the child. But the legal fiction that there can only be two parents was always maintained, possibly due to the fear that non-exclusivity of parental status would lead to hampered decisionmaking among the adults and thus thwart state efforts to make parents the primary providers of services and discipline to minors.

Developments in foster parenting and the explosion of step-parenting continued this trend of parental exclusivity. No third party could gain a permanent, legally recognized relationship with a child absent an extraordinary intervention by the courts or by the permanent withdrawal of the natural parents from the child's life. These biological, or "real," parents were given an almost unbeatable presumption in their favor when it came to contested custody and parenting cases, and when supplanted by nonbiological parents, they were made to disappear in order to re-create the illusion of a "biological" family. Thus this western tradition dictated that there could be only one of each type of parent, although other societies freely experimented with polygyny.[21]

---

20. *See, e.g.,* Hill, *supra* note 13, at 391-93; RUSSELL SCOTT, THE BODY AS PROPERTY (1981); Lori B. Andrews, *My Body, My Property*, 16 HASTINGS CENTER REP., Oct. 1986, at 28.

The same issue has arisen with regard to the use of a patient's spleen cells in the development of a commercially valuable cell line. Moore v. Regents of the University of California, 249 Cal. Rptr. 494 (1988). Thus, the progenitors of a frozen, in vitro embryo may be treated as property owners in some contexts, *see* York v. Jones, 717 F.2d Supp. 421 (E.D. Va. 1989), Del Zio v. Columbia Presbyterian Medical Center (unreported; New York 1987), and as prospective parents in others *see* Davis v. Davis, 842 S.W.2d 588 (Tenn. 1992), but at the moment of birth the offspring is no longer property of any sort. *See also* MARY ANN GLENDON, THE NEW FAMILY AND THE NEW PROPERTY (1981).

21. MARILYN STRATHERN, REPRODUCING THE FUTURE: ESSAYS ON ANTHROPOL-

DISCARDING BIOLOGICAL RELATIONSHIPS TO FURTHER THE CONTRACTUAL MODEL OF THE FAMILY

At the same time, though, this seeming fascination with biology had a strong competitor — the need to find substitute parents when genetic linkages were missing or inconvenient. Adoption, a statutory creation not existing at common law[22] though long taking place informally or with private legislation,[23] is evidence of a strong social tradition that recognizes the purely social and psychological dimensions of parenting, even in the absence of biological ties. Yet even with adoption, adoptive parents may acquire parental status with respect to a particular child only after termination of the parental rights of the child's biological parents, particularly those of the natural mother. The "presumption of biology" serves as an irrebuttable legal presumption that the birth mother of the child is its legal mother and that adoption can take place only consequent to a termination of the parental rights of the birth mother.[24]

In early Rome and in other ancient cultures adoption served a primarily religious function associated with ensuring a legitimate male heir to carry out sacred obligations.[25] Even after the religious overtones vanished, civil law countries viewed adoption principally as a vehicle for perpetuating the adoptive parent's name and property rather than as a means of benefiting the adoptee.[26] The English common law did not recognize adoption at all; England finally legalized it by statute in 1926.[27] A more cynical explanation, therefore, of the romanticization of genetic linkages between father and child, and the degree to which adoption is structured to re-create families with clear lines of succession from a single father, rests on the needs of men to conserve their property for the benefit of only a few children, those to whom they are truly related by blood and whom they have, in a sense, contracted to sire.[28]

In the United States, adoption began as a means for privatizing the cost of maintaining orphans. It only later became grounded in child welfare, and that welfare was generally defined as re-creation of a biological-style family unit for the child to enter. Although Americans have always farmed out children in some fashion, adoption as known today did not

---

OGY, KINSHIP, AND THE NEW REPRODUCTIVE TECHNOLOGIES (1992).

22. Smith v. Organization of Foster Families, 431 U.S. 816, 845-46 (1977).

23. IRVING J. SLOAN, THE LAW OF ADOPTION AND SURROGATE PARENTING 5-11 (1988).

24. See, e.g., Lori B. Andrews, Surrogate Motherhood: Should the Adoption Model Apply?, 7 CHILDREN'S LEGAL RTS. J. Fall 1986 1, 13; PHILLIPPE ARIES, CENTURIES OF CHILDHOOD: A SOCIAL HISTORY OF FAMILY LIFE (1962).

25. Stephan B. Presser, The Historical Background of the American Law of Adoption, 11 J. FAM. L. 443 (1971).

26. See, e.g., Fred L. Kuhlman, Intestate Succession By and from the Adopted Child, 28 WASH. U. L.Q. 221 (1943); Leo Albert Huard, The Law of Adoption: Ancient and Modern, 9 VAND. L. REV. 743, 745 (1956); Presser, supra note 25.

27. The Adoption of Children Act, 1926, 16 & 17 Geo. 5, ch. 29.

28. See Presser, supra note 25.

fully emerge until the mid-nineteenth century when general adoption legislation was introduced on a wave of social welfare reform.[29] Before then child placement in this country was an informal affair. Upon the death of one or both parents, a child was simply "put-out" for a suitable blood relative, usually designated in the decedent's will, to raise. Orphaned or abandoned children without family connection and too young for apprenticeship went to public facilities until they were useful enough to be either "bound-out" (indentured or apprenticed) or sent to uninvestigated homes.[30] Although some attention was paid to the child's well-being, placement mainly served to privatize the cost of the child's education and care, while providing inexpensive labor to the adults taking in the child.[31]

By the nineteenth century, the economic atmosphere tempted many adoptive parents to take advantage of a child's labor without returning much by way of education and succor.[32] Christian reformers, through religiously affiliated private agencies, began to shift the focus of their efforts toward the placement of infants and young children in homes where they would be treated more like family members than servants.[33] Adoption statutes soon followed suit, reflecting a slow shift in public attitudes from the notions of apprenticeship and service to the notion that child placement should primarily serve the welfare of the dependent child.

Modern adoption statutes are replete with statements that make it clear that the primary focus of today's adoption laws is the well-being of the adopted child. The requirement of many modern adoption statutes that prospective adoptive parents pass a rigorous screening process before the adoption is finalized illustrates this concern.[34] In the case of the out-of-wedlock infant given to strangers for adoption, society generally deems it in the adoptee's best interests to make him a full-fledged member of his adoptive family, as though he had been born into his adoptive family.

Furthermore, it is widely believed that an adoptee's retention of ties with his biological family can undermine the psychological aspect of this assimilation. Thus, courts have described adoption statutes as "giving the adopted child a 'fresh start' by treating him as the natural child of the adoptive parent,"[35] in essence a "substitution of the adoptive in place of the natural family and severance of legal ties with the child's natural family."[36] And in the 1993 gestational surrogacy case *Johnson v. Calvert,*[37]

---

29. *Id.*

30. *See, e.g.,* ARTHUR W. CALHOUN, 1 A SOCIAL HISTORY OF THE AMERICAN FAMILY (1917); Presser, *supra* note 25.

31. Laslett, *The Family as a Public and Private Institution, in* INTAMACY, FAMILY, AND SOCIETY (Skolnick & Skolnick eds., 1974).

32. *See, e.g.,* HOMER FOLKS, THE CARE OF DESTITUTE, NEGLECTED, AND DELINQUENT CHILDREN 64-65 (1902); Presser, *supra* note 25.

33. Presser, *supra* note 25.

34. Office of Technology Assessment of the Congress of the United States, INFERTILITY: MEDICAL AND SOCIAL CHOICES (1988) [hereinafter *OTA* 1988].

35. In Re Estates of Donnelly, 81 Wash. 2d 430, 436 (1972).

36. Crumpton v. Mitchell, 303 N.C. 657, 664 (1981).

which will be discussed more extensively *infra*, the California Supreme Court wrote that:

> We decline to accept the contention of amicus curiae the American Civil Liberties Union (ACLU) that we should find the child has two mothers. Even though rising divorce rates have made multiple parent arrangements common in our society, we see no compelling reason to recognize such a situation here. The Calverts are the genetic and intending parents of their son and have provided him, by all accounts, with a stable, intact, and nurturing home. To recognize parental rights in a third party with whom the Calvert family has had little contact since shortly after the child's birth would diminish Crispina's role as mother.[38]

Thus, once created by statute, adoption was designed to use law to re-create the image of biological family unit. It required that the biological parents be permanently removed from the child's life and the adoptive parents substituted for them,[39] a policy that would be followed in the 1990s by the permanent removal of inconvenient genetic or gestational parents. It was not possible for the child to be adopted without the natural parents relinquishing all parental rights and responsibilities. Under law, they became legal strangers.[40]

DISCARDING BIOLOGICAL RELATIONSHIPS TO FURTHER MARITAL STABILITY AND MAINTAIN BIOLOGICAL APPEARANCES

The other important purpose to be served whenever deviating from biological definitions of the family was the preservation of the heterosexual marital unit. Thus, many states preserved English tradition and passed laws that created a presumption of paternity on the part of a mother's husband. Indeed, the husband did not have to be physically present at the time of conception.[41] The Supreme Court recognized the importance of this policy by pointing out in *Michael H. v. Gerald D.* that if a husband, not physically incapable, was within 'the four seas of England' during the period of gestation, the court would not listen to evidence casting doubt on his paternity.[42]

Common law went so far as to deny the biological father the opportunity to assert his own paternity of a child born to a woman married to another man,[43] although it could be asserted *against* him by the mother or her husband. This generally remains true today,[44] even though forensic

---

37. 19 Cal. Rptr. 2d 494 (1993).

38. *Id* at 499 n. 8.

39. Martha Minow, *The Free Exercise of Families*, 1991 U. ILL. L. REV. 925.

40. JOHN T. DEMPSEY, THE FAMILY AND PUBLIC POLICY: THE ISSUE OF THE 1980'S (1981).

41. MARTHA A. FIELD, SURROGATE MOTHERHOOD 189 n.11 (1988).

42. Michael H. v. Gerald D., 491 U.S. 110, (1989), citing Blackstone's Commentaries 456, (Chitty ed. 1826).

43. Hill, *supra* note 13, at 373.

44. *Id*.

uses of DNA testing now enable paternity determinations to be made with great accuracy.[45]

Thus, the biological progenitor of a child does not enjoy a constitutional right to establish paternity for his own pleasure or to seek any form of legal recognition of the relationship if the mother of the child is married to another man, even where he has actively sought to establish a relationship with the child. In *Michael H. v. Gerald D.*,[46] a plurality of the Supreme Court held that a state may constitutionally deny a man parental rights with respect to a child he fathered during a liaison with the wife of another man, since it is the marital family that traditionally has been accorded a protected liberty interest, as reflected in the historic presumption of legitimacy of a child born into such a family. In this way, biological reality gives way to strong public policy considerations: that a child not be stigmatized by illegitimacy; that a husband should not be cuckolded against his will; that an adulterer not enjoy the fruits of his sin; and that the appearance of a biological family unit be maintained whenever possible.

The conflicting interests here — the child's interest in having a recognized mother and father, men's interests in avoiding unwanted responsibility for non-biological children, and men's interests in having access to biological children — are difficult to reconcile in a coherent fashion. Neither biology nor contractual relationship is the clear trump. What *is* clear, however, is that these interests must be sorted out within the paradigm of a two parent, heterosexual marital parenting unit. The solution of declaring both the husband and the progenitor as fathers is simply not available. The Uniform Parentage Act makes these policy considerations quite evident.[47]

Thus, the genetic relationship between father and child is considered secondary to the public policy of maintaining the integrity of "traditional" marriage and of rearing children, as often as possible, within such confines. Where no such "traditional" family is available, however, as is the case when the child is born to a mother who is single or part of a lesbian couple, the law *does* permit the biological father to assert his paternal rights, *even* if he clearly stated his intention prior to conception to have no relationship to the child. This has been the case, for example, with sperm donors.[48] The Supreme Court has elevated this principle to a constitutional level.[49] Thus, a man achieves constitutional protection as parent of

---

45. Office of Technology Assessment of the Congress of the United States, Genetic Witness 99 (1991) [hereinafter *OTA 1991*].

46. 491 U.S. 110 (1989).

47. The Uniform Parentage Act is a model statute covering issues of parental identification and custody rights.

48. Jhordan C. v. Mary K., 224 Cal. Rptr. 530 (1986).

49. *See, e.g.*, Lehr v. Robertson, 463 U.S. 248 (1983); Caban v. Mohammed, 441 U.S. 380 (1979); Quilloin v. Walcott, 434 U.S. 246 (1978); Stanley v. Illinois, 405 U.S. 645 (1972).

his child by virtue of the genetic relationship alone *if* there is no substitute male parent and he does not otherwise appear to waive the right.[50]

With the advent of artificial insemination by donor (AID) services, courts and legislatures faced a fresh challenge. The procedure posed squarely the problem of determining whether genetic mixing without sexual intercourse constituted an affront to the marriage. Early on, courts held that it did, likening AID to adultery,[51] although that trend was later reversed.[52] Second, courts were called on to determine whether genetic parentage, by itself, would be recognized under law as equivalent to legal parentage. As in non-adulterous situations of nonmarital sexual intercourse, the answer generally was "yes". Without a husband available to substitute for the genetic father, biological linkage created legal parenthood.[53]

But where the recipient of the donor semen is married, the presumption of spousal paternity comes into play, just as it does in situations of true adultery.[54] Over half the states have passed laws specifically stating that a donor is not to be considered the legal father of a child conceived by a married woman.[55] But if the woman is not married, she is either denied access to the service entirely, or the donor is potentially considered the legal father, despite the fact that she is resorting to AID specifically because she does not want the genetic father to have a legal status vis-a-vis the child. The hope is illusory that the magical desexualization of conception by using a syringe rather than intercourse will yield the protection of the law against unwanted intrusions by the genetic father.

---

50. Katherine T. Bartlett, *Rethinking Parenthood as an Exclusive Status: The Need for Legal Alternatives When the Premise of the Nuclear Family Has Failed*, 70 VA. L. REV. 879 (1984); John T. Wright, Note, *Caban v. Mohammed: Extending the Rights of Unwed Fathers*, 46 BROOK. L. REV. 95 (1979).

> The significance of the biological connection is that it offers the natural father an opportunity that no other male possesses to develop a relationship with his offspring. If he grasps that opportunity and accepts some measure of responsibility for the child's future, he may enjoy the blessings of the parent-child relationship and make uniquely valuable contributions to the child's development. Lehr v. Robertson, 463 U.S. 248, 262 (1983).

"The biological connection between father and child is unique and worthy of constitutional protection if the father grasps the opportunity to develop that biological connection into a full and enduring relationship." Adoption of Kelsey S., 4 Cal. Rptr. 2d 615, 627 (1992).

51. Doornbos v. Doornbos, 23 U.S.L.W. 2308 (1954), *appeal dismissed*, 12 Ill. App. 2d 473 (1956).

52. Walter Wadlington, *Artificial Conception: The Challenge for Family Law*, 69 VA. L. REV. 465 (1983); Lori B. Andrews, *The Stork Market: The Law of the New Reproductive Technologies*, 70 A.B.A.J., Aug. 1984 at 50.

53. Daniel I. Wikler, *The Family as Social Construct: Dilemmas of Kinship Determinations in Artificial Insemination*, paper at the United Nations University WIDER Institute conference on Women, Equality, and Reproductive Technology (Helsinki, August 1992); OTA 1988, *supra* note 34.

54. OTA 1988, *supra* note 34.

55. *Id.*

THE PROBLEM OF DECEPTIVE APPEARANCES

At least with ordinary AID by married women, appearances of a typical, biologically-related family can be maintained by discarding the inconvenient genetic parent. Not so with contract motherhood (more commonly known as surrogate motherhood). The wife of the genetic father, who intends to rear the child, is visibly un-pregnant. Therefore, she is disfavored as compared to the biological mother.[56] For example, the New Jersey Supreme Court held that Mary Beth Whitehead (now Gould), the genetic and gestational mother of a child conceived with semen from Bill Stern, was still the legal mother of the child, the surrogacy contract notwithstanding. Bill Stern was the legal father, based on his biological relationship, despite the existence of Mary Beth's husband as a potential competitor for the title based on presumptions of husband paternity. And Mrs. Stern was left without any legal relationship to the child, despite the fact that she would be the child's custodial maternal figure.[57] The result was prescient as well as self-fulfilling; in disputed cases, contract mothers generally retain parental status but lose custody.[58]

DEFINING BIOLOGICAL RELATIONSHIPS

The effort to give biological relationships precedence over contractual and intention-based relationships (outside of a few special instances) is probably based on administrative considerations as much as on philosophical ones. A biological delineation of family seems to provide a bright-line definition, and presumably offers history and common sense as its policy underpinnings without any further explanation. But biology is not nearly as clearly defined as the law imagines; the recent separation of biological motherhood into its genetic and gestational components demonstrates the point. And when commentators begin to argue whether the genetic mother or the gestational mother should be granted the title "biological," it is usually argued in terms of which one fulfills the relevant "biological" function. But the "relevant" function here is the one which gives biology its entitlement to primacy, thus forcing a more explicit discussion of exactly what emotional or psychological or administrative goals are being furthered and exalted by current family law. This exercise is precisely why the advent of compartmentalized reproduction has led to the opportunity to re-examine assumptions, values, and the very definition of "family" to be used by American law.

The courts have confronted conflicts between a genetic mother and a gestational mother only twice, both times favoring the genetic over the gestational mother.[59] In the first case, *Smith v. Jones*,[60] the proceeding

---

56. Andrews, *supra* note 24.
57. In re Baby M, 537 A.2d 1227, 1253 (1988).
58. R. Alta Charo, *United States: Surrogacy*, in LAW REFORM AND HUMAN REPRODUCTION 223 (Sheila A. M. McLean ed., 1992).
59. *See, e.g., id.*; John A. Robertson, *Technology and Motherhood: Legal and Ethi-*

was a "set-up" to allow the egg donor to adopt the child, and, in accordance with the surrogate agreement, the surrogate did not contest the ruling. In the second, *Johnson v. Calvert*, the trial and appellate courts found that the definition of a "biological" relationship is that of genetic linkage.[61]

The reasons for favoring a genetic model of the family have already been discussed. But there are arguments to be made that where a conflict arises between genetic and gestational relationships for women, gestation should prevail. These include arguments based on prenatal and postnatal bonding, the harmful effects to the birth mother of forcibly removing the child, the physical involvement of the birth mother in bringing the child to term, and the administrative difficulties presented by a world in which no hospital and no physician can securely hand a newborn up from the birth mother's loins to her arms.

It would be simple enough, then, to state that the woman giving birth is the sole biological, and therefore legal, mother. This maintains appearances. And it would effectively protect the egg donation programs that are beginning to flourish in states such as California, where women seek to use substituted gametes in the same way that men have done since the advent of AID. Those programs require that, as with sperm donation, the female gamete donor vanish into the mists of legal fictions.

But it would appear that this is not the approach of the California courts. In the *Johnson* case, the California appellate court held that a woman giving birth may be nothing more than a glorified wet nurse, and the child's real mother is the woman whose egg was used for the conception.[62]

The attorney for the gestational contract mother, Anna Johnson, said his client wanted only "a profound parental relationship" with the boy she gave birth to more than two years ago.[63] Sensing that his best chance was to argue that his client was the "natural" mother, who is given preference under California law in cases of disputed custody, Johnson's attorney argued that "the term 'natural mother' means the woman who gave birth. Crispina [Calvert, the female progenitor] is not the mother."[64]

A lawyer for the Calverts argued that state statutory guidelines for determining parentage in the context of paternity suits clearly mandate that the genetic parents be declared legal parents. "We can't deny that

---

cal Issues in Human Egg Donation, 39 CASE W. RES. L. REV. 1 (1989).

60. No. 85-532014 DZ (Mich. Cir. Ct. Mar. 14, 1986).

61. *Johnson*, 19 Cal. Rptr. 2d 494.

62. A woman named Crispina Calvert had usable ova but no uterus. So she had one of her eggs fertilized with her husband's semen and hired a second woman, Anna Johnson, to carry the pregnancy to term. When a dispute broke out after birth, an Orange County Superior Court judge ruled that the Calverts were the "genetic, biological and natural" father and mother and entitled to retain custody." Harriet Chiang, *Surrogate Mother Custody Case Argued in State High Court*, S.F. CHRON. Feb. 3, 1993, at A5.

63. *Id.*

64. *Id.*

Anna Johnson had an important role, but does that confer a legal prescription that she is a parent?" asked the lawyer; "I think not."[65] But Johnson's lawyer responded by arguing that "[i]t is the relationship between the birth mother and her baby that is legally protected. It tortures the English language to say that a woman (like Mrs. Calvert) who was never pregnant and never gave birth meets the traditional definition of the term mother."[66]

Nonetheless, the California appellate court upheld the trial court's conclusions, characterizing the woman who gave birth as merely a "foster parent" for the "natural" mother whose egg had been used. It never confronted the implications of its ruling for California's flourishing egg donation practices, in which genetic mothers expect to be treated as legal strangers from their genetic offspring, while birth mothers using purchased eggs expect to be treated as legal parents of their offspring.

The continued viability of the "traditional" family unit, one that mimics what happens in nature, was very much on the minds of the California Supreme Court justices when they heard oral argument on the case. Several seemed leery of the child ending up with a father and two legally recognized mothers. "Here we could have a genetic parent . . . and a gestational parent," said Justice Panelli. "Is that the traditional family unit?"[67] Chief Justice Malcolm Lucas deplored the prospect of growing up with both a "mother" and a "genetic progenitor."[68] And the court-appointed lawyer for the child argued: "The minor in this case can be served only by being raised in the traditional, two-parent family. To declare (Johnson) a parent would complicate the child's life — and has never been recognized under law."[69]

One justice, however, did seem intent on examining the broader issues, asking whether it is possible to have two biological mothers. She also suggested during oral argument that one thing "seems to be forgotten in this tug-of-war. . . . What importance should be given to the child's best

65. Philip Hager, *Justices Cool to Orange County Surrogate Mother's Case*, L.A. TIMES, Feb. 3, 1993, at A1.

66. *Id.*

67. *Id.*

68. *Id.*

69. This same fear of disrupting the definition of the "traditional" family unit led the New York State Bar Association's House of Delegates in February 1993 to reject a recommendation by the Special Committee on Biotechnology and the Law. The house defeated a resolution that called for expanding the definition of "parent" in the Domestic Relations Law to include both the genetic and gestational mothers in surrogate births. Delegates, including several from the Trusts and Estates Section, were concerned that the proposal could have unexpected consequences in other fields of law. Several asked whether a child born through surrogacy would be entitled to inherit through both mothers. Limited New York precedent indicates that, unlike in California, the gestational mother would be the only woman recognized as the legal mother. Gary Spencer, *House of Delegates Puts Off Resolutions on AIDS Victims*, N.Y.L. JOURNAL, Feb. 1, 1993, at sec. State Bar Meeting pg. 1.

interests?"[70] But the Calverts' attorney responded that the language of the Uniform Parentage Act, which defines a parent in terms of genetic linkages, already incorporates a child's best interests, i.e. that it is in a child's best interest to be considered the child of his or her genetic parents. The attorney did not comment, however, on the degree to which spousal paternity presumptions and adoption would therefore presumably not serve a child's best interests.[71]

So What is a "Natural" Parent After All?

The dilemma faced by the California appellate court, who insisted upon a single definition of "natural" mother but found that none will fit the needs of both egg donation programs and gestational surrogacy programs, is that it tried to move toward a contractual model of the family without having fully abandoned the old biological models. In fact, it is the very power of genetic relationships that is driving infertile people and the courts to find ways to regularize surrogacy and AID.[72]

One of the reasons given by Bill Stern in the *Baby M* case for his decision to hire a contract mother was that his family had been wiped out in the Holocaust, and he wished to have blood relations with someone, somewhere. Egg donation is sought by women who want desperately to have the experience of being pregnant and giving birth to the child whom they will raise. AID is used so that women with infertile husbands can nonetheless have children to whom they are genetically related.

But in order to make this possible within the strait-jacketed confines of the western, heterosexual marriage, it is necessary that we simultaneously de-value the genetic and gestational relationships of the men and women who give or sell their gametes or their capability for gestation. Those biological connections must be considered less valuable than the contract these people signed when they became donors or surrogates. Unfortunately, the very fact that the infertile persons or couples who sought their services did not seek adoption to begin with testifies to the enormous significance of that biological tie. And the agreement the infertile partners of these biological parents have made to raise these children as their own testifies to the parallel significance of contractual agreements to take on these children as their own.

So if we insist upon a preference for "natural" parents, perhaps the definition of "natural" mother depends not upon biology but upon psychology — the intent to take the baby home. After all, what could be more "unnatural" than a woman who denies her own child? Consider two stories from Australia. In the first, Linda K. agreed to give a child to her sister. She gestated and gave birth to a child conceived with her infertile

---

70. Hager, *supra* note 65, at A1.
71. *Id.*
72. William J. Wagner, *The Contractual Reallocation of Procreative Resources and Parental Rights: The Natural Endowment Critique,* 41 Case W. Res. L. Rev. 1 (1990).

sister's egg. As she, the gestational mother, relinquished the child to the infertile sister who was the child's genetic mother, she denied feeling as if she was giving up her own baby girl: "I always considered myself her aunt."[73] By contrast, Carol C. donated eggs to her infertile sister so the sister could become pregnant and give birth to a child of whom the infertile sister would be the gestational and rearing mother. Reflecting on her relationship with the resulting children, who were her genetic offspring, Carol said "I could never regard the twins as anything but my nephews."[74] The two births occurred in Melbourne within weeks of each other.

But if the definition of the natural mother depends primarily upon the intention to take care of the resulting child, then another California court decision, in the *Moschetta* case, makes no sense. Cynthia and Robert Moschetta hired a woman to act as a contract mother because Mrs. Moschetta was infertile. The contract mother, Elvira Jordan, was impregnated with Mr. Moschetta's semen, and relinquished the child at birth to the hiring couple. Mrs. Moschetta cared for the baby at home for seven months, until the day Mr. Moschetta walked out on the marriage, taking the baby with him. In a three-way custody battle between Mr. Moschetta, Mrs. Moschetta, and the "surrogate," the California court promptly threw out the application of the one parent who had actually taken care of the child, day in and day out, for over half a year. Mrs. Moschetta, the court explained, was not the child's natural or (yet) adoptive parent, and therefore had no rights at all.[75] An argument can be made for the moral priority of this intended mother; but for her and her husband, and their desire to have a child, there would be no infant and no need for Solomonic decisions.

The *Moschetta* case is reminiscent of controversies concerning foster care, where the Supreme Court has said: "[n]o one would seriously dispute that a deeply loving and interdependent relationship between an adult and a child in his or her care may exist even in the absence of blood relationship." Nevertheless, "the usual understanding of 'family' implies biological relationships, and most decisions treating the relation between parent and child have stressed this element."[76] "In the end," states one commentator,

> the Court appeared to create a distinction based on natural law, arguing
> that the relationship between foster parent and child is a creation of the

73. Charo, *supra* note 58, at 247.

74. *Id.* at 248.

75. Matt Lait, *Judge Orders Co-Custody in Surrogate Case; Parenthood: Mother, Biological Father, Who is Legally Separated From His Wife, Will Share in Upbringing of the 15-Month-Old Girl*, L.A. TIMES, Sept. 27, 1991, at A3; Matt Lait, *Toupee Snatched as Emotions Soar in Custody Case; Courts: Woman Seeking to Maintain Ties to Baby Lashes out at Her Estranged Husband During Testimony in Suit Brought by the Child's Surrogate Mother*, L.A. TIMES, Sept. 5, 1991, at B1.

76. Smith v. Organization of Foster Parents, 431 U.S. 816, 843 (1977).

state, whereas the biological relationship between parent and child is grounded in a "liberty interest in family privacy [which] has its source, and its contours . . . not in state law, but in intrinsic human rights, as they have been understood in 'this Nation's history and tradition.' " While marriage traditionally has been the most important type of relationship, ascription of paternal rights also may depend upon the type of nonmarital relationship.[77]

Shaping the Family to Conform to Public Policy Needs

Another possible explanation of all these seemingly inconsistent precedents is that courts are assigning parental status primarily to protect societal or child interests. Thus, the genetic father in the *Michael H.* case,[78] who is both a psychological and biological father, is denied parental status because the mother's husband provides a substitute who fills important policy needs. Single women who become pregnant via intercourse or AID, regardless of the original intentions of the genetic father, are faced with court decisions declaring the donors to be the legal fathers. If such women are married, however, their husbands can substitute for the genetic father and provide the necessary camouflage. Egg donation poses no problem, as the egg donor simply vanishes in the face of the gestational mother who uses the egg to create a child for herself to rear.[79] But where there are competing claims made to motherhood, based on psychological, gestational, and genetic factors, the maternal status seems to be assigned to the woman who has two out of three characteristics, a kind of "⅔" rule.

Carol C. from Australia, for example, may be genetically a mother, but she is not the "natural" (i.e. "legal") mother because it was her sister who wanted children and brought the twins to term.[80]

"[U]nder our analysis," stated the California Supreme Court, "in a true "egg donation" situation, where a woman gestates and gives birth to a child formed from the egg of another woman with the intent to raise the child as her own, the birth mother is the natural mother under California law."[81] And Mrs. Calvert in the *Johnson* case is the "natural" mother because she is genetically linked *and* she was the first one who wanted the child, thus having a "two-thirds" claim on the baby:

> Because two women each have presented acceptable proof of maternity, we do not believe this case can be decided without enquiring into the parties' intentions as manifested in the surrogacy agreement. . . . We conclude that although the [California legislation based upon the Uni-

---

77. Hill, *supra* note 13, at 381 (quoting *Smith*, 431 U.S. at 845 and Moore v. City of E. Cleveland, 431 U.S. 494, 503 (1977)).

78. See text accompanying footnote 42, *supra*.

79. Usually the gestational mother seeks to rear with a husband, who may or may not be the genetic father of the child, depending on whether donor semen was used.

80. See text accompanying footnote 72, *supra*.

81. *Johnson*, 19 Cal. Rptr. 2d at 500, n. 10.

form Parentage] Act recognizes both genetic consanguinity and giving birth as means of establishing a mother and child relationship, when the two means do not coincide in one woman, she who intended to procreate the child — that is, she who intended to bring about the birth of a child that she intended to raise as her own -- is the natural mother under California law."[82]

Finally, the *Baby M* and *Moschetta* cases demonstrate that where there is a woman who has a genetic and gestational relationship to a child, another woman's intentions and desires will be irrelevant, even if it was those desires that initiated the sequence of events leading to conception and birth.

Looked at this way, it is evident that there is nothing sacred about either genetic *or* gestational linkages, or, for that matter, about psychological linkages. All are accommodated only to the extent that they are consistent with an overriding public policy in favor of placing children in homes with two parents, of different gender, and married to one another if at all possible.[83]

This, then, opens the door to an explicit examination of *which* forms of biological relationship define "natural" parenting, *which* public policies are important enough to supplant our innate preference for favoring biological definitions of parenthood, and *why* we prefer when possible to place children in "traditional" homes, even at the expense of the interests of their genetic and gestational parents. Justice Kennard, dissenting in the *Johnson* case, argued:

> For each child, California law accords the legal rights and responsibilities of parenthood to only one "natural mother." When, as here, the female reproductive role is divided between two women, California law requires courts to make a decision as to which woman is the child's natural mother, but provides no standards by which to make that decision. The majority's resort to "intent" to break the "tie" between the genetic and gestational mothers is unsupported by statute, and in the absence of appropriate protections in the law to guard against abuse of surrogacy arrangements, it is ill-advised. To determine who is the legal mother of a child born of a gestational surrogacy arrangement, I would apply the

---

82. *Id.*

83. If an egg donor and a contract gestational mother were used to produce a child to be adopted by a biologically unrelated woman who intended from the beginning to be the rearing parent, we would finally pit biology against intention in its purest form. Assuming that donor semen was used and the rearing mother and both biological mothers are unmarried, thus eliminating the possibilities of preferences for a married couple as custodial parents, it is not clear at all how a California court would determine maternity, though the general prejudice in favor of biology, and of genetic definitions of biology, would probably weight the dice. Indeed, the *Johnson* opinion hints at the reluctance to award parental status on intention alone: "In what we must hope will be the extremely rare situation in which neither the gestator nor the woman who provided the ovum for fertilization is willing to assume custody of the child after birth, a rule recognizing the intending parents as the child's legal, natural parents should best promote certainty and stability for the child." *Johnson*, 19 Cal. Rptr. 2d at 501.

standard most protective of child welfare — the best interests of the child.[84]

But while courts hold that primary custody should be granted to the parent who would best serve the interests of the child, these principles are not supposed to operate to remove a child from a fit parent merely to enhance the child's life chances.[85] So if both of the biological mothers, one genetic and one gestational, are fit mothers, then deciding between them based on the best interests of the child is to deny that *either* woman should be treated as a biological mother, from whom no child could be taken unless she was shown to be unfit.

This then returns us to the question of biological primacy in gestational surrogacy. If one and only one woman must be chosen to be the "natural" parent, whom should it be? A majority of American courts, newspapers, and academic commentators have already adopted the term "natural" or "biological" mother to mean "genetic" mother, and write of conflicts between genetic and gestational mothers as that of "nature versus nurture."[86] And perhaps it shouldn't surprise us, since many of these judges and commentators are men whose only possible biological links are genetic. They can never have "morning" sickness in the afternoon or swollen ankles in the eighth month, and so may find it difficult to relate to the physiological (read: biological) phenomena that are solely related to the fact of the pregnancy, not the genetic link between parent and child. In a man's world, biology begins and ends with the DNA chains that link one generation to another.

In a woman's world, however, pregnancy is indisputably a biological fusing of fetal and maternal bodies, health, and well-being. The imposition of a male definition on a uniquely female biological experience would almost be a bad feminist joke if it didn't have such potentially troubling consequences for women's liberties. Names are a form of classification that shape substantive rights. When Mary Beth Whitehead, a genetic and gestational parent, was called a "surrogate" instead of a "mother," the infamous *Baby M* case was already halfway decided, regardless of whether a pre-conception parenting contract should be enforceable. In the words of courts and commentators, a pregnant woman may be no more than a walking womb, a human incubator working on behalf of a future child. A month before the birth, one Michigan court declared that "plaintiff Mary Smith is the mother of the child to be born to defendant Jane Jones on or about July 1987."[87] In other words, a woman can be pregnant and already a legal stranger to the unborn child within her.

---

84. *Johnson*, 19 Cal. Rptr. 2d at 507 (Kennard, J., dissenting).

85. William Ruddick, *Parents and Life Prospects, in* HAVING CHILDREN: PHILO-SOPHICAL AND LEGAL REFLECTIONS ON PARENTHOOD 123 (Onora O'Neill & William Ruddick eds., 1979).

86. The implication here is that nine months of pregnancy is not biological or natural, but is some kind of extended baby-sitting job.

87. Smith v. Jones, No. 85-532014 DZ (Mich. Cir. Ct. Mar. 14, 1986).

In a country that has seen prosecutors, hospital lawyers, and judges use court orders to stop pregnant women from smoking or to force them to undergo caesarean sections, it is frightening to imagine what could happen when it is not strangers but the "natural" and "legal" parents of an unborn child still in another's womb who are trying to ensure the gestational mother, this "foster parent," does everything the way they would have done it.[88] A pregnant woman's sense of fused biological well-being may stand little chance against a legal property interest that others have in the fetus still within her body.

Thus, there are strong public policy arguments to be made in favor of a gestational definition of motherhood. And just as genetic parenthood has yielded to public policy in the cases of illegitimacy, AID, and adoption, so too could genetic maternity yield to gestational maternity. California's *Johnson* decision that a gestational mother can be no more than a foster parent to her own child is almost without precedent in the world. Only Israel, bound by unique aspects of religious identity law, has adopted a genetic definition of motherhood. Every other country that has examined the problem — including the United Kingdom, Germany, Switzerland, Bulgaria, and even South Africa with its race-conscious legal structure — has concluded for historical, ethical, or administrative reasons that the woman who gives birth is the child's mother.[89]

MAKE ROOM FOR DADDY. . . AND PAPA, AND MOMMY, AND MAMA. . .

But in fact, there is a better solution than choosing *between* competing biological mothers, or *between* genetic and social fathers. We've already entered an era of "crazy making," where courts are re-examining the prejudice against polygamy when reviewing adoption requests by certain Mormon families,[90] and are granting visitation rights to step-parents and the gay and lesbian partners of biological parents.[91] The next step would be to toss out legal fictions altogether and recognize in court what has already happened in the physical world. Some children have three biological parents, not two. Some children have two biological mothers, not one. Acknowledging that two women are biologically related to the same child, that both women are "natural" mothers, does not necessarily determine which will have superior claims to raise the child. As every divorced parent in America knows, biology alone does not dictate custody.

Hundreds of children, most in San Francisco, New York, and other urban centers, grow up with multiple parents, usually due to arrange-

---

88. R. Alta Charo, *Mandatory Conception in the United States*, 339 LANCET 1104-05 (May 2, 1992).

89. OTA 1988, *supra* note 34.

90. Adoption of W.A.T., 808 P.2d 1083 (Utah 1991).

91. Martha Minow, *Redefining Families: Who's In and Who's Out*, 62 COLO. L. REV. 269 (1991).

ments among gay and lesbian couples and their friends of the opposite sex who were involved in the conception and birth. The lovers of the biological mother and father frequently take an active role in rearing children. Private contracts attempt to spell out relative degrees of involvement. Such co-parents argue that their children, far from being confused by the unusual circumstances, actually benefit from being exposed to a wider range of adult influences. These families are more significant than their numbers suggest because they challenge the foundation of laws based on the heterosexual, nuclear-family model.[92]

A year ago, a group called Prospective Queer Parents was founded, which holds brunches that some participants have affectionately dubbed "sperm-and-egg mixers." "On the second Sunday of every month, about two dozen gay men and lesbians interested in finding co-parents gather to eat, chat . . . and scope out each other's genes." "Our family arrangement is in many ways radical and visionary, since we're a bunch of four queers," one participant said. "But in other ways, we're a very traditional family — we value longevity, and struggling through for the long haul."[93]

Although the logistics can be complicated, co-parents reportedly say that their real problems stem from a legal system that fails to certify their families. As a result, the nonbiological parents in co-parenting arrangements often worry about their legal relationship to the child, and may even resort to judicial efforts to cement their relationships in situations where more legally secure parties would negotiate.[94]

Thus, resolutions of cases concerning the opportunity of a lesbian woman to adopt her lover's biological child and thereby become a second, legally recognized mother are of great importance.[95] A probate judge ruled in June 1992, for example, that Vermont's adoption law does not allow someone who is not married to a legal, custodial parent to become a second, adoptive parent of the legal parent's children.[96]

Vermont does allow single persons to adopt children, and the companion of a lesbian biological mother argued that she met the prerequisites. However, a separate provision of adoption law states that, except for adoption by step-parents, the parental rights of a biological parent are terminated once an adoption is granted. Without recognition of homosexual marriage, there can be no "step-parent" adoption by a gay companion of a biological parent.[97] Despite this obstacle, though, family law is yielding. As of September 1993, California, the District of Columbia, Alaska, Vermont, New York, Texas, and Washington have taken the radical step

---

92. Tuller, *supra* note 2.
93. *Id.*
94. *Id.*
95. Betsy Liley, *Lesbian Custody Case Goes to the Vermont Supreme Court*, GANNETT NEWS SERVICE, Feb. 3, 1993.
96. *Id.*
97. *Id.*

of approving homosexual adoption in a manner that creates two parents of the same sex.[98]

Perhaps it is time to take a great leap in family law. We could recognize that all biological relationships — genetic and gestational — are irrevocable. The emotional and medical significance of the bonds cannot be undone by signing a contract or adoption papers. The thousands of children who have wondered about the biological parents who gave them up for adoption or the sperm donors used to conceive them already know this. The numerous possibilities the Human Genome Initiative has identified for using a biological parent's medical history to help in the diagnosis or treatment of even late-onset disorders in the adopted-out children also testifies to this.

At the same time, the voluntary social responsibilities we take on when we adopt children are equally permanent, and no less profound. That is why so many adopted children, though they may wonder about their biological parents, take no action to find them. Forced by society to choose among various adults, these adopted children understand that the most important parent is the one who tries to stay around.

Why not give these children a break? Once a parent enters into a child's life, whether by virtue of genes, gestation, or declaration, there is an unbreakable bond of psychology and history between the two. Crispina Calvert, Anna Johnson, Elvira Jordan, Cynthia Moschetta, Linda K., Carol C., and Mary Beth Whitehead are all mothers to their children, just as Robert Moschetta, Michael H., and Bill Stern are fathers to their children. Even for those whose parents are absent due to contract, abandonment, or involuntary events there is a mutual tie of emotion, of wondering how the other is doing, and of moral responsibility.

In an age when courts have been forced to manage the untidy families created by divorce and remarriage, it is simply not enough to argue that it will be difficult to organize a regime of family law that accommodates the permanency of both contractual and biological (both genetic and gestational) ties. And having admitted already that step-parents and grandparents are indeed real family members, what legitimate obstacle remains to accepting the adults who enter family arrangements via group marriage or homosexual marriage? Surely we can be creative enough to create a new category, somewhere between custodial parent and legal stranger, that captures these relationships.

Certainly the administrative and emotional complications of recognizing as permanent all biological and contractual ties are daunting. Nothing better demonstrates this point than the case of Kimberly Mays, whose biological parents were unwittingly separated from her, and whose attempts to form a relationship fourteen years later were eventually rebuf-

---

98. Mat Boot, *Bay State Court Approves Adoption by Homosexuals*, CHRISTIAN SCI. MONITOR, Sept. 13, 1993, at 8; Hollace Weiner, *Texas Decision Extends Rights of Gays: Companion of Mom Allowed to Adopt Child*, PHOENIX GAZETTE, Sept. 7, 1993, at A7.

fed by both their biological daughter and her rearing father. But this case is, thankfully, rare and unusual in its details. Empirical research on polygamous families, families with homosexual parents, and other nontraditional families may yet demonstrate that it *is* possible to recognize more than two adults, while also maintaining clear lines of authority and responsibility. While courts and legislatures may see the need to determine who has a primary role in raising the child, there may well be no need to cut these other people out entirely. Indeed, from the child's point of view, it may simply be wrong to do so.

It has been said that you can never be too rich or too thin. Shall we add, perhaps, that you can never have too many parents to love you?

Part III
Contractual Reproduction: Gamete Donation and Surrogacy Arrangements

[5]

BIOETHICS AND FATHERHOOD

*Daniel Callahan**

I. INTRODUCTION

For most of the rest of our culture, the twin issues of the meaning of masculinity (or maleness, depending on your tastes), and the significance of fatherhood are well-developed topics of public discussion. Whether as a response to feminism, on the one hand, or to independent uncertainties about what it means to be a male, on the other, the question of masculinity attracts considerable attention. While fatherhood was not exactly a neglected topic in years past, there seems little doubt that the nasty phenomena of more and more single-parent families, mainly headed by females, and a growing number of absent and neglectful fathers, has given the issue a fresh urgency. What does it mean to be a father? What is the importance of the father for the nurturing of children? What can be done to encourage and assist more responsible fatherhood? What is the relationship between fatherhood and masculinity?

These are interesting and important questions, and timely as well. One would, however, never guess that from reading the literature of bioethics. For whatever reason, that literature, when it focuses on gender at all, is almost exclusively interested in women. And when it focuses on parenthood, it almost exclusively focuses on motherhood. While the general topics of reproductive choices and artificial means of reproduction have had a central place in bioethics, the literature and debate have usually centered on women's choices or women's role in such things as surrogate motherhood and *in vitro* fertilization. Fathers and fatherhood are just absent from the discussion altogether.

The absence of fatherhood in the debate is puzzling, especially since the topic of artificial means of reproduction is a central one in the field. My surmise is that, because those means of reproduction depend so heavily upon anonymous male sperm

---

* Director, The Hastings Center, Briarcliff Manor, New York.

donations, and since such donations are rarely questioned for their moral propriety, there has been no need or place to talk about fathers. They just don't really count in that brave new world of reproduction. I will return later to that topic. Of more general importance is whether fatherhood can be given a fresh look and a reinvigorated role in bioethics.

At the heart of the problem and future of parenthood, and thus of the most basic and indispensable kind of human nurturing, is a *relationship*, of men, women, and children bound together. Professionals seem to have lost a sense of and feel for that relationship—of the way men, women, and children need and best flourish in the company of the other. Instead, professionals have done conceptually what society has been doing legally and socially—treating men, women, and children as separate and distinguishable, with their own needs and rights. Thus we now speak easily of women's rights, and children's rights, and (hardly surprising, even if amusing) we have seen the growth of a men's rights movement. Doubtless there are some good reasons for this fragmenting development, the most important being the way earlier generations were prone to stack the family relationship, and its ground rules, too heavily in favor of men; or, where children were concerned, to treat them too much as the property of their parents, not as persons in their own rights.

But it is time for some reintegration. The fragmentation is, unless corrected in the long run, going to be harmful for men, women, and children, both individually and in their relationship. A revived and reinvigorated place for fathers and the institution of fatherhood is as good a place as any to begin. I want to develop three points: (1) biological fatherhood carries with it permanent and nondispensable duties; (2) the rapid and widespread acceptance of artificial insemination donors was much too thoughtless and casual, but for just that reason symbolic of the devaluation of fatherhood; and (3) feminism as a movement has hurt both men and children, but also women, by its tendency to substantively displace fathers from a central role in the making of procreation decisions.

II. The Duties of Fatherhood

I begin here with the most simple and primitive of moral axioms, rarely articulated as such but as undeniable as anything can possibly be in ethics. The axiom is this: Human beings bear a moral responsibility for those voluntary acts that have an impact on the lives of others; they are morally accountable for such acts. I will not discuss the many nuances and problems that this axiom raises: what counts as "voluntary," how great must be the impact upon others, and which effects of actions on others are morally more or less important.

In the case of biological fatherhood those nuances will not ordinarily be of great importance. From this moral axiom I will argue that given the obvious importance of procreation in bringing human life into existence, fathers have a significant moral responsibility for the children they voluntarily procreate. What human action could be more important than that which creates new life, the burden of which the newly born person must live with for the rest of his or her life? What causal connection could be more direct than biological procreation, without which human existence would not be possible? A father can hardly be held wholly responsible for *what* a child becomes—much will depend upon circumstances—but a father can be held responsible with the mother for the fact the child comes to be at all.

One philosopher has advanced the notion that our only serious moral obligations are those we voluntarily impose upon ourselves, as in specific contracts.[1] There cannot be, she says, involuntary obligations. This is not the place to debate the full implications of such a theory—which must systematically close its eyes to what it means to live in a community with other people—but it is pertinent to make a single point. Unless a male is utterly naive about the facts of procreation, to engage in voluntary sexual intercourse is to be responsible for what happens as a result. To enter into a contract with another is, at the least, to undertake a voluntary activity with a known likely outcome. Sexual intercourse for an informed male is fairly close to that, so even on a contract theory of moral obligation, intercourse shares many critical features with a contract. Society, curiously, seems to

---

1. Judith J. Thompson, *A Defense of Abortion*, 1 PHIL. & PUB. AFF. 47, 65 (1971).

have been faster in establishing the moral and causal links between drinking and driving than between sexual activity and pregnancy. But that may be because society prefers to think that accidental, unwanted pregnancies come more from contraceptive ignorance and failure than from the sexual activities that require them; the former is a more comforting thought to sustain the sexual revolution.

From my moral axiom, therefore, and from what we know about the biology of human procreation, I believe there is no serious way of denying the moral seriousness of biological fatherhood and the existence of moral duties that follow from it. The most important moral statement might be this: Once a father, always a father. Because the relationship is biological rather than contractual, the natural bond cannot be abrogated or put aside. I conclude, that just as society cannot put aside the biological bond, so neither ought it put aside the moral bond, the set of obligations that go with that biological bond. If there are to be moral duties at all, then the biological bond is as fundamental and unavoidable as any that can be imagined.[2] Does this mean that each and every father has a full set of moral obligations toward the children he procreates? My answer is yes—unless he is mentally or financially incompetent to discharge those duties. To treat the matter otherwise is to assume that fatherhood *is* some kind of contractual relationship, one that can be set aside by some choice on the part of the father, or the mother and father together, or on the part of the state. This position does not preclude allowing one person to adopt the child of another, to play the role of father with a legal sanction to do so. This arrangement, however, is legitimate only when there are serious obstacles standing in the way of the biological father playing that role himself. Even then, however, he remains the biological father, and should the alternative arrangements for the child fail, he is once again responsible, and responsible whether he likes it or not, accepts it or not. The obligation stems from his original, irreversible act of procreation; so too is his moral obligation irreversible.

Imagine the following scenario. A father has, through the assorted legal ways society allows fathers to turn over their

2. James L. Nelson, *Parental Obligations and the Ethics of Surrogacy: A Causal Perspective*, 5 PUB. AFF. Q. 49 (1991).

parental authority to another, legally ceased to act as a father and someone else is caring for the child. But imagine that the other person fails to adequately act as a father; fails, that is, to properly care for and nurture the child. The child then returns to the father and says: "You are still my father biologically; because of you I exist in this world. I need your help and you are obliged to give it to me." I have never been able to imagine even *one* moral reason why a father in that circumstance could disclaim responsibility, and disclaim it if, even in principle, there was someone else available who could take care of the child. A father is a father is a father.

III. FATHERHOOD AND ARTIFICIAL INSEMINATION

I find it remarkable that, with hardly any public debate at all, the practice—indeed, institution—of artificial insemination by an anonymous male donor so easily slipped in. What could society have been thinking about? In this section I will argue that it is fundamentally wrong and should have no place in a civilized, much less a supposedly liberal society. It is wrong for just the reasons I have sketched in Section II about the moral obligations that go with fatherhood. A sperm donor whose sperm is successfully used to fertilize an ovum, which ovum proceeds through the usual phases of gestation, is a *father*. Nothing more, nothing less. He is as much a father biologically as the known sperm inseminator in a standard heterosexual relationship and sexual intercourse.

If he is thereby a biological father, he has all the duties of any other biological father. It is morally irrelevant that (1) the donor does not want to act as a father, (2) those who collect his sperm as medical brokers do not want him to act as a father, (3) the woman whose ovum he is fertilizing does not want him to act as a father, and (4) society is prepared to excuse him from the obligations of acting as a father. Fatherhood, because it is a biological condition, cannot be abrogated by personal desires or legal decisions. Nor can the moral obligations be abrogated either, unless there are reasons why they *cannot* be discharged, not simply that no one wants them to be discharged. Just as a "surrogate mother" is not a "surrogate" at all but a perfectly real and conventional biological mother, so also is a sperm donor whose sperm results in a child a perfectly real and conventional biological father.

Why was it decided to set all that aside? Why was it deemed acceptable for males to become fathers by becoming sperm donors but then to relieve them *totally* of all responsibility of being fathers, leaving this new father ignorant of who his child is and the child ignorant of who the father is? I was not present at that great cultural moment, but two reasons seem to have been paramount.

First, it was introduced under medical auspices and given a medical legitimation. Artificial Insemination by a Donor ("AID"), one author wrote, is "medically indicated in instances of the man's sterility, possible hereditary disease, rhesus incompatibility, or in most cases of oligospermia."[3] "Medically indicated?" But it does not cure anyone's disease—not some other would-be father who is sterile, or the woman who receives the sperm who is perfectly capable of motherhood without donated sperm. What is cured, so to speak, is a couple's desire to have a child; but medicine does not ordinarily treat relational problems (save in psychotherapy), so there is no reason to call the matter medical at all. Moreover, of course, since artificial insemination only requires a single syringe, inserted in a well-known place, there is nothing "medical" even about the procedure.

As Daniel Wikler has nicely pointed out, the professional dominance of doctors in the history of AID is a perfect case of the medicalization of a nonmedical act, and the establishment of a medical monopoly and legitimization as a result.[4] Just how far this medicalization has gone can be seen by the very language used to describe the procedure: "[Artificial Insemination] is of two basic types: homologous, when the semen is obtained from the husband (AIH); and heterologous, when the semen is acquired from a donor (AID)."[5] I wonder how many males, working pleasurably to produce some sperm, understood themselves to be engaged in a heterologous activity? There is very little that medical science cannot dress up with a technical term.

---

3. Mark S. Frankel, *Reproductive Technologies: Artificial Insemination*, 4 ENCYCLO-PEDIA OF BIOETHICS 1439, 1444 (Warren T. Reich ed., 1978).

4. Daniel Wikler & Norma J. Wikler, *Turkey-baster Babies: The Demedicalization of Artificial Insemination*, 69 MILBANK Q. 5, 8 (1991).

5. *See* Frankel, *supra* note 3, at 1444.

The second reason for ready acceptance was probably that, in the name of helping someone to have a child, society seems to be willing to set aside any existing moral restraints and conventions. Perhaps in an underpopulated world, whose very existence is threatened by low birth rates, a case for artificial procreation might be made.

But it is hard to see why, in our world, where the problem of feckless and irresponsible male procreators is far more of a social crisis, society lets that one pass. One can well understand the urge, often desperate, to have a child. But it is less easy to understand an acceptance of the systematic downgrading of fatherhood brought about by the introduction of anonymous sperm donors. Or perhaps it was the case that fatherhood had already sunken to such a low state, and male irresponsibility was already so accepted, that no one saw a problem. It is as if everyone argued: Look, males have always been fathering children anonymously and irresponsibly; why not put this otherwise noxious trait to good use?

As a symbol of male irresponsibility—and a socially sanctioned symbol at that—one could hardly ask for anything better than artificial insemination with the sperm of anonymous donors. It raises male irresponsibility to the high level of a praised social institution, and it succeeds in getting males off the hook of fatherhood and parenthood in a strikingly effective and decisive way. The anonymity is an especially nice touch; no one will know who did what, and thus there can never be any moral accountability. That is the kind of world all of us have wished we could live in from time to time, especially in its sexual subdivision. From the perspective of the sperm donor, if the child's life turns out poorly, the donor will neither know about that nor inconveniently be called upon to provide help, fatherly help. Home free!

IV. FEMINISM AND FATHERHOOD

As a movement, feminism has long had a dilemma on its hands. If women are to be free of the undue coercion and domination of males, they must establish their own independent sphere of activities and the necessary social and legal rights to protect that sphere. Women cannot and should not leave their fate in the hands of males, much less their reproductive fates. Meanwhile, feminists have also deplored feckless, irresponsible males who leave women in the lurch. Yet if males are to be encouraged to act more responsibly, to take seriously their duties to women and children, then they must be allowed to share the right to make decisions in those domains that bear on their activities and responsibilities. Males, moreover, have rights corresponding to their duties; they should be empowered to do that which their moral duties require of them.

For the most part, this dilemma has been resolved by the feminist movement in favor of stressing the independence of females from male control. This is evident in two important respects. First, in the abortion debate there has been a firm rejection of the claim that males should be either informed that a woman is considering an abortion or that the male should have a right to override her decision. The male should, in short, have neither a right to information nor choice about what happens to the conception.

Second, in its acceptance of single-parent procreation and motherhood, for both heterosexual and lesbian women, some branches of feminism have in effect declared fathers biologically irrelevant and socially unnecessary. Since this kind of motherhood requires, as a necessary condition, some male sperm (provided *in vitro* or *in vivo*), it has not been possible to dispense altogether with males. No such luck. But it has been possible to hold those males who assist such reproduction free of all responsibility for their action in providing the sperm. The only difference between the male who impregnates a woman in the course of sexual liaison and then disappears, and the man who is asked to disappear voluntarily after providing sperm, is that the latter kind of irresponsibility is, so to speak, licensed and legitimated. Indeed, it is treated as a kindly, beneficent action. The effect on the child is of course absolutely identical—an unknown, absent father.

Both of these moves seem understandable in the short run, but profoundly unhelpful to women in the long run. It is under-standable why women would not want their abortion decision to depend upon male permission. They are the ones who will have to carry the child to term and nurture, as mothers, the child thereafter. It is no less understandable why some women want children without fathers. Some cannot find a male to marry but do not want to give up motherhood altogether; they view this as a course of necessity, a kind of lesser evil. Other women, for reasons of profound skepticism about males, or hostility toward them, simply want children apart from males altogether.

Please note that I said these motives are "understandable." I did not say they are justifiable. What is short-sighted about either of these choices is that, by their nullification of the moral obligations that ought to go with biological fatherhood, they contribute to the further infantilization of males, a phenomenon already well advanced in our society, and itself a long-standing source of harm for women.

If the obligations of males to take responsibility for the children they have procreated is sharply limited due to women deciding whether to grant males any rights, then males quickly get the message. That message is that the ordinary moral obligations that go with procreation are contingent and dispensable, not nearly as weighty as those of women. For even the most advanced feminists do not lightly allow women who have knowingly chosen to become mothers to jettison that obligation. Mothers are understood to be mothers forever, unlike fathers, who are understood to be fathers as long as no one has declared them free of responsibility. If you are a sperm donor, of course, that declaration can readily be had.

What social conditions are necessary to have the responsibilities of fatherhood taken seriously? The most obvious, it would seem, is a clear, powerful, and consistent social message to fathers: You are responsible for the lives of the children you procreate; you are always the father regardless of legal dispensations; only the gravest emergencies can relieve you of that obligation; you will be held liable if you fail in your duties; and, you will be given the necessary rights and prerogatives required to properly discharge your duties. Only recently has there been a concerted effort, long overdue, to require fathers to make good on child-support agreements. And only recently, and interestingly, has the importance of biological parenthood been sufficiently recognized to lower some of the barriers erected to keep adopted children from discovering the identity of their biological parents, including fathers.

Those feminists who believe that fathers should have no role in abortion decisions should reconsider that position or at least add some nuance. There are probably good reasons to not legally require that fathers be informed that the mother is considering an

744 UTAH LAW REVIEW [1992: 735

abortion; the possibilities of coercion and continuing stress thereafter are real and serious. But that is no reason to dispense with a *moral* requirement that the fathers be informed and their opinion requested if there are no overpowering reasons not to. The fetus that would be aborted is as much their doing as that of the mother, and the loss to the father can obviously be considerable. Acting as if the only serious consequences are for the woman is still another way of minimizing the importance of fatherhood.

Far too much is made of the fact that the woman actually carries the fetus. That does not make the child more hers than his, and in the lifetime span of procreation, childbearing, and child-rearing, the nine-month period of gestation is a minute portion of that span. Only very young parents who have not experienced the troubles of teenage children or an adult child's marital breakup could think of the woman's pregnancy as an especially significant or difficult time compared with other phases of parenthood.

Fathers, in short, have a moral right to know that they are fathers and to have a voice in decisions about the outcome of pregnancy. To deny males such a right is also to reject the very concept of paternal responsibility for one's procreative actions. The right to be a father cannot rest upon someone else's decision to grant such a right; that is no right at all. If the right to be a father is that poorly based, then there will be no better basis for upholding the moral obligations of fathers, or holding them accountable for their actions. I see no possibility of having it both ways. Society often asserts as a general principle that rights entail obligations. In this case, I am arguing the converse: If society wants obligations taken seriously, rights must be recognized.

The argument for a father's moral right to knowledge and choice does not entail a corresponding legal right to force a woman to bear a child against her will. There are a number of prudential and practical reasons not to require legal notification that a woman plans to have an abortion or to require the father's permission. Such a requirement, I suspect, would be both unworkable and probably destructive of many marital relationships. But as a moral norm, this requirement is perfectly appropriate. It puts moral pressure on women to see the need to inform fathers they are fathers, and to withhold such knowledge only when there are serious moral reasons to do so.

Women should, in general, want to do everything possible to encourage fathers to take their role and duties seriously. Women, and the children they bear, only lose if men are allowed to remain infantile and irresponsible. The attempt to encourage more responsible fatherhood and the sharing of childrearing duties while simultaneously promoting the total independence of women in their childbearing decisions only sends a mixed message: Fathers should consider themselves responsible, but not too much; and they should share the choices and burdens of parenthood, but more the latter than the former; and all parents are created equal, but some are more equal than others.

I have mainly laid the emphasis so far on abortion decisions. But the same considerations apply when women, heterosexual or lesbian, make use of donated sperm deliberately to have a single-parent child. Women have been hurt throughout history by males who abandon their parental duties, leaving to women the task of raising the children. A sperm donor is doing exactly the same thing. The fact that he does it with social sanction does not change the outcome; one more male has been allowed to be a father without taking up the duties of fatherhood. Indeed, there is something symbolically destructive about using anonymous sperm donors to help women have children apart from a permanent marital relationship with the father.

For what action could more decisively declare the irrelevance of fatherhood than a specific effort to keep everyone ignorant? A male who would be a party to such an arrangement might well consider himself some kind of altruistic figure, helping women to get what they want. He would in reality be part of that grand old male tradition of fatherhood without tears, that wonderful fatherhood that permits all of the pleasures of procreation but none of its obligations. Women who use males in this way, allowing them to play once again that ancient role in a new guise, cannot fail to do harm both to women and parenthood.

V. PARENTHOOD, FAMILIES, AND RELATIONSHIP

A great deal of fun is made these days of those old-fashioned families of the 1950s, especially the television versions, where the emphasis was placed on the family as a unit. They are spoofed in part because they failed to account for all of the families in those days that were simply not like that. Fair enough. They are derided as well because they often treated the women as empty-headed creatures good for nothing other than cleaning up after the kids and keeping father happy. And sometimes they are attacked because they did not present those fathers as strong leaders and role models for children. Rather, they portrayed fathers as weak and childish, capable of manipulation by wives and children.

But what the old-fashioned families saw clearly enough is that parenthood is a set of relationships, a complex web of rights, privileges, and duties as well as the more subtle interplay of morality in intimate relationships. Feminists have been prone to pose the problem of procreative rights as principally a female problem. Traditionalists have been wont to view fatherhood as a role of patriarchical hegemony. Both are wrong, however, because they fail to see the complexity of the relationship or to place the emphasis in the right place. Both mothers and fathers, as individual moral beings, have important roles as well as the rights and duties that go with those roles.

Those roles, most importantly, are conditioned by, and set in a context of, their mutuality. Each needs and is enriched by the role of the other. The obligations of the one are of benefit to the other; indeed, the mutuality of their obligations amplifies all of them. A mother can better be a mother if she has the active help of a father who takes his duties seriously. Likewise, the father will be a better father with the help of an equally serious mother. The child will, in turn, gain something from both of them, both individually and as a pair. It is important, therefore, that society return fatherhood to center stage not only for the sake of fathers, who will be forced to grow up, but also for mothers, who will benefit from a more mature notion of what fatherhood and parenthood are.

[6]

Legal Issues in Human Egg Donation and Gestational Surrogacy

John A. Robertson, J.D.

One of the fastest growing areas of assisted reproduction is human egg donation. Over 100 American in vitro fertilization (IVF) programs now offer the procedure,[1] and thousands of women suffering from ovarian dysfunction or who are at an advanced reproductive age are potential candidates. Egg donation raises several ethical and legal issues that need attention if it is to be used in a productive and beneficial way.

In egg donation, a woman's ovaries are stimulated with hormones, multiple eggs are removed, and the eggs are fertilized in vitro with the sperm of the partner of a woman who cannot herself produce viable eggs. The fertilized eggs or embryos are then placed in the uterus of the recipient (whose cycle has been synchronized with that of the donor) or cryopreserved for use by the recipient in a later cycle. If successful, the transferred embryos implant, and the recipient gives birth to a child that she and her husband then rear. Unless the egg donor is a friend or family member, the egg donor ordinarily has no contact with the recipient or offspring.

Medically, egg donation offers great hope to thousands of women who cannot themselves produce healthy or viable eggs. Many of these women have premature ovarian failure or have been surgically castrated. Others are of advanced reproductive age and have a poor prognosis of fertility with other therapies. For example, women over 40 have a higher success rate with donor oocytes than with IVF using their own eggs.[2] Indeed, a recent report

suggests that women in their late 40s or even early 50s can deliver children after egg donation.[2]

While the donor may be another woman going through IVF who donates extra eggs, the advent of cryopreservation of embryos has reduced the supply of donor eggs from this source. Increasingly egg donations come from friends or family members that the recipient herself recruits, or from anonymous donors recruited by the center providing the service. In the latter case, the donors are extensively screened, and usually paid from $1200 to $2000 for their services.

Egg donation thus appears to be a medically safe and effective way to produce children for women who cannot themselves produce healthy eggs. It has a higher success rate for this group of patients than other therapies. It also replicates more closely than does donor sperm or surrogacy the biologic ties that usually exist between parents and offspring. Egg donation enables each rearing parent to have a biologic connection with offspring, with only the female genetic connection missing.

Because egg donation is still relatively new, a full assessment of its effects on offspring, donors, infertile couples, and society cannot now be made. Nevertheless, it is reasonable to assume that its net effects will be good for all the participants. Given the existing acceptability of IVF and of donor insemination, the combination of IVF and gamete donation in the form of egg donation should also be ethically and legally acceptable.

University of Texas School of Law, Austin, Texas

Reprint requests: Mr. Robertson, University of Texas School of Law, 727 E. 26th Street, Austin, TX 78705

With the exception of four states, however, there is no legislation or court decision that now directly addresses egg donation and thus clarifies whether the parties' intentions to exclude the egg donor from all rearing rights and duties in offspring will have legal effect. Some states also have laws against buying and selling human organs and tissue that could restrict payments to egg donors. Nor is it clear whether donors who are injured in the course of donation must bear those costs or whether other parties can be held responsible. A variety of other legal questions arise, from the offspring's right to have information about her genetic mother to questions about whether egg donation to women who are past the normal age of childbearing can be banned.

While these uncertainties present no insuperable barrier to performing egg donation, they do require that physicians, hospitals, couples, donors, and others involved in egg donation pay careful attention to how they conduct the practice. The following discussion identifies the main legal issues that need attention and suggests reasonable steps to deal with current legal uncertainty. Until the law is clarified by legislation or judicial decision, egg donation programs that are conducted with full disclosure of existing risks and uncertainties should be legally acceptable, with the caveats discussed below.

REARING RIGHTS AND DUTIES

A major legal issue with egg donation concerns rearing rights and duties in offspring. In almost all instances the intent of the parties is to have the sperm provider and the recipient be the rearing father and mother for all purposes, and for the donor to have no rearing rights and duties at all. This goal will exist even if friends or family members act as egg donors. Egg donation thus attempts to replicate the situation that ordinarily occurs with donor sperm to a married couple, in which the consenting husband is the legal father for all purposes and an anonymous donor has no rearing rights or duties.

A problem, however, for recipients and donors at the present time is that only Oklahoma, Texas, Florida, and Virginia[3–5a] have yet recognized such intentions as legally determinative of rearing rights and duties in offspring. Until legislators or judges address this issue, participants in egg donation in other states will lack certainty that their preconception intentions will be legally binding. They must be fully informed of this uncertainty and should execute consent forms and releases that clearly state their intentions and acknowledge the uncertainty they face.

The absence of legislation, however, does not mean that the express intentions of the parties will not be honored if a legal dispute arises over rearing rights and duties in children born of egg donation. In sperm donation, for example, the intention of the parties to exclude the sperm donor and assign all rearing rights and duties to the consenting husband is recognized by statute or court decisions in over 30 states.[6] A court faced with a dispute over rearing rights and duties in egg donation is likely to follow the donor sperm model, as do the egg donation laws in Oklahoma, Texas, Virginia, and Florida, and give legal effect to the intention of the parties.

Consider, for example, two types of disputes that could arise over rearing rights and duties with egg donation. One would be where the donor as genetic mother later attempts to assert some rearing rights. Since ordinarily a sperm donor would not have the legal right to play a parenting role, it is hard to see why an egg donor should have any greater claim. She explicitly waived or relinquished her parental rights in providing the egg, just as a sperm donor does, and a later change of mind should not give her any greater right of access to her genetic offspring than a sperm donor has. Although she did undergo ovarian stimulation and surgical retrieval to provide the eggs, she would not have had the experience of pregnancy and childbirth that distinguishes the claim of surrogate mothers who in some states may retain rearing rights despite their promise to relinquish custody after birth. Fairness requires that the original intentions of the parties, on which all relied, be followed.

In the absence of a statute giving effect to agreements to exclude the genetic mother from rearing, only a state that defined motherhood in genetic but not gestational terms might regard the matter differently. In *Anna J v Mark C*, a case involving a gestational surrogate who wanted to play a rearing role after birth, the California Court of Appeals did hold that motherhood, like fatherhood, was to be determined on genetic grounds.[7] In that decision the court held that a gestational surrogate was not the "mother" of the child that she carried and gave birth to, because the egg was provided by another woman. If that rationale for the decision had been affirmed, an egg donor, like the woman providing the egg for surrogate gestation, would have been the "mother" under California law and thus have standing to seek visitation or custody of resulting children.

However, this rationale did not survive the California Supreme Court's affirmation of the decision.[8] That court excluded the gestational surrogate from any rearing role and awarded sole custody of the child to the contracting couple, on the grounds that explicitly did not also apply to egg donation, thus removing the potential legal barrier to egg donation that the Court of Appeals decision appeared to create.

SEMINARS IN REPRODUCTIVE ENDOCRINOLOGY   Volume 13, Number 3   August 1995

Yet even under a purely genetic definition of motherhood, it would not follow that the egg donor—the genetic mother—would be entitled to visit the child or have any other rearing role when she had agreed at the time of donation to relinquish all rearing rights and duties in offspring born of her donated eggs. Doctrines of waiver and best interests of the child would still control. If she had not asserted her claim before or shortly after birth, she would most likely be found to have waived it, as unmarried fathers who do not assert any rearing right soon after birth are held to do.[9] Even if waiver doctrines did not apply and the case was decided solely in terms of the child's best interests, it will be difficult to show that the child's interests are best served by having a nongestational, genetic parent involved in rearing a child when the parties had reached a contrary agreement at the time at which the eggs were donated.

In the final analysis, the resolution of this issue will depend on society's view of the importance of genetic vs gestational motherhood and the importance of the parties' preconception intentions. In a state without egg donor legislation, a very risk-averse couple could have the donor terminate her parental rights after the child is born and then have the recipient/gestational mother adopt her husband's child in a stepparent adoption. As a general rule, however, such steps are unnecessary until there are court decisions that give the egg donor the right to assert parental claims after birth. Given the original intentions of the parties, the gestational role of the recipient, and sperm donation practices, such court decisions are unlikely to occur.

A second type of dispute would arise if attempts were made to hold the egg donor liable after birth for child support or other rearing obligations toward her genetic child. Because egg donors ordinarily intend to be excluded from any rearing role, they will want legal protection from later rearing obligations. One can imagine a scenario where the recipient dies after birth, or where the couple undergoes hardships that make it impossible for them to support the child. Either they or the state then seek to hold the donor as genetic mother responsible for child support.

Until state law makes clear that egg donors lose all rearing rights and duties, there is always some risk that such a duty could be imposed, but it is highly unlikely. The situation is unlike the situation of sperm donation to a single woman where the donor has occasionally been held responsible for child support when no rearing father existed.[10] Here the donation is to a woman who intends to gestate, rear, and be completely responsible for the child's welfare. Holding the egg donor liable for support in this situation would deter egg donation to married and single women alike. Followed to its logical conclusion, it would also make doctors who assist reproduction by single women potentially liable for child support.

Although it is highly unlikely that such a duty would be imposed, the donor needs to be fully informed of this uncertainty. If she is very risk-averse, she could demand that the recipient couple agree to hold her harmless for any financial obligation that might arise from the birth of such a child, but this guarantee might not be worth much if they or the state need to turn to her for child support. Alternatively, she could terminate her parental rights at birth and have the recipient adopt the child to make clear that she has no parental obligations. Except for the most risk-averse donors, however, this step is unnecessary as a general rule until a court decision holds egg donors liable for later obligations. Judicial decisions that create duties contrary to the original intentions of the parties are as unlikely to occur as decisions that create rights in the donor contrary to the original agreement of the parties.

Questions about rearing rights and duties could also affect questions of inheritance. Donor sperm legislation usually makes the consenting husband the legal father for all purposes and the donor the father for none, so that devises to one's "children" or "heirs," or to children under intestacy statutes would, in the case of a deceased husband, go to the children born of sperm donation, while in the case of the deceased donor they would not.[11] A similar result might be reached in states without donor sperm legislation, though the question has not yet arisen. Of course, either party could make specific bequests to make sure that certain individuals did or did not take from their estate.

A similar result would probably be reached in legislation establishing rearing rights and duties in offspring of egg donation. The child would be the "heir" or "child" of the recipient and not of the donor, unless a specific bequest were made. Until such legislation is passed, however, it is unclear whether the offspring of egg donation are children of the donor, of the recipient, or of both under intestacy statutes or general devises to one's "children" or "heirs." To avoid problems and make sure that intentions are honored, both recipients and donors should specify in their wills by name or relation persons whom they wish to share in their estate.

Finally, it should be noted that there may be instances of egg donation in which the donor and the recipient agree to share in parenting rights and duties.[12] While this will not be the usual case, and may not even be known to the physician providing the service, persons who plan such arrangements should execute agreements that make very clear what their mutual rights and obligations are. There is no guarantee that their agreements will be honored, and they should understand these limitations in proceeding.

RISKS TO DONORS

Egg donors face both psychosocial and physical risks of harm from participation in egg donation. The psychosocial risk is that they will wish more contact with resulting offspring than they are able to have, and thus feel cut off from their genetic offspring. There is also the risk that women who wish to have no contact with offspring may later be faced with offspring seeking them out or demands for child support. Donors should be fully informed that they might have different feelings about donation at a later point, and about the legal uncertainties that, in the absence of legislation or court decision, exist about determining rearing rights and duties by preconception agreement. As noted, the most likely scenario is that donors will be totally excluded from any contact or relationship with any offspring, no matter how much they later desire it, if they had so agreed at the time of donation. In addition, even though they cannot be guaranteed that they will not have unwanted contact or later obligations, the chances of that occurring appear to be small.

Donors also face physical risks. Unlike sperm donors who are asked to be abstinent and then masturbate into a jar, egg donors will have their ovaries stimulated with hormones to produce multiple eggs, which will then be surgically retrieved, either by transvaginal ultrasound-guided aspiration or by laparoscopy. Several days of injections will also be necessary. Risks of complications or infection, while small, do exist. These include hyperstimulation syndrome, infection, etc. They are the same risks that candidates for IVF undergo.

Although the complication rate with ovarian stimulation and egg retrieval is very small, it is possible that some egg donors will be injured in the process. An important legal question is to determine who will be responsible for the medical and other costs of such injures. Potential donors need to be fully informed of the risks that they face and also to be told who will bear responsibility for the costs of any injuries that occur.

One possibility would be to have the donor assume the costs of these risks. Just as human subjects of biomedical research bear the costs of any injuries sustained in the research process,[13] egg donors could also be asked to bear the cost. The risk of incurring these costs is part of what they are providing as egg donors. If so, it should be made clear to them that they are bearing that cost. However, the cost is limited to the cost of non-negligently caused injuries

because they cannot waive their right to recovery for negligence that causes their injuries.[13] If they clearly understand that they are bearing these costs, their assumption of that risk has a reasonable chance of protecting the program and recipient couple from liability for non-negligently caused injuries that result from the participation as egg donors.

An alternative solution is to have the program assume all or some portion of the costs of any non-negligently caused injuries to donors. Because such costs would ultimately be passed on to recipient couples, they should also be clearly informed of the extent, if any, to which they will be responsible for the donor's medical and other costs. The program cannot hold them liable unless they have specifically agreed to assume those costs. For their own protection they need to be informed of this risk and set limits on their exposure.

The best solution to this problem would be to have the program that recruits the donor purchase a short-term health insurance policy to cover any medical costs that she incurs as a result of the donation. Programs that do not themselves recruit donors but that retrieve eggs from donors identified by the recipient should also provide such insurance. The cost of this insurance would be paid by the program or the recipient, and would be the extent of their responsibility for non-negligently caused injuries. Such a limitation should be clearly explained to potential donors and recipients, so that they are fully aware of their rights and responsibilities.

THE LEGALITY OF PAYING DONORS

Unless a couple seeking an egg donor has a friend or family member willing to donate, the main source of donor eggs is likely to be anonymous strangers recruited for that purpose. Although they will have mixed motives, including altruism and the desire to have genetic offspring without gestational or rearing burdens, women may be unwilling to donate unless they are paid for their efforts, which are not inconsiderable. Without payment to donors, many women may be denied access to egg donation.

While some ethicists have objected to paying women for their eggs on the ground that it is exploitive and commodifies offspring, there is no clear consensus that such payments are unethical. Since sperm donors are paid, it would be discriminatory to ban payment to egg donors, who undergo greater burdens. Nor is it clear that paying for eggs is exploitative or coercive of women. The amounts paid are not so large relative to the time and effort involved that they are likely to induce women to undergo unacceptable risks. Experience also indicates that most women who volunteer are not poor or minor-

SEMINARS IN REPRODUCTIVE ENDOCRINOLOGY   Volume 13, Number 3   August 1995

ities. Finally, the transaction can be structured as paying for their physical services rather than for the eggs themselves, which reduces the risk that the transaction will be viewed as one involving the sale of children.

An important issue is whether federal and state laws that ban buying and selling organs for transplant also apply to paying egg donors. In response to fears that persons would sell living or cadaveric organs for transplant, the federal government and several states passed laws making it a crime (with penalties ranging from felony to misdemeanor) to buy or sell organs.[14] Although the intent of these laws was not to apply to sperm and egg donation, their language in some cases is drawn so broadly that the sale of eggs could be covered as prohibited.

The main threat here is from state law. The 1986 Federal Organ Transplant Act, which prohibits the acquisition, receipt, or transfer of "any human organ for valuable consideration for use in human transplantation," defines "human organ" in such a way that sperm and ova are clearly excluded.[15] Only Louisiana expressly prohibits "the sale of a human ovum."[16] However, prohibitions in Texas, Ohio, California, and several other states are less narrowly defined than the federal law and leave open the possibility that the sale of ova and even sperm is criminally banned.

The Texas statute, for example, defines human organ to include "the human kidney, liver, heart ... or any other human organ or tissue, but does not include hair or blood, blood components (including plasma), blood derivatives, or blood reagents."[17] The question turns then on whether ova are "tissue." Under a standard dictionary definition of tissue—"a collection of similar cells and the intercellular substances surrounding them"[18]—the contents of one follicle would not be tissue, even if cumulus and follicular fluid is also aspirated, because only the egg is donated. On the other hand, the legislature failed to exclude sperm and ova as it did blood and blood products, and in a broad sense ova could be viewed as tissue. The Ohio statute raises similar issues.[19]

A law in Nevada bans the sale of specified organs and "any other part of the human body except blood."[20] Are oocytes a "part of the human body" or are they products of the body? Either interpretation is possible.

Another kind of ambiguity arises in California[21] and South Dakota[22] statutes that make it a crime to receive, sell, transfer, or promote the transfer of "any human organ, for purposes of transplantation, for valuable consideration." Human organ is defined as "the human kidney, liver, heart ... or any other human organ or nonrenewable or nonregenerative tissue except plasma and sperm." Because the statute

explicitly excludes sperm and plasma but not ova, and ova, strictly speaking, are nonrenewable or nonregenerative, one could conclude that ova are included within the definition of "human organ." However, one could also reasonably argue that ova are not tissue, or that they are renewable tissue because a donor has a large supply of ova. One or more cycles of egg donation will not deplete the eggs available for the donor until she herself reaches menopause.

Finally, one can question whether California-type statutes ban payments to egg donors because egg donation is not for the purpose of "transplantation." Transplantation implies insertion of an organ or tissue in another person to replace a missing function. But eggs are not transplanted. Rather, they are fertilized in vitro, and then the cleaving embryo is placed in the uterus. Transfer of an embryo to the uterus followed by implantation and pregnancy is thus not "transplantation" of an organ or tissue. Indeed, in some cases the donated eggs will not produce embryos, and all embryos may not be transferred to the uterus, much less successfully implant therein.

These examples of state statutes banning the sale of organs show that the definition of organ as "tissue" or "any other body part" opens the door to the possibility that sale of ova is included in the statutory ban, particularly when it is not included in certain exceptions. However, an arguably more persuasive reading of these laws would exclude sperm and ova from them. They were written with sale of solid organs in mind, sperm and ova are functionally renewable, and it is very doubtful that the donated ova and sperm are then "transplanted." Moreover, including the sale of sperm and ova would raise constitutional problems, both of vagueness and procreative liberty, and statutes are generally construed to avoid doubts about their constitutionality.

Despite these uncertainties, physicians, couples, and donors in states with laws that could be interpreted to ban payment for egg donation might still reasonably proceed with paid egg donation when that is the only way to recruit suitable donors. While the risk of prosecution cannot be totally eliminated, it appears to be small. No prosecutions have yet been brought. If prosecution did occur, the participants would have a strong defense that the statute is unconstitutionally vague in that a reasonable person could not tell whether ova are included in the prohibition.[23,24] In addition, if they honestly believed that ova were not covered, they would also lack the specific intent to violate the law required in most cases for criminal liability. They could also attack the law as an unconstitutional interference with the right of infertile married couples to form a family with the help of an egg donor.[25]

To reduce the risks of prosecution even further, the relationship between the donor and the program or recipient should be structured as one in which they are paying for the services of the donor in undergoing the procedures necessary to produce the eggs, rather than the eggs themselves. Thus payment should depend on the number and kind of procedures undergone and not be calibrated to the production of eggs or of any number of eggs. The agreement should state that payment is to compensate the donor for her time and services and not for the eggs. It should also state that the donor is free to back out at any point, that she will be paid for any procedures undergone, including egg retrieval, even if she decides at the last minute not to relinquish her rights in retrieved eggs. Skillful writing of the contract/agreement with the donor will reduce the risk, which may already be small, that the participants will be prosecuted for, much less found guilty of, unlawful sale of organs or tissue under state law.

In any event, even if these laws do apply, there would still be room to pay donors their medical and other expenses. The statutes in question do allow for reimbursement of the donor's "expenses of travel, housing and lost wages."[17] Thus some fee to the donor would be possible if time off work were required, even if this did pose an upper limit. Also, such restrictions would permit one couple to pay the expenses of another couple going through IVF with the understanding that they would share the resulting eggs harvested. This would seem to be the paying of expenses necessary to produce the donation, and not a payment for the eggs themselves.

ISSUES OF OFFSPRING WELFARE

Egg donation, like other assisted reproductive techniques, raises questions about the impact on offspring. Legal duties aside, there is a strong ethical obligation to pay attention to how these procedures will affect the children who are produced as a result. Programs should be run and structured to minimize harm to offspring.

This duty creates a paradox, however. But for the assisted reproductive procedure in question, the child would never be born. Thus even if a procedure leads to a child with a novel set of parents, it is still not possible to say that the child is harmed by having two female parents because the child would not otherwise have been born, and the resulting parenting arrangement or confusion does not produce such dire consequences that the child would have been better off never having been born at all.

Even if one rejects this analysis generally, it is not easy to argue that egg donation creates such a confusing parenting situation that the child is clearly harmed irreparably just by being born in this way. After all, in the ordinary case the child will be reared by two biologic parents, which distinguishes egg donation from surrogacy and donor sperm. Of all collaborative reproductive arrangements, egg donation is closest to the norm of two parents contributing genes, gestation, and rearing. Indeed, a ban on egg donation on the ground that it harms offspring because it splits genetic and gestational parentage would not rise to the level of compelling interest necessary to justify infringing the fundamental right to procreate.[17,25]

This is true even if eggs are donated to an unmarried woman or to a woman who is past the normal outer limit of menopause—say, to a woman in her 50s. Providing donor eggs to a single woman is no different than providing her with donor sperm or, indeed, than a single woman engaging in coital reproduction. In each case a woman decides to conceive and give birth to a child knowing that there will not be a rearing male partner. Yet few people would now argue, particularly in the case of an economically stable woman, that birth to a single woman is such a detriment to the child that it should not have been born at all. Physicians treating infertility may decide not to participate in such situations, but they would not be acting unethically or illegally if they did. Indeed, a law that outlawed such assistance would be subject to attack on both equal protection and due process grounds, for it would deny an infertile unmarried woman the same rights that a married person has.

Similarly, the use of donor eggs with a woman past the normal age of childbearing is not clearly harmful to the child either. Such cases will be relatively infrequent, but they will occur and may garner wide media attention when they do, as occurred with the 1993 birth of twins in Britain to a 59-year-old recipient of donor eggs.[26–28] Having an older mother does deviate from past practices and traditional views of motherhood, but men have been able to reproduce late in life. To deny women this opportunity when a technology permits it would seem to be discriminatory on gender grounds. Even if the child's mother dies at an earlier age than usual, the child is not so worse off that it would have been better that it had not been born at all. Again, individual programs or practitioners may choose not to offer egg donation to older recipients, but it would not be unethical to do so, and could not, given constitutional rights of equal protection and procreative liberty, legally be banned in the United States.

Even though egg donation cannot itself be banned to protect offspring, it should be conducted in ways that will respect their interests. The most important measure here is to keep confidential records about donor identity and characteristics so that offspring

SEMINARS IN REPRODUCTIVE ENDOCRINOLOGY   Volume 13, Number 3   August 1995

may later, if the law or changes in social policy permit, learn the identity of their genetic mother and even have contact with her if that can be arranged in a mutually satisfactory way. Recognition of the child's right to have information about or even learn the identity at some later point of its genetic mother does not also mean that the egg donor will have other rearing duties imposed against her wishes.

At present their is no law that requires that such records be kept or that enables offspring of sperm or egg donation to ever learn who their genetic parents are. While some state adoption laws allow the confidentiality of records to be pierced for good cause, there is no existing provision for offspring of gamete donation, and no records may be available if there were.[29,30] Whether and to what extent children should be informed of how they were born will have to depend on the families that raise them. Disclosure cannot and should not be legislated. But if state law does permit or require disclosure, or the parties otherwise agree to disclosure, it will be necessary to have records of donors and recipients available.

It is thus essential that donors be informed of the extent to which anonymity will be preserved and records kept so that later contact or information, if mutually desired or otherwise required by state law, can be arranged.

GESTATIONAL SURROGACY

Gestational surrogacy allows women with intact ovaries who lack uterine capacity or ability to gestate to have and rear biologically related offspring. A surrogate agrees to have the embryo formed with the egg and sperm of another couple to be placed in her uterus, where she will gestate it, bring it to term, and then relinquish it to the hiring couple for rearing.

The intention of the parties in gestational surrogacy is for the persons who provided egg and sperm for creation of the embryo, who are the child's genetic parents, to rear, and for the surrogate, who has no parental genetic tie to offspring, to have no role in rearing. When sisters, mothers, other family members, or friends serve as surrogates, the rearing role might be different. By contrast, in full surrogacy the surrogate is artificially inseminated with husband sperm, gestates and gives birth to a child of which she is also the genetic mother, and then relinquishes it to the father and his partner for rearing.

Although many ethical questions have been raised about surrogacy and society has not yet placed a clear imprimatur of approval on the practice, gestational surrogacy is not legally prohibited. The main legal issues concern whether gestational surrogates can be paid beyond their expenses, whether the surrogate loses all rearing rights and duties, what goes on the birth certificate, whether the couple or physician can be liable for injuries to the surrogate, and how issues of conflict about management of the pregnancy are handled.

Payment

A major issue is whether gestational surrogates may be paid for their services. Unless a sister, friend, or family member is willing to act as surrogate, it will be necessary to pay surrogates to obtain their services. Yet some persons have argued that payment is unethical because it might commodify surrogates and offspring or create coercive inducements to poorer women to serve in this role. The counterargument is that the money is paid to a surrogate for her services, not for selling a baby; she is freely and knowingly choosing; she has a right to sell her gestational services; and there is no evidence that offspring or women are viewed or treated as objects.

The legality of paying for gestational surrogate services remains uncertain, except in those few states that have explicitly banned or permitted payment. In other states the legality of paying surrogates will depend on the scope of state bans on baby-selling or paying for more than medical expenses in adoptions. In the Baby M case, the New Jersey Supreme Court held that such statutes prohibit paying fees to full surrogates. Even if other states follow that precedent in the case of full surrogacy, it does not follow that New Jersey or other states will treat gestational surrogacy the same way. For the gestational surrogate, who is not carrying her own genetic child, is more clearly being paid for her gestational services. Indeed, in many jurisdictions she may not have to go through an adoption proceeding to relinquish rearing rights to offspring born of the surrogate arrangement. Finally, a ban on paying a gestational surrogate might unconstitutionally interfere with the procreative liberty of infertile couples who have no alternative way to reproduce.[30]

Rearing Rights and Duties

Ethical and legal commentators are split on whether a gestational surrogate should be able to retain custody or otherwise be involved in rearing of the child that she delivers. Because preconception and prenatal agreements to relinquish coitally conceived children for adoption are invalid, some commentators have argued that surrogacy contracts should be as well. They claim that a surrogate should always be free to change her mind for a specified period after birth because of the intense bond she has developed with the fetus and the labor and delivery that she has experienced. Others have argued that her agreement should be enforceable because of the reliance interests of the hiring couple and the need to treat men and women equally in holding them to their contracts.

Legally, the situation is uncertain. The Baby M case held that the preconception agreement with a full surrogate was not enforceable. Several states passed laws in the aftermath of Baby M giving the surrogate mother a period of time after birth to change her mind. Unfortunately, most of those statutes do not make clear whether they also extend to gestational surrogacy, thus leaving the question open to dispute and litigation. In the few cases involving gestational surrogates that have reached the courts, the courts have tended to side with the contracting couple on the theory that parentage is defined genetically. Thus the California Supreme Court in *Johnson v Calvert* interpreted California statutes defining parentage as making the hiring couple the parents and giving the gestational surrogate no parental rights. Because the hiring couple has entrusted their embryo(s) to the surrogate in reliance on her promise to gestate and relinquish at birth, it is likely that other courts and jurisdictions will follow *Johnson v Calvert* when similar situations arise. Until there are legislation or clear precedents in effect, however, there will be some uncertainty about the legal status of enforcing the promise of gestational surrogates to relinquish at birth.

Birth Certificates

The question of who is the legal mother also arises in the question of whose name should be listed as mother on the birth certificate. Trial courts in Michigan and Texas have ordered the genetic mother's name to be entered in proceedings prior to birth in which all parties agree. However, the point has never been settled by an appellate court, and practice concerning birth certificates varies from state to state.

Liability for Surrogate Injuries

Just as the parties in egg donation should be clear about who bears the cost of any injury that the egg donor suffers in the stimulation and retrieval cycle, so the parties should be clear about who bears the risk of injuries to the surrogate. A gestational surrogate might reasonably request that she be compensated for any medical expenses and lost earnings

that result from injuries suffered as a result of her surrogacy. She should also be informed of the extent to which the couple providing the embryo have been screened for human immunodeficiency syndrome, cytomegalovirus, and other diseases that could be transmitted to her. A federal appeals court held in *Stiver v Parker* that physicians running a surrogate program could be liable to a surrogate who contracted cytomegalovirus allegedly as a result of insemination with the hiring husband's sperm that had not been adequately screened for this disease.[31] The cost of injuries should be clearly explained and laid out in advance. As with egg donors, a fair arrangement would have the hiring couple purchase a supplemental health insurance policy to cover her medical expenses during pregnancy.

Control of Surrogate's Behavior during Pregnancy

As gestational surrogacy increases in frequency, conflicts over the surrogate's behavior during pregnancy will arise. The two most important issues here are the surrogate's refusal to undergo prenatal diagnosis or abort in the case of a serious genetic defect, and questions of drug and alcohol use during pregnancy.

Many hiring couples may request that the surrogate undergo prenatal diagnosis and abort in the case of a serious or otherwise specified genetic defect. If the surrogate refuses to do so, contract provisions may require that the surrogate then assume responsibility for the child, and even be liable for damages to the couple for any injury they have suffered as a result. Although the surrogate could not be physically forced to undergo amniocentesis, much less abortion, because of the involuntary bodily intrusions that would be involved, that barrier would not necessarily apply to requiring the surrogate to pay damages to the couple for breach of her agreement to abort in certain circumstances. In cases where the surrogate's intentional or negligent prenatal conduct causes a child who could have been born healthy to be born with disabilities, damage remedies may also be possible.

CONCLUSION

Egg donation and gestational surrogacy are both promising techniques for treating infertility, but they both lack the legal infrastructure necessary to provide the participants with certainty about the legal consequences of this collaborative form of assisted reproduction. Legislation, judicial decision, and

SEMINARS IN REPRODUCTIVE ENDOCRINOLOGY Volume 13, Number 3 August 1995

standard practice will eventually cure these uncertainties.

In the meantime, interested parties need not refrain from participation in human egg donation and gestational surrogacy, but they should be fully aware of the areas of uncertainty that exist and take steps to minimize undesired consequences. In the final analysis, full disclosure, free and informed consent, and respect for the interests of all parties will be the best protection for physicians, couples, donors, and surrogates who participate in these practices.

REFERENCES

1. Sauer MV, Paulson RJ: Understanding the current status of oocyte donation in the United States: What's really going on out there? Fertil Steril 58:16–18, 1992
2. Sauer MV, Paulson RJ, Lobo RA: Reversing the natural decline in human fertility: An extended clinical trial of oocyte donation to women of advanced reproductive age. JAMA 268:1275–1279, 1992
3. Okla Stat Ann 10 §544 (1991)
4. Tex. SB 512, 73rd Leg, RS (1993)
5. S2082, 1993 Reg Sess, Florida Laws (1993)
5a. VA Code Ann (Michie 1995) §§20–156 to 165
6. United States Congress, Office of Technology Assessment: *Infertility: Medical and Social Choices.* Washington, DC: U.S. Government Printing Office, 1988, pp 242–249
7. 286 Cal Rptr 369 (Cal App 4 Dist 1991)
8. 822 P2d 1317, 4 Cal Rptr 2d 170 (1992)
9. *Lehr v Robertson,* 463 US 248 (1983)
10. *Jhordan C v Mary K,* #A27810 (Cal Ct App 1986)
11. Tex Fam Code Ann §12.03 (Vernon 1986)
12. Robertson JA: Ethical and legal issues in human egg donation. Fertil Steril 52:353–363, 1989
13. President's Commission for the Study of Ethical Problems in Medicine and Biomedical and Behavioral Science Research: *Compensating for Research Injuries.* Washington, DC: U.S. Government Printing Office, 1982, pp 81–98
14. Note: Regulating the sale of human organs. Virginia Law Rev 71:1015, 1985
15. Prohibition of Organ Purchases, 42 USCA #274(e)
16. La Civ Code Ann Art 9:122 (Supp 1987)
17. Texas Health and Safety Code Ann, §48.02 (West 1989)
18. *Stedman's Medical Dictionary.* 22nd ed., 1972
19. Ohio Rev Code Ann S 2108.11, 2108.12 (Baldwin 1980)
20. Nev Rev Stat #201.460 (1991)
21. Cal Penal Code #367f (West 1988)
22. SD Codified Laws Ann-S 34-26-42
23. *Margaret S v Edwards,* 794 F2d 994 (5th Cir 1986)
24. *Lifchez v Hartigan,* 735 F Supp 1361 (ND Ill 1990)
25. Robertson JA: Technology and motherhood: Ethical and legal issues in human egg donation. Case Western Reserve Law Rev 39:1–38, 1989
26. Schmidt W: Birth to a 59-year-old generates an ethical controversy in Britain. New York Times December 29, 1993
27. Associate Press: 53-year-old grandmother gives birth to premature test-tube twins. Austin American-Statesman November 11, 1992
28. People Magazine May 8, 1992
29. Robertson JA: Embryos, families and procreative liberty: The legal structure of the new reproduction. South Calif Law Rev 59:942–1039, 1986
30. Robertson JA: *Children of Choice: Freedom and the New Reproductive Technologies.* Princeton, NJ: Princeton University Press, 1994
31. 975 F2d 261 (6th Cir 1992)

[7]
Surrogate Motherhood as Prenatal Adoption

Bonnie Steinbock

The recent case of "Baby M" has brought surrogate motherhood to the forefront of American attention. Ultimately, whether we permit or prohibit surrogacy depends on what we take to be good reasons for preventing people from acting as they wish. A growing number of people want to be, or hire, surrogates; are there legitimate reasons to prevent them? Apart from its intrinsic interest, the issue of surrogate motherhood provides us with an opportunity to examine different justifications for limiting individual freedom.

In the first section of this article, I examine the Baby M case and the lessons it offers. In the second section, I examine claims that surrogacy is ethically unacceptable because it is exploitive, inconsistent with human dignity, or harmful to the children born of such arrangements. I conclude that these reasons justify restrictions on surrogate contracts, rather than an outright ban.

Baby M

Mary Beth Whitehead, a married mother of two, agreed to be inseminated with the sperm of William Stern and to give up the child to him for a fee of $10,000. The baby (whom Ms. Whitehead named Sara, and the Sterns named Melissa) was born on March 27, 1986. Three days later, Ms. Whitehead took her home from the hospital and turned her over to the Sterns.

Then Ms. Whitehead changed her mind. She went to the Sterns' home, distraught, and pleaded to have the baby temporarily. Afraid that she would kill herself, the Sterns agreed. The next week, Ms. Whitehead informed the Sterns that she had decided to keep the child, and threatened to leave the country if court action was taken.

At that point, the situation deteriorated into a cross between the Keystone Kops and Nazi stormtroopers. Accompanied by five policemen, the Sterns went to the Whitehead residence armed with a court order giving them temporary custody of the child. Ms. Whitehead managed to slip the baby out of a window to her husband, and the following morning the Whiteheads fled with the child to Florida, where Ms. Whitehead's parents lived. During the next three months, the Whiteheads lived in roughly twenty different hotels, motels, and homes to avoid apprehension. From time to time, Ms. Whitehead telephoned Mr. Stern to discuss the matter: he taped these conversations on advice of counsel. Ms. Whitehead threatened to kill herself, to kill the child, and to falsely accuse Mr. Stern of sexually molesting her older daughter.

At the end of July 1986, while Ms. Whitehead was hospitalized with a kidney infection, Florida police raided her mother's home, knocking her down, and seized the child. Baby M was placed in the custody of Mr. Stern, and the Whiteheads returned to New Jersey, where they attempted to regain custody. After a long and emotional court battle, Judge Harvey R. Sorkow ruled on March 31, 1987, that the surrogacy contract was valid, and that specific performance was justified in the best interests of the child. Immediately after reading his decision, he called the Sterns into his chambers so that Mr. Stern's wife, Dr. Elizabeth Stern, could legally adopt the child.

This outcome was unexpected and unprecedented. Most commentators had thought that a court would be unlikely to order a reluctant surrogate to give up an infant merely on the basis of a contract.[1] Indeed, if Ms. Whitehead had never surrendered the child to the Sterns, but had simply taken her home and kept her there, the outcome undoubtedly would have been different. It is also likely that Ms. Whitehead's failure to obey the initial custody order angered Judge Sorkow, and affected his decision.

The decision was appealed to the New Jersey Supreme Court, which issued its decision on February 3, 1988. Writing for a unanimous court, Chief Justice Wilentz reversed the lower court's ruling that the surrogacy contract was valid. The court held that a surrogacy contract that provides money for the surrogate mother, and that includes her irrevocable agreement to surrender her child at birth, is invalid and unenforceable. Since the contract was invalid, Ms. Whitehead did not relinquish, nor were there any other grounds for terminating, her parental rights. Therefore, the adoption of Baby M by Dr. Stern was improperly granted, and Ms. Whitehead remains the child's legal mother.

The court further held that the issue of custody is determined solely by the child's best interests, and it agreed with the lower court that it was in Melissa's best interests to remain with the Sterns. However, Ms. Whitehead, as Baby M's legal as well as natural mother, is entitled to have her own interest in visitation considered. The determination of what kind of visitation rights should be granted to her, and under what conditions, was remanded to the trial court.

The distressing details of this case have led many people to reject surrogacy altogether. Do we really want police officers wrenching infants from their mothers' arms, and prolonged custody battles when surrogates find they are unable to surrender their children, as agreed? Advocates of surrogacy say that to reject the practice wholesale, because of one unfortunate instance, is an example of a "hard case" making bad policy. Opponents reply that it is entirely reasonable to focus on the worst potential outcomes when deciding public policy. Everyone can agree on at least one thing: this particular case seems to have been mismanaged from start to finish, and could serve as a manual of how not to arrange a surrogate birth.

First, it is now clear that Mary Beth Whitehead was not a suitable candidate for surrogate motherhood. Her ambivalence about giving up the child was recognized early on, although this information was not passed on to the Sterns.[2] Second, she had contact with the baby after birth, which is usually avoided in "successful" cases. Typically, the adoptive mother is actively involved in the pregnancy, often serving as the pregnant woman's coach in labor. At birth, the baby is given to the adoptive, not the biological mother. The joy of the adoptive parents in holding their child serves both to promote their bonding and to lessen the pain of separation of the biological mother.

At Ms. Whitehead's request, no one at the hospital was aware of the surrogacy arrangement. She and her husband appeared as the proud parents of "Sara Elizabeth Whitehead," the name on her birth certificate. Ms. Whitehead held her baby, nursed her, and took her home from the hospital—just as she would have done in a normal pregnancy and birth. Not surprisingly, she

thought of Sara as her child, and she fought with every weapon at her disposal, honorable and dishonorable, to prevent her being taken away. She can hardly be blamed for doing so.[3]

Why did Dr. Stern, who supposedly had a very good relation with Ms. Whitehead before the birth, not act as her labor coach? One possibility is that Ms. Whitehead, ambivalent about giving up her baby, did not want Dr. Stern involved. At her request, the Sterns' visits to the hospital to see the newborn baby were unobtrusive. It is also possible that Dr. Stern was ambivalent about having a child. The original idea of hiring a surrogate was not hers, but her husband's. It was Mr. Stern who felt a "compelling" need to have a child related to him by blood, having lost all his relatives to the Nazis.

Furthermore, Dr. Stern was not infertile, as was stated in the surrogacy agreement. Rather, in 1979 she was diagnosed by two eye specialists as suffering from optic neuritis, which meant that she "probably" had multiple sclerosis. (This was confirmed by all four experts who testified.) Normal conception was ruled out by the Sterns in late 1982, when a medical colleague told Dr. Stern that his wife, a victim of multiple sclerosis, had suffered a temporary paralysis during pregnancy. "We decided the risk wasn't worth it," Mr. Stern said.[4]

Ms. Whitehead's lawyer, Harold J. Cassidy, dismissed the suggestion that Dr. Stern's "mildest case" of multiple sclerosis determined the Sterns' decision to seek a surrogate. He noted that she was not even treated for multiple sclerosis until after the Baby M dispute had started. "It's almost as though it's an afterthought," he said.[5]

Judge Sorkow deemed the decision to avoid conception "medically reasonable and understandable." The Supreme Court did not go so far, noting that Dr. Stern's "anxiety appears to have exceeded the actual risk, which current medical authorities assess as minimal."[6] Nonetheless, the court acknowledged that her anxiety, including fears that pregnancy might precipitate blindness and paraplegia, was "quite real." Certainly, even a woman who wants a child very much may reasonably wish to avoid becoming blind and paralyzed as a result of pregnancy. Yet is it believable that a woman who really wanted a child would decide against pregnancy *solely* on the basis of *someone else's* medical experience? Would she not consult at least one specialist on her *own* medical condition before deciding it wasn't worth the risk? The conclusion that she was at best ambivalent about bearing a child seems irresistible.

This possibility conjures up many people's worst fears about surrogacy: that prosperous women, who do not want to interrupt their careers, will use poor and educationally disadvantaged women to bear their children. I will return shortly to the question of whether this is exploitive. The issue here is psychological: what kind

Volume 16: 1–2, Spring 1988

of mother is Dr. Stern likely to be? If she is unwilling to undergo pregnancy, with its discomforts, inconveniences, and risks, will she be willing to make the considerable sacrifices that good parenting requires? Ms. Whitehead's ability to be a good mother was repeatedly questioned during the trial. She was portrayed as immature, untruthful, hysterical, overly identified with her children, and prone to smothering their independence. Even if all this is true—and I think that Ms. Whitehead's inadequacies were exaggerated—Dr. Stern may not be such a prize either. The choice for Baby M may have been between a highly strung, emotional, overinvolved mother, and a remote, detached, even cold one.[7]

The assessment of Ms. Whitehead's ability to be a good mother was biased by the middle-class prejudices of the judge and of the mental health officials who testified. Ms. Whitehead left school at fifteen, and is not conversant with the latest theories on child rearing: she made the egregious error of giving Sara teddy bears to play with, instead of the more "age-appropriate," expert-approved pans and spoons. She proved to be a total failure at patty-cake. If this is evidence of parental inadequacy, we're all in danger of losing our children.

The Supreme Court felt that Ms. Whitehead was "rather harshly judged" and acknowledged the possibility that the trial court was wrong in its initial award of custody. Nevertheless, it affirmed Judge Sorkow's decision to allow the Sterns to retain custody, as being in Melissa's best interests. George Annas disagrees with the "best interests" approach. He points out that Judge Sorkow awarded temporary custody of Baby M to the Sterns in May 1986, without giving the Whiteheads notice or an opportunity to obtain legal representation. That was a serious wrong and injustice to the Whiteheads. To allow the Sterns to keep the child compounds the original unfairness: "justice requires that reasonable consideration be given to returning Baby M to the permanent custody of the Whiteheads."[8]

But a child is not a possession, to be returned to the rightful owner. It is not fairness to all parties that should determine a child's fate, but what is best for her. As Chief Justice Wilentz rightly stated, "The child's interests come first: we will not punish it for judicial errors, assuming any were made."[9]

Subsequent events have substantiated the claim that giving custody to the Sterns was in Melissa's best interests. After losing custody, Ms. Whitehead, whose husband had undergone a vasectomy, became pregnant by another man. She divorced her husband and married Dean R. Gould last November. These developments indicate that the Whiteheads were not able to offer a stable home, although the argument can be made that their marriage might have survived if not for the strains introduced by the court battle and the loss of Baby M. But

even if Judge Sorkow had no reason to prefer the Sterns to the Whiteheads back in May 1986, he was still right to give the Sterns custody in March 1987. To take her away then, at nearly eighteen months of age, from the only parents she had ever known would have been disruptive, cruel, and unfair to her.

Annas' preference for a just solution is premised partly on his belief that there *is* no "best interest" solution to this "tragic custody case." I take it that he means that however custody is resolved, Baby M is the loser. Either way, she will be deprived of one parent. However, a best-interests solution is not a perfect solution. It is simply the solution that is on balance best for the child, given the realities of the situation. Applying this standard, Judge Sorkow was right to give the Sterns custody, and the Supreme Court was right to uphold the decision.

The best-interests argument is based on the assumption that Mr. Stern has at least a *prima facie* claim to Baby M. We certainly would not consider allowing a stranger who kidnapped a baby and managed to elude the police for a year to retain custody on the grounds that he was providing a good home to a child who had known no other parent. However, the Baby M case is not analogous. First, Mr. Stern is Baby M's biological father and, as such, has at least some claim to raise her, which no non-parental kidnapper has. Second, Mary Beth Whitehead *agreed* to give him their baby. Unlike the miller's daughter in *Rumpelstiltskin,* the fairy tale to which the Baby M case is sometimes compared, she was not forced into the agreement. Because both Mary Beth Whitehead and Mr. Stern have *prima facie* claims to Baby M, the decision as to who should raise her should be based on her present best interests. Therefore we must, regretfully, tolerate the injustice to Ms. Whitehead, and try to avoid such problems in the future.

It is unfortunate that the court did not decide the issue of visitation on the same basis as custody. By declaring Ms. Whitehead-Gould the legal mother, and maintaining that she is entitled to visitation, the court has prolonged the fight over Baby M. It is hard to see how this can be in her best interests. This is no ordinary divorce case, where the child has a relation with both parents that it is desirable to maintain. As Mr. Stern said at the start of the court hearing to determine visitation, "Melissa has a right to grow and be happy and not be torn between two parents."[10]

The court's decision was well-meaning but internally inconsistent. Out of concern for the best interests of the child, it granted the Sterns custody. At the same time, by holding Ms. Whitehead-Gould to be the legal mother, with visitation rights, it precluded precisely what is most in Melissa's interest, a resolution of the situation. Further, the decision leaves open the distressing possibility that a Baby M situation could happen again. Legislative efforts should be directed toward ensuring that this worst-case scenario never occurs.

Should Surrogacy Be Prohibited?

On June 27, 1988, Michigan became the first state to outlaw commercial contracts for women to bear children for others.[11] Yet making a practice illegal does not necessarily make it go away: witness black-market adoption. The legitimate concerns that support a ban on surrogacy might be better served by careful regulation. However, some practices, such as slavery, are ethically unacceptable, regardless of how carefully regulated they are. Let us consider the arguments that surrogacy is intrinsically unacceptable.

Paternalistic Arguments

These arguments against surrogacy take the form of protecting a potential surrogate from a choice she may later regret. As an argument for banning surrogacy, as opposed to providing safeguards to ensure that contracts are freely and knowledgeably undertaken, this is a form of paternalism.

At one time, the characterization of a prohibition as paternalistic was a sufficient reason to reject it. The pendulum has swung back, and many people are willing to accept at least some paternalistic restrictions on freedom. Gerald Dworkin points out that even Mill made one exception to his otherwise absolute rejection of paternalism: he thought that no one should be allowed to sell himself into slavery, because to do so would be to destroy his future autonomy.

This provides a narrow principle to justify some paternalistic interventions. To preserve freedom in the long run, we give up the freedom to make certain choices, those that have results that are "far-reaching, potentially dangerous and irreversible."[12] An example would be a ban on the sale of crack. Virtually everyone who uses crack becomes addicted and, once addicted, a slave to its use. We reasonably and willingly give up our freedom to buy the drug, to protect our ability to make free decisions in the future.

Can a Dworkinian argument be made to rule out surrogacy agreements? Admittedly, the decision to give up a child is permanent, and may have disastrous effects on the surrogate mother. However, many decisions may have long-term, disastrous effects (e.g., postponing childbirth for a career, having an abortion, giving a child up for adoption). Clearly we do not want the state to make decisions for us in all these matters. Dworkin's argument is rightly restricted to paternalistic interferences that protect the individual's autonomy or ability

to make decisions in the future. Surrogacy does not involve giving up one's autonomy, which distinguishes it from both the crack and selling-oneself-into-slavery examples. Respect for individual freedom requires us to permit people to make choices they may later regret.

Moral Objections

Four main moral objections to surrogacy were outlined in the Warnock Report.[13]

1) It is inconsistent with human dignity that a woman should use her uterus for financial profit.
2) To deliberately become pregnant with the intention of giving up the child distorts the relationship between mother and child.
3) Surrogacy is degrading because it amounts to child-selling.
4) Since there are some risks attached to pregnancy, no woman ought to be asked to undertake pregnancy for another in order to earn money.[14]

We must all agree that a practice that exploits people or violates human dignity is immoral. However, it is not clear that surrogacy is guilty on either count.

EXPLOITATION

The mere fact that pregnancy is *risky* does not make surrogate agreements exploitive, and therefore morally wrong. People often do risky things for money; why should the line be drawn at undergoing pregnancy? The usual response is to compare surrogacy and kidney-selling. The selling of organs is prohibited because of the potential for coercion and exploitation. But why should kidney-selling be viewed as intrinsically coercive? A possible explanation is that no one would do it, unless driven by poverty. The choice is both forced and dangerous, and hence coercive.[15]

The situation is quite different in the case of the race-car driver or stuntman. We do not think that they are *forced* to perform risky activities for money: they freely choose to do so. Unlike selling one's kidneys, these are activities that we can understand (intellectually, anyway) someone choosing to do. Movie stuntmen, for example, often enjoy their work, and derive satisfaction from doing it well. Of course they "do it for the money," in the sense that they would not do it without compensation; few people are willing to work "for free." The element of coercion is missing, however, because they enjoy the job, despite the risks, and could do something else if they chose.

The same is apparently true of most surrogates.

"They choose the surrogate role primarily because the fee provides a better economic opportunity than alternative occupations, but also because they enjoy being pregnant and the respect and attention that it draws."[16] Some may derive a feeling of self-worth from an act they regard as highly altruistic: providing a couple with a child they could not otherwise have. If these motives are present, it is far from clear that the surrogate is being exploited. Indeed, it seems objectionably paternalistic to insist that she is.

HUMAN DIGNITY

It may be argued that even if womb-leasing is not necessarily exploitive, it should still be rejected as inconsistent with human dignity. But why? As John Harris points out, hair, blood, and other tissue is often donated or sold; what is so special about the uterus?[17]

Human dignity is more plausibly invoked in the strongest argument against surrogacy, namely, that it is the sale of a child. Children are not property, nor can they be bought or sold.[18] It could be argued that surrogacy is wrong because it is analogous to slavery, and so is inconsistent with human dignity.

However, there are important differences between slavery and a surrogate agreement.[19] The child born of a surrogate is not treated cruelly or deprived of freedom or resold; none of the things that make slavery so awful are part of surrogacy. Still, it may be thought that simply putting a market value on a child is wrong. Human life has intrinsic value; it is literally priceless. Arrangements that ignore this violate our deepest notions of the value of human life. It is profoundly disturbing to hear in a television documentary on surrogacy the boyfriend of a surrogate say, quite candidly, "We're in it for the money."

Judge Sorkow accepted the premise that producing a child for money denigrates human dignity, but he denied that this happens in a surrogate agreement. Ms. Whitehead was not paid for the surrender of the child to the father: she was paid for her willingness to be impregnated and carry Mr. Stern's child to term. The child, once born, is his biological child. "He cannot purchase what is already his."[20]

This is misleading, and not merely because Baby M is as much Ms. Whitehead's child as Mr. Stern's. It is misleading because it glosses over the fact that the surrender of the child was part—indeed, the whole point—of the agreement. If the surrogate were paid merely for being willing to be impregnated and carrying the child to term, then she would fulfill the contract upon giving birth. She could take the money *and* the child. Mr. Stern did not agree to pay Ms. Whitehead merely to *have* his child, but to provide him with a child. The New Jersey Supreme Court held that this violated New Jersey's laws prohibiting the payment or acceptance of money in connection with adoption.

One way to remove the taint of baby-selling would be to limit payment to medical expenses associated with the birth or incurred by the surrogate during pregnancy (as is allowed in many jurisdictions, including New Jersey, in ordinary adoptions).[21] Surrogacy could be seen, not as baby-selling, but as a form of adoption. Nowhere did the Supreme Court find any legal prohibition against surrogacy when there is no payment, and when the surrogate has the right to change her mind and keep the child. However, this solution effectively prohibits surrogacy, since few women would become surrogates solely for self-fulfillment or reasons of altruism.

The question, then, is whether we can reconcile paying the surrogate, beyond her medical expenses, with the idea of surrogacy as prenatal adoption. We can do this by separating the terms of the agreement, which include surrendering the infant at birth to the biological father, from the justification for payment. The payment should be seen as compensation for the risks, sacrifice, and discomfort the surrogate undergoes during pregnancy. This means that if, through no fault on the part of the surrogate, the baby is stillborn, she should still be paid in full, since she has kept her part of the bargain. (By contrast, in the Stern–Whitehead agreement, Ms. Whitehead was to receive only $1,000 for a stillbirth).[22] If, on the other hand, the surrogate changes her mind and decides to keep the child, she would break the agreement, and would not be entitled to any fee or to compensation for expenses incurred during pregnancy.

The Right of Privacy

Most commentators who invoke the right of privacy do so in support of surrogacy.[23] However, George Annas makes the novel argument that the right to rear a child you have borne is also a privacy right, which cannot be prospectively waived. He says:

> [Judge Sorkow] grudgingly concedes that [Ms. Whitehead] could not prospectively give up her right to have an abortion during pregnancy.... This would be an intolerable restriction on her liberty and under *Roe v. Wade*, the state has no constitutional authority to enforce a contract that prohibits her from terminating her pregnancy.

But why isn't the same logic applicable to the right to rear a child you have given birth to? Her constitutional rights to rear the child she has given birth to are even stronger since they involve even more intimately, and over a lifetime, her privacy rights to reproduce and rear a child in a family setting.[24]

Absent a compelling state interest (such as protecting

a child from unfit parents), it certainly would be an intolerable invasion of privacy for the state to take children from their parents. But Baby M has two parents, both of whom now want her. It is not clear why only people who can give birth (i.e., women) should enjoy the right to rear their children.

Moreover, we do allow women to give their children up for adoption after birth. The state enforces those agreements even if the natural mother, after the prescribed waiting period, changes her mind. Why should the right to rear a child be unwaivable before, but not after, birth? Why should the state have the constitutional authority to uphold postnatal, but not prenatal, adoption agreements? It is not clear why birth should affect the waivability of this right or have the constitutional significance that Annas attributes to it.

Nevertheless, there are sound moral and policy, if not constitutional, reasons to provide a postnatal waiting period in surrogate agreements. As the Baby M case makes painfully clear, the surrogate may underestimate the bond created by gestation and the emotional trauma caused by relinquishing the baby. Compassion requires that we acknowledge these findings, and not deprive a woman of the baby she has carried because, before conception, she underestimated the strength of her feelings for it. Providing a waiting period, as in ordinary postnatal adoptions, will help protect women from making irrevocable mistakes, without banning the practice.

Some may object that this gives too little protection to the prospective adoptive parents. They cannot be sure that the baby is theirs until the waiting period is over. While this is hard on them, a similar burden is placed on other adoptive parents. If the absence of a guarantee serves to discourage people from entering surrogacy agreements, that is not necessarily a bad thing, given all the risks inherent in such contracts. In addition, this requirement would make stricter screening and counseling of surrogates essential, a desirable side-effect.

Harm to Others

Paternalistic and moral objections to surrogacy do not seem to justify an outright ban. What about the effect on the offspring of such contracts? We do not yet have solid data on the effects of being a "surrogate child." Any claim that surrogacy creates psychological problems in the children is purely speculative. But what if we did discover that such children have deep feelings of worthlessness from learning that their natural mothers deliberately created them with the intention of giving them away? Might we ban surrogacy as posing an unacceptable risk of psychological harm to the resulting children?

Feelings of worthlessness are harmful. They can prevent people from living happy, fulfilling lives. However,

a surrogate child, even one whose life is miserable because of these feelings, cannot claim to have been harmed by the surrogate agreement. Without the agreement, the child would never have existed. Unless she is willing to say that her life is not worth living because of these feelings, that she would be better off never having been born, she cannot claim to have been harmed by being born of a surrogate mother.[25]

Elsewhere I have argued that children can be *wronged* by being brought into existence, even if they are not, strictly speaking, *harmed*.[26] They are wronged if they are deprived of the minimally decent existence to which all citizens are entitled. We owe it to our children to see that they are not born with such serious impairments that their most basic interests will be doomed in advance. If being born to a surrogate is a handicap of this magnitude, comparable to being born blind or deaf or severely mentally retarded, then surrogacy can be seen as wronging the offspring. This would be a strong reason against permitting such contracts. However, it does not seem likely. Probably the problems arising from surrogacy will be like those faced by adopted children and children whose parents divorce. Such problems are not trivial, but neither are they so serious that the child's very existence can be seen as wrongful.

If surrogate children are neither harmed nor wronged by surrogacy, it may seem that the argument for banning surrogacy on grounds of its harmfulness to the offspring evaporates. After all, if the children themselves have no cause for complaint, how can anyone else claim to reject it on their behalf? Yet it seems extremely counter-intuitive to suggest that the risk of emotional damage to the children born of such arrangements is not even relevant to our deliberations. It seems quite reasonable and proper—even morally obligatory—for policy-makers to think about the possible detrimental effects of new reproductive technologies, and to reject those likely to create physically or emotionally damaged people. The explanation for this must involve the idea that it is wrong to bring people into the world in a harmful condition, even if they are not, strictly speaking, harmed by having been brought into existence.[27] Should evidence emerge that surrogacy produces children with serious psychological problems, that would be a strong reason for banning the practice.

There is some evidence on the effect of surrogacy on the other children of the surrogate mother. One woman reported that her daughter, now seventeen, who was eleven at the time of the surrogate birth, "is still having problems with what I did, and as a result she is still angry with me." She explains: "Nobody told me that a child could bond with a baby while you're still pregnant. I didn't realize then that all the times she listened to his heartbeat and felt his legs kick that she was becoming attached to him."[28]

A less sentimental explanation is possible. It seems likely that her daughter, seeing one child given away, was fearful that the same might be done to her. We can expect anxiety and resentment on the part of children whose mothers give away a brother or sister. The psychological harm to these children is clearly relevant to a determination of whether surrogacy is contrary to public policy. At the same time, it should be remembered that many things, including divorce, remarriage, and even moving to a new neighborhood, create anxiety and resentment in children. We should not use the effect on children as an excuse for banning a practice we find bizarre or offensive.

Conclusion

There are many reasons to be extremely cautious of surrogacy. I cannot imagine becoming a surrogate, nor would I advise anyone else to enter into a contract so fraught with peril. But the fact that a practice is risky, foolish, or even morally distasteful is not sufficient reason to outlaw it. It would be better for the state to regulate the practice, and minimize the potential for harm, without infringing on the liberty of citizens.

References

1. See, for example, "Surrogate Motherhood Agreements: Contemporary Legal Aspects of a Biblical Notion," *University of Richmond Law Review*, 16 (1982): 470; "Surrogate Mothers: The Legal Issues," *American Journal of Law & Medicine*, 7 (1981): 338, and Angela Holder, *Legal Issues in Pediatrics and Adolescent Medicine* (New Haven: Yale University Press, 1985), 8: "Where a surrogate mother decides that she does not want to give the baby up for adoption, as has already happened, *it is clear that no court will enforce a contract entered into before the child was born* in which she agreed to surrender her baby for adoption." Emphasis added.

2. Had the Sterns been informed of the psychologist's concerns as to Ms. Whitehead's suitability to be a surrogate, they might have ended the arrangement, costing the Infertility Center its fee. As Chief Justice Wilentz said, "It is apparent that the profit motive got the better of the Infertility Center." In the matter of Baby M, Supreme Court of New Jersey, A-39, at 45.

3. "[W]e think it is expecting something well beyond normal human capabilities to suggest that this mother should have parted with her newly born infant without a struggle. . . . We . . . cannot conceive of any other case where a perfectly fit mother was expected to surrender her newly born infant, perhaps forever, and was then told she was a bad mother because she did not." Id.: 79.

4. "Father Recalls Surrogate Was 'Perfect,'" *New York Times*, Jan. 6, 1987, B2.

5. Id.

6. In the matter of Baby M, supra note 2, at 8.

7. This possibility was suggested to me by Susan Vermazen.

8. George Annas, "Baby M: Babies (and Justice) for Sale," *Hastings Center Report*, 17, no. 3 (1987): 15.

9. In the matter of Baby M, supra note 2, at 75.

10. "Anger and Anguish at Baby M Visitation Hearing," *New York Times*, March 29, 1988, 17.

11. *New York Times*, June 28, 1988, A20.

12. Gerald Dworkin, "Paternalism," in R.A. Wasserstrom, ed., *Morality and the Law* (Belmont, Cal.: Wadsworth, 1971); reprinted in J. Feinberg and H. Gross, eds., *Philosophy of Law*, 3d ed. (Belmont, Cal.: Wadsworth, 1986), 265.

13. M. Warnock, chair, *Report of the Committee of Inquiry into Human Fertilisation and Embryology* (London: Her Majesty's Stationery Office, 1984).

14. As summarized in J. Harris, *The Value of Life* (London: Routledge & Kegan Paul, 1985), 142.

15. For an argument that kidney-selling need not be coercive, see B.A. Brody and H.T. Engelhardt, Jr., *Bioethics: Readings and Cases* (Englewood Cliffs, N.J.: Prentice-Hall, 1987), 331.

16. John Robertson, "Surrogate Mothers: Not So Novel after All," *Hastings Center Report*, 13, no. 5 (1983): 29; citing P. Parker, "Surrogate Mother's Motivations: Initial Findings," *American Journal of Psychiatry*, 140 (1983): 1.

17. Harris, supra note 14, at 144.

18. Several authors note that it is both illegal and contrary to public policy to buy or sell children, and therefore contracts that contemplate this are unenforceable. See B. Cohen, "Surrogate Mothers: Whose Baby Is It?," *American Journal of Law & Medicine*, 10 (1984): 253; "Surrogate Mother Agreements: Contemporary Legal Aspects of a Biblical Notion," *University of Richmond Law Review*, 16 (1982): 469.

19. Robertson makes a similar point, supra note 16, at 33.

20. In re Baby "M," 217 N.J. Super. 372, 525 A.2d 1157 (1987).

21. Cohen, supra note 18. See also Angela Holder, "Surrogate Motherhood: Babies for Fun and Profit," *Law, Medicine & Health Care*, 12 (1984): 115.

22. Annas, supra note 8, at 14.

23. See, for example, Robertson, supra note 16, at 32; and S.R. Gersz, "The Contract in Surrogate Motherhood: A Review of the Issues," *Law, Medicine & Health Care*, 12 (1984): 107.

24. Annas, supra note 8.

25. For discussion of these issues, see D. Parfit, "On Doing the Best for Our Children," in M.D. Bayles, ed., *Ethics and Population* (Cambridge, Mass.: Schenkman, 1976); M.D. Bayles, "Harm to the Unconceived," *Philosophy & Public Affairs*, 5 (1976): 292; J. Glover, *Causing Death and Saving Lives* (Harmondsworth, Eng.: Penguin, 1977), 67; John Robertson, "In Vitro Conception and Harm to the Unborn," *Hastings Center Report*, 8 (1978): 13; J. Feinberg, *Harm to Others* (Oxford: Oxford University Press, 1984), 95.

26. Bonnie Steinbock, "The Logical Case for 'Wrongful Life'," *Hastings Center Report*, 16, no. 2 (1986): 15.

27. For the distinction between being harmed and being in a harmful state, see Feinberg, supra note 25, at 99.

28. "Baby M Case Stirs Feelings of Surrogate Mothers," *New York Times*, March 2, 1987, B1.

[8]

DEBRA SATZ

Markets in Women's Reproductive Labor

Much of the evolution of social policy in the twentieth century has occurred around conflicts over the scope of markets. To what extent, under what conditions, and for what reasons should we limit the use of markets?[1] Recently, American society has begun to experiment with markets in women's reproductive labor. Many people believe that markets in women's reproductive labor, as exemplified by contract pregnancy,[2] are more problematic than other currently accepted labor markets. I will call this the asymmetry thesis because its proponents believe that there ought to be an asymmetry between our treatment of reproductive labor and our treatment of other forms of labor. Advocates of the asymmetry

Many people were helpful during the "gestation" of this essay. I especially wish to thank Elizabeth Anderson, Richard Arneson, Michael Bratman, Jiwei Ci, Rachel Cohon, John Dupré, Howard Eilberg-Schwartz, John Ferejohn, Geoff Garrett, Margo Horn, Andrew Levine, Susan Okin, Margaret Jane Radin, Richard Terdiman, Mark Tunick, Jacob Weiner, Elisabeth Wood, and the Editors of *Philosophy & Public Affairs* for their detailed comments. Versions of this article were read at a Stanford Political Theory Seminar and the Stanford Feminist Theory Seminar; I am grateful for discussions with all of the participants. Research on this article was supported by a Stanford University Humanities Center Fellowship and an NEH Summer Grant.

1. See Karl Polanyi, *The Great Transformation* (Boston: Beacon Press, 1970); Gosta Esping-Andersen, *Politics Against Markets: The Social Democratic Road to Power* (Princeton: Princeton University Press, 1985); Michael Walzer, *Spheres of Justice: A Defense of Pluralism and Equality* (New York: Basic Books, 1983); Richard M. Titmuss, *The Gift Relationship: From Human Blood to Social Policy* (New York: Pantheon Books, 1971); Margaret Jane Radin, "Market-Inalienability," *Harvard Law Review* 100 (1987): 1849–1937; Viviana A. Zelizer, "Human Values and the Market: The Case of Life Insurance and Death in Nineteenth Century America," *American Journal of Sociology* 84 (1978): 591–610.

2. I will use the terms *contract pregnancy* and *pregnancy contract* in place of the misleading term *surrogacy*. The so-called surrogate mother is not a surrogate; she is the biological and/or gestational mother. In this article, I do not make any assumptions about who is and who is not a "real" mother.

Legal and Ethical Issues in Human Reproduction

Philosophy & Public Affairs

thesis hold that treating reproductive labor as a commodity, as something subject to the supply-and-demand principles that govern economic markets, is worse than treating other types of human labor as commodities. Is the asymmetry thesis true? And, if so, what are the reasons for thinking that it is true?

My aims in this article are to criticize several popular ways of defending the asymmetry thesis[3] and to offer an alternative defense. Other foundations for an argument against contract pregnancy are, of course, possible. For example, several of the arguments that I examine in this article have sometimes been raised in the context of more general anti-commodification arguments. I do not examine such general arguments here. Instead, I focus my discussion on those arguments against contract pregnancy that *depend* on the asymmetry thesis. I believe that the asymmetry thesis both captures strong intuitions that exist in our society and provides a plausible argument against contract pregnancy.

Many feminists hold that the asymmetry thesis is true because women's reproductive labor is a special kind of labor that should not be treated according to market norms. They draw a sharp dividing line between women's reproductive labor and human labor in general: while human labor may be bought and sold, women's reproductive labor is intrinsically not a commodity. According to these views, contract pregnancy allows for the extension of the market into the "private" sphere of sexuality and reproduction. This intrusion of the economic into the personal is seen as improper: it fails to respect the intrinsic, special nature of reproductive labor. As one writer has put it, "When women's labor is treated as a commodity, the women who perform it are degraded."[4]

Below, I argue that this is the wrong way to defend the asymmetry thesis. While I agree with the intuition that markets in women's reproductive labor are more troubling than other labor markets, in this article

---

3. See Elizabeth S. Anderson, "Is Women's Labor a Commodity?" *Philosophy & Public Affairs* 19, no. 1 (Winter 1990): 71–92; Christine Overall, *Ethics and Human Reproduction: A Feminist Analysis* (Boston: Allen and Unwin, 1987); Mary Warnock, *A Question of Life: The Warnock Report on Human Fertilisation and Embryology* (Oxford: Basil Blackwell, 1985); Martha Field, *Surrogate Motherhood: The Legal and Human Issues* (Cambridge, Mass.: Harvard University Press, 1988); Gena Corea, *The Mother Machine* (New York: Harper and Row, 1985); Carole Pateman, *The Sexual Contract* (Stanford: Stanford University Press, 1988). Not all of the arguments against contract pregnancy in these texts depend on the asymmetry thesis.

4. Anderson, "Women's Labor," p. 75.

Markets in Women's Reproductive Labor

I develop an alternative account of why this should be so. My analysis has four parts. In the first part, I criticize the arguments against the commodification of women's reproductive labor that turn on the assumption that reproductive labor is a special form of labor, part of a separate realm of sexuality. I argue that there is no distinction between women's reproductive labor and human labor generally, which is relevant to the debate about contract pregnancy. Moreover, I argue that the sale of women's reproductive labor is not *ipso facto* degrading. Rather, it becomes "degrading" only in a particular political and social context.[5] In the second part, I criticize arguments in support of the asymmetry thesis that appeal to norms of parental love. Here, the asymmetry between reproductive labor and labor in general is taken to derive from a special bond between mothers and children: the bond between a mother and her child is different from the bond between a worker and his product. In response, I argue that the bond between mothers and children is more complicated than critics of contract pregnancy have assumed and that, moreover, contract pregnancy does not cause parents to view children as commodities. The third part of the article examines an argument that stresses the potential negative consequences of contract pregnancy for children. While this argument has some merit, I argue that it is unpersuasive.

The first three parts of the article argue that the various reasons given in the literature for banning contract pregnancy on the basis of its asymmetry with other forms of labor are inadequate. Nonetheless, most people think that there should be some limits to commodification, and there does seem to be something more problematic about pregnancy contracts than other types of labor contract. The question is, what is the basis for and the significance of these intuitions? And what, apart from its agreement with these particular intuitions, can be said in favor of the asymmetry thesis?

In the fourth part of my article, I argue that the asymmetry thesis is true, but that the reason it is true has not been properly understood. The asymmetry thesis should be defended on external and not intrinsic or essentialist grounds. The conditions of pervasive gender inequality in our society are primary to the explanation of what is wrong with contract

5. I believe that my argument can also be applied to the case of prostitution, but I do not pursue that point in this article.

pregnancy. I claim that the most compelling objection to contract pregnancy concerns the background conditions of gender inequality that characterize our society. Markets in women's reproductive labor are especially troubling because they reinforce gender hierarchies in a way that other accepted labor markets do not. My defense of the asymmetry thesis thus rests on the way that contract pregnancy reinforces asymmetrical social relations of gender domination in American society. However, not all of the features of contract pregnancy that make it troubling concern gender inequality. Contract pregnancy may also heighten racial inequalities[6] and have harmful effects on the other children of the gestational mother.[7] In addition, the background conditions of economic inequality that characterize our society raise questions about the equal status of the contracting parties. I do not address these points in detail here. However, these latter considerations would have to be addressed in order to generate a complete argument against contract pregnancy.

I. THE SPECIAL NATURE OF REPRODUCTIVE LABOR

A wide range of attacks on contract pregnancy turn out to share a single premise, viz., that the intrinsic nature of reproductive labor is different from that of other kinds of labor. Critics claim that reproductive labor is not just another kind of work; they argue that unlike other forms of labor, reproductive labor is not properly regarded as a commodity. I will refer to this thesis as the essentialist thesis, since it holds that reproductive labor is *essentially* something that should not be bought and sold.

In contrast to the essentialist thesis, modern economic theories tend to treat the market as "theoretically all encompassing."[8] Such theories tend to treat all goods and capacities as exchangeable commodities, at least in principle.[9] Economists generally base their defense of markets as distributive mechanisms on three distinct ideas.

6. See Anita Allen, "Surrogacy, Slavery and the Ownership of Life," *Harvard Journal of Law and Public Policy* 13 (1990): 139–49.

7. See Amy Z. Overvold, *Surrogate Parenting* (New York: Pharos, 1988); Elizabeth Kane, *Birth Mother* (San Diego: Harcourt Brace Jovanovich, 1988).

8. Radin, "Market-Inalienability," p. 1859. Radin refers to this view as "universal commodification."

9. The theoretical assumption that everything is commodifiable characterizes a range of modern economic theories. It is found in both liberal welfare economics and in the conservative economics of the Chicago School. In welfare economics, there are technical reasons

Markets in Women's
                                       Reproductive Labor

First, there is the idea that markets are good for social welfare. Indeed, the fundamental theorem of welfare economics states that every competitive (market) equilibrium is Pareto optimal.[10] A Pareto optimum is a distribution point at which, given the initial distribution of resources, no individual can become better off (in view of her preferences) without at least one other individual becoming worse off. The so-called converse theorem of welfare economics states that every Pareto optimum is a competitive equilibrium.

Second, there is the idea that markets promote freedom. The agent of economic theory is a free, autonomous chooser.[11] Markets enhance her capacities for choosing by decentralizing decision-making, decentralizing information, and providing opportunities for experimentation. Markets also place limits on the viability of unjust social relationships by providing avenues for individual exit, thereby making the threat of defection a credible bargaining device.

Third, there is the idea that excluding a free exchange of some good, as a matter of principle, is incompatible with liberal neutrality. Liberalism requires state neutrality among conceptions of value. This neutrality constrains liberals from banning free exchanges: liberals cannot mandate that individuals accept certain values as having "intrinsic" or ulti-

---

for this assumption: Walrasian equilibrium theory, as generalized by Arrow and Debreu, depends on there being markets in everything, including futures, uncertainty, and public goods. In order to demonstrate the existence of a general equilibrium, all goods must be included in the equations.

The economists of the Chicago School argue that most things should be treated as commodities. They start with the assumption that rational human beings make their choices according to economic principles. Gary Becker, for example, has claimed that all human behavior can be understood in terms of maximizing efficiency, market equilibrium, and stable preferences. Becker's work uses these assumptions to explain criminal punishment, marriage, childbearing, education, and racial discrimination. See Becker, *The Economic Approach to Human Behavior* (Chicago: University of Chicago Press, 1976). (For criticisms of the application of Walrasian equilibrium theory to certain domains, see Joseph Stiglitz, "The Causes and Consequences of the Dependence of Quality on Price," *Journal of Economic Literature* 25 [1987]: 1–48; Louis Putterman, "On Some Recent Explanations of Why Capital Hires Wage Labor," in *The Economic Nature of the Firm*, ed. Putterman [Cambridge: Cambridge University Press, 1986]; Samuel Bowles and Herbert Gintis, "Contested Exchange: New Microfoundations for the Political Economy of Capitalism," *Politics and Society* 18 [1990]: 165–222.)

10. The first welfare theorem holds only under specific conditions, for example, where external economies and diseconomies are absent.

11. See Milton Friedman, *Capitalism and Freedom* (Chicago: University of Chicago Press, 1962).

mate worth.[12] Liberals can, of course, seek to regulate exchanges so that they fall within the bounds of justice. But any argument prohibiting rather than regulating market activity is claimed to violate liberal neutrality.[13]

If we accept the logic of the economic approach to human behavior, we seem led to endorse a world in which everything is potentially for sale: body parts, reproductive labor, children, even persons.[14] Many people are repulsed by such a world. But what exactly is the problem with it? Defenders of the essentialist thesis provide the starting point for a counterattack: not all human goods are commodities. In particular, human reproductive labor is improperly treated as a commodity. When reproductive labor is purchased on the market, it is inappropriately valued.

The essentialist thesis provides support for the asymmetry thesis. The nature of reproductive labor is taken to be fundamentally different from that of labor in general. In particular, proponents of the essentialist thesis hold that women's reproductive labor should be respected and not used.[15] What is it about women's reproductive labor that singles it out for a type of respect that precludes market use?

Some versions of the essentialist thesis focus on the biological or naturalistic features of women's reproductive labor: (1) Women's reproductive labor has both a genetic and a gestational component.[16] Other forms of labor do not involve a genetic relationship between the worker and her product. (2) While much human labor is voluntary at virtually every step, many of the phases of the reproductive process are involuntary. Ovulation, conception, gestation, and birth occur without the conscious direction of the mother. (3) Reproductive labor extends over a period of approximately nine months; other types of labor do not typically necessitate

12. See Will Kymlicka, "Rethinking the Family," *Philosophy & Public Affairs* 20, no. 1 (Winter 1991): 95–96.

13. In *Birthpower* (New Haven: Yale University Press, 1989) Carmel Shalev develops a powerful defense of contract pregnancy that draws on considerations of liberty, welfare, and liberal neutrality. She argues that it is a matter of the "constitutional privacy" of individuals to define legal parenthood in terms of their prior-to-conception intentions; that contract pregnancy will empower women and improve their welfare by unleashing a new source of economic wealth; and that the market is neutral between competing conceptions of human relationships.

14. See Robert Nozick, *Anarchy, State and Utopia* (New York: Basic Books, 1974), p. 331.

15. See Anderson, "Women's Labor," p. 72.

16. In cases of in vitro fertilization, reproductive labor is divided between two women.

Markets in Women's
Reproductive Labor

a long-term commitment. (4) Reproductive labor involves significant restrictions of a woman's behavior during pregnancy; other forms of labor are less invasive with respect to the worker's body.

These characteristics of reproductive labor do not, however, establish the asymmetry thesis: (1) With respect to the genetic relationship between the reproductive worker and her product, most critics object to contract pregnancy even where the "surrogate" is not the genetic mother. In fact, many critics consider "gestational surrogacy"—in which a woman is implanted with a preembryo formed in vitro from donated gametes—more pernicious than those cases in which the "surrogate" is also the genetic mother.[17] In addition, men also have a genetic tie to their offspring, yet many proponents of the asymmetry thesis would not oppose the selling of sperm. (2) With respect to the degree to which reproductive labor is involuntary, there are many forms of work in which workers do not have control over the work process; for example, mass-production workers cannot generally control the speed of the assembly line, and they have no involvement in the overall purpose of their activity. (3) With regard to the length of the contract's duration, some forms of labor involve contracts of even longer duration, for example, book contracts. Like pregnancy contracts, these are not contracts in which one can quit at the end of the day. Yet, presumably, most proponents of the essentialist thesis would not find commercial publishing contracts objectionable. (4) With regard to invasions into the woman's body, nonreproductive labor can also involve incursions into the body of the worker. To take an obvious example, athletes sign contracts that give team owners considerable control over their diet and behavior, allowing owners to conduct periodic tests for drug use. Yet there is little controversy over the sale of athletic capacities.[18] Sales of blood also run afoul of a noninvasiveness condition. In fact, leaving aside the genetic component of reproductive labor, voluntary military service involves features 2 through 4; do we really want to object to such military service on *essentialist* grounds?

Carole Pateman suggests a different way of defending the asymmetry thesis as the basis for an argument against contract pregnancy. Rather than focusing on the naturalistic, biological properties of reproductive

17. See Katha Pollitt, "When Is a Mother Not a Mother?" *The Nation*, 31 December 1990, p. 843.
18. See Orlando Patterson, *Slavery and Social Death* (Cambridge, Mass.: Harvard University Press, 1982) for comparisons between slaves and athletes.

labor, she argues that a woman's reproductive labor is more "integral" to her identity than her other productive capacities. Pateman first sketches this argument with respect to prostitution: "Womanhood, too, is confirmed in sexual activity, and when a prostitute contracts out use of her body she is thus selling herself in a very real sense. Women's selves are involved in prostitution in a different manner from the involvement of the self in other occupations. Workers of all kinds may be more or less 'bound up in their work,' but the integral connection between sexuality and sense of the self means that, for self-protection, a prostitute must distance herself from her sexual use."[19]

Pateman's objection to prostitution rests on a claim about the intimate relation between a woman's sexuality and her identity. It is by virtue of this tie, Pateman believes, that sex should not be treated as an alienable commodity. Is her claim true? How do we decide which of a woman's attributes or capacities are essential to her identity and which are not? In particular, why should we consider sexuality more integral to self than friendship, family, religion, nationality, and work?[20] Yet we allow commodification in each of these spheres. For example, rabbis or priests may view their religion as central to their identity, but they often accept payment for performing religious services, and hardly anyone objects to their doing so. Does Pateman think that *all* activities that fall within these spheres and that bear an intimate relationship to a person's identity should be inalienable?

Pateman's argument in the above passage appears to support the asymmetry thesis, by suggesting that a woman's sexuality is *more* intimately related to her identity than her other capacities. Yet she provides no explicit argument for this suggestion. Indeed, at times, her argument seems intended not so much to support the asymmetry thesis as to support a more general thesis against alienating those activities that are closely tied to the identity of persons. But this more general argument is implausible. It would not allow individuals to sell their homes or their paintings or their book manuscripts or their copyrights.

A similar argument about the close connection between sexuality and identity underlies the objection to contract pregnancy raised by the British government–commissioned Warnock Report on Human Fertilisation

19. Pateman, *The Sexual Contract*, p. 207.
20. Freudian theory, with its emphasis on "natural" drives, might give us such reasons, but Pateman does not explicitly endorse such a theory.

Markets in Women's
Reproductive Labor

and Embryology. The Warnock Report links reproductive labor to a person's dignity, claiming that "it is inconsistent with human dignity that a woman should use her uterus for financial profit."[21] But why is selling the use of a woman's uterus "undignified" while selling the use of images of her body in a television commercial is not?

The Warnock Report's argument implicitly rests on the assumption that women's sexuality and reproduction belong to a sacred, special realm. In the words of another author, it is a realm "worthy of respect."[22] Even if this is so, however, the idea of respect alone cannot guarantee the conclusion that reproductive labor should not be treated as a commodity. We sometimes sell things that we also respect. As Margaret Radin puts it, "we can both know the price of something and know that it is priceless."[23] For example, I think that my teaching talents should be respected, but I don't object to being paid for teaching on such grounds. Giving my teaching a price does not diminish the other ways in which my teaching has value.

This point undermines Pateman's argument as well. For although Pateman would not endorse the idea that sexuality is part of a private realm, she does believe that it bears a special relationship to our identities and that by virtue of that relationship it should be inalienable. But we sometimes sell things intimately tied to our identities, without ceasing to be the people that we are. For example, as I suggested above, a person's home may be intimately tied to her identity, but she can also sell it without losing her sense of self.[24]

Finally, I believe that it is a mistake to focus, as does the Warnock Report, on maintaining certain cultural values without examining critically the specific social circumstances from which those values emerge. Thus, the view that selling sexual or reproductive capacities is "degrading" may reflect society's attempts to control women and their sexuality.

21. Warnock, *A Question of Life*, p. 45.

22. See Anderson, "Women's Labor," p. 72.

23. Margaret Jane Radin, "Justice and the Market Domain," in *Markets and Justice*, ed. John W. Chapman and J. R. Pennock (New York: New York University Press, 1989), p. 175.

24. However, I believe that there should be limits on the sale of housing: poor people should not be displaced from their homes for someone else's profit. But in this case, as in contract pregnancy, I think that markets should be limited by considerations of equality. For an interesting alternative approach, see Margaret Jane Radin, "Residential Rent Control," *Philosophy & Public Affairs* 15, no. 4 (Fall 1986): 350–80.

At the very least, the relations between particular views of sexuality and the maintenance of gender inequality must be taken into account. This is especially important insofar as one powerful defense of contract pregnancy rests on its alleged consequence of empowering poor women.[25] Indeed, there is something hypocritical in the objection to contract pregnancy as "degrading," when the fundamental background conditions of social inequality—many of which are at least equally "degrading"—are ignored.

II. The Special Bonds of Motherhood

Sometimes what critics of pregnancy contracts have in mind is not the effect of such contracts on the relationship between reproductive labor and a woman's sense of self or her dignity, but its effect on her views (and ours) of the mother-fetus and mother-child bond. On this view, what is wrong with commodifying reproductive labor is that by relying on a mistaken picture of the nature of these relationships, it degrades them. Further, it leads to a view of children as fungible objects. In part 1 of this section I examine arguments against contract pregnancy based on its portrayal of the mother-fetus bond; in part 2 I examine arguments based on contract pregnancy's portrayal of the mother-child bond.

1. Mothers and Fetuses

Some critics of contract pregnancy contend that the relationship between a mother and a fetus is not simply a biochemical relationship or a matter of contingent physical connection. They claim that the relationship between a mother and a fetus is essentially different from that between a worker and her material product. The long months of pregnancy and the experience of childbirth are part of forming a relationship with the child-to-be. Elizabeth Anderson makes an argument along these lines. She suggests that the commodification of reproductive labor makes pregnancy an alienated form of labor for the women who perform it: selling her reproductive labor alienates a woman from her "normal" and justified emotions.[26] Rather than viewing pregnancy as an evolving relation-

25. Radin calls our attention to the problem of the "double bind": under current conditions of inequality, there are negative external effects of both banning and allowing pregnancy contracts. See Radin, "Market-Inalienability," p. 1917.
26. Anderson, "Women's Labor," p. 81.

Markets in Women's Reproductive Labor

ship with a child-to-be, contract pregnancy reinforces a vision of the pregnant woman as a mere "home" or an "environment."[27] The commodification of reproductive labor thus distorts the nature of the bond between the mother and the fetus by misrepresenting the nature of a woman's reproductive labor. What should we make of this argument?

Surely there is truth in the claim that pregnancy contracts may reinforce a vision of women as baby machines or mere "wombs." Recent court rulings with respect to contract pregnancy have tended to acknowledge women's contribution to reproduction only insofar as it is identical to men's: the donation of genetic material. The gestational labor involved in reproduction is explicitly ignored in such rulings. Thus, Mary Beth Whitehead won back her parental rights in the "Baby M" case because the New Jersey Supreme Court acknowledged her genetic contribution.[28]

However, as I will argue in Section IV below, the concern about the discounting of women's reproductive labor is best posed in terms of the principle of equal treatment. By treating women's reproductive labor as identical to men's when it is not, women are not in fact being treated equally. But those who conceptualize the problem with pregnancy contracts in terms of the degradation of the mother-fetus relationship rather than in terms of the equality of men and women tend to interpret the social practice of pregnancy in terms of a maternal "instinct," a sacrosanct bonding that takes place between a mother and her child-to-be. However, not all women "bond" with their fetuses. Some women abort them.

Indeed, there is a dilemma for those who wish to use the mother-fetus bond to condemn pregnancy contracts while endorsing a woman's right to choose abortion. They must hold that it is acceptable to abort a fetus, but not to sell it. While the Warnock Report takes no stand on the issue of abortion, it uses present abortion law as a term of reference in considering contract pregnancy. Since abortion is currently legal in England, the Report's position has this paradoxical consequence: one can kill a fetus, but one cannot contract to sell it.[29] One possible response to this

27. See Orange County Superior Court Judge Richard Parslow's ruling in which he referred to birth mother Anna Johnson as a "home" for an embryo and not a "mother." *New York Times*, 23 October 1990.

28. *In the Matter of Baby M*, 537 A.2d 1227 (N.J. 1988).

29. Michael Bratman has suggested that the analogy between abortion and contract

objection would be to claim that women do not bond with their fetuses in the first trimester. But the fact remains that some women never bond with their fetuses; some women even fail to bond with their babies after they deliver them.

Additionally, are we really sure that we know which emotions pregnancy "normally" involves? While married women are portrayed as nurturing and altruistic, society has historically stigmatized the unwed mother as selfish, neurotic, and unconcerned with the welfare of her child. Until quite recently, social pressure was directed at unwed mothers to surrender their children after birth. Thus, married women who gave up their children were seen as "abnormal" and unfeeling, while unwed mothers who failed to surrender their children were seen as selfish.[30] Such views of the mother-fetus bonding relationship reinforce this traditional view of the family and a woman's proper role within it.

2. *Mothers and Children*

A somewhat different argument against contract pregnancy contends that the commodification of women's reproductive labor entails the commodification of children. Once again, the special nature of reproduction is used to support the asymmetry thesis: the special nature of maternal love is held to be incompatible with market relations. Children should be loved by their mothers, yet commercial surrogacy responds to and promotes other motivations. Critics argue that markets in reproductive labor give people the opportunity to "shop" for children. Prospective womb-infertile couples will seek out arrangements that "maximize" the value of their babies: sex, eye color, and race will be assessed in terms of market considerations.[31] Having children on the basis of such preferences

---

pregnancy breaks down in the following way. In contract pregnancy, a woman gets pregnant with the intention of giving up the child. There is presumably no analogous intention in the case of abortion: few women, if any, intentionally get pregnant in order to have an abortion. Critics of contract pregnancy might claim that intentionally conceiving a child either to give it up for money or to abort it is immoral. I am not persuaded by such arguments. If abortion is murder, then it is so regardless of the intentions involved. My own view is that the best argument in favor of the right to abortion makes no reference to intentions, but concerns the consequences of abortion restrictions for women, restrictions that, moreover, directly burden only women.

30. See Adrienne Rich, *Of Women Born: Motherhood as Experience and Institution* (New York: Norton, 1976).

31. See Radin, "Market-Inalienability," p. 1927.

reflects an inferior conception of persons. It brings commercial attitudes into a sphere that is thought to be properly governed by love.

What are the reasons that people seek to enter into contract pregnancy arrangements? Most couples or single people who make use of "surrogates" want simply to have a child that is "theirs," that is, genetically related to them. In fact, given the clogged adoption system, some of them may simply want to have a child. Furthermore, the adoption system itself is responsive to people's individual preferences: it is much easier, for example, to adopt an older black child than a white infant. Such preferences may be objectionable, but no one seriously argues that parents should have no choice in the child they adopt nor that adoption be prohibited because it gives rein to such preferences. Instead, we regulate adoption to forbid the differential payment of fees to agencies on the basis of a child's ascribed characteristics. Why couldn't contract pregnancy be regulated in the same way?

Critics who wish to make an argument for the asymmetry thesis based on the nature of maternal love must defend a strong claim about the relationship between markets and love. In particular, they must claim that even regulated markets in reproductive services will lead parents to love their children for the wrong reasons: love will be conditional on the child's having the "right" set of physical characteristics. While I share the view that there is something wrong with the "shopping" attitude in the sphere of personal relations, I wonder if it has the adverse effects that the critics imagine. Individuals in our society seek partners with attributes ranging from a specified race and height to a musical taste for Chopin. Should such singles' advertisements in magazines be illegal? Should we ban dating services that cater to such preferences? Isn't it true that people who meet on such problematic grounds may grow to love each other? I suspect that most parents who receive their child through a contract pregnancy arrangement will love their child as well.

Even if contract pregnancy does not distort our conception of personhood per se, critics can still associate contract pregnancy with baby-selling. One popular argument runs: In contract pregnancy women not only sell their reproductive services, but also their babies. Because baby-selling is taken to be intrinsically wrong, this type of argument attempts to use an analogy to support the following syllogism: If baby-selling is wrong, and contract pregnancy is a form of baby-selling, then contract pregnancy is wrong. The Warnock Report, for example, makes this charge.[32] Suppose that we grant, as seems plausible, that baby-selling is wrong (perhaps on essentialist grounds). Is this argument successful?

It is important to keep in mind that pregnancy contracts do not enable fathers (or prospective "mothers," women who are infertile or otherwise unable to conceive) to acquire children as property. Even where there has been a financial motivation for conceiving a child, and whatever the status of the labor that produced it, the *child* cannot be treated as a commodity. The father cannot, for example, destroy, transfer, or abandon the child. He is bound by the same norms and laws that govern the behavior of a child's biological or adoptive parents. Allowing women to contract for their reproductive services does not entail baby-selling, if we mean by that a proxy for slavery.

Anderson has argued that what makes contract pregnancy a form of baby-selling is the way such contracts treat the "mother's rights over her child."[33] Such contracts mandate that the mother relinquish her parental rights to the child. Furthermore, such contracts can be enforced against the mother's wishes. Anderson argues that forcing a woman to part with her child and to cede her parental rights by sale entails treating the child as a mere commodity, as something that can be sold. Even if this is true, it does not necessarily lead to the conclusion that pregnancy contracts should be banned. There are many similarities between contract pregnancy and adoption. Like adoption, pregnancy contracts could be regulated to respect a change of mind of the "surrogate" within some specified time period; to accord more with an "open" model in which all the parties to the contract retain contact with the child; or by making pregnancy contracts analogous to contracts that require informed consent, as in the case of medical experiments. Pregnancy contracts could be required to provide detailed information about the emotional risks and costs associated with giving up a child.[34]

Finally, some writers have objected to pregnancy contracts on the ground that they must, by their nature, exploit women. They point to the fact that the compensation is very low, and that many of the women who agree to sell their reproductive labor have altruistic motivations. Anderson writes, "A kind of exploitation occurs when one party to a transaction is oriented toward the exchange of 'gift' values, while the other party

32. Warnock, *A Question of Life*, p. 45.
33. Anderson, "Women's Labor," p. 78.
34. I owe this suggestion to Rachel Cohon.

121   *Markets in Women's*
                                 Reproductive Labor

operates in accordance with the norms of the market exchange of commodities."[35]

Two responses are possible to this line of argument. First, even if it is
the case that all or most of the women who sell their reproductive labor
are altruistically motivated,[36] it is unfair to argue that the other parties to
the contract are motivated solely in accord with market values. The couples who use contract pregnancy are not seeking to make a profit, but to
have a child. Some of them might even be willing to maintain an "extended family" relationship with the "surrogate" after the child's birth.
Second, even if an asymmetry in motivation is established, it is also present in many types of service work: teaching, health care, and social work
are all liable to result in "exploitation" of this sort. In all of these areas,
the problem is at least partially addressed by regulating compensation.
Why is contract pregnancy different?

III. THE CONSEQUENCES OF CONTRACT PREGNANCY FOR CHILDREN

Susan Okin makes an argument against contract pregnancy that is
based on its direct consequences for children, and not on the intrinsic
features of reproductive labor or the bonds of motherhood. She argues
that the problem with pregnancy contracts is that they do not consider
the interests of the child.[37] Okin thus focuses on a different aspect of the
concern that contract pregnancy leads us to adopt an inferior understanding of children. She points not to the conception itself, but to its
consequences for children. The asymmetry, then, between reproductive
labor and other forms of labor is based on the fact that only in the former
are the child's interests directly at stake.

Putting aside the difficult question of what actually constitutes the
child's best interests,[38] it is not certain that such interests will always be

35. Anderson, "Women's Labor," p. 84.
36. Philip Parker, "Motivation of Surrogate Mothers: Initial Findings," *American Journal
of Psychiatry* 140 (1983): 117–18. I am grateful to Elizabeth Anderson for bringing this
article to my attention.
37. Susan Okin, "A Critique of Pregnancy Contracts: Comments on Articles by Hill, Merrick, Shevory, and Woliver," *Politics and the Life Sciences* 8 (1990): 205–10.
38. See Jon Elster, *Solomonic Judgements* (Cambridge: Cambridge University Press,
1989) for a discussion of the difficulties of ascertaining the best interests of the child. Elster
is also skeptical of the idea that the best interests of the child should necessarily prevail in
custody disputes.

served by the child's remaining with its biological parents. Some children may be better off separated from their biological parents when such parents are abusive. No one would claim that children should always remain with their biological parents. Nevertheless, I agree with Okin that one problem with pregnancy contracts lies in their potential for weakening the biological ties that give children a secure place in the world.[39] If it can be shown that pregnancy contracts make children more vulnerable, for example, by encouraging parental exit, then such a consideration might contribute to calls for restricting or prohibiting such contracts.[40] Such an argument will have nothing to do with the special nature of reproductive labor, nor will it have to do with the special biological relationship between a parent and a child. It will remain valid even where the child bears no genetic relation to its parents. Children are vulnerable and dependent, and this vulnerability justifies the moral obligations parents have toward them. While this objection can be used to support the asymmetry thesis, it is important to note that asymmetrical vulnerabilities are found throughout the social world; they are not unique to the spheres of the family, sex, and reproduction. The same principles that will mandate against pregnancy contracts will also mandate against the use of child labor and argue for helping the disabled and the aged.

Nonetheless, this objection does point out an asymmetry between reproductive labor and other forms of labor. Can it be used to justify prohibiting contract pregnancy? One of the difficulties with evaluating pregnancy contracts in terms of their effects on children is that we have very little empirical evidence of these effects. The first reported case of a pregnancy contract in the United States occurred in 1976.[41] Even with the more established practice of artificial insemination, no research is available on the effects of donor anonymity on the child. Nor do we know how different family structures, including single-parent and alternative families and adoption, affect children. We should be wary of prematurely making abstract arguments based on the child's best interests without

39. Anderson raises this point as well. See "Women's Labor," p. 80.
40. We must be careful in considering the scope of this argument. Divorce and adoption, for example, may weaken the ties between children and parents, but very few people would be willing to give the state the right to forbid divorce or adoption on such grounds.
41. D. Gelman and E. Shapiro, "Infertility: Babies by Contract," *Newsweek*, 4 November 1985.

any empirical evidence. Moreover, in the case of families whose life situation may be disapproved of by their community, we may have moral reasons for overriding the best interests of an individual child.[42] For example, if the child of a single or lesbian mother were to suffer discrimination, I do not think that this would justify removal of the child from the mother. Thus, while pregnancy contracts may threaten the interests of children, this is not yet established; nor is this consideration by itself a sufficient reason for forbidding such contracts.

IV. REPRODUCTIVE LABOR AND EQUALITY

In the preceding three sections I have argued that the asymmetry thesis cannot be defended by claiming that there is something "essential" about reproductive labor that singles it out for different treatment from other forms of labor; nor by arguing that contract pregnancy distorts the nature of the bonds of motherhood; nor by the appeal to the best interests of the child. The arguments I have examined ignore the existing background conditions that underlie pregnancy contracts, many of which are objectionable. In addition, some of the arguments tend to accept uncritically the traditional picture of the family. Such arguments take current views of the maternal bond and the institution of motherhood as the baseline for judging pregnancy contracts—as if such views were not contested.

If we reject these arguments for the asymmetry thesis, are we forced back to the view that the market is indeed theoretically all-encompassing? Can we reject contract pregnancy, and defend the asymmetry thesis, without claiming either that reproductive labor is essentially not a commodity, or that it necessarily degrades the bonds between mothers and children, or that it is harmful to children?

I think that the strongest argument against contract pregnancy that depends upon the asymmetry thesis is derived from considerations of gender equality. It is this consideration that I believe is tacitly driving many of the arguments; for example, it is the background gender inequality that makes the commodification of women's and children's attributes especially objectionable. My criticism of contract pregnancy centers on the hypothesis that in our society such contracts will turn

42. See Elster, *Solomonic Judgements*, pp. 148ff.

women's labor into something that is used and controlled by others[43] and will reinforce gender stereotypes that have been used to justify the unequal treatment of women.

Contrary to the democratic ideal, gender inequality is pervasive in our society. This inequality includes the unequal distribution of housework and child care that considerably restricts married women's opportunities in the work force; the fact that the ratio between an average full-time working woman's earnings and those of her average male counterpart is 59.3:100,[44] and the fact that divorce is an economically devastating experience for women (during the 1970s, the standard of living of young divorced mothers fell 73%, while men's standard of living following divorce rose 42%).[45] These circumstances constitute the baseline from which women form their preferences and make their "choices." Thus, even a woman's choice to engage in commercial surrogacy must be viewed against a background of unequal opportunity. Most work done by women in our society remains in a "female ghetto": service and clerical work, secretarial work, cleaning, domestic labor, nursing, elementary school teaching, and waitressing.

I assume that there is something deeply objectionable about gender inequality. My argument is that contract pregnancy's reinforcing of this inequality lies at the heart of what is wrong with it. In particular, reproduction is a sphere that historically has been marked by inequality: women and men have not had equal influence over the institutions and practices involved in human reproduction. In its current form and context, contract pregnancy contributes to gender inequality in three ways:

1. Contract pregnancy gives others increased access to and control over women's bodies and sexuality. In a provocative book, Carmel Shalev argues that it is wrong to forbid a woman to sell her reproductive capac-

43. Of course, pregnancy contracts also give another woman, the adoptive mother, control over the body of the surrogate mother. The important point here is that in a society characterized by gender inequalities, such contracts put women's bodies at the disposal of others.

44. This figure compares the earnings of white women and white men. In 1980, black and Hispanic women earned, respectively, 55.3% and 40.1% of white men's earnings. See Sara M. Evans and Barbara Nelson, *Wage Justice: Comparable Worth and the Paradox of Technocratic Reform* (Chicago: University of Chicago Press, 1989).

45. Lenore J. Weitzman, *The Divorce Revolution: The Unexpected Social and Economic Consequences for Women and Children in America* (New York: The Free Press, 1985), p. 323.

Markets in Women's
                                          Reproductive Labor

ities when we already allow men to sell their sperm.[46] But Shalev ignores a crucial difference between artificial insemination by donor (AID) and a pregnancy contract. AID does not give anyone control over men's bodies and sexuality. A man who elects AID simply sells a product of his body or his sexuality; he does not sell control over his body itself. The current practices of AID and pregnancy contracts are remarkably different in the scope of intervention and control they allow the "buyer." Pregnancy contracts involve substantial control over women's bodies.[47]

What makes this control objectionable, however, is not the intrinsic features of women's reproductive labor, but rather the ways in which such control reinforces a long history of unequal treatment. Consider an analogous case that has no such consequence: voluntary (paid) military service, where men sell their fighting capacities. Military service, like contract pregnancy, involves significant invasions into the body of the seller; soldiers' bodies are controlled to a large extent by their commanding officers under conditions in which the stakes are often life and death. But military service does not *directly* serve to perpetuate traditional gender inequalities.[48] The fact that pregnancy contracts, like military contracts, give someone control over someone else's body is not the issue. Rather, the issue is that in contract pregnancy the body that is controlled belongs to a woman, in a society that historically has subordinated women's interests to those of men, primarily through its control over her sexuality and reproduction.

Market theorists might retort that contract pregnancy could be regulated to protect women's autonomy, in the same way that we regulate other labor contracts. However, it will be difficult, given the nature of the

46. Shalev, *Birthpower.*

47. A man who buys women's reproductive labor can choose his "surrogate"; he does not legally require his wife's permission; pregnancy contracts include substantial provisions regulating the surrogate's behavior. Such provisions include agreements concerning medical treatment, the conditions under which the surrogate agrees to undergo an abortion, and regulation of the surrogate's emotions. Thus, in the case of Baby M, Mary Beth Whitehead consented to refrain from forming or attempting to form any relationship with the child she would conceive. She agreed not to smoke cigarettes, drink alcoholic beverages, or take medications without written consent from her physician. She also agreed to undergo amniocentesis and to abort the fetus "upon demand of William Stern, natural father" if tests found genetic or congenital defects. See "Appendix: Baby M Contract," *Beyond Baby M*, ed. Dianne Bartels (Clifton, N.J.: Humana Press, 1990).

48. This is not to imply that voluntary military service is not objectionable on other grounds, a question that I cannot discuss here.

interests involved, for such contracts not to be very intrusive with respect to women's bodies in spite of formal agreements. The purpose of such contracts is, after all, to produce a healthy child. In order to help guarantee a healthy baby, a woman's behavior must be highly controlled.[49]

Moreover, if the pregnancy contract is a contract for reproductive labor, then, as in other types of labor contracts, compliance—what the law terms "specific performance"—cannot be enforced. For example, if I contract to paint your house, and I default on my agreement, you can sue me for breaking the contract, but even if you win, the courts will not require me to paint your house. Indeed, this is the salient difference between even poorly paid wage labor and indentured servitude. Thus, by analogy, if the woman in a pregnancy contract defaults on her agreement and decides to keep the child, the other parties should not be able to demand performance (that is, surrender of the child); rather, they can demand monetary compensation.[50]

This inability to enforce performance in pregnancy contracts may have consequences for the *content* of such contracts that will make them especially objectionable. Recall that such contracts occur over a long period of time, during which a woman may undergo fundamental changes in her willingness to give up the child. The other parties will need some mechanism to ensure her compliance. There are two mechanisms that are likely to produce compliance, but both are objectionable: (a) The contract could be set up so that payment is delivered to the woman only after the child is born. But this structure of compensation closely resembles baby-selling; it now looks as if what is being bought is not the woman's services, but the child itself. Thus, if baby-selling is wrong, then we should be very troubled by the fact that, in order to be self-enforcing, contract pregnancy must use incentives that make it resemble baby-selling. (b) The contract could mandate legal and psychological counseling for a woman who is tempted to change her mind. Given that it is hard to imagine in advance what it means to surrender a child, such counseling

49. There is already legal precedent for regulating women's behavior in the "best interests" of the fetus. A Massachussetts woman was charged with vehicular homicide when her fetus was delivered stillborn following a car accident. See Eileen McNamara, "Fetal Endangerment Cases on the Rise," *Boston Globe*, 3 October 1989; cited in Lawrence Tribe, *Abortion: The Clash of Absolutes* (New York: Norton, 1990).

50. This analogy may be complicated by the fact that the other parties to the contract may have at least some biological relationship to the child.

could involve a great deal of manipulation and coercion of the woman's emotions.[51]

2. Contract pregnancy reinforces stereotypes about the proper role of women in the reproductive division of labor. At a time when women have made strides in labor force participation, moving out of the family into other social spheres, pregnancy contracts provide a monetary incentive for women to remain in the home.[52] And, while some women may "prefer" to stay at home, we need to pay attention to the limited range of economic opportunities available to these women, and to the ways in which these opportunities have shaped their preferences. Under present conditions, pregnancy contracts entrench a traditional division of labor—men at work, women in the home—based on gender.

Additionally, pregnancy contracts will affect the way society views women: they will tend to reinforce the view of women as "baby machines."[53] It is also likely that they will affect the way women see themselves. Insofar as the sale of women's reproductive capacities contributes to the social subordination of women, and only of women, there are antidiscrimination grounds for banning it.

3. Contract pregnancy raises the danger, manifested in several recent court rulings, that "motherhood" will be defined in terms of genetic material, in the same way as "fatherhood." Mary Beth Whitehead won back parental rights to Baby M on the basis of her being the genetic "mother." On the other hand, Anna Johnson, a "gestational" surrogate, lost such rights because she bore no genetic relationship to the child.[54] These court rulings establish the principle of parenthood on the basis of genetic contribution. In such cases, women's contribution to reproduction is recognized only insofar as it is identical to that of men. Genes alone are taken to define natural and biological motherhood. By not taking wom-

51. Anderson also makes this point. See "Women's Labor," pp. 84ff.

52. This is not to imply that the current sexual division of labor, in which women are disproportionately involved in unpaid domestic work, is just.

53. See Corea, *The Mother Machine*.

54. Anita Allen, in "Ownership of Life," has pointed to the disturbing possibilities contract pregnancy poses for racial equality. In cases like *Johnson v. Calvert*, where the gestator (surrogate), Johnson, was a black woman and the Calverts were white and Filipina, it is difficult to imagine a judge awarding the baby to Johnson. For example, there are almost no adoption cases in which a healthy white infant is placed with black parents. In his ruling in *Johnson v. Calvert*, Judge Parslow referred to Johnson as the baby's "wet nurse." Any full assessment of contract pregnancy must consider the implications of the practice for women of color.

en's actual gestational contributions into account, the courts reinforce an old stereotype of women as merely the incubators of men's seeds.[55] In fact, the court's inattention to women's unique labor contribution is itself a form of unequal treatment. By defining women's rights and contributions in terms of those of men, when they are different, the courts fail to recognize an adequate basis for women's rights and needs. These rulings place an additional burden on women.[56]

Given its consequences for gender inequality, I think that the asymmetry thesis is true, and that pregnancy contracts are especially troubling. Current gender inequality lies at the heart of what is wrong with pregnancy contracts. The problem with commodifying women's reproductive labor is not that it "degrades" the special nature of reproductive labor, or "alienates" women from a core part of their identities, but that it reinforces a traditional gender-hierarchical division of labor. A consequence of my argument is that under very different background conditions, in which men and women had equal power and had an equal range of choices, such contracts would be less objectionable.[57] For example, in a society in which women's work was valued as much as men's and in which child care was shared equally, pregnancy contracts might serve primarily as a way for single persons, disabled persons, and same-sex families to have children. Indeed, pregnancy contracts and similar practices have the potential to transform the nuclear family. We know too little about possible new forms of family life to restrict such experiments on a priori grounds; but in our society, I have argued that there are consequentialist reasons for making this restriction.

At the same time, there are potential caveats to the acceptability of a regulated form of pregnancy contract even under conditions of gender equality: (1) the importance of background economic inequality;[58] (2)

---

55. The medieval church held that the male implanted into the female body a fully formed homunculus (complete with a soul). See Barbara Ehrenreich and Deidre English, *Witches, Midwives and Nurses: A History of Women Healers* (Old Westbury, N.Y.: Feminist Press, 1973).

56. For a perceptive discussion of the ways in which the social treatment of difference has been used to perpetuate inequalities, see Martha Minow, *Making All the Difference* (Ithaca, N.Y.: Cornell University Press, 1990).

57. Of course, under different conditions, the importance of genetically based ties between parents and children might decline.

58. According to a 1987 study by the U.S. Office of Technology Assessment, the typical clients of surrogate parenting agencies are white; 64% have annual incomes of over

Markets in Women's
                                        Reproductive Labor

the effect of the practice on race equality; (3) the need to ensure the
woman's participation in the overall purpose of the activity; (4) the need
to ensure that the vulnerable—children—are protected. We know very
little about the prerequisites for psychologically healthy children. We
know very little about the effects of pregnancy contracts on parental exit
or on the other children of the birth mother.[59] For this reason, even under more ideal circumstances, there is reason to be cautious about the
potential use of such contracts. For the time being, I believe that pregnancy contracts should be discouraged. This can be done by making
such contracts unenforceable in the courts. Furthermore, in contested
cases, the courts should recognize no distinction between genetic and
gestational "surrogates" with respect to parental rights. Finally, broker-
age of pregnancy contracts should be illegal. These proposals aim to discourage contract pregnancy and to strengthen the position of the "surrogate," who is the most economically and emotionally vulnerable party
in any such arrangement.

V. CONCLUSION: WAGE LABOR, REPRODUCTIVE LABOR, AND EQUALITY

In this article, I have analyzed various grounds for forbidding markets in
women's reproductive labor. While I rejected most of these grounds, including the essentialist thesis, the opposing approach of market theorists
misses the point that there are noneconomic values that should con-
strain social policy. Market theorists, in representing all of human behavior as if it were a product of voluntary choice, ignore the fact of unequal power in the family and in the wider society.

While market theorists often defend their approach in terms of the values of liberty, welfare, and neutrality, they abstract away from the in-
egalitarian social context in which an individual's preferences are
formed. But how preferences are formed, and in the light of what range
of choices,[60] has a great deal to do with whether or not acting on those
preferences is liberty- and welfare-enhancing.[61] Under some circum-

---

$50,000. By contrast, 66% of the "surrogates" reported annual incomes of less than
$30,000.

59. See n. 7 above.

60. I am indebted to Elisabeth Wood for many discussions about the importance of the
"range of choice" in evaluating social practices.

61. Cass Sunstein has criticized the tendency of a wide range of political views to take
preferences as given, without attention to the background conditions that shaped them.

stances, for example, it could be welfare-enhancing to sell oneself into slavery.[62]

What about liberal neutrality? Market theorists may claim that the asymmetry thesis is a violation of liberal neutrality: it imposes a standard of gender equality on free exchanges. Furthermore, it may seem biased—distinguishing activities that harm women from those that harm everyone. The issue of neutrality is a difficult matter to assess, for there are many interpretations of neutrality. At the very least, however, two considerations seem relevant. First, why should existing distributions serve as the standard against which neutrality is measured? I have argued that it is a mistake to assume that the realm of reproduction and sexuality is "neutral"; it is a product (at least in part) of the unequal social, political, and economic power of men and women. Second, most liberals draw the line at social practices such as slavery, indentured servitude, labor at slave wages, and the selling of votes or political liberties. Each of these practices undermines a framework of free deliberation among equals. If such restrictions violate viewpoint "neutrality," then the mere violation of neutrality does not seem objectionable.

Contract pregnancy places women's bodies under the control of others and serves to perpetuate gender inequality. The asymmetries of gender—the fact of social relations of gender domination—provide the best foundation for the asymmetry thesis. However, not all of the negative consequences of contract pregnancy involve its effects on gender inequality. I have also referred to its possible effects on children, and to the problematic form that such contracts will have to take to be self-enforcing. In addition, a full assessment of the practice would have to consider both its potential for deepening racial inequality and the unequal bargaining power of the parties to the contract. Some of these features of pregnancy contracts are shared with other labor contracts. Indeed, there is an important tradition in social philosophy that argues that it is precisely these shared features that make wage labor itself unacceptable. This tradition emphasizes that wage labor, like contract pregnancy, places the productive capacities of one group of citizens at the service and under the control of another. Unfortunately, there has been little attention in political philosophy to the effects of gender and class in-

See his "Preferences and Politics," *Philosophy & Public Affairs* 20, no. 1 (Winter 1991): 3–34.

62. See Patterson, *Slavery and Social Death*, for a discussion of such circumstances.

Markets in Women's
                                        Reproductive Labor

equality on the development of women's and workers' deliberative capacities or on the formation of their preferences. We have to ask: What kinds of work and family relations and environments best promote the development of the deliberative capacities needed to support democratic institutions?

Part IV
Reprogenetics

Part IV
Reprogenetics

[9]

Prenatal Genetic Testing and Screening: Constructing Needs and Reinforcing Inequities

Abby Lippman*

This Article considers the influence and implications of the application of genetic technologies to definitions of disease and to the treatment of illness. The concept of "geneticization" is introduced to emphasize the dominant discourse in today's stories of health and disease and the social construction of biological phenomenon is described. The reassurance, choice and control supposedly provided by prenatal genetic testing and screening are critically examined, and their role in constructing the need for such technology is addressed. Using the stories told about prenatal diagnosis as a focus, the consequences of a genetic perspective for and on women and their health care needs are explored.

I. INTRODUCTION

During the past two decades, numerous techniques have been developed that allow geneticists to assess the physical status of the fetus during a woman's pregnancy. The variety of prenatal diagnostic techniques[1] and detectable/diagnosable fetal conditions continues to expand. These screening and testing procedures are already the most widespread application of genetic technology to humans.

This paper, part of an ongoing project, explores the genetic stories[2] told about health and disease today, the storytellers and the

---

* Associate Professor, Dep't of Epidemiology & Biostatistics, McGill University. Prenatal diagnosis, the focus of much of this paper, is troublesome for all women, users and critics alike. In no way do I intend my remarks about it to reflect on women who have considered or undergone testing; criticism of the technologies is not to be read as criticisms of them. Women considering childbearing today face agonizing issues I was fortunate enough not to have to confront, and I can only admire their resilience and strength.

[1] See *infra* notes 20-26 and accompanying text for a discussion of these techniques.

[2] In this Article, the word "stories" is not used to suggest that what is said is not true (this may or may not be the case). Rather it is used in a literary, not a legal, sense to capture the idea that how scientists present their observations and study results is no different from how novelists present *their* interpretations of the external world. "Raw" material is shaped and interpreted to convey a message by both groups, with their constructions reflecting the pre-

16   AMERICAN JOURNAL OF LAW & MEDICINE VOL. XVII NOS. 1 & 2 1991

cirumstances in which these stories are told. In this Article, I first discuss how disease categories and biomedical practices are constructed within their cultural context, and provide some technical information regarding prenatal diagnosis. I then examine the stories constructed about genetic testing and screening; the particular assumptions upon which they are grounded;[3] and the necessarily problematic nature of applications of these genetic technologies with respect to perceptions of pregnancy and the health care needs of women considering childbearing. I demonstrate how the approach implicit in the use of genetic technology is as much a cultural and social activity as it is scientific. Specifically, I examine why prenatal diagnosis is made available, discussing some of the rationales usually presented for its use, and explore how a "need" for prenatal diagnosis is currently constructed. I then consider how existing health, health care beliefs and North American social stratifications situate prenatal technologies and how these activities may themselves influence health and health care inequities.

II. HEALTH AND DISEASE AND THE STORIES TOLD ABOUT THEM

In today's western world, biomedical and political systems largely define health and disease, as well as normality and abnormality.[4] They also determine the individuals to whom each term will be applied. Western biomedicine does not just describe a pre-existing biological reality, but is grounded in particular social and cultural assumptions.[5]

---

vailing social/cultural context. Further, to the degree that the same story is repeated and becomes accepted and used, it will itself begin to shape this context.

[3] I attempt, in this way, to enter "an old text from a new critical direction." A. RICH, *When We Dead Awaken*, in ON LIES, SECRETS AND SILENCE 35 (1979). I consider how stories about prenatal diagnosis both reflect and affect the social process of geneticization, how they emerge from existing cultural values at the same time as they interactively influence this very culture, altering our values, redefining our reality. *See infra* notes 101-40 and accompanying text. Using the biomedical and social science literature, and switching analogies, I want to create a "femmage," a "sister concept" to the collage, wherein a composite describing these stories is created from multiple sources. *See* S. PRICE, PRIMITIVE ART IN CIVILIZED PLACES 4 (1989) (quoting Meyer & Shapiro, *Waste Not, Want Not: An Inquiry into What Women Saved and Assembled*, 4 HERESIES 66-69 (1978)).

[4] It should be emphasized that the priority given to matters of health is historically dependent and determined on a local level. These issues may not warrant political, economic or scientific attention in all places or at all times. A malady that is diagnosed and treated as a prevalent disease in one country may be diagnosed and treated completely differently in another country. *See generally* L. PAYER, MEDICINE & CULTURE (1988).

[5] *See* THE PROBLEM OF MEDICAL KNOWLEDGE: EXAMINING THE SOCIAL CONSTRUCTION OF MEDICINE (P. Wright & A. Treacher eds. 1982) [hereinafter THE PROBLEM OF MEDICAL KNOWLEDGE]; M. LOCK & D. GORDON, *Relationship Between Society, Culture, and Biomedicine: Introduction to the Essays*, in BIOMEDICINE EXAMINED 11, 11-18 (M. Lock & D. Gordon eds. 1988); Taussig, *Reification and the Consciousness of the Patient*, 14 SOC. SCI. & MED. 3, 3 (through reification, "disease is recruited into serving the ideological needs of the social order"); Young, *The Anthropologies of Illness and Sickness*, 2 ANN. REV. ANTHROPOLOGY 257 (1982) [hereinafter *The*

No strictly objective and value-free view of the biological world exists. Any attempt to explain or order it will be shaped by the historical and cultural setting within which it occurs.[6]

Although there is a biological reality to disease, biological processes take on particular forms in different human groups and in different periods of time.[7] Disorders and disabilities are not merely physiological or physical conditions with fixed contours. Rather, they are social products with variable shapes and distributions. Defining and studying these categories and the people assigned to them is necessarily subjective, reflecting how those with power at any particular historical time construct them as problems.

In studying the distribution of health and disease, any one of the factors influencing their occurrence (social and physical environments, economic conditions, heredity, personal behaviors, health services, etc.) may be chosen for attention and investment of resources. This choice and its subsequent expression in public policies and private practices reflect the assumptions, vested interests and ideologies of the investigators and those funding them.[8] Because "disease is socially mutable" and medical responses are "maleable,"[9] there is abundant raw material from which to create metaphors and stories describing health and disease. The same observations may be taken as evidence to construct very different hypotheses or stories.[10]

Today's stories about health and disease both in professional journals[11] and mass circulation magazines[12] are increasingly told in the lan-

Anthropologies of Illness and Sickness]; Young, *When Rational Men Fall Sick: An Inquiry into Some Assumptions Made by Medical Anthropologists,* 5 CULTURE MED. & PSYCHOLOGY 317 (1981) [hereinafter *When Rational Men Fall Sick*]; *see also* Young, *Rational Men and the Explanatory Model Approach,* 6 CULTURE, MED. & PSYCHOLOGY 57 (1982) [hereinafter *Rational Man and the Explanatory Model Approach*] (containing Young's replies to comments directed toward *When Rational Men Fall Sick, supra*).

[6] *See generally* S. TESH, HIDDEN ARGUMENTS: POLITICAL IDEOLOGY AND DISEASE PREVENTION POLICY 3 (1988) ("there is an inextricable interrelationship between facts and values, both in the search for the causes of disease and in the process of developing the best preventive policy").

[7] *See* Laurell, *Social Analysis of Collective Health in Latin America,* 28 SOC. SCI. & MED. 1183 (1989); M. LOCK, *Mind, Matter and Middle Age: Ideologies for the Second Sex, to be published in* ANALYSIS IN MEDICAL ANTHROPOLOGY (S. Lindenbaum & M. Lock eds.).

[8] *See* Winner, *Is There Any Light Under Our Bushel? Three Modest Proposals for S.T.S.,* 10 BULL. SCI. TECH. & SOC'Y 12 (1990).

[9] Woolhandler & Himmelstein, *Ideology in Medical Science: Class in the Clinic,* 28 SOC. SCI. & MED. 1205, 1206 (1989).

[10] *See generally* H. LONGINO, SCIENCE AS SOCIAL KNOWLEDGE: VALUES AND OBJECTIVITY IN SCIENTIFIC INQUIRY (1990).

[11] *E.g.,* Chui, Wong & Scriver, *The Thalassemias and Health Care in Canada: A Place for Genetics in Medicine,* 144 CANADIAN MED. ASS'N J. 21 (1991); Koshland, *The Rational Approach to the Irrational,* 250 SCIENCE 189 (1990); Stead, Senner, Reddick & Lofgren, *Racial Differences in Susceptibility to Infection by Mycobacterium Tuberculosis,* 322 NEW ENG. J. MED. 422, 426 (1990); Watson, *The Human Genome Project: Past, Present, and Future,* 248 SCIENCE 44 (1990).

18   AMERICAN JOURNAL OF LAW & MEDICINE VOL. XVII NOS. 1 & 2 1991

guage of genetics. Using the metaphor of blueprints,[13] with genes and DNA fragments presented as a set of instructions, the dominant discourse describing the human condition is reductionist, emphasizing genetic determination. It promotes scientific control of the body, individualizes health problems and situates individuals increasingly according to their genes. Through this discourse, which is beginning seriously to threaten other narratives, clinical and research geneticists and their colleagues are conditioning how we view, name and propose to manage a whole host of disorders and disabilities. Though it is only one conceptual model, "genetics" is increasingly identified as *the* way to reveal and explain health and disease, normality and abnormality. Baird, for example, sees the "major determinants" of disease as internal genetic factors.[14]

This conditioning directs how intellectual and financial resources are applied to resolve health problems.[15] More critically, it profoundly influences our values and attitudes. To capture this process, I use the term "geneticization."[16] Although most neologisms confuse rather

---

[12] *E.g.*, Alexander, *The Gene Hunt*, TIME, Mar. 20, 1989, at 52; Beers, *The Gene Screen*, VOGUE, June 1990, at 236, 237; Montgomery, *The Ultimate Medicine*, DISCOVER, Mar. 1990, at 60; Schmeck, *Battling the Legacy of Illness*, N.Y. TIMES GOOD HEALTH MAGAZINE, Apr. 28, 1990, at 36.

[13] *See* Council for Responsible Genetics, *Position Paper on Genetic Discrimination*, 3 ISSUES REPRODUCTIVE & GENETIC ENGINEERING 287 (1990) (criticizing the "blueprint" notion); Newman, *Idealist Biology*, 31 PERSPECTIVES BIOLOGY & MED. 353, 361 (1988) (DNA is one component of a "complex dynamical system," not a "command center" that is impervious to environmental input); Rose, *Human Perfectability*, 2 LANCET 1380, 1380-81 (1984) (emphasizing the effects of environment on DNA). *See generally* G. LAKOFF & M. JOHNSON, METAPHORS WE LIVE BY (1980).

[14] Baird, *Genetics and Health Care: A Paradigm Shift*, 33 PERSPECTIVES BIOLOGY & MED. 203, 203-04 (1990).

[15] *See* Lippman, *Genetics and Public Health: Means, Goals and Justices, to be published in* AM. J. HUM. GENETICS (1991) [hereinafter *Genetics and Public Health*]; Lippman, Messing & Mayer, *Is Genome Mapping the Way to Improve Canadians' Health?*, 81 CANADIAN J. PUB. HEALTH 397, 398 (1990) (noting that "undirected" studies of, for instance, "environmental protection against genotoxicants or of nutritional supplementation during pregnancy," will suffer financially because funds are going to human genome mapping).

[16] A. Lippman, La "Geneticization" de la Vie (unpublished manuscript presented at Seminaire, Lalonde-les-Maures, France, May, 1990). A few years ago, in an article only recently rediscovered, Edlin described a process he called "geneticizing" to refer to the tendency to label as "genetic" diseases and disorders "of possible polygenic-multifactorial origin" for which there was, in fact, "scant or no genetic evidence." Edlin, *Inappropriate Use of Genetic Terminology in Medical Research: A Public Health Issue*, 31 PERSPECTIVES BIOLOGY & MED. 47, 48 (1987). He argued that geneticizing led to premature categorization of diseases as genetic, and caused research funds to be allocated to genetic research to the detriment of other research. *Id.* at 48. I have deliberately chosen not to resurrect his term, since the processes I want to describe go beyond those that he emphasized. In this regard, too, the concept of geneticization goes beyond Yoxen's discussion of the "construction" of genetic disease. Yoxen, *Constructing Genetic Diseases*, in THE PROBLEM OF MEDICAL KNOWLEDGE, *supra* note 5, at 144. Apparently, the term "geneticism" was used even earlier in an essay by Sir Peter Medawar also to describe the inappropriate genetic labeling of variations between peo-

than clarify, enlarging our lexicon to interpret human genetics is appropriate. A new canon deserves a new vocabulary.

Geneticization refers to an ongoing process by which differences between individuals are reduced to their DNA codes, with most disorders, behaviors and physiological variations defined, at least in part, as genetic in origin. It refers as well to the process by which interventions employing genetic technologies are adopted to manage problems of health. Through this process, human biology is incorrectly equated with human genetics,[17] implying that the latter acts alone to make us each the organism she or he is.

Duster captures much of this in describing how prevailing social concerns of our age are leading us to see things through a genetic "prism."[18] "Geneticization" goes further, however, and poses genetics as the source of illumination itself, not merely one of the ways in which it might be refracted.

Prenatal diagnosis, already designated as a "ritual" of pregnancy, at least for white, middle-class women in North America, is the most widespread application of genetic technology to humans today.[19] It provides a central activity around which to explore geneticization and the health stories told in its language.

III. PRENATAL DIAGNOSIS: A TECHNICAL AND A SOCIAL CONSTRUCTION

Of all applied genetic activities, prenatal diagnosis is probably most familiar to the general population and is also the most used. Prenatal diagnosis refers to all the technologies currently in use or under development to determine the physi(ologi)cal condition of a fetus

ple. Medawar, *The Genetic Improvements of Man*, 18 AUSTRALASIAN ANNALS MED. 317, 319 (1969).

[17] *See* R. HUBBARD, THE POLITICS OF WOMEN'S BIOLOGY 52 (1990) (noting that in a less individualized society than ours, people might find many aspects of biology "more interesting than heredity, genes and . . . DNA"); Murphy, *The Logic of Medicine*, 66 AM. J. MED. 907, 908 (1979) (warning against a "narrow concern with single genes" that "destroys our vision of the human organism").

[18] T. DUSTER, BACKDOOR TO EUGENICS 2 (1990). Duster defines the "prism of heritability" as a "way of perceiving traits and behaviors that attributes the major explanatory power to biological inheritance." *Id.* at 164. In this definition, he is very close to Edlin's "geneticizing." *See supra* note 16. However, only when Duster notes, but without detailed development of the theme, that labels will determine how we choose to respond to a problem, does he begin to incorporate all that I place under the rubric of geneticization. The concept of geneticization explicitly makes this an essential part of the process.

[19] Rapp, *The Power of "Positive" Diagnosis: Medical and Maternal Discourses on Amniocentesis*, in CHILDBIRTH IN AMERICA: ANTHROPOLOGICAL PERSPECTIVES 103, 105 (K. Michaelson ed. 1988) [hereinafter CHILDBIRTH IN AMERICA]. *See generally* R. BLATT, PRENATAL TESTS: WHAT THEY ARE, THEIR BENEFITS AND RISKS, AND HOW TO DECIDE WHETHER TO HAVE THEM OR NOT (1988).

20   AMERICAN JOURNAL OF LAW & MEDICINE VOL. XVII NOS. 1 & 2 1991

before birth. Until recently, prenatal diagnosis usually meant amniocentesis,[20] a second trimester procedure routinely available for women over a certain age (usually thirty-five years in North America),[21]
for Down syndrome detection. Amniocentesis is also used in selected
circumstances where the identification of specific fetal genetic disorders
is possible.[22] Now, in addition to amniocentesis, there are chorionic
villus sampling (CVS)[23] tests that screen maternal blood samples to detect a fetus with a neural tube defect or Down syndrome, and ultrasound screening.[24] Despite professional guidelines to the contrary,[25]

---

[20] In amniocentesis, a hollow needle is inserted through a woman's abdomen and into the
amniotic sac in order to remove a small sample of the fluid that surrounds the developing
fetus. The procedure is usually preceded by an ultrasound examination to document the age
of the fetus and its location so that an appropriate site for insertion of the amniocentesis
needle can be chosen. The fluid that is removed — amniotic fluid — contains cells from the
fetus that, if allowed to divide in the laboratory, can then be analyzed. In particular, one can
count the number of chromosomes in the cells, determine fetal sex and carry out biochemical
and specific genetic analyses on these cells. Amniocentesis is performed at about sixteen to
twenty weeks' gestation, the second trimester of pregnancy: before this time not enough fluid
or enough cells are available. Once a fluid sample has been obtained, there is a further three
to four week wait for the analyses to be completed and results to be available, since it takes
this long to grow a sufficient number of cells for study. Thus, if a fetus is found to be affected
with the condition for which testing was done and the woman chooses to abort the pregnancy,
the abortion is not induced until about the twentieth week, which is halfway through the pregnancy. *See* E. NIGHTINGALE & M. GOODMAN, BEFORE BIRTH: PRENATAL TESTING FOR GENETIC
DISEASE 32-35 (1990) [hereinafter BEFORE BIRTH]. Recent technical developments that allow
diagnoses to be made following amplification of the genetic material in a single cell can
shorten considerably the time needed to obtain results. *See infra* note 23 and accompanying
text.

[21] *See infra* note 67 and accompanying text for a discussion of the social, rather than biological, bases for categorizing women over 35 as "at risk."

[22] Over 150 "single gene" disorders can now be detected, and testing may be carried out
for women who have a documented family history of one of these or who are otherwise known
to be at increased risk. Testing is not carried out for these disorders without specific indications. *See generally* Antonarakis, *Diagnosis of Genetic Disorders at the DNA Level*, 320 NEW ENG. J.
MED. 153 (1989) (reviewing recent progress in identifying single gene disorders).

[23] In chorionic villus sampling (CVS), a small tube (catheter) is inserted through the va-
gina and cervix. It is then advanced, under ultrasound guidance, until it reaches the placenta,
from which a small amount of tissue (chorionic villi) is removed. Some obstetricians now
obtain a sample through a needle inserted into the abdomen instead. Any chromosomal or
biochemical disorder can, in theory, be diagnosed with tissues obtained by CVS, because the
cells of the fetus and placenta (which are formed from chorionic villi) are genetically the same.
See Vekemans & Perry, *Cytogenic Analysis of Chorionic Villi: A Technical Assessment*, 72 HUM. GE-
NETICS 307 (1986). This procedure was first used successfully in China as early as 1975 to
determine fetal sex. Tietung Hosp. Dep't of Obstetrics & Gynecology, *Fetal Sex Prediction by
Sex Chromatin of Chorionic Villi Cells During Early Pregnancy*, 1 CHINESE MED. J. 117 (1975). CVS
can be done as early as eight or nine weeks after a woman's last menstrual period and, while
the results of tests carried out on the placental tissue can be available within hours, a two or
three day waiting period is usually required. *See* BEFORE BIRTH, *supra* note 20, at 35-36. If a
woman chooses to abort the pregnancy following CVS, the abortion can be carried out in the
first trimester. Finally, CVS does not appear more likely to cause a spontaneous abortion than
amniocentesis. Canadian Collaborative CVS - Amniocentesis Clinical Trial Group, *Multicentre
Randomised Clinical Trial of Chorion Villus Sampling and Amniocentesis*, 1 LANCET 1, 4 (1989).

[24] During an ultrasound examination, high frequency sound waves are projected into the

ultrasound screening is performed routinely in North America on almost every pregnant woman appearing for prenatal care early enough in pregnancy. And although ultrasound is not usually labeled as "prenatal diagnosis," it not only belongs under this rubric but was, I suggest, the first form of prenatal diagnosis for which informed consent is not obtained.[26]

Expansion of prenatal diagnosis techniques, ever widening lists of identifiable conditions and susceptibilities, changes in the timing of testing and the populations in which testing is occurring, and expanding professional definitions of what should be diagnosed *in utero*, attest to this technology's role in the process of geneticization.[27] But these operational characteristics alone circumscribe only some aspects of prenatal diagnosis. Prenatal diagnosis as a social activity is becoming

---

uterus; the sound waves that are reflected back are resolved visually to allow one to "see" the fetus on a television-like display screen. A. OAKLEY, THE CAPTURED WOMB: A HISTORY OF THE MEDICAL CARE OF PREGNANT WOMEN 155-68 (1984).

[25] *See* BEFORE BIRTH, *supra* note 20, at 31-32. A consensus development conference in the United States recently recommended reserving the use of ultrasound for pregnancies that may require it for specific medical reasons. PUB. HEALTH SERV., U.S. DEP'T OF HEALTH & HUM. SERVS., CONSENSUS DEVELOPMENT CONFERENCE: DIAGNOSTIC ULTRASOUND IMAGING IN PREGNANCY 11 (National Inst. of Health Publication No. 667, 1984). This recommendation is clearly not being followed and, at present, in many major North American teaching hospitals, almost all pregnant women are referred for two "routine" ultrasound examinations — one before the twentieth week and one in the third trimester — for purposes of dating the pregnancy, even though the benefits of such a policy have not been established. Even more frequent scans are considered routine in France. As a specific tool for prenatal diagnosis, ultrasound can be used to identify certain malformations such as neural tube defects, cleft lip, or limb shortening in fetuses known to be at risk for one of these abnormalities. It can also be used to identify fetal sex. Most subtle malformations will not be identified when ultrasound is applied routinely on a non-diagnostic basis, however; the detailed examination that would be necessary requires more than the time that is usually allowed (or the machinery that is employed) when the primary goal is pregnancy dating. Nevertheless, some fetal problems can be diagnosed and their recognition may influence subsequent decisions about how pregnancy is managed.

[26] *See* Chervenak, McCullough & Chervenak, *Prenatal Informed Consent for Sonogram*, 161 AM. J. OBSTETRICS & GYNECOLOGY 857, 860 (1989); Lippman, *Access to Prenatal Screening: Who Decides?*, 1 CANADIAN J. WOMEN L. 434 (1986) [hereinafter *Who Decides?*]. Chervenak and colleagues have recently called attention to the issue of informed consent for ultrasound, but their conclusions are troublesome. They consider the pregnant woman "the patient's fiduciary," the "patient" to them being the fetus. Chervenak, McCullough & Chervenak, *supra*, at 858. This suggests that the consent process they propose will be coercive.

It is also worth noting that ultrasound is no longer the only genetic technology applied without prior consent. Screening for carriers of hemoglobin disorders, for example, is also done unbeknownst to the individuals being tested in certain jurisdictions. *See* Rowley, Loader, Sutera & Walden, *Do Pregant Women Benefit from Hemoglobinopathy Carrier Detection?*, 565 ANNALS N.Y. ACADEMY SCIENCES 152, 153 (1989) [hereinafter Rowley]. These authors noted that consent for sickle cell and other hemoglobinopathies was not obtained because: "Consent for screening was not routinely sought; providers agreed that obtaining timely informed consent required counseling approaching that to be provided to identified carriers and many providers declined to participate if they had to obtain it." Rowley, *supra*, at 153.

[27] *See generally Who Decides?*, *supra* note 26, at 434.

22   AMERICAN JOURNAL OF LAW & MEDICINE VOL. XVII NOS. 1 & 2 1991

an element in our culture and this aspect, which has had minimal attention, will be examined in depth.

A. PRENATAL DIAGNOSIS AND THE DISCOURSE OF REASSURANCE

Contemporary stories about prenatal diagnosis contain several themes, but these generally reflect either of two somewhat different models.[28] In the "public health" model, prenatal diagnosis is presented as a way to reduce the frequency of selected birth defects.[29] In the other, which I will call the "reproductive autonomy" model, prenatal diagnosis is presented as a means of giving women information to expand their reproductive choices.[30] Unfortunately, neither model fully captures the essence of prenatal diagnosis. In addition, neither acknowledges the internal tension, revealed in the coexistence of quite contradictory constructions of testing that may be equally valid: 1) as an assembly line approach to the products of conception, separating out those products we wish to develop from those we wish to discontinue;[31] 2) as a way to give women control over their pregnancies, respecting (increasing) their autonomy to choose the kinds of children they will bear;[32] or 3) as a means of reassuring women that enhances their experience of pregnancy.[33]

The dominant theme throughout the biomedical literature, as well as some feminist commentary, emphasizes the last two of these constructions.[34] A major variation on this theme suggests, further, that

---

[28] *Id.*

[29] *See, e.g.,* Kolker, *Advances in Prenatal Diagnosis: Social-psychological and Policy Issues,* 5 INT'L J. TECH. ASSESSMENT HEALTH CARE 601 (1989); *see also* Dalgaard & Norby, *Autosomal Dominant Polycystic Kidney Disease in the 1980s,* 36 CLINICAL GENETICS 320, 324 (1989) (placing importance on "selective reproduction prevention").

[30] *See* PRESIDENT'S COMM'N FOR THE STUDY OF ETHICAL PROBLEMS IN MEDICAL AND BIOMEDICAL AND BEHAVIORAL RESEARCH, SCREENING AND COUNSELING FOR GENETIC CONDITIONS: THE ETHICAL, SOCIAL, AND LEGAL IMPLICATIONS OF GENETIC SCREENING, COUNSELING, AND EDUCATION PROGRAMS 55 (1983) [hereinafter PRESIDENT'S COMM'N] ("In sum, the fundamental value of genetic screening and counseling is their ability to enhance the opportunities for the individual to obtain information about their personal health and childbearing risks and to make autonomous and noncoerced choices based on that information.").

[31] *See* B. ROTHMAN, RECREATING MOTHERHOOD: IDEOLOGY AND TECHNOLOGY IN A PATRIARCHAL SOCIETY 21 (1989) (describing the "commodification of life, towards treating people and parts of people . . . as commodities . . . . We work hard, some of us, at making the perfect product, what one of the doctors in the childbirth movement calls a 'blue ribbon baby.' "). *See also* Ewing, *Australian Perspectives on Embryo Experimentation: An Update,* 3 ISSUES REPRODUCTIVE & GENETIC ENGINEERING 119 (1990); Rothman, *The Decision to Have or Not to Have Amniocentesis for Prenatal Diagnosis,* in CHILDBIRTH IN AMERICA, *supra* note 19, at 92, 92-98. ·

[32] *See* Hill, *Your Morality or Mine? An Inquiry into the Ethics of Human Reproduction,* 154 AM. J. OBSTETRICS & GYNECOLOGY 1173, 1178-80 (1986).

[33] *See generally* ROYAL COLLEGE OF PHYSICIANS OF LONDON, PRENATAL DIAGNOSIS AND GENETIC SCREENING: COMMUNITY AND SERVICE IMPLICATIONS (1989).

[34] *See, e.g.,* WOMEN'S RIGHTS LITIGATION CLINIC, REPRODUCTIVE LAWS FOR THE 1990s: A BRIEFING HANDBOOK (1987); *Who Decides?, supra* note 26, at 438.

through the use of prenatal diagnosis women can avoid the family distress and suffering associated with the unpredicted birth of babies with genetic disorders or congenital malformations, thus preventing disability while enhancing the experience of pregnancy.[35] Not unlike the approach used to justify caesarean sections,[36] prenatal diagnosis is constructed as a way of avoiding "disaster."

The language of control, choice and reassurance certainly makes prenatal diagnosis appear attractive. But while this discourse may be successful as a marketing strategy,[37] it relates a limited and highly selected story about prenatal diagnosis. Notwithstanding that even the most critical would probably agree prenatal diagnosis *can be* selectively reassuring[38] (for the vast majority of women who will learn that the fetus does not have Down syndrome or some other serious diagnosable disorder), this story alone is too simplistic. It does not take account of why reassurance is sought, how risk groups are generated and how eligibility for obtaining this kind of reassurance is determined. Whatever else, prenatal diagnosis *is* a means of separating fetuses we wish to develop from those we wish to discontinue. Prenatal diagnosis does approach children as consumer objects subject to quality control.

This is implicit in the general assumption that induced abortion will follow the diagnosis of fetal abnormality.[39] This assumption is reinforced by the rapid acceptance of CVS, which allows prenatal diagnosis to be carried out earlier and earlier in pregnancy when termination of a fetus found to be "affected" is taken for granted as less problematic.[40] The generally unquestioned assumption that pre-implantation diagno-

---

[35] McDonough, *Congenital Disability and Medical Research: The Development of Amniocentesis*, 16 WOMEN & HEALTH 137, 143-44 (1990). McDonough notes that three rationales for amniocentesis emerged from her survey: "The procedure offered those at risk the possibility of 'health' . . . . [it] provided parents with reassurance and avoided abortion . . . . [and it] prevent[ed] disease and disability." *Id.*

[36] *See, e.g.*, McClain, *Perceived Risk and Choice of Childbirth Service*, 17 SOC. SCI. & MED. 1857, 1862 (1983).

[37] There is no evidence that control, autonomy and reassurance are actually enhanced and not merely assumed to occur. In fact, there have been very few in-depth studies in this area, and the conclusions of these investigations seem to vary with the orientation of the investigator. Studies reported in the social science and feminist literature suggest that prenatal diagnosis removes control; studies reported in the biomedical literature are interpreted to show how reassurance is provided. For an overview of these studies, see Lippman, *Research Studies in Applied Human Genetics: A Quantitative Analysis and Critical Review of Recent (Biomedical) Literature, to be published in* AM. J. MED. GENETICS (1991). Much more ethnographic work in this area is required.

[38] *See infra* text accompanying notes 48-51 for a reconstruction of the notion of reassurance.

[39] *See supra* notes 31-32 and accompanying text.

[40] This issue is discussed in A. Lippman, Led Astray by Genetic Maps (speech given, Ottawa, Canada, 1991). Treatment, often said to be a goal of early identification of affected fetuses, becomes even less likely with CVS. Pharmaceutical companies will not be motivated

24   AMERICAN JOURNAL OF LAW & MEDICINE VOL. XVII NOS. 1 & 2 1991

sis is better than prenatal diagnosis also undermines a monotonic reassurance rhetoric.[41] With pre-implantation (embryo) diagnosis, the selection objective is clear: only those embryos thought to be "normal" will be transferred and allowed to continue to develop.[42] Thus, embryo destruction is equated with induced abortion.[43] In perhaps the most blatant example, Brambati and colleagues have proposed the combined use of *in vitro* fertilization, gamete intrafallopian transfer, chorionic villus sampling and fetal reduction to "avoid pregnancy termination among high risk couples" [sic], and have stated that the "fetus was reduced" when describing a situation in which this scenario actually occurred.[44]

Thus, while no single storyline is inherently true or false, the reassurance discourse appears to mask essential features of genetic testing and screening that are troubling. Reassurance — for pregnant women or for geneticists[45] — notwithstanding, the story is more complex. Prenatal diagnosis necessarily involves systematic and systemic selection of fetuses, most frequently on genetic grounds.[46] Though the word

---

to invest in developing treatments for conditions that "need not occur." Rarely will they base business decisions on their social worth rather than on their financial value.

This situation contains elements of an unusual conflict. Increasingly, geneticists are promising to have treatments available for a wide range of disorders and, for some conditions, therapeutic developments have occurred which make them far more benign than previously. The promises, and the available examples, are likely to to be sufficiently persuasive that women "at-risk" may either make use of prenatal diagnosis less frequently or see less reason to abort an affected fetus than today. Yet, at the same time, the very availability of prenatal diagnosis and abortion may be seen as justifications for *not* investing in the further development of these therapies that parents will have been led to expect. *Cf.* Varekamp, Suurmeijer, Bröcker-Vriends, Van Dijck, Smit, Rosendaal & Briët, *Carrier Testing and Prenatal Diagnosis for Hemophilia: Experiences and Attitudes of 549 Potential and Obligate Carriers*, 37 AM. J. MED. GENETICS 147, 153 (1990) [hereinafter Varekamp] (noting decrease in hemophilia screening as treatment capabilities increased).

[41] *See* Bell, *Prenatal Diagnosis: Current Status and Future Trends*, in HUMAN GENETIC INFORMATION: SCIENCE, LAW & ETHICS 18-36 (Ciba Foundation Series 1990). *See also* Kolker, *supra* note 29, at 612 (prevention is "clearly cheaper than providing services for those with genetic disorders"); Modell, *Cystic Fibrosis Screening and Community Genetics*, 27 J. MED. GEN. 475, 476 (1990) ("undesirable [diseases] may be all but eradicated"); Dalgaard & Norby, *supra* note 29, at 323-24 ("access to selective reproductive prevention" is important).

[42] S. WYMELENBERG, SCIENCE AND BABIES: PRIVATE DECISIONS, PUBLIC DILEMMAS 130 (1990).

[43] In fact, some consider the combined procedures of *in vitro* fertilization and embryo diagnosis to be "ethically better" than prenatal diagnosis for detecting problems because it "avoids" abortion. *See* Michael & Buckle, *Screening for Genetic Disorders: Therapeutic Abortion and IVF*, 16 J. MED. ETHICS 43 (1990). *But see* J. TESTART, LE MONDE DIPLOMATIQUE 24 (1990) (suggesting that it is the very need to consider abortion ("de terribles responsabilités) that is perhaps the best safeguard against ordinary eugenics ("l'eugenisme ordinaire")).

[44] Brambati, Formigli, Tului & Simoni, *Selective Reduction of Quadruplet Pregnancy at Risk of B-Thalassemia*, 336 LANCET 1325, 1326 (1990).

[45] If nothing else, it is certainly preferable for their public image if geneticists are seen as reassuring women, rather than selecting their offspring.

[46] Much of importance has been written about the link between prenatal diagnosis and

"eugenics" is scrupulously avoided in most biomedical reports about prenatal diagnosis, except when it is strongly disclaimed as a motive for intervention, this is disingenuous.[47] Prenatal diagnosis presupposes that certain fetal conditions are intrinsically not bearable. Increasing diagnostic capability means that such conditions, as well as a host of variations that can be detected *in utero*, are proliferating, necessarily broadening the range of what is not "bearable" and restricting concepts of what is "normal." It is, perhaps, not unreasonable to ask if the "imperfect" will become anything we can diagnose.[48]

While the notion of reassurance has been successfully employed to justify prenatal testing and screening as responses to the problems of childhood disability, we need to question both the sufficiency and the necessity of its linkage to prenatal diagnosis. At best, reassurance is an acquired, not an inherent, characteristic of prenatal diagnosis. Even if testing provides "reassurance," it is of a particular and limited kind. For example, although the fetus can be shown not to have Down syndrome, most disabilities only manifest themselves after birth. Further, it is not the (only) way to achieve a global objective of "reassuring" pregnant women. Indeed, it may even be counterproductive. This becomes clear if one reconstructs the notion of reassurance. Assuming it is an acceptable objective of prenatal care, are there ways to reassure pregnant women desiring "healthy" children that do not lead to genetic testing and control?

Data from the United States Women, Infants and Children program leave little doubt that "low technology" approaches providing essential nutritional, social and other supportive services to pregnant women will reduce the low birth weight and prematurity responsible for most infant mortality and morbidity today.[49] Providing an adequate diet to the unacceptably large number of pregnant women living below the poverty line would clearly "reassure" them that their babies were developing as well as the babies of wealthier women. Similarly, alloca-

---

eugenics; this dialogue, despite its importance, will not be repeated here. *See generally* T. DUSTER, *supra* note 18; R. HUBBARD, *supra* note 17; Degener, *Female Self-determination Between Feminist Claims and "Voluntary" Eugenics, Between "Rights" and Ethics,* 3 ISSUES REPRODUCTIVE & GENETIC ENGINEERING 87 (1990); Hubbard, *Eugenics: New Tools, Old Ideas,* 13 WOMEN & HEALTH 225 (1987).

[47] This point is not merely an argument of critics of prenatal diagnosis. Shaw, a geneticist-lawyer who strongly defends the principle of fetal protection, has written that "any counselor who explains reproductive alternatives and offers a prenatal test to a counselee is a practicing eugenicist and any couple who chooses to avoid having babies with chromosome abnormalities or deleterious mutant genes is also practicing eugenics." Shaw, *Letter to the Editor: Response to Hayden: Presymptomatic and Prenatal Testing,* 28 AM. J. MED. GENETICS 765, 765-66 (1987).

[48] Rothschild, *Engineering Birth: Toward the Perfectability of Man?,* in 2 SCIENCE, TECHNOLOGY AND SOCIAL PROGRESS 93 (S. Goldman ed. 1989).

[49] *See* Anon, *WIC Program Shows Major Benefits,* NATION'S HEALTH, Dec. 1990, at 3.

26   AMERICAN JOURNAL OF LAW & MEDICINE VOL. XVII NOS. 1 & 2 1991

tion of funds for home visitors, respite care and domestic alterations would "reassure" women that the resources required to help them manage their special needs were readily available without financial cost, should their child be born with a health problem. It would also be "reassuring" to know that effective medication and simplified treatment regimes were available or being developed for prevalent disorders. Reassurances such as these may be all that many pregnant women want. Not only would these alternative approaches provide "reassurance" with respect to (and *for*) fetal disability, they would diminish a woman's feeling of personal responsibility for a child's health, rather than "exacerbate" it as does prenatal diagnosis.[50]

Genes may contribute to the distribution of low birth weight and prematurity in North America, and likely some investigators will seek their location and the order of their DNA base sequences on the human gene map. The social and economic inequalities among women with which they are associated,[51] however, are already well "mapped"; the "location" of women who are at increased risk is well known; the "sequences" of events leading to excessively and unnecessarily high rates of these problems have been well described. From this perspective, *gene* mapping and sequencing may be irrelevant as a source of reassurance in view of the most pressing needs of pregnant women. Even if genes were shown to be related to these problems, it must be remembered that the individuals to whom reassurance will be provided, as well as the concerns chosen for alleviation, rest on social, political and economic decisions by those in power. Such choices require continued analysis and challenge.

B. CONSTRUCTING THE "NEED" FOR PRENATAL DIAGNOSIS

While reassurance has been constructed to justify health professionals' offers of prenatal diagnosis, genetic testing and screening have also been presented in the same biomedical literature as responses to the "needs" of pregnant women. They are seen as something they "choose." What does it mean, however, to "need" prenatal diagnosis, to "choose" to be tested?[52] Once again, a closer look at what appear to

---

[50] *See* Farrant, *Who's for Amniocentesis? The Politics of Prenatal Screening,* in THE SEXUAL POLITICS OF REPRODUCTION 96, 120 (H. Homans ed. 1985) [hereinafter THE SEXUAL POLITICS OF REPRODUCTION].

[51] *See* Yankauer, *What Infant Mortality Tells Us,* 80 AM. J. PUB. HEALTH 653 (1990).

[52] While those in need are identified explicitly as (certain) pregnant women, it is worth noting that clinical geneticists, themselves, have a need for this technology, too. For instance, when a child is born with a malformation, geneticists likely feel most "helpful" when prenatal diagnosis, a technological palliative for the pains of etiologic ignorance, can be offered. Saying that the malformation is not likely to happen again, given the usually low empiric recurrence risks associated with most of these problems, is not nearly as comforting for genetic counselors as is offering *in utero* detection. Counselors "need" this technique for the satisfac-

be obvious terms may illuminate some otherwise hidden aspects of geneticization and the prenatal diagnosis stories told in its voice.

We must first identify the concept of need as itself a problem and acknowledge that needs do not have intrinsic reality. Rather, needs are socially constructed and culture bound, grounded in current history, dependent on context and, therefore, not universal.

With respect to prenatal diagnosis, "need" seems to have been conceptualized predominantly in terms of changes in capabilities for fetal diagnoses: women only come to "need" prenatal diagnosis after the test for some disorder has been developed. Moreover, the disorders to be sought are chosen exclusively by geneticists.[53] In addition, posing a "need" for testing to reduce the probability a woman will give birth to a child with some detectable characteristic rests on assumptions about the value of information, about which characteristics are or are not of value and about which risks should or should not be taken. These assumptions reflect almost exclusively a white, middle-class perspective.[54]

This conceptualization of need is propelled by several features of contemporary childbearing.[55] First, given North American culture, where major responsibility for family health care in general, for the fetus she carries and for the child she births, is still allocated to a woman,[56] it is generally assumed that she must do all that is

---

tory performance of their jobs no less than they believe a family "needs" prenatal diagnosis to prevent the birth of a second affected child.

[53] *See* Lippman, *Prenatal Diagnosis: Reproductive Choice? Reproductive Control?*, [hereinafter *Reproductive Choice?*] in THE FUTURE OF HUMAN REPRODUCTION 182, 187 (C. Overall ed. 1989) [hereinafter THE FUTURE OF HUMAN REPRODUCTION] (consideration of prenatal diagnosis as a professional resource).

[54] *See* Nsiah-Jefferson, *Reproductive Laws, Women of Color and Low Income Women* in REPRODUCTIVE LAWS FOR THE 1990s 17, 17-58 (S. Cohen & N. Taub eds. 1988) [hereinafter REPRODUCTIVE LAWS FOR THE 1990s] (discussing potential areas of cultural conflict in genetic counseling).

[55] There is an extensive literature on "medicalization" in general and on the medicalization of pregnancy and childbirth *per se* in which this discussion is rooted and from which it derives guidance. *See, e.g.*, A. OAKLEY, *supra* note 24, at 275. ("The medicalization of everyday life is a phenomenon described in many radical and liberal critiques of medicine."); *id.* at 276 ("For both birth and death normal signs have become neon lights flagging risks which demand and validate medical intervention."); Raymond, *Feminist Ethics, Ecology, and Vision*, in TEST-TUBE WOMEN 427, 427-37 (R. Arditti, R. Klein & S. Minden eds. 1984) [hereinafter TEST-TUBE WOMEN]; I. ZOLA, *Healthism and Disabling Medicalization*, in I. ILLICH, I. ZOLA, J. MCKNIGHT, J. CAPLAN & H. SHAIKEN, DISABLING PROFESSIONS 41 (1977); Zola, *In the Name of Health and Illness: On Some Socio-Political Consequences of Medical Influence*, 9 SOC. SCI. & MED. 83, 85-87 (1975) (noting that control by medical value not achieved through political means but by "medicalization"); Zola, *Medicine as an Institution of Social Control*, 20 SOCIOLOGY REV. 487 (1972); *see also* Lewin, *By Design: Reproductive Strategies and the Meaning of Motherhood*, in SEXUAL POLITICS OF REPRODUCTION, *supra* note 50, at 123, 123-38 (1985) (women "must adapt" to "motherhood" but can also approach it as "active strategists").

[56] *See* Oakley, *Smoking in Pregnancy: Smokescreen or Risk Factor? Towards a Materialist Analysis*, 11 SOCIOLOGY HEALTH & ILLNESS 311 (1989).

28   AMERICAN JOURNAL OF LAW & MEDICINE VOL. XVII NOS. 1 & 2 1991

recommended or available to foster her child's health. At its extreme, this represents the pregnant woman as obligated to produce a healthy child. Prenatal diagnosis, as it is usually presented, falls into this category of behaviors recommended to pregnant women who would exercise their responsibilities as caregivers.[57] Consequently, to the extent that she is expected generally to do everything possible for the fetus/ child, a woman may come to "need" prenatal diagnosis, and take testing for granted. Moreover, since an expert usually offers testing, and careseekers are habituated to follow through with tests ordered by physicians,[58] it is hardly surprising that they will perceive a need to be tested.[59] With prenatal diagnosis presented as a "way to avoid birth defects," to refuse testing, or perceive no need for it, becomes more difficult than to proceed with it.[60] This technology perversely creates a burden of not doing enough, a burden incurred when the technology is *not* used.[61]

A second feature, related to the first, is that women generally, and

---

[57] *See* Farrant, *supra* note 50, at 96; Oakley, *supra* note 56, at 311.

[58] *See* R. HATCHER & H. THOMPSON, SATISFACTION WITH OBSTETRICAL CARE AMONG CANADIAN WOMEN (Health Servs. Res. Unit, Department of Community Health, Queen's Univ., Kingston, Ontario 1987) (results of a survey showing pregnant women's reluctance to question medical authority).

[59] *See* Lippman, *supra* note 53, at 182. Physicians may pressure women into being tested, even using false information to do so. Marteau, Kidd, Cook, Michie, Johnston, Slack & Shaw, *Perceived Risk not Actual Risk Predicts Uptake of Amniocentesis*, 96 BRIT. J. OBSTETRICS & GYNAECOLOGY 739 (1989).

[60] *See* Hubbard & Henifin, *Genetic Screening of Prospective Parents and of Workers: Some Scientific and Social Issues*, 15 INT'L J. HEALTH SERVS. 231 (1985); Rothman, *The Meaning of Choice in Reproductive Technology*, in TEST-TUBE WOMEN, *supra* note 55, at 23. I have previously discussed the "burden" of decisionmaking in the context of genetic counseling and a similar "burden" would seem to exist here. *See* Lippman-Hand & Fraser, *Genetic Counseling I: Parents' Perceptions of Uncertainty*, 4 AM. J. MED. GENETICS 51, 58-63 (1979) [hereinafter *Genetic Counseling I*]; Lippman-Hand & Fraser, *Genetic Counseling II: Making Reproductive Choices*, 4 AM. J. MED. GENETICS 73 (1978) [hereinafter *Genetic Counseling II*]. This theme is present in contemporary literature as demonstrated by Goldstein's reference to the "momentous decision" that childbearing now involves. R. GOLDSTEIN, THE MIND-BODY PROBLEM 200 (1983).

Hubbard and Henifin, in fact, identify a "new Catch-22" wherein participating in a genetic screening program may lead to a person's being identified as a "genetic deviant," but failure to participate (or to abort a fetus diagnosed with a disorder *in utero*) may lead to her being labeled as a "social deviant." Hubbard & Henifin, *supra*, at 231-48.

[61] The degree of this burden is demonstrated by the frequency with which women queried about their reasons for having prenatal diagnosis say that they "had no choice." Sjögren & Uddenberg, *Decision Making During the Prenatal Diagnostic Procedure*, 8 PRENATAL DIAGNOSIS 263 (1988). *See* Kirejczyk, *A Question of Meaning? Controversies About the NRT's in the Netherlands*, 3 ISSUES REPRODUCTIVE & GENETIC ENGINEERING 23 (1990) (individuals often accept a medical technique because of fear that they might later regret not having done so); *see also* A. FINGER, PAST DUE: A STORY OF DISABILITY, PREGNANCY AND BIRTH (1990); Beck-Gernsheim, *From the Pill to Test-Tube Babies: New Options, New Pressures in Reproductive Behavior*, in HEALING TECHNOLOGY: FEMINIST PERSPECTIVES 23 (1988) [hereinafter HEALING TECHNOLOGY]; Rapp, *Moral Pioneers: Women, Men and Fetuses in a Frontier of Reproductive Technology*, 13 WOMEN & HEALTH 101 (1987).

pregnant women specifically, are bombarded with behavioral direc-tives[62] that are at least as likely to foster a sense of incompetence as to nourish a feeling of control.[63] It is therefore not surprising that a search for proof of competence is translated into a "need" for testing; external verification takes precedence over the pregnant woman's sense of herself. Evidence that the fetus is developing as expected may pro-vide some women with a sense that all is under control (although this suggestion has not been studied empirically to the best of my under-standing). Personal experience is set aside in favor of external and measured evidence.[64] Moreover, given that a pregnant woman is more and more frequently reduced to a "uterine environment,"[65] and looked upon as herself presenting dangers to the fetus (especially if she eats improperly, smokes, drinks alcoholic beverages, takes medications, etc.), being tested becomes an early warning system to identify whether this "environment" is adequate. Women who share these suspicions and doubt that they can have a healthy baby without professional aid are likely to subject themselves to tests that are offered.[66]

Third, prenatal diagnosis will necessarily be perceived as a "need" in a context, such as ours, that automatically labels pregnant women thirty-five years and over a "high risk" group.[67] Although this risk la-

---

[62] B. ROTHMAN, *supra* note 31, at 92-97. Women are expected to behave in accordance with norms set up by those in power. *See* Rodgers, *Pregnancy as Justifications for Loss of Judicial Autonomy*, in THE FUTURE OF HUMAN REPRODUCTION, *supra* note 53, at 174.

[63] *See, e.g.*, Fleischer, *Ready for Any Sacrifice? Women in IVF Programmes*, 3 ISSUES REPRODUC-TIVE & GENETIC ENGINEERING 1 (1990) (referring to a "code of good conduct" pregnant wo-men ought to follow); *see also* M. DE KONINCK & F. SAILLANT, ESSAI SUR LA SANTÉ DES FEMMES (Conseil du Statut de la femme 1981); A. QUÉNIART, LE CORPS PARADOXAL: REGARDS DE FEM-MES SUR LA MATERNITÉ (1988); Simkin, *Childbearing in Social Context*, 15 WOMEN & HEALTH 5 (1989) (all discussing the ideology of risk and behavioral expectations in pregnancy).

[64] *See* B. ROTHMAN, *supra* note 31, at 92; Leuzinger & Rambert, *"I Can Feel It — My Baby Is Healthy:" Women's Experiences with Prenatal Diagnosis in Switzerland*, 1 ISSUES REPRODUCTIVE & GENETIC ENGINEERING 1153 (1988).

[65] *Cf.* Levran, Dor, Rudak, Nebel, Ben-Shlomo, Ben-Rafael & Mashiach, *Pregnancy Potential of Human Oocytes — The Effect of Cryopreservation*, 323 NEW ENG. J. MED. 1153, 1154 (1990) [hereinafter Levran]; Sauer, Paulson & Lobo, *A Preliminary Report on Oocyte Donation Extending Reproductive Potential to Women Over 40*, 323 NEW ENG. J. MED. 1157, 1159 (1990).

[66] *See generally* R. BLATT, *supra* note 19; A. Lippman, *supra* note 40.

[67] *See* Fuhrmann, *Impact, Logistics and Prospects of Traditional Prenatal Diagnosis*, 36 CLINICAL GENETICS 378, 380 (1988). This categorization is more a cultural than biological creation. *See* Bourret, *Le temps, l'espace en Génétique: Intervention Médicale et Géographique Sociale du gène*, 6 SCI-ENCES SOCIALES ET SANTÉ 171 (1988); A. Lippman, The Geneticization of Health and Illness: Implications for Social Practice (manuscript in preparation based on presentation at National Ass'n for Science, Tech. & Soc'y, Washington, D.C., Feb. 2, 1991). It reflects prevailing ideas about the kinds of children women should have and when the probability for them is or is not diminished. *See* Finkelstein, *Biomedicine and Technocratic Power*, HASTINGS CENTER REP. 1990, at 13, 14-16; *see also infra* note 86 for a discussion of the role of genetics in creating these ideas.

Age has thus become more than an event, a birthday; it has been redefined as a marker, a risk, although nothing inherent in it makes it so. *See* Fuhrmann, *supra*, at 380 (35 is the crucial age in North America); J. Moatti, J. Lanoë, C. LeGalés, H. Gardent, C. Julian & S. Aymé,

30   AMERICAN JOURNAL OF LAW & MEDICINE   VOL. XVII NOS. 1 & 2 1991

beling is, itself, socially rather than biologically determined,[68] women informed that they are "at-risk" may find it hard to refuse prenatal diagnosis or other measures that are advertised to be risk-reducing. Once again, however, this "need" does not exist apart from the current context that created it by categorizing homogeneously those thirty-five and older who are pregnant as "at-risk." Mere identification of one's self as a member of a "high risk" group may influence the interpretation of an absolute risk figure[69] and the acceptance of a test. In this light, the additional screening and testing possibilities generated by genome projects are likely to expand greatly the ranks of those deemed "needy."[70] As the number of factors or people labeled as risks or at-risk increases, so, too, will offers of intervention.[71]

Fourth, as prenatal diagnosis becomes more and more routine for women thirty-five years and older in North America, the risks it seems to avoid (the birth of a child with Down syndrome) appear to be more ominous,[72] although the frequency of Down syndrome has not

---

Economic Assessment of Prenatal Diagnosis in France (unpublished manuscript presented at Joint Meeting of European Health Economic Societies, Barcelona, Spain, Sept. 21-23, 1989) (age 38 in France); Sjögren & Uddenberg, *supra* note 61, at 263 (age 37 in Sweden). This age marker may even serve to stigmatize the "older" woman. *See* Hubbard & Henifin, *supra* note 60, at 238 (1985). Further discussion of the arbitrariness of age 35 as a criterion for access to prenatal diagnosis can be found in *Who Decides?*, *supra* note 26, at 434; Vekemans & Lippman, *Letter to the Editor: Eligibility Criteria for Amniocentesis*, 17 Am. J. Med. Genetics 531 (1986).

[68] The many ways in which the concept of "risk" is itself a cultural creation, unfortunately, cannot be given the attention they deserve here. However, it is useful to recall that the data used to assign people to risk categories reflects the information we choose to collect, and the problems that interest the collector. Alexander & Keirse, *Formal Risk Scoring*, in 1 Effective Care in Pregnancy and Childbirth 345, 346-47 (I. Chalmers & M. Keirse eds. 1989). It is also important to note that changes in the nature and number of things counted as risks are more prevalent than changes in the actual number of people "at-risk"; and that even using the term "risk" to describe an event or experience is politically and socially dependent. *Cf.* L. Winner, The Whale and the Reactor: A Search for Limits in an Age of High Technology 142 (1986) (discussing risks versus hazards).

[69] *See* Botkin, *Prenatal Screening: Professional Standards and the Limits of Parental Choice*, 75 Obstetrics & Gynecology 875 (1990); Shiloh & Sagi, *Effect of Framing on the Perception of Genetic Recurrence Risks*, 33 Am. J. Med. Genetics 130 (1989).

[70] A. Lippman, *supra* note 40. Human genome projects comprise the organized and directed international and national programs to map and sequence all human genes. Some of these genes will be associated with recognizable disorders; others will be associated with biological variations of varying and mostly unknown consequence. *See generally* McKusick, *Mapping and Sequencing the Human Genome*, 320 New Eng. J. Med. 910 (1989); Watson, *supra* note 11 at 44. Differences between people will be identified, and while knowing the location and composition of human genes will add to our information about the latter, it will not reveal how the person with these genes will "turn out." *See supra* notes 13-14 and accompanying text for a critical discussion of the limits of the genetic model.

[71] *Cf.* Vallgarda, *Increased Obstetric Activity: A New Meaning to "Induced Labor?"*, 43 J. Epidemiology & Community Health 48, 51 (1989) (hypothesizing that, among other factors, the availability of new technologies such as electronic fetal monitoring leads to an increased number of interventions by practitioners).

[72] This may be an example of what Tversky and Kahnemann have called the "availability" heuristic. Tversky & Kahneman, *Availability: A Heuristic for Judging Frequency and Probability*, 5

changed. This, too, may have a framing effect, generating a "need" for prenatal testing among women in this age group. Interestingly, however, this perception may inadvertantly influence both the implementation and efficiency of proposed screening programs designed to supplement risk estimates based on maternal age with information from maternal blood samples.[73] Having been socialized during the past fifteen to twenty years to view age thirty-five and over as the entry card to prenatal diagnosis, and convinced that once past this birthday they are "at risk," how will women beyond this age respond when blood test results remove them statistically from those in "need" of prenatal diagnosis? Will there be lingering doubts, and their sequelae, or will it be as easy to remove a risk label as it has been to affix one? What about the younger women who will have become prematurely aged (that is, eligible "by age" for prenatal diagnosis though not yet thirty-five)? As the title of a recent book phrases it, are pregnancy screening and fetal diagnosis *Calming or Harming?*[74] We neither have the data necessary to answer this question, nor do we give priority to studies that would be informative.[75] Instead, we proceed as if calming were a foregone conclusion. Programmatic changes such as these, no less than those subsequent to developments in genomics, underline how risk groups and needs are generated and constructed.

Fifth, on the collective level, prenatal diagnosis is generally presented as a response to the public health "need" to reduce unacceptably high levels of perinatal mortality and morbidity associated with perceived increases in "genetic" disorders. This reduction is of a special kind, in that prenatal diagnosis does not *prevent* the disease, as is

---

COGNITIVE PSYCHOLOGY 207 (1973). That is, having become familiar through constant reference to it and to prenatal diagnosis, Down syndrome may be perceived by the general population as "worse" and as more frequent than it is statistically.

[73] Until recently, the frequency of births of children with Down syndrome to women of different ages was the sole basis for estimating individual risks. Within the past few years, investigators have identified certain substances in blood samples from pregnant women that show a statistical association with the chromosomal status of the fetus. This additional information is now beginning to be used in conjunction with maternal age to estimate risks for Down syndrome. In some cases these data will increase a woman's putative risk above that associated with her age alone; in others, it will decrease it. When the numerical value of this risk equals or surpasses that associated with maternal age 35 alone, ("35-equivalent"), prenatal diagnosis is generally offered. *See* Wald & Cuckle, *AFP and Age Screening for Down Syndrome,* 31 AM. J. MED. GENETICS 197 (1988).

[74] J. GREEN, CALMING OR HARMING? A CRITICAL REVIEW OF PSYCHOLOGICAL EFFECTS OF FETAL DIAGNOSIS ON PREGNANT WOMEN (Galton Inst. 2d Series 1990). In this context, the notion of "iatrogenic anxiety" would seem pertinent. This anxiety may develop when laboratory analyses reveal chromosomal variations never before reported whose significance is unknown. The prevalence of iatrogenic anxiety among women being tested may be substantial, but its extent is currently unknown.

[75] *See* Lippman, *supra* note 37.

32   AMERICAN JOURNAL OF LAW & MEDICINE VOL. XVII NOS. 1 & 2 1991

usually claimed.[76] Yet, even this "need," ostensibly based on "hard" data demonstrating the size of these problems, is constructed. For example, geneticists say "their" kinds of diseases are increasing as the prevalence of infectious diseases decreases, making genetic intervention seem appropriate. But others construe the same data as evidence of an increase in the "new morbidity" of pediatrics (developmental delays, learning difficulties, chronic disease, emotional and behavioral problems, etc.), the problems of concern in *their* specialty.[77] Clearly, what one counts, emphasizes and treats as "evidence,"[78] depends on what one seeks as well as on the background beliefs generating the search. The numbers are then tallied, justifying a "need" to do something.[79]

Moreover, unacceptably high rates of morbidity generate all sorts of "needs."[80] Reducing these solely to biomedical problems hides the range of potential responses that might be considered.

Viewing needs and demands as cultural creations within a social context leads to doubts that assumptions of "free choice" with respect to the actual use of prenatal diagnosis are appropriate. It also clarifies why it is not fruitful to think that there may be a conflict between women who want prenatal diagnosis and critics who do not want them to have it. Not only does this polarization misinterpret the critics' position, it fails to recognize, for example, that prenatal diagnosis cannot really be a choice when other alternatives are not available,[81] or that accepting testing as "needed" may be a way for a woman to justify going through what is a problematic experience for her. Society does not truly accept children with disabilities or provide assistance for their nurturance. Thus, a woman may see no realistic alternative to diagnosing and aborting a fetus likely to be affected.

---

[76] *See, e.g.*, Modell, *Cystic Fibrosis Screening and Community Genetics*, 27 J. MED. GENETICS 475 ("Cystic fibrosis . . . is fast becoming preventable . . . . [because] [t]he gene in which mutation can lead to CF . . . has recently been identified . . . [This creates] an imminent need to set up population screening for CF carriers.").

[77] *See, e.g.*, N. ZILL & C. SCHOENBORN, DEVELOPMENTAL, LEARNING, AND EMOTIONAL PROBLEMS: HEALTH OF OUR NATION'S CHILDREN 190 (National Center for Health Statistics, Nov., 1990).

[78] *See* H. LONGINO, SCIENCE AS SOCIAL KNOWLEDGE: VALUES AND OBJECTIVITY IN SCIENTIFIC INQUIRY 38, 38-48 (1990).

[79] *See* Armstrong, *The Invention of Infant Mortality*, 8 SOCIOLOGY HEALTH & ILLNESS 211 (1986) (the idea of infant mortality was created by new measuring tools in statistics); Armstrong, *Use of the Genealogical Method in the Exploration of Chronic Illness: A Research Note*, 30 SOC. SCI. & MED. 1225 (1990) (how increases in chronic disease are constructed).

[80] Children with malformations and medical disorders will always be born, and avoiding their birth via prenatal diagnosis does not address the issue of preventing these problems or of ameliorating their effects on the child or the family. The former will require interventions that reduce environmental mutagens and teratogens, for example; the latter elicits interventions which have already been discussed. *See supra* text accompanying notes 42-44.

[81] *See* R. HUBBARD, *supra* note 17, at 198.

Parallel to the creation of a woman's "need" for prenatal diagnosis is the development of health professionals' "need" for technological solutions to problems of malformation. Thus, geneticists increasingly choose to use and develop prenatal diagnosis to deal with problems of malformation excluding, if not precluding, consideration of other approaches. They "need" to employ these technologies, and in doing so they establish professional norms about how much is needed. Individual decisions about when a woman needs testing accumulate, and rapidly establish new standards for the profession.[82] The routine use of ultrasound to monitor all pregnancies is probably the most obvious example. Regardless of the driving forces for dependency on this technology, the result is the construction of a particular "need": the basic "need" to know the gestational age of the fetus; the additional "need" to demonstrate that the pregnancy is progressing "normally." And the "needs" grow.

"Needs" for prenatal diagnosis are being created simultaneously with refinements and extensions of testing techniques themselves.[83] In popular discourse — and with geneticists generally silent witnesses — genetic variations are being increasingly defined not just as problems, but, I suggest, as problems for which there is, or will be, a medical/technical solution. With but slight slippage these "problems" come to be seen as *requiring* a medical solution. This again hides the extent to which even "genetic" disease is a social/psychological experience as much as it is a biomedical one.[84] This process is likely to accelerate as gene mapping enlarges the numbers of individuals declared eligible for genetic testing and screening. Given the extent of human variation, the possibilities for constructing "needs" are enormous.

C. PRENATAL DIAGNOSIS AND THE SOCIAL CONTROL OF ABORTION AND PREGNANCY

The third element in the prenatal discourse that I will consider here stems from the often told story that testing is an option that increases women's reproductive choices and control. This claim has had

---

[82] *See* Beck-Gernsheim, *supra* note 61, at 28-29 ("It is characteristic that new technologies, once available, produce new standards of what we ought to have."); Lippman, *supra* note 53, at 182 (discussing professional establishment of criteria for testing and physicians' desires to comply with perceived medical standards).

[83] These techniques are likely to be driven by financial considerations of the pharmaceutical companies developing them. *See, e.g.*, D. NELKIN & L. TANCREDI, DANGEROUS DIAGNOSTICS: THE SOCIAL POWER OF BIOLOGICAL INFORMATION 33-36 (1989); A. Lippman, *supra* note 40; *cf.* Note, *Patents for Critical Pharmaceuticals: The AZT Case*, 17 AM. J.L. & MED. 145 (1991) (analyzing the validity of pharmaceutical companies' claims that without a federally-granted monopoly, they would not have the incentive to research and develop orphan drugs).

[84] *See* Shiloh, Waisbren & Levy, *A Psychosocial Model of a Medical Problem: Maternal PKU*, 10 J. PRIMARY PREVENTION 51 (1989).

34   AMERICAN JOURNAL OF LAW & MEDICINE VOL. XVII NOS. 1 & 2 1991

much attention in the literature and I will examine it only with respect
to how some features of prenatal diagnosis do increase control, but allocate it to someone other than a pregnant woman herself. This is most
apparent in the context of abortion.[85]

Without doubt, prenatal diagnosis has (re)defined the grounds for
abortion[86] — who is justified in having a pregnancy terminated and why
— and is a clear expression of the social control[87] inherent in this most
powerful example of geneticization. Geneticists and their obstetrician
colleagues are deciding which fetuses are healthy, what healthy means
and who should be born, thus gaining power over decisions to continue
or terminate pregnancies that pregnant women themselves may not always be permitted to make.

To the extent that specialists' knowledge determines who uses prenatal diagnosis and for what reasons, geneticists determine conditions
that will be marginalized, objects of treatment or grounds for abortion.[88] Prenatal diagnosis is thus revealed as a biopolitical as well as a
biomedical activity.[89] For example, an abortion may only be "legal" in
some countries if the fetus has some recognized disorder,[90] and the
justifying disorder only becomes "recognizable" because geneticists
first decide to screen for it. Fuhrmann suggests that in Europe, in fact,
geneticists significantly influenced legislators establishing limits within
which abortion would be at all permissible, by arguing that access to
abortion be maintained through a gestational age that reflected when
results from amniocentesis might be available.[91] One wonders where

---

[85] For thorough analyses of the question of women's control, see generally Rapp, *Chromosomes and Communication: The Discourse of Genetic Counseling*, 2 MED. ANTHROPOLOGY Q. 143 (1988).

[86] In fact, the availability of amniocentesis "influenced legislation so that the upper limit of gestational age for legally tolerated termination of pregnancy was adjusted to the requirements of second trimester prenatal diagnosis in several countries." Fuhrmann, *supra* note 67, and 378. Evidently, geneticists can accomplish what women's groups cannot: a revisioning of abortion.

[87] The term "social control" is used in accord with its original use to embrace "the widest range of influence and regulation imposed by society upon the individual." D. GORDON, *Clinical Science and Clinical Expertise: Changing Boundaries Between Art and Science in Medicine*, in BIOMEDICINE EXAMINED, *supra* note 5, at 257.

[88] *Reproductive Choice?, supra* note 53, at 187-192.

[89] Finkelstein, *supra* note 65, at 14-16.

[90] Fetal abnormality as grounds for abortion is of fairly recent vintage, having first become "legal" in the United States in 1967 in response to a rubella epidemic. The Canadian Medical Association gave its approval the same year. Beck, *Eugenic Abortion: An Ethical Critique*, 143 CANADIAN MED. ASS'N J. 181, 181-84 (1990). Today, members of the general population as well as physicians regularly and strongly agree that fetal abnormality is a justification for abortion. *See* Annas, *The Supreme Court, Privacy and Abortion*, 321 NEW ENG. J. MED. 1200 (1989); Breslau, *Abortion of Defective Fetuses: Attitudes of Mothers of Congenitally Impaired Children*, 49 J. MARRIAGE FAMILY 839 (1987); Varekamp, *supra* note 40, at 147.

[91] *See* Fuhrmann, *supra* note 67, at 383-84. A recent example of the use of genetics to set social policy in this area is the position taken by the American Society of Human Genetics with

limits might have been placed had first trimester chorionic villus sampling been available *before* amniocentesis? Would they have been more restrictive?

Other potential participants in what should be an intensely personal matter for "control" include insurance companies and governments.[92] If either funds genetic screening programs or covers the cost of treatment for conditions diagnosable *in utero*, they may claim a say in determining which tests are carried out and what action the results entail.[93] Recently circulated reports about a health maintenance organization planning to withdraw medical coverage for a woman who could have avoided the birth of a child with cystic fibrosis if she had "chosen" to abort the pregnancy after the prenatal diagnosis was made, gives substance to concerns about changes in the locus of control.[94] While this kind of abuse of power grabs headlines — and gets discounted as something regulations can prevent — there are more subtle forms of control that achieve the same ends and actually result from seemingly benevolent regulations and public policies. For example, newborn screening for Phenylketonuria (PKU) is carried out in the United States with universal approval. However, in only four states are health insurers required to cover the cost of the special foods children with PKU need.[95] What choices/control does a woman have in this context? What are her options if prenatal diagnosis for PKU is offered? It would not be unreasonable to believe that a pregnant woman who learns that the fetus has the genes for PKU and does not see this as a reason for abortion may feel compelled to terminate her pregnancy because she could not herself finance the special diet her child would require after

---

respect to possible restrictions on abortion under consideration in various parts of the United States. This professional group has proposed as model legislation

that any pregnant female whose pregnancy has not reached the point of viability and who has been informed by a licensed or certified health care professional that her fetus (or fetuses) is/are likely to have a serious genetic or congenital disorder shall have the right, among other options, to choose to terminate her pregnancy. This right shall extend to situations where the female is at significantly increased risk for bearing a child with a serious disorder for which precise prenatal diagnosis is not available.

Letter from Phillip J. Riley to the author. The merits for/against this position aside, it certainly demonstrates how geneticists seek to influence the resolution of fundamentally political, legal (and ethical) problems.

[92] Nsiah-Jefferson, *supra* note 54, at 31-37, 39-41.

[93] Billings, *Genetic Discrimination: An Ongoing Survey*, GENEWATCH, May 1990, at 7-15.

[94] *See* Billings, Kohn, de Cuevas & Beckwith, *Genetic Discrimination As a Consequence of Genetic Screening, to be published in* AM. J. HUM. GENETICS (1991); *see also* Gostin, *Genetic Discrimination: The Use of Genetically Based Diagnostic and Prognostic Tests by Employers and Insurers*, 17 AM. J.L. & MED. 109 (1991).

[95] Brody, *A Search to Ban Retardation in a New Generation*, N.Y. Times, June 7, 1990, at B9, col. 1 (citing Carol Kaufman) (the four states are Massachusetts, Montana, Texas and Washington). PKU reflects an inability to metabolize phenylalanine properly. It can be controlled by dietary restrictions.

36   AMERICAN JOURNAL OF LAW & MEDICINE VOL. XVII NOS. 1 & 2 1991

birth. Such pressures (explicit and implicit) exerted on a woman to abort a pregnancy following the prenatal diagnosis of some problem that makes her unable to keep a pregnancy she wants reveals another way in which social control over abortion may be genetically based.

Policy decisions establish control, too, in the guise of guidelines for seemingly straightforward features of prenatal screening and testing programs. For example, it has been shown that parents' decisions about pregnancy termination for the same chromosome abnormality are influenced by whether or not fetal anomalies are visualized on ultrasound.[96] Even *who* does the counseling associated with prenatal diagnosis can influence what a woman does after learning of a fetal chromosome abnormality;[97] rates of induced abortion are higher when obstetricians relate the results of testing than when geneticists do.[98] Similarly, the interval between prenatal diagnosis counseling and testing is of consequence. This is demonstrated clearly in the reported association between the rates of amniocentesis utilization and the interval between counseling and testing: the shorter the interval, the greater the use.[99] Pressure from state policies establishing when (as well as how)[100] genetic counseling will be provided to screening program participants may be covert, but this does not prevent it from being controlling. In sum, prenatal testing and screening may provide control. But for whom? To what ends? For whose benefit?

IV. THE CONTEXT OF GENETICIZATION

I now turn from the specific stories being told about prenatal diag-

---

[96] Drugen, Greb, Johnson & Krivchenia, *Determinants of Parental Decisions to Abort for Chromosomal Abnormalities*, 10 PRENATAL DIAGNOSIS 483 (1990).

[97] *See Genetic Counseling I, supra* note 60, at 51; *Genetic Counseling II, supra* note 60, at 73; Harper & Harris, *Editorial: Medical Genetics in China: A Western View*, 23 J. MED. GENETICS 385, 386-388 (1986) (noting role of "genetic counselor as arbiter for permission to have additional children in China" or to abort child); Rapp, *supra* note 85, at 143 (analyzing messages conveyed in genetic counseling discourse); *see also* Puck, *Some Considerations Bearing on the Doctrine of Self-Fulfilling Prophecy in Sex Chromosome Aneuploidy*, 9 AM. J. MED. GENETICS 129 (1981) (noting use of term "syndrome" in prenatal diagnosis).

[98] Holmes-Seidle, Ryynanen & Lindenbaum, *Parental Decisions Regarding Termination of Pregnancy Following Prenatal Detection of Sex Chromosome Abnormality*, 7 PRENATAL DIAGNOSIS 239, 241-243 (1987). *See also* Robinson, Bender & Linden, *Decisions Following the Intrauterine Diagnosis of Sex Chromosome Aneuploidy*, 34 AM. J. MED. GENETICS 552 (1989). This raises an interesting question for the future as screening is further routinized and moves increasingly from geneticists to obstetricians.

[99] Lorenz, Botti, Schmidt & Ladda, *Encouraging Patients to Undergo Prenatal Genetic Testing Before the Day of Amniocentesis*, 30 J. REPRODUCTIVE MED. 933 (1985).

[100] As possibilities for screening and testing expand, so, too, will the need to provide genetic counseling services to participants. The size of the resources required to do this appropriately may be enormous, if existing models for genetic counseling are to be followed. *See* Fraser, *Genetic Counseling*, 26 AM. J. HUM. GENETICS 636 (1974). The consequences may also be enormous — however the programs are designed.

nosis to the circumstances in which they are being told, attempting to show the interactions between content and context. The links are numerous and the required analysis substantial. I shall concentrate here on the existence of the connections rather than on their critique. My overall thesis is that characteristics (political, economic, social) of the North American society in which prenatal diagnostic technologies have been developed determine how these techniques will influence how we define individual health, health care and the health care system. The same technology will have different consequences in different societies, so that exploring the characteristics of the system in which it is introduced is important.[101] The critical characteristics derive from current stratifications of North American society and the inequities with which they are associated.[102] These influence (and are influenced by) the use of prenatal technology in ways that laws, regulations or even ethical codes for screening and testing alone do not — and probably cannot — address.

A. IS THE "PLAYING FIELD" LEVEL?

Access to, a perceived need for and the use of either health care providers or the health care system vary markedly between people. The outcomes of these encounters (or of their non-occurrence) also are quite variable. A person with certain signs, characteristics or features may be referred to different people/services/systems for help.[103] Variations in the perspective and nature of the "help," along with variations in people's approach to and use of these different services, mean that disease and illness are labeled and socialized differentially according to where one becomes situated.[104] The definition of and help offered for

---

[101] Kranzberg, *The Uses of History in Studies of Science, Technology and Society*, 10 BULL. SCI. TECH. & SOC. 6 (1990). These technologies are not neutral objects waiting for us to make good or evil use of them. Rather, the "politics embodied in material things" from the very start, Winner, *supra* note 8, at 12, give them "valence" and make it essential to understand the social context in which a new device or practice is offered. Bush, *Women and the Assessment of Technology: To Think, To Be; To Unthink, To Free*, in MACHINA EX DEA: FEMINIST PERSPECTIVES ON TECHNOLOGY 154, 154-56 (J. Rothschild ed. 1983) [hereinafter MACHINA EX DEA]. The context, itself, not only influences the technologies we choose to develop but also presupposes certain approaches to their use. In turn, the use of any given technology will change the context, will change us. Technology is like a "new organism insinuating itself and altering us irrevocably." Boone, *Bad Axioms in 'Genetic Engineering*, HASTINGS CENTER REP., Aug.-Sept. 1988, at 9.

[102] This issue is presented in fairly general terms here without the in-depth consideration that is being (and will be) developed elsewhere in the context of my larger project.

[103] Waxler, *The Social Labeling Perspective on Illness and Medical Practices*, in THE RELEVENCE OF SOCIAL SCIENCE TO MEDICINE 283 (L. Eisenberg & A. Kleinman eds. 1980); *The Anthropologies of Illness and Sickness*, *supra* note 5, at 257; *Rational Men and The Explanatory Model Approach*, *supra* note 5, at 57.

[104] A recent example is the differential in rates of substance abuse reporting during pregnancy to public health authorities in Florida, with poor women being reported more often

38   AMERICAN JOURNAL OF LAW & MEDICINE VOL. XVII NOS. 1 & 2 1991

the same "sickness" or characteristic will vary according to an individual's economic and social power. This variability distributes inequities in health problems and their resolution.

Moreover, since health-related naming and helping activities occur in a cultural/political context where restraints on options vary with a person's place in the society, "life choices,"[105] presented as ways to manage or avert health problems, will not be randomly distributed.[106] This certainly includes a "choice" of asking for or accepting information obtainable through genetic screening tests. Again, societal differences, no less than individual psychological ones, underlie these differential behaviors.

Life circumstances, broadly defined, establish an individual's place in society. They act, therefore, as powerful restraints on health options from identification of a problem to approaches, by self or others, to its resolution, and they influence possible options, expectations and responses.[107] These dynamics establish the inequities, the contours/terrain of the society (the so-called "playing field"), that will modulate the impact of genetic screening and testing just as the latter may themselves landscape the "playing field" and its inequities. To illustrate this, I shall consider in very broad terms how two stratifications — gender and class — shape and are shaped by genetic testing and screening.[108] Although these are inseparably linked, I shall arbitrarily isolate each one to clarify the discussion.

B. GENDER

Prenatal testing and screening represent techniques applied to women. How, when, why and by whom they are applied will be condi-

---

than others. Chasnoff, Landress & Barrett, *The Prevalence of Illicit Drug or Alcohol Use During Pregnancy and Discrepancies in Mandatory Reporting in Pinellas County, Florida*, 322 NEW ENG. J. MED. 1202 (1990). *See also* L. WHITEFORD & M. POLAND, *Introduction*, in NEW APPROACHES TO HUMAN REPRODUCTION 1 (L. Whiteford & M. Poland eds. 1989).

[105] *See* Townsend, *Individual or Social Responsibility for Premature Death? Current Controversies in the British Debate About Health*, 20 INT'L J. HEALTH SERVS. 373, 382-84 (1990) (noting that life style is not just a matter of choice, and presenting an analysis of the many forces that shape what we too easily call choice); *cf.* Rosén, Hanning & Wall, *Changing Smoking Habits in Sweden: Towards Better Health, But Not for All*, 19 INT'L J. EPIDEMIOLOGY 316 (1990) (providing example of where education contributes to increased inequities in health).

[106] *Rational Men and the Explanatory Model Approach*, *supra* note 5, at 57.

[107] *See* Kickbusch, *Self-Care in Health Promotion*, 29 SOC. SCI. & MED. 125 (1989).

[108] Other stratifications of consequence here based on ability, race, etc. are considered elsewhere. *See generally* A. Lippman, *supra* note 40; T. DUSTER, *supra* note 18 (emphasizing racial and ethnic strata). In addition, inequities attached to genetic screening and testing relating to employment discrimination, insurance refusals and racial prejudice, for example, have been considered in detail elsewhere and these situations will not be reviewed specfically here. *See, e.g.*, T. DUSTER, *supra* note 18; N. HOLTZMAN, PROCEED WITH CAUTION: PREDICTING GENETIC RISKS IN THE RECOMBINANT DNA ERA (1989); Billings, *supra* note 93, at 7, 15; Council for Responsible Genetics, *supra* note 13, at 287.

tioned by prevailing attitudes about women, their bodies and their roles. Because the world in which genetic and other reproductive technologies are developing is gendered, it would be naive to think that these technologies can escape gendered use.[109] In this world, women are disadvantaged, generally powerless, and frequently socialized to follow authority and acquiesce in certain norms surrounding maternity and motherhood.[110] Furthermore, because a child's disability is viewed as a private problem for the family, the gendered attribution of responsibilities for family health to women obligates them to deal with it alone whether by avoiding, reducing or managing disability. Prenatal diagnosis in such a context can hardly be "neutral."

Perhaps the most dramatic consequence of gender stratification for prenatal diagnosis is the (potential) use of genetic screening and testing to identify and select fetuses on the basis of their sex alone. Being female is of less value than being male, and the fetuses that are least valued are those most likely to be aborted.[111] Though generally condemned by North American geneticists,[112] and commonly considered unlikely when "selection" entails a second trimester abortion, the availability of chorionic villus sampling resurrects the problem anew, as if the timing of abortion were the (only) problematic aspect.[113] Because this use of prenatal diagnosis as a tool *against* women has had much attention in the literature, with one commentator calling it "previctimization,"[114] it will not be considered further here other than to emphasize that "sex selection" is problematic no matter when it is carried out, whether or not it requires some technological assistance, and that preconceptional selection differs from postconceptional selection only with respect to process, not principles.[115] However done, it

---

[109] Some even suggest that they have been developed and used specifically to maintain gendered distinctions and increase patriarchal power. *See, e.g.*, Morgan, *Of Woman Born? How Old Fashioned! — New Reproductive Technologies and Women's Oppression*, in THE FUTURE OF HUMAN REPRODUCTION, *supra* note 53, at 60; Rowland, *Reproductive Technologies: The Final Solution to the Woman Question?*, in TEST-TUBE WOMEN, *supra* note 55, at 356.

[110] *See* L. WHITEFORD & M. POLAND, NEW APPROACHES TO HUMAN REPRODUCTION 1, 8-9 (1989); Raymond, *Reproductive Gifts and Gift Giving: The Altruistic Woman*, HASTINGS CENTER REP., Nov.-Dec., 1990 at 7; *see also supra* note 61.

[111] *See, e.g.*, M. WARREN, GENDERCIDE: THE IMPLICATIONS OF SEX SELECTION (1985); Hoskins & Holmes, *Technology and Prenatal Femicide*, in TEST-TUBE WOMEN, *supra* note 55, at 237; Rothschild, *supra* note 48, at 107.

[112] *E.g.*, Fletcher, *Is Sex Selection Ethical?*, in RESEARCH ETHICS 333 (K. Berg & K. Tranoy eds. 1983); Wertz & Fletcher, *Ethics and Medical Genetics in the United States: A National Survey*, 29 AM. J. MED. GENETICS 815, 821 (1988) (Table V).

[113] *Who Decides?*, *supra* note 26, at 434; *Reproductive Choice?*, *supra* note 53, at 182.

[114] Raymond, *Introduction*, in THE CUSTOM-MADE CHILD? WOMEN CENTERED PERSPECTIVES 177 (H. Holmes, B. Hoskins & M. Gross eds. 1981) (defining previctimization as "the spectre of women being destroyed and sacrificed before even being born").

[115] *See generally* G. COREA, R. KLEIN, J. HANMER, H. HOLMES, B. HOSKINS, M. KISHWAR, J. RAYMOND, R. ROWLAND & R. STEINBACHER, MAN-MADE WOMEN: HOW NEW REPRODUCTIVE

40   AMERICAN JOURNAL OF LAW & MEDICINE VOL. XVII NOS. 1 & 2 1991

can only reinforce gender-based inequities.

Another consequence, less immediately obvious, is how the current applications of prenatal diagnosis are subtly entangled with another long-standing problematic for women: aging.[116] Not only has the availability of prenatal diagnosis and professionally imposed limits on access to testing created the "social category"[117] of "the older woman at risk," considered above,[118] but, not unlike cosmetic surgery or estrogen replacement regimens, testing has been presented as another way for women to circumvent features of aging,[119] with prenatal diagnosis supposedly a tool *for* women. The increasing probability of chromosomal nondisjunction associated with increases in a woman's age[120] can be managed, just as can other bodily changes associated with "getting older." The biological "failure" causing Down syndrome can be controlled and "older" women need not be "less fit"[121] for childbearing, just as wrinkles of the skin or hot flashes can be controlled. "Old enough" to warrant control is getting younger all the time.[122] When age, whether chronological or "equivalent,"[123] is used as a principal criterion for prenatal diagnosis, it appears to be essential for defining a woman (and women in general). Age-based strata come to be seen strictly as fixed "facts" of life, camouflaging the extent of their social production.[124]

TECHNOLOGIES AFFECT WOMEN (1987); Hanmer, *Reproductive Technology: The Future for Women?*, in MACHINA EX DEA, *supra* note 101, at 183, 191 ("The questions of social scientists imply that sex predetermination is an accepted and acceptable idea. It is just a matter of finding out which method is preferred and when and how many children are desired."); Rowland, *Technology and Motherhood: Reproductive Choice Reconsidered*, 12 SIGNS 512 (1987).

[116] *Cf.* E. MARTIN, THE WOMAN IN THE BODY: A CULTURAL ANALYSIS OF REPRODUCTION (1987).

[117] D. NELKIN & L. TANCREDI, *supra* note 83, at 17 (testing creates social categories "in order to preserve existing social arrangements and to enhance the control of certain groups over others").

[118] *See supra* notes 67-71 and accompanying text.

[119] These circumventions pale in comparison to the variety of pharmaceutical and surgical methods that can be applied to remove all age limits on the possibility of pregnancy for a woman. *See, e.g.*, Levran, *supra* note 65, at 1153; Sauer, Paulson & Lobo, *supra* note 63, at 1157.

[120] Hook, Cross & Schreinemachers, *Chromosomal Abnormality Rates at Amniocentesis and in Live-Born Infants*, 249 J. A.M.A. 2034 (1983).

[121] Hubbard & Henifin, *supra* note 60, at 238.

[122] R. HUBBARD, *supra* note 17; Hubbard, *Personal Courage Is Not Enough: Some Hazards of Childbearing in the 1980s*, in TEST-TUBE WOMEN, *supra* note 55, at 331, 339.

When amniocentesis was first introduced, 40 years was the age cut-off. This has dropped to 35 in North America, and recommendations that it be lowered further have been made. PRESIDENT'S COMM'N, *supra* note 30, at 81; Crandell, Lebherz & Tabsh, *Maternal Age and Amniocentesis: Should This Be Lowered to 30 Years?*, 6 PRENATAL DIAGNOSIS 237, 241 (1986).

[123] *See supra* note 73.

[124] *See* Rindfuss & Bumpass, *Age and the Sociology of Fertility: How Old Is Too Old?*, in SOCIAL DEMOGRAPHY 43 (K. Taueber, L. Bumpass & J. Severt eds. 1978) (providing an overview of social definitions of childbearing age).

Existing gender (and age) strata mean that procreation-linked testing and screening cannot but be *of* major consequence to women (irrespective of any consequences it may have *for* them).[125] Thus, the *geneticization* of pregnancy is following a trajectory similar to — but perhaps even more alienating than — that described and analyzed eloquently by others studying the medicalization of pregnancy.[126] Once again, those with great power — physicians -- control powerful technologies to monitor, regulate and even obliterate the female body when they situate a fetus in conflict with a pregnant woman in the provision of obstetric care.[127] With dramatic images obtained by ultrasound, a presentation of the pregnant woman as a fetal container,[128] a uterine environment,[129] perhaps even a "fetal abuser"[130] gains force. Once again, an underlying ideological premise that women's inadequacy can threaten the success of reproduction justifies some technological intervention, and this time the "inadequacy" is innate. Purposefully or not, prenatal testing and screening reinforce stereotyped gender definitions of women and traditional values regarding their behavior. It would be particularly unfortunate, therefore, if realistic and serious concerns about increasing threats to women's already fragile abortion rights were to silence no less realistic and serious concerns about the place of prenatal diagnosis in a gendered society.

C. ECONOMIC CLASS

Morbidity patterns associated with all aspects of procreation (fertility, abortion, pregnancy or birthing, for example) have repeatedly been

---

[125] Its impact on their experience of pregnancy is enormous but will not be considered here. *See* Beeson, *Technological Rhythms in Pregnancy*, in CULTURAL PERSPECTIVES ON BIOLOGICAL KNOWLEDGE 145 (T. Duster & K. Garrett eds. 1984); A. Lippman, *supra* note 40; *see also* B. ROTHMAN, THE TENTATIVE PREGNANCY: PRENATAL DIAGNOSIS AND THE FUTURE OF MOTHERHOOD (1986).

[126] *See generally* K. MICHAELSON, *Childbirth in America: A Brief History and Contemporary Issues*, in CHILDBIRTH IN AMERICA, *supra* note 19, at 1; A. OAKLEY, *supra* note 24; Fraser, *Selected Perinatal Procedures: Scientific Bases for Use and Psycho-social Effects. A Literature Review*, 117 ACTA OBSTETRICA ET GYNECOLOGICA SCANDANAVIA 6, 6 (Supp. 1983); O'Reilly, *Small "p" Politics: The Midwifery Example*, in THE FUTURE OF HUMAN REPRODUCTION, *supra* note 53, at 159.

[127] Board of Trustees, American Med. Ass'n, *Legal Interventions During Pregnancy. Court-Ordered Medical Treatments and Legal Penalties for Potentially Harmful Behavior by Pregnant Women*, 264 J. A.M.A. 2663 (1990); Landwirth, *Fetal Abuse and Neglect: An Emerging Controversy*, 79 PEDIATRICS 508 (1987) (discussing tension between fetal interests and maternal rights to privacy and self-determination).

[128] Petchesky, *Fetal Images: The Power of Visual Culture in the Politics of Abortion*, in REPRODUCTIVE TECHNOLOGIES: GENDER, MOTHERHOOD AND MEDICINE 57 (M. Stanworth, ed. 1987).

[129] Morgan, *supra* note 109, at 65. For recent use of this term in the context of scientific studies, see *supra* note 65 and accompanying text.

[130] *See* Robertson, *Procreative Liberty and the Control of Conception, Pregnancy, and Childbirth*, 69 VA. L. REV. 405, 438-43 (1983); Shaw, *The Potential Plaintiff: Preconceptional and Prenatal Torts*, in 2 GENETICS AND THE LAW 225 (A. Milunsky & G. Annas eds. 1980).

Legal and Ethical Issues in Human Reproduction

shown to be influenced by a woman's economic circumstances.[131] As previously noted, these circumstances are created and result from general class- and power-based inequities that determine how illness is named and treated (by self or others).[132] A woman's social (political) status will also lead inescapably to "classist" effects in the use of genetic testing, screening and the resulting information. Most simply, varying circumstances (and psychological differences) cause individuals to react to offers of testing and screening unequally, and differentials in the use of genetic services have repeatedly been observed.[133] For example, from the time amniocentesis first became available, utilization rates of prenatal diagnosis among women thirty-five and over have been associated with a woman's socioeconomic status: those with more education or wealth undergo amniocentesis more often than women with less schooling or income. This is true even in Canada where there is no direct financial charge for testing.[134] Whatever the exact reason,[135] the potential consequences of this distribution are similar. One is the possibility of a substantial socially-created alteration in the epidemiology of chromosomal disorders: Down syndrome, which heretofore was generally unrelated to sociodemographic factors might no longer be so in the future. To the extent that use of prenatal diagnosis is class-specific, and abortion of fetuses with trisomy 21 the general pattern, so, too, will be the prevalence of this condition among births. Similarly, with "routine" prenatal care automatically including an ultrasound examination of a woman early in her pregnancy, children with neural tube defects may be born increasingly out of proportion to women whose circumstances prevent early prenatal care — the poor and the powerless.[136]

---

131 *E.g.*, Lazarus, *Poor Women, Poor Outcomes: Social Class and Reproductive Health*, in CHILD-BIRTH IN AMERICA, *supra* note 19, at 39; Silins, Semenciw, Morrison, Lindsay, Sherman, Mao & Wigle, *Risk Factors for Perinatal Mortality in Canada*, 133 CANADIAN MED. ASS'N J. 1214 (1985) (listing social class as risk factor in stillbirths and infant deaths up to seven years of age); Yankauer, *Editorial: What Infant Mortality Tells Us*, 80 AM. J. PUB. HEALTH 653 (1990).

132 *See supra* text accompanying notes 104-07.

133 Beeson, *supra* note 125, at 145; Roghmann, Doherty, Robinson, Nitzkin & Sell, *The Selective Utilization of Prenatal Genetic Diagnosis: Experiences of a Regional Program in Upstate New York During the 1970s*, 21 MED. CARE 1111, 1122 (1983) (concluding that in use of prenatal genetic testing, "[t]he primary factor appears to be emotional acceptance by the patient . . . . [but] [l]ack of knowledge, financial barriers, earlier prenatal care, and cooperation from the primary care sector are important"); Sokal, Byrd, Chen, Goldberg & Oakley, *Prenatal Chromosomal Diagnosis: Racial and Geographic Variation for Older Women in Georgia*, 244 J. A.M.A. 1355 (1980) (study showing that 15% of Georgia women 40 years and older underwent prenatal chromosomal diagnosis; use ranged from 60% among whites in two large urban counties to 0.5% among blacks outside Augusta and Atlanta health districts).

134 Lippman-Hand & Piper, *Prenatal Diagnosis for the Detection of Down Syndrome: Why Are So Few Eligible Women Tested?*, 1 PRENATAL DIAGNOSIS 249, 250 (1981).

135 Professional underreferral seems to be a factor in underutilization of prenatal diagnosis. *Id.* at 255.

136 I do not suggest that all women *should* have an ultrasound exam early in a "normal" pregnancy but merely point out what one of the effects of such a policy might be.

Leaving aside important questions about the priority to assign to this or any other sophisticated prenatal genetic screening program in a society that does not guarantee access to adequate prenatal care for all women, establishing such programs on today's "playing field" may be more likely to reinforce than to reduce existing inequalities in the distribution of health problems.[137] The failure to reduce inequalities in health among social groups during the past forty years, despite the proliferation of other biomedical developments during this interval,[138] strengthens this concern.

The conditions of this playing field also, and unfortunately, mean that posing "access" as an *isolated* problem of prenatal diagnosis may produce failure to grapple fully with the issue of who is (or can get) tested. If access is defined merely as having sufficiently affordable and geographically available services, class-based inequities will likely persist. Comparable availability does not automatically lead to equity, especially when individuals start off unequally. If nothing else, inequities in the distribution of information will keep the poor excluded in a class-stratified society.[139] "Access" may not even be a meaningful feature when the allocation of resources and services is controlled by those who develop and employ them, rather than by those on whom they are used.

With respect to genetic screening, particularly those programs likely to follow gene mapping, the "bumps" in the playing field deriving from class strata based on occupation may be of special pertinence, especially for women. The unequal distribution of workplace hazards by type of activity and the continued existence of female employment ghettos, combined with persisting racial discrimination, mean that some women will be seen as "more" eligible for certain genetic screening tests than others. To the extent that one finds what one is looking for, the identification of only certain groups of workers as "susceptible" to some putative workplace hazard might be used as a supposedly sci-

---

[137] Bowman, *Legal and Ethical Issues in Newborn Screening*, 83 PEDIATRICS 894, 895 (Supp. 1989) ("If we ask poor mothers to participate in newborn screening programs and do not fight for universal prenatal care, equitable health care delivery, education, and adequate housing and food, then we are coconspirators in health deception."); Lippman, Messing & Mayer, *supra* note 15, at 398; Lippman, *supra* note 15; Lippman, *supra* note 67.

[138] Acheson, *Public Health — Edwin Chadwick and the World We Live In*, 336 LANCET 1482, 1483 (1990) (United Kingdom study suggesting that inequalities in health are present everywhere).

[139] *Cf.* Stewart, *Access to Health Care for Economically Disadvantaged Canadians: A Model*, 81 CANADIAN J. PUB. HEALTH 450, 452-53 (1990) (advocating education as one of four strategies to increase health care access for the poor). Omitted from discussion here, since it is being treated in detail elsewhere, is the marketing of susceptibility screening as a form of preventive medicine and its failure to acknowledge the historical, political and economic determinants of health (by its focus on individuals) or the constraints on behavioral choice created by class (and other) stratifications. Lippman, *supra* note 67.

44   AMERICAN JOURNAL OF LAW & MEDICINE VOL. XVII NOS. 1 & 2 1991

entific justification for workplace discrimination.[140] Occupational segregation, no less than racial or residential segregation, is entangled
with differential perceptions of the acceptability and "appropriate" applicability of genetic testing. Will testing level — or build up further —
"bumps"?

V. CONCLUSION

There are an unlimited number of ways to tell stories about health
and disease, and an extensive vocabulary exists for telling them. Yet
today, an increasing number of these stories are being told in the same
way and with the same language: genetics, genes and genetic technologies. These genetic presentations of health, disease and ways to deal
with them are grounded in the political and social context of the storytellers. My concern has been to decipher some of the stories about prenatal genetic screening and testing, and to reveal alternative
constructions and interpretations to those already written.

Prenatal testing and screening, as has been repeated throughout
this text, are most often presented as ways to decrease disease, to spare
families the pain of having a disabled child and to enhance women's
choice. The best-selling stories about them speak of reassurance,
choice and control. As has also been suggested, this discourse presents
a child born with some disorder requiring medical or surgical care as
(exhibiting) a "failure."[141] This failed pregnancy theme is reinforced
in counseling provided to these families when counselors emphasize
how most fetuses with an abnormality abort spontaneously during
pregnancy, are "naturally selected," as it were, and how prenatal testing is merely an improvement on nature.

Just as there are several ways to construe reassurance, choice and
control, the birth of a child with a structural malformation or other
problem, "genetic" or otherwise, can be presented in other than biomedical terms. Is the story claiming that the pregnancy has malfunc-
tioned (by not spontaneously aborting),[142] resulting in a baby with a
malformation, any "truer" than the story suggesting that *society* has mal-
functioned because it cannot accommodate the disabled in its midst?[143]

---

[140] *See* Andrews & Jaeger, *Confidentiality of Genetic Information in the Workplace*, 17 AM. J.L. &
MED. 75 (1991).

[141] Dunstan, *Screening for Fetal and Genetic Abnormality: Social and Ethical Issues*, 25 J. MED.
GENETICS 290 (1988).

[142] Dunstan thus sees genetic screening and "selective abortion" as a "rationalized adjunct to natural processes" in which "defective products" (babies) are "discard[ed] spontaneously." *Id.* at 292.

[143] For a full development of these ideas, see Asch, *Reproductive Technology and Disability*, in
REPRODUCTIVE LAWS FOR THE 1990s, *supra* note 54, at 69; Asch & Fine, *Shared Dreams: A Left
Perspective on Disability Rights and Reproductive Rights*, in WOMEN WITH DISABILITIES 297 (M. Fine
& A. Asch eds. 1988).

Social conditions are as enabling or disabling as biological conditions. Why are biological variations that create differences between individuals seen as preventable or avoidable while social conditions that create similar distinctions are likely to be perceived as intractable givens?[144]

While "many people don't believe society has an obligation to adjust to the disabled individual,"[145] there is nothing inherent in malformation that makes this so. Consequently, arguing that social changes are "needed" to enable those with malformations to have rich lives is not an inherently less appropriate approach. Actually, it may be more appropriate, since malformation, a biomedical phenomenon, requires a social translation to become a "problem." Expanding prenatal diagnostic services may circumvent but will not solve the "problem" of birth defects; they focus on disability, not on society's discriminatory practices.[146] They can, at best, make only a limited contribution to help women have offspring free of disabilities, despite recent articles proposing prenatal diagnosis and abortion as ways to "improve" infant mortality and morbidity statistics.[147] Thus, as sociopolitical decisions about the place of genetic testing and screening in the health care system are made, it will be important to consider how problems are named and constructed so that we don't mistakenly assume the story told in the loudest voice is the only one — or that the "best seller" is best.

Unarguably, illness and disability *are* "hard" (difficult) issues,[148]

---

[144] There would seem to be similar assumptions beneath the transformation of problems with dirty workplaces into problems with women workers who may become pregnant. *See, e.g.*, Bertin, *Women's Health and Women's Rights: Reproductive Health Hazards in the Workplace*, in HEALING TECHNOLOGY, *supra* note 61, at 289, 297 (advocating legislation requiring safe workplaces and prohibiting sterility requirements); Woolhandler & Himmelstein, *supra* note 9, at 1205.

[145] Levin, *International Perspectives on Treatment Choice in Neonatal Intensive Care Units*, 30 Soc. SCI. & MED. 901, 903 (1990) (citation omitted).

[146] For a further discussion on this, see McDonough, *supra* note 35, at 149.

[147] Powell-Griner & Woolbright, *Trends in Infant Deaths from Congenital Anomalies: Results from England and Wales, Scotland, Sweden and the United States*, 19 INT'L J. EPIDEMIOLOGY 391, 397 (1990) (probable that level of infant mortality will be influenced by prenatal screening and selective abortion); Saari-Kemppainen, Karjalainen, Ylostalo & Heinonen, *Ultrasound Screening and Perinatal Mortality: Controlled Trial of Systematic One-Stage Screening in Pregnancy*, 336 LANCET 387, 391 (1990) (Researchers of ultrasound screening in Helsinki, Finland concluded that "[t]he decrease in perinatal mortality of about half in this trial can be explained mainly by the detection of major fetal anomalies by ultrasound screening and the subsequent termination of these pregnancies.").

[148] Lippman, *supra* note 15. *See* A. FINGER, *supra* note 61; P. Kaufert, The Production of Medical Knowledge: Genes, Embryos and Public Policy (paper presented at *Gender, Science and Medicine II* conference, Toronto, Ontario, Nov. 2, 1990). Moreover, illness and disability are *hard* (i.e., difficult) issues partly because society defines them as such, in its decisions about how (not) to allocate resources to deal with them. Unfortunately, since resources are always "scarce," the programs or projects that do (not) get supported will merely be those which policymakers choose (not) to fund. No specific choice is inherent in the limited budgets available, although the requirement that choices be made is. In choosing how to deal with health problems, budget limitations may sometimes be secondary to limitations in our visions about

46   AMERICAN JOURNAL OF LAW & MEDICINE VOL. XVII NOS. 1 & 2 1991

and no one wants to add to the unnecessary suffering of any individual. But being "hard" neither makes illness or disability totally negative experiences,[149] nor does it mean they must all be eliminated or otherwise managed exclusively within the medical system. Women's desire for children without disability warrants complete public and private support. The question is how to provide this support in a way that does no harm.

To date, support has been constructed to comprise genetic screening and testing. This construction is, in many ways, a result of the current system of health-care delivery in North America and the economic pressures on it. At a time when cost-containment is a dominant theme and a primary goal of policy makers, identifying those with, or susceptible to, some condition and preventing the occurrence of the anticipated condition seem to "make sense." It coincides, too, with the risk-benefit approach currently applied to most social and environmental problems.[150] It corresponds with middle-class attitudes toward planning, consumers' rights and quality. But while this approach seems to "make sense," it does not suffice as a justification for the use of these technologies. Though it is more than twenty years since the first fetal diagnosis of Down syndrome by amniocentesis, we do not yet know the full impact of prenatal testing and screening on women's total health, power and social standing.

When amniocentesis was introduced, abortion subsequent to a diagnosis of fetal abnormality was presented as a temporary necessity until treatment for the detected condition could be devised.[151] Advocates assumed that this would soon be forthcoming. With time, however, the gap between characterization and treatment of disease has widened.[152] New information from efforts at gene mapping will certainly increase the ability to detect, diagnose and screen, but not to treat. A human gene map will identify variations in DNA patterns. Genes that "cause" specific disease, as well as those associated with increased susceptibility to specific disorders, will be found. Simultaneously, prenatal screening and testing are evolving in a context where a "genetic approach" to public health is gaining great favor.[153] All the variations that will be mapped can become targets of prenatal testing. Which targets will be selected in the quest for improved public health? And who will deter-

---

what to do. And, in choosing how to approach (even) "hard" issues, genetic prevention is but one possibility.

[149] Asch, *Reproductive Technology and Disability, supra* note 143, at 70.

[150] *Cf.* L. WINNER, *supra* note 68.

[151] *See* Friedmann, *Opinion: The Human Genome Project — Some Implications of Extensive "Reverse Genetic" Medicine,* 46 AM. J. HUM. GENETICS 407, 412 (1990).

[152] *Id.* at 411.

[153] Lippman, Messing & Mayer, *supra* note 15, at 397.

mine that they have been reached? Given the extraordinary degree of genetic variability within groups of people, what does "genetic health" actually mean — and does it matter?

For society, genetic approaches to health problems are fundamentally expensive, individualized and private. Giving them priority diminishes incentives to challenge the existing system that creates illness no less than do genes. With prenatal screening and testing in particular, the genetic approach seems to provide a "quick fix" to what is posed as a biological problem, directing attention away from society's construction of a biological reality *as* a problem and leaving the "conditions that create social disadvantage or handicap . . . largely unchallenged."[154]

Justice in the domain of health care has several definitions, but only one is generally employed in contemporary choice-and-control stories of genetic screening and testing. In these stories, justice is defined by the extent to which testing and screening programs are available and accessible to all women.[155] Distributive justice is the goal: fair treatment requires access for all.

This definition seems insufficient. Access involves more than availability, even broadly defined. Not all individuals can respond similarly even to universally "available" services and, even if they can, unfairness and injustice may continue. Thus, perhaps we need to introduce other concepts of justice when thinking about prenatal testing and how these programs contribute to, or diminish, fairness in health and health care for women (and others). Do they ensure good for the greatest number (social justice)[156] given all the causes of perinatal morbidity and mortality? Do they recognize and seek to correct past discrimination (corrective justice) given current and historically-based inequities in health? Will they level the playing field for women, for the poor?

One approach to justice is not necessarily better than another. In fact, depending on the circumstances, each one might be seen as "better." We need to keep these multiple routes to fairness in mind as we determine those to whom we wish to be fair and that for which fairness will be sought. For instance, human relationality may be as worthy of guarantees and respect as human autonomy;[157] "individual good" is not always synonymous with "common good," though social responsi-

---

[154] McDonough, *supra* note 35, at 149.

[155] *See, e.g.*, Cunningham & Kizer, *Maternal Serum Alpha-Fetoprotein Screening: Activities of State Health Agencies: A Survey*, 47 AM. J. HUM. GENETICS 899 (1990) (arguing that state health agencies must accept that genetic services constitute a public health responsibility).

[156] Lippman, *supra* note 15. *Cf.* Shannon, *Public Health's Promise for the Future: 1989 Presidential Address*, 80 AM. J. PUB. HEALTH 909 (1990) (need for public health programs to promote social justice).

[157] Ryan, *The Argument for Unlimited Procreative Liberty: A Feminist Critique*, HASTINGS CENTER REP., July-Aug. 1990, at 6 (cautioning that human relationships must not be overlooked in the argument for an unlimited right to procreate).

48   AMERICAN JOURNAL OF LAW & MEDICINE VOL. XVII NOS. 1 & 2 1991

bility need not become paternalism. There are choices to be made and the choices will reflect our values and ideology. How we choose our culture (by the routes we take) is no less problematic than how we choose our children, and consequences from both will be among our legacies.[158]

Addressing these choices will itself be "hard," and will require we recognize and grapple with disjunction[159] between goals and needs — perhaps even "rights" — on the social and on the individual levels. What seems to be appropriate or best for the individual may not be so for the collectives to which we all belong.[160] We need urgently to address these contradictions now, using our energies to situate, understand and maybe even in some way resolve them, rather than keep them at the periphery of our vision. We must confront the possible need to choose between what is unfortunate and what is unfair in the distribution and reduction of risks to health and well-being. We must also acknowledge how our compassion for an individual's situation may harm women's health in general if addressing private needs dislocates provisions required for the public or solidifies existing inequities in women's position. This disjunction is not unique to genetic screening and testing,[161] but is certainly echoed with force in this area.

This disjunction will make dialogue about the place of prenatal diagnosis in women's health care especially difficult (and, on occasion, tense). However, this only underscores the need to avoid premature closure of discussion and to avoid reducing it to sterile debates be-

---

[158] *See* R. CHADWICK, *Having Children*, in ETHICS, REPRODUCTION AND GENETIC CONTROL 3 (R. Chadwick ed. 1987) (prenatal diagnosis is not only a private matter); *see also* Edwards, *The Importance of Genetic Disease and the Need for Prevention*, 319 PHIL. TRANSACTIONS ROYAL SOC'Y LONDON 211 (1988). Edwards identifies the "conveyance of our genetic material from one generation to the next with the minimum of damage" as the "biggest public health problem facing our species." *Id.* at 112. I adapt his comments as a further reminder of the essential interconnections between genes and culture: mutations cause genetic damage and we do make social and political choices that influence the rate of mutation.

[159] I thank Margrit Eichler for suggesting this term and apologize if my use distorts her concept inappropriately.

[160] *Cf.* Danis & Churchill, *Autonomy and the Commonweal*, HASTINGS CENTER REP., Jan.-Feb. 1991, at 25 (suggesting we can no longer avoid the conflict between individual wishes and societal needs and proposing, though with respect to other technologies, that we consider the concept of "citizenship" in attempting to accommodate both levels); *see also* Fox, *The Organization, Outlook and Evolution of American Bioethics: A Sociological Perspective*, in SOCIAL SCIENCE PERSPECTIVES ON MEDICAL ETHICS 201 (G. Weisz ed. 1990) [hereinafter SOCIAL SCIENCE PERSPECTIVES].

[161] Given that even viewing private and public as alternatives reflects our prior western beliefs that these are necessarily distinct spheres, it is of interest that the notion of disjuncture seems to echo the lingering historical debate between "healers" and "hygienists" about the best way to deal with health problems. Generally, heroism in healing has had more appeal than the supposedly less glamorous work of the hygienist. *See* Loomis & Wing, *Is Molecular Epidemiology a Germ Theory for the End of the Twentieth Century?*, 19 INT'L J. EPIDEMIOLOGY 1 (1990).

tween "pros" and "cons." The issue is *not* between experts promoting technology and Luddites trying to retard science. It is not between women who "want" prenatal diagnosis and women who don't want "them" to have it. It is not a dispute between advocates of prenatal diagnosis who are seen as defending women's already fragile rights to abortion and critics who are said to be fueling "right to life" supporters seeking to impose limits on women (and their choices).[162] All of these themes are being played out, but to focus on them is to create false polarities and to trivialize the possible advantages and disadvantages of these technologies when trying to deal with women's health concerns. Moreover, it incorrectly decontextualizes these technologies, severing their essential relatedness to time and place and isolating them from the broader health and social policy agenda of which they are a part.

Consequently, it is imperative that we continue to listen to the stories being told about prenatal testing and screening with a critical ear, situate them in time and place, question their assumptions, demystify their language and metaphors and determine whether, and to what extent, they can empower women. These technologies warrant social analysis.[163] Not to examine repeatedly the tales and their tellers will be to abdicate responsibility to the generations that present and future genetic screening and testing programs will, or will not, allow to be born. A perspective that makes us responsible for the future effects of our current activities, the well-intentioned and the unintended, may stimulate the imaginative re-vision required so that we consider not just "where in the world" we are going with the new genetics,[164] but where we want to go and whether we in fact want genetics to lead us there.†

---

[162] Important to understanding this idea is the distinction between "fetalists" and "feminists." Raymond, *Fetalists and Feminists: They are Not the Same*, in MADE TO ORDER: THE MYTH OF REPRODUCTIVE AND GENETIC PROGRESS 58 (P. Spallone & D. Steinberg eds. 1987). "Feminist positions on the NRTs [new reproductive technologies] highlight the explicit subordination and manipulation of women and their bodies that are involved in these reproductive procedures . . . . [while f]etalists are concerned with what they express as the 'violence' done to the conceptus, embryo, or fetus in procedures such as IVF." *Id.* at 60-61.

[163] In fact, we must be careful not to assume that all the social implications are ethical ones and to acknowledge that even deciding *what* the moral/ethical questions are is not "value free." This is especially important because bioethical analyses tend to emphasize individual rights rather than the "mutual obligations and interdependence" that may be critical determinants. G. WEISZ, *Introduction*, in SOCIAL SCIENCE PERSPECTIVES, *supra* note 160, at 1, 3.

[164] Fletcher, *Where in the World Are We Going with the New Genetics?*, 5 J. CONTEMP. HEALTH L. POL'Y 33 (1989).

† This paper, and the larger project from which it derives, would have been impossible without the support (emotional and intellectual) of an especially generous and thoughtful number of friends and colleagues who have nurtured my work and ideas (and, not infrequently, me) during the past several years. Some of these individuals are personal friends; others I've either met only recently or know only through their writing because of our common interests in and concern about the impact on women or reproductive and genetic technologies. Among the latter, Peggy McDonough, Christine Overall, Rayna Rapp, Janice Raymond and Barbara Katz Rothman have been of particular influence. In many ways, this

paper represents a synthesis of much of what they and I have said or written on various occasions in our interconnecting and overlapping commentaries. I have tried to disentangle who said/wrote what first so as to give credit where it is due, but I fear I have not always been successful. This means that the initiator of some argument or the coiner of some phrase may not be appropriately acknowledged in what follows. I request forgiveness for these citational lapses and count on those whose work I have unconsciously adopted and adapted without credit to point them out.

I extend special gratitude, too, to Louise Bouchard, Myriam Marrache and Marc Renaud, colleagues at the Université du Montréal who helped me think through some aspects of this project during its earliest stages in its — and their — mother tongue.

I have benefitted in many ways from my friends Gwynne Basen, Margrit Eichler, Patricia Kaufert, Karen Messing and Louise Vandelac. Their insightful ideas and comments have given depth and breadth to my own thinking about the issues discussed here, and their constant support has kept me going. Friendship with these very special women has enriched my life enormously.

The same is true of Ruth Hubbard, who graciously and thoughtfully shared her wisdom and provided encouragement. She was first to introduce many of the issues and concerns I address and her presence is apparent throughout this text. Her proposal that I use the opportunity of this paper to pull together several partial manuscripts I had been carrying around, on paper and in my head, was, moreover, just the stimulus needed to get me going at a time when this project was stalled and likely to remain so forever. But, while she is responsible for the process, any shortcomings in the product are mine alone.

There are others whom I would also like to thank: Marion Kaplan, the "best friend" everyone should have who, with Irwin, was an extravagent donor of bed and board during my sojourn in New York; the staff at the Hastings Center for their hospitality and the occasion to get carried away in their library during my month there as a visiting international scholar in 1989; Ryk Edelstein and Bill Swetland, who made emergency house calls when my limited word processing skills made manuscript drafts mysteriously disappear; Zeba Hashmi who put up with multiple document conversions trying to harmonize her WP 5.0 with my 4.2 as we created the text and its multiple annotations; the Social Sciences and Humanities Research Council of Canada for providing funds to support research assistants for project-related studies that allowed me to meet and work with Fern Brunger, a graduate student who held my hand during my first steps in the world of critical medical anthropology, and provided clear evidence of how the best learning is a two-way street; the National Health Research Development Program of Health and Welfare Canada for a Scholar Award that provides my personal support; and finally, but perhaps most of all and with much love, Christopher and Jessica for being in my life.

[10]

Ethical Issues and Practical Problems in Preimplantation Genetic Diagnosis

Jeffrey R. Botkin

Preimplantation genetic diagnosis (PGD) is a new method of prenatal diagnosis that is developing from a union of in vitro fertilization (IVF) technology and molecular biology. Briefly stated, PGD involves the creation of several embryos in vitro from the eggs and sperm of an interested couple. The embryos are permitted to develop to a 6-to-10-cell stage, at which point one of the embryonic cells is removed from each embryo and the cellular DNA is analyzed for chromosomal abnormalities or genetic mutations.[1] An embryo or several embryos found to be free of genetic abnormalities are subsequently transferred to the woman's uterus for gestation. Embryos found to carry a genetic abnormality are discarded or frozen. Extra normal embryos may be frozen for future transfer or donation to another couple.

The rationale for this approach to prenatal diagnosis is straight-forward: "Preimplantation diagnosis for some couples at risk of transmitting inherited disorders to their children is an alternative to prenatal diagnosis and recurrent abortion."[2] But, as with other forms of prenatal diagnosis, the use of PGD need not be restricted to couples at high risk for inherited disorders. No doubt, continued developments in molecular biology will permit a detailed genetic analysis of a potential child for a wide range of conditions, susceptibilities and, perhaps, behavioral tendencies before gestation even begins.

As an alternative to an existing clinical practice, the ethics of PGD can be considered in reference to prenatal diagnosis using better established techniques such as amniocentesis and chorionic villous sampling (CVS)—hereafter termed "traditional" prenatal diagnosis. Because PGD does not involve abortion, it has been offered as a less

morally problematic alternative to prenatal diagnosis. I will argue that PGD does circumvent the problem of abortion, but it raises an interesting array of other practical and ethical issues. A primary conclusion is that PGD will not provide a solution to some of the most serious ethical concerns in prenatal diagnosis.

The emphasis of this discussion will be on the ethically relevant distinctions between PGD and traditional prenatal diagnostic techniques, and I will not develop in detail the many ethical issues involved with prenatal diagnosis in general. I also will not address the ethical issues raised by storage of embryos or the potential use of normal or abnormal embryos for research purposes—both of which are relevant to PGD.

Is there a demand for PGD?

As a backdrop to the discussion of this technology, we should consider the extent to which PGD might be utilized as an alternative to traditional prenatal diagnosis. Utilization will depend as much, or more, on the complexity of the procedures as it will on its perceived ethical advantages. The basic notions of placing eggs and sperm in a dish, testing the resulting embryos and transferring the healthy ones to a receptive uterus are, in principle, quite simple and elegant. Yet the retrieval of multiple eggs, the growing of embryos, the complexities of their analysis, and the subsequent induction of an initially fragile pregnancy require remarkable dedication by a couple and collaboration of a small army of physicians, scientists, and technicians. Willy Lissens et al. describe PGD:

> Preimplantation diagnosis is ... a procedure requiring the multidisciplinary collaboration of a clinical IVF unit, a laboratory IVF unit with micromanipula-

Journal of Law, Medicine & Ethics, 26 (1998): 17–28.
© 1998 by the American Society of Law, Medicine & Ethics.

Volume 26:1, Spring 1998

tion facilities, a molecular biology and cytogenetics laboratory, and a clinical genetics unit. Most centres still consider [PGD] an experimental method and request and advise follow-up prenatal diagnosis in cases of pregnancy.[3]

But this orchestrated creation is not a one-shot deal for most couples—two or more cycles of egg retrieval, testing, and implantation usually are required to establish a successful pregnancy. For any individual couple, PGD involves months of time, multiple drugs, invasive procedures, a team of subspecialists at a center for reproductive medicine, and it requires the will to endure the failures of implantation or the loss of early pregnancies. Once a pregnancy is established, subsequent traditional prenatal diagnosis is still recommended to check the accuracy of the process.

Related to the complexity and physical burdens and risks of the procedures are their costs. PGD remains experimental, meaning there is no established set of services provided, and there is yet to emerge a literature on its associated costs. However, there is literature on the cost of IVF for infertile couples. In a 1994 article, Peter Neumann et al. estimate that the total direct and indirect cost of IVF per cycle of egg retrieval ranges from $67,000 for the first cycle to $114,000 for the sixth cycle. In a 1997 publication, Bradley Van Voorhis et al. calculate the cost per delivery of IVF in 71 couples to be $43,000 per delivery of an infant.[4] Assuming PGD is on the same order of magnitude, it is an extraordinarily expensive intervention. It is likely that customers for PGD will have to pay for this service out-of-pocket because it is unlikely that insurance carriers or government funding agencies will cover these costs given the nonessential nature of this intervention, the cheaper alternatives, and the controversial nature of prenatal diagnosis in general. Currently, 85 percent of the costs of IVF are not covered by insurance in the United States.[5] Many individuals using PGD to date have their costs covered by the experimental programs developing the technology.

The market demand for PGD will depend on several factors: (1) the number of people interested in prenatal diagnosis; (2) the proportion of those interested who would strongly desire to avoid abortion; and (3) the proportion of those reluctant to consider abortion who would be willing to meet the monetary and nonmonetary costs of PGD procedures. Remarkably, despite these apparent constraints on its appeal, Yuri Verlinski notes that most experimental PGD cycles at present are being done for maternal age–related chromosomal aneuploidy (trisomy 21, trisomy 18, and so forth).[6] For many or most of these older couples, PGD probably is being used as an adjunct to IVF for infertility. PGD by older women outside the context of infertility is an unlikely market due to two considerations. First, the risk of bearing a child with a chromosomal aneuploidy

for, say, a forty-year-old women, is approximately 2.5 percent.[7] Second, the efficiency of IVF declines significantly with age.[8] Richard Legro et al. summarize the literature, which indicates that the pregnancy rate per cycle is 5 percent or less in women over forty years of age. Assuming future costs will not be covered by experimental programs or insurance, it is unlikely that many older mothers will be willing to undergo multiple interventions at high cost to address a modest risk that can otherwise be addressed through CVS or amniocentesis (or, perhaps, through adoption). To be more specific, how many women would spend $40,000 for a procedure with a 5 percent success rate to ensure an outcome that would occur 97.5 percent of the time anyhow? Traditional prenatal diagnosis, counseling, and pregnancy termination would avoid the same outcome at a cost of under $3,000,[9] and this full expense would occur only if a pregnancy is achieved and a fetus with an abnormality is detected.

Further, for a number of genetic conditions, there has been a marked ambivalence about the use of prenatal diagnosis in some populations—cystic fibrosis (CF) and sickle cell disease are notable examples because they are the most common genetic conditions in Caucasians and African Americans, respectively. In 1991, a prospective trial of population screening for sickle cell disease found that less than half of those couples identified as at risk pursued prenatal diagnosis.[10] Further, for those couples who pursued prenatal diagnosis and learned of an affected fetus, a termination rate of 39 percent was documented in a 1987 survey of U.S. and Canadian centers performing prenatal diagnosis for sickle cell disease.[11] If these attitudes remain prevalent in the African American community, utilization of PGD for sickle cell disease is likely to be unusual. The ability to do prenatal testing for CF in recent years is being met with limited interest in the United States on the part of at-risk families.[12] The reluctance of many at-risk couples to use prenatal diagnosis and to terminate pregnancies for these conditions is due, in part, to a reluctance to abort a pregnancy—precisely the issue addressed by PGD. But this ambivalence about selective termination is more complex than this one issue of a reluctance to abort per se. Additional dimensions include cultural attitudes about the use of prenatal diagnosis in general, the presence of other options, such as having no more children, and concerns about what abortion may imply for the value of the life of an existing affected child.

These limitations suggest that PGD in the *commercial* market will be a boutique service for the foreseeable future, even if the efficiency rates increase considerably. It is questionable whether many couples will believe that the added benefits of PGD will justify its costs and other burdens. This raises the broader question of whether the development of this extraordinary technology is born more of consumer demand for an alternative to prenatal diagnosis, or more of a technical fascination with the manipulation of human life, albeit for justifiable reasons. The relevance of this question comes, in part, from wondering how we will respond if we build it and they do not come. There will be other uses for PGD, beyond that for serious genetic disabilities, that may emerge as attractive if this powerful technology has limited use for its currently designated purpose. Alternatives uses, such as for genetic enhancement, will be discussed below.

The purpose of PGD

Despite reasons to question the future demand for this technology, there is at least a clarity of purpose for PGD compared with more established prenatal diagnostic techniques. The literature on traditional prenatal diagnosis offers a variety of potential purposes for these interventions. One purpose is to reduce the risk of bearing a child with an unwanted genetic condition or congenital malformation. This purpose is the same for PGD, although this purpose must be clearly focused and understood by clients. With all prenatal diagnostic approaches, the reduction in risk applies only to the conditions being evaluated by the technology. PGD does not guarantee that the child will be free of genetic or congenital conditions (a "perfect" baby), only that the child will be free of conditions for which testing is done. Two points are relevant here. First, the current literature is reassuring that the use of PGD does not appear to cause an increase in the risk congenital malformation in the resulting child—a reasonable concern because the procedure removes a substantial portion of the mass of the developing embryo. Joe Simpson and Inge Liebaers reviewed the literature in 1996 and report that pregnancy outcome data suggest that the prevalence of congenital malformation in infants following IVF with or without micromanipulation is about 3 to 4 percent, that is, the same as that in the general population.[13] So although PGD does not appear to increase the overall risk, it does not decrease it below the general population level. Of course, it is important to emphasize that reduction of risk to the population level may look quite good to couples at high risk of bearing a child with a specific genetic condition.

The point here is that couples undergoing PGD should have the clear understanding that the child retains the same base-line risk of a congenital abnormality as children in the general population. More specifically, PGD is not useful for predicting congenital malformations or diseases that do not have an identified genetic basis. For couples who will not consider abortion, PGD alone will not reduce the risk of bearing a child with conditions such as spina bifida, anencephaly, encephalocele, omphalocele, hypoplastic left heart, bladder extrophy, renal agenesis, or many other conditions, because these malformations often do not have their origins in single-gene defects or in detectable chromosomal aberrations. It is interesting to note that Asangla Ao et al. report that more than 50 percent of the couples who underwent PGD for CF in their series did not want additional prenatal diagnostic evaluations of the fetus beyond routine ultrasound.[14] Such decisions may be quite reasonable, as long as the couples understand the limitations of PGD technology.

Another purpose often mentioned for prenatal diagnosis is simply to provide couples with information about the pregnancy. This is a more neutral goal for prenatal diagnostic services consistent with the nondirective tradition of genetic counseling. Because this goal appears less problematic than goals that entail abortion, it may be promoted in patient information materials or in physician-patient encounters. Nancy Press and Carol Browner's work demonstrates how issues surrounding pregnancy termination were not explicitly mentioned in materials and initial encounters in the alpha-fetoprotein screening program in California.[15] Many women did not understand that the principal implication of a decision to be screened was a decision about abortion if an affected child was detected. At the public policy level, it remains a challenge to decide whether prenatal screening programs are a success when at-risk couples are identified and informed of the risk, or whether success requires a significant reduction in the number of affected children born to screened couples. In the prospective screening trial for hemoglobinopathies noted above, 18,907 women were screened to identify 810 carrier women, leading to one pregnancy termination (for hemoglobin H disease). The women generally were grateful for the information—a success. Nevertheless, the limited use of the information by the women indicates that the program was largely a failure in terms of reducing the incidence of serious hemoglobinopathies—at least for the pregnancies followed in the study.

These clinical and policy problems associated with trying to provide neutral information as a purpose for prenatal diagnosis are not relevant to PGD. It would make little sense to go through IVF procedures and genetic analyses only to be nondirective about which embryos to place in the uterus. The purpose of PGD is not simply to inform couples about the genetic nature of their embryos. The explicit purpose is also to transfer healthy embryos and to discard those destined to be affected. Once a couple has chosen PGD, nondirectiveness is no longer relevant.

Similarly, a third purpose often claimed for prenatal diagnosis is that it permits parents to prepare for the birth of an affected child. Several scholars question whether emotional preparation by parents can be effective prior to actually holding and experiencing the child.[16] Nevertheless, the claim is plausible, particularly for conditions requiring immediate surgical interventions that would be facilitated by delivery at a tertiary center. In any case, this purpose for prenatal diagnosis is not relevant to PGD.

Volume 26:1, Spring 1998

Embryo diagnosis would not be necessary or appropriate as a mechanism to prepare for the birth of an affected child.

The explicit purpose of PGD involves the unstated assumption that couples will experience a relative psychological benefit through PGD by discarding embryos to achieve a healthy child, as compared with the abortion of an affected fetus. However, the psychological reactions to PGD remain to be evaluated. What are the psychological implications of going through IVF for this purpose and discarding affected embryos or cryopreserving others for an indefinite fate? With time, do these embryos become lost children in their parents' minds? How often do women think about the children that might have been? How often do they challenge their own adequacy as parents—inadequacy suggested, perhaps, by a need to undergo a gauntlet of procedures before accepting a child? Do the moral distinctions between PGD and selective termination remain clear with time? Alternatively, for the majority of couples, do the lost embryos remain defective tissue or simple cells unworthy of emotional weight? In one study of couples' attitudes at a time immediately prior to undergoing IVF concerning the status of the embryo, 25 percent of them stated they considered the embryo to be a child. Of note, however, 30 percent of the couples preferred destruction of extra embryos (including many who considered the embryo to be a child), while 92 percent would tolerate their destruction.[17] Of course, this research does not address how couples feel *after* such a choice has been made. Although we would not anticipate the profound psychological effects associated with miscarriages or other perinatal losses[18] to be induced by PGD, a careful evaluation of the effects will be essential as this technology emerges.

It is worth emphasizing here that virtually all couples who go through PGD will discard embryos or leave others in frozen limbo, while, at most, 50 percent of couples for any given genetic condition will be faced with an abortion decision per pregnancy. When traditional prenatal diagnosis is done for advanced maternal age, the great majority of older women will not face an abortion decision. So, if there are any adverse psychological impacts from embryo selection, they may be more prevalent than the psychological impacts of traditional prenatal diagnosis.

A significant issue to be addressed in the ethics of PGD, therefore, is the psychological welfare of those who go through the rather arduous process, including those who endure multiple cycles, those with early spontaneous abortions, and those who never carry a child to term, in addition to the successful outcomes. In contrast to the large volume of literature on the conceptual, philosophical, and legal issues associated with assisted reproduction and prenatal diagnosis, the literature on the psychological and behavioral implications of these technologies is relatively scant. The federal government does not support human embryo research directly, but a clear role exists for pro-

grams like the Ethical, Legal and Social Implications branch of the National Human Genome Research Institute to evaluate the personal implications of this and other new forms of prenatal genetic testing.

Ethical issues

An initial set of ethical issues to consider are ones that are shared by other forms of prenatal diagnosis and selective termination. These include the destruction of prenatal life, defining the appropriate uses of the technology, the broader social effects of prenatal diagnosis for those with disabilities, allocation of resource issues, and informed consent concerns. PGD presents some new and interesting ethical concerns in each of these familiar domains. Following this discussion, I turn briefly to two new issues that are raised by PGD alone: germ-line gene therapy and genetic enhancement.

Destruction of prenatal life

The advantage of PGD over traditional prenatal diagnosis hinges largely on the ethical distinction between discarding an affected embryo and aborting an affected fetus. The range of positions on the moral status of prenatal life will be familiar to most readers. The conservative position, consistent with the position taken by the Catholic church, is that all prenatal life post-fertilization is of full and equal moral status to that of all other persons.[19] Under this conception, no distinction exists between discarding an embryo and aborting a fetus—both are morally unacceptable. The opposite position, characterized by the arguments of Michael Tooley,[20] is the claim that moral status is conferred by cognitive traits that are probably lacking in newborns, and clearly absent in fetuses and embryos. Under this conception, fetuses and embryos are equal in their lack of significant moral standing. However, the majority of scholars and official bodies who have addressed the issue have adopted positions within a broad center ground. These positions are similar in that they maintain that all prenatal human life should be afforded a special moral status, but a moral status that is not equal to that of a full-fledged person. Further, these views typically hold that the relative moral status is influenced by the developmental status of the embryo or fetus. Some commentators argue that development is a seamless continuum, therefore, the moral status of the embryo and fetus increases incrementally with development.[21] However, the predominant set of arguments confer moral status based on the achievement of certain milestones in the developmental process that have moral significance. Developmental milestones that have been promoted as conferring increased (although not necessarily full) moral status for the developing human include formation of the primitive streak at 14 days, "quickening" at about 18 weeks, development of "brain life" at about 20 to 22 weeks, a sapient or sentient state emerging at about 22 to 24 weeks, and viability at 23 to 24 weeks of gestation.[22] As Carson Strong notes, this developmental conception of moral status is in agreement with widely held moral intuitions that intrauterine devices are morally acceptable even though they destroy the preimplantation embryo, that early abortion is better than late abortion, and that infanticide is wrong.[23] The recent partial birth abortion debate also illustrates the heightened ethical concern over pregnancy termination as the fetus approaches term.

The National Institutes of Health's Human Embryo Research Panel in 1994, in its review of the moral status of the embryo, observed that only the conservative position attributed personhood and full moral status to the preimplantation embryo.[24] Other philosophical positions, the panel concluded, accord the preembryo either limited or no moral status. The panel preferred not to adopt any single criterion as determinative of the moral status of the embryo, but rather what it called a "pluralistic approach."

> As gestation continues, the further development of human form, the onset of a heartbeat, the development of the nervous system leading to brain activity and with this at least some of the physical basis for future sentience, relational presence to the mother, and capacity for independent existence all counsel toward according an increasing degree of protectability.[25]

Broad recognition of this pluralistic approach in our society provides solid support for the claim that the fetus has greater moral standing than the preimplantation embryo does. A preference by individual couples for discarding embryos versus terminating a fetus is ethically justified through reference to this widely accepted social standard. Therefore, PGD is ethically acceptable on this basis as a method of prenatal diagnosis and selective termination. Conversely, however, given the debatable nature of the moral status of prenatal life and the burdens and expense of PGD, it obviously cannot be claimed that PGD is ethically *obligatory* as a method of prenatal diagnosis in contrast to more traditional methods.

One further point on the moral status of the preimplantation embryo deserves emphasis. For those who hold the conservative position, PGD will be seen as *more* ethically problematic than traditional prenatal diagnosis. PGD requires the creation of numerous embryos for each live birth produced. In a recent report by Ao et al., twelve couples utilized PGD to screen for CF. The couples produced 137 embryos, of which 26 were transferred to a woman's uterus and 5 births resulted.[26] The loss of prenatal life was substantially greater through PGD than would have resulted had the twelve at-risk couples pursued tradi-

tional prenatal diagnosis and selective termination. Clearly, PGD does not resolve the ethical concerns in prenatal diagnosis for many who have fundamental objections to abortion—indeed, it makes the situation considerably worse.

Setting limits on the use of PGD

In general, there is social support for prenatal diagnosis for so-called "serious" conditions, including conditions like Tay-Sachs disease, spina bifida, CF, sickle cell disease, hemophilia, muscular dystrophy, and a number of others. There is also a general conviction that prenatal diagnosis and abortion for "trivial" or minor conditions is ethically troubling,[27] although a number of professionals and commentators[28] would permit such use of prenatal diagnosis based on a respect for parental autonomy in reproductive matters. Gender selection is often used as an extreme example of selective abortion for frivolous reasons. Nevertheless, the majority of U.S. geneticists surveyed by Dorothy Wertz and John Fletcher in 1985 would either perform prenatal diagnosis for a couple who did not want a fifth daughter or refer them to a colleague who would.[29] Therefore, with traditional prenatal diagnosis, a conflict in social values arises between a reluctance to validate termination of a fetus for a less than a serious medical condition and a desire to respect parental autonomy in this most intimate of enterprises.

This fundamental problem with traditional prenatal diagnosis will be exacerbated by the rapid increase in genetic tests for a wide range of conditions, including late-onset conditions, conditions with a limited impact on health, and, possibly, behavioral or physical characteristics that fall within the normal range. This is not to suggest that genes play a predominant role in complex human behaviors and characteristics. Increasingly, it could be found that, for all but the simplest genetic conditions, dozens or hundreds of genes interact with each other and with thousands of biochemical and environmental agents over extended periods of time to produce the phenotype. Such complexity could frustrate any meaningful predictions based on genetic tests alone. Richard Strohman argues that much of the contemporary interest in genetic testing will collapse as our overly deterministic genetic paradigm progressively fails.[30] Nevertheless, we only may need a popular *perception* of genetic determinism, fueled by creative marketing and weak regulation, to move poorly predictive tests from the lab into the clinic.

If, indeed, an extensive battery of genetic tests become available for prenatal diagnosis, what tests should be offered to couples and what tests should professionals provide on request? Should we draw a line, indicating which tests should and should not be provided by an ethical practitioner? Several general positions on the "line-drawing" question are beginning to emerge. John Robertson con-

Volume 26:1, Spring 1998

cedes the morally problematic nature of prenatal diagnosis for "minor" conditions, but argues that our respect for procreative liberty should be paramount, at least until some definitive harm is demonstrated from unfettered use.[31] Robertson places no limits on the parents' ability to obtain prenatal testing for any condition. Strong advocates use of prenatal diagnosis for all diseases or susceptibilities to diseases, but not for nondisease conditions.[32] Strong's analysis places a heavy emphasis on the value of nondirectiveness in prenatal diagnostic services, suggesting that line drawing between disease categories undermines this important value. In contrast, Stephen Post, Peter Whitehouse, and I have argued that minor and late-onset conditions do not justify testing.[33] Angus Clark supports prenatal diagnosis only for the most serious conditions.[34] Adrienne Asch, although deeply troubled by the termination of embryos and fetuses for disabling conditions, believes that a policy of line drawing would be enormously detrimental to those in the disabled community who fall below the line.[35] She, therefore, opposes line drawing, but would couple prenatal diagnosis with better education, emphasizing a fuller understanding of life's prospects with a disabled child. The Institute of Medicine has taken the position that "prenatal diagnosis not be used for minor conditions or characteristics."[36] These positions illustrate a balancing of a number of considerations, including the moral status of the embryo and fetus, the limits of professional authority, the limits, if any, of our respect for parental autonomy, and the impact of individuals with disabilities on the family and society. Also to be considered in this dilemma is the impact of prenatal diagnosis on those who live with disabilities and the impact of broad choice on the parent-child relationship. Much more work needs to be done on this line-drawing question for prenatal diagnosis in general to achieve some resolution at a societal level.

PGD will serve to complicate this dilemma by reducing the concern over one significant element in the equation—abortion. The technology, by its very design, offers each couple a range of choices in offspring. Choice in offspring through PGD is not contingent on abortion. Whether to transfer an affected embryo is not a dilemma with PGD, because this is its explicit purpose; but other more subtle choices are made possible by the technology. Imagine a couple who has 8 embryos in vitro, 2 of which are homozygous for CF, 2 are heterozygous, and 4 are neither carriers nor affected (termed *homozygous normal*). At the request of the parents, the embryos are sexed and three of the four homozygous normal embryos are female and both of the heterozygous embryos are male. The couple desires a son, so the homozygous normal male embryo is split—one-half (now a viable embryo itself) is implanted and the other is cryopreserved along with the other unaffected embryos.

Is there a problem with this scenario? No embryos have been destroyed on the basis of gender and the couple fulfills its wishes. Does this form of gender selection strike us as less problematic than gender selection by abortion? After all, the couple has quite a few embryos from which to choose—a primary choice has been made to discard the affected embryos, but why not choose the specific one to be implanted on the basis of secondary characteristics? By producing a number of embryos with each cycle and by eliminating the moral hurdle of abortion in the selection of offspring, PGD facilitates a broad range of possibilities for selecting the biologic characteristics of children.

If we are entering an age of genetic testing for a wide range of conditions, the extensive analysis of potential children may be a popular application. One example of a particularly interesting development is the chip technology in which tens of thousands of DNA fragments are imbedded in a glass slide that is used to analyze a target DNA sample.[37] It is anticipated that these chips will enable a DNA sample to be evaluated for tens of thousands or hundreds of thousands of mutations or alleles. Backed by a powerful computer, it may be possible to correlate the results of such a DNA analysis with complex physical or psychological traits in individuals. For example, assuming intelligence has some genetic components, correlating a DNA chip analysis of, say, 100,000 random coding sites in the genome with traditional IQ scores may reveal patterns of results that are associated with higher or lower IQ scores in healthy individuals. Note that such a "test" can function with no true knowledge about the genetic influences on IQ. The same kind of testing might be used for any physical or psychological characteristic for which there are objective measures and any meaningful genetic contributions. As noted, these tests need not be very predictive to be adopted by some couples who want the very best that their sperm, eggs, and money can provide.

If such genetic tests are perceived as useful for predicting the physical and psychological characteristics of future children, some couples may pursue PGD for no other reason than to select their ideal embryo. This could well be a growth industry in the coming century for couples who can afford it.

For those who are uneasy with this notion, the challenge is to articulate the ethical problem with this approach to child bearing when abortion is no longer a concern (and assuming one does not hold the conservative position with respect to the moral weight of embryo destruction). One consistent criticism of prenatal diagnosis is the message of rejection that it sends to people with disabilities. It is feared that prenatal diagnosis will lead to heightened intolerance of disability as forces are marshaled to eliminate those embryos and fetuses with disabilities rather than to develop a society in which the disabled can live as welcomed partners. If prenatal diagnosis and PGD specifically were to have a significantly negative effect on the millions of disabled individuals in society, this would be a powerful argument for limiting or discouraging its use, at least for less than serious medical conditions.

The speculative nature of this concern, both in terms of whether people will use PGD or traditional prenatal diagnosis for a broad range of conditions, and whether such use will produce additional discrimination for the disabled, makes this concern difficult to weigh as a moral issue. There is no evidence of this kind of effect to date on a broad scale, despite the use of prenatal diagnosis for several decades. In contrast, individuals with disabilities have never had *more* social support than they do today, as reflected in the sentiment and substance of the Americans with Disabilities Act.[38] Certainly, more social support is still due, but a generally improved social stature for the disabled has occurred in recent decades in parallel with the development and use of prenatal diagnostic techniques. Changes in technology, economics, and attitudes could adversely change the situation for the disabled in the future, but current experience indicates that society can simultaneously promote respect and opportunity for the disabled while enabling couples to prevent the birth of a disabled child through prenatal diagnosis.

However, distinctions may be made in the future between those disabled from genetic conditions that are detectable prenatally and the majority of the disabled who have limitations from a broad range of other causes (injury, stroke, infection, and so forth). Given the potential power of PGD to select the genetic characteristics of future children, it could promote societal expectations of "perfectibility" in children, thus fostering a more narrow intolerance of those disabled from genetic and congenital etiologies and, perhaps, of the parents who choose to have such a child. This is a serious concern that deserves scrutiny and persistent efforts to combat discriminatory attitudes toward the disabled.

It is likely, however, that broad changes in social attitudes concerning perfectibility and disability will be affected more by prenatal diagnostic techniques that may have much greater appeal than will PGD. For example, techniques that will enable the isolation of fetal cells from maternal blood samples early in pregnancy, in conjunction with medications to terminate early pregnancies privately and relatively painlessly, are more likely to have widespread utilization than PGD. There are even developments that may enable the determination of fetal sex through a maternal urine test.[39] I suspect that any new approaches that make prenatal diagnosis accurate and selective termination substantially easier early in pregnancy would be widely adopted. For whatever benefits this technology may bring, widespread use could significantly reduce societal tolerance for "less than perfect" babies.

A second concern raised by the use of PGD to select against minor conditions (or for desirable characteristics) is the potential effect such control might have on the parent-child relationship. As noted, PGD facilitates the selection of children, as compared with traditional prenatal diagnosis, because it offers a range of choices with each set of embryos produced rather than the single choice of accepting or terminating an established pregnancy.

The most compelling argument from my perspective as a pediatrician is the adverse effect detailed selection may have on the parent-child relationship, whether by PGD or traditional prenatal diagnosis. Parents always have had hopes and expectations at the birth of a child, but these are layered on the knowledge that children will grow up and in directions over which they ultimately will have little control. We have all lived through our own parents' expectations and we all understand how supportive and damaging these can be. What would it mean for parents to have very specific expectations for a child based in prenatal testing and selection?

From the age of nine months onward when an infant begins to crawl, her project becomes increasingly one of independence. Her parents' project, in contrast, is one of control, indoctrination, and education to protect, to prepare, to bypass the mistakes made by others (often their own), and to fulfill their own conception of a life of value. This tension between the child's striving for independence and the parents' need for nurturing is fundamental to the parent-child relationship. Ultimately, we establish ourselves as independent—often to be quite different from what our parents had in mind. But remarkably, there need be no love lost in this clash of projects, although there sometimes is. For the most part, we continue to love our children (and our parents) as they are.

What influence could PGD technology have on this most important relationship? How might the knowledge that a child was deliberately selected for her biological characteristics affect how an individual regards her parents, how her parents regard her, and how she regards herself? Could the selection enhance the expectations of parents and alter the child's self-perception of strengths and weaknesses? Would children be strongly channeled in directions of the parents' choosing? To what extent would children resent such an intrusion on their own autonomy? Oscar Wilde observed: "Children begin by loving their parents. After a time they judge them. Rarely, if ever, do they forgive them." I suspect that the greater the power parents have over the biological nature of their children, the more this observation will hold true. This is not because the child would be directly harmed by the biological selection, but because the selection may well come with a stifling set of expectations.[40] The question is whether the child's future autonomy—her right to an "open future"[41]—will be sacrificed through an uncompromising respect for parental liberty in reproductive decisions.

My purpose here is to outline ethical concerns over the unfettered use of PGD that extend beyond the destruction of embryos alone. These concerns over the parent-child relationship are quite speculative and there is certainly no data as yet to support or refute these possibilities. Nevertheless, the fundamental importance of the parent-child relationship suggests that a burden of justification must rest with parents or professionals who would use PGD for the selection of offspring for characteristics other than significant health conditions. Parental desires to use technology in the fine-grained selection of children must be justified through claims of legitimate interest. Parents traditionally have had only a *prima facie* right to liberty in reproductive decisions—not an absolute right in the face of potential countervailing harms.

Further, in response to Strong's concern about undermining nondirectiveness through limitations on services, it should be noted that nondirectiveness in genetic services traditionally relates what couples should do with information provided to them through diagnostic services, not to what services are offered. Women under the age of thirty-five have not been routinely offered amniocentesis due to the professional judgment that the benefits do not outweigh the risks in younger women. Whether the geneticist provides prenatal diagnosis to a younger woman who requests it usually is based on individual factors in the patient-professional relationship. Geneticists do not reflexively acquiesce to such requests based on a respect for nondirectiveness. Similarly, the identification of the gene associated with CF in 1989 has not led to the offering of CF carrier screening in the general population, due to broad social and professional concerns.[42] The practice of medicine in general is characterized by professional judgment on what services are offered in specific clinical circumstances. Once couples are provided with information about the embryo or fetus, then nondirectiveness is relevant to their decision over their response. Therefore, undertaking an analysis of the benefits and harms of what services should be *offered* or *provided* in PGD is quite consistent with contemporary practice in medical genetics and medicine more generally.

Why would parents want to select the biological characteristics of their children, beyond a selection against conditions causing significant disability? Is there a convincing rationale for such an intervention? If the claim is that such selections ultimately will make the resulting children happier with their lives, then the credibility of this claim can be challenged. Each of us can point to a number of biological characteristics that have influenced our lives favorably and unfavorably, but this provides little evidence for what characteristics our children will find beneficial or harmful in their lives as they unfold in very different ways, times, and places. Do we know which biological characteristics promote a contented life? If we were to look in detail at a list of genetic characteristics of a set of infants, would we presume to predict which children would experience the most fulfilling lives, by whatever definition we choose?

We probably do have a list of traits that would make our children more *competitive* in contemporary society, but success in competition and contentment are two very different things. There is less moral force to the claim that parents should be supported in their efforts to gain competitive advantage for their children, particularly when competitive advantage remains possible through traditional means such as education, wealth, and hard work.

The parents themselves may imagine that they would be happier if they could select just the right child. But, as I have argued, the very act of selection may mitigate against an ideal relationship, assuming that such a relationship derives in large measure from unqualified love and support. Tom Murray writes:

> The quest for perfection has been spurred by a desire to escape the limitations and especially the hurts that mark indelibly our existence as finite, embodied, independent beings. The danger in that quest is that we can become so attracted to some suprahuman idea or entity that we lose sight of, or even come to have contempt for, the actual flawed and vulnerable human beings with whom we live.[43]

Perhaps these fears of corrupted relationships belie a cynical view of human nature. Perhaps parents and professionals will not use PGD technology for "frivolous" selections, or perhaps such selections will have no adverse impacts on complex relationships. But despite the infancy of PGD technology, there are inklings of problems already. Ao et al., reporting on PGD for CF, state:

> A maximum of two embryos were transferred to each patient. In some cases, carrier embryos were transferred where only one embryo was diagnosed as normal after discussion with the patients. If more than two embryos were diagnosed as normal, two embryos were selected for transfer on the basis of morphology and advanced stages of development.[44]

Stated differently, heterozygous embryos were considered to be flawed in some way and there was a preference not to transfer them. CF heterozygotes are healthy and normal in all respects, so the decision not to implant heterozygotes unless necessary is, I suspect, what J.A. Raeburn has termed "technological stigmatization."[45] As the power of the diagnostic technology expands in PGD, circumventing the abortion problem may make the price of technological stigmatization appear deceptively small.

It is essential that the appropriate uses and misuses of this technology be debated and defined. This is perhaps the greatest ethical challenge raised by PGD. At present, concerns over the impact on those with disabilities and the impact on the parent-child relationship suggest a limited

The Journal of Law, Medicine & Ethics

use of PGD (and other prenatal diagnostic approaches) for significant health concerns. (This conclusion does not necessitate legal prohibitions on some uses of the technology, only the development of standards for which tests should be offered and/or provided by the ethical practitioner.) PGD avoids the problem of abortion, but it heightens more subtle and longer-term concerns over the limits of parental control over the biological nature of their children.

Allocation of resources

The substantial cost of PGD will make it well beyond the means of most couples. Insurance and government programs like Medicaid are unlikely ever to cover the costs because, as noted previously, 85 percent of the costs of IVF are not covered by insurance in the United States and substantially less costly means of prenatal diagnosis than PGD exist. The discrepancies in the use of prenatal diagnosis between urban white women and other women in the United States are well known. This discrepancy represents both financial and cultural differences. If, or when, PGD becomes commercially available on a broad scale, it is likely to be used almost exclusively by affluent couples. (Less affluent couples who are infertile and who have their IVF costs covered by insurance may also be able to use PGD if they can afford the additional marginal costs of the genetic analysis.)

The extent to which the anticipated lack of wide availability is an ethical problem hinges on the extent to which PGD addresses important needs, or the extent to which PGD produces additional social advantages for the well-to-do. At present, the advantages of PGD are not substantial enough to require an equitable distribution in society. However, if the technology is widely used in decades hence to enhance the offspring of the well-to-do in some meaningful way (or if they are widely perceived to be enhanced), then arguments for an equitable distribution will have much stronger sway.[46]

Research context

Reproduction decisions are some of the most emotionally laden of any in life. The very existence of IVF has been termed coercive for infertile couples.[47] If this is the feeling of many who use IVF technology, then it suggests that the manipulation of couples who are struggling with reproductive concerns is a real possibility. What are couples told about the risks, burdens, and possibilities of success with PGD? The literature on PGD explicitly states that it is an experimental intervention, yet the literature reveals few acknowledgments of institutional review board (IRB) review. Are these projects being subject to peer review and this fact being omitted from the publications, or is there no peer review of many PGD programs?

The purpose of IRB review is both to evaluate the ethics

of the protocol and to help assure that the informed consent process is adequate and balanced. Given the value-laden context of PGD, peer review through an IRB is highly desirable to ensure appropriate human subject protections. Many PGD programs may not be required to undergo IRB review if they are not federally supported or regulated, or if they are not part of an institution that requires IRB review of all human subject research. One solution to this problem is passage of federal legislation to require peer review for human subject concerns for all human subjects research.[48] Absent new federal legislation, voluntary submission of PGD protocols to an IRB would reassure subjects and colleagues of the integrity of this work. As an additional incentive, journal editorial boards should strongly consider requiring IRB review for publication of this innovative work using human subjects.

Issues unique to PGD: germ-line gene therapy and genetic enhancement

PGD could be a component of two controversial interventions that are not relevant to traditional prenatal diagnosis: germ-line gene therapy and genetic enhancement. The ability to manipulate the in vitro embryo will greatly facilitate the insertion of genetic material, either to treat a medical condition or, potentially, to enhance its genetic characteristics. Such gene therapy is germ-line therapy because the genetic insertion into an individual embryonic cell (or zygote), which is then grown as a separate embryo, would result in the transformation of all of the cells in the resulting individual, including the gametes. PGD could be used prior to and after insertion of genetic material in order first to identify a suitable embryo and then to evaluate the success of the genetic transfer.

Germ-line gene therapy has been the subject of a growing volume of literature, even though gene therapy in general has proven to be much more difficult than originally hoped. Leroy Walters and Judy Palmer outline eight arguments from the literature against germ-line gene therapy.[49] The most compelling, at least for this purpose, is that the emergence of PGD has virtually eliminated the need for germ-line therapy. For many medical conditions in which genetic mutations produce structural or developmental abnormalities from early in gestation, successful therapy and prevention will require that the genetic material be inserted either into the gamete(s) of the parents or into the early embryo. In this circumstance, the gene therapy becomes germ-line as a by-product of the primary therapeutic intent. However, in the foreseeable future, the difficulty of reliably introducing a stable, functional genetic element into in vivo human eggs and sperm will be very difficult to surmount.[50] In contrast, the possibility of introducing functional genes into an in vitro zygote or embryo seems quite reasonable in the foreseeable future.

Volume 26:1, Spring 1998

The basic question is why a couple would bother to treat an affected embryo with gene therapy when they could simply discard any affected embryos and transfer the ones destined to be healthy. Because embryos have little moral stature, there is no mandate to rescue them with gene therapy. Further, the failure of the gene therapy protocol would result in miscarriage or a choice over abortion later in the pregnancy, both highly undesirable in comparison with discarding the affected embryo in the first place. The only rational reasons to undertake gene therapy in an embryo would be (1) if a couple were opposed to discarding or freezing embryos, in which case PGD technology is unlikely to be attractive at the outset, or (2) if a couple were both homozygous for a recessive condition, say, a couple both of whom had sickle cell disease. This latter possibility hardly seems a solid basis for the development of an experimental gene therapy intervention for human embryos, particularly if gene therapy were developed to where somatic gene therapy could treat the affected children.

The only plausible reason to insert genetic material into embryos would be for genetic enhancement. PGD to select the best embryo followed by insertion of advantageous genetic material would be the most logical method to produce genetic enhancement. The ethics of genetic enhancement is complex and beyond the scope of this paper. Suffice it to say that, in my view, some forms of genetic enhancement may be justifiable, in principle. An enhancement of the immune system to assist in fighting infectious diseases and/or to reduce the risk of cancer or autoimmune diseases may be an example of a justifiable intervention.[51] Enhancement of other characteristics like intelligence or physical stature or coordination, assuming such things will ever be possible, are much more problematic. In any case, enhancement created through embryo manipulation (including PGD) rather than enhancement of fetuses or children brings no new concerns to the debate, other than those created by potential differences in risk or efficacy. Research in PGD could facilitate the development of genetic enhancement, so it is imperative that we clearly articulate the appropriate uses of the technology.

Conclusions

First, PGD is ethically permissible for its primary purpose, that is, to offer couples at high risk of bearing a child with a significant genetic condition the opportunity to have a healthy child without resorting to selective abortion.

Second, PGD currently is inefficient, burdensome, and expensive. When the costs are not being subsidized by research protocols, few couples are likely to find PGD attractive for its primary purpose.

Third, as with other forms of prenatal diagnosis, socially sanctioned uses need to be defined through broad social discourse. The option to avoid aborting a fetus

through PGD does not justify the selection of embryos for less than serious genetic conditions. The definition of _serious_ in this context needs much more work.

Fourth, research on the psychological effects of PGD is essential to validate the implicit claim that couples fare better through PGD than they would through prenatal diagnosis and selective termination.

Fifth, IRB review of PGD protocols should be strongly encouraged on a voluntary basis, or mandated by federal legislation, and documented in published articles.

And, sixth, PGD provides a logical avenue for genetic enhancement, but ethical concerns over enhancement possibilities do not invalidate PGD for its contemporary use.

PGD provides a new opportunity for couples who desire prenatal diagnosis, but who want to avoid abortion of an affected fetus. Yet the potential power of this technology to manipulate human embryos raises a host of new concerns about the nature of the parent-child relationship and the limits of our biological control over succeeding generations. It remains to be determined whether this is a good trade of ethical concerns.

Acknowledgments

An earlier version of this paper was presented at a meeting titled "Introducing Innovation into Practice: Technical and Ethical Analyses of Preimplantation Genetic Diagnosis and Intracytoplasmic Sperm Injection Technologies," which was sponsored by the National Advisory Board on Ethics in Reproduction and the National Institute of Child Health and Human Development on June 18, 1997. I am grateful to participants in the conference, and to Jay Jacobson, M.D., Leslie Francis, J.D., Ph.D., and Margaret Battin, Ph.D., for their suggestions. My thanks also to Sara Taub for her assistance with the research. This work was supported, in part, by a grant from the National Human Genome Research Institute (Grant No. P50 HG00199).

References

1. W. Lissens et al., Review, "Preimplantation Diagnosis of Inherited Disease," _Journal of Inherited and Metabolic Disease,_ 19 (1996): 709–23; and J.C. Harper, "Preimplantation Diagnosis of Inherited Disease by Embryo Biopsy: An Update of the World Figures," _Journal of Assisted Reproduction and Genetics,_ 13, no. 2 (1996): 90–95.

2. I. Soussis et al., "Pregnancies Resulting from Embryos Biopsied for Preimplantation Diagnosis of Genetic Disease: Biochemical and Ultrasonic Studies in the First Trimester of Pregnancy," _Journal of Assisted Reproduction and Genetics,_ 13, no. 3 (1996): at 254.

3. Lissens et al., _supra_ note 1, at 719.

4. See B.J. Van Voorhis et al., "Cost-Effectiveness of Infertility Treatments: A Cohort Study," _Fertility and Sterility,_ 67 (1997): 830–36.

5. See J.A. Collins et al., "An Estimate of the Cost of In Vitro Fertilization Services in the United States in 1995," _Fertil-_

The Journal of Law, Medicine & Ethics

ity and Sterility, 64 (1995): 538–45.

6. See Y. Verlinsky, "Preimplantation Genetic Diagnosis," *Journal of Assisted Reproduction and Genetics*, 13, no. 2 (1996): 87–89.

7. See L.Y.F. Hsu, "Prenatal Diagnosis of Chromosomal Abnormalities," in A. Milunsky, ed., *Genetic Disorders and the Fetus: Diagnosis, Prevention and Treatment* (New York: Plenum, 1986): at 118.

8. See R.S. Legro et al., "ART in Women 40 and Over: Is the Cost Worth It?," *Journal of Reproductive Medicine*, 42 (1997): 76–82.

9. See T.A. Lieu, S.E. Watson, and A.E. Washington, "The Cost-Effectiveness of Prenatal Carrier Screening for Cystic Fibrosis," *Obstetrics and Gynecology*, 84 (1994): 903–12.

10. See P.T. Rowley et al., "Prenatal Screening for Hemoglobinopathies: A Prospective Regional Trial," *American Journal of Human Genetics*, 48 (1991): 439–46.

11. See P.T. Rowley, "Prenatal Diagnosis for Sickle Cell Disease: A Survey of the United States and Canada," *Annals of the New York Academy of Science*, 565 (1989): 48–52.

12. See D.C. Wertz et al., "Attitudes Toward the Prenatal Diagnosis of Cystic Fibrosis: Factors in Decision Making among Affected Families," *American Journal of Human Genetics*, 50 (1992): 1077–85; and I. Jedlicka-Kohler, M. Gotz, and I. Eichler, "Utilization of Prenatal Diagnosis for Cystic Fibrosis over the Past Seven Years," *Pediatrics*, 94 (1994): 13–16.

13. See J.L. Simpson and I. Liebaers, "Assessing Congenital Anomalies after Preimplantation Genetic Diagnosis," *Journal of Assisted Reproduction and Genetics*, 13, no. 2 (1996): 170–76.

14. A. Ao et al., "Clinical Experience with Preimplantation Genetic Diagnosis of Cystic Fibrosis (ΔF508)," *Prenatal Diagnosis*, 16 (1996): 137–42.

15. See N.A. Press and C.H. Browner, "'Collective Fictions': Similarities in Reasons for Accepting Maternal Serum Alpha-Fetoprotein Screening among Women of Diverse Ethnic and Social Class Backgrounds," *Fetal Diagnosis and Therapy*, 8, Supp. 1 (1993): 97–106.

16. See J.A. Boss, *The Birth Lottery: Prenatal Diagnosis and Selective Abortion* (Chicago: Loyola University Press, 1993): at 77–78.

17. See C. Laruelle and Y. Engler, "Psychological Study of In Vitro Fertilization-Embryo Transfer Participants' Attitudes Toward the Destiny of Their Supernumerary Embryos," *Fertility and Sterility*, 63 (1995): 1047–50.

18. See I.G. Leon, "Psychodynamics of Perinatal Loss," *Psychiatry*, 49 (1986): 312–24.

19. See Congregation for the Doctrine of Faith, "Instruction on Respect for Human Life in Its Origin and on the Dignity of Procreation," *Origins*, 16 (1987): 701.

20. See M. Tooley, *Abortion and Infanticide* (New York: Oxford University Press, 1983).

21. See N.C. Gillespie, "Abortion and Human Rights," *Ethics*, 87 (1977): 237–43.

22. See B. Steinbock, *Life Before Birth: The Moral and Legal Status of Embryos and Fetuses* (New York: Oxford University Press, 1992): at 43–88; and C. Strong, *Ethics in Reproductive and Perinatal Medicine: A New Framework* (New Haven: Yale University Press, 1997): at 41–62.

23. See Strong, *id.*

24. See Ad Hoc Group of Consultants to the Advisory Committee to the Director, National Institutes of Health, *Report of the Human Embryo Research Panel* (Bethesda: National Institutes of Health, 1994): at 38.

25. *Id.* at 30.

26. See Ao et al., *supra* note 14.

27. See L.B. Andrew et al., Committee on Assessing Genetic Risks, Division of Health Sciences Policy, Institute of Medicine, eds., *Assessing Genetic Risks: Implications for Health and Social Policy* (Washington, D.C.: National Academy Press, 1994): at 105; and Council on Ethical and Judicial Affairs, American Medical Association, "Ethical Issues Related to Prenatal Genetic Testing," *Archives of Family Medicine*, 3 (1994): 633–42; and D.C. Wertz and J.C. Fletcher, "Fatal Knowledge? Prenatal Diagnosis and Sex Selection," *Hastings Center Report*, 19, no. 3 (1989): 21–27.

28. See, for example, J.A. Robertson, *Children of Choice: Freedom and the New Reproductive Technologies* (Princeton: Princeton University Press, 1996).

29. See Wertz and Fletcher, *supra* note 27.

30. See R.C. Strohman, "The Coming Kuhnian Revolution in Biology," *Nature Biotechnology*, 15 (1997): 194–200.

31. See J.A. Robertson, "Genetic Selection of Offspring Characteristics," *Boston University Law Review*, 76 (1996): at 421.

32. See Strong, *supra* note 22, at 133–58.

33. See S.G. Post, J.R. Botkin, and P. Whitehouse, "Selective Abortion for Familial Alzheimer Disease?," *Obstetrics and Gynecology*, 79 (1992): 794–98; and J. Botkin, "Fetal Privacy and Confidentiality," *Hastings Center Report*, 25, no. 5 (1995): 32–40.

34. A. Clarke, "Is Non-Directive Counseling Possible?," *Lancet*, 338 (1991): 998–1001.

35. See A. Asch, "Reproductive Technology and Disability," in S. Cohen and N. Taub, eds., *Reproductive Laws for the 1990's* (Clifton: Humana Press, 1998): 69–124.

36. See Andrews et al., *supra* note 27.

37. See D.W. Ross, "DNA on a Chip," *Archives of Pathology and Laboratory Medicine*, 120 (1996): 604–05; C. Eng and J. Vijg, "Genetic Testing: The Problems and the Promise," *Nature Biotechnology*, 15 (1997): 422–26; and A. Marshall and J. Hodgson, "DNA Chips: An Array of Possibilities," *Nature Biotechnology*, 16 (1998): 27–31.

38. Americans with Disabilities Act of 1990, 42. U.S.C. §§ 12101–12113 (1994).

39. See Anonymous, "Fetal Gender Testing," *Nature Biotechnology*, 15 (1997): 700.

40. See G. McGee, "Parenting in an Era of Genetics," *Hastings Center Report*, 27, no. 2 (1997): 16–22.

41. See D.S. Davis, "Genetic Dilemmas and the Child's Right to an Open Future," *Hastings Center Report*, 27, no. 2 (1997): 7–15.

42. See NIH Workshop on Population Screening for Cystic Fibrosis Gene, "Statement from the National Institutes of Health Workshop on Population Screening for Cystic Fibrosis Gene," *N. Engl. J. Med.*, 323 (1990): 70–71; Committee on Obstetrics, Fetal and Maternal Medicine, American College of Obstetricians and Gynecologists, "American College of Obstetricians and Gynecologists Committee Opinion: Current Status of Cystic Fibrosis Carrier Screening" (Washington, D.C.: American College of Obstetricians and Gynecologists, 1991); and L. Biesecker et al., "General Population Screening for Cystic Fibrosis Is Premature," *American Journal of Human Genetics*, 50 (1992): 438–39.

43. See T.H. Murray, *The Worth of a Child* (Berkeley: University of California Press, 1996): at 136.

44. See Ao et al., *supra* note 14.

45. See J.A. Raeburn, Commentary, "Preimplantation Diagnosis Raises a Philosophical Dilemma," *British Medical Journal*, 311 (1995): 540–41.

46. See M.J. Mehlman and J.R. Botkin, *Access to the Ge-*

Volume 26:1, Spring 1998

nome: The Challenge to Equality (Washington, D.C.: Georgetown University Press, 1998).

47. See P. Lauritzen, "What Price Parenthood?," *Hastings Center Report,* 20, no. 2 (1990): 38–46.

48. See Advisory Committee on Human Radiation Experiments, *Final Report: The Advisory Committee on Human Radiation Experiments* (Washington, D.C.: U.S. Government Printing Office, 1995): at 825, Recommendation 13.

49. See L. Walters and J.G. Palmer, *The Ethics of Human Gene Therapy* (New York: Oxford University Press, 1997).

50. The technical difficulties of inserting functional genetic material into in vivo eggs and sperm are significant. Primary oocytes are produced from cell division while the woman is still

a fetus herself and the meiotic divisions occur near the time of ovulation and fertilization. Because the insertion of genetic material generally requires an actively dividing cell, primary oocytes are a difficult target in their dormant state. The challenge with sperm is to insert successfully the genetic material into virtually 100 percent of billions on billions of sperm stem cells. Further, the insertion must be in a stable fashion that leaves the sperm functional and otherwise unimpaired. Given the limited success to date with any gene therapy, prospects for such success in humans are not on the horizon.

51. See E.T. Juengst, "Can Enhancement Be Distinguished from Prevention in Genetic Medicine?," *Journal of Medicine and Philosophy,* 22, no. 2 (1997): 125–42.

[11]

TWO MODELS OF HUMAN CLONING

John A. Robertson*

I. INTRODUCTION

Progress in the science of mammalian cloning has made it increasingly likely that human cloning will soon be technically feasible. The birth of Dolly, the sheep cloned from the mammary cells of an adult ewe, was announced in February 1997.[1] By July 1998, scientists in Hawaii had succeeded in cloning several generations of mice, considered by many scientists to be a much harder feat.[2] In December 1998, Japanese scientists reported that they had cloned eight calves from cells gathered from a slaughterhouse.[3] That same month, a South Korean team announced—though without supporting publication—that they had cloned a human cell from an infertile woman to the four cell stage.[4]

Although none of the scientists conducting cloning research claimed an interest in cloning humans, the techniques used to clone sheep, cows, and mice could easily be adapted to human beings.[5] After

---

Vinson and Elkins Chair in Law, University of Texas School of Law; B.A., Dartmouth College, 1964; J.D., Harvard Law School, 1968.

1. See Ian Wilmut, *Dolly's False Legacy*, TIME, Jan. 11, 1999, at 74, 74.

2. See T. Wakayama et al., *Full-Term Development of Mice from Enucleated Oocytes Injected with Cumulus Cell Nuclei*, 394 NATURE 369, 369 (1998).

3. See Gina Kolata, *Japanese Scientists Clone a Cow, Making Eight Copies*, N.Y. TIMES, Dec. 9, 1998, at A8.

4. See Sheryl WuDunn, *South Korean Scientists Say They Cloned a Human Cell*, N.Y. TIMES, Dec. 17, 1998, at A12. Another group, Advanced Cell Technology, Inc., announced that it had combined a human nucleus with a cow egg and activated it to the four cell stage. Considerable skepticism, however, has greeted that report. See Eliot Marshall, *Claim of Human-Cow Embryo Greeted with Skepticism*, 282 SCI. 1390, 1390-91 (1998).

5. The Wilmut team in Scotland appears driven by the desire to "pharm" domestic animals through transgenic modification to produce drugs or other valuable substances in their milk. See Elizabeth Pennisi, *After Dolly, a Pharming Frenzy*, 279 SCI. 646, 646 (1998). The work with mice in Hawaii seems aimed at getting identical generations of mice to improve the reliability of laboratory research, and to extend the reach of transgenic mice. See Wakayama et al., *supra* note 2, at 369. The Japanese work may be directed at reproducing "exact copies of animals that are superb producers of milk or meat." Kolata, *supra* note 3, at A8.

610 HOFSTRA LAW REVIEW [Vol. 27:609

research to determine which cloned human somatic cells most reliably progress to the blastocyst stage, transfer to the uterus to produce a cloned human being could occur. The cloning procedure would remove the nucleus from a human somatic cell, deprogram it, place it an enucleated oocyte, activate it by electrofusion, and then transfer the activated embryo to a uterus for implantation and eventual birth.[6] Whether such a transfer ever should occur, however, is a highly controversial question.

Although one could envisage several plausible uses for cloning once it were shown to be safe and legal, the initial public reaction to the prospect of human cloning has been decidedly negative.[7] For many people the very idea of human cloning has seemed odd or even baffling—or perhaps too familiar as an example of the narcissism and urge for power that realism teaches us too often motivates people. There is a risk that some persons might try to clone themselves or third parties without regard to the effect on resulting children or society at large. As a result, three states and several countries have banned human cloning, and several bills to outlaw cloning are pending in Congress.[8]

In this situation, it is well to heed the admonition of the visionary poet William Blake that "[o]ne Law for the Lion [and] Ox is oppression."[9] Just as the law should take account of differences in the subjects which it regulates, so public policy toward cloning and genetic engi-

---

6. *See* 1 NATIONAL BIOETHICS ADVISORY COMM'N, CLONING HUMAN BEINGS: REPORT AND RECOMMENDATIONS OF THE NATIONAL BIOETHICS ADVISORY COMMISSION 19-20 (1997) [hereinafter CLONING HUMAN BEINGS].

7. *See, e.g., The Clone Age*, A.B.A. J., July 1997, at 68, 68 (presenting a roundtable discussion on the implications of human cloning); Bill Hoffmann, *Pope Condemns Human Cloning*, N.Y. POST, Feb. 8, 1999, at 18 (quoting the Pope as sharing in the "'firm condemnation of human cloning'"); Leon R. Kass, *The Wisdom of Repugnance*, NEW REPUBLIC, June 2, 1997, at 17, 25 ("[H]uman cloning is unethical in itself and dangerous in its likely consequences."); Paul Recer, *Sheep Cloner Says Cloning People "Inhumane"—Senator Disagrees*, ASSOCIATED PRESS POL. SERV., Mar. 13, 1997, *available at* 1997 WL 2508493 (reporting testimony of Dr. Ian Wilmut and Dr. Harold Varmus before the United States Senate, March 12, 1997, regarding the banning of human cloning research).

8. *See, e.g.*, Human Cloning Prohibition Act, S. 1601, 105th Cong. § 301(a) (1998) ("It shall be unlawful for any person or entity, public or private, in or affecting interstate commerce, to use human somatic cell nuclear transfer technology."); Human Cloning Prohibition Act, H.R. 923, 105th Cong. § 2(a) (1997) ("It shall be unlawful for any person to use a human somatic cell for the process of producing a human clone."); *see also* 2 CLONING HUMAN BEINGS, *supra* note 6, at F-23 to 27 (outlining bills introduced in 11 states and three competing federal bills restricting human cloning); *Clinton Seeks to Ban Human Cloning but Not All Experiments*, N.Y. TIMES, June 10, 1997, at C4 (reporting that Australia, Britain, Denmark, Germany, and Spain have banned cloning).

9. WILLIAM BLAKE, SELECTED POETRY AND PROSE OF WILLIAM BLAKE 134 (Northrop Frye ed., 1953).

neering generally should take account of the different ways in which these techniques might be used, some of which might be beneficial and valuable, while others could be abusive and harmful.

This Article argues that a rational public policy toward human cloning should acknowledge the different goals that cloning might serve, and fashion policy according to the demands of each area. Two distinctions are important here. First is the distinction between therapeutic and reproductive cloning. The second distinction arises within the area of reproductive cloning, and asks whether the proposed cloning is a response to reproductive failure or is being used as a way for fertile individuals to choose the genome of offspring.

II. THERAPEUTIC CLONING

An essential policy distinction is between cloning to obtain tissue or organs for transplant and cloning for reproductive purposes. The cloning technique in each case is the same, but therapeutic cloning clones a person's cells to the blastocyst stage with no intent to transfer the cloned cells and resulting embryo to the uterus, as would occur with reproductive cloning.[10] Embryonic stem ("ES") cells would then be removed from the embryo in order to obtain cells or tissue for research and eventually transplantation.[11] Reproductive cloning, on the other hand, clones a person's cells with the intent of placing the resulting embryo in the uterus in order to bring about the birth of a child with that genome.[12]

Therapeutic cloning has received a big boost from the recent announcement of the in vitro culture of human stem cells derived from the inner cell mass of blastocysts donated by couples undergoing in vitro fertilization ("IVF") treatment for infertility and from cultured primordial germ cells retrieved from aborted fetuses.[13] The ability to isolate and grow human ES cells in the laboratory so that lines of immortal ES cells are created holds great promise for research and therapy.

The research uses of human ES cells include in vitro studies of normal and abnormal human embryogenesis, human gene discovery,

---

10. *See* 1 CLONING HUMAN BEINGS, *supra* note 6, at 29-33.

11. *See id.*

12. *See id.* at 31; John A. Robertson, *Liberty, Identity, and Human Cloning*, 76 TEX. L. REV. 1371, 1378-82 (1998).

13. *See* Michael J. Shamblott et al., *Derivation of Pluripotent Stem Cells from Cultured Human Primordial Germ Cells*, 95 PROC. OF THE NAT'L ACAD. SCI. 13,726, 13,726-31 (1998); James A. Thomson et al., *Embryonic Stem Cell Lines Derived from Human Blastocysts*, 282 SCI. 1145, 1145-47 (1998).

and drug and teratogen testing.[14] Potential clinical applications are as a renewable source of cells for tissue transplantation, cell replacement, and gene therapy.[15] For example, if human ES cells could be directed to differentiate into particular tissues and immunologically altered to prevent rejection after engraftment, they could treat or cure thousands of patients who now suffer from diabetes, neurodegenerative disorders, spinal cord injury, heart disease, and other illnesses.[16]

The growth of human ES cells in culture is a first, but necessary step toward development of cell replacement therapies.[17] Future work will have to develop ways to derive human ES cells efficiently and reliably, and then identify growth factors to direct them into lineage-restricted differentiation in ways that will provide the large numbers of pure populations of cells that will be necessary for transplantation.[18] Finally, clinical research using ES-derived cells will be needed to determine under what conditions they are therapeutic for the many conditions which they could potentially help.[19] Of major importance will be tailoring stem cells genetically to avoid attack by a patient's immune system.[20]

One way to achieve histocompatability with a recipient's immune system would be to derive ES cells from embryos created through nuclear transfer cloning of the recipient's own cells.[21] The nucleus of a somatic cell would be removed and fused with an enucleated donor egg.[22] After activation, the resulting embryo would be cultured in the laboratory to the blastocyst stage, when ES cells could be removed by microsurgery from the inner cell mass, and cultured in turn to provide the kind of tissue needed for the patient.[23] Retrieval of ES cells would

---

14. *See* Eliot Marshall, *A Versatile Cell Line Raises Scientific Hopes, Legal Questions*, 282 SCI. 1014, 1015 (1998).

15. *See* 1 CLONING HUMAN BEINGS, *supra* note 6, at 29-30; Robertson, *supra* note 12, at 1380.

16. *See* Marshall, *supra* note 14, at 1015.

17. *See id.* at 1014 (describing the research conducted by James Thomson, in which embryonic stem cells were successfully cultivated in a lab dish); Shamblott et al., *supra* note 13, at 13,726 (detailing the process of deriving pluripotent stem cells, indicating that growth of cells in a culture is the first stage of the process); Thomson et al., *supra* note 13, at 1145 (indicating that the culture of embryos is the first stage in developing an embryonic stem cell line).

18. *See* Shamblott et al., *supra* note 13, at 13,730; Thomson et al., *supra* note 13, at 1146-47.

19. *See* Eliot Marshall, *Britain Urged to Expand Embryo Studies*, 282 SCI. 2167, 2167 (1998).

20. *See* Robertson, *supra* note 12, at 1380-81; Thomson et al., *supra* note 13, at 1147.

21. *See* Marshall, *supra* note 19, at 2167; Robertson, *supra* note 12, at 1380-81.

22. *See* Robertson, *supra* note 12, at 1374.

23. *See id.* at 1380-81.

destroy the embryo, so there is no possibility then of transfer to the uterus.[24] The tissue resulting from in vitro culture of the ES cells will have the exact nuclear genome as the recipient, and thus should avoid rejection or the need for immunosuppression upon transplant to that patient.[25]

The development of ES cell technology to obtain cell or tissue replacement will require considerably more research before the need to test histocompatibility through nuclear transfer therapeutic cloning would arise. However, if the field progresses as expected, such cloning may eventually be needed. Therapeutic cloning might also be needed to obtain ES cells that have been genetically altered to reduce the antigenecity of the cells so that they would be compatible with different segments of the population.[26]

As research with ES cells ripens into a promising field of research, two ethical problems will have to be overcome for its full promise to be realized.[27] One is resolution of issues about embryo status and research, so that ethical conflict about the value of embryos does not block further ES cell research. Ethical issues in embryo research are implicated because of the need to destroy embryos in order to obtain ES cells from the inner cell mass of human blastocysts. Although embryo research is legal in all but a few states in the United States, Congress has enacted laws against federal funding of embryo research, and no overall regulatory structure for carrying out such research now exists.[28] ES cell science could continue with private funding alone, but it would advance more rapidly if Congress lifted the ban on federal funding and instituted a regulatory scheme for all ES cell research.

Once policymakers recognize that researchers may ethically use embryos not intended for transfer to derive ES cells, they should also recognize that spare embryos donated by infertile couples undergoing IVF treatment for infertility may not suffice for some kinds of essential ES cell research or therapy. For example, research that aims at making tissue derived from human ES cells compatible with the immune systems of recipients may require that researchers create embryos for re-

---

24. See id. at 1381 n.53.

25. See id. at 1380-81.

26. See Thomson et al., supra note 13, at 1147 ("Strategies to prevent immune rejection of the transplanted cells need to be developed but could include banking ES cells with defined major histocompatibility complex backgrounds or genetically manipulating ES cells to reduce or actively combat immune rejection.").

27. For a discussion of the embryonic stem cell controversy, see John A. Robertson, Ethics and Policy in Embryonic Stem Cell Research, KENNEDY INST. ETHICS J. (forthcoming June 1999).

28. See 144 CONG. REC. H11,147 (daily ed. Oct. 19, 1998).

search, with no intent to transfer to the uterus, rather than rely on spare donated embryos.[29] Creation of research embryos would also be essential to see if ES cells derived from embryos created by nuclear transfer cloning of a potential recipient's own cells would avoid rejection problems.

A second set of ethical problems involves clearly separating therapeutic from reproductive cloning. Because the techniques involved with therapeutic cloning are the same techniques that would be involved in reproductive cloning, opponents of the latter might argue that no therapeutic cloning should be permitted because it will inevitably lead to reproductive cloning. The fear is that once cloned human embryos are created in the laboratory, there will be no way to stop scientists or physicians from acceding to a person's request to have the cloned embryos placed in her uterus so that a cloned child may be born.

A slippery slope, however, from therapeutic to reproductive cloning is not inevitable. The mere possibility that the latter could occur is not a sufficient ground to ban the former when there are compelling reasons to undertake therapeutic cloning. Although both kinds of cloning require the cloning of human cells to the embryonic or blastocyst stage, it is a much more significant step to transfer that embryo or blastocyst to the uterus of a woman willing to carry an implanted cloned human embryo to term. If the latter is deemed unethical or undesirable, reproductive cloning could be made illegal without also prohibiting therapeutic cloning or running a great risk that such a ban would be widely ignored.

Distinctions between acceptable and unacceptable uses of a practice or technique are often made in public policy. The risk that acceptable practice A might lead to unacceptable practice B is a reason to draw a bright line between the two practices, not to prohibit A because it could lead to some instances of B. For example, guns are sold for legal purposes, even though there is a risk that purchasers will use them for illegal ends as well. Spare embryos may be donated for research even though such a practice could lead to attempts to sell embryos for research. Because a line between the two can be so clearly drawn, therapeutic cloning should not be banned just because reproductive cloning is prohibited.[30]

---

29. *See* Robertson, *supra* note 27; Robertson, *supra* note 12, at 1380-81.

30. Although reputable physicians would observe the law, a small number of persons might violate it. In any case, once cloning science has progressed to the point that human cloning is feasible, legal bans on therapeutic cloning are unlikely to stop disreputable scientists from cloning humans somewhere in the world.

The distinction between reproductive and therapeutic cloning has been accepted in previous policy recommendations and laws. The National Institutes of Health Human Embryo Research Panel ("HERP") recognized such a distinction in ES cell research in 1994.[31] Although it found that embryo research involving reproductive cloning was not acceptable for federal funding,[32] it did find that funding of nuclear transfer cloning in order to get genetically identical tissue from ES cells warranted further review.[33] With regard to therapeutic cloning it noted that, because no gametes were combined, such therapeutic cloning was a preferable way to obtain histocompatible tissue than fertilizing an oocyte specifically for that purpose.[34] It strongly implied that when there was a clearer need to proceed with therapeutic cloning research, it should be acceptable for federal funding even if federal funding of embryo research aimed at reproductive cloning was prohibited.[35]

In the United Kingdom, a recent public consultation on human cloning carefully distinguished between therapeutic and reproductive cloning.[36] The consultation recommended strongly against reproductive cloning, and urged that legislation be enacted so that the existing ban by the Human Fertilisation and Embryology Authority ("HFEA") on licensing reproductive cloning would become statutory, and not subject to administrative reversal.[37] At the same time, however, it recommended that regulations be issued to permit embryos to be used in studies of therapeutic cloning to replace damaged tissue or organs.[38]

The effort to pass laws in the United States against cloning has also, to some extent, taken account of this distinction. Several bills have been introduced in Congress to ban cloning.[39] A number of them define

---

31. *See* 1 NATIONAL INSTITUTES OF HEALTH, REPORT OF THE NIH HUMAN EMBRYO RESEARCH PANEL 76 (1994).

32. *See id.* at 80-81.

33. *See id.* at 79-80.

34. *See id.*

35. *See id.*

36. *See* Human Genetics Advisory Comm'n, Cloning Issues in Reproduction, Science, and Medicine (visited Feb. 24, 1998) <http://www.dti.gov.uk/hgac/papers/papers_d.htm>.

37. *See id.* ¶ 9.2.

38. *See id; see also* Marshall, *supra* note 19, at 2167-68 (reviewing the recommendations from the Human Genetics Advisory Commission for a new law banning reproductive cloning, but permitting therapeutic cloning).

39. *See* Prohibition on Cloning of Human Beings Act of 1998, S. 1611, 105th Cong.; Prohibition on Cloning of Human Beings Act of 1998, S. 1602, 105th Cong.; Human Cloning Prohibition Act, S. 1601, 105th Cong. (1998); Human Cloning Prohibition Act of 1998, S. 1599, 105th Cong.; Human Cloning Prohibition Act, S. 1574, 105th Cong. (1998); Human Cloning Research Prohibition Act, H.R. 3133, 105th Cong. (1998); Human Cloning Prohibition Act, H.R. 923, 105th Cong. (1997); Human Cloning Research Prohibition Act, H.R. 922, 105th Cong. (1997); S. 368,

prohibited cloning as the placement in the uterus of cells or embryos cloned by any means, thus clearly banning reproductive cloning but leaving therapeutic cloning legal.[40] At the state level, three states have passed laws against human cloning.[41] However, two of the three states (California and Rhode Island) prohibit only reproductive cloning, and do not limit therapeutic cloning or the research that could lead to it.[42] The third state—Michigan—has written its law more broadly to include therapeutic cloning as well.[43] Such a broad ban is more difficult to justify, and may not have been a considered decision by Michigan legislators.

In sum, the question of therapeutic cloning through nuclear transfer to produce ES cells compatible with the immune system of a prospective recipient for research or therapy is ethically controversial primarily because it requires the creation of embryos for research or therapy, and only secondarily because it involves cloning *per se*. Cloning to get ES cells for research or therapy involves issues of respect for embryos, and not the issues of identity, copying, and selection and shaping of persons which make reproductive cloning so troubling. Once the embryo research issues are resolved, there should be little opposition to therapeutic cloning as long as the line between therapeutic and reproductive cloning is clearly drawn.

III. REPRODUCTIVE CLONING

While there is increasing recognition that therapeutic cloning should be acceptable to obtain ES cells for research or therapy, there is strong sentiment that no form of reproductive cloning should be permitted.[44] As noted, the public consultation in the United Kingdom that

---

105th Cong. (1997).

40. *See* S. 1611 § 498C(b)(1); S. 1602 § 498C(b)(1); S. 1574 § 3(c).

41. *See* CAL. HEALTH & SAFETY CODE § 24185 (West Supp. 1998); 1998 Mich. Pub. Acts 108 (codified in MICH. COMP. LAWS §§ 333.20165, 333.16274, 333.20197); R.I. GEN. LAWS §§ 23-16.4-1 to -4 (1998).

42. *See* CAL. HEALTH & SAFETY CODE § 24185; R.I. GEN. LAWS § 23-16.4-1.

43. *See* 1998 Mich. Pub. Acts 108 (codified in MICH. COMP. LAWS § 333.16274).

44. *See, e.g.*, 1 CLONING HUMAN BEINGS, *supra* note 6, at 104 ("[I]t is morally unacceptable for anyone in the public or private sector . . . to attempt to create a child using somatic cell nuclear transfer cloning."); George J. Annas, *Why We Should Ban Human Cloning*, 339 NEW ENG. J. MED. 122, 125 (1998) ("We can (and should) take advantage of this opportunity to distinguish the cloning of cells and tissues from the cloning of human beings by somatic nuclear transplantation and to permit the former while prohibiting the latter." (footnote omitted)); Kass, *supra* note 7, at 26 ("[E]mbryonic research may proceed if and only if it is preceded by an absolute and effective ban on all attempts to implant into a uterus a cloned human embryo . . . to produce a living child."); Chris Meehan, *Cloning Pioneer Opposed to Work on Humans*, GRAND RAPIDS PRESS, Jan. 15,

urged authorization of research in therapeutic cloning also recommended that the current administrative ban on cloning be made legislative, so that it would not depend upon a statutory body like the HFEA.[45] California, Michigan, and Rhode Island have already passed laws that prohibit reproductive cloning, as have several nations.[46] Both Congress and international bodies have also called for prohibition on cloning human beings.[47] Even if many nations or American states should decide to permit therapeutic cloning, there is strong sentiment that no cloned embryos should ever be transferred to the uterus, so that they might implant and be born.[48]

The strong prohibition against reproductive cloning rests largely on the view that a resulting child would be an identical copy of the nuclear deoxyribonucleic acid ("DNA") source, and would suffer in its identity, freedom, and right to be treated as a separate individual with dignity.[49] Accompanying this view is the sense that no person could rationally wish to clone unless it were to gain some illegitimate or unethical control over the identity of offspring, a power which is likely to hurt the child, family, and society.[50]

Yet such views, which have largely driven the human cloning debate to date, are unduly overbroad, and do not take account of important distinctions in the circumstances in which persons might choose to un-

1998, at A1 (quoting Dr. Ian Wilmut, who successfully cloned Dolly as stating: "'It's quite appalling to me to think someone is seriously thinking about using this technology to produce people' . . . .").

45. *See supra* notes 36-38 and accompanying text.

46. *See supra* notes 41-43 and accompanying text; *see also* Heidi Forster & Emily Ramsey, *Legal Responses to the Potential Cloning of Human Beings*, 32 VAL. U. L. REV. 433, 455-57 (1998) (reviewing European bans on the cloning of humans).

47. *See* COUNCIL OF EUROPE: DRAFT ADDITIONAL PROTOCOL TO THE CONVENTION ON HUMAN RIGHTS AND BIOMEDICINE ON THE PROHIBITION OF CLONING HUMAN BEINGS WITH EXPLANATORY REPORT AND PARLIAMENTARY ASSEMBLY OPINION (adopted Sept. 22, 1997), *reprinted in* 36 INT'L LEGAL MATERIALS 1415, 1417 (1997) (declaring that the members of the States of the Council of Europe, the other States, and the European Community signatories have agreed that "[a]ny intervention seeking to create a human being genetically identical to another human being, whether living or dead, is prohibited"); *supra* notes 38-39 and accompanying text.

48. *See supra* notes 6-7 and accompanying text; *see also* George J. Annas, *Human Cloning: A Choice or an Echo?*, 23 U. DAYTON L. REV. 247, 268-73 (1998) (recounting the progression of anti-cloning legislation in the United States).

49. *See* Annas, *supra* note 48, at 272 (recounting that the primary reason for banning human cloning, articulated in the early 1970s by Hans Jonas, is that "cloning is a crime against the clone, the crime of depriving the clone of his or her 'existential right to certain subjective terms of his being'").

50. *See* Katheryn D. Katz, *The Clonal Child: Procreative Liberty and Asexual Reproduction*, 8 ALB. L.J. SCI. & TECH. 1, 17 (1997) (describing the view that clones will be treated as a "genetically engineered class of subnormal human beings . . . developed for nefarious purposes"); Robertson, *supra* note 12, at 1404.

dertake reproductive cloning. Recalling Blake's dictum about the importance of relevant distinctions,[51] the quality of the ethical, legal, and social debate about human cloning would be greatly enhanced if it took account of two different models or types of human reproductive cloning. The two models are distinguishable by whether the parties seeking to clone are able to reproduce sexually by coital or assisted reproduction. Model 1 uses of cloning would cover cases in which an infertile couple resorts to reproductive cloning because it is the only way for it to have a child genetically or biologically related to the rearing partners. Model 2 uses would cover cases where an individual or couple could reproduce sexually but prefer to forego sexual reproduction in order to have a child with the nuclear DNA of one of them or a third person.

In my view, a strong case can be made for allowing cloning in cases of reproductive failure (Model 1) when it is the only technique available to achieve the reproductive goal of having and rearing children with whom one has a genetic kinship relationship. Model 2 cloning, on the other hand, lacks that rationale, and thus would have to be defended on the basis of a more general right to use positive means to select the genome of offspring whom one rears.[52] Although arguments can be made for such a right, at the present time they appear to be much weaker than the argument for Model 1 cloning. As a result, public policy should permit Model 1 cloning without fearing that Model 2 uses would necessarily or automatically follow.

IV. MODEL ONE: CLONING TO OVERCOME REPRODUCTIVE FAILURE

The strongest case for human reproductive cloning is for persons who are not able to reproduce sexually, and who thus face the prospect of having no genetically-related children to rear. Not all persons faced with this limitation would clone to achieve that connection, even if cloning were safe and legal, but a subset of them doubtlessly would.[53] Based on prevailing conceptions of procreative freedom, persons who opt for reproductive cloning in order to establish an otherwise unavail-

---

51. *See supra* note 9 and accompanying text.

52. *See generally* John A. Robertson, *Genetic Selection of Offspring Characteristics*, 76 B.U. L. REV. 421 (1996).

53. Richard and Eric Posner make the mistake of assuming that all infertile persons would choose cloning to deal with their infertility when other treatments and alternatives are available to help them have children. *See* Eric A. Posner & Richard A. Posner, *The Demand for Human Cloning*, *in* CLONES AND CLONES: FACTS AND FANTASIES ABOUT HUMAN CLONING 233, 233-39 (Martha C. Nussbaum & Cass R. Sunstein eds., 1998) [hereinafter CLONES AND CLONES].

able genetic connection with offspring should have a presumptive right to use that technique.[54] That right should be denied them only if substantial harm from cloning to have genetically-related children for rearing could be shown.

That argument assumes that reproduction is an important source of value and meaning for individuals, and that state efforts to limit reproduction require compelling justification.[55] It assumes that reproduction is valued because rearing and genetic transmission occur together (even though each may have personal importance separately). On this view, genetic transmission *tout court*—reproduction without rearing—is reproduction that lacks the full extent of meaning that comes with rearing or social connection with one's offspring, and should not be protected to the same extent that genetic transmission and rearing combined are.[56] Conversely, rearing a child with whom one has no genetic or biologic kinship connection may be important and meaningful, but it is not reproductive, and is not included at the present time in the category of rights or values that are distinctively "reproductive."[57]

Who is included in the group of those who might plausibly choose cloning as the only way of achieving the goal of having genetic or biologically-related offspring to rear? The strongest candidates are a subset of persons who are gametically infertile—one or both partners lacks viable gametes for reproduction.[58] Note that this group does not include the many infertile couples whose infertility is due to nongametic factors, and thus who might benefit from IVF and embryo transfer, intrauterine inseminations ("IUI") with partner sperm, intracytoplasmic sperm injections ("ICSI"), gestational surrogacy, and the other forms of assisted reproduction that are now available to infertile persons.[59]

---

54. *See* Robertson, *supra* note 12, at 1388-1403.

55. For a further discussion of reproductive freedom, see JOHN A. ROBERTSON, CHILDREN OF CHOICE: FREEDOM AND THE NEW REPRODUCTIVE TECHNOLOGIES 29-40 (1994).

56. A person thus has no fundamental right simply to transmit genes, or to acquire children for rearing without genetic transmission. For example, a constitutional right to hire women to conceive children and then turn over for adoption has not been recognized. *See id.* at 108-09.

57. *See id.* at 142-45. Some persons might challenge these limits, and to some extent the categories are in flux. As a matter of positive law and ethical analysis, however, there is still an important distinction between claiming a right to rear or adopt and a right to reproduce.

58. *See generally* Marjorie Maguire Shultz, *Reproductive Technology and the Intent-Based Parenthood: An Opportunity for Gender Neutrality*, 1990 WIS. L. REV. 297, 333-46 (describing reproduction techniques available for the biologically infertile).

59. For further discussion of infertility treatments, see OFFICE OF TECH. ASSESSMENT, U.S. CONGRESS, ARTIFICIAL INSEMINATION: PRACTICE IN THE UNITED STATES 8-11 (1988) [hereinafter ARTIFICIAL INSEMINATION] (discussing that the overwhelming majority of those seeking and obtaining artificial insemination are married couples with male reproductive problems); 1 U.S. DEPT. OF HEALTH & HUMAN SERVS., CENTERS FOR DISEASE CONTROL & PREVENTION, NATIONAL

Persons infertile due to gametic factors face the prospect of going childless, adopting, or using the services of sperm or egg donors. Couples vary, of course, in their willingness to choose a particular option because of the distinct costs and benefits of each alternative. Many couples, for example, might try to have a child through egg or sperm donation, because gamete donation will provide a genetic connection with the child for at least one of the parties.[60] In sperm donation, the rearing father has no genetic connection but the rearing mother, who has provided the egg and gestates, does.[61] In egg donation, the rearing mother has a gestational but not a genetic connection, while the rearing father has provided the sperm.[62] In embryo donation, the rearing father and mother have no genetic connection, but the rearing mother has the biologic relationship of gestation.[63]

It is plausible that some persons who are gametically infertile would choose to clone one of the partners rather than choose the other options facing them. The most likely candidates would be couples in which there is severe male infertility—oligospermia or azoospermia—for whom IUI, IVF, or even ICSI, which utilize the male partner's sperm, will not work.[64] Having no sperm at all, such couples face childlessness, adoption, or resort to a sperm donor. If cloning were available, some who might have gone childless, adopted, or chosen donor sperm might decide to have a child through cloning the husband's cells. Cloning is a plausible option because it would provide a genetic or biologic tie between each rearing partner and their child, albeit a lesser genetic

---

CENTER FOR CHRONIC DISEASE PREVENTION & HEALTH PROMOTION, 1995 ASSISTED REPRODUCTIVE TECHNOLOGY SUCCESS RATES, NATIONAL SUMMARY AND FERTILITY CLINIC REPORTS 6, 35 (1997) [hereinafter 1 FERTILITY CLINIC REPORTS] (reporting on the use of assisted reproductive technology to treat infertility).

60. It is estimated that over 30,000 children are born each year as a result of donor sperm. *See* ARTIFICIAL INSEMINATION, *supra* note 59, at 3. In 1996, about 4000 egg donor cycles occurred, with 2500 children born as a result. *See* U.S. DEPT. OF HEALTH & HUMAN SERVS., CENTERS FOR DISEASE CONTROL & PREVENTION, NATIONAL CENTER FOR CHRONIC DISEASE PREVENTION & HEALTH PROMOTION, 1996 ASSISTED REPRODUCTIVE TECHNOLOGY SUCCESS RATES, NATIONAL SUMMARY AND FERTILITY CLINIC REPORTS 35 (1998).

61. *See* Robertson, *supra* note 12, at 1390 n.90.

62. *See id.*; John A. Robertson, *Oocyte Cytoplasm Transfers and the Ethics of Germ-Line Intervention*, 26 J.L. MED. & ETHICS 211, 214 (1998).

63. *See* Lori B. Andrews & Lisa Douglass, *Alternative Reproduction*, 65 S. CAL. L. REV. 623, 631 (1991); Robertson, *supra* note 12, at 1390 n.90.

64. "Oligospermia" or "oligozoospermia" is defined as "a subnormal concentration of spermatozoa in the penile ejaculate." STEDMAN'S MEDICAL DICTIONARY 1083, 1084 (25th ed. 1990). "Aspermia" or "azoospermia" is defined as the "[a]bsence of living spermatozoa in the semen; failure of spermatogenesis." *Id.* at 162.

role for the wife.[65] In such a case, the wife would provide the egg which would be enucleated to receive the husband's deprogrammed nucleus (instead of a sperm) and then activated by electrofusion and placed in her uterus for gestation and childbirth. She would have contributed an egg, including cytoplasm and mitochondrial DNA ("mtDNA"), as well as gestation to the child, while her husband would have provided nuclear DNA.[66]

It is unclear how many persons facing total male gametic infertility would choose cloning rather than sperm donation, adoption, or childlessness. Given the deeply engrained desire to have and rear one's genetic or biologic offspring, it is likely that some persons in this group would choose to clone the husband.[67] Cloning, however, has its own uncertainties and drawbacks, including the willingness of a wife to give up a nuclear genetic tie with children in favor of her husband having such a connection. A couple would have to weigh these disadvantages against the alternative options for having a related child to rear. If they did, some couples are likely to find that the desire for a male genetic tie with children is so strong that it outweighs those drawbacks and would opt for cloning the husband if cloning were safe and legal.[68]

The need to consider cloning as a way to establish a genetic connection with children is not limited to physical infertility. Couples who are both carriers for autosomal recessive genetic disease face a one in four risk of having a child with Tay Sachs disease, cystic fibrosis, sickle cell anemia, or other severe illnesses.[69] Although some of those couples

---

65. The wife's genetic contribution through providing the egg consists of the mitochondrial deoxyribonucleic acid ("mtDNA") found in the cytoplasm of the egg, which codes only for a series of mitochondrial proteins and ribonucleic acids. *See* GÜNTHER KAHL, DICTIONARY OF GENE TECHNOLOGY 289 (1995). The mother transmits her mtDNA through the cytoplasm of her ovum to all of her offspring. *See* TEXTBOOK OF INTERNAL MEDICINE 2301 (William N. Kelley et al. eds., 3d ed. 1997). Males never transmit their mtDNA. *See id.*

66. If the wife does not contribute an egg, she may still choose to gestate, thereby providing a biological connection to the child. If the wife contributes the enucleated egg but she does not gestate, her genetic contribution will be provided by her mtDNA. *See* TEXTBOOK OF INTERNAL MEDICINE, *supra* note 65, at 2301. In either case, she would still have a biologic or genetic connection to the child that she and her husband will rear.

67. *See* Andrews & Douglass, *supra* note 63, at 626-28 (discussing the value of genetic and biological links); Rochelle C. Dreyfuss & Dorothy Nelkin, *The Jurisprudence of Genetics*, 45 VAND. L. REV. 313, 320 (1992).

68. Where the wife lacks viable eggs, cloning her cells would give her but not her husband a genetic connection with the child that she gestates and they rear. Egg donation, on the other hand, would give the husband a genetic connection (his sperm would be used to fertilize the donated egg) and the wife the biologic connection of gestation. *See supra* notes 62-64 and accompanying text; *see also* Andrews & Douglass, *supra* note 63, at 628 (discussing how infertility affects men and women differently).

69. *See* LOIS WINGERSON, UNNATURAL SELECTION: THE PROMISE AND THE POWER OF

will not reproduce at all or adopt, others will conceive coitally and either take the risk of having an affected child or undergo prenatal diagnosis and abort or discard embryos. Couples unwilling to take any of these options might also consider sperm or egg donation. If cloning were safe and legal, however, some couples in that subset might choose to clone one of the partners. Because the wife could provide the egg and gestate, they might decide to clone the husband's cells, thus assuring a biologic or genetic connection between each of them and the offspring whom they rear.

Other potential cases of cloning also involve gametic infertility—the need for an egg or embryo donor.[70] The idea of cloning the wife instead of using an egg donor would leave the husband with no genetic connection with the child, when both he and his wife would have a biologic connection if they received an egg donation, which was fertilized with his sperm and carried to term by his wife.[71] Where both partners suffer from gametic infertility but the wife could gestate, the couple could benefit from an embryo donation or separate egg and sperm donations that are then combined. Some couples in this group might choose to clone the husband's cells in order to produce a child that is genetically related to the husband and biologically related to the wife who has gestated.[72]

Couples who suffer from gametic infertility, who are seeking to have children to rear to whom they are genetically or biologically-related, may plausibly argue that cloning one of the partners is part of their constitutional right to reproduce.[73] If so, their choice to form a family by cloning should not be restricted unless the practice were highly likely to cause substantial harm to children or others.

Claims of harm from reproductive cloning have largely rested on consequentialist grounds, though deontological/symbolic objections have also been noted.[74] The main consequentialist harm is to resulting

---

HUMAN GENE RESEARCH 6, 38 (1998) (explaining the genetic transmission of diseases such as Tay-Sachs, Huntington's disease, and cystic fibrosis).

70. *See* Shultz, *supra* note 58, at 311-12 (describing the causes for impaired production of female gametes, such as lack of egg production and blockage of the fallopian tubes).

71. Probably few persons who are candidates for egg donation would exclude a male genetic tie unless they had or were not interested in a male mate. *See infra* notes 117-24 and accompanying text (discussing lesbian cloning).

72. Persons in that situation might choose to clone a third party instead of one of themselves. If they do so, however, they would not, unless they choose to clone a very close relative, be achieving a genetic connection with the resulting child whom they rear.

73. *See* Robertson, *supra* note 12, at 1388-1403.

74. *See, e.g.*, Dan W. Brock, *Cloning Human Beings: An Assessment of the Ethical Issues Pro and Con*, in CLONES AND CLONES, *supra* note 53, at 141, 151-55 (1998) (outlining moral ar-

children, who, it is said, will be harmed as a result of being born the clone of another, say of the male parent, or a third party of known phenotype whose DNA was chosen precisely in order to obtain those same characteristics.[75] The fear is that the child will be confused with the DNA source and expected to act accordingly, thereby denying her autonomy and a unique identity. Alternatively, parents who resort to cloning may be more intent on using the child as a means to establish a genetic connection than in caring for her own welfare, and set unrealistic expectations that the child will have difficulty meeting.

In my view, neither the consequentialist nor deontological/symbolic arguments are sufficient to justify infringement of the presumptive right of married couples to have and rear genetically-related children in cases of Model 1 reproductive cloning.[76] Because gametically infertile parents will have resorted to cloning as the only way of establishing a genetic or biologic relation with their children, they are less interested in having the child be a genetic copy of the husband than that the child be genetically related to him. While they too could fall prey to expecting the child to be an exact copy of the nuclear DNA source, they are less likely to expect that the child would develop or be like the DNA source than if they had sought to clone in order to choose the child's genome (Model 2). A responsible cloning policy would require that reproductive physicians not provide cloning to infertile couples until they have thoroughly understood that the resulting child, while having a close physical resemblance to the DNA source, will have been gestated and reared in a very different uterine and family setting, and thus is likely to be phenotypically different in significant ways.[77] Given that parents are generally interested in having healthy, genetically-related children to rear, most infertile couples who resort to cloning to establish a genetic connection with the children they rear are likely to have their cloned children's best interests at heart and will treat

---

guments against human cloning); Robertson, *supra* note 12, at 1382-86 (explaining the various moral objections made by opponents of cloning).

75. *See* 1 CLONING HUMAN BEINGS, *supra* note 6, at 72-74; Annas, *supra* note 48, at 248 ("[C]reating a clone in your own image is to curse your child by condemning it to be only an echo."); Robertson, *supra* note 12, at 1418-19. Ian Wilmut, the creator of Dolly, has argued: "[I]t would be difficult for families created in this way to provide an appropriate environment for the child. . . . In making a copy of oneself or some famous person, a parent is deliberately specifying the way he or she wishes that child to develop." Wilmut, *supra* note 1, at 74.

76. For a more complete analysis of why those arguments are insufficient, see Robertson, *supra* note 12, at 1404-52.

77. *See* Leon Eisenberg, *Are Cloned Sheep Really Like Humans*, 340 NEW ENG. J. MED. 471 (1999).

them as separate individuals with their own interests and identity, just as other couples who seek infertility treatment do. Of course, raising a child who is one's later born nuclear DNA twin may pose special problems, but there is good reason to think that couples, who after counseling and preparation for these problems decide to proceed with cloning, will be competent, loving parents who are devoted to their child's unique identity and welfare, despite its cloned origin.

Others have argued that reproductive cloning would have bad consequences for society as a whole, in that it would lead to an emphasis on eugenics rather than chance in reproduction, and that it will ultimately reduce genetic diversity by greatly increasing the number of persons who reproduce by cloning.[78] The threat of eugenics is a charge more justly laid at the feet of those who undertake Model 2 cloning, for Model 1 cloning aims at a relational not a eugenic goal. As noted, the purpose of Model 1 reproductive cloning is not to choose the best or most adaptive genome, but merely a genome that is related by kinship to the rearing parents.

The further consequentialist claim that Model 1 uses of cloning would drive out sexual reproduction and thus reduce genetic diversity appears at present to be highly speculative and implausible. Such a claim draws on the debate in evolutionary biology about the evolutionary or natural selection advantages of sexual reproduction—the question of why did sex evolve.[79] The question arises because asexual reproduction (cloning), which relicates one hundred percent of an organism's genes,[80] appears to be more efficient in replicating genes than sexual reproduction, which replicates just fifty percent of the reproducer's genes. Sexual reproduction, however, appears to be a more successful evolutionary strategy than asexual reproduction because of the genetic diversity it produces. Through recombination of genes in the formation of gametes and then in fertilization itself, sexually reproducing species are able to select for advantages over parasites and microorganisms that might end their life before reproduction occurs, and then to respond to selective adaptation of those organisms in turn.[81] Genetic recombination

---

78. "Eugenics," a term first introduced by British scientist Sir Francis Galton, is described as the science of improving the human race by the careful selection of parents. *See* DANIEL KEVLES, IN THE NAME OF EUGENICS: GENETICS AND THE USES OF HUMAN HEREDITY 3-4 (1985).

79. *See* Bernice Wuethrich, *Why Sex? Putting Theory to the Test*, 281 SCI. 1980, 1980 (1998).

80. The following account ignores mtDNA contributions, for they would arise only in human cloning.

81. The battle or "arms race" for advantage between host and parasite is often referred to as the Red Queen problem. Although hosts and parasites are constantly evolving to outwit the previ-

also removes harmful mutations more easily than asexual reproduction. A single mutation affecting an asexually reproducing population could lead to the entire population going extinct.[82]

If sexual reproduction has such clear advantages as a reproductive strategy, as undoubtedly it does, then cloning appears to be evolutionary suicide for a species. Richard and Eric Posner, in a provocative essay entitled *The Demand for Human Cloning*, explore such a claim. They argue that allowing the infertile to clone themselves "could have the radical consequence of eventually eliminating sexual reproduction," apparently regardless of whether Model 2 uses of reproductive cloning also occur.[83] Their argument rests on the assumption that infertility is inherited, and that all persons with heritable infertility would choose to clone rather than use other means that might enable them to have biologically related children to rear.[84] On that assumption the number of persons with inherited infertility would increase in each generation (as they clone themselves rather than forego reproduction). Since the Posners assert that "[p]eople can clone themselves faster than they can produce children through sexual reproduction,"[85] they propose that the birthrate of the infertile would then increase so rapidly that, regardless of the actual rate of inherited infertility, "[i]nfertility will spread like a virus . . . and eventually drive off fertility."[86] As a result, human genetic diversity in the long run would be decreased, and future generations who were clones would be more susceptible to parasites and other diseases that had evolved to outwit the immunological defenses of the current generation of persons who, because cloning had come to dominate, would not through sexual reproduction have evolved in turn.[87]

Neither the Posners' thought-experiment nor the biological research on which they implicitly draw is a sufficient basis to deny those

ous adaptational advantage of the other, neither gains an advantage for long, just as the Red Queen in Lewis Carroll's *Alice in Wonderland* is constantly moving but getting nowhere. *See* MATT RIDLEY, THE RED QUEEN: SEX AND THE EVOLUTION OF HUMAN NATURE 61-64 (1993); Wuethrich, *supra* note 79, at 1980.

82. *See* Wuethrich, *supra* note 79, at 1980.

83. Posner & Posner, *supra* note 53, at 235.

84. *See id.*

85. *Id.* at 255.

86. *Id.* at 256. They appear to be relying on the work of researchers such as evolutionary biologist Curtis Lively who has argued that, all other things being equal, in a population of one million sexually reproducing snails and a single asexual female mutant in which the sexually reproducing females and their progeny always produce a male and a female, and the asexual mutant and her progeny always have two daughters, asexuals would replace their sexual counterparts in about 52 generations. *See* Wuethrich, *supra* note 79, at 1980.

87. *See* Posner & Posner, *supra* note 53, at 256-57.

infertile couples who wish to resort to cloning the right to do so.[88] The Posners reach their conclusion by making two assumptions that appear highly counterfactual. One is their odd assertion that one could produce a child more quickly by cloning than by sexual reproduction.[89] If true, this would lead to infertile clones being produced much more quickly than fertile persons created by sexual reproduction. But this assumption is clearly wrong because in either case nine months of gestation would be necessary to produce a new individual.[90]

Secondly, they incorrectly assume that all infertility would lead to a demand for cloning rather than to a demand for the other treatments and alternatives for dealing with infertility.[91] They appear to assume that all infertility, even heritable infertility, is the gametic infertility for which reproductive cloning might be a valid option, when many kinds of heritable infertility, whether cervical, uterine, or gametic in origin, could be successfully treated by assisted reproduction or other techniques that do not involve cloning.[92] Infertile couples who can achieve genetic or biologic reproduction with conventional noncoital or assisted reproductive techniques are no more likely to forego a genetic connection with both partners simply because cloning is legal and safe than are fertile couples. If so, they are engaged in a form of Model 2 reproductive cloning.

The Posners also err in thinking that persons with gametic or nongametic infertility that cannot be treated by conventional methods would always choose cloning over childlessness, adoption, or gamete donation.[93] Because of the special meanings and complications raised by cloning, only a (small) subset of this group of infertile couples is likely to choose cloning as the solution to their reproductive problem. If so few infertile persons are likely to choose Model 1 reproductive cloning, then it is also unlikely that their cloned offspring and all later cloned progeny would invariably do so in turn. Thus the Posners have not shown that any use of reproductive cloning by gametically infertile couples is so likely to lead to such a high rate of cloning that human

---

88. To their credit, the Posners do not suggest that government prohibition of cloning on that basis would be justified. *See id.* at 258.

89. *See id.* at 255.

90. This claim may simply be an error on their part, for the preceding paragraph acknowledges that cloning will still require a womb and nine months gestation. *See id.* at 254.

91. *See id.* at 252. For purposes of this discussion we may assume that the infertility at issue is genetic, and thus heritable in the next generation.

92. For example, intrauterine inseminations, in vitro fertilization, or intracytoplasmic sperm injections might work for the couple. *See supra* note 58-59 and accompanying text.

93. *See* Posner & Posner, *supra* note 53, at 252.

asexual reproduction, with its long-term harmful effects for the species, will come to replace sexual reproduction in any conceivably relevant future time period.

Similar problems arise with the species suicide argument even when it is freed from the Posners' particular version of it. Biologists making such projections assume that every asexually reproducing organism and its progeny and their progeny in turn will reproduce asexually, thereby eventually outstripping organisms of that species that reproduce sexually.[94] But human reproduction is driven by social and cultural factors beyond biology. It is reasonable to think that only some persons who are gametically infertile would choose to clone themselves. Nor is there good reason to think that their cloned progeny or their cloned progeny's clones in turn would always resort to cloning to have and rear children, a condition essential to the biologic doomsayer's argument. Finally, even if the clones of clones always did asexually reproduce, the species effects are too distant in the future—fifty-two generations of human reproduction is more than 1000 years[95]—to function as an acceptable justification for interfering with an infertile couple's procreative liberty now. The potential consequentialist effects of human reproductive cloning simply do not add enough weight to consequentialist concerns about effect on children to justify interference with the right of couples who are gametically infertile to have genetically-related children to rear by cloning.

V.   MODEL TWO: CLONING TO SELECT OFFSPRING GENOME WHEN NO REPRODUCTIVE FAILURE

If the argument is strong for human reproductive cloning in the case of gametic failure or equivalent condition, the case for reproductive cloning when sexual reproduction is feasible appears much weaker. In that case cloning is unnecessary to achieve the valued experience of having and rearing genetically-related children, but is chosen in order to have a child with a particular genome or relationship to rearers.[96] Drawing a distinction between the two types of reproductive uses is

---

94. *See supra* note 86 (discussing the theory of Curtis Lively).

95. I assume that four generations of human reproduction would occur in a 100 year period, a not unreasonable assumption for the reproductive patterns of relatively well-off individuals in developed countries who are most likely to have access to cloning technology.

96. The relationship sought might be that of being "father" to one's later-born identical twin. In any event, not all genomes sought to be replicated are available for cloning, and the consent of the deoxyribonucleic acid ("DNA") source would most likely be necessary. *See* Robertson, *supra* note 12, at 1446-48.

crucial because it is Model 2 uses that have generated the most frightening images of human cloning.

May Model 2 uses be prohibited even if Model 1 uses are permitted? In considering this question, we must focus on Model 2 uses where a couple seeking to clone would rear the child whose genome they have selected.[97] This limitation would exclude entrepreneurs who bring together eggs, desirable genomes, and gestation to satisfy a demand for high quality children for adoption, because they would not themselves be rearing. In addition, neither the broker nor her clients would be making a procreative choice, because neither of them would have a genetic connection with the resulting child. There is no fundamental right to acquire children for rearing when there is no biologic/genetic connection with that child.[98]

The question of a right to engage in Model 2 uses of reproductive cloning then arises only with couples who are interested in rearing children but who choose cloning over sexual reproduction in order to have them. They are not claiming a right to reproduce *per se*, but rather a right to select, control, or shape offspring characteristics in the course of reproduction—a right to engage in reprogenetics.[99] Indeed, reproductive cloning is highly controversial because it presents the first practical opportunity to engage in positive rather than negative reprogenetics. It thus raises issues of prebirth genetic selection of offspring characteris-

---

97. We need not discuss the case of a single person who could reproduce sexually but who chooses to clone. If fertile couples have no right to clone, nor would fertile unmarried individuals. Similarly, if single males do not have the right to hire egg donors and surrogate mothers in order to gain a child to rear, infertile single males would have no right to acquire a child to rear through cloning themselves or another. Thus physically fertile persons who are unmarriageable, such as the excessively narcissistic, the psychotic, mentally retarded, persons with severe disabilities, pedophiles, and sociopaths, would not have a right to clone themselves. The Posners think that this group would find cloning attractive because it would do away with the need for a mate to reproduce. *See* Posner & Posner, *supra* note 53, at 248. Because they could achieve that goal by sexual reproduction through use of an egg donor and surrogate, it is unclear how cloning offers them any advantage, for they could not clone without a woman's assistance—a barrier to their reproduction similar to the need to find a mate.

98. *See supra* note 56-57 and accompanying text.

99. "Reprogenetics" describes the use of genetic selection techniques in human reproduction. *See* LEE SILVER, REMAKING EDEN: CLONING AND BEYOND IN A BRAVE NEW WORLD 8, 15, 77-79 (1997). Rearing by that couple is also assumed. If no rearing is intended, then the claim to procreative freedom is extremely weak, for procreation is usually a protected freedom because of the experiences and meaning that attend rearing one's offspring. *See supra* notes 55-56 and accompanying text. Just as reproduction or genetic transmission *tout court* has no particular legal or ethical standing, so cloning just to produce a child who will exist elsewhere in the world, but with no parenting or other relationship with the person initiating the cloning, should have little standing as a legal or moral right.

tics that will be the focus of ethical, legal, and social debate for some time to come.[100]

At the outset, it must be noted that such choices would be extremely rare just because they deviate so substantially from dominant cultural understandings of reproduction and having children. People want to procreate, i.e., transmit their genes to a new generation, which can transmit them in turn, and have some rearing role with their progeny.[101] This transmission occurs by sexual reproduction, with each mate transmitting fifty percent of nuclear DNA. Only if sexual reproduction between the two is not possible might they consider sexual reproduction with one of the partners only, as might occur with sperm or egg donation, or with neither, as occurs in embryo donation.[102] In negotiating which partner will lose the genetic connection with offspring, some couples might find reproductive cloning an acceptable solution, as where the husband provides nuclear DNA and the wife cytoplasm, mtDNA, and gestation, as opposed to the use of donor sperm, in which the gestating wife provides the egg and the rearing husband has no genetic connection at all.

But if sexual reproduction is possible,[103] and the partners nevertheless choose to clone one of themselves or a third party (and then gestate), then it is not the kinship connection alone which they seek, but rather a particular kind of genome or genetic relationship with the child. Core Model 2 claims arise when the couple that could reproduce sexually chooses to clone one of the partners out of sheer narcissism or desire to have a copy of oneself, or when, for eugenic reasons, they choose to clone another person in order to provide their child with that person's genes. The situation would arise if a married couple chose to clone the husband, say, rather than engage in coital reproduction to have a child.

---

100. Development of techniques of prebirth genetic modification of offspring will increase the pressure for answers to these questions. *See* Robertson, *supra* note 52, at 421.

101. *See* Andrews & Douglass, *supra* note 63, at 626-28. Such rearing is valued in most Western developed countries, even if not all reproductive partners share childrearing burdens equally.

102. People who want to reproduce and rear children assume that they will need a mate to do so. The technical ability to clone oneself without the need of a man, which cloning would make possible for women, does not mean that many people will want to use those techniques. The social meaning of reproducing and rearing offspring will still be perceived and constructed around having a mate and reproducing sexually. Thus only infertile people who cannot achieve a genetic or biologic connection with children whom they will rear are likely to consider cloning as a feasible way to form a family.

103. I am assuming that the subjects have a mate, putting aside for the moment the question of cloning when there is not a mate, because males at least would still need a woman for eggs and gestation.

Or if the couple sought to clone a third person, whether a member of the family, a celebrity, or a person with a desirable genome, when they could reproduce sexually.

Two cases of cloning when sexual reproduction is possible should be excluded from the core instances of Model 2 cloning that cause concern. One would be the wish of a fertile couple to clone their child, whether living or dead, in order to have a twin of that child. If the child is living, this wish might arise from the desire to have as lovely or attractive a child as the first, rather than risk a child with a different genome. If the child is dead or dying, it might be to retain as much of that child as possible in the world by continuing him genetically in a later-born clone or twin of that child. Whatever one thinks of these choices, they can be distinguished from more dubious Model 2 uses because the couple would be rearing a child with genes of both rearing parents, and not the clone of one of them or an unrelated other.

A second case would be to produce a child who is a close tissue match with an existing child so that the later child could serve as a tissue or organ donor for the first child. Although some persons criticize the practice as too overtly using the child as a means to the well-being of others, defenders have pointed to the positive results in the widely-publicized Ayala case in which a couple opted to reverse a vasectomy and conceive in order to produce a child who could serve as a bone marrow donor to a leukemic daughter.[104] There the new child was clearly valued and respected for herself, even if the need for a histocompatible bone marrow donor for her sister was the immediate impetus for her conception.[105] Indeed, if parents are free to achieve this goal coitally, it would be very difficult to deny them the right to achieve this goal through cloning, especially when sexual conception runs a much greater risk than cloning that the second child's tissue would not match the first. As with other instances of cloning one's child, one would be having and rearing a child whose genes come from both rearing partners, not only one of them or a third party. In any event, progress in therapeutic cloning and ES cell technology would make this Model 2 use of reproductive cloning unnecessary.[106]

---

104. *See* ROBERTSON, *supra* note 55, at 214-17; *see also Baby Is Conceived to Save Daughter*, N.Y. TIMES, Feb. 17, 1990, at 10 (reporting that the Ayalas would not have another child if it was not for their other child's leukemia, but maintaining that they would love their baby); Anastasia Toufexis, *Creating a Child to Save Another*, TIME, Mar. 5, 1990, at 56, 56 (reporting the Ayalas' situation and raising some ethical considerations concerning the conception of one child to save another).

105. *See* ROBERTSON, *supra* note 55, at 215.

106. If embryonic stem cell technology develops as hoped, it will be rare that an embryo

More troubling Model 2 uses of reproductive cloning would arise when one of the partners wishes to have and rear a clone of himself or herself or a desirable third person. In the case of cloning one of the partners, say the husband, the goal would be to replicate the husband genetically, so that he will be rearing his identical nuclear twin, and the wife would be bearing and rearing a younger version of her husband. This might be done out of narcissism on the husband's part or a desire to maximize the chance that his genes will continue in the world. Cloning will pass almost 100% of his genes to a new generation rather than the 50% that occurs with sexual reproduction.[107] In the case of cloning in order to have a child with the genome of a third party, the couple may do so in order to honor or preserve the genes of that person (say if they themselves did not want to reproduce), or because they wanted their child to have as good a chance in life as possible, and so have tried to give her a highly desirable set of genes as based on the phenotype of the DNA source.

Such cases of reproductive cloning, when sexual reproduction is otherwise feasible, are difficult to understand within our current conceptions of reproduction, family, and parenting. The case of cloning oneself when otherwise fertile would give a genetic connection between the clone source and the child who is reared and the wife who is a minor genetic parent and gestator (if the wife who gestates has provided the cytoplasm and mtDNA). But it is hard to empathize with and therefore respect a couple's desire to clone one of themselves when they could reproduce sexually, even though the desire to clone is understandable if they have no other way to establish a genetic connection with their child. Indeed, it seems so odd as to approach the pathologically obsessive, and suggests that the rearing father (identical nuclear twin) might be so overidentified with rearing a younger version of himself that he

---

cloned from an existing child's cells would have to be transferred to the uterus and a child be born to obtain the needed tissue.

107. *See* Posner & Posner, *supra* note 53, at 235 (positing such cloning as a rational response for those who want their genes preserved or passed on because cloning passes on 100% of their genes, and not just 50% as occurs in sexual reproduction). Although most people might find it difficult to find women to provide the egg and gestation for this purpose, those with wealth and/or good genes might easily be able to do so. The Posners conclude that

cloning would benefit mainly wealthy women with good genes and to a lesser extent wealthy men with good genes. One would therefore expect, if human cloning were feasible and permitted, a growing concentration of wealth and highly desired heritable characteristics at the top end of the distribution of these goods and fewer marriages there.

Id. at 247.

could have unrealistic expectations for the child.[108] Whether or not the child, who could not otherwise have been born but as his rearing father's twin, is thereby harmed, the practice seems too far removed from current conceptions of reproduction and parenting to deserve protection as an aspect of procreative liberty, in the way that cloning in the case of reproductive failure does.[109]

Similarly, the idea of cloning a third party with a desirable phenotype, when a couple could sexually reproduce, also is hard to understand or accept in terms of conventional understandings of parenting, family, and kinship. In this case, there would be no nuclear genetic connection with either the rearing husband or wife, though the wife might have provided the enucleated egg and gestated. If they want the celebrity status of having and rearing a younger version of that celebrity, one could question whether they are interested in the child for herself.[110] A claim that they wanted to give their child the best possible chance in life by assuring it good genes appears to reflect a purely eugenic intent, because they are choosing to have a child whose nuclear DNA does not derive from them. Again, even if one could not show consequentialist harm, the choice is so far removed from conventional understandings of reproduction, family, and kinship, that it is difficult to credit it as an exercise of procreative liberty as commonly understood.

Both the narcissistic and eugenic uses of cloning when sexual reproduction is possible—"[c]opying . . . as a means by which parents can have the child of their dreams," as Wilmut puts it[111]—go far beyond current understandings of the freedom to have genetically-related children for rearing. Some degree of negative selection may now enter into the latter decision, for example, through carrier, embryo, and fetal screening to prevent the birth of a child with severe genetic disease.[112] A parent in those cases might sincerely claim that they would not have reproduced at all if they could not take steps to assure a healthy birth. Similarly,

---

108. Of course, the father could say: "I know that my clone would not be exactly like me because [it was] gestated and reared in a different environment, but I want a special relationship with my child, and will be more committed if he is my younger identical twin than my child by sexual reproduction," thereby arguing that he would not reproduce at all unless able to clone himself. For a similar argument and a response to it, see Robertson, *supra* note 52, at 438-39.

109. *See* Robertson, *supra* note 12, at 1404-09.

110. The Posners give the example of Humbert Humbert wishing to clone and presumably rear Lolita. *See* Posner & Posner, *supra* note 53, at 259 n.14. (referencing VLADIMIR NABOKOV, LOLITA (1955)). In this case the person instigating the cloning might truly love the resulting child, but in a way that would not be good for that child.

111. Wilmut, *supra* note 1, at 76.

112. *See* Robertson, *supra* note 52, at 432-35.

when germline gene therapy or other forms of prebirth genetic modification becomes available, they could argue that they would not have children unless they could engage in genetic modification. Cases of genetic modification, however, still have both rearing parents genetically connected to the child whose genome they have modified in order to protect her health or well-being.[113]

In short, the claim to use reproductive cloning in lieu of sexual reproduction hardly seems to be an aspect of procreative freedom as conventionally understood, even though cloning in the case of reproductive failure does fit those understandings. Nor would its denial greatly limit sexual reproduction or cloning in other circumstances. One can formulate coherent views of procreative freedom without including the right to choose the entire genome of one's child when sexual reproduction is otherwise possible.

How long this conception of procreation and procreative liberty will continue to prevail is another matter. As with other reprogenetic questions, answers that define or reconstitute our conceptions of procreation, kinship, and family will be provided as we confront and make those choices. If future attitudes and value commitments change with scientific advances, much greater freedom to select and shape offspring genomes may be recognized, including the freedom to rear a clone of oneself or of another person even when sexual reproduction is feasible. At present, however, cloning in lieu of sexual reproduction does not appear to be part of procreative liberty as we now understand or define it. Once human cloning is shown to be safe and effective, policy for the immediate future should permit cloning in cases of reproductive failure without also authorizing it when sexual reproduction is possible.

VI. HOMOSEXUAL CLONING

The distinction between Model 1 and Model 2 reproductive cloning also illuminates questions of homosexual cloning. Gays and lesbians have a special interest in reproductive cloning because of the discrimination which they have experienced in their efforts to have and rear children.[114] Indeed, homosexual groups were among the first proponents of cloning, perceiving cloning as a way to control their reproduction

---

113. Cases of intentional diminishment are a different matter, though the parents might still claim that diminishing the child's capacity for hearing, for example, will benefit her if her parents are deaf, and she will be raised in a deaf environment. *See* Robertson, *supra* note 52, at 438-39, 464-67.

114. *See* William N. Eskridge, Jr. & Edward Stein, *Queer Clones, in* CLONES AND CLONES, *supra* note 53, at 95, 95-96.

free of homophobic discrimination in their efforts to form families.[115] For lesbians, it offered the unique advantage of reproduction without the need of a male, which is an important goal for some lesbians. It also allowed a woman to reproduce alone, for she herself could provide the mtDNA and cytoplasm, nuclear DNA, and gestation needed to produce a child.[116] The appeal of cloning to gay males is less clear. It may be based less on grounds of feasibility as in the case of lesbians, and more on the wish to select the genome of the child.

A. *Lesbian Cloning*

I will assume that lesbians have the same right to reproduce that other women, single or married, have, i.e., the right to have genetically-related children to rear.[117] Lesbian cloning poses the question of whether their right to clone to form families exists even if homosexual women have the same access to men or sperm banks that married heterosexual couples do. If they do have access to sperm, a single lesbian or lesbian couple who is fertile could each contribute biologically to the birth of a child via sexual reproduction.[118] If the woman is single, she could have artificial insemination with donor sperm, and then gestate and rear her child, with or without involvement of the genetic father.[119] If she has a lesbian partner, one of them could be inseminated and then gestate, with both sharing rearing. In some states the nonbiologic rearing partner could adopt the child and thus legally establish rearing rights and duties.[120] If both partners wanted a biologic connection, they could undergo IVF, with one partner providing the egg and the other gestation. In that case presumably each would be considered the legal mother if that were

---

115. *See* Anita Manning, *Pressing a "Right" to Clone Humans: Some Gays Foresee Reproduction Option*, USA TODAY, Mar. 6, 1997, at D1.

116. *See* Eskridge & Stein, *supra* note 114, at 98-99.

117. Gay males also have the same rights to reproduce and rear as male heterosexuals have.

118. If she is infertile due to uterine or health factors, she would need someone else to gestate to produce a genetically-related child. If she were gametically infertile, she could receive an egg donation and then gestate. Only in that latter case would she need to clone herself in order to have a genetic connection with offspring.

119. This would depend upon the agreement between the woman and the sperm source and applicable state laws. *See, e.g.,* Adoption of Tammy, 619 N.E.2d 315, 316 (Mass. 1993) (describing the adoption surrender signed by the biological father of the daughter of a lesbian couple); *see also* Alexa E. King, *Solomon Revisited: Assigning Parenthood in the Context of Collaborative Reproduction*, 5 UCLA WOMEN'S L.J. 329, 361-65 (1995) (providing an overview of contractual parenting arrangements).

120. *See, e.g.,* Adoption of Tammy, 619 N.E.2d at 316; *In re* Adoption of Two Children by H.N.R., 666 A.2d 535, 536 (N.J. Super. Ct. App. Div. 1995); *In re* Jacob, 660 N.E.2d 397, 398 (N.Y. 1995); *In re* Adoption of B.L.V.B., 628 A.2d 1271, 1272 (Vt. 1993).

their clear preconception agreement for that arrangement.[121]

Although fertile lesbians have no physical impediment to sexual reproduction and increasingly no social impediment either, it would be a mistake to view all cases of a fertile lesbian's decision to engage in reproductive cloning as a Model 2 rather than a Model 1 use of cloning. In the case hypothesized, the decision to clone is not so much to have a child with a particular genome as it is to have a child free of sperm or gametes outside the lesbian relationship. In addition, reproductive cloning would enable each partner to contribute genetically to the child whom they would both rear (one providing the nuclear DNA and the other cytoplasm and mtDNA, with either of them gestating), which is not now possible even when one partner provides the egg and the other partner gestates.[122] If the woman were single, she could reproduce by herself by providing the egg in which the nucleus of one of her somatic cells is placed, and then bear the resulting embryo to term.[123]

The normative question presented by a lesbian's choice to clone rather than reproduce sexually is whether her desire to reproduce without male involvement should be respected as much as any desire to have and rear genetically-related children. If a woman's wish to have children without male gametes is valued as an essential part of her procreation, then the need to clone herself, whether she is alone or with a partner, can plausibly be viewed as a case of reproductive failure. She cannot then reproduce without a man sexually, and thus must resort to cloning, just as a gametically infertile heterosexual couple that wishes to have genetic children to rear might choose cloning of the husband over anonymous sperm donation. In neither case would sexual reproduction enable them to produce a genetically-related child to rear.

The case of a single lesbian deserves similar treatment. A gay woman would have no need to clone in order to have genetically-related

---

121. There would be no reason to prefer the gestational over the genetic mother when there was an agreement for both to be rearing mothers. *But see* Johnson v. Calvert, 851 P.2d 776, 787 (Cal. 1993) (holding that a gestational surrogate who carries an implanted embryo containing none of her genetic material to term is not the "natural mother" of the resulting child under California law).

122. The possibility of sharing mtDNA and nuclear DNA may limit the desire to create a chimera made from clones of each, if that procedure were ever safe and legal, in order to produce a child sharing the genes of each partner. *See* SILVER, *supra* note 99, at 180-82; Eskridge & Stein, *supra* note 114, at 96-97. The creation—much less acceptance—of human chimeras is more distant in the future than is reproductive cloning, and may never be a practical alternative for lesbians or gay men who want to reproduce with a same-sex partner.

123. Similarly, a single, fertile, heterosexual woman who wishes to reproduce without donor sperm might choose to clone herself in order to procreate. *See* Katz, *supra* note 50, at 57-58. (raising the fears that men, as agents of reproduction, could become superfluous).

children because through artificial insemination or coitus she could conceive and then gestate a child. A single woman who did not want a male source of sperm, even anonymous donor sperm from a commercial sperm bank, might elect to clone herself. If her choice to eschew male gametes is respected as an essential part of her reproduction, she would be in the same position as an infertile heterosexual couple who decides to clone instead of using an anonymous sperm donor.[124]

In these cases the choice to clone is to establish a genetic connection between the child and rearing parent without male involvement, not to have a child with a particular genome as such. If the choice to eschew male involvement deserves respect, then the situation is very much like that of an infertile heterosexual couple who clones the husband to provide him with a genetic connection to the child whom he rears, and not because of a desire *per se* to replicate another individual. Lesbian cloning to avoid male involvement might then be perceived as an instance of Model 1 reproductive cloning, the equivalent of reproductive failure because sexual reproduction is not feasible.

B. Gay Male Cloning

It is much harder to view gay male cloning as a Model 1 use where sexual reproduction is not physically or socially available than it is to view lesbian cloning in that light. Instead, it appears to be a case of sexually fertile individuals choosing to clone in order to obtain or select a child with a particular genome and relationship to the rearing parent. No man, whether gay or straight, can reproduce sexually or by cloning without the assistance of a woman to provide an egg and gestate.[125] Nor is it possible for each male partner to contribute biologically to the child in the way that each lesbian partner could, with one partner providing mtDNA and cytoplasm and gestating, and the other providing nuclear

124. If a single lesbian has the right to clone herself, it may be difficult to bar a single, heterosexual, fertile woman from doing so as well, unless the preference to procreate by cloning oneself rather than use donor sperm carries more weight when it derives from a lesbian ideology or belief system than when it springs from the convenience of not having to risk having a child with a genetic father who might later claim rearing rights. Of course, the clone source's own father would be the genetic father of the clone of the woman, though his social role, if any, would most likely be that of grandfather rather than father.

125. *See* Robertson, *supra* note 62, at 214-15. The use of bovine eggs to receive nuclear transfer, as has been suggested for therapeutic cloning, is unlikely to work here, and faces social and other objections, such as mixing animal and human. *See* Rebecca Dresser, *Ethical and Legal Issues in Patenting New Animal Life*, 28 JURIMETRICS J. 399, 415 (1988) (finding that patenting critics are alarmed by the prospect of the creation of animal-human creatures).

DNA.[126] If a woman's cooperation must in any case be obtained to provide an egg and gestation, cloning alone will not enable a man to produce a child who has no alternative feasible way to have a genetic child to rear. If so, he cannot claim that cloning is necessary for him to have and rear genetically-related children because sexual reproduction also requires that help. Nor can he justify the choice to clone as the lesbian can on the grounds of aversion to reproduction with the opposite sex. If he is to reproduce at all, he will need the assistance of a woman.

The use of cloning by gay males would thus seem to be a case of seeking to have a child with a particular genome rather than having a child who is genetically connected at all.[127] In most instances, one could hypothesize that the DNA chosen would be that of the individual himself, perhaps in part to increase the chances that the child will be gay and thus perpetuate gay culture.[128] If so, it would raise the question of the right to choose children's nuclear genomes regardless of the ability to reproduce sexually—the issue discussed above in the context of cloning one of the partners when there is no reproductive failure. If single or married heterosexuals do not have the right to clone themselves or others when they can reproduce sexually, it is hard to see why gay males would have a greater right to clone. In neither case is cloning necessary for their reproduction to occur. Of course, if heterosexuals are permitted to clone when there is no reproductive failure, then homosexuals should be free to do so as well.

VII. CONCLUSION

Public policy regarding human cloning should avoid painting with the broad brush that has characterized much of the public discussion to date. A rational approach requires recognition of distinctions between therapeutic and reproductive cloning, and within reproductive cloning, between cloning in cases of reproductive failure and cloning to select the genome of offspring when sexual reproduction is possible.

---

126. *See* Eskridge & Stein, *supra* note 114, at 96-97. A chimera created with the genes of two different males would make each a genetic father of the child, but such a procedure is too distant in the future to be a practical option. *See* SILVER, *supra* note 99, at 180-82.

127. The case of a gay, *infertile* male would be different. He could argue that he needs to clone in order to have a genetically-related child to rear. If single, infertile, heterosexual males have the right to clone themselves, then it follows that homosexual males should as well, for one cannot meaningfully distinguish their interest in having genetically-related children for rearing or their ability to rear based on their sexual orientation.

128. *See* Eskridge & Stein, *supra* note 114, at 104. The genetic or inherited component of homosexuality is unclear, although some studies show that it may be responsible for 20 percent to 38 percent of homosexuality.

With therapeutic cloning, the main ethical issues arise from conflicts over the status and respect owed preimplantation human embryos, and not from cloning *per se*. Those ethical issues involve questions of whether embryos have rights or interests, when they may be discarded or destroyed, and whether they may be created solely for research or therapeutic purposes. If ES cell science progresses as hoped, answers to those questions will largely determine the extent to which therapeutic cloning occurs.

With regard to reproductive cloning, the chief question is whether any instance of it should ever be permitted. The strongest case for reproductive cloning arises in cases of gametic failure, where a married couple has no other way than cloning to have a genetic kinship relation with the child whom they rear. In that case, the key question is whether a couple who chooses to clone one of the spouses could still be responsible parents who are committed to the autonomy, individuality, and well-being of the resulting child. A plausible case, based on the interests that parents ordinarily have in the well-being of their children, can be made that couples who choose to clone in these circumstances could responsibly and lovingly rear the children who result from nuclear cloning of their own DNA.

The case for reproductive cloning where there is no reproductive failure, however, is at present much weaker. Under conventional understandings of reproduction, parenting, and kinship, it is difficult to understand why a couple that could reproduce sexually would nevertheless choose to clone one of themselves or a third party (other than a previous child). While they might claim that they would have a family only if they could clone, and then can demonstrate that they would be responsible rearing parents if they did so, their claim roams too far from current understanding of the values that make reproduction such an important right to merit the same respect that cloning in the case of reproductive failure deserves. As progress in reprogenetics occurs and attitudes and values change, however, those conceptions of acceptable reproduction might change as well.

The idea of reproductive cloning is likely to be contested for some time to come. Even if cloning by gametically infertile married couples is accepted in carefully limited circumstances, contests over the use of reproductive cloning by unmarried persons and homosexuals will continue. In resolving those disputes, the distinction between the two models of human reproductive cloning presented in this Article may prove useful.

Part V
Limits to Procreative Liberty

[12]

STERILIZATION OF MENTALLY RETARDED PERSONS: REPRODUCTIVE RIGHTS AND FAMILY PRIVACY

ELIZABETH S. SCOTT*

Sterilization is one of the most frequently chosen forms of contraception in the world;[1] many persons who do not want to have children select this simple, safe, and effective means of avoiding unwanted pregnancy. For individuals who are mentally disabled, however, sterilization has more ominous associations. Until recently, involuntary sterilization was used as a weapon of the state in the war against mental deficiency. Under eugenic sterilization laws in effect in many states, retarded persons were routinely sterilized without their consent or knowledge.[2]

---

* Associate Professor and Director, Center for the Study of Children and the Law, University of Virginia School of Law. J.D. 1977, University of Virginia.

My interest in the impact of the sterilization reform laws on families arose out of my association with the Forensic Psychiatry Clinic at the University of Virginia, an interdisciplinary clinic associated with the Law School and Medical School. This clinic has frequently conducted psychological evaluations of mentally disabled persons whose parents sought sterilization under Virginia's reform law. My observation of these individuals and their families has influenced my thinking on these issues. Several examples in this article are taken from Forensic Psychiatry Clinic cases.

I would like to thank my colleagues Kenneth Abraham, Richard Bonnie, Nancy Ehrenreich, Gary Melton, John Monahan, Gary Peller, and Walter Wadlington for their helpful comments on earlier drafts of this article. Special thanks are due to Robert Scott. I also thank Cathy Basham, John D'Amico, Margaret Rice, and Amy Nickell for research assistance.

1. See Isaacs, *Reproductive Rights—1983: An International Survey,* 14 COLUM. HUM. RTS. L. REV. 311, 328 (1983) (90 to 100 million couples worldwide choose sterilization as a method of contraception). In the United States, sterilization is the most popular form of birth control for couples over thirty, and it rivals the Pill as a method of contraception for all couples. *Id.*

Salpingectomy (tubal ligation) is a surgical procedure by which the fallopian tubes are tied and severed. There are many different methods of performing tubal ligation, ranging from abdominal incisions to laparoscopy, a microsurgical procedure. See R. HATCHER, F. GUEST, F. STEWART, G. STEWART, J. TRUSSELL, S. CEREL & W. CATES, CONTRACEPTIVE TECHNOLOGY 1986-1987, at 283-93 (1986) [hereinafter CONTRACEPTIVE TECHNOLOGY]. Vasectomy, the most effective means of male fertility control, is a surgical excision of the vas deferens (a duct that carries sperm). *Id.* at 104, 281-83.

2. For a discussion of the eugenic sterilization movement of the early twentieth century, see *infra* notes 10-13 and accompanying text. See generally Lombardo, *Three Generations, No Imbeciles, New Light on* Buck v. Bell, 60 N.Y.U. L. REV. 30, 31 (1985). It is estimated that almost 64,000 persons had been involuntarily sterilized under state eugenic sterilization laws by 1963. The practice was most prevalent in California (20,108 sterilizations), Virginia (7162 sterilizations), and North Carolina (6297 sterilizations). EUGENIC STERILIZATION app. at 1 (J. Robitscher ed. 1973). In Conservatorship of Valerie N., 40 Cal. 3d 143, 152, 707 P.2d 760, 765, 219 Cal. Rptr. 387, 392 (1985), the California Supreme Court noted that California led the nation in eugenic sterilization. This factor may have influenced the legislature's enactment of a law barring the sterilization of

STERILIZATION   807

Sterilization law has undergone a radical transformation in recent years.[3] Influenced by a distaste for eugenic sterilization and a desire to redress past injustices, the emerging law seeks to protect the interests of mentally disabled persons by erecting formidable barriers to sterilization. The policy goals of this reform movement are commendable. However, in its singleminded effort to prevent erroneous sterilizations, the law departs from what would be its underlying objectives: to protect where possible the individual's right to make her[4] own reproductive decisions and to ensure that any decision made by others will best protect her interests.

Current law purports to protect the individual's reproductive rights, but the focus is one-sided. Although the law protects the "right to procreate," it does so by unnecessarily burdening the reciprocal right not to procreate. The option of sterilization—seen as a legitimate exercise of the right of reproductive privacy when chosen by the normal person—may be unavailable to the retarded person. Despite rhetorical emphasis on the importance of reproductive autonomy, the paternalistic stance of the law improperly limits the freedom of some persons who may be capable of making their own reproductive choices. In many states, only a court acting as decisionmaker is deemed capable of protecting disabled persons from those who would violate their rights.

The assumption that the law's overriding purpose is to protect the right to procreate arises from the historical and political context of the

---

incompetents. CAL. PROB. CODE § 2356(d) (1981). This statutory provision was struck down in *Valerie N.*

3. The sterilization law reform movement is largely embodied in a series of judicial opinions beginning in 1980 with the Washington Supreme Court case of *In re* Guardianship of Hayes, 93 Wash. 2d 228, 239, 608 P.2d 635, 641 (1980). *See infra* notes 33-36 and accompanying text. *See also* Ruby v. Massey, 452 F. Supp. 361, 369 (D. Conn. 1978); *In re* C.D.M., 627 P.2d 607, 614 (Alaska 1981); *Valerie N.*, 40 Cal. 3d at 160, 707 P.2d at 771-72, 219 Cal. Rptr. at 399; *In re* A.W., 637 P.2d 366, 370 (Colo. 1981); Wentzel v. Montgomery Gen. Hosp., Inc., 293 Md. 685, 703, 447 A.2d 1244, 1254 (1982), *cert. denied,* 459 U.S. 1147 (1983); *In re* Moe, 385 Mass. 555, 559, 432 N.E.2d 712, 716 (1982); *In re* Penny N., 120 N.H. 269, 271-72, 414 A.2d 541, 543 (1980); *In re* Grady, 85 N.J. 235, 258-62, 426 A.2d 467, 479-81 (1981); *In re* Sallmaier, 85 Misc. 2d 295, 297, 378 N.Y.S.2d 989, 991 (Sup. Ct. 1976); *In re* Terwilliger, 304 Pa. Super. 553, 564-68, 450 A.2d 1376, 1382-84 (1982); *In re* Guardianship of Eberhardy, 102 Wis. 2d 539, 578-79, 307 N.W.2d 881, 899 (1981). Several states have enacted reform statutes in recent years. *See* CONN. GEN. STAT. ANN. § 45-78y(b) (West Supp. 1986); ME. REV. STAT. ANN. tit. 34-B, §§ 7001-7017 (Supp. 1986); OR. REV. STAT. § 436.305(3) (1983); UTAH CODE ANN. § 64-10-8(4) (1986); VT. STAT. ANN. tit. 18, § 8705 (Supp. 1986); VA. CODE ANN. §§ 54-325.10 to .12 (1982). For a discussion of the reform laws, see *infra* notes 31-58 and accompanying text.

4. This article uses the feminine pronoun to refer to the mentally retarded person for whom sterilization is proposed because it appears that the issue arises much more frequently with females than with males. For example, all cases cited *supra* note 3 involved females. Furthermore, some of the analysis, such as that involving the intrusiveness of hysterectomy, applies only to females. Nonetheless, much of the analysis applies to both males and females.

reform movement. It is not based on a careful analysis of the retarded person's interest in reproductive autonomy and how this interest may be affected by her disability. There is an understandable reluctance to undertake such analysis; even asking the question implies differences in the interests of retarded and nonretarded people. However, the failure to discern the actual interests at stake can lead to erroneous decisions contrary to the normative objective of the law.

This article focuses on parents' efforts to obtain sterilization of their mentally retarded children. As a result of the trend toward deinstitutionalization, a growing number of mentally disabled individuals live with their parents. Because current law reacts primarily to the state's historical wrongful treatment of institutionalized persons,[5] it is not sufficiently responsive to the needs of retarded individuals who live with their families.[6]

Part I of the article describes the current law and explores how its paternalistic approach fails to protect the interests of mentally disabled persons when their parents propose sterilization.[7] Part II develops an alternative approach, which I will call the "autonomy model."[8] This model is developed primarily through an analysis of the effects of mental disability on three dimensions of the disabled person's reproductive interest—avoiding unwanted pregnancy, having children, and making autonomous choices. Part III explores the implications of the autonomy model for the formulation of an optimal sterilization rule.[9] The model suggests that the law should maximize individual and family autonomy and minimize paternalistic intervention by the state. The goal of protecting the retarded person's interests is largely achieved by choosing the appropriate decisionmaker; in most cases this will be the individual herself or her parents. Under this approach, the court's role in most cases is limited to deciding whether the individual has the capacity to make her own choices or whether her parents must make the decision for her.

---

5. Many eugenic sterilization laws, directed toward institutionalized patients, authorized the director of such facilities to make the decision or to petition a court. In Ruby v. Massey, 452 F. Supp. 361 (D. Conn. 1978), a Connecticut law that permitted sterilization only of mentally disabled individuals in institutions was struck down on equal protection grounds. *Id.* at 367-69. Some laws required sterilization as a precondition to release from state institutions. *See, e.g.,* Buck v. Bell, 274 U.S. 200, 204 (1927).

6. Indeed, most of the judicial opinions developing the paternalism model involved efforts by a parent or guardian to sterilize a child cared for at home. *See, e.g., In re* Grady, 85 N.J. 235, 240-42, 251, 426 A.2d 467, 469-70, 475 (1981); *In re* Sallmaier, 85 Misc. 2d 295, 296-97, 378 N.Y.S.2d 989, 989-90 (Sup. Ct. 1976).

7. *See infra* notes 10-61 and accompanying text.

8. *See infra* notes 62-139 and accompanying text.

9. *See infra* notes 140-80 and accompanying text.

I. CURRENT STERILIZATION LAW: A PATERNALISM MODEL

A. The Context of Reform.

Three factors have stimulated and shaped the reform of sterilization law: the discrediting of the eugenic theory, the development of the constitutional doctrine of reproductive privacy, and the changing conception of mental retardation. The vigilant stance of current law is largely a response to the unsavory history of eugenic sterilization in this country.[10] During the first half of this century, laws in many states authorized sterilization of mentally deficient persons and others believed to be societal burdens.[11] These laws were based largely on eugenic theory, which enjoyed considerable popularity in the progressive era. The theory posited that intelligence and most personality traits are genetically based and are predictably inherited by children from their parents.[12] The objective of

---

10. *See In re* Moe, 385 Mass. 555, 559, 432 N.E.2d 712, 717 (1982) ("We are well aware of the sordid history of compulsory eugenic sterilization laws in the United States."); *Grady,* 85 N.J. at 245, 426 A.2d at 472 ("[W]e have serious doubts about the scientific validity of eugenic sterilization."); *In re* Guardianship of Hayes, 93 Wash. 2d 228, 236, 608 P.2d 635, 640 (1980) ("[T]he theoretical foundation for eugenic sterilization as a method of improving society has been disproved."). Rejection of compulsory sterilization laws on scientific and social policy grounds has had broad support in the legal literature since the 1960's. *See* Burgdorf & Burgdorf, *The Wicked Witch is Almost Dead:* Buck v. Bell *and the Sterilization of Handicapped Persons,* 50 TEMP. L.Q. 995, 1033-34 (1977); Ferster, *Eliminating the Unfit—Is Sterilization the Answer?,* 27 OHIO ST. L.J. 591, 619-25 (1966); Murdock, *Sterilization of the Retarded: A Problem or a Solution?,* 62 CALIF. L. REV. 917, 934-35 (1974); Sherlock & Sherlock, *Sterilizing the Retarded: Constitutional, Statutory, and Policy Alternatives,* 60 N.C.L. REV. 943, 980-83 (1982).

11. Sterilization laws were directed at the mentally retarded, mentally ill, epileptic, and criminal populations. Indiana passed the first involuntary sterilization law in 1907. Act of March 9, 1907, ch. 215, 1907 IND. ACTS 377 (repealed 1963). By 1925, twenty-three states had passed eugenic sterilization laws. Cynkar, Buck v. Bell: *"Felt Necessities" v. Fundamental Values?,* 81 COLUM. L. REV. 1418, 1433 (1981). As late as 1966, twenty-six states had eugenic sterilization laws. Ferster, *supra* note 10, at 596. State courts often upheld sterilization laws using two police power justifications—that of preventing the birth of defective children and that of lowering the public welfare expense of supporting children whose parents could not support them. *See In re* Simpson, 180 N.E.2d 206, 208 (Ohio P. Ct. 1962); Ferster, *supra* note 10, at 609.

Some sterilization laws were used to punish habitual criminals and rapists. A Washington statute authorizing the sterilization of convicted rapists was upheld in State v. Feilen, 70 Wash. 65, 66, 126 P. 75, 76 (1912). The United States Supreme Court, however, struck down an Oklahoma statute allowing sterilization of habitual criminals in Skinner v. Oklahoma *ex rel.* Williamson, 316 U.S. 535, 542-43 (1942). Some statutes had paternalistic objectives and authorized sterilization if it was in the best interest of the individual and society. Virginia's sterilization statute was enacted in part to alleviate fears that institutionalized individuals returning to society would produce children. *See* Act of March 20, 1924, ch. 394, 1924 VA. ACTS 569, 569 (amended and recodified 1968).

12. The eugenic movement was an outgrowth of Mendelian genetics. The eugenicists, building upon Mendel's findings about the hereditability of physical traits, argued that intelligence, personality, and even character traits such as dishonesty, criminality, and laziness were directly "transmitted." *See* H. LAUGHLIN, EUGENIC STERILIZATION IN THE UNITED STATES 369 (1922). Furthermore, certain traits were associated with racial or national groups. *Id.* at 372-92 (listing "human traits which have been shown to follow definite rules of inheritance"). This view served as the basis for the Nazi eugenic policies. The accepted view was that defectives were reproducing

the eugenic sterilization laws was to protect and improve society by preventing reproduction by those who might produce defective offspring.[13]

In 1927, the Supreme Court in *Buck v. Bell*[14] upheld Virginia's ster-

---

more quickly than normal people, thus posing a significant threat to society. For an excellent historical account of the eugenic movement, see Cynkar, *supra* note 11, at 1420-35.

13. *See* H. LAUGHLIN, *supra* note 12, at 369 ("[D]efectives who are practically certain to breed principally defectives, owe a debt to the community that can be discharged only by an adequate guarantee that they shall not contribute to the next generation."). The following quote reveals the threat to society that eugenicists thought the mentally retarded posed:

> The past few years have witnessed a striking awakening of professional and popular consciousness of the widespread prevalence of feeblemindedness and its influence as a source of wretchedness to the patient himself and to his family, and as a causative factor in the production of crime, prostitution, pauperism, illegitimacy, intemperance, and other complex social diseases. . . . The feebleminded are a parasitic, predatory class, never capable of self-support or of managing their own affairs. . . . They cause unutterable sorrow at home and are a menace and danger to the community. . . . Feebleminded women are almost invariably immoral and if at large usually become carriers of venereal disease or give birth to children who are as defective as themselves. . . . Every feebleminded person, especially the high-grade imbecile, is a potential criminal, needing only the proper environment and opportunity for the development and expression of his criminal tendencies.

S. DAVIES, SOCIAL CONTROL OF THE FEEBLEMINDED 56 (1923), *quoted in* Cynkar, *supra* note 11, at 1424-25.

A 1934 law review note, arguing for a sterilization law in Kentucky, also reflects this perception of societal threat: "Since time immemorial, the criminal and defective have been the 'cancer of society.' Strong, intelligent, useful families are becoming smaller and smaller; while irresponsible, diseased, defective families are becoming larger. The result can only be race degeneration." Note, *A Sterilization Statute for Kentucky?*, 23 KY. L.J. 168, 168 (1934), *quoted in* Burgdorf & Burgdorf, *supra* note 10, at 998.

14. 274 U.S. 200, 207 (1927). Prior to *Buck v. Bell*, most courts struck down sterilization statutes as unconstitutional. *See* Davis v. Berry, 216 F. 413, 417 (S.D. Iowa 1914) (cruel and unusual punishment grounds), *rev'd as moot*, 242 U.S. 468 (1917); Williams v. Smith, 190 Ind. 526, 528, 131 N.E. 2, 2 (1921) (due process grounds); Haynes v. Lapeer, 201 Mich. 138, 145, 166 N.W. 938, 941 (1918) (equal protection grounds); *see also* Burgdorf & Burgdorf, *supra* note 10, at 1000-01 nn.44-48; Ferster, *supra* note 10, at 593-94 nn.11-12.

Buck v. Bell is often cited to illustrate the abuses of eugenic sterilization policy. *Bell* was the test case for Virginia's new sterilization law. Carrie Buck was a 17 year-old girl who had been committed to a state institution for the epileptic and feebleminded after giving birth to an illegitimate daughter. The Virginia law required that institutionalized patients be sterilized for eugenic and therapeutic reasons as a condition of release. *See* Cynkar, *supra* note 11, at 1437-38. Subsequent historical research has suggested that neither Carrie, her mother, nor Carrie's daughter (who was an infant at the time of the "diagnosis") were "imbeciles" as characterized by Justice Holmes in his much quoted proclamation, "[t]hree generations of imbeciles are enough." *Bell*, 274 U.S. at 207. Indeed, it has been reported that Carrie's daughter was on the second grade honor roll before dying at age eight. *See* Lombardo, *supra* note 2, at 61. It seems probable that the moralistic impulses of the eugenicists influenced the categorization of this family as feebleminded. *See* Cynkar, *supra* note 11, at 52-53. Carrie and her mother both produced children out of wedlock. The testimony of Dr. Priddy, the director of the institution, also suggests that sterilization was viewed as a way to achieve social control over the poor: "[T]hese people belong to the shiftless, ignorant, and worthless class of anti-social whites of the South . . . [about whom] it is impossible to get intelligent and satisfactory data . . . ." Lombardo, *supra* note 2, at 51-52. *See also* Cynkar, *supra* note 11, at 1439 (discussing use of sterilization as method for controlling poverty).

This harsh tone may obscure the fact that eugenic policies were not viewed as oppressive infringements on individual rights, but as tools of social reform. Eugenicists attributed most social

ilization law against constitutional challenge and implicitly accepted the validity of eugenic theory. Even at that time, however, the scientific merit of the theory was controversial;[15] it has since been largely discredited.[16] Reports of widespread sterilization in Nazi Germany led to increased criticism of eugenic sterilization laws. By the 1960's, involuntary sterilization was frequently characterized as an unjustified intrusion by the state on individual liberty and privacy.[17] The reform law that has

---

problems to heredity; they linked crime, prostitution, and poverty to mental deficiency. Progressives therefore embraced these policies as state action designed to improve society, arguing that if afflicted individuals were prevented from reproducing, society's ills would disappear. Justice Holmes was articulating the accepted liberal view in endorsing the eugenic rationale.

15. *See* Cynkar, *supra* note 11, at 1420-35. It appears, though, that Buck's attorney, Whitehead, never fully briefed this issue for argument before the Court. It was only in the petition for rehearing (following a storm of public protest over Holmes's opinion) that Whitehead included the strongest arguments against the sterilization law—questioning for the first time the "scientific" propositions espoused by eugenic theories. Some have pointed to this sequence of events to support the allegation that *Bell* was a "friendly suit." Lombardo, *supra* note 2, at 57.

16. Researchers in genetics increasingly disassociated themselves from the eugenic movement as scientific understanding of genetics became more sophisticated in the 1920's and 1930's. In 1936, the American Neurological Association Committee for the Investigation of Eugenical Sterilization issued a statement opposing eugenic sterilization and challenging its scientific premises. *See* Ferster, *supra* note 10, at 602-03. In 1937, a committee of the American Medical Association also adopted this position. *Id.* at 603. The critical scientific fallacy underlying the sterilization laws is that "conditions such as *feeblemindedness* lump together cases having no genetic component with those in which there may be a partial or complete genetic contribution." Moorhead, *Views of a Geneticist on Eugenic Sterilization,* in EUGENIC STERILIZATION, *supra* note 2, at 115. For an interesting history of the eugenics movement, see Kevles, *The Annals of Eugenics,* NEW YORKER, Oct. 8, 1984, at 51; Oct. 15, 1984, at 52; Oct. 22, 1984, at 92; Oct. 29, 1984, at 51.

This is not to say that intelligence does not have a hereditary component. Most modern experts agree that genetic factors significantly influence intelligence and that there is, in general, a relationship between children's and parents' intelligence. Scarr-Salapatek, *Genetics and the Development of Intelligence,* 4 CHILD DEV. RES. 1 (1975). Psychological studies indicate that both heredity and environment can influence intelligence. The most impressive evidence for some genetic determination of intelligence comes from studies of adopted children. Professor Munzinger critically evaluated studies of adopted children and found that five studies (involving 351 families) showed that the average correlation between the parents' and their adopted children's IQs was 0.19. B. MARTIN, ABNORMAL PSYCHOLOGY 567 (1977). He found a significantly greater correlation between the intelligence level of the same children and their biological parents. *Id.*

17. The development of the doctrine of reproductive privacy in the 1960's and 1970's has affected the constitutional analysis of sterilization laws. Since eugenic sterilization laws infringe a fundamental right, these laws are subject to strict scrutiny rather than the rational-basis review engaged in by Justice Holmes in *Bell.* *See* Roe v. Wade, 410 U.S. 113, 155 (1973); Skinner v. Oklahoma *ex rel.* Williamson, 316 U.S. 535, 541 (1942). The Virginia statute in *Bell* probably would not meet this heightened scrutiny given the dubious validity of eugenic theory. Indeed, several courts authorizing parens patriae sterilization have assumed that *Bell* is constitutionally suspect. *See In re* A.W., 637 P.2d 366, 368 (Colo. 1981); *In re* Grady, 85 N.J. 235, 246, 426 A.2d 467, 472 (1981).

Even if the state could establish that involuntary sterilization was necessary to promote a compelling state interest, the statute in *Bell* might fall under the "least restrictive alternative" doctrine. In Shelton v. Tucker, 364 U.S. 479 (1960), the Supreme Court stated this doctrine as follows: "Even though the governmental purpose be legitimate and substantial, that purpose cannot be pursued by means that broadly stifle fundamental personal liberties when the end can be more narrowly

emerged in recent years represents a vehement rejection of the philosophy and policy of the eugenic movement.[18] It is explicitly designed to protect the interests of the retarded person rather than those of society.

A second impetus to reform has been the development of the constitutional doctrine of reproductive privacy.[19] A principal reason why courts and legislatures have been concerned about protecting the reproductive rights of retarded persons[20] is that reproductive rights in general

---

achieved. The breadth of legislative abridgment must be viewed in the light of less drastic means for achieving the same basic purpose." *Id.* at 488 (footnote omitted). *See generally* Hoffmann & Faust, *Least Restrictive Treatment of the Mentally Ill: A Doctrine in Search of Its Senses,* 14 SAN DIEGO L. REV. 1100 (1977).

Numerous commentators have criticized eugenic sterilization and Justice Holmes's opinion in *Bell* from a constitutional perspective. *See* Sherlock & Sherlock, *supra* note 10, at 954; Zenoff, *Reappraisal of Eugenic Sterilization Laws,* 10 CLEV.-MARSHALL L. REV. 149, 159-60 (1961); Note, *Eugenic Sterilization Statutes: A Constitutional Re-Evaluation,* 14 J. FAM. L. 280, 297 (1975).

18. Twenty-eight eugenic sterilization statutes were reported in 1956. *See* O'Hara & Sanks, *Eugenic Sterilization,* 45 GEO. L.J. 20, 42 (1956). Many of these have been repealed since the 1960's. *See* CAL. WELF. & INST. CODE § 7254 (West Supp. 1972) (repealed 1972); ME. REV. STAT. ANN. tit. 34, § 2462 (1978) (repealed 1981); OKLA. STAT. ANN. tit. 43A, § 341 (West 1979) (repealed 1983). Today only a few states have police-power sterilization laws. *See* MISS. CODE ANN. § 41-45-1 (1972); N.C. GEN. STAT. § 35-36 (1984); S.C. CODE ANN. § 44-47-10 (Law. Co-op. 1976); W. VA. CODE § 27-16-1 (1980).

19. A series of Supreme Court opinions beginning with Griswold v. Connecticut, 381 U.S. 479, 485 (1965) (striking down law banning use of contraceptives), developed the modern doctrine of reproductive privacy. Several decisions have struck down restrictions on the use and sale of contraceptives and on a woman's right to choose abortion. *See, e.g.,* Thornburgh v. American College of Obstetricians & Gynecologists, 106 S. Ct. 2169, 2182 (1986) (women have constitutionally protected right to abortion; state regulation may not intimidate women into continuing pregnancies); City of Akron v. Akron Center for Reproductive Health, Inc., 462 U.S. 416, 452 (1983) (city cannot impose restrictive requirements on abortion or determine that all minors under age 15 are too immature to make abortion decision); Bellotti v. Baird, 443 U.S. 622, 651 (1979) (plurality opinion) (mature minors have right to make abortion decisions without parental consent); Carey v. Population Servs. Int'l, 431 U.S. 678, 694 (1977) (law prohibiting sale of contraceptives to anyone under age 16 restricts reproductive privacy); Planned Parenthood v. Danforth, 428 U.S. 52, 69-70 (1976) (states cannot give husband or parents veto over wife's or daughter's abortion decision by requiring consent); *Roe,* 410 U.S. at 164-66 (women have right to terminate pregnancy through abortion until viability); Doe v. Bolton, 410 U.S. 179, 201 (1973) (requirement that abortions be performed in hospitals and approved by a hospital committee unduly restricts reproductive privacy); Eisenstadt v. Baird, 405 U.S. 438, 443 (1972) (making contraceptives unavailable to single women infringes reproductive privacy).

Aside from the uncertain scientific basis of eugenic theories, there has been a vehement rejection on ethical grounds of the *policy* that less intelligent members of society should not be allowed to reproduce.

20. The judicial opinions dealing with parens patriae sterilization repeatedly emphasize the importance of protecting the retarded person's constitutional right of reproductive privacy. *See* Conservatorship of Valerie N., 40 Cal. 3d 143, 161, 707 P.2d 760, 772, 219 Cal. Rptr. 387, 399 (1985) (incompetent women have procreative choice that is recognized as fundamental right); *see also In re* Moe, 385 Mass. 555, 563-64, 432 N.E.2d 712, 719 (1982) (decision to bear child at heart of constitutionally protected right to privacy); *Grady,* 85 N.J. at 250, 426 A.2d at 474 (inability to make reproductive decisions should not result in forfeiture of constitutional right); *In re* Guardianship of Hayes, 93 Wash. 2d 228, 234, 608 P.2d 635, 639 (1980) (sterilization implicates right to privacy and fundamental right to procreate).

have been accorded a special status in recent years. The right of normal adults and mature minors[21] to avoid unwanted pregnancy through abortion, contraception, and (for adults) sterilization[22] is well ·established. The right to procreate, in contrast, has received little attention, probably because it has seldom been challenged.[23] The development of the doctrine of reproductive privacy casts substantial doubt on the continued validity of involuntary sterilization laws like the one upheld in *Buck v. Bell.*[24] There is general consensus that mentally disabled persons should, to the extent that their disability allows, enjoy the same right of reproductive privacy as normal people.[25]

---

21. *See supra* note 19.

22. The Supreme Court has not addressed the issue of the right of normal adults to obtain sterilization. Lower courts, however, have expanded the right of reproductive privacy to include the right to obtain sterilization. *See* Hathaway v. Worcester City Hosp., 475 F.2d 701, 706 (1st Cir. 1973) (hospital policy banning sterilization violates equal protection clause because surgical procedures of equal risk are permitted); Ponter v. Ponter, 135 N.J. Super. 50, 55, 342 A.2d 574, 577 (1975) (married woman has constitutional right to obtain sterilization without husband's consent).

Normal minors are generally not permitted to obtain sterilization. *See, e.g.,* COLO. REV. STAT. § 27-10.5-128(1) (1982); VT. STAT. ANN. tit. 18, § 8705(a) (Supp. 1986). The enormous cost of error justifies some restriction on reproductive autonomy. Unlike abortion and contraception, the minor can postpone the sterilization decision with minimal cost.

23. *See* Robertson, *Procreative Liberty and the Control of Conception, Pregnancy, and Childbirth,* 69 VA. L. REV. 405, 406 (1983). Professor Robertson provides a comprehensive analysis of the right to procreate in the context of modern reproductive technology. He defines three dimensions of the right—conception, gestation and birth, and rearing.

The only Supreme Court decision that specifically affirms the right to procreate is Skinner v. Oklahoma *ex rel.* Williamson, 316 U.S. 535 (1942). The Court did not analyze the substance of the right but described it as essential to the "survival of the race." *Id.* at 541.

24. Nonetheless, constitutional analysis of the reform law is complicated by two factors. The application of the doctrine of reproductive privacy to persons with questionable capacity for autonomous decisionmaking is unclear to the extent that the right of reproductive privacy is the right to control reproductive decisions. Furthermore, unlike eugenic law, the reform law is designed to promote the mentally retarded person's interest (by making the option of sterilization available); it is not inherently an infringement by the state on a fundamental right. As noted above, the right to choose sterilization is itself constitutionally protected. *See supra* note 22. Thus the application of strict scrutiny is unclear.

25. Reform advocates tend to define the retarded person's interest in reproductive privacy solely in terms of the right to procreate. In Foy v. Greenblott, 141 Cal. App. 3d 1, 9-10, 190 Cal. Rptr. 84, 90 (1983), a severely retarded woman became pregnant and had a child. She sued her conservator for negligence in failing to prevent the pregnancy and birth through contraception or abortion. The court rejected the claim on the ground that her conservator would have interfered with her right of reproductive privacy by taking such measures. *Id.* at 9, 190 Cal. Rptr. at 89-90.

Many courts that have examined sterilization laws have likewise emphasized the disabled woman's fundamental right to procreate. *See In re* Truesdell, 63 N.C. App. 258, 267, 304 S.E.2d 793, 799 (1983) ("[S]terilization not only affects the individual's fundamental right to procreate, . . . it forever deprives the individual of that basic liberty."). In Conservatorship of Valerie N., 40 Cal. 3d 143, 707 P.2d 760, 219 Cal. Rptr. 387 (1985), Chief Justice Bird, dissenting, argued to uphold California's statutory ban on the sterilization of individuals under a conservatorship on the grounds of the right to procreate. *Id.,* at 183, 707 P.2d at 788, 219 Cal. Rptr. at 415 (Bird, C.J., dissenting). Bird argued that the mentally disabled person does not have the right to be sterilized because that right is premised on the ability to make a decision. *Id.* According to Bird, the mentally disabled

The view that the mentally retarded person should exercise her rights to the fullest extent possible reflects a changing conception of mental retardation. A cognitive developmental approach has to some extent supplanted the medical model of mental retardation that emphasizes unalterable organic brain pathology.[26] With the application of cognitive developmental theory to the functioning of mentally retarded persons, there has been a corresponding appreciation that the designation "mentally retarded" applies to individuals who exhibit a broad range of deficiencies.[27]

---

person does have an unrestricted right to procreate, because she has the right to retain "the biological capabilities with which . . . she was born into this world." *Id.* at 181, 707 P.2d at 786, 219 Cal. Rptr. at 413. *See generally* Price & Burt, *Sterilization, State Action and the Concept of Consent,* 1 L. & PSYCHOLOGY REV. 57, 63-65 (1975) (characterizing third-party consent to sterilization as a deprivation of the individual's rights).

Some laws assume that the retarded person's interest in reproductive choice is like that of the normal person, and that the law's role is to remove the barrier created by her disability. The New Jersey Supreme Court articulated this view: "Lee Ann does not have the ability to make a choice between sterilization and procreation. . . . But her inability should not result in the forfeit of this constitutional interest. . . . [T]he decision . . . 'should not be discarded solely on the basis that her condition prevents her conscious exercise of the choice.' " *In re* Grady, 85 N.J. 235, 250, 426 A.2d 467, 474 (1981) (quoting *In re* Quinlan, 70 N.J. 10, 41, 355 A.2d 647, 664, *cert. denied,* 429 U.S. 922 (1976)).

26. *See* E. SCHULMAN, FOCUS ON THE RETARDED ADULT: PROGRAMS AND SERVICES 34-94 (1980). Schulman traces the historical development of conceptions of mental disability and corresponding public policy responses. The medical model of retardation dominated in the late nineteenth and early twentieth centuries. This model described and classified several organic causes of retardation including brain injury and chromosomal and genetic abnormalities such as Down's Syndrome, Tay Sachs disease, microcephaly, and hydrocephaly. The medical approach is useful in understanding severe retardation; persons with Wechsler IQs below 39 are almost always in the organically impaired category. *See* R. MACKLIN & W. GAYLIN, MENTAL RETARDATION AND STERILIZATION 13-14 (1981). But organic pathology does not explain the causes of disability in most mildly retarded persons; only 25% of mildly retarded persons are organically impaired. The remaining 75% may simply be comprised of individuals whose intelligence level is at the lower end of a continuum. *See* E. SCHULMAN, *supra,* at 55. *But see* B. MARTIN, *supra* note 16, at 570-74 (describing the extent to which mild retardation has organic causes).

Professor Zigler and others developed the cognitive developmental approach that applies Piaget's theories to the functioning of mentally retarded persons. *See* Zigler, *Mental Retardation: Current Issues and Approaches,* 2 REV. CHILD DEV. RES. 107, 111-13 (1966). Piaget postulated that human intelligence developed in a series of adaptive stages occurring in childhood and adolescence. See H. KAPLAN & B. SADOCK, MODERN SYNOPSIS OF COMPREHENSIVE TEXTBOOK OF PSYCHIATRY 57 (3d ed. 1981). Disabled persons progress through the developmental stages at a slower rate than normal children and fail to attain the higher developmental stages. The stage of cognitive development attained correlates with the level of mental retardation. *See id.* at 852.

27. A retarded person is classified by comparing her behavior to a particular age group's behavior using factors such as academic skill, social responsiveness, responsibility, and vocational performance. The classification may change as the retarded person develops or as society's expectations change. *See* H. KAPLAN & B. SADOCK, *supra* note 26, at 853. Four commonly used classifications of mental retardation have been recognized by the American Psychiatric Association's Diagnostic and Statistic Manual of Mental Disorders. *See id.* at 851. These classifications are based on the Weschler Intelligence Quotient of the affected person. The four classifications are:

Custodial programs that segregate and warehouse retarded persons are no longer endorsed by professionals. Today, programs for mentally retarded persons pursue the goal of "normalization"—the development of skills that enable the individual to live as independently and self-sufficiently as possible.[28] Issues of sexual autonomy are an important aspect

---

(1) *Mild—IQ 51 to 70.* Mildly retarded individuals can usually master basic academic skills. Adults are capable of living independently or semi-independently in the community. *See id.* at 852. Mildly retarded persons may need slight assistance such as health care reminders or help in purchasing clothes. They are coordinated, can navigate their neighborhood, can communicate and understand complex verbal concepts, and can perform semi-skilled or low skill jobs. *See* H. GROSSMAN, CLASSIFICATION IN MENTAL RETARDATION (1983). Mildly retarded individuals handle sexual impulses and urges normally and can develop appropriate adaptive skills through education. *See* R. MONAT, SEXUALITY AND THE MENTALLY RETARDED 6 (1982).

(2) *Moderate—IQ 36 to 50.* Many individuals functioning at this level can learn self-help, communication, social, and simple occupational skills, but only limited academic or vocational skills. *See* H. KAPLAN & B. SADOCK, *supra* note 26, at 852. Moderately retarded persons perform personal hygiene tasks, possess gross and fine motor coordination, use complex sentences, and read simple prose material; they may initiate activities and conscientiously perform simple household tasks. *See id.* Moderately retarded persons can learn sexual responsibility, but self-experimentation is common. *See* R. MONAT, *supra,* at 15.

(3) *Severe—IQ 20 to 35.* Severely retarded persons require continuing and close supervision, but may perform self-help and simple work tasks. *See* H. KAPLAN & B. SADOCK, *supra* note 26, at 851-52. They can usually prepare simple foods and perform uncomplicated household tasks. Severely retarded persons may use sentences and understand verbal communication, but they profit most from systematic habit training. *See id.* They do not control sexual impulses well but conditioning can alter their behavior to some extent. There is a limited ability to predict or foresee the consequences of their sexual behavior. *See* R. MONAT, *supra,* at 3-4.

(4) *Profound—IQ 0 to 20.* Profoundly retarded persons require continuing and close supervision, but some may be able to perform simple self-help tasks. They often have handicaps and require total life-support systems. *See* H. KAPLAN & B. SADOCK, *supra* note 26, at 851-52. Profoundly retarded persons do not perform all personal hygiene tasks and generally use only simple language. *See id.* Their sexual reactions are predominantly impulsive, they cannot easily engage in sexual activity on a reciprocal level, and they often masturbate in a harmful or excessive way. *See* R. MONAT, *supra,* at 4, 24-25.

28. Professor Nirje is the leading proponent of normalization. He defined the concept as "making available to the mentally subnormal patterns and conditions of everyday life which are as close as possible to the norms and patterns of the mainstream of society." Nirje, *Symposium on "Normalization": The Normalization Principle—Implications and Comments,* 16 BRIT. J. MENTAL SUBNORMALITY 62, 62 (1970). *See also* Wolfensburger, *The Principle of Normalization and Its Implication to Psychiatric Services,* 127 AM. J. PSYCHIATRY 291, 291-97 (1970). Normalization has become the primary objective of programs for the retarded.

The two central components of normalization are deinstitutionalization and educational mainstreaming. Experts generally agree that mentally retarded persons attain fuller development in community settings rather than in institutions. Retarded children develop better when they live with their families and are reared by their parents. Adults may also thrive in a well-functioning family; however, a residence for retarded adults may alternatively provide companionship and support. *See* E. SCHULMAN, *supra* note 26, at 256-83.

The normalization approach also emphasizes educational mainstreaming. The federal law dealing with the education of handicapped individuals supports this normalization principle. *See* 20 U.S.C. § 1412(5) (1982) (state must provide "procedures to assure that, to the maximum extent appropriate, handicapped children . . . are educated with children who are not handicapped").

of the normalization trend;[29] freedom and privacy in social and sexual relationships may be as important to mentally disabled persons as to others. Furthermore, marriage and parenthood are realistic options for some mildly disabled persons who, with appropriate training, may be capable of fulfilling those roles.[30] Sterilization is viewed as rarely desirable because many mentally retarded persons are presumed to have at least a potential interest in having children.

Many mildly retarded persons have been "mainstreamed" into regular classrooms. *See* E. SCHULMAN, *supra* note 26, at 65.

Implicit in the concept of normalization is the notion that mentally retarded persons should enjoy the same legal rights as others to the extent that they are able to do so. In an official statement in 1973, the American Academy of Mental Deficiency emphasized that "[m]entally retarded citizens are entitled to enjoy and exercise the same rights as are available to nonretarded citizens, to the limits of their ability to do so." *Rights of Mentally Retarded Persons: An Official Statement of the American Academy of Mental Deficiency,* MENTAL RETARDATION, Oct. 1973, at 56, 56-57. *See also* Wald, *Basic Personal and Civil Rights,* in THE PRESIDENT'S COMMITTEE ON MENTAL RETARDATION, THE MENTALLY RETARDED CITIZEN AND THE LAW 3 (1976).

Some commentators argue that zealous commitment to the principle of normalization in education may not help seriously impaired persons because the quality of the individual's educational experience depends on factors other than physical placement. *See, e.g.,* Vitello, *Cautions on the Road to Normalization,* MENTAL RETARDATION, Oct. 1974, at 39, 40.

29. The notion that mentally disabled persons are sexual beings is only recently gaining acceptance among professionals who work with this population. In the past, dealing with sexual behavior was viewed as a "problem"; usually, preventing sexual contact among residents or participants in programs/placements for mentally retarded persons was standard policy. Mentally retarded persons have traditionally been deemed incapable of controlling sexual impulses, a view that is clearly erroneous as applied to mildly retarded persons. *See* E. SCHULMAN, *supra* note 26, at 298. Today, as part of the normalization trend, sex education is an important part of programs for mentally retarded persons. Helping the individual deal with sexual issues in a positive and socially appropriate manner has become the objective of many programs. *See* S. HAARIK & K. MENNINGER, SEXUALITY, LAW, AND THE DEVELOPMENTALLY DISABLED PERSON 151 (1981); R. MONAT, *supra* note 27, at 46-49; E. SCHULMAN, *supra* note 26, at 292-312.

30. Historically, many states have statutorily prohibited or restricted marriage by mentally retarded persons. *See* Note, *The Right of the Mentally Disabled to Marry: A Statutory Evaluation,* 15 J. FAM. L. 463, 487-507 (1977). States have begun to repeal these statutes because of a growing awareness that some mentally retarded persons may successfully marry and rear children. *See* Shaman, *Persons Who Are Mentally Retarded: Their Right to Marry and Have Children,* 12 FAM. L.Q. 61, 84 (1978); Note, *Retarded Parents in Neglect Proceedings: The Erroneous Assumption of Parental Inadequacy,* 31 STAN. L. REV. 785, 804 (1979).

Mental retardation professionals generally support normalization; however, many are still concerned about the capability of mentally retarded persons to be parents. Indeed, one goal among professionals has been to promote normal relationships that are not burdened by the possibility of pregnancy. *See* E. SCHULMAN, *supra* note 26, at 301-03. There is growing recognition, however, that some mentally disabled persons can function as parents. *See* Rosenberg & McTate, *Intellectually Handicapped Mothers: Problems and Perspectives,* CHILDREN TODAY, Jan.-Feb. 1982, at 24. Authorities seem to require that mentally retarded parents provide a higher standard of care than that generally expected of normal parents. *See* Murphy, Coleman & Abel, *Human Sexuality in the Mentally Retarded,* in TREATMENT ISSUES AND INNOVATIONS IN MENTAL RETARDATION 614 (J. Matson & F. Andrasik eds. 1983). Recently there has been a focus on supportive services and training in parenting skills for mentally retarded persons. *See* Madsen, *Parenting Classes for the Mentally Retarded,* 17 MENTAL RETARDATION 195, 195 (1979); Rosenberg & McTate, *supra,* at 24.

STERILIZATION   817

B. Current Sterilization Law.

The preceding factors have stimulated the reform of sterilization law in recent years. A few jurisdictions have banned sterilization of incompetent persons altogether.[31] Under most reform laws, however, the state may authorize sterilization under its parens patriae authority if certain conditions are met.[32] Many of these laws follow a model derived from a Washington Supreme Court case, *In re Guardianship of Hayes*.[33] *Hayes* requires a two-part inquiry. First, the court must determine whether the individual is competent to make an informed medical decision about sterilization.[34] This inquiry seeks to protect the autonomy interest of the

---

31. *See* COLO. REV. STAT. § 27-10.5-128(2) (Supp. 1985) ("No person with developmental disabilities who has not given consent shall be sterilized."). In 1981, the Colorado Supreme Court carved out an exception to allow sterilization of mentally retarded minors. *See In re* A.W., 637 P.2d 366, 375 (Colo. 1981). A California law prohibiting sterilization of all persons under conservatorship, CAL. PROB. CODE § 2356 (1981), was struck down in 1985 in Conservatorship of Valerie N., 40 Cal. 3d 143, 160-61, 707 P.2d 760, 771-72, 219 Cal. Rptr. 387, 398-99 (1985). Several courts have effectively banned sterilization by refusing to allow sterilization in the absence of statutory authority. *See infra* note 32. Federal law prohibits government funding of the sterilization of minors and incompetents. *See* Relf v. Weinberger, 372 F. Supp. 1196, 1201 (D.D.C. 1974) (Secretary of HEW has no authority to fund sterilization of minors or mentally incompetent persons who are incompetent to consent to the operation); 42 C.F.R. § 50.207 (1985) (prohibiting federally assisted family-planning projects from funding hysterectomies performed solely for the purpose of sterilization).

32. During the 1960's and 1970's, many states repealed eugenic sterilization laws, often without making alternative provisions for sterilization of incompetents. Courts generally rejected petitions to obtain sterilization of mentally retarded persons because of the absence of statutory authority. *See* Wade v. Bethesda Hosp., 337 F. Supp. 671, 673-74 (S.D. Ohio 1971); Hudson v. Hudson, 373 So. 2d 310, 312 (Ala. 1979); Guardianship of Kemp, 43 Cal. App. 3d 758, 761-62, 118 Cal. Rptr. 64, 66-67 (1974); A.L. v. G.R.H., 163 Ind. App. 636, 638, 325 N.E.2d 501, 502 (1975), *cert. denied,* 425 U.S. 936 (1976); Holmes v. Powers, 439 S.W.2d 579, 580 (Ky. Ct. App. 1968); *In re* M.K.R., 515 S.W.2d 467, 470 (Mo. 1974); Frazier v. Levi, 440 S.W.2d 393, 394 (Tex. Civ. App. 1969). *But see In re* Sallmaier, 85 Misc. 2d 295, 297-98, 378 N.Y.S.2d 989, 991 (Sup. Ct. 1976); *In re* Simpson, 180 N.E.2d 206, 208 (Ohio P. Ct. 1962).

In 1978, the United States Supreme Court held that judicial immunity protected an Indiana judge who had authorized the sterilization of a young woman in the absence of statutory authority. Stump v. Sparkman, 435 U.S. 349, 356 (1978). Immunity applied because the judge's decision was not in the "clear absence of all jurisdiction," although the judge may have erred or exceeded his authority. *Id.* at 356-57.

Although *Stump* does not directly affirm judicial authority, it opened the path for a series of decisions recognizing the parens patriae power to order the sterilization of mentally disabled persons in the absence of statutory authority.

Several states have enacted statutory provisions that sanction parens patriae sterilization of incompetents. *See* statutes cited *supra* note 3. Most recent laws are grounded in the state's parens patriae authority; earlier laws, in contrast, were usually based on the police power.

33. 93 Wash. 2d 228, 608 P.2d 635 (1980).

34. The *Hayes* court explained that:

[T]he judge must first find by clear, cogent and convincing evidence that the individual is (1) incapable of making his or her own decision about sterilization, and (2) unlikely to develop sufficiently to make an informed judgment about sterilization in the foreseeable future.

Id. at 238, 608 P.2d at 641.

competent person who has no need for a surrogate decisionmaker.[35] If the court determines that the person is incompetent, it must then consider specific factors and decide whether sterilization is in the person's best interest.[36]

Most laws following the *Hayes* decision embody strict procedural and substantive requirements that create a strong presumption against sterilization. These laws presume that there is a conflict of interest between the child and the parent in this context and consequently exclude parents from any role in the decision.[37] A court makes the sterilization decision in a formal "semi-adversarial" proceeding.[38] The retarded indi-

---

35. Some states follow *Hayes* and require a threshold determination of the person's competency to make the sterilization decision before considering whether nonconsensual sterilization is appropriate. *See In re* C.D.M., 627 P.2d 607, 612 (Alaska 1981); Wentzel v. Montgomery Gen. Hosp., Inc., 293 Md. 685, 702, 447 A.2d 1244, 1253 (1982), *cert. denied,* 459 U.S. 1147 (1983); *In re* Moe, 385 Mass. 555, 566, 432 N.E.2d 712, 721 (1982); *In re* Grady, 85 N.J. 235, 264, 426 A.2d 467, 483 (1981); *In re* Terwilliger, 304 Pa. Super. 553, 565, 450 A.2d 1376, 1383 (1982); COLO. REV. STAT. § 27-10.5-130 (Supp. 1985); CONN. GEN. STAT. ANN. § 45-788 (West 1981); ME. REV. STAT. ANN. tit. 34-B, § 7005 (Supp. 1986); OR. REV. STAT. § 436.225(3) (1985); UTAH CODE ANN. § 64-10-2 (1986); VT. STAT. ANN. tit. 18, § 8707 (Supp. 1986); VA. CODE ANN. § 54-325.9 (1982). Although many laws state that the first determination is incompetency, only a few clearly stop the inquiry if competency is found. *See* CONN. GEN. STAT. ANN. § 45-78W (West 1981); ME. REV. STAT. ANN. tit. 34-B, § 7008 (1986). A few states permit sterilization on a general finding of incompetency. *See In re* Penny N., 120 N.H. 269, 271, 414 A.2d 541, 543 (1980) ("The court must [find] that the ward is 'incapacitated' . . . and suffers a 'developmental disability' . . . ."); MINN. STAT. ANN. § 252 A.11-13 (West 1982) (conservatee may be sterilized upon best interest finding).

36. *See Hayes,* 93 Wash. 2d at 237, 608 P.2d at 640.

37. The parent's petition generally triggers the appointment of a guardian ad litem to represent the child's interests. *See Grady,* 85 N.J. at 252, 426 A.2d at 475 (incompetents are best protected by independent judicial decisionmaking, not parents' good faith decision); *Hayes,* 93 Wash. 2d at 236, 608 P.2d at 640 (parents' interests cannot be presumed to be identical to those of child).

Some laws characterize the court's role as deciding whether to authorize the parent/guardian to consent to sterilization; however, this does not signify any abdication to parental decisionmaking authority in terms of relaxed procedural or substantive standards. *See, e.g., Wentzel,* 293 Md. at 701, 447 A.2d at 1254 (guardian's decision authorized only if sterilization is medically necessary).

38. *See C.D.M.,* 627 P.2d at 612 (procedural due process requires full judicial hearing with medical testimony and guardian ad litem to represent incompetent); *Grady,* 85 N.J. at 252, 426 A.2d at 475 (independent judicial decisionmaking best protects interests of incompetents). Most laws specify a range of procedural protections such as representation by counsel and expert evaluation of the retarded person. *See Wentzel,* 293 Md. at 703, 447 A.2d at 1253 (independent medical, psychological, and social evaluations by competent professionals); *Hayes,* 93 Wash. 2d at 238, 608 P.2d at 641 (comprehensive medical, psychological, and social evaluation); COLO. REV. STAT. § 27-10-5-130(1) (Supp. 1985) (appointment of two mental health professionals to perform evaluations); CONN. GEN. STAT. ANN. § 45-78t (West 1981) (appointment of counsel); IDAHO CODE § 39-3903(a),(d) (1985) (appointment of two physicians); ME. REV. STAT. ANN. tit. 34-B, § 7008.2 (Supp. 1986) (appointment of not less than two disinterested mental health experts); MINN. STAT. ANN. § 252A.13.4 (West 1982) (appointment of counsel and written medical, social, and psychological evaluations); UTAH CODE ANN. § 64-10-8(2) (1986) (appointment of counsel); VT. STAT. ANN. tit. 18, § 8710 (Supp. 1986) (appointment of counsel); VA. CODE ANN. § 54-325.12.B (1982) (independent medical, social, and psychological evaluations).

Some laws accord other procedural protections such as notice of the proceedings, the right to cross-examine witnesses, and the right to pursue an appeal. *See Moe,* 385 Mass. at 566-67, 432

vidual is represented by an attorney, usually a guardian ad litem, who may be directed to oppose the parents' petition for sterilization.[39] Most of the reform laws allow a court to order sterilization only upon findings based on clear and convincing evidence.[40]

In addition to procedural restrictions, these laws employ rigorous substantive criteria to guide the court's deliberations. Some require inquiries into whether the individual is able to reproduce[41] and whether she

---

N.E.2d at 721 (adequate notice, opportunity to be heard, and pursuit of appeal); *Grady,* 85 N.J. at 264, 426 A.2d at 482 (appointment of guardian ad litem and opportunity to present proofs and cross-examine); *Terwilliger,* 304 Pa. Super. at 565, 450 A.2d at 1383 (same); COLO. REV. STAT. § 27-10.5-129(2), (3) (1982) (notice, presence at proceeding, and opportunity to cross-examine); CONN. GEN. STAT. ANN. §§ 45-78s to 78y(a) (West Supp. 1986) (notice, opportunity to testify and cross-examine); ME. REV. STAT. ANN. tit. 34-B, §§ 7007.3, 7008.1 (Supp. 1986) (opportunity to present evidence, call witnesses, and cross-examine); OR. REV. STAT. §§ 436.255(2), 436.275(2), 436.315 (1983) (appointment of counsel on appeal and opportunity to present evidence and cross-examine witnesses); VT. STAT. ANN. tit. 18, §§ 8709(c), 8711, 8714 (Supp. 1986) (notice and right to appeal); VA. CODE ANN. § 54-325.11.2 (1982) (notice of proceedings and appointment of counsel).

39. *See, e.g., Moe,* 385 Mass. at 567, 432 N.E.2d at 721.

40. In *In re* A.W., 637 P.2d 366, 373-75 (Colo. 1981), the Colorado Supreme Court interpreted COLO. REV. STAT. § 15-14-312 (Supp. 1986) to allow court-ordered sterilization upon a showing of clear and convincing evidence. The law of Maine specifically requires "clear and convincing evidence that sterilization is in the best interest of the person being considered for sterilization." ME. REV. STAT. ANN. tit. 34-B, § 7013(4) (Supp. 1986). In Wentzel v. Montgomery Gen. Hosp., Inc., 293 Md. 685, 447 A.2d 1244 (1982), *cert. denied,* 459 U.S. 1147 (1983), the Maryland Supreme Court held that section 13-702 of the Maryland Estates and Trusts Code empowered the court to adopt standards that would ensure the ward's best interest regarding proposed sterilization. The New Hampshire Supreme Court ruled that under a statute mandating court approval of guardian-requested sterilization, N.H. REV. STAT. ANN. § 464-A:25I(c) (1983), the guardian must present clear and convincing proof that the ward is incapacitated, and that the guardian is acting in the best interest of the ward. *In re* Penny N., 120 N.H. 269, 271-72, 414 A.2d 541, 543 (1980). The proponent of a sterilization in New Jersey must show by clear and convincing evidence that the person to be sterilized lacks the capacity to consent or withhold consent. *See Grady,* 85 N.J. at 265, 426 A.2d at 483. The Pennsylvania Supreme Court required "proof by clear and convincing evidence that sterilization is in the best interest of the incompetent." *Terwilliger,* 304 Pa. Super. at 564, 450 A.2d at 1382. Virginia statutory law requires a court to determine "by clear and convincing evidence" that a child is incapable of making a decision before that court can order sterilization. VA. CODE ANN. § 54-325.10 (1982). In order for *any* incompetent in Virginia to be sterilized, the statutory elements must be shown by clear and convincing evidence. VA. CODE ANN. § 54-325.12 (1982). The Washington Supreme Court stated that the requirements for a court-ordered sterilization must be proven by "clear, cogent and convincing evidence." *Hayes,* 93 Wash. 2d at 238-39, 608 P.2d at 641.

41. *See In re* C.D.M., 627 P.2d 607, 613 (Alaska 1981) ("[I]t must then be established that the incompetent is capable of reproduction . . . ."); *Terwilliger,* 304 Pa. Super. at 566, 450 A.2d at 1383 ("[T]he person for whom sterilization is requested must be proven capable of reproduction."); *Hayes,* 93 Wash. 2d at 238, 608 P.2d at 641 ("The judge must find that the individual is . . . physically capable of conceiving . . . ."); CONN. GEN. STAT. ANN. § 45-78p(d) (West Supp. 1986) ("no evidence of infertility"); ME. REV. STAT. ANN. tit. 34-B, § 7011 (West Supp. 1986) (petition for sterilization must include a "medical statement assessing the physiological capability of the person to procreate"); N.C. GEN. STAT. § 635-39 (1984) (petition for involuntary sterilization must state whether patient is likely to procreate).

Some courts seem to presume reproductive capacity from the existence of regular monthly periods and the absence of contrary medical evidence. *See Grady,* 85 N.J. at 266, 426 A.2d at 483; *In re*

is "imminently" likely to engage in sexual activity.[42] The petitioner will be asked to demonstrate that less drastic forms of contraception have been tried and are not feasible.[43] The court must also assess the individual's capacity to care for a child.[44] Some states require a determination that sterilization is medically essential to preserve the life or the physical or mental health of the individual.[45] In some states, the court must also inquire into the disabled person's understanding of reproductive functions and the relationship between sexual intercourse, pregnancy, and childbirth.[46] Some laws direct the court to consider the psychological trauma associated with sterilization and alternatively with pregnancy

---

Truesdell, 63 N.C. App. 258, 283, 304 S.E.2d 793, 808 (1983), *aff'd as modified,* 313 N.C. 421, 329 S.E.2d 630 (1985). Other courts require further affirmative medical proof. *See In re* Debra B., 495 A.2d 781, 783 (Me. 1985) (mother's sterilization petition denied because she failed to present clear and convincing evidence to prove that 26 year-old daughter was capable of procreation). Such requirements may involve an intrusive medical examination to prove reproductive capacity (or postponing the sterilization initiative until the person has become pregnant).

42. *See Moe,* 385 Mass. at 570, 432 N.E.2d at 722; *Terwilliger,* 304 Pa. Super. at 567, 450 A.2d at 1384; *Hayes,* 93 Wash. 2d at 238, 608 P.2d at 641; CONN. GEN. STAT. ANN. § 45-78p(d)(4) (West Supp. 1986); UTAH CODE ANN. § 64-10-8(1)(d) (1983); VT. STAT. ANN. tit. 18, § 8711(c)(3)(B) (Supp. 1986); VA. CODE ANN. § 54-325.12.A.1 (1982). *But see Grady,* 85 N.J. at 266, 426 A.2d at 483 (no need to show likelihood of pregnancy).

43. Many laws require that all less drastic (nonpermanent) contraceptive methods be unworkable and that there be no alternative to sterilization. *See C.D.M.,* 627 P.2d at 613; *In re* A.W., 637 P.2d 366, 376 (Colo. 1981); *Moe,* 385 Mass. at 569, 432 N.E.2d at 722; *Grady,* 85 N.J. at 266, 426 A.2d at 483; *Hayes,* 93 Wash. 2d at 237, 608 P.2d at 640; CONN. GEN. STAT. ANN. § 45-78p(d)(1) (West Supp. 1986); GA. CODE ANN. § 31-20-3(c)(2) (1985); ME. REV. STAT. ANN. tit. 34-B, § 7013(5)(a) (Supp. 1984); MINN. STAT. § 252A.13.4 (1982); VT. STAT. ANN. tit. 18, § 8711(a)(3)(E) (Supp. 1986); VA. CODE § 54-325.12.A.2 (1982); W. VA. CODE § 27-16-1 (1980).

44. *See C.D.M.,* 627 P.2d at 613; *Moe,* 385 Mass. at 569, 432 N.E.2d at 722; *Grady,* 85 N.J. at 266, 426 A.2d at 483; *Terwilliger,* 304 Pa. Super. at 567, 450 A.2d at 1384; *Hayes,* 93 Wash. 2d at 238, 608 P.2d at 641; CONN. GEN. STAT. ANN. § 45-78p(d)(6) (West Supp. 1983); OR. REV. STAT. § 436.205(e); VT. STAT. ANN. tit. 18, § 8711(c)(3)(C) (Supp. 1986); VA. CODE ANN. § 54-325.12.A.4 (1982); W. VA. CODE § 27-16-1(3) (1980).

45. *See A.W.,* 637 P.2d at 375; *Moe,* 385 Mass. at 569 n.10, 432 N.E.2d at 722 n.10; CONN. GEN. STAT. ANN. § 45-78p(d)(8) (West Supp. 1983); ME. REV. STAT. ANN. tit. 34-B, § 7013.5 (Supp. 1984). Colorado requires this finding to protect the individual's health and "fundamental procreative rights." *A.W.,* 637 P.2d at 376. Courts in Maryland must make a finding of medical necessity and also determine whether sterilization is in the individual's best interest. *See* Wentzel v. Montgomery Gen. Hosp., Inc., 293 Md. 685, 703, 447 A.2d 1244, 1253-54 (1982), *cert. denied,* 459 U.S. 1147 (1983).

In Conservatorship of Valerie N., 40 Cal. 3d 143, 169, 707 P.2d 760, 777, 219 Cal. Rptr. 387, 404 (1985), the California Supreme Court seemed to require medical necessity because of the absence of a statute. The court directed, pending legislative action, that the procedures for approving intrusive medical procedures for conservatees be applied to sterilization.

In general, the "medical necessity" requirement treats sterilization like other medical procedures for incompetents. However, sterilization is also a *reproductive* option which normal persons choose for reasons other than health promotion. The New Jersey Supreme Court has rejected a required showing of "medical necessity" as too restrictive of the rights of the retarded person. *See Grady,* 85 N.J. at 262-63, 426 A.2d at 481.

46. *See Grady,* 85 N.J. at 266, 426 A.2d at 483; *Terwilliger,* 304 Pa. Super. at 567, 450 A.2d at 1384.

and childbirth.[47] Additionally, an inquiry into the individual's preferences about sterilization may be required, although her objection is not determinative.[48] The *Hayes* decision and some later laws require findings that medical science is not on the verge of breakthroughs that will correct the individual's disability or make reversible sterilization available.[49] These various criteria create formidable substantive barriers to the sterilization of mentally retarded persons.[50]

Current law explicitly or implicitly excludes some variables from the court's consideration, such as the state's interest in protecting society from the genetic and financial burden of children produced by retarded persons.[51] The parents' interest in protecting their child from unwanted

---

47. *See Grady,* 85 N.J. at 266, 426 A.2d at 483; *Terwilliger,* 304 Pa. Super. at 567, 450 A.2d at 1384; *Hayes,* 93 Wash. 2d at 238-39, 608 P.2d at 641-42; ME. REV. STAT. ANN. tit. 34-B, § 7013.3.B (Supp. 1986); OR. REV. STAT. § 436.205(1) (1985).

48. Several laws specify that the retarded person has a right to be present at the hearing and further direct the court to inquire about the person's wishes and gain impressions about her competency. *See C.D.M.,* 627 P.2d at 613 n.17 (weight given the individual's preferences varies according to ability to comprehend); *A.W.,* 637 P.2d at 375 (person's wish not to be sterilized weighs heavily against authorizing the procedure); *Wentzel,* 293 Md. at 703, 447 A.2d at 1253 (court must allow full opportunity for individual to express views); *Grady,* 85 N.J. at 265, 426 A.2d at 482 (same); *Terwilliger,* 304 Pa. Super. at 565-66, 450 A.2d at 1383 (judge must meet with individual, but not necessarily at hearing); *Hayes,* 93 Wash. 2d at 238, 608 P.2d at 641 (court must elicit individual's views before ordering sterilization); ME. REV. STAT. ANN. tit. 34-B, § 7011.9 (Supp. 1986) (court must consider the person's attitudes or desires regarding sterilization before sanctioning the procedure); UTAH CODE ANN. § 64-10-8(3) (1986) (record must include the person's views on issue of sterilization); VA. CODE ANN. § 54-325.11.5 (1982) (court must elicit and thoroughly consider the child's views on sterilization).

49. *See Moe,* 385 Mass. at 570, 432 N.E.2d at 722; *Grady,* 85 N.J. at 266, 426 A.2d at 483; *Terwilliger,* 304 Pa. Super. at 567, 450 A.2d at 1384; IDAHO CODE § 39-3901(e) (1985); UTAH CODE ANN. § 64-10-8(1)(a) (1986); VT. STAT. ANN. tit. 18, § 8711(c)(3)(D) (Supp. 1986); VA. CODE ANN. § 54-325.11.4 (1982).

50. Indeed, this is the intention. Several courts state clearly that sterilization of an incompetent is seldom in her best interest. For example, the Washington Supreme Court has stated that there is a "heavy presumption against sterilization . . . that must be overcome by the person . . . requesting sterilization." *Hayes,* 93 Wash. 2d at 239, 608 P.2d at 641. *See also C.D.M.,* 627 P.2d at 612 (advocates of sterilization bear heavy burden of proving that sterilization is in the incompetent's best interest).

It is interesting to note the similarity between the procedural and substantive requirements of the recent parens patriae laws and the remaining police-power laws. *Compare* statutes cited *supra* note 3 *with* GA. CODE ANN. § 31-20-3(a) (1985); IDAHO CODE § 39-3901(a) (1985); N.C. GEN. STAT. § 35-39(3) (1984).

The police-power laws require these protections because sterilization is viewed as a deprivation of the fundamental right to procreate. It is clear that parens patriae laws are grounded in the same notion. Thus, despite rhetoric about the exercise of reproductive choice, *see Grady,* 85 N.J. at 247-51, 426 A.2d at 473-74, reform laws treat sterilization as an infringement on the person's rights just as do the police-power laws.

51. *See Grady,* 85 N.J. at 262 n.8, 426 A.2d at 481 n.8 (court should consider "only the best interests of the incompetent person, not the interests or convenience of society"). *Grady* rejected the use of sterilization to promote genetic objectives or to prevent the birth of children who would be a burden to society. The Colorado Supreme Court has stated that sterilization is to be allowed only if

pregnancy or in avoiding the inconvenience associated with menstrual hygiene is also excluded from consideration.[52] Finally, the disabled individual's interest in promoting family stability by reducing the stress associated with her care may not be considered.

The substantive criteria that guide the decisionmaker are formulated into four kinds of legal rules. The *Hayes* opinion adopts the most common approach, which could be termed a "mandatory criteria" rule; under this type of rule a court can authorize sterilization only if several specific findings are clearly made.[53] This rule places a significant burden on the petitioner, limits judicial discretion, and makes it difficult to establish the desirability of sterilization. The "discretionary best interest" standard is a more flexible rule; instead of requiring specific findings, it directs judges to consider and weigh designated criteria in determining whether sterilization is in the incompetent person's best interest.[54] A few

---

"medically essential" and has emphasized that only the interests of the person herself, and not those of society or her parents, are to be considered. *A. W.*, 637 P.2d at 376. *See also Terwilliger,* 304 Pa. Super. at 564, 450 A.2d at 1382 ("[A] court should consider *only* the interests of the individual . . . .").

52. Some laws require parents to demonstrate their good faith and concern for their child's best interest. *See C.D.M.,* 627 P.2d at 613 (court must examine motivation behind petition); *Wentzel,* 293 Md. at 704-05, 447 A.2d at 1254 ("[T]he welfare of society or the convenience or peace of mind of the ward's parents or guardian plays no part."); *In re* Penny N., 120 N.H. 269, 271, 414 A.2d 541, 543 (1980) ("[T]he court must be satisfied that . . . the applicants have demonstrated their good faith and that their concern is for the best interests of the ward."); CONN. GEN. STAT. ANN. § 45-78p(d)(7) (West Supp. 1986) (applicants' "primary concern" must be best interest of the incompetent).

53. *See Hayes,* 93 Wash. 2d at 238-39, 608 P.2d at 641. This kind of law in effect restricts the discretion of the judge; the legislature or appellate court designating the criteria determines the sterilization decision. As a legal decision principle, it may be easier to apply than the discretionary best interest standard, *see infra* note 54, because it incorporates fewer factual variables. However, the rule as applied may not result in decisions that benefit the individual for whom sterilization is proposed. Thus, costs of error are high. The analysis in Parts II and III of this article suggests that this kind of rule may offer the greatest risk of error. *See generally* Ehrlich & Posner, *An Economic Analysis of Legal Rulemaking,* 3 J. LEGAL STUD. 257, 267-71 (1974) (discussing correlation of costs to variations in precision of legal rules). For an analysis of variations in types of decision principles in child custody law, see Scott & Derdeyn, *Rethinking Joint Custody,* 45 OHIO ST. L.J. 455 (1984).

54. *See Penny N.,* 120 N.H. at 271, 414 A.2d at 543; *Terwilliger,* 304 Pa. Super. at 564-67, 450 A.2d at 1383-84; CONN. GEN. STAT. ANN. § 45-78y(b) (West Supp. 1986); MINN. STAT. § 252A.13.4 (1982); OR. REV. STAT. § 436.305(1) (1985); VT. STAT. ANN. tit. 18, § 8712(c) (Supp. 1986).

Even under the discretionary best interest standard, most laws require the court to make a finding of whether the individual is competent to make the sterilization decision. If the individual is incompetent, these laws require the court to consider several substantive criteria and decide whether there is clear and convincing evidence that sterilization is in the person's best interest. Error under this standard may occur if the court fails accurately to weigh the various criteria in the decision. Maryland requires a finding of medical necessity but *also* directs the court to weigh several factors in determining whether sterilization is in the person's best interest. *Wentzel,* 293 Md. at 702-03, 447 A.2d at 1253-54. Thus, a finding that sterilization is in the person's best interest would not suffice; sterilization must also be a medical necessity. The requirement of a best-interest finding seems su-

states have adopted the "substituted judgment" approach first proposed by the New Jersey Supreme Court in *In re Grady*.[55] *Grady* directs the court to consider the *Hayes* criteria and any other relevant factors in order to make the decision that the disabled person would make for herself if she were competent.[56] Finally, a few jurisdictions simply prohibit the sterilization of anyone found by the court to be incompetent to give informed consent to the medical procedure.[57]

On a functional level, the various legal rules seem to promote different objectives. A rule prohibiting sterilization without the subject's informed consent apparently aims to protect only the right to procreate. Sterilization is by definition a violation of this right, regardless of the person's preferences. At the other extreme, the substituted judgment standard attempts, at least in theory, to approximate the choice that the

---

perfluous, since a procedure that is medically necessary would arguably always be in the person's best interest.

55. 85 N.J. 235, 426 A.2d 467 (1981).

56. *Id.* at 264-67, 426 A.2d at 482-83. *See also In re* Moe, 385 Mass. 555, 565-71, 432 N.E.2d 712, 720-23 (1982); UTAH CODE ANN. § 64-10-8(4) (1986). The substituted judgment doctrine has frequently been used in cases involving medical decisions for individuals who have become incompetent. Many of these decisions involve attempts to withdraw life-sustaining treatment from terminally ill patients. The landmark case is *In re* Quinlan, 70 N.J. 10, 355 A.2d 647, *cert. denied,* 429 U.S. 922 (1976). The New Jersey Supreme Court held that a 21 year-old woman in a persistent vegetative state had a right, which her father as her appointed guardian could exercise on her behalf, to withdrawal of life-sustaining treatment. *Id.* at 41-42, 355 A.2d at 664. The objective of the substituted judgment approach is for the decisionmaker to "step into the shoes" of the incompetent in order to make a decision that subjectively reflects what the individual's values and preferences would be were she competent. *Id.* In theory, the decision may reflect subjective idiosyncratic values and need not be the one that objectively reflects the person's best interest.

Courts have applied the substituted judgment approach in cases involving individuals who have never been competent. *See* Superintendent of Belchertown State School v. Saikewicz, 373 Mass. 728, 750-51, 370 N.E.2d 417, 430 (1977) (chemotherapy withheld from profoundly retarded 67 year-old man). The application of the substituted judgment approach is problematic because it requires the surrogate decisionmaker to discern the competent values and preferences of a never-competent person.

By establishing objective criteria to aid in approximating the disabled person's best interest, the cases applying the substituted judgment approach implicitly recognize the pitfalls of a subjective inquiry. *See Grady,* 85 N.J. at 266-67, 426 A.2d at 483 (determination based on a range of factors, including incompetency). In this way, despite the rhetoric, the substituted judgment approach is similar to the discretionary best interest approach. The Wisconsin Supreme Court accurately characterized the effort to reach the sterilization decision that the incompetent retarded person would make taking into account anything that would have been relevant to her including her incompetency as "legal legerdemain." *In re* Guardianship of Eberhardy, 102 Wis. 2d 539, 566, 307 N.W.2d 881, 893 (1981).

A presidential commission recommended that courts apply an objective best interest standard to surrogates' decisions to withdraw life-sustaining treatment from persons who had never been competent, although the commission endorsed the substituted judgment approach for persons who had once expressed competent preferences. PRESIDENT'S COMM'N FOR THE STUDY OF ETHICAL PROBLEMS IN MEDICINE AND BIOMEDICAL AND BEHAVIORAL RESEARCH, SUBSTANTIVE AND PROCEDURAL PRINCIPLES OF DECISIONMAKING FOR INCAPACITATED PATIENTS 179-88 (1983).

57. *See supra* note 31.

individual would make if she were competent. Between these two extremes are laws that attempt to protect the individual's interest in procreation from parental or state interference.[58] Despite variation, however, the reform laws are all based on a paternalism model. The model protects the mentally disabled person by establishing a heavy presumption against sterilization and by requiring a judicial decisionmaker.

C. *The Limits of Good Intentions: Some Problems with the Paternalism Model.*

The rigorously protective approach of the paternalism model may seem to offer a desirable level of protection when parents propose sterilization. The irreversibility of the medical procedure in itself justifies caution. Given the abuses of the past and lingering biases toward mentally retarded persons, a rule that constrains the surrogate decisionmaker by a strong presumption against sterilization would seem to be justified.

Some retarded persons, however, may be hurt by laws based on the paternalism model because that model places the interest in procreation above all other interests, including the interest in avoiding pregnancy. Like other people, a retarded person may have an interest in engaging in a sexual relationship without fear of pregnancy. This objective could often be most satisfactorily implemented through sterilization, but that option usually will be unavailable under current law. Current law also unnecessarily restricts the individual's interest in reproductive autonomy. Although accorded rhetorical deference, this interest is protected only if the individual is found to be intellectually capable of making the medical decision. If the person is found to be incompetent, a court decides whether sterilization is in her best interest. Yet it seems possible that some persons who may be incapable of informed *medical* decisions may be capable of meaningful *reproductive* choices (to produce a child or avoid pregnancy). The basis of the restricted conception of individual autonomy under the paternalism model is unclear. It may derive from a desire to protect vulnerable individuals from those who threaten their right to procreate. Alternatively, it may be based on a simplistic analysis of the mentally disabled person's interest in reproductive autonomy.

---

58. The case law and commentary discuss two seemingly contradictory objectives of sterilization law. On the one hand, sterilization is authorized as a means of facilitating reproductive choice. On the other hand, sterilization is characterized as a deprivation of a fundamental right. *See supra* note 20. This characterization is the basis of the general requirement that the criteria supporting sterilization be established by clear and convincing evidence. Courts cite Addington v. Texas, 441 U.S. 418 (1979), which required a clear and convincing standard in civil commitment proceedings because a deprivation of liberty was involved. This analogy suggests that sterilization is viewed by some courts as deprivation of procreative capacity rather than a widely used contraceptive option that could be made available through a surrogate.

Another problematic aspect of this model is the presumed conflict of interest in all cases between parent and child. Because every disabled person is assumed to have an interest in procreation that conflicts with her parents' effort to obtain sterilization, parental or family interests are excluded from the decision calculus. This approach may protect the mildly disabled person who may have an interest in making her own choices about reproduction. But it could be harmful for the more severely retarded person. Parents who care for a severely disabled child assume a substantial burden. It is not clear that the law serves the interest of such a person by augmenting that burden, especially if the presumed interest in procreation in fact does not exist. It is also not clear that a surrogate will be a better decisionmaker than the parents, who presumably know and love the child.

It is unlikely that sterilization, the contraceptive choice of many normal persons, is only infrequently desirable for retarded persons. Yet sterilization will rarely be ordered in many states because most parents will be unable to meet the rigid criteria set out in the sterilization laws.[59] These laws erect obstacles to sterilization in order to protect a possible interest in procreation,[60] yet they do not grapple directly with the basic question: How can it be determined whether a given individual has this interest? In the absence of such an inquiry, it is unclear whether the purported safeguards serve an actual protective function or whether they simply burden the petitioning parent and ultimately the affected individual.[61]

II. The Interests of the Retarded Person in Sterilization: An Autonomy Model

This Part develops an alternative approach to sterilization of retarded persons, premised on the primacy of individual and family autonomy. First it explores the interest in reproductive autonomy and the extent to which mental retardation affects the ability to make a meaningful decision to have children or to avoid pregnancy. It then examines the residual interests that may be important for the severely disabled person

---

59. *See supra* notes 37-50 and accompanying text.

60. *See supra* note 58.

61. By way of example, consider the blanket requirement that temporary alternatives be tried and found unworkable. This requirement assumes that the person may have an interest in having children in the future (and that a nonpermanent form of contraception is therefore desirable) without inquiry into whether or not she actually does. A more extreme example is the rule that authorizes sterilization only if it is a medical necessity. Such a requirement virtually forecloses sterilization for contraceptive purposes. It presumes that sterilization benefits the individual only if mandated by critical health needs; otherwise, preserving reproductive capacity is presumed to be of primary importance.

who is incapable of autonomous reproductive choice—interests involving medical risks and benefits, human dignity, and stable family life.

A. *Reproductive Autonomy and the Impact of Mental Disability.*

Analysis of reproductive autonomy[62] focuses on the individual's substantive interest in producing children or avoiding pregnancy as well as on her interest in controlling the decision. It might seem artificial to examine each interest separately and to distinguish the mentally retarded person's interest in making her own decisions from the underlying substantive choices themselves. A retarded person's disability, however, can differentially affect her interest in alternative outcomes because the decision to procreate and the decision not to procreate each require different intellectual capabilities. Furthermore, a person who is unable to make an autonomous choice about reproduction might nonetheless have an interest in the substance of the decision made by others for her.[63] Thus, a separate analysis of each dimension of the reproductive autonomy interest is indicated.

1. *The Interest in Preventing Reproduction.* The Supreme Court decisions that recognize a woman's right to make contraception and abortion decisions[64] are based on a right not to procreate.[65] Married individuals have a legally sanctioned right to cohabit without producing unwanted children.[66] Unmarried persons and minors may not have the right to engage in sexual activity, but they do have the right to avoid the

---

62. *See infra* note 92. Reproductive autonomy is the constitutionally protected interest individuals have in private autonomous decisions about whether or not to have a child. *See* Roe v. Wade, 410 U.S. 113, 153 (1973) (fundamental right to choose abortion); Griswold v. Connecticut, 381 U.S. 479, 484-86 (1965) (fundamental right of marital privacy located in "penumbras" of first, third, fourth, and ninth amendments). Reproductive privacy is an important aspect of a more general constitutional right of privacy that extends to decisions about marriage and childrearing, and more broadly to protection of bodily integrity and avoidance of personal disclosures. In Whalen v. Roe, 429 U.S. 589 (1977), the Supreme Court described the right of privacy as encompassing both an "interest in avoiding disclosure of personal matters" and a distinct interest in "independence in making certain kinds of important decisions." *Id.* at 599-60. *See generally* L. TRIBE, AMERICAN CONSTITUTIONAL LAW 921-34 (1978) (tracing development of right to privacy in reproduction decisions).

63. This is also true of many decisions made for children. Children have an interest in the substantive decisions their parents or the state make concerning their health and safety, even though they are disabled from making autonomous choices themselves and thus have no recognized autonomy interest.

64. *See supra* note 19.

65. Although the Court has characterized the right of reproductive privacy as the right to decide whether or not to bear a child, *see* Eisenstadt v. Baird, 405 U.S. 438, 453 (1972), Professor Robertson correctly points out that the interest at stake in abortion and contraceptive cases is the interest in *avoiding* conception and childbirth. *See* Robertson, *supra* note 23, at 405-06.

66. *See* Griswold v. Connecticut, 381 U.S. 479, 481-86 (1965).

potential costs of sexual intercourse.[67]

These costs are varied and substantial. If a woman does not want to become pregnant or give birth, the pain, discomfort, medical risk, and lasting physical and emotional effects of the experience are substantial burdens. For an unmarried female, pregnancy can be an embarrassing social disability. Responsibility for an unwanted child can entail substantial financial costs and may limit the social, career, and educational opportunities available to the parent.

The mentally retarded person may have an interest in avoiding pregnancy that is comparable to that of the normal person. She might want to avoid the costs of sexual freedom—the physical burden of pregnancy and the discomfort of childbirth. She might also derive a benefit from avoiding the psychological burden caused by the birth of a child who is unwanted or for whom she cannot care. The stress of parental responsibility and the negative effect on social, educational, and employment opportunities are costs that are as onerous for the retarded individual as for others.

2. *The Interest in Procreation.* In defining the constitutional doctrine of reproductive privacy, the Supreme Court has seldom focused directly on the right to procreate.[68] Nonetheless, the importance and constitutionally protected status of this right are clear. The Court has described procreation as a "basic civil right of man."[69] The right is protected by the constitutional tradition of family privacy and supported by a strong historical tradition.[70] Despite recent concerns about population

---

67. The Supreme Court has never struck down a state statute proscribing sexual activity between unmarried persons. However, the Court did strike down a Massachusetts law that limited access to contraceptives. *See Eisenstadt,* 405 U.S. at 454-55. In Carey v. Population Servs. Int'l, 431 U.S. 678 (1977), the Court held that a New York law restricting sale of nonprescription contraceptives to minors was unconstitutional. The Court noted, however, that the Constitution "does not bar state regulation of the sexual behavior of minors." *Id.* at 694 n.17. The Court stated in *Eisenstadt* that it would be unreasonable to believe that the legislature intended to "prescribe pregnancy as punishment for fornication." *Eisenstadt,* 405 U.S. at 448. The Court has recently recognized that protection of sexual privacy outside of marriage may be restricted in nature. In Bowers v. Hardwick, 106 S. Ct. 2841 (1986), it rejected the challenge of an adult homosexual arrested under a Georgia antisodomy law for engaging in consensual sexual activity in his home. *Id.* at 2843. Because the opinion emphasized the homosexual nature of the activity, its broader application is unclear.

68. Professor Robertson points out that this right has seldom been subject to state regulation; for this reason, perhaps, it has seldom been examined and is "ill-defined." *See* Robertson, *supra* note 23, at 406.

69. Skinner v. Oklahoma *ex rel.* Williamson, 316 U.S. 535, 541 (1942). *Skinner* struck down, on equal protection grounds, an Oklahoma law that authorized sterilization of some but not all habitual criminals.

70. Because of our strong tradition of family privacy, many would reject the notion of state interference in a couple's freedom to have a child. Other countries have overtly discouraged procre-

control, the right to procreate remains relatively unambiguous[71]—in contrast to the right not to procreate, which in the abortion context is limited by the interest of the fetus. Indeed, direct restrictions on reproduction have been tolerated only when applied to mentally disabled persons through involuntary sterilization laws.

Procreation as a "basic civil right" is closely linked to the doctrine of family privacy and the right of parents to rear their children. In *Stanley v. Illinois,*[72] the Supreme Court held that an unmarried natural father who was rearing his children had a constitutionally protected parental interest. The Court implicitly linked this parental interest to procreative rights, stating that "[t]he Court has frequently emphasized the importance of the family. The rights *to conceive and raise* one's children have been deemed 'essential.' "[73] Earlier, in *Meyer v. Nebraska,*[74] the Court defined the rights "to marry, establish a home and bring up children"[75] as liberties protected by the fourteenth amendment. In contrast, the parental interest of one who has reproduced without assuming parental responsibilities is given minimal legal and constitutional recognition. In *Lehr v. Robertson,*[76] the Court held that a natural father who had as-

---

ation in pursuit of policies of population control. The Chinese government offers "one-child" awards that are available upon sterilization or a promise not to have additional children. These awards take the form of cash payments and the payment of the child's medical, educational, and nursery expenses. These "one-child" awards also may take the form of time off from work and increased pensions. The Chinese government imposes penalties upon parents who have more than one child and these penalties become more severe as more children are born. *See* Goodstadt, *China's One-Child Family,* 8 POPULATION & DEV. REV. 37, 48 (1982).

71. The reduction in the size of the American family in recent years may be attributed to economics and better contraception but not to coercive governmental policies. *See* Mintz & Kellogg, *Recent Trends in American Family History,* 81 HOUS. L. REV. 789 (1984).

72. 405 U.S. 645 (1972). In *Stanley,* the Court struck down an Illinois statute that allowed removal, without a hearing, of the children of an unmarried father from the father's custody upon the mother's death. *Id.* at 658. The Court affirmed the father's interest in the "children he has sired and raised." *Id.* at 651.

73. *Id.* (emphasis added).

74. 262 U.S. 390 (1923). *Meyer* was the first decision to suggest a constitutionally protected interest in family privacy. The Court struck down a Nebraska law restricting the use of foreign languages in schools; part of the Court's rationale was that the law restricted parental authority. *Id.* at 400.

75. *Id.* at 399.

76. 463 U.S. 248, 263-64 (1983). *Lehr* is consistent with the legal trend that began with *Stanley.* In general, the courts have held that an unmarried father's relationship with his child is to be accorded substantial legal protection if the father has assumed parental responsibility. The Supreme Court did state in *Lehr,* however, that the "mere existence of a biological link does not merit equivalent constitutional protection." *Lehr,* 463 U.S. at 261. The *Lehr* Court characterized the natural father's genetic link as an "opportunity" to assume a unique relationship with the child. If he fails to do so, he loses his parental rights. *Id.* at 262.

Because a natural mother undergoes pregnancy and gives birth, she may be accorded a superior legal status over a natural father. *See Lehr,* 463 U.S. at 260 n.16. Nonetheless, she may lose this

STERILIZATION

sumed no responsibility for his child was not entitled to notice of the child's adoption by the mother's husband.

The right to procreate is the right to produce one's own children to rear. The right presumes and indeed requires an intention as well as an ability to assume the role of parent. Without this purpose and capacity, the "right" is limited to a right to conceive, carry, and bear a child.[77] To be sure, these components of the reproductive process may have independent value to the individual. For example, a man might wish to donate sperm to perpetuate his lineage even though the children conceived will remain unknown to him. A woman might want to act as a surrogate mother because she finds pregnancy and childbirth to be meaningful and satisfying experiences. But neither of these desires, legitimate though they may be, implicates a fundamental right. Indeed, debate concerning the constitutional implications focuses on the reproductive rights of the prospective *rearing* parents.[78] It is the objective of rearing the child—of establishing a family—that elevates the right to procreate to a lofty status.

---

status if she fails to care for the child. *See infra* notes 80-81; *see also* Caban v. Mohammed, 441 U.S. 380 (1979); Quilloin v. Walcott, 434 U.S. 246 (1978).

77. Professor Robertson describes three aspects of the right to procreate: conception, gestation and birth, and childrearing. Robertson, *supra* note 23, at 408-10. In contrast to the view expressed in this article, Professor Robertson values each aspect of the right to procreate independently and suggests that the benefit derived from conception or gestation should not be sacrificed because the person lacks the ability to raise a child. *Id.* at 413.

78. Surrogate mother contracts, in particular, have been controversial. *See* Robertson, *Surrogate Mothers: Not So Novel After All,* HASTINGS CENTER REP., Oct. 1983, at 28; Wadlington, *Artificial Conception: The Challenge for Family Law,* 69 VA. L. REV. 465, 479-82 (1983). Some courts have rejected surrogate mother contracts as contrary to public policy "because they involve an exchange of money for the baby." Doe v. Kelley, 106 Mich. App. 169, 173-74, 307 N.W.2d 438, 441 (1981), *cert. denied,* 459 U.S. 1183 (1983). The cases focus on the contracting couple's argument that the contract should be upheld to protect their constitutional right of reproductive privacy. *See, e.g.,* Surrogate Parenting Assocs. v. Commonwealth *ex rel.* Armstrong, 704 S.W.2d 209, 212 (Ky. 1986) ("The decision whether or not to beget or bear a child is at the very heart . . . of constitutionally protected choices."). Professor Robertson argues that infertile couples have a right to participate in noncoital cohabitative arrangements such as surrogate contracts. Robertson, *supra* note 23, at 428. The infertile couple may have no other means to exercise a decision to have a child except through some noncoital arrangement. This argument is only compelling, however, if the couple desires a child to rear. No one argues that the surrogate mother is exercising her right to procreate by becoming pregnant through a surrogate arrangement.

Artificial insemination by a donor (AID) is characterized not as an exercise of the donor's reproductive rights, but as a means of providing the mother with a child. *See Surrogate Parenting Assocs.,* 704 S.W.2d at 211-12. This characterization is appropriate because the donor has no intention of assuming parental responsibilities. Many states have passed laws protecting the donor from fatherly responsibilities not contemplated at the time of the contract. The Uniform Parentage Act provides that the husband of the woman inseminated with the donor's sperm is the natural/legal father. *See* U.P.A. § 5 (1986); *see also* CAL. CIV. CODE § 7005 (West 1983); MICH. COMP. LAWS ANN. § 700.111(2) (West 1980). Indeed, the sperm donor's status as natural father only becomes legally relevant in the rare instance when he seeks to assume parental responsibilities. *See, e.g.,* C.M. v. C.C., 152 N.J. Super. 160, 167-68, 377 A.2d 821, 824-25 (1977).

Traditional family law also implicitly supports this analysis of the limited nature of the right to procreate. The law favors biological parents over mere caretakers, recognizing the interest that natural parents have in pregnancy, childbirth, and the genetic link to future generations.[79] However, biological parents who cannot or will not fulfill their responsibilities as parents lose the legal protection created by their status. For example, abandonment of a child is grounds for termination of parental rights in every state.[80] Similarly, parental neglect or abuse that is not remediable and that results in intolerably poor child care will also result in state intervention to remove the child and limit or extinguish the natural parent's legal interest in the child.[81]

Historically, it was commonly believed that mentally retarded persons were per se unable to fulfill their responsibilities as parents. Even today, many child protection statutes list mental retardation as a factor supporting a finding of unfitness.[82] This presumption of incompetency

---

79. There has traditionally been a legal presumption favoring natural parents in custody disputes with third parties, even if the nonparent has been the child's primary caretaker. *See* Spence-Chapin Adoption Serv. v. Polk, 29 N.Y.2d 196, 201, 274 N.E.2d 431, 434, 324 N.Y.S.2d 937, 941-42 (1971). Only if the natural parent is unfit will custody go to a nonparent over a parent. *See* Bennett v. Jeffreys, 40 N.Y.2d 543, 545-46, 356 N.E.2d 277, 280-81, 387 N.Y.S.2d 821, 823-24 (1976). The Kansas Supreme Court struck down a statutory provision favoring the child's "psychological parent" as a violation of the natural parents' fundamental right to custody. Sheppard v. Sheppard, 230 Kan. 146, 153-55, 630 P.2d 1121, 1127-28 (1981), *cert. denied,* 455 U.S. 919 (1982). Many statutes, however, give the state very broad authority to intervene in families and remove children for abuse and neglect. *See, e.g.,* CAL. WELF. & INST. CODE § 300 (West Supp. 1986).

80. Abandonment statutes generally specify a period of time after which the state may terminate the parent's rights. *See, e.g.,* MISS. CODE ANN. § 93-15-103(3)(a) (Supp. 1985) (six months if child is under age three; one year if child is over age three); MONT. CODE ANN. §§ 41-3-102(3)(d), 41-3-609(1)(b) (1985) (six months); UTAH CODE ANN. § 78-3a-48(1)(b) (Supp. 1986) (six months); VA. CODE ANN. § 16.1-283(D) (Supp. 1986) (six months).

81. The state may terminate parental rights if the parents are unable or unwilling to remedy the conditions or behavior that led to the child's removal. Unless the parents' behavior presents a serious threat to the child, or is clearly not remediable, most states require that before termination can be ordered, services be provided to assist in remediation and the parent be given an opportunity to rectify the conditions that led to removal. *See, e.g.,* MONT. CODE ANN. § 41-3-609(1)(c)(i), (ii) (1985); VA. CODE ANN. § 16.1-283(C)(2)(b) (Supp. 1986); WASH. REV. CODE ANN. § 13.34.130(2)(a) (Supp. 1986). Many states require that the social service agency submit a foster-care plan providing for remedial services to facilitate the child's return. *See, e.g.,* VA. CODE ANN. § 16.1-281 (Supp. 1986); WASH. REV. CODE ANN. § 13.34.130(2) (Supp. 1986).

If, after a reasonable period of time, parents have not demonstrated progress such as would make the child's return feasible, the state may hold a hearing to terminate the parents' rights and free the child for adoption. *See, e.g.,* VA. CODE ANN. §§ 16.1-283(A), (C)(2) (Supp. 1986). The Supreme Court has acknowledged the seriousness of this deprivation by requiring a clear and convincing standard of proof. *See* Santosky v. Kramer, 455 U.S. 745, 747-48 (1982).

82. *See* KAN. STAT. ANN. § 38-1583(b)(1) (Supp. 1985); MISS. CODE ANN. § 93-15-103(3)(d)(i) (Supp. 1985); MO. ANN. STAT. § 211.447.2(2)(a) (Vernon Supp. 1986); S.C. CODE ANN. § 20-7-1572(6) (Law. Co-op. 1976); VA. CODE ANN. § 16.1-283(B)(2) (Supp. 1986).

Courts have frequently based withdrawal of custody or termination of parental rights on parents' mental retardation. *See In re* Jeannie Q., 32 Cal. App. 3d 288, 298-302, 107 Cal. Rptr. 646,

has been challenged by growing evidence that some mildly retarded individuals may be able to function as adequate parents.[83] Under my analysis, these individuals may have a protected interest in procreation.

The retarded person's interest in having children is more closely linked to her intellectual and functional ability than is her interest in avoiding pregnancy. A severely disabled person may have no affirmative interest at all in producing offspring, if conception, gestation, birth, and childrearing have no meaning to her. A less-impaired person may enjoy pregnancy or express a childlike interest in the notion of having her own child, but may be unable to care for a child due to her disability.[84] A mildly retarded person may have an interest in reproduction that approximates that of the normal individual; she may desire children of her own and may be capable of caring for them.[85] This article takes the position that the individual who is capable of caring for a child has a legally protectable interest in procreation, and that the individual who lacks this capability does not.[86]

653-57 (1973) (state withdrawal of retarded mother's custody of five children upheld because mother's IQ was 61 and two children showed evidence of malnutrition); *In re* Devine, 81 Ill. App. 3d 314, 319-20, 401 N.E.2d 616, 620-21 (1980) (termination of parental rights upheld where father's IQ was 63, mother's IQ was 55, and children had been neglected); *In re* McDonald, 201 N.W.2d 447, 449-53 (Iowa 1972) (termination of parental rights upheld where father's IQ was 74, mother's IQ was 47, and mother was unable to cope with typical child-care problems); State v. C.N.S., 319 S.E.2d 775, 780-82 (W. Va. 1984) (termination of mentally retarded parents' rights upheld without probationary period because there was no reasonable likelihood of improvement); *In re* C.M., 556 P.2d 514, 519 (Wyo. 1976) (termination of parental rights upheld since retarded parents would require full-time assistance).

    83. *See supra* note 30. Several commentators have challenged the notion that mental retardation creates a presumption of parental unfitness. *See* Shaman, *supra* note 30, at 72-73; Wald, *supra* note 28, at 14-15; Note, *The Law and the Problem Parent: Custody and Parental Rights of Homosexual, Mentally Retarded and Incarcerated Parents,* 16 J. FAM. L. 797 (1978); Note, *Low Intelligence of the Parent: A New Ground for State Interference with the Parent-Child Relationship?,* 13 J. FAM. L. 379 (1974).

    Some courts in recent years have viewed the capabilities of mentally retarded parents in more positive light. *See, e.g., In re* Montgomery, 62 N.C. App. 343, 303 S.E.2d 324 (1983) (order terminating parental rights of mentally retarded parents overturned; although parents could not provide some economic needs, they were providing for daily care and were able to summon help in emergency situations), *rev'd,* 311 N.C. 101, 111, 316 S.E.2d 246, 253 (1984); *see also In re* L. Children, 131 Misc. 2d 81, 499 N.Y.S.2d 587 (N.Y. Fam. Ct. 1986) (child-care agency's petition to terminate mother's parental rights dismissed because agency had not made diligent efforts to encourage and stengthen parental relationship and evidence failed to establish that mental retardation would preclude mother from caring for child).

    84. For example, W., an individual evaluated at the Forensic Psychiatry Clinic at the University of Virginia, was a severely retarded 15 year-old girl whose mother had recently had a baby. W. treated her brother like a doll and required constant supervision when she played with him. After her brother was born, she frequently expressed a wish for her own baby.

    85. *See supra* notes 29-30 and accompanying text.

    86. Onora O'Neill argues that the right to procreate should be contingent on a willingness and ability to rear or to delegate childcare responsibilities. *See* O'Neill, *Begetting, Bearing and Rearing,* in HAVING CHILDREN 26 (O. O'Neill & W. Ruddick eds. 1979). I would argue that the parent who

Under this analysis, severely retarded individuals who are not capable of fulfilling the basic responsibilities of parenthood do not have a legally protectable interest in procreation. The meaning of procreation for such a person is limited to the satisfaction she might derive from conception, pregnancy, and birth and from producing a child who will be cared for by others. The absence of a legally protectable interest in procreation does not, however, mean that nonconsensual sterilization is always appropriate for such a person. It does suggest that the decisionmaker should not exaggerate the retarded person's interest in procreation when determining whether sterilization is appropriate.

The analysis proposed here, which focuses on the retarded person's ability to fulfill the basic responsibilities of parenthood rather than on some absolute right to procreate, is consistent with current legal policy regarding contraception and abortion for retarded persons. Despite strong pronouncements in the sterilization context about the mentally disabled person's "right to procreate," it is clear that most states permit restrictions on the exercise of this right by retarded individuals who are unable to function as parents. Little controversy arises when a parent seeks to prevent a mentally disabled child from becoming pregnant.[87] Even in those states where sterilization is barred, parents and guardians can consent to contraception and even abortion for incompetent persons.[88] These laws acknowledge that the incompetent person's interest in

---

delegates some responsibility due to a physical disability (for example, a quadraplegic parent) may have an interest in reproduction and parenting if she is still able to guide the child's upbringing. However, the person who cannot fulfill any important dimension of the parental role has at most an ephemeral interest in reproduction—one that does not merit legal recognition.

87. It is arguable that parents may not responsibly ignore a legitimate risk that their mentally disabled child may become pregnant. *Cf.* Foy v. Greenblott, 141 Cal. App. 3d 1, 8-14, 190 Cal. Rptr. 84, 89-93 (1983) (institutionalized individual who became pregnant unsuccessfully sued facility responsible for her care for failure to provide contraception). Normalization policies assume mentally retarded persons will use contraceptives when engaging in sexual activity.

88. The California Supreme Court declared unconstitutional a law that prohibited sterilization of a conservatee with the conservator's consent, but that permitted the conservator to consent to contraception and abortion. *See* Conservatorship of Valerie N., 40 Cal. 3d 143, 707 P.2d 760, 219 Cal. Rptr. 387 (1985). The court stated:

> At present her conservators may, on Valerie's behalf, elect that she not bear or rear children. As means of avoiding the severe psychological harm which assertedly would result from pregnancy, they may choose abortion should she become pregnant; they may arrange for any child Valerie might bear to be removed from her custody; and they may impose on her other methods of contraception, including isolation from members of the opposite sex. They are precluded from making, and Valerie from obtaining the advantage of, the one choice that may be best for her, and which is available to all women competent to choose— contraception through sterilization.

Id. at 161, 707 P.2d at 771, 219 Cal. Rptr. at 398-99. Parents and guardians of mentally retarded persons are generally authorized to consent to contraceptive and other medical treatment subject to specific exclusions such as sterilization, psychosurgery, or electroshock treatment. *See* MONT. CODE ANN. § 72-5-321(2)(c) (1985); OHIO REV. CODE ANN. § 5122.271(c) (Anderson Supp. 1985); UTAH CODE ANN. § 75-5-312(1)(c) (1978).

STERILIZATION

avoiding pregnancy is more important than a theoretical interest in reproduction. Only sterilization law, responding to its unsavory history, seems to support an unqualified interest in procreation without regard to the person's capacity to fulfill the responsibilities of parenthood.

Defining the level of incompetency in parenting skills that signals the absence of a protectable interest in procreation will undoubtedly be a difficult and inexact process.[89] An erroneous decision to sterilize is probably more costly than an erroneous decision not to sterilize.[90] Therefore, the risk of error should be tipped in the direction of optimism about the individual's potential parenting capacity. But if the retarded person is so severely and irremediably impaired that she could never provide a child with minimally adequate care,[91] and if the state would therefore be justified in terminating her parental rights were she ever to have a child, then she has no protectable interest in procreation.

3. *Personal Autonomy and the Right to Make Reproductive Choices.* The importance of the principle of personal autonomy in defining the relationship between the individual and the state is well established in our constitutional and legal tradition.[92] Legal protection of the freedom of the individual to make personal choices about religious practice, expression of opinion, place of residence, and employment is grounded in the value of personal autonomy. Few decisions are more important to the individual than the decision whether or not to have children. Thus, inherent in the substantive interests in producing and rearing one's own children and, alternatively, in avoiding the burdens of reproduction is the individual's interest in exercising *control* over repro-

---

89. *See infra* notes 142-43 and accompanying text.

90. Sterilization by vasectomy or salpingectomy may be reversible, although this factor should not enter the decisionmaking process because it is not predictable.

91. It is the irremediable quality of the impairment that distinguishes the retarded person from others who have failed at parenting. The fact that the normal parent has repeatedly had children removed from her custody may be persuasive evidence of an inability to provide minimally adequate care. Her inadequacy as a parent, however, is not necessarily irremediable; her theoretical future interest in procreation and in bodily integrity would make involuntary sterilization unacceptable.

92. John Stuart Mill's *On Liberty* is the classic political philosophy treatise on autonomy. State control over individual action is legitimate, in Mill's view, only if necessary to prevent harm to others. J. MILL, ON LIBERTY 77-79 (1859). In American constitutional law, the principle of autonomy is the basis of many of the protections in the Bill of Rights. It inheres in the broader right of privacy which includes both notions of autonomy and freedom from disclosure of personal facts. *See* Whalen v. Roe, 429 U.S. 589, 598-600 (1977). Justice Stevens has described the individual's "interest in independence in making certain kinds of important decisions" as central to the right of privacy. *Id.* at 599-600. For an examination of the evolution and contours of the broader constitutional rights of privacy and personhood, see L. TRIBE, *supra* note 62, at 886-990. *See also* Note, *A Taxonomy of Privacy: Repose, Sanctuary, and Intimate Decision,* 64 CALIF. L. REV. 1447 (1976).

DUKE LAW JOURNAL [Vol. 1986:806]

ductive decisions.[93]

The Supreme Court's opinions on abortion and contraception emphasize the constitutional status of the right to make reproductive decisions free from state interference.[94] The Court has recognized that this interest is held by competent adults[95] as well as minors who are capable of making their own decisions.[96] Neither the parents of a mature minor nor a husband may veto a woman's right to make an autonomous choice to obtain an abortion or continue the pregnancy.[97]

Until recently, mental disability was the basis for a blanket presumption of incompetency. Even libertarians such as John Stuart Mill assumed that retarded persons as a class (like children) were not to be regarded as autonomous persons.[98] In contrast, modern commentators

---

93. The Supreme Court has stated that "[i]f the right of privacy means anything, it is the right of the *individual,* married or single, to be free from unwarranted governmental intrusion into matters so fundamentally affecting a person as the decision whether to bear or beget a child." Eisenstadt v. Baird, 405 U.S. 438, 453 (1972).

94. *See id.*; Carey v. Population Servs. Int'l, 431 U.S. 678, 684-85 (1977).

95. The Supreme Court focused on protection of marital privacy in striking down Connecticut's ban on contraceptive use in Griswold v. Connecticut, 381 U.S. 479, 485-86 (1965). The Court later held that the right extended to single persons. *Eisenstadt,* 405 U.S. at 452-55.

96. The Supreme Court has restricted the traditional authority of parents to make medical decisions for their children because of the critical and urgent nature of the abortion decision and the potential conflict of interest between parent and child. *See* City of Akron v. Akron Center for Reproductive Health, Inc., 462 U.S. 416, 439-40 (1983); H.L. v. Matheson, 450 U.S. 398, 405 (1981); Bellotti v. Baird, 443 U.S. 622, 643-44 (1979) (plurality opinion); Planned Parenthood v. Danforth, 428 U.S. 52, 74 (1976). In *Bellotti,* a plurality found that a minor was entitled to a judicial proceeding to show that she was "mature enough and well enough informed to make her abortion decision . . . independently of her parents' wishes." *Bellotti,* 443 U.S. at 643. The Court has never defined "maturity," and commentators have speculated whether it connotes competency to make an informed medical decision, or some more general notion of maturity. *See* Scott, *Adolescent's Reproductive Rights: Abortion, Contraception, and Sterilization,* in CHILDREN, MENTAL HEALTH AND THE LAW 140 (1983). Even a young minor cannot be presumed incompetent to make her own decisions. In *City of Akron,* the Court struck down an ordinance requiring parental consent to abortion for minors under age fifteen. *City of Akron,* 462 U.S. at 452.

The Court acknowledged traditional parental interests, however, when it upheld a Utah statute requiring physicians to give notice to parents when they perform abortions on minors. *Matheson,* 450 U.S. at 411-13. Justice Powell, concurring, specifically left open the question whether this requirement would apply to mature minors. *Id.* at 414.

97. *See Danforth,* 428 U.S. at 69.

98. Mill argued that the only appropriate reason for interfering with individual freedom is to avoid harm to others. He would not tolerate paternalistic intervention in decisions by "mature and rational human beings," even if the paternalistic act would protect one from self-harm. *See* J. MILL, *supra* note 92, at 77-79. He specifically excluded children, and by implication mentally disabled persons. *Id.* at 22 ("Those who are still in a state to require being taken care of by others must be protected against their own actions as well as against external injury."). For commentary on the implications of Mill's philosophy for the mentally disabled, see Monahan, *John Stuart Mill on the Liberty of the Mentally Ill: A Historical Note,* 134 AM. J. PSYCHIATRY 1428 (1977). *See also* Feinberg, *Legal Paternalism,* 1 CAN. J. PHIL. 105 (1971). Feinberg explains that autonomous actions and decisions must be "fully voluntary" and "chosen." *Id.* at 111. Chosen actions require deliberation—a process that requires time, information, and highly developed rational faculties. *Id.* A deci-

have challenged the presumption that mentally retarded persons are not able to make legally relevant decisions.[99] Some observers have gone a step further and have suggested that disabled persons may benefit from the exercise of legal rights even if they do not fully comprehend the decisions they make.[100]

The law has come to reflect these changing attitudes in some respects. Mentally disabled persons are no longer presumed by the law to be incompetent, unless they are subject to a guardianship.[101] Furthermore, some guardianship laws are structured so that the guardian has authority over only a limited range of decisions that are clearly beyond the capability of the disabled person.[102]

---

sion is not a chosen action if it is made without an understanding of its meaning and consequences. *Id.* at 110-11.

Traditionally, mentally retarded persons were deemed incapable of making rational choices. Their decisions were not chosen and, hence, not autonomous. The use of a surrogate decisionmaker therefore did not violate autonomy. *See* T. BEAUCHAMP & J. CHILDRESS, PRINCIPLES OF BIOMEDI- CAL ETHICS 63-64, 70-74 (1983). To the extent that the mentally disabled person *is* capable of rational choice, of course, autonomous decisions are possible and the traditional approach is invalid.

99. *See, e.g.,* Wikler, *Paternalism and the Mildly Retarded,* 8 PHIL. & PUB. AFF. 377 (1979). Wikler asserts that relative intellectual inferiority does not provide a general justification for pater- nalistic intervention because otherwise the liberty of normal people could be restricted and they could be subject to the superior decisionmaking of the intellectually gifted. *Id.* at 380. Other au- thors have criticized a general incompetency standard as applied to medical decisions. *See* C. LIDZ, A. MEISEL, E. ZERUBAVEL, M. CARTER, R. SESTAK & L. ROTH, INFORMED CONSENT: A STUDY OF DECISIONMAKING IN PSYCHIATRY 221 (1984); Meisel, *The "Exceptions" to the Informed Consent Doctrine: Striking a Balance Between Competing Values in Medical Decisionmaking,* 1979 WIS. L. REV. 413, 440-42.

100. John Garvey describes several theories that would justify ascribing constitutional freedoms (by which he means rights that involve choices) to persons with a limited capacity to make choices. Garvey, *Freedom and Choice in Constitutional Law,* 94 HARV. L. REV. 1756, 1762 (1981). Insofar as it ascribes freedoms without regard to competency in order to preserve human dignity, a laissez faire model offers the most expansive protection. Although Garvey does not support the laissez faire approach, he uses it to challenge traditional presumptions of incompetency. *Id.* at 1765. He also identifies an instrumentalist approach, which emphasizes that the exercise of freedom may promote the individual's development and welfare. *Id.* at 1768. Garvey argues that a surrogate deci- sionmaker is needed if the choice involves significant risk or if the person is incapable of making any choice. The disabled person can exercise freedoms free from state interference through a surrogate who is close to the individual. *Id.* at 1778. Only if a concerned surrogate is lacking is the individual subject to state authority.

101. Most laws provide that a court can appoint a guardian only after a competency hearing. The statutes make provision for notice, the right to counsel, and the right to cross-examine. *See* MINN. STAT. ANN. §§ 252A.03-.10 (West 1982); N.Y. SURR. CT. PROC. ACT § 1750 (Supp. 1986); N.C. GEN. STAT. §§ 35-1.8 to 1.20 (1984); W. VA. CODE § 27-11-1 (1986), § 44-10A-1 (1982). For an overview and critique of plenary guardianship, see Frolik, *Plenary Guardianship: An Analysis, a Critique and a Proposal for Reform,* 23 ARIZ. L. REV. 599 (1981). *See also* Webster, *A Study of Guardianship in North Dakota,* 60 N.D.L. REV. 45 (1984).

102. For example, a limited guardianship may give the guardian authority only to make medical or financial decisions. *See* MINN. STAT. ANN. § 252A.11 (West 1982); N.Y. SURR. CT. PROC. ACT § 1751 (Supp. 1986); N.C. GEN. STAT. § 35-1.34 (1984); W. VA. CODE § 44-10A-2 (1982). For a good overview with an emphasis on limited guardianship, see Sherman, *Guardianship: Time for a*

DUKE LAW JOURNAL [Vol. 1986:806]

Broad presumptions regarding the incompetency of mentally disabled persons are not appropriate because competency can vary in two ways. First, competency can vary according to the person's level of impairment. The capacity of the mildly retarded person to make most legally relevant decisions may approximate that of a normal person. Second, competency will depend on the decision to be made; a given individual might be competent to make some decisions but incompetent to make others.[103]

Even for persons who are otherwise deemed incompetent, a presumption of incompetency is inappropriate when reproductive decisions are involved. The Supreme Court has recognized that individuals who are not legally autonomous for some purposes can nonetheless have a constitutionally protected interest in reproductive autonomy. The Court has consistently held that a minor who is capable of a mature abortion decision need not obtain the consent of her parents or the state.[104] The traditional legal presumption favoring parental authority yields in this situation because of the importance of the child's interest in reproductive privacy and the potential conflict of interest between parent and child. A decision made on the minor's behalf by a surrogate decisionmaker is acceptable only if the minor is actually incapable of making her own decision.

In some sense, the retarded individual for whom sterilization is proposed is in a similar position. She might be capable of making the reproductive decision, even if she is subject to a guardianship for other purposes.[105] Like the adolescent seeking abortion, the retarded individ-

---

Reassessment, 49 FORDHAM L. REV. 350 (1980). *See also* Note, *Limited Guardianship for the Mentally Retarded,* 8 N.M.L. REV. 231 (1978).

103. Thus, an individual might be capable of driving a car and managing simple finances, but incapable of making an informed medical decision. This suggests the importance of basing the determination about competency on an individualized assessment of the person's ability to make the specific decision or perform the specific function in question. Ruth Macklin and Willard Gaylin identify three variables as relevant to determining competency: (1) the type of decision, (2) age and transient emotional or motivational variables, and (3) potential for training for future competency. R. MACKLIN & W. GAYLIN, *supra* note 26, at 59.

104. *See supra* note 96. The comparison between minors and mentally disabled persons is instructive. Minors are subject to a blanket presumption that they are incompetent to make most decisions, but the restriction on minors' autonomy is of a limited duration and consequently the deprivation of rights may be less costly. Thus, individualized determinations regarding competency on most specific issues may simply be too cumbersome and inefficient. *See generally* Weithorn, *Children's Capacities in Legal Contexts,* in CHILDREN, MENTAL HEALTH AND THE LAW 25 (1984).

The exception carved out for minors' abortion decisionmaking is justified in part because the decision cannot be postponed and it is critically important to the minor's life. Unlike most other health care decisions, the parents' objective cannot be presumed to be promotion of the health of the child.

105. Most current laws require a determination about the individual's competency to make the sterilization decision—regardless of whether she is subject to a guardianship. *See supra* notes 34-35.

ual who is actually competent to exercise meaningful choice should have a legally protected interest in reproductive autonomy.

What then constitutes meaningful reproductive choice? Three distinct decisions are involved, each of which requires a different level of competency and intellectual functioning. First, a disabled individual may be capable of making a meaningful decision to have a child. Second, she may be competent to make the separate decision to forgo having a child. Finally, if she has competently made the basic reproductive decision, she may be capable of implementing that choice through an informed medical decision regarding sterilization or other forms of birth control.

The autonomy interest of the mentally retarded person in deciding whether to have a child is obscured under laws based on the paternalism model because of the requirement of a threshold inquiry into whether the person is competent to make an informed medical decision about sterilization. If she is not, the law presumes that she is incapable of making the reproductive decision and that a surrogate (the court) must weigh her interests and make the decision for her.[106] The ability to make an informed medical decision involves a level of cognitive functioning that many mentally retarded persons lack.[107] However, a person who is unable to make this implementing decision might nonetheless be capable of making the underlying decision to have or to forgo having a child.[108] This decision is fundamentally different from the medical sterilization decision and requires different capabilities. By specifying competency to make the medical decision as the threshold requirement, laws based on the paternalism model distort and even foreclose the inquiry into the individual's ability to make the decision whether to have a child.

Under the autonomy model, competency to make a meaningful choice to procreate rests on the individual's ability to fulfill the basic responsibilities of parenthood. A mildly impaired person may have this ability regardless of whether she is legally competent to make medical decisions regarding sterilization. Her interest in making her own repro-

---

In a few states, a sterilization decision can be based on a general designation of incompetency. *See In re* Penny N., 120 N.H. 269, 271, 414 A.2d 541, 543 (1980).

106. *See supra* notes 34-35 and accompanying text.

107. *See supra* note 26 and accompanying text; *see also infra* notes 112-18 and accompanying text (discussing cognitive capacity needed for medical decisionmaking).

108. My colleague Ken Abraham suggests that individuals who are unable to make medical decisions will not be competent parents because such individuals would be unable to make informed medical decisions for their children. The point is well taken; however, if a parent could accomplish all other critical parental tasks, some mechanism could be devised to compensate for this disability.

Moreover, the distinction between the two types of competency is useful for analytical purposes. The most important inquiry in determining the individual's interest in reproductive autonomy is whether she will ever want a child. The medical competency issue obscures this inquiry.

ductive decisions should be legally protected. On the other hand, a severely disabled person's childlike wish for a baby does not signify a meaningful choice. A decision to have a child is, most importantly, a decision to become a parent—to assume a role that requires a minimal level of competency. If the individual lacks this capability and the state would predictably intervene to remove any child produced in order to protect it, then the choice to have a child is not a legally protectable exercise in personal autonomy.[109] Thus, the interest in autonomy is derivative of the underlying interest in having children. If the retarded individual lacks the ability to exercise the substantive interest, she lacks the interest in making the choice.[110]

The disabled person also may be capable of making an autonomous decision not to have a child. She may clearly express a stable preference not to have a child based on a desire not to assume the burdens of pregnancy or the responsibilities of rearing a child. Unlike the decision to procreate, the decision to avoid pregnancy involves an underlying substantive interest that does not itself require a minimal level of competency.[111] Thus, the ability to make the decision to avoid pregnancy rests solely on a capacity for rational decisionmaking and not on any underlying functional capability. Rationality may be measured by the clarity and consistency of the expressed preference not to have a child. The preference may be to prevent pregnancy in the immediate future or it may directly or indirectly reflect a desire not to have children.

The individual who is competent to make her own reproductive choice may also be competent to implement that choice by making the medical decision about sterilization or other contraceptive options. With respect to the contraception decision, her autonomy interest has two dimensions. First, the decision is an exercise of reproductive autonomy. She is making a decision about whether to permanently or temporarily prevent pregnancy through a chosen medical procedure. Second, the competent individual has an overlapping but distinct interest in maintaining control over health care decisions. She has an interest in weighing the benefits and risks to her health of various medical and surgical

109. In theory, a person who is incapable of parenting because of mental disability may be capable of making a "rational" decision to procreate reflecting a basic understanding of what it means to have a child—costs, benefits, risks, etc. That decision has little meaning, however, if she could never function as a parent. In reality, it is probable that few will lack the functional capability while possessing the cognitive decisional ability.

110. The underlying interest itself often defines the individual's interest in control over making the decision. For example, minors do not have the freedom to make the decision to marry because they are deemed incapable of assuming the responsibility of marriage. They lack the underlying substantive interest and therefore lack the interest in making the decision.

111. Indeed, avoiding pregnancy may promote the physical, psychological, and social welfare of a profoundly impaired person. *See* H. KAPLAN & B. SADOCK, *supra* note 26, at 852.

procedures and reaching a decision whether or not to undergo a given treatment.[112] Applying the preferred legal standard, competency to give (or withhold) informed consent to a medical procedure is based on an appreciation of the nature and purpose of the procedure, its risks and benefits, and its consequences in comparison with available alternatives.[113]

Some individuals who are capable of making a meaningful reproductive decision will not be capable of making the medical decision necessary to implement the underlying choice.[114] It has been suggested that informed medical decisionmaking requires the ability to engage in formal operational thinking. According to Piaget, this is the highest stage of cognitive development and is achieved by normal individuals between the ages of eleven and fourteen.[115] At this stage one has the capability to conceptualize several abstract possibilities and consider the consequences of various courses of action.[116] Many mentally disabled persons lack this capability and are thus unable either to appreciate the consequences,

---

112. Commentators have argued that the informed consent requirement for medical treatment is also based on protecting personal autonomy. The individual must understand the procedure, its risks, benefits, and alternatives in order to control what will be done to her body. *See* Capron, *Informed Consent in Catastrophic Disease Research and Treatment,* 123 U. PA. L. REV. 340, 364-76 (1974).

In a leading case defining the contours of modern informed consent law, Natanson v. Kline, 186 Kan. 393, 350 P.2d 1093 (1960), the Kansas Supreme Court stated: "Anglo-American law starts with the premise of thorough-going self-determination. It follows that each man is considered to be master of his own body, and he may, if he be of sound mind, expressly prohibit the performance of life-saving surgery, or other medical treatment." *Id.* at 406-07, 350 P.2d at 1104.

113. There are several standards of competency to make medical decisions. Under the lowest standard, a competent individual is one who is capable of expressing a preference. A second standard focuses on whether the decision itself is rational; if it is, it is deemed competent. Some commentators have suggested that this standard is typically used in psychiatric hospitals. The decision to accept treatment is deemed competent; to refuse treatment suggests incompetency. *See* Meisel, *supra* note 99, at 443-45. A third standard looks at the rationality of the decisionmaking process. The fourth and prevailing standard is the so-called appreciation standard, which measures the patient's inferential as well as factual understanding or recall. *See* Weithorn, *Developmental Factors and Competence to Make Informed Treatment Decisions,* CHILDREN & YOUTH SERVICES, Spring-Summer 1982, at 85, 89-95. Several commentators have suggested that appreciation requires the ability to think abstractly and draw inferences about the implications of the proposed treatment. *See* Applebaum & Roth, *Clinical Issues in the Assessment of Competency,* 138 AM. J. PSYCHIATRY 1462, 1463-65 (1981); Weithorn, *supra* note 104, at 35.

114. The Forensic Psychiatry Clinic at the University of Virginia, for example, evaluated a woman, B., age 35 with one child, who had over a number of years consistently said that she wanted "no more babies." Attempts to use birth control pills and an IUD had caused substantial medical problems. Her competency to make the sterilization decision was questionable, however, because she could not think abstractly about permanence and about not being able to change her mind in the future.

115. *See* H. KAPLAN & B. SADOCK, *supra* note 26, at 58-59.

116. *See* Weithorn, *supra* note 104, at 37. Weithorn and Campbell conducted research on the competency of normal children to make medical decisions. They found that, by age 14, minors reasoned about medical decisions much like adults. *See* Weithorn & Campbell, *The Competency of*

risks, and benefits of sterilization or to weigh the alternatives.[117] If the individual is incapable of giving informed consent to contraceptive treatment, her reproductive decision may be undermined.[118] Therefore, the law should facilitate her reproductive choice through a surrogate who can consent to the medical procedure for her.

The retarded person who is competent to make autonomous reproductive and medical decisions should not be subject to paternalistic supervision. In light of the overriding interest in personal autonomy, the individual should be free to weigh whatever other interests are subjectively important to her, regardless of what an objective decisionmaker would consider to be in her best interest. For example, she is free to choose to have a child even if a medical condition makes this decision risky. If her decision is competent, its wisdom should not be scrutinized.

4. *Summary.* In contrast to the paternalism model, the autonomy model defines the interest in reproductive autonomy both more precisely and more expansively by focusing on the person's capability to make the reproductive choice. The mentally retarded person has an interest in reproductive autonomy if she is capable of making a meaningful decision about whether or not to have a child. Her interest in a meaningful choice to procreate is derived from her substantive interest in reproduction. If she is capable of rearing a child, her interest in procreation and in the decision to have children is indistinguishable from that held by the normal person. Her interest in the decision not to have children rests on her ability to make a meaningful choice to avoid pregnancy. The individual who is capable of making an autonomous reproductive choice might or might not be capable of making the implementing medical decision; this requires the cognitive ability to give or withhold informed consent to the medical procedure.

Children and Adolescents to Make Informed Treatment Decisions, 53 CHILD DEV. 1589, 1595-96 (1982); *see also supra* note 26.

117. Persons who are more than mildly retarded are unlikely to have this capability. It is unclear whether mildly retarded persons would be able to engage in these cognitive processes. *See* R. MACKLIN & W. GAYLIN, *supra* note 26, at 59-62. The cognitive developmental approach to mental retardation suggests by definition that mentally retarded persons do not reach the highest stage of cognitive development—formal operational thinking. *See supra* note 26 and accompanying text. I am reluctant to engage in such a broad categorization, however, given the variations in conceptualizing both mental retardation and competency.

118. The individual described *supra* note 114 is a good example. Sterilization was not allowed because she was capable of caring for her child, and thus could not meet one of the mandatory criteria under Virginia law. *See* VA. CODE ANN. § 54-325.13(4) (1982).

B. *Residual Interests of the Severely Retarded Person.*

Some mentally disabled persons are not competent to make reproductive decisions for themselves. A decision about sterilization made on behalf of an individual in this category violates no interest in reproductive autonomy; when a person is incapable of making her own decision, others must determine whether sterilization is in her best interest.[119] Sterilization is not necessarily the appropriate choice simply because the individual has no meaningful interest in reproduction, and therefore has a presumptive interest in avoiding pregnancy. The desirability of the procedure may depend on nonreproductive considerations such as medical risks and benefits, human dignity, privacy, and family continuity and stability.

1. *Medical Risks and Benefits.* The person who is unable to make her own medical decisions has an interest in a decision about contraception that most effectively promotes her medical needs. Risk, convenience, comfort, intrusiveness, and effectiveness are variables that may be relevant in treatment choice. One option is long-term use of birth control pills. However, this practice is generally not advised for normal women; its medical risks are now being studied.[120] Use of an intrauterine device also entails substantial risk;[121] indeed, most models have been

---

119. The term "best interest" is often associated with a judicial decisionmaker exercising the state's parens patriae authority. This article uses the term to encompass decisions by parents as well. The law's objective is for the decisionmaker, whether court or parent, to make the sterilization decision that is best for the incompetent person.

120. Oral contraceptives such as the Pill must be taken on a regular schedule and may present several risks to the user including heart disease, diabetes, thrombophlebitis, and hypertension. *See* CONTRACEPTIVE TECHNOLOGY, *supra* note 1, at 49-50, 56-61. *But see* Sattin, Rubin, Wingo, Webster & Ory, *Oral Contraceptive Use and the Risk of Breast Cancer,* 315 NEW ENG. J. MED. 405 (1986) (study finding no correlation between long-term use of oral contraceptives and breast cancer). Minor side effects such as weight gain and frequent headaches are also possible. *See* CONTRACEPTIVE TECHNOLOGY, *supra* note 1, at 55-56.

121. IUDs are inserted into the uterus and prevent an embryo from attaching to the uterine wall. The principle risks associated with IUDs are: discomfort, increased bleeding, spontaneous expulsion, increased frequency of urine and pelvic infection, and pregnancy failures. *See* CONTRACEPTIVE TECHNOLOGY, *supra* note 1, at 202-10.

Concerns about the safety of the IUD have grown in recent years and the device may not be available in the future. Some commentators feel that for nulliparous women (women who have never been pregnant), the use of an IUD may double the risk of tubal infertility in comparison with other methods of contraception. *See* Cramer, Schiff, Schoenbaum, Gibson, Balisle, Albrecht, Stillman, Berger, Wilson, Stadel & Seibel, *Tubal Infertility and the Intrauterine Device,* 312 NEW ENG. J. MED. 941, 947 (1985). A.H. Robins, Inc., producer of the Dalkon Shield, has incurred massive liability in a class action settlement with women seriously injured by this device. Robins filed a Chapter 11 bankruptcy petition after incurring liability of $1.1 billion in litigation costs with 5,000 suits pending. Another manufacturer of IUDs, G.D. Searle & Co., is facing potentially disastrous litigation. Over 600 suits were pending as of October 1985. *See* Glaberson, *Did Searle Close Its Eyes?,* BUS. WK., Oct. 14, 1985, at 120. Both Searle and Ortho Pharmaceutical Corp. have removed

withdrawn from the market. This risk is increased if the physician uses a general anesthetic while inserting the device (a common practice with severely retarded women because the patient may otherwise resist the procedure).[122] The experimental drug Depo-Provera is another form of contraception used for retarded women.[123] Again, the effects of long-term use are unclear. Finally, if ineffective (perhaps less risky) birth control options are chosen, the risks associated with pregnancy, abortion, and childbirth must be considered.[124] None of these contraceptive options is a clearly superior *medical* alternative to salpingectomy or other nonintrusive forms of sterilization.[125] Thus, the individual's interest in the optimal medical decision may be promoted as well by nonintrusive forms of sterilization as by the available contraceptive alternatives.

Laws based on the paternalism model fail to separate the individual's reproductive interest from her interest in the medical decision. Be-

---

their IUDs from the market. The only IUD currently being sold in the United States is a little-used device that releases hormones in much the same way as the Pill. Dulea, *Liability Crisis Complicates Contraception,* N.Y. Times, May 19, 1986, at B8, col. 1.

122. Insertion of an IUD may be difficult with a retarded woman as some pain is involved, which she may not understand. Some gynecologists use general anesthesia when performing this procedure because of concern that perforation or other injury will result if the woman is agitated. *See* Melton & Scott, *Evaluation of Mentally Retarded Persons for Sterilization: Contributions and Limits of Psychological Consultation,* 15 PROF. PSYCHOLOGY: RES. & PRAC. 34, 42 (1984).

Professors La Veck and de la Cruz, writing before the risks of IUDs became known, recommended the IUD as the optimal contraceptive option for mentally retarded women since it requires no motivation or intellectual skills. *See* La Veck & de la Cruz, *Contraception for the Mentally Retarded: Current Methods and Future Prospects,* in HUMAN SEXUALITY AND THE MENTALLY RETARDED 96-97 (F. de la Cruz & G. La Veck eds. 1973).

123. Depo-Provera is a substituted progesterone that suppresses ovulation. It is effective for three months when injected intramuscularly. The Food and Drug Administration has not yet approved Depo-Provera for contraceptive use in the United States because it causes breast tumors in beagles. *See* R. HATCHER & G. STEWART, CONTRACEPTIVE TECHNOLOGY 1982-1983, at 66-67 (1982). Use of the drug also causes minor side effects such as disruption of normal menstruation and irregular and unpredictable bleeding. The woman may experience weight gain and a delayed return of fertility once treatments are stopped. *See id.* at 67.

124. The medical risk, pain, and anxiety associated with pregnancy and birth may be greater for one who does not understand the process and cannot look forward to the fruits of the effort. Abortion has some risks that increase as the term of the pregnancy progresses. Second trimester abortions have risks comparable to the risks of childbirth. *See id.* at 7. For teens, childbirth has five times the mortality/morbidity rate of a first trimester abortion. *Id.*

125. Some forms of tubal ligation may be performed on an outpatient basis. It leaves minute scars, involves minimal discomfort, and allows for a rapid recovery with a quick return to normal activity, including sex. The most popular form of tubal ligation is laparoscopy, which involves extremely rare risks of hemorrhage, electric shock, perforation of organs, puncture of blood vessels and skin, and internal burns. The current mortality rate for the laparascopic procedure is 10 deaths per 100,000 procedures. *See id.* at 195-96.

The only complications associated with vasectomy, an outpatient procedure, are skin discoloration, swelling, pain, and hematoma (a mass of clotted blood from injured blood vessels in loose connective tissues of the scrotum). Hematomas usually occur in less than one percent of all vasectomies. *See id.* at 190.

cause sterilization extinguishes reproductive capacity, it is presumed to be inherently more intrusive and "drastic" than any nonpermanent form of contraception, and is only allowed as a last resort. However, for the person who has no interest in having children, some forms of sterilization are no more "drastic" in a medical sense than other contraceptive options. For the severely disabled person who lacks a potential interest in having children, assessment of sterilization as a treatment alternative should be made independently of the interest in reproduction itself.

However, more intrusive forms of sterilization, such as hysterectomy, are not comparable in a medical sense to other contraceptive options. Some parents might seek hysterectomy[126] for a severely retarded daughter because she has difficulty managing menstrual hygiene tasks or because she experiences distress with menstrual periods.[127] In this situation, the threat to the retarded person's interest in the optimal medical decision is greatly increased because the procedure is major surgery and involves enhanced medical risk. Furthermore, medical judgment may not serve its traditional protective function. Physicians can generally be relied on to recommend the treatment that best promotes the patient's medical welfare with minimal risk. However, a gynecologist might recommend a hysterectomy for a severely retarded young woman, based not on the woman's gynecological needs, but on an evaluation of her intellectual capabilities, an issue on which gynecologists have little expertise. To the extent that risk is incurred beyond that indicated by her medical needs, intrusiveness is increased and justification of the decision on the ground that it promotes the patient's interests becomes more difficult.[128]

---

126. Although hysterectomy is 100% effective as a method of birth control, some authorities flatly state that because of the risks, hysterectomy is never appropriate for contraceptive purposes. *See* Amirikia & Evans, *Ten-year Review of Hysterectomies: Trends, Indications, and Risks,* 134 AM. J. OBSTETRICS & GYNECOLOGY 431, 432-33 (1979) (study of 6400 hysterectomies described significant complications including infection (4.7%), bleeding (1.4%), risks from transfusion (12%), bladder and bowel injury (0.6%), thromboembolisms (0.6%) and death (0.26%)). Usually hysterectomies are only performed for sterilization purposes when there are other gynecologic problems present as well. *See* M. SAIDI & C. ZAINIE, FEMALE STERILIZATION: A HANDBOOK FOR WOMEN 44 (1980). Many current laws implicitly discourage hysterectomies by requiring that the sterilization procedure chosen be the least restrictive alternative. *See, e.g.,* VA. CODE ANN. § 54-325.12 (1982).

127. Research indicates that moderately retarded persons with proper training can manage all aspects of menstrual hygiene. Severely retarded women can learn all aspects except initiation. *See* Hamilton, Allen, Stephens & Davall, *Training Mentally Retarded Females to Use Sanitary Napkins,* MENTAL RETARDATION, Feb. 1969, at 40, 43; *see also* Melton & Scott, *supra* note 122, at 42-43.

128. A major surgical procedure with significant medical risk may be medically necessary to save the person's life or restore her health. It is the discrepancy between the nonautonomous patient's medical needs and the risk associated with the procedure that raises concerns about whether her welfare is promoted.

An analogous problem arises in medical research on incompetents and children. If an individual is not competent to consent to the risks of research, the procedure may represent an unwarranted

2. *Human Dignity and Privacy.* The severely disabled person who is incapable of autonomous choice has an interest in being treated with human dignity and in avoiding unnecessary intrusions into her privacy by those who make the sterilization decision for her.[129] Her dignity interest is threatened if she is subjected to a medical procedure against her will. Furthermore, protection of privacy requires that personal inquiry and disclosure in the decisionmaking process be limited, and that only those persons whose participation is needed to make a good decision be involved.[130]

Some individuals who are not capable of making their own reproductive decisions will object to a proposed sterilization. Such objection can reflect varying levels of comprehension and may have several sources. The individual might adhere to a childlike wish for a baby. She might be afraid of doctors, hospitals, or pain. Whatever the source of her protest, the medical procedure will be more offensive to her dignity then if she were agreeable. In general, any objection reflecting basic understanding signifies that the procedure intrudes on the individual's dignity. Although the protest should not necessarily determine the outcome, it does reflect an interest of the individual that should be considered in any decision designed to promote her welfare.[131]

In general, the severely retarded person has a reduced expectation of personal privacy. Others are involved in intimate decisions affecting her life, including medical decisions, to a greater extent than is the case with the normal person. Even if she is capable of making her own decisions,

---

bodily intrusion because its purpose is not solely health promotion. *See* Kaimowitz v. Michigan Dep't of Mental Health, 42 U.S.L.W. 2063, 2063 (Mich. Cir. Ct. July 10, 1973) (involuntarily committed patient cannot consent to experimental "high risk-low benefit" psychosurgery).

129. The notion of "respect for persons" extends beyond respect for individual autonomy to a recognition of the humanity of nonautonomous persons. In Kantian terms, persons should not be treated as a means to another end. *See* T. BEAUCHAMP & J. CHILDRESS, *supra* note 98, at 7.

130. The Supreme Court has described two dimensions of the right of privacy: independence in making important personal decisions, and freedom to prevent disclosure of personal facts. *See* Whalen v. Roe, 429 U.S. 589, 599-600 (1977). The incompetent person lacks the first dimension, but this does not mean that the second dimension should routinely be disregarded. Many current laws require judges, attorneys, and others to scrutinize the mentally retarded person's competency, parenting ability, sexual activities, reproductive capacity, and contraceptive practices. *See supra* notes 35-48 and accompanying text. Such scrutiny is justified only if it serves some beneficial purpose.

131. Federal regulations governing medical research involving children recognize that an incompetent person's agreement or objection to a medical procedure may be significant. *See* 45 C.F.R. §§ 46.401-.409 (1985). These regulations require the parents' permission and the minor's *assent* for most types of research. Assent is not defined, but Professor Weithorn has described it as knowledgeable agreement. Weithorn, *Children's Capacities to Decide About Participation in Research,* IRB, Mar.-Apr. 1983, at 1, 2. Weithorn suggests that children become capable of assent at age six. *Id.* at 5. If a child capable of assent protests, the protest will be respected unless the research offers the child a direct health benefit that is otherwise unavailable. 45 C.F.R. § 46.408(a) (1985).

STERILIZATION

she will be allowed to do so only after intrusive scrutiny of her competency.[132] Although most medical decisions will involve only her parents or guardian and a physician, the sterilization decision often involves an expanded group of participants. The potential for infringement of her privacy interest is great if the law requires rigorous procedural protections and substantive findings.[133] Under the paternalism model, both individual and family privacy are largely ignored in the process of evaluating the desirability of sterilization. Although some intrusion on privacy is necessary, this interest should not be unnecessarily sacrificed.[134]

3. *The Interest of the Retarded Person in Family Stability.* Many parents abandon or institutionalize their mentally retarded children when the disability becomes apparent or burdensome;[135] others place their children in foster care. The disabled person whose parents have accepted the responsibility of caring for her at home is very likely better off than one subjected to any of these alternatives; she has a substantial interest in continued care by her parents. Family stability is thus an interest held by the child as well as the parents. This stability may be affected by the level of stress that attends the burden of caring for a retarded child.[136] It can be threatened by concerns about the child's sexuality. The welfare of a severely retarded person who has no interest in reproduction may be promoted if her parents' concerns about pregnancy

---

132. Note the parallel here to the procedures set forth in Bellotti v. Baird, 443 U.S. 622, 643-44 (1979) (plurality opinion), for determining the maturity of the minor who seeks an abortion. For a discussion of *Bellotti,* see *supra* note 96.

133. *See supra* notes 37-50 and accompanying text.

134. Application of the least restrictive alternative doctrine is relevant to intrusions into personal privacy. *See* Hoffman & Foust, *Least Restrictive Treatment of the Mentally Ill: A Doctrine in Search of its Senses,* 14 SAN DIEGO L. REV. 1100, 1102-03 (1977). Any infringement of a constitutionally protected interest should be restricted to that necessary to accomplish the legitimate purpose. *Id.* at 1101. This doctrine has been applied to involuntary treatment of mentally ill patients. *Id.* at 1102. Civil commitment law in many states includes a directive that the least restrictive treatment be utilized. *Id.* at 1112.

135. The normalization trend has encouraged parents to rear their mentally retarded children at home. *See supra* note 28. Nonetheless, family stress may increase as the child grows older, and may ultimately prompt a decision to remove the child from the home. For boys, concern among neighbors about aggressiveness may be a problem. *See* E. SCHULMAN, *supra* note 26, at 100. For girls, the parents' dominant concern may be pregnancy.

136. For a discussion of the stresses involved for parents and siblings who live with a retarded child, see E. SCHULMAN, *supra* note 26, at 96-125. *See also* J. GREENFELD, A CHILD CALLED NOAH: A FAMILY JOURNEY (1972) (personal account of father of autistic child). Families with a mentally disabled child frequently experience marital and financial stress. *See* Dunlap & Hollinsworth, *How Does a Handicapped Child Affect the Family? Implications for Practitioners,* 26 FAM. COORDINATOR 286 (1977); Sherman & Cocozza, *Stress in Families of the Developmentally Disabled: A Literature Review of Factors Affecting the Decision to Seek Out-of-Home Placements,* 33 FAM. REL. 95 (1984).

are alleviated. Her interest in family stability is substantial and therefore may warrant legal protection.

The individual's interest in family stability should become legally relevant with respect to the sterilization decision only if the individual is so seriously impaired that she will never be capable of making her own reproductive decisions. For example, a mildly retarded young woman whose parents respond to her promiscuous behavior by seeking sterilization might have an interest in reducing family stress; if sterilization is proscribed, her parents might respond with abusive treatment, unreasonable restrictions of her freedom, or even relinquishment of their parental role. However, this young woman will one day be independent and might at that time want to have children.[137] Thus her future capability to make decisions for herself precludes legal consideration of her present interest in family continuity. Using sterilization to promote family stability is as offensive here as it would be in the case of a promiscuous normal adolescent.

C. *The Autonomy Model and the Deficiencies of Current Law.*

The analytic framework developed in this Part suggests that current law falls short of its objective of promoting sterilization decisions that reflect the interests of mentally disabled persons. The preoccupation with correcting the abuses of the past in combination with a superficial analysis of the interests at stake has engendered significant distortions. Three problems result from the paternalism model's presumption that the primary interest at stake is the interest in procreation. First, in its effort to protect the mentally retarded person from wrongful sterilization, the law unduly restricts her right of self-determination. As I have shown, if only persons competent to make the medical decisions are deemed capable of making reproductive decisions for themselves, some persons who do have an interest in autonomy will find themselves subject to the authority of another decisionmaker. That is, an individual who is capable of deciding the more basic issue—whether or not to have a child—will sometimes, in the name of protection, be subject to a surrogate decisionmaker.

---

137. This situation was presented in Stump v. Sparkman, 435 U.S. 349 (1978). In that case, a mother, prompted by concern over her teenage daughter's promiscuity, successfully petitioned a judge for the daughter's sterilization. The daughter was described as "somewhat retarded," although she was promoted each year with her public school class. *Id.* at 351. She was told that the surgical procedure was an appendectomy and did not learn that she had been sterilized until she married and found that she was unable to become pregnant. *Id.* at 353. The daughter sued her mother and the judge who authorized the procedure. The Supreme Court upheld the judicial immunity of the judge, who had authorized the sterilization absent statutory authority. *Id.* at 364.

Second, laws based on the paternalism model treat sterilization as an infringement of the right to procreate rather than as a means of exercising the right not to procreate.[138] It is ironic that a legal rule designed to protect mentally disabled persons impairs the fundamental right to avoid pregnancy—a right that others can exercise freely. Laws premised on a strong presumption that every retarded person has an interest in procreation make consideration of the interest in avoiding pregnancy very difficult in some cases.

Finally, current law ignores the interest in family stability that the severely disabled person shares with her parents. Under the paternalism model, the parents' interest in convenience, reduced anxiety, and family stability is not only deemed irrelevant to the decision, but is presumed to conflict with the child's interest. This presumption is valid if an interest in procreation exists. If no such interest exists, however, ignoring the importance of family stability for the severely retarded person may well lead to a decision *contrary* to her best interest.

The analysis proposed here offers an alternative conception of the interests of the mentally retarded person for whom sterilization is proposed. The autonomy model defines the interests of the mentally disabled person in making her own reproductive decisions more broadly and more precisely than does the paternalism model. The competent person's interest in independent decisionmaking rests on her ability to make the underlying reproductive choice, whether or not she can implement that choice through a medical decision. The model suggests that the individual who is not capable of making autonomous reproductive decisions has an interest in preserving family stability, and that this interest will be promoted by state deference to parental authority.[139] Thus, in contrast to the paternalism model, which offers elaborate substantive criteria, the autonomy model identifies the correct allocation of decisionmaking authority as the means of advancing the retarded person's interests. The autonomy model indicates that the interests of the mentally retarded person will be best protected by a legal rule that limits protective state intervention and supports private decisionmaking by the individual or, if she is incompetent to make the reproductive decision, by her parents. The next Part examines the implications of the autonomy model for the formulation of an optimal legal rule.

---

138. *See supra* note 50.

139. The person incapable of making her own choices has an interest in having parents make decisions for her and in avoiding state interference. In analyzing the child's interest in parental authority under the constitutional family privacy doctrine, Garvey aptly asserts that "[c]onstitutional liberties protect children in the exercise of choices that their parents have made for them." Garvey, *supra* note 100, at 1782.

III. APPLICATION OF THE AUTONOMY MODEL

A. *Protecting Meaningful Choice—The Retarded Person as Decisionmaker.*

Devising a legal rule that protects the expansively defined autonomy interest of the competent retarded individual is more difficult than it might first appear. The autonomy model suggests that three separate inquiries are relevant: an inquiry into the individual's competency to make the decision to have children, an inquiry into her competency to avoid pregnancy, and an inquiry into her competency to elect sterilization.

The examination of competency is further complicated in this context by the unique relevance of the person's *future* competency and interest in autonomous choice. Because sterilization extinguishes reproductive capacity and moots the issue of reproductive choice, the law should preserve the disabled person's potential interest in making her own decisions if she might become competent in the future. Thus a determination of incompetency may require an evaluation of future functioning that is necessarily speculative in nature.

Because incompetency may be due to developmental factors, potential competency is particularly important if the mentally retarded person is a minor. To guard against error, sterilization might be restricted to adults.[140] However, because severely retarded minors have a strong interest in family continuity, they may particularly benefit from legal support for parental authority; a policy that proscribes their sterilization may not serve their interests. Despite uncertainty, it is possible to make a determination that some severely disabled minors will never have the capacity to make reproductive decisions independently.

A person also has an interest in preserving future options if she is competent but currently has no expressed preferences. Thus, the retarded person who is potentially a capable parent should not be sterilized on the ground that she has expressed no desire for children. Only her stable long-term desire not to have children should be implemented through sterilization.

When parents propose sterilization for a mentally retarded child, an evaluation by an expert in mental retardation is necessary. One source of erroneous sterilization decisions in the past was reliance on the attending physician's opinion that sterilization was medically appropriate. This

---

140. In most states, normal minors may not obtain sterilization because of the permanency of the procedure. Sterilization laws directed at mentally disabled persons require a determination of future incompetency, *see supra* note 34, thereby distinguishing the mentally retarded minor from other presumably incompetent normal minors.

Vol. 1986:806]   *STERILIZATION*   849

physician was usually a gynecologist with little or no expertise in assessing the functional capabilities of mentally disabled persons. Some current laws attempt to remedy this problem by requiring psychiatric, psychological, or "social" evaluation of the retarded individual.[141] However, little guidance is given regarding the focus of the evaluation or the required expertise of the evaluator. Most physicians, including psychiatrists, have very limited expertise in mental retardation; most psychologists have only marginally more., A specific designation of expertise and training in mental retardation would promote more accurate assessments of competency than are likely to result under current law.

The determination of whether the disabled individual has the ability to make her own reproductive decisions should begin with an evaluation of her interest in procreation. Then, if she does not want children, the competency of this choice must be assessed. If her decision to avoid pregnancy is competently made, further inquiry is necessary to determine whether she is capable of making the informed medical decision to implement her reproductive choice. The discussion that follows examines the implications of positive and negative findings of competency.

1. *Parenting Capacity and Reproductive Choice.* The autonomy model presumes an interest in procreation, unless the individual would be so limited in her parenting ability that the state would be justified in terminating her parental rights should she ever have a child. Thus, under the autonomy model, the individual who is capable of functioning as a minimally adequate parent will not be sterilized unless she competently chooses never to have children. Making a determination about parenting ability will admittedly be difficult unless the person has had substantial experience being with children.[142]

A person has the minimal capacity to function as a parent if she would be able to meet a child's most basic needs. Thus, a parent must be able to understand the child's basic nutritional requirements and protect

---

141. *See supra* note 38.

142. The assessment of present competency to make a decision is potentially a highly reliable judgment. It can be compared with determinations about competency of criminal defendants to stand trial. *See* R. ROESCH & S. GOLDING, COMPETENCY TO STAND TRIAL (1980). Much more uncertain are evaluations that predict how someone will function or act in the future. *See* J. MONAHAN, PREDICTING VIOLENT BEHAVIOR: AN ASSESSMENT OF CLINICAL TECHNIQUES (1981); Melton & Scott, *supra* note 122, at 39.

Several types of inquiry may be useful in assessing potential parental competency. An assessment of the person's actual and potential ability to care for herself is important because the person who cannot provide for her own nutritional, health, and safety needs cannot assume responsibility for another person. The individual's experience in caring for her own children, her siblings, or neighborhood children is also significant. Problem-solving hypotheticals involving typical child care issues may also be useful.

the child from physical harm. She must be able to discern illness and know how to obtain medical help; she should also be able to express affection and provide adequate supervision of the child's daily routine.

The retarded person's interest in having children, however, should not be contingent on her ability to perform other functions usually associated with being a "good" parent.[143] If she must demonstrate a more sophisticated capability to provide intellectual stimulation or meet the child's emotional needs, she will be subject to standards of competency in parenting that are not applied to others. Although good parents typically provide an intellectually stimulating environment, many normal parents do not. Horizontal equity thus dictates that nothing more than a standard of minimal adequacy be required.

The individual who is not capable of functioning as a parent has no interest in procreation and the choice to have children is not available to her. Arguably, she might have the capability to choose among alternatives for avoiding pregnancy; if so, her competent preferences should be respected. It is unlikely, however, that a person who is incapable of being a minimally adequate parent because of mental retardation will have the cognitive ability to consider contraceptive alternatives and make an informed medical decision.[144] If she is incompetent, a decision will be made for her by her parents or (in some cases) by a court.

2. *Protecting the Decision to Avoid Pregnancy: Reproductive Choice and the Medical Decision.* A mentally disabled person may clearly and unambiguously express a desire not to have children. If she understands the implications of the decision and if it is made without coercive influence, her expressed preference should be respected by the law as a com-

---

143. The findings of research assessing the parental capability of mentally disabled persons are mixed. This research involves only parents who are mildly or moderately retarded. Some observers have suggested that the children of mentally retarded parents may suffer from a lack of intellectual stimulation. *See* E. SCHULMAN, *supra* note 26, at 302. An early study of mentally disabled parents found that 42% provided adequate care for their children's physical needs, 32% provided marginal care, and 26% provided care warranting removal. *See* Mickelson, *The Feebleminded Parent: A Study of 90 Family Cases,* 51 AM. J. MENTAL DEFICIENCY 644, 645 (1947). Some researchers have observed that although mentally retarded parents may not provide care meeting "middle class" standards, most do provide adequate care. *See* Murphy, Coleman & Abel, *Human Sexuality in the Mentally Retarded,* in TREATMENT ISSUES AND INNOVATIONS IN MENTAL RETARDATION 615 (J. Matson & F. Andrasik eds. 1983).

Support services may be available to provide parents with training and assistance. *See* Mickelson, *supra,* at 644. Rosenberg and McTate reported that mildly retarded persons who participated in parent training programs were able to improve their parenting skills. Rosenberg & McTate, *supra* note 30, at 24, 37.

144. If such a hypothetical person existed, her interest might be characterized as an interest in controlling the *health care* decision, rather than an interest in controlling the *reproductive* decision. In any event it would be a restricted exercise of autonomy since she is not free to choose the alternative of having children.

petent and meaningful reproductive choice. Evaluation of the competency of this decision should focus on the consistency, clarity, and stability of the expressed choice and on the extent to which the decision is an independent one.

If the disabled person is found to be making a meaningful decision to terminate permanently her ability to have children, an examination of her competency to make an informed medical decision regarding sterilization should follow. The predominant standard defining competency to make medical decisions, and the one applicable to sterilization decisions, is the appreciation standard.[145] This standard requires an inquiry into whether the individual has an inferential and factual understanding of the procedure's purpose, consequences, risks, and benefits, as well as an appreciation of the contraceptive alternatives available to her.

The evaluation of competency should focus on the person's understanding of the following: (a) the contraceptive purpose of sterilization, (b) the nature of the procedure (the incision, hospitalization, use of anesthesia), (c) the permanence of reproductive incapacity following sterilization, (d) the risks associated with the procedure (pain, possible infection or other complications), and (e) the availability and important characteristics of nonpermanent forms of contraception.[146] The individual must be provided with sufficient information about the proposed sterilization to make an informed decision; a finding of incompetency should be based not on a lack of knowledge, but only on incapacity to understand the necessary information.

The doctrine of informed consent requires that the decision be voluntary as well as competent and informed.[147] Given the potential conflict of interest between parent and child, the dependence of the individual on her parents, and the observed suggestibility of retarded persons, parental overbearance may be a significant possibility. Therefore, the independence of the individual's preferences as well as the extent to which her choices have been influenced by others must be determined.

A determination regarding the individual's competency to make the medical decision should be made as accurately, but as unobtrusively, as possible. A nonjudicial review of the finding that the person has competently decided on sterilization may often be desirable; however, it should be undertaken in such a way as to minimize intrusion into the person's

---

145. *See supra* note 113 and accompanying text.

146. *See* Melton & Scott, *supra* note 122, at 38-39. The most critical factor and the one most mentally disabled persons are unlikely to understand is irreversibility. *See infra* note 149.

147. *See* Meisel, Roth & Lidz, *Toward a Model of the Legal Definition of Informed Consent*, 134 AM. J. PSYCHIATRY 285, 286 (1977).

privacy.[148] Further inquiry is warranted only if competency to make the medical decision is questionable.

Some persons may be capable of making a competent decision not to have children but incapable of making an informed medical decision. A person who is unable to think abstractly about decisionmaking in the remote future might not fully understand that sterilization results in permanent infertility; she may, however, have unambiguously stated over an extended period of time that she does not want to have children. This person may be making a meaningful reproductive choice never to have children; the inference can be drawn that permanence is desired. Nonetheless, in those states that follow the paternalism model, her inability to understand the concept of permanence would preclude a competent medical decision and thus foreclose the possibility of sterilization, particularly if she already has children.[149]

3. *Protecting Against Erroneous Decisions.* The more expansive recognition of the autonomy interest of retarded persons under the autonomy model may arguably increase the risk of erroneous decisions to sterilize. The acquiescent or well-coached person might erroneously be characterized as making a meaningful decision to opt for sterilization. An error of this kind is particularly costly if the person has an interest in procreation.[150]

A few safeguards will reduce this risk. A comprehensive evaluation of the individual's decision by an expert in mental retardation is essential.[151] If the person is incompetent to make the medical decision, a determination that sterilization is the optimal means of implementing her competent reproductive choice should be made. If she is potentially a competent parent, sterilization is usually appropriate only if a normal person in similar circumstances would choose this alternative.[152] A mechanism should be provided to review the findings of competency and to determine the appropriateness of sterilization to implement the choice. Given the reproductive interest at stake, a judicial proceeding may be warranted. A less costly and less intrusive alternative would be review

---

148. *See supra* notes 129-30, 174.

149. For example, the patient described *supra* note 114 had consistently said for years that she wanted "no more babies." There was no indication that she would ever change her mind. She could not, however, think abstractly and hypothetically about how she might feel in the distant future. When asked "What if you should change your mind in ten years?," she would only repeat the assertion that she wanted a boyfriend and "no more babies."

150. *See supra* note 90.

151. Many current sterilization laws require evaluation by an expert. *See supra* note 38.

152. *See supra* notes 83-87.

by a committee modeled on a hospital ethics committee.[153] Finally, since informed consent to the medical procedure must be provided by some competent person, the parents' consent should be required.

4. *Summary.*   When parents seek to have their child sterilized, an expert in mental retardation should examine the child and assess her capacity to make reproductive choices for herself. First, the expert should assess her interest in having children. If she has the ability to provide minimally adequate care for a child, no further inquiry is needed; sterilization should be proscribed *unless* she expresses a clear and independent preference not to have children. If she lacks an interest in procreation, the choice to have children will be unavailable to her. In most cases, a decision will be made for her as an incompetent.

    If the individual expresses a preference not to have children, the second stage of inquiry begins with an examination of her capacity to make this decision autonomously. If her preference represents a rational choice, examination of her ability to make the implementing informed medical decision should follow. If she is competent, she should be treated like a normal person. If she is not, further assessment may be needed to probe the stability and consistency of her decision and to determine whether sterilization represents an appropriate medical response. Some independent review of these latter decisions is advisable.

B. *The Incompetent Individual: Who Decides?*

    Analysis under the autonomy model indicates that the range of individuals who are competent to make reproductive decisions is broader than current law recognizes. Some persons, however, will have no interest in procreation and will be unable to make their own reproductive choices. Under the paternalism model, they will be subject to courts as decisionmakers; their parents are legally disqualified because of a presumed conflict of interest. The autonomy model indicates that the se-

---

153. For a discussion of the function of hospital ethics committees and the recommended role of this type of committee when parents make decisions for incompetents, see *infra* note 174 and accompanying text.

    There are three situations in which some kind of independent review of the competency determination may be indicated:

    1) The retarded person is found competent to make the medical decision and chooses sterilization.

    2) The retarded person is found competent to make the reproductive but not the medical decision, her decision is never to have children, and sterilization appears to best implement her choice.

    3) The retarded person is incompetent to make the reproductive decision and her parents seek authority to make the sterilization decision.

In choosing the kind of review process, interests in individual and family privacy as well as accuracy are relevant. *See supra* notes 120-37 and accompanying text.

verely impaired individual lacks an interest in having children; in such case there is no significant conflict of interest and a legal rule promoting family privacy and supporting parental authority will best protect her interests. Paternalistic judicial intervention should occur only when necessary to ensure that the retarded individual's rights are not violated.

It is for good reason that the law traditionally recognizes parents as decisionmakers for children.[154] No one else knows the child as well or cares about her as much as do her parents. Although most adults no longer need their parents to make decisions for them, the rationale supporting parental authority can still be valid with respect to incompetent adults.[155] For children and for many incompetent adults, substitution of a nonparent as decisionmaker is beneficial only if there is a serious conflict of interest between parent and child.[156]

---

154. There is a strong tradition of legal support for parents' authority to make decisions for their children and to generally direct their upbringing. The Supreme Court has recognized the constitutional status of the interest in family privacy, and has upheld parental authority against state intervention in several decisions. *See* Wisconsin v. Yoder, 406 U.S. 205, 234 (1972) (right of Amish parents to withdraw children from school at age 14, though legal minimum age was 16); Pierce v. Society of Sisters, 268 U.S. 510, 534 (1925) (statute requiring that all children be sent to public schools unreasonably interfered with the "liberty of parents and guardians to direct the upbringing and education of children under their control"); Meyer v. Nebraska, 262 U.S. 390, 399 (1923) (statute forbidding the teaching of foreign languages before the eighth grade unreasonably interfered with the right to "establish a home and bring up children").

The state may intervene to protect children if the parents' decisions or conduct threatens harm to the child. *See* Prince v. Massachusetts, 321 U.S. 158, 166 (1944) (statute prohibiting minor from selling newspapers and prohibiting adult from furnishing minor with newspapers did not infringe fourteenth amendment protected liberty). The state's parens patriae interest in the welfare of children supports state intervention in cases of abuse and neglect.

There has been a considerable amount of scholarly commentary on the tension between family privacy and the state's interest in protecting children. *See* J. GOLDSTEIN, A. FREUD & J. SOLNIT, BEFORE THE BEST INTERESTS OF THE CHILD 28-133 (1979); R. MNOOKIN, CHILD, FAMILY AND STATE 29-64 (1978); Wald, *Children's Rights: A Framework for Analysis,* 12 U.C. DAVIS L. REV. 225, 281 (1979). In the first half of this century the rise of the juvenile court system and social work movement created enthusiasm for state intervention to protect children. *See generally* M. LEVINE & A. LEVINE, A SOCIAL HISTORY OF HELPING SERVICES 46-47 (1970); A. PLATT, THE CHILD SAVERS: THE INVENTION OF DELINQUENCY 45 (1977). But modern commentators have challenged the notion that children benefit when the state intervenes to protect them from their parents. *See* J. GOLDSTEIN, A. FREUD & J. SOLNIT, *supra,* at 9; Chambers, *The "Legalization" of the Family: Toward a Policy of Supportive Neutrality,* 18 U. MICH. J.L. REF. 805, 817 (1985); Mnookin, *Foster Care—In Whose Best Interest?,* 43 HARV. EDUC. REV. 599, 622-26 (1973); Wald, 27 STAN. L. REV. 985, 987-89 (1975).

In recent years there has also been a recognition that the child herself may have an interest in controlling decisions, particularly reproductive decisions, that affect her life. *See supra* note 104. Thus, legal policy dealing with children may on some issues have to balance three interests: the state's parens patriae interest, the parents' (and child's) interest in family privacy, and the child's autonomy interest. *See* Garvey, *Child, Parent, State and the Due Process Clause: An Essay on the Supreme Court's Most Recent Work,* 51 S. CAL. L. REV. 769 (1978).

155. *See infra* notes 171-72 and accompanying text.

156. *See infra* notes 160-69 and accompanying text.

1. *Examining the Conflict of Interest.* A constricted range of interests are at stake for a severely disabled person when her parents propose sterilization. This person will never function as a parent. Meaningful decisions about reproduction or about the medical means for avoiding pregnancy are beyond her capabilities. Thus, no interest in self-determination or in reproduction is potentially in conflict with her parents' interest in seeking sterilization. The severely retarded person does, however, have an interest in avoiding pregnancy. The physical strain of pregnancy and the discomfort, pain, and risk of childbirth are burdens to be avoided when the individual cannot enjoy or adequately care for a baby. Indeed, when a severely retarded young woman is at risk of becoming pregnant, few question either her interest in avoiding pregnancy or her parents' authority to protect her by employing *some* form of contraception. Beyond this, the severely impaired person has an interest in avoiding unnecessary medical risk; any surgical or medical procedures should be beneficial to her, and risk, discomfort, and intrusiveness should be minimized. She also has a right to be treated with dignity. Her objections should be taken seriously, and her privacy should not be unduly sacrificed. Finally, her interest in family functioning will often be implicated because sterilization of the severely retarded person can lighten the burden of responsibility on her parents or contribute to their determination to continue to care for her at home.

For persons who will never have an interest in reproduction, a substantial conflict of interest with their parents is likely only if the parents seek to have a hysterectomy performed. The convenience to parents of avoiding menstrual hygiene care may clash with the child's interest in avoiding the substantial risk and intrusiveness that attends this surgical procedure. If the parents propose a less intrusive form of sterilization for their severely impaired child, no significant conflict of interest is apparent. Indeed, this child and her parents have a mutual interest in avoiding the child's pregnancy and promoting family stability. Furthermore, the child's interest in minimizing medical risk is served as well, or nearly as well, by sterilization as it would be by alternative contraceptive options.

2. *The Costs of Withholding Parental Authority.* The rigorous procedural and substantive requirements under current law impose formidable costs on the family, in terms of money, time expended, and psychological stress. In most states, parents seeking sterilization will have to hire an attorney to pursue their objective.[157] They may have to pay for

---

157. Most parents will need the assistance of a lawyer to file the petition and present supporting evidence. Although most laws provide for the appointment of a guardian ad litem for the child, none provides the parent with legal assistance.

mental health evaluations and will often be forced to miss time from work. Furthermore, to the extent that the procedure imposes burdensome requirements and particularly if it has an adversarial character, it will predictably create greater tension within a family unit already subject to considerable stress.

Many parents who have struggled with the burden of caring for a severely disabled child will understandably resent a judicial proceeding that is premised on the notions that they are pursuing their own interest in seeking their child's sterilization and that a judge can better decide what is best for their child. If sterilization is denied because rigorous substantive requirements are not met, the parents' frustration can have a disruptive effect on their ability to care for the child. For some parents, fear that their child may become pregnant will severely strain their ability to cope with the difficulties of caring for a retarded child. Sterilization may be a means of preserving family functioning by helping parents meet their responsibilities; they may view it as an alternative to institutionalization or foster care.[158]

For severely impaired individuals whose parents propose a nonintrusive type of sterilization, judicial scrutiny serves only one useful purpose. A check is needed to ensure that the individual actually lacks any reproductive autonomy interest. It is possible to accomplish this objective with less cost to the family and the disabled person than is the case under current law. Indeed, as I shall argue below, some individuals can receive adequate protection with no judicial proceeding.

Along with costly procedural protections, current law imposes burdensome substantive barriers. These include requirements that no temporary form of contraception be workable, that the individual be currently engaging in sexual activity, and that sterilization be necessary to preserve the physical or mental health of the individual. These criteria are based on the assumption that a significant reproductive interest is threatened by the sterilization initiative. As applied to a category of persons without this interest, these requirements become superfluous and serve to thwart parental efforts without offering a corresponding benefit to the child. Thus, they can ultimately do more harm than good to the disabled person.

The preservation of family functioning and the minimization of stress are as important to the severely disabled person as to her parents. To the extent that the procedural and substantive requirements under

---

158. In cases evaluated at the Forensic Psychiatry Clinic at the University of Virginia, parents often expressed frustration and resentment at the expense and complex legal requirements for sterilization and occasionally have said that they would give up custody if sterilization were not possible.

current law place additional stress on the family, they represent a cost to the subject of the sterilization initiative as well as to her parents.

3. *The Constitutional Parameters: Parental Authority and Children's Reproductive Rights.* The traditional legal authority of parents to make medical decisions for their children rests, in part, on a presumption that parents are motivated to promote their children's interests. If parental authority conflicts with an important interest of the child's, it should be withdrawn.

Courts and commentators, emphasizing the potential for a conflict of interest, have suggested that the retarded person's constitutional interest in reproductive privacy is not protected unless parental authority is withdrawn.[159] It might be thought that the autonomy model violates this interest by allowing parents to make the sterilization decision for severely impaired children. Yet the critical interest in reproductive autonomy that mandates protection is absent in these cases and consequently there is no substantial ground for withdrawal of parental authority.

The Supreme Court has examined constitutional challenges to parental authority to make sensitive medical decisions for the child in two contexts—abortion and psychiatric hospitalization. In both areas, an important interest of the child may conflict with the parents' interest, and the presumption underlying parental authority—that parents will act in their child's best interest—is called into question. These cases are often pointed to by those who support withdrawal of parental authority in the sterilization context. However, an examination of the Court's analysis in the abortion and psychiatric hospitalization cases supports the contention that a constitutional challenge to parental authority to make the decision to sterilize a severely retarded child has little merit.

a. *The Abortion Rights of Minors.* The mature minor who seeks an abortion is making a meaningful reproductive choice that should be respected. Indeed, under my analysis, this recognition should not be contingent on her capacity to give informed consent to the medical procedure. Unless undue coercion is involved, her decision not to continue the pregnancy warrants the withdrawal of traditional parental authority.[160]

The abortion cases present a situation in which parents and child are in actual disagreement over the decision to abort, or in which the child is

---

159. *See In re* C.D.M., 627 P.2d 607, 614 (Alaska 1981); *In re* A.W., 637 P.2d 366, 370 (Colo. 1981); *In re* Grady, 85 N.J. 235, 264, 426 A.2d 467, 482 (1981); Murdock, *supra* note 10, at 932-34; Price & Burt, *supra* note 25, at 69-70; Sherlock & Sherlock, *supra* note 10, at 955.

160. A determination that she is too immature to make this decision may lead to the paradoxical result that her pregnancy should continue and the immature minor should become a mother.

reluctant to consult her parents because she fears conflict.[161] Furthermore, other interests besides health are at stake here and a congruence of interests between parent and child cannot be presumed. Therefore, the traditional presumption that parents will make medical decisions that promote their child's health must be set aside. It is the possible conflict of interest and probable conflict in fact between parent and child over a matter of critical importance to the child's life, as well as the assumption that the child is mature and making a rational choice, that justifies the withdrawal of parental authority.

In *Planned Parenthood v. Danforth,* [162] the Court rejected the notion that absolute parental authority over a minor's abortion decision could be justified on the basis of an interest in preserving family stability:

> It is difficult . . . to conclude that providing a parent with absolute power to overrule a determination, made by the physician and his minor patient, to terminate the patient's pregnancy will strengthen the family unit. Neither is it likely that such veto power will enhance parental authority . . . where the minor and the nonconsenting parent are so fundamentally in conflict and the very existence of the pregnancy already has fractured the family structure.[163]

A mildly disabled individual whose parents seek sterilization has an interest in making autonomous reproductive choices similar to that of a minor contemplating abortion. However, the analogy is not applicable to a retarded person who is so disabled that she lacks the ability to make the decision. These cases typically arise in a context that differs substantially from that of the teenager seeking an abortion without her parents' knowledge. If the child is significantly retarded, it is probable that her parents have initiated the procedure; the child's response is likely to be incomprehension or assent. Since the child has no interest in reproduction, there is no potential conflict of interest with her parents unless an intrusive sterilization procedure is proposed. The overt, or at least implicit, family conflict inherent in the abortion context is absent here. Thus, the sterilization decision is not made in the context of the "fractured" family structure discerned by the Court in *Danforth*. Indeed, the sterilization initiative might represent an effort by the parents to preserve

---

161. In a study of 1170 teenagers who obtained abortions, the Alan Guttmacher Institute found that approximately 55% reported that their parents were aware of their decision to abort. Of those whose parents did not know, 23% said they would not have gone to an abortion clinic if they had been required to tell their parents; 40% of these said they would have obtained an illegal abortion. *See* Torres, Forrest & Eisman, *Telling Parents: Clinic Policies and Adolescents' Use of Family Planning and Abortion Services,* 12 FAM. PLAN. PERSP. 284 (1980). Some studies have suggested that minors overestimate the negativity of parents' reactions. *See* Furstenburg, *The Social Consequences of Teenage Parenthood,* 8 FAM. PLAN. PERSP. 148 (1976). Nonetheless, fears can affect the minor's behavior.

162. 428 U.S. 52 (1976).

163. *Id.* at 75.

family functioning and thereby continue to meet their responsibilities to-ward their retarded child, an objective that surely promotes the interest of the retarded person.

    b. *The Analogy to Psychiatric Hospitalization.* The efforts of par-ents to obtain sterilization for their retarded child are also analogous to the efforts of parents seeking to have their reluctant child committed to a psychiatric hospital. Involuntary psychiatric hospitalization is a coercive medical intervention and the interests of the parents can conflict with a constitutionally protected liberty interest held by the resisting child. In *Parham v. J.R.,* [164] however, the Supreme Court upheld a Georgia statute that authorized parents to place their minor children in psychiatric hos-pitals, refusing to require a "formal adversary pre-admission hearing" to protect the child's liberty interest.[165] The Court stated that "[t]he fact that a child may balk at hospitalization . . . does not diminish the par-ents' authority to decide what is best for the child."[166]

    As Justice Brennan pointed out in his dissenting opinion in *Parham,* a significant conflict of interest is possible in this situation. The parents' decision to hospitalize might be motivated by a desire to relieve the fam-ily of the burden of a disruptive child. Justice Brennan argued that the child whose parents seek to surrender custody to a state mental institu-tion has, in effect, been "ousted from his family."[167] The hospital may serve as a "dumping ground" for children whose parents either cannot or will not continue to care for them.[168] Policy reasons for maintaining pa-rental authority—supporting the preservation of the family unit and pro-tecting family privacy—are less compelling in this situation.

    The parents' decision to sterilize can pose a greater threat to a po-tentially competent child's constitutionally protected interests than does the decision to hospitalize; sterilization is permanent while psychiatric hospitalization may be of limited duration. However, if the child is not potentially capable of reproductive choice, she is less at risk than the child for whom hospitalization is sought. Parents seeking sterilization are not trying to "dump" their retarded child. Their initiative may well

---

    164. 442 U.S. 584 (1979). For a critical analysis of this case, see Melton, *Family and Mental Hospital as Myths: Civil Commitment of Minors,* in CHILDREN, MENTAL HEALTH AND THE LAW 1983, at 151 (1983).

    165. *Parham,* 442 U.S. at 603.

    166. *Id.* at 604.

    167. *Id.* at 631 (Brennan, J., dissenting).

    168. *Id.* at 629 ("The National Institute of Mental Health recently found that only 36% of patients below age 20 who were confined in St. Elizabeth's Hospital actually required such hospitali-zation."). The literature does not support the majority's positive view of state mental hospitals and their potential benefits to the unwilling minor whose parents seek her admission. *See* Melton, *supra* note 164, at 158-59.

be an effort to facilitate her continued care at home. Thus, potential conflicts of interest would seem less probable in this situation than when psychiatric hospitalization is proposed.

Preserving parental authority to make the sterilization decision for severely impaired children does not inherently violate a constitutionally protected interest. The critical reproductive interest that mandates protection in abortion cases and in sterilization cases involving less disabled persons is absent. Furthermore, the potential for conflict would appear to be less threatening than when psychiatric hospitalization is sought by parents—a decision that the Court has found may be appropriately made by parents and doctors without judicial intervention.[169] Thus, some retention of parental authority in these cases should pass constitutional muster.

The interest of both parent and child in family privacy has itself been accorded constitutional protection on both libertarian and utilitarian grounds.[170] Sound legal policy limits state intervention in family affairs to situations in which there is a real threat of harm to the child or in which there is a significant conflict of interest. A parental decision to sterilize a severely retarded child for contraceptive purposes by a nonintrusive procedure falls within the traditional legal and constitutional protections. Expansive paternalistic intervention by the state that does not protect the child is not a valid exercise of parens patriae authority.

Parents who seek sterilization of adult children may seem less clearly suitable as decisionmakers. Traditional parental authority ex-

---

169. The Georgia law upheld in *Parham* required independent review by the medical director of the facility of the appropriateness of the admission. What the Court rejected was the need for formal adversary hearings, which the Court characterized as "time-consuming procedural minuets." *Parham*, 442 U.S. at 605. The Court found that requiring a hearing would be disruptive to the family and would discourage parents from seeking needed treatment. *Id.* at 605.

170. *See supra* note 154. Libertarian support for family privacy is the extension to the family unit of a belief in the primacy of the *individual* under the due process clause of the fourteenth amendment. Within the family, parents are the natural decisionmakers for their minor children. For an analysis of parental authority to make medical decisions for children, see Goldstein, *Medical Care for the Child at Risk: On State Supervention of Parental Authority*, 86 YALE L.J. 645 (1977).

The utilitarian position emphasizes not so much the inviolability of the parents' liberty interest as it does the insubstantial quality of the state interest that justifies intervention. The proposition that children are generally better off if the state does not interfere with the family is supported by three arguments. First, it is uncertain when parental conduct will harm children. Second, the intervention may be harmful because it disrupts the child's life and family ties. Finally, the alternative placement offered by the state may be harmful to the child because it is unclear that children benefit from foster-care placements. In sum, family privacy should receive legal support because parens patriae intervention may do more harm than good. Compared with the libertarian, the utilitarian more readily accepts increased state intervention if it is demonstrably beneficial to children. *Compare* J. GOLDSTEIN, A. FREUD, A. SOLNIT & S. GOLDSTEIN, IN THE BEST INTERESTS OF THE CHILD (1986) (libertarian approach) *with* Mnookin, *supra* note 154 (utilitarian approach).

tends only to minors, unless a guardianship has been established.[171] Furthermore, the interest in family continuity is often less compelling, since most adult children can be expected to leave home at some point.[172] Nonetheless, parental authority should be maintained in cases involving severely retarded adults who have been cared for by parents since childhood. One can assume that these parents know their child better than anyone else and that they are most concerned with her interests. If a surrogate is needed, there is no reason to believe that a court will make better decisions than parents in cases in which no apparent conflict of interest exists. Even if the disabled individual may eventually leave home to live more independently—an objective which loving parents might promote—the parents are still the best decisionmakers for their incompetent child.

   4. *Safeguarding Against Erroneous Decisions.* The primary barrier to recognizing parental authority to make sterilization decisions is the concern that person in question will be erroneously classified as lacking an interest in reproductive autonomy. The principal justification for judicial intervention is that it reduces error and provides optimal protection of that interest. Although this protective approach imposes significant costs on an already burdened family, it may seem necessary to ensure that an accurate evaluation of the individual's capacities is made.

   Under the autonomy model, there are two ways to reduce error without unduly sacrificing of family privacy. The first, discussed above, is to ensure that determinations regarding competency are made by an expert.[173] The second involves linking the scope of judicial intervention to the level of disability. Error can be reduced by increasing the level of scrutiny and procedural protection in cases in which there exists an enhanced possibility that the individual has a reproductive interest.

   Mentally disabled persons who will require lifelong care clearly lack the capacity to care for a child. They also have a greater interest in family continuity and stability than do those who are less disabled. Thus, only minimal procedural requirements are desirable. If a reliable clinical evaluation shows that the person lacks the capacity to care for herself, little risk is created by avoiding a judicial proceeding altogether and permitting the sterilization to be performed upon parental request and authorization.

---

   171. *See supra* notes 101-02 and accompanying text.

   172. An objective for many retarded adults is to live in a home or apartment with a few other disabled persons with minimal assistance and supervision. *See* E. SCHULMAN, *supra* note 26, at 65.

   173. *See supra* note 151 and accompanying text.

In the case of a less disabled person who is potentially capable of caring for herself, but who clearly lacks an interest in reproduction, judicial review is desirable if the procedural costs to the individual and her family are outweighed by the potential for reducing error. Alternatively, procedural costs might be reduced without unduly sacrificing accuracy by using a less formal review forum similar to a hospital ethics committee.[174] Such a committee could undertake nonadversarial review of the expert's evaluation to ensure that it is competent, independent, and based on all relevant information. The committee could consult with other experts or with the parents. Such a nonjudicial review mechanism would protect family privacy and stability to a greater degree than would a judicial proceeding.

If the disability is less severe, the possibility of underestimating the interest in reproductive choice becomes greater, and the costs of procedural protections become more acceptable. Thus, if the findings of the expert raise any ambiguity about the individual's potential interest in reproductive choice, judicial review is warranted.

---

174. Institutional Review Boards (IRBs) review proposals for research involving human subjects with the objective of protecting the subjects from undue harm and ensuring informed consent. Federal regulations require IRB approval of virtually all federally funded research. *See* 45 C.F.R. § 46.103 (1985). The committee must be diverse in membership and must include members from diverse disciplines and different medical specialties. *See id.* § 46.107. *See generally* N. HERSHEY & R. MILLER, HUMAN EXPERIMENTATION AND THE LAW 47 (1976); R. LEVINE, ETHICS AND REGULATION OF CLINICAL RESEARCH 321-63 (1986). For an analysis of ethics committees and the law, see Capron, *Legal Perspectives on Institutional Ethics Committees,* 11 J.C. & U.L. 417 (1985).

Ethics committees have been established in other areas to review or make recommendations regarding medical decisions. For example, Infant Care Review Committees (ICRCs) assist in decisionmaking about critically ill newborns. The current applicable HHS regulation recommends that any health care provider receiving federal assistance establish an ICRC. 45 C.F.R. § 84.55(a) (1985). The regulation includes an advisory model making the committee responsible for: (1) recommending institutional policies concerning the withholding or withdrawal of life-sustaining treatment for seriously ill newborns, (2) providing advice when life-sustaining treatment is in question, and (3) reviewing situations where life-sustaining medical or surgical treatment has been withdrawn. HHS recommends that the IRCRs include members from varied backgrounds such as doctors, nurses, hospital administrators, lawyers, disability group representatives, and community members. HHS also recommends that a medical staff member serve as chairperson. *Id.* § 84.55(f). In Bowen v. American Hosp. Ass'n, 106 S. Ct. 2101 (1986), the Supreme Court upheld parental authority to elect to withhold life-sustaining treatment from seriously ill newborns and invalidated four subsections of section 84.55, including the subsection that required health care institutions receiving federal funds to post notice that treatment could not be withheld from handicapped infants solely because of their handicap. 45 C.F.R. § 84.55(b) (1985). Subsections (a) and (f) were not challenged, however. *See Bowen,* 106 S. Ct. at 2106 n.4. The American Academy of Pediatrics adopted guidelines for Hospital Infant Bioethics Committees in April 1984. *See American Academy of Pediatrics Guidelines for Infant Bioethics Committees,* 11 J.C. & U.L. 433 (1985).

A sterilization-review committee might include mental retardation experts, gynecologists, psychologists, attorneys, parents, and mental disability advocates. The committee should review the professional assessment of competency, not decide whether sterilization is in the individual's best interest. In performing its review, it may be necessary for the committee to speak directly with the individual and her parents, although this may have significant privacy costs. *See supra* notes 129-30.

Mandatory judicial review may also be indicated if the person protests the sterilization in any meaningful way, regardless of her level of disability.[175] The incompetent person's protest should not be a bar to her parents' decision. Nonetheless, it would justify mandatory judicial scrutiny of her lack of competency.

The autonomy model contemplates a considerably more limited judicial role than does the paternalism model. Decisions made outside the judicial process will often better serve the interests of the disabled person. For the seriously disabled individual, family privacy and stability will be promoted by as simple a review process as is consistent with an accurate assessment of her interests. For the clearly competent or potentially competent person, judicial review should only be triggered, if at all, when sterilization is proposed as a means to implement the choice to avoid pregnancy by a person who lacks the capacity to make the medical decision.

There are only two situations under the autonomy model in which it is appropriate for courts to actually decide whether sterilization is in the best interest of the incompetent disabled person.[176] The first is when the parents seek a hysterectomy for their child; the second is when the parents who are seeking sterilization of their child have not assumed primary responsibility for her care. In both instances, the autonomy model indicates that the interests of the individual are such that the parents can no longer be presumed to be the best decisionmaker.

a. *The Special Case of Hysterectomy.* Judicial scrutiny is appropriate if a hysterectomy is sought because this operation subjects the individual to major surgery that is not required for gynecological reasons.[177] Parents may seek a hysterectomy for a number of reasons. Usually they desire to end their daughter's menstrual cycles because they believe that she is unable to manage menstrual hygiene tasks. Some parents may seek a hysterectomy because their daughter experiences physical or psychological problems during menstruation.[178] Finally, parents may propose a

---

175. Some threshold of understanding may be required before judicial review is triggered; a young child or seriously retarded person may protest a medical procedure without comprehension. The review is a mechanism to ensure that the individual has not been wrongly classified as one who lacks reproductive interests. Responding to the protest by invoking the judicial process signifies that the individual's objection is respected. For an analysis of the importance of process to human dignity, see Mashaw, *Administrative Due Process: The Quest for a Dignitary Theory,* 61 B.U.L. REV. 885 (1981).

176. *See supra* notes 154-56 and accompanying text.

177. *See supra* note 126 and accompanying text.

178. Parents often report that their retarded daughters are unduly distressed during their periods and are consequently difficult to manage at home and at school. Some may even react self-destructively. Thus, in some families, the girl's period may cause considerable disruption each month. In

hysterectomy for their own and their daughter's convenience, even if the child experiences few problems with menstruation. They may reason that since their disabled daughter will never want to have children, a hysterectomy is a desirable way to avoid the monthly "hassle" of menstruation.[179] In light of the significant medical risks involved, few normal women would consider undergoing a hysterectomy purely for convenience. Therefore, a decision to subject an incompetent individual to this procedure cannot be justified on such relatively minor grounds.

The important inquiry when a hysterectomy is proposed is whether the problems associated with the menstrual periods substantially interfere with the individual's functioning and well-being and, if they do, whether they are subject to remediation. Parents (and even teachers) often underestimate the potential for training mentally disabled girls to manage menstrual hygiene tasks and thus may exaggerate the burden.[180]

b. *Petitioning Parents Who Have Relinquished Care of Their Child.* The case for supporting parental authority to make the sterilization decision is considerably weakened if the parents have put the child in an institution or surrendered custody to a state agency. These parents may lack the intimate concern for and knowledge about the child which, in the case of custodial parents, supports the presumption that the parents will act to promote the child's interest. Furthermore, there is less reason to support the authority of parents who have not assumed the burdensome responsibility of care for the disabled child. Moreover, some parents in this situation may petition for sterilization because of pressure from the facility where the child resides. Finally, the retarded person's interest in family continuity and harmony is not great in this context.

Although there is less reason to support parental authority in these cases, it does not necessarily follow that a court will always be a better decisionmaker. A court, however, is less likely than the parents to be subject to external pressures or be influenced by a conflict of interest in this context. A judicial decisionmaker is arguably preferable because there is no compelling argument that the child's interest is better protected by preserving parental authority. The court should make the decision that a reasonable and concerned parent would make to promote the

---

one Forensic Psychiatry Clinic case, E.'s mother reported that she was required to miss three or four days of work each month when her severely retarded daughter had her period because E.'s teacher and sitter found E.'s inability to manage menstrual hygiene tasks so offensive that they urged E.'s mother to keep her at home during these times.

179. In several of the Forensic Psychiatry Clinic cases, doctors advised parents to seek hysterectomy despite the absence of serious problems. *See supra* note 126 and accompanying text. Parents sometimes seemed unaware that hysterectomy is major surgery.

180. *See supra* note 127.

child's welfare. Considerations may include the likelihood of sexual activity and risk of pregnancy, the relative benefits to this individual of alternative forms of contraception, and the individual's expressed or anticipated preferences.

IV. CONCLUSION

The undisputed objective of sterilization law is to promote decisions that reflect the interests of the disabled person. The autonomy model proposed in this article offers a more accurate and precise definition of these interests than does the paternalism model that forms the foundation of current law. The paternalism model limits the mentally disabled person's freedom through the erection of formidable barriers to sterilization. These barriers are justified by a strong presumption that the individual has a pervasive interest, not in autonomy, but in procreation. By clarifying the substantive interest in procreation as an interest in producing a child to rear, the autonomy model promotes a direct examination of whether the person in fact has this interest. If the person cannot rear a child, she lacks this interest and the law should take into account those interests that she retains. These residual interests include interests in optimal medical decisions, in human dignity and privacy, and in family stability.

The desire to correct the abuses of the past is admirable. We should only take care that in pursuing this goal, we do not create a new set of problems for the future. In contrast to current law, the autonomy model accords substantial deference to personal and family autonomy. The model reveals that the law's objectives are best met by leaving the sterilization decision to the retarded person who is competent to make her own reproductive choices, with only as much intervention as is necessary to facilitate her decisions. For retarded persons who cannot make their own decisions, parents—not courts—are the best surrogates.

[13]

HARMING FUTURE PERSONS: OBLIGATIONS TO THE CHILDREN OF REPRODUCTIVE TECHNOLOGY

PHILIP G. PETERS, JR.*

Two paradigms dominate contemporary ethical and legal debate about the risks posed to children who owe their lives to reproductive technology. One asks whether the children have lives so tragic that life itself is harmful. The other approach asks whether children so conceived are likely to enjoy a minimally decent existence. Although the two approaches have quite different analytic foundations, they share one crucial trait. Each concludes that children who owe their lives to reproductive technology are harmed only when that technology causes genuinely catastrophic injuries.

Because these conventional paradigms define harmful conduct exclusively by reference to the magnitude of the injuries suffered, they sometimes lead to indefensible conclusions. In Italy, for example, authorities recently shut down a Florentine sperm bank that was selling the sperm of a man infected with hepatitis C and genital herpes to fertility clinics throughout Italy.[1] The sperm bank's failure to screen its donors posed unnecessary risks to would-be mothers and their children. Under conventional analysis, however, no harm was done to any of the children affected by the sperm bank's failure to screen

---

* Ruth L. Hulston Professor of Law, University of Missouri-Columbia. J.D., University of California at Berkeley, 1976; A.B., Harvard University, 1972. I am grateful for the comments of John Robertson, Bonnie Steinbock, Melinda Roberts, Len Riskin, and Chris Guthrie; for the assistance of Cheryl Poelling and Cindy Shearrer; and for the generous financial support of the Myers Memorial Faculty Research Fellowship and the Fred J. Young Faculty Research Fellowship.

1. *See Diseased sperm forces fertility clinics to close*, ST. LOUIS POST-DISPATCH, Nov. 30, 1997, at A5. Both diseases can also be transmitted to the mothers via the sperm.

376 *SOUTHERN CALIFORNIA INTERDISCIPLINARY LAW JOURNAL*

because their only alternative to life with their illnesses was nonexistence. Better screening would not have improved their health. Instead, it would have resulted in the birth of a different child. Under conventional analysis, therefore, no harm was done by the failure to screen unless the affected children would have been better off never existing at all.

This conclusion defies common sense. Better screening would have avoided needless suffering. Responsible clinics already know this. They screen. Yet, conventional analysis cannot account for their concern. Because it focuses exclusively on the magnitude of the injuries suffered by the children actually born, conventional analysis overlooks the possibility that individuals using reproductive technology could reduce future injuries by conceiving *other children* who would suffer less. These injuries are avoidable by the substitution of one child for another.

Because conventional analysis looks only for individual victims, it ignores the harm that can be inflicted on future children as a class when irresponsible reproductive choices are made. Although the narrow focus of conventional thinking is appropriate in legal actions for *compensatory damages*, where proof of harm to the individual plaintiff is essential, it needs supplementation when the issue is whether future generations would benefit from *public health regulation*.

This Article explores an alternative way of determining whether an existence-inducing act is harmful to future children. The methodology proposed here focuses on the choices available to providers and parents who engage in reproductive conduct. When they choose a risky route over a safer one (perhaps, because it is more profitable, less risky to the mother, or more likely to result in conception), they threaten the welfare of future children.

Imagine, for example, a fertility clinic that implants more embryos than its competitors in order to maximize its success rate, even though this policy increases the number of dangerous multiple births. Or imagine a woman who is able to conceive naturally but chooses to clone herself despite the risks of using old DNA. These choices may cause unnecessary future suffering. Contrary to conventional analysis, the harmfulness of these choices does not turn exclusively on the magnitude of the injury inflicted. Harm can also be caused by the use of a dangerous procedure when a safer one is available.

Part I of this paper reviews the contemporary reproductive settings in which these issues currently arise and introduces the debate over harmfulness. Part II examines the conventional ways of identifying harmful reproductive conduct. Parts III and IV then propose and explore a class-based method of identifying harm to future children that focuses on the choices made by parents and providers. The likely criticisms are answered in Part V.

I. THE CONTEMPORARY CONTEXT

For decades, ethicists and legal scholars have debated the moral implications of the unknown dangers that new reproductive technologies pose to future children. First, artificial insemination prompted this discussion; later, it was in vitro fertilization and surrogacy.[2] Recently, two events have brought this issue back to prominence. First, the birth of the McCaughey septuplets and the Chukuri octuplets has renewed fears that unregulated fertility treatments would expose many parents and children to the risks of multiple pregnancies.[3] Second, Dr. Ian Wilmut cloned a sheep named Dolly, producing an ethical and regulatory frenzy over the prospect of human cloning.[4]

According to the National Center of Health Statistics, the number of triplets has more than tripled since the 1970s, and fertility treatments account for most of this increase.[5] Fertility drugs, for example, induce women to produce more than one egg in a single cycle.[6] And fertility clinics routinely implant more than one embryo when they perform in vitro fertilization and other similar procedures. As a result, both of these fertility treatments increase the risk of multiple pregnancy. In fact, 75% of the triplets, 90% of the quadruplets, and all of the quintuplets are born to women under treatment for fertility problems.[7]

---

2. *See* Philip G. Peters, Jr., *Protecting the Unconceived: Nonexistence, Avoidability, and Reproductive Technology*, 31 Ariz. L. Rev. 487, 490-92 (1989) (reviewing the debates and collecting citations).

3. *See* Barbara Carton, *Agonizing Decision: Multiple Pregnancies Are Often Pared Back in "Fetal Reduction,"* Wall St. J., Nov. 21, 1997, at A1.

4. *See* Cloning Human Beings: Report and Recommendations of the National Bioethics Advisory Commission 3-8 (1997) [hereinafter NBAC Report].

5. *See* Daney Q. Haney, *In Fertility Field, Septuplets are Failure Multiplied*, USA Today, Nov. 21, 1997, at 3A.

6. *See* Ellen Goodman, *Standards Will Help Reduce Multiple Birth Catastrophes*, Columbia Daily Trib., Dec. 4, 1997, at 6A.

7. *See* Carton, *supra* note 3, at A6.

378 *SOUTHERN CALIFORNIA INTERDISCIPLINARY LAW JOURNAL*

Unfortunately, multiple births are associated with an increased incidence of blindness, learning defects, lung problems, and other ailments.[8] Quintuplets are twelve times more likely to die in infancy. And many of the survivors will have serious medical problems.[9] For this reason, the United Kingdom has placed a limit on the number of embryos that may be transplanted at one time.[10] "Does the mother have the right," asks Dr. John Balint, "to expose these little creatures to the risk of marked prematurity, with the risk of cerebral hemorrhage, bowel infarctions, lung complications and so forth?"[11] Should a woman whose fertility drugs have produced too many eggs wait until "the bus is not so full,"? asks ethicist Thomas Murray.[12]

Like multiple pregnancies, cloning too may pose risks to the safety of future children. Although this risk probably is not the major source of the widespread uneasiness about human cloning, it is the risk most widely agreed upon and, thus, provided the articulated basis for the National Bioethics Advisory Commission's (NBAC) recommendation that a three-to-five year moratorium be placed on human cloning.

Within twenty-four hours of the announcement that Dolly had been cloned using a technique known as somatic cell nuclear transfer, President Clinton called for a moratorium on human cloning research.[13] A few months later, the NBAC issued its report, recommending that the cloning technique used to clone Dolly be temporarily banned.[14] The NBAC's recommendation "was based almost entirely on safety considerations: the high likelihood of failure and a

---

8. *See id.* at A1; Geoffrey Cowley and Karen Springer, *Multiplying the Risks: More Group Births Mean More Preemies and, Often, More Problems*, NEWSWEEK, Dec. 1, 1997, at 66. Multiple pregnancies also place financial, emotional, and physical burdens on parents that could harm the welfare of both the parents and the children. *See Fertility Experts Decry Multiple Births: One Healthy Baby is the Goal, They Say,* ST. LOUIS POST-DISPATCH, Nov. 21, 1997, at A8 [hereinafter *One Healthy Baby*].

9. *See* Carton, *supra* note 3, at A6.

10. The maximum currently is three and may soon be reduced to two. *See* Carton. *supra* note 3, at A6. Boston's Beth Israel Deaconess Medical Center sets a limit of three embryos and the American Society for Reproductive Medicine recommends a maximum of four embryos for women aged 35-40 and five for older women. *See id.*

11. Carton. *supra* note 3. at A6.

12. Goodman. *supra* note 6. Physicians often urge women to wait a month. But doing so increases the costs. *See One Healthy Baby, supra* note 8 at A8. *See also* John McCormick & Barbara Kantrowitz. *The Magnificent Seven,* NEWSWEEK. Dec. 1, 1997. at 58, 61.

13. *See* John A. Robertson. *Wrongful Life, Federalism, and Procreative Liberty: A Critique of the NBAC Cloning Report,* 38 JURIMETRICS 69 (1997).

14. *See* NBAC Report. *supra* note 4. The Commission's proposal would apply only to the cloning that uses the technique reportedly used to clone Dolly: somatic cell nuclear transfer. *See*

consequent high rate of miscarriage, and the unknown risk of developmental abnormalities in the offspring."[15] President Clinton sent Congress legislation to outlaw the cloning of humans for at least five years.[16] When Dr. Richard Seed announced his plans to establish a center for the cloning of humans,[17] President Clinton renewed his call for a prohibition.[18]

In recommending a temporary prohibition on the cloning of adult human cells to create new human beings, the NBAC expressed its belief that dangers to cloned children make cloning morally unacceptable at the present time.[19] It said:

> The prospect of creating children through somatic cell nuclear transfer has elicited widespread concern, much . . . in the form of fears about harms to the children who may be born as a result. There are concerns about possible physical harms from the manipulations of ova, nuclei, and embryos which are parts of the technology, and also about possible psychological harms, such as a diminished sense of individuality and personal autonomy.... *Virtually all people agree that the current risks of physical harm to children associated with somatic cell nuclear transplantation cloning justify a prohibition at this time on such experimentation.*[20]

The Commission specifically rejected the argument that cloned children are only harmed if they would be better off unborn.

> This metaphysical argument, in which one is forced to compare existence with non-existence, is problematic. Not only does it require us to compare something unknowable—non-existence—with something else, it also can lead to absurd conclusions if taken to its logical extreme. For example, it would support the argument that there is no degree of pain and suffering that cannot be inflicted on a child, provided that the alternative is never to have been conceived.[21]

---

id. at 1, 13, 33. The Commission did not make any proposals dealing with cloning by embryo-splitting.

15. Bonnie Steinbock, *The NBAC Report on Cloning Human Beings: What It Did—and Did Not—Do*, 38 JURIMETRICS 39-41 (1997).

16. *See Clinton Attacks Physicist's Intention to Clone Humans; President Calls the Plan by a Chicago Scientist "Profoundly Troubling,"* ST. LOUIS POST-DISPATCH, Jan. 11, 1998, at A3 [hereinafter *Profoundly Troubling*].

17. *See Scientist Makes Plans to Clone a Person*, ST. LOUIS POST-DISPATCH, Jan. 7, 1998, at A7.

18. *See Profoundly Troubling, supra* note 16, at A3.

19. *See* NBAC REPORT, *supra* note 4, at 63-65, 79-82.

20. *Id.* at 63 (emphasis added).

21. *Id.* at 66.

380 *SOUTHERN CALIFORNIA INTERDISCIPLINARY LAW JOURNAL*

The Commission concluded that the wrongful life approach was not administrable and would lead to absurd results.

As John Robertson has subsequently noted, the Commission's analysis is vulnerable to several criticisms. For example, the Commission's analysis arguably relies on the very comparison that it says is impossible. If it is better for cloned children not to be born, suggests Robertson, then the Commission has implicitly concluded that nonexistence is preferable.[22] Robertson also notes the Commission's mistaken belief that the wrongful life approach would never permit intervention on behalf of suffering children. In truth, the wrongful life model would favor intervention whenever the anticipated suffering is so severe that nonexistence would be better.[23] Robertson could also have included one additional criticism: the Commission did not articulate or defend an alternative conception of harmfulness that would support its conclusions.[24]

Still, one cannot think about the risks posed by existence-inducing technologies without sharing the Commission's intuitions that the wrongful life paradigm misses something important in our understanding of harmful conduct. The conduct of the Italian sperm bank is just one example of conduct whose harmfulness is not captured by conventional analysis. The same can be said of the fertility clinic that implants an unreasonable number of embryos or the physician who is

---

22. Robertson, *supra* note 13, at 76. There is no evidence, Robertson suggests, "that feared harms of cloning would cause such physical or psychological suffering that the child's very existence would be a wrongful one." *Id.* at 74. Robertson also makes several other cogent points in his criticism of the Commission's recommendation. He notes, for example, that the Commission's reasoning would also make it unethical to knowingly give natural birth to children who are not fully healthy, physically or psychologically. *Id.* at 73-74.

23. *See id.* at 75-76. Robertson also persuasively rebuts the Commission's contention that this comparison is "metaphysical." He notes that the comparison is made from the standpoint of the living child. *See id.* at 75. As I and others have noted, this test of harmfulness really calls for a comparison between the benefits of life and the burdens of life, a judgment that we routinely permit severely ill patients and their proxies to make. *See, e.g.,* Nora K. Bell & Barry M. Loewer, *What is Wrong with "Wrongful Life" Cases,* 10 J. MED. & PHIL. 127, 138 (1985); Joel Feinberg, *Wrongful Life and the Counterfactual Element in Harming,* 4 SOC. PHIL. & POL'Y 145, 158-59, 161-67 (1986); Michael B. Kelly, *The Rightful Position in "Wrongful Life" Actions.* 42 HASTINGS L.J. 505, 518 n.58 (1991); Philip G. Peters, Jr., *The Illusion of Autonomy at the End of Life: Unconsented Life Support and the Wrongful Life Analogy,* UCLA L. REV. 673. 698-99 (1998).

24. As Robertson notes, "Either the conclusion that it is unethical because of harm to children should be rejected, or some other basis for the ethical claim established." Robertson, *supra* note 13, at 76. This Article accepts his challenge to offer another basis.

willing to clone children for individuals who could have conceived naturally. This essay attempts to outline an analytic framework for the intuition that choices of this kind can be harmful.

II. CONVENTIONAL CONCEPTIONS OF HARM

Under conventional legal analysis, to cause harm is to make someone worse off than she would otherwise have been.[25] In tort law, this conception of harm is embodied in the "but for" test of causation-in-fact.[26] In most cases, the application of this test is quite straightforward. A driver who strikes a pedestrian has harmed the pedestrian. A physician who carelessly prescribes drugs that injure a pregnant patient and her fetus has harmed both of them. These simple examples involve the infliction of harm that could fairly be described as *ordinary harm*.

When a disputed act is *existence-inducing*, however, its harmfulness is typically more difficult to measure.[27] Assume, for example, that a fertility clinic's failure to adequately screen its egg donors results in an unnecessarily high incidence of genetic disabilities among the resulting children. Under conventional analysis, no harm has been caused by failure to screen unless the children actually born have lives that are worse than the alternative—never existing at all. Only in those rare circumstances where the injuries are so catastrophic that life itself is harmful can the failure to screen be said to have made these children worse off than they would otherwise have been. Even a clinic's failure to screen for HIV infection may not rise to this level.

---

25. *See, e.g.*, James S. Fishkin, *Justice Between Generations: The Dilemma of Future Interests, in* 4 SOCIAL JUSTICE: BOWLING GREEN STUDIES IN APPLIED PHILOSOPHY 23, 24 (Michael Bradie & David Braybrooke eds., 1992). For a masterful and comprehensive study of the notion of harming, see JOEL FEINBERG, HARM TO OTHERS (1984).

26. *See, e.g.*, Turpin v. Sortini, 643 P.2d 954 (1982); PROSSER AND KEETON ON TORTS 266 (5th ed. 1984).

27. Sometimes, however, even existence-inducing activities can inflict ordinary harm. A fertility clinic that carelessly stores frozen embryos, causing injuries that could have been avoided, causes ordinary harm to the injured child. Indeed, Melinda Roberts persuasively argues that ordinary harm also occurs in some contexts mistakenly assumed to be governed by the wrongful life paradigm. For example, multiple cloning may injure the genetically-identical children by depriving them of their individuality, *see*, Mona S. Amer, *Breaking the Mold: Human Embryo Cloning and its Implications for a Right to Individuality*, 43 UCLA L. REV. 1659, 1677-84 (1996) (proposing that cloning be limited to a single success). It could have been avoided by cloning only one child. *See* Melinda Roberts, *Human Cloning: A Case of No Harm Done?*, 21 J. MED. AND PHIL. 537, 545 (1996). *See also* Melinda Roberts, *Present Duties and Future Persons: When are Existence-Inducing Acts Wrong?*, 14 LAW & PHIL. 297, 324-26 (1995).

382 *SOUTHERN CALIFORNIA INTERDISCIPLINARY LAW JOURNAL*

As John Robertson notes, a person with HIV infection may have "years of life that are good for her."[28]

In wrongful life tort actions, American courts have wholeheartedly endorsed this way of analyzing the harmfulness of existence-inducing acts. They have uniformly concluded that mistakes, such as negligent sterilization,[29] which lead to the birth of a child with disabilities do not harm that child unless her life is worse than not existing at all.[30] In the rest of this paper, I will refer to this demanding test of harmfulness as the *wrongful life* approach.

If similar logic is used to ascertain the state's interest in regulating reproductive technology on behalf of future children, then the interests of those children will rarely, if ever, be taken into account. The risks associated with reproductive technology will very rarely be so catastrophic that life itself is harmful.

Bonnie Steinbock and others, including this author, have argued that the nonexistence threshold as traditionally construed is too strict and that persons who engage in existence-inducing conduct ought to provide the resulting children with a minimally-decent existence.[31]

---

28. JOHN A. ROBERTSON, CHILDREN OF CHOICE 76 (1994).

29. *See, e.g.*, Fassoulas v. Ramey, 450 So.2d 822 (Fla. 1984).

30. *See, e.g.*, Gleitman v.Cosgrove, 227 A.2d 689, 692 (N.J. 1967); Stewart v. Long Island College Hosp., 296 N.Y.S.2d 41, 44-45 (1968), *modified*, 313 N.Y.S.2d 502 (App. Div. 1970). Nearly all courts have refused to recognize a tort cause of action on behalf of the affected children. Some courts do not trust the jury's ability to calculate damages based on this comparison between life and nonexistence. *See, e.g.*, Gleitman v. Cosgrove, 227 A.2d 689, 692 (N.J. 1967); Becker v. Schwartz, 386 N.E.2d 807, 812 (N.Y. 1978). Other courts worry that recognition of such a claim would impugn the sanctity of life. *See, e.g.*, Blake v. Cruz, 690 P.2d 315, 321 (Idaho 1984); Siemieniec v. Lutheran Gen. Hosp., 512 N.E.2d 691, 702 (Ill. 1987); Smith v. Cote, 513 A.2d 314, 352 (N.H. 1986). *See also* DAVID HEYD, GENETHICS 30 (1992) (arguing that wrongful life suits are improper because it is not possible to compare life to nonexistence because there is no value to nonexistence). These judicial conclusions were mistaken. *See* Philip G. Peters, Jr., *The Illusion of Autonomy at the End of Life: Unconsented Life Support and the Wrongful Life Analogy*, 45 UCLA L. REV. 673 (1998); Philip G. Peters, Jr., *Protecting the Unconceived: Nonexistence, Avoidability, and Reproductive Technology*, 31 ARIZ. L. REV. 487, 502 (1989).

31. *See, e.g.*, Michael Bayles, *Harm to the Unconceived*, 5 PHIL. & PUB. AFF. 292, 302 (1976); Cynthia B. Cohen, *"Give Me Children or I Shall Die!" New Reproductive Technologies and Harm to Children*, HASTINGS CENTER REP., March-April 1996. 19, 24; Fred Feldman, *Justice, Desert, and the Repugnant Conclusion*, 7 UTILITAS 189, 196 (1995); E. Haavi Morreim, *The Concept of Harm Reconceived: A Different Look at Wrongful Life*, 7 LAW AND PHIL. 3 (1988); Peters, *supra* note 2, at 542-45; Bonnie Steinbock and Ron McClamrock, *When is Birth Unfair to the Child?*, 24 HASTINGS CENTER REP., Nov.-Dec. 1994. at 15, 21; Bonnie Steinbock, *The Logical Case for "Wrongful Life,"* HASTINGS CENTER REP., April 1986, 15, 19. *See also* Matthew Hanser, *Harming Future People*, 19 PHIL. & PUB. AFFAIRS 47 (1990) (arguably supporting a minimum quality of life). This modification of the wrongful life threshold of harmfulness is intuitively appealing. However, defending it is a difficult assignment. After all, the resulting children have lives that are beneficial on balance even if they do not meet some ideal minimum

This method of identifying the interests of future children broadens the range of cognizable harm, but only marginally. A "decent minimum" requirement continues to limit the notion of harmful conduct to reproductive behavior that causes catastrophic injury. Although this alternative to the wrongful life approach usefully expands the concept of harmful conduct, it fails to explain why the behavior of the Italian sperm bank seems irresponsible. For that, another notion of harmfulness is needed—one that focuses on the choices available to the actor, rather than the absolute magnitude of the injury to the child.

III. MAXIMIZING THE WELL-BEING OF FUTURE CHILDREN

By focusing exclusively on the presence or absence of harm to the children actually born, conventional analysis completely ignores the possibility that individuals using reproductive technology could reduce future injuries by conceiving *other children* who would suffer less. These are injuries that are *avoidable by substitution* of one child for another.[32] Behavior of this kind causes future generations to suffer unnecessarily and, accordingly, threatens their collective welfare.

---

quality of life. *See, e.g.,* DEREK PARFIT, REASONS AND PERSONS 364 (1984); ROBERTSON, *supra* note 28, at 75-76, 122; Melinda Roberts, *Present Duties and Future Persons: When are Existence-Inducing Acts Wrong?,* 14 LAW & PHIL. 297, 302-33 (1995); James Woodward, *The Non-Identity Problem,* 96 ETHICS 804, 815 n.12 (1986). The articles cited here employ a variety of strategies to justify this shift in the threshold. In addition, Ronald Green, the Interim Director of the Office of Genome Ethics at the National Institute of Health's National Center for Human Genome Research, offers a more unique benchmark. He suggests that children are owed a quality of life equal to that of others in the child's birth cohort. Ronald Green, *Parental Autonomy and the Obligation Not to Harm One's Child Genetically,* 25 J. LAW, MED. & ETHICS 5, 8-9 (1997). *See also* MICHAEL BAYLES, MORALITY AND POPULATION POLICY 3 (1980) (advocating a duty not to make it unlikely that future generations will have an equivalent quality of life). Under contemporary conditions, that promises to be a more robust obligation than a decent minimum. Because his proposal uses average well-being as its benchmark, it has some superficial similarities to the proposal made in this essay. Fundamentally, however, his approach is quite different as the obligation he discusses does not appear to arise out of, or depend upon, the availability of safer reproductive options. Taking a quite different route, James Woodward has argued that children can be wronged when parents have children knowing that they cannot fulfill their parental obligations to the children. *See* Woodward, *supra* at 815; James Woodward, *Reply to Parfit,* 97 ETHICS 800 (1986). While Woodward's thesis is intriguing, it is quite narrow in its application. He concedes that there would be no obligation not to have children who will be well cared-for. It would not apply to impairments that do not arise out a failure to meet parental obligations. As a result, his thesis would not reach the cases of the sperm clinic or Dr. Seed.

32. *See* Peters, *supra* note 2, at 510. *See also* Dan W. Brock, *The Non-Identity Problem and Genetic Harms—The Case of Wrongful Handicaps,* 9 BIOETHICS 269, 273 (1995).

384 *SOUTHERN CALIFORNIA INTERDISCIPLINARY LAW JOURNAL*

Such behavior is exemplified by a fertility clinic that implants more embryos than its competitors in order to maximize its success rate and, thus, its business, even though this policy increases the number of dangerous multiple pregnancies. Likewise, a woman who is able to conceive naturally, but chooses to clone herself despite the risks of using old DNA is taking avoidable risks with her future children. Any injuries caused by these choices could have been avoided.

The harmfulness of these acts lies not in magnitude of the injury, but in the decision to take a risky route to reproduction when a safer one was available. The conventional model of harming overlooks this kind of harmful conduct because it does not make a specific child worse off. If the safer route had been chosen, a different child would have been born. Because conventional analysis requires an individual victim, it overlooks the fact that the collective welfare of future children is impaired by decisions of this kind. Although conventional wisdom's insistence on proof of harm to a specific individual is appropriate in actions for *compensatory damages*, this narrow notion of harming should not be relied upon by legislatures and administrative agencies contemplating *public health regulation*.

A. PARFIT'S IMPATIENT MOTHER

The English moral philosopher Derek Parfit offers the provocative story of a woman who is advised by her doctor not to become pregnant until she gets over a temporary illness that causes birth defects.[33] Although she could wait two months for the condition to pass, she ignores his advice and conceives a child who suffers the deformity. Intuitively, her choice was a harmful one. Yet, if she had waited, *another child* would have been born. The child actually born would not have existed. Because that child's only alternative to living with this deformity was nonexistence, conventional wrongful life analysis tells us that no harm was done unless life with her disability is worse than never existing at all.[34]

This conclusion assaults our common sense. The unacceptability of this conclusion is reinforced by comparing it with the conclusion that would be reached if, instead, the mother had possessed the power

---

33. Derek Parfit, *On Doing the Best for Our Children*, in ETHICS & POPULATION 100 (Michael D. Bayles ed., 1976). Parfit also uses the example of a 14-year-old girl who chooses to have a child rather than to wait. PARFIT, *supra* note 31, at 358-59.

34. *See, e.g.*, Parfit, *supra* note 33, at 101; Bayles, *supra* note 31, at 297; Joel Feinberg, *Wrongful Life and the Counterfactual Element in Harming*, 4 SOC. PHIL. & POL'Y 145, 168-69.

to prevent the birth defects by taking medication during her pregnancy.[35] In that event, her failure to take the medication would unquestionably constitute harmful conduct because the child actually born could have been born without these injuries. These vastly different conclusions simply do not pass a moral gut test.[36] Both mothers had an equal opportunity to avoid human misery. Both caused unnecessary human suffering.[37]

The inadequacy of the traditional model is further illustrated by comparing its conclusions in the case of unscreened sperm with those that result when a sperm clinic negligently stores its sperm. Under traditional notions of harmfulness, the negligent storage of sperm causes ordinary harm because reasonable care could have prevented injury to the resulting children. By contrast, the failure to screen for infected sperm, because it changes the identify of the resulting children, is harmless unless the injuries caused are so catastrophic that life itself is harmful. Once again, two similarly culpable choices have dramatically different implications under conventional theory—implications that are not consistent with common norms of responsible behavior.

The conclusions dictated by conventional analysis in these two examples reveal the need for supplementation. Conventional analysis overlooks the harm caused to future children as a class when a dangerous means of reproduction is chosen in lieu of a safer one. Choices of this kind cause unnecessary suffering. Parents intuitively understand this idea. They avoid reproduction while on powerful drugs. Many screen themselves or their embryos for genetic abnormalities.

Even Dr. Richard Seed, the notorious physician who purportedly plans to clone humans in the near future, understood the power of this moral perspective. His initial proposal would ostensibly have restricted access to cloning to couples who were *both* infertile. Why would he impose such a narrow restriction? Dr. Seed understood that cloning would be more vulnerable to criticism if used by couples with access to less controversial reproductive options, such as artificial

---

35. *See* Parfit, *supra* note 33, at 103. Syphilis might be one such condition. *See* Robertson & Schulman, *Pregnancy and Prenatal Harm to Offspring: The Case of Mothers With PKU*, Hastings Center Rep., Aug./Sept. 1987, at 26. By contrast, AIDS also presents a risk of infected offspring, but the absence of treatment makes the risk unavoidable for the mother who wishes to bear her own child. *See id.* at 31.

36. *See* Peters, *supra* note 2, at 513-14.

37. *See* Feinberg, *supra* note 34, at 178. Parfit calls this the "no-difference view." Parfit, *supra* note 31, at 367-68.

386 *SOUTHERN CALIFORNIA INTERDISCIPLINARY LAW JOURNAL*

insemination or egg donation. By excluding these couples, he reduced his vulnerability to the charge that his plans would harm future children by substituting a more risky procedure for a less risky one.

B. THEORETICAL FOUNDATIONS

A prima facie duty to minimize suffering finds its strongest support in utilitarian theory.[38] Derek Parfit, for example, recognized that having the happier child would maximize social utility. Table 1 illustrates this utilitarian implication.

Table 1

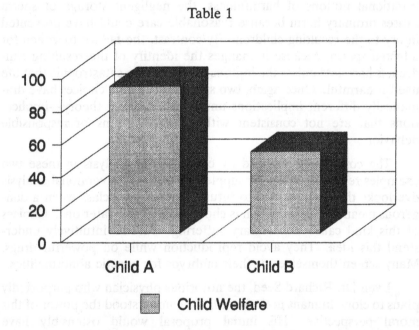

Assume, for example, that Option A is to conceive a child naturally and Option B is to clone a child. If cloning is reasonably believed on balance to threaten the welfare of the resulting child more than natural conception,[39] then Option A maximizes the well-being of

38. Parfit felt that an appeal to "rights" could never solve cases like the failure to delay pregnancy because no specific individual is made worse off. Parfit said that the wrong in these cases is not "person affecting." PARFIT, *supra* note 31, at 378. Fishkin describes the analysis in these cases as "identity independent." Fishkin, *supra* note 25, at 26. He notes that this method of assessing interests is, in this sense, anonymous. *See id.*

39. Cloning may confer some benefits as well as some burdens. *See* Susan M. Wolf, *Ban Cloning? Why NBAC is Wrong*, 27 HASTINGS CENTER REP., Sept.-Oct. 1997, at 12-13 (cloning

the anticipated child. From a utilitarian standpoint, therefore, Option A is better for future children.[40]

Derek Parfit articulated a principle that he called the "Q" to capture this insight.[41]

> If in either of two outcomes the same number of people would ever live, it would be bad if those who live are worse off or have a lower quality of life than those who would have lived.[42]

Translated into simpler language, Q exhorts providers and would-be parents to have the child who will suffer least.

A prima facie obligation to avoid unnecessary suffering is also consistent with the method of moral reasoning associated with John Rawls[43] and sometimes called Ideal Contractualism.[44] This approach identifies binding moral obligations by asking whether they would be chosen by people who are under a veil of ignorance and, thus, are unaware whether they would bear the brunt of the chosen principles. I believe that people under the veil would agree, all other things being equal, that parents and the individuals who assist them should try to have the children who will suffer least. Although Parfit and others have suggested that we cannot imagine a future in which we do not exist, I believe that we can and that most people would prefer that their welfare be maximized if they are to be born at all.[45] Put differently, they would favor the avoidance of unnecessary suffering.

Indeed, it is remarkable that so obvious a proposition has not already become a part of the fabric of academic thinking about reproductive decisionmaking. Yet, only the American philosopher Dan

---

could spare children the difficulties of having an anonymous genetic parent as they would if donor egg or sperm were used).

40. Whether it is absolutely better would turn on the utilities to other persons, like parents, of the choice between Option A and Option B. The point of this analysis is that child welfare should constitute a component of overall utility analysis.

41. PARFIT, *supra* note 31, at 360.

42. Parfit also called this principle "The Same Number Quality Claim." *Id.*

43. JOHN RAWLS, A THEORY OF JUSTICE (1971).

44. *See* PARFIT, *supra* note 31, at 391.

45. However, Parfit disagrees. He assumes that we cannot imagine a history in which we do not exist. PARFIT. *supra* note 31, at 392. *See also* Jan Narveson, *Moral Problems of Population, in* ETHICS AND POPULATION 59, 78 (Michael D. Bayles ed., 1976) (finding the prospect "perfectly mind-boggling"). Parfit reports that other writers assume that we would choose a history that maximizes the future population, as long as the lives lived are worth living. *Id.* Narveson. however, assumes that our inability to imagine that we would not exist would lead us to maximize average utility and a better quality of life for those who do exist. *Id.*

388 *SOUTHERN CALIFORNIA INTERDISCIPLINARY LAW JOURNAL*

Brock[46] has endorsed Parfit's model and applied it to reproductive technology.[47] Thus far, no legislator has publicly relied upon this conception of harmful conduct to defend the regulation of reproductive technology. Perhaps that is because legislators feel free to rely on their personal moral barometers without the need for a philosophical defense. Yet this reliance leaves them open to criticisms that their position is unprincipled. Furthermore, reliance on untutored intuitions will tempt legislators to assume that all the burdens imposed by a reproductive technology are harmful. However, that is not the lesson of Q. The harmfulness identified by this model lies in the choice of a dangerous option over a safer one. As a result, no conclusions about the harmfulness of a person's choices can be reached until the alternatives realistically available to the decisionmaker have been identified and examined.

In this respect, the NBAC's analysis of cloning was too blunt. The propriety of taking the risks associated with cloning turns on the alternatives available to the parents. The case for permitting cloning despite its risks will be strongest when the would-be parents are both infertile and ineligible to adopt.[48] It will also be strong when both carry the genes for horrible birth defects. It will be weakest when a would-be parent is fertile and simply insists on having an identical child or a child cloned from some famous public figure.

Under the expanded conception of harmful conduct proposed here, a three-step inquiry will be needed to determine whether regulatory action is appropriate. The first step is to identify the parenting options realistically available to the affected parents and clinicians. The second is to compare the advantages and disadvantages of each alternative from the perspective of the resulting children.[49] Finally,

---

46. Dan W. Brock, *The Non-Identity Problem and Genetic Harms—The Case of Wrongful Handicaps*, 9 BIOETHICS 269, 271 (1995).

47. A few other philosophers have hinted that they endorse a similar idea in the context of population policy. *See, e.g.*, Gregory Kavka, *The Paradox of Future Individuals*, 11 PHIL. & PUB. AFFAIRS 93, 105 n.24 (1981); Woodward, *supra* note 31, at 806-07.

48. Whether adoption should be treated as an available option and, if so, whether parental interests in genetically-related children would justify refusal to adopt are examples of the interesting second-generation questions arising out of a duty to do the best you can.

49. It is important to emphasize that this analysis requires an honest appraisal of the burdens and benefits of the reproductive methods under scrutiny. Some controversial reproductive technologies, such as cloning, may actually offer advantages to the affected children that could potentially offset the burdens associated with the technology. Studies of genetically identical twins, for example, suggest that this relationship can confer significant emotional benefits. *See* Susan M. Wolf, *Ban Cloning? Why the NBAC is Wrong*, HASTINGS CENTER REP., Sept.-Oct. 1997, at 12, 13. Cloning may bestow some of the same benefits. *See id.*

the interests of future children must be balanced against the rights and interests of parents and providers. Only then can a final decision about regulatory action be made.

It is crucial to emphasize that this proposal does not dictate or even support state intervention every time a harmful choice is made. The interests of future children must be examined alongside the rights and interests of parents, providers, and the community as a whole.[50] Those rights and interests will vary with the circumstances. Other principles, like procreative liberty and maternal bodily autonomy will often override the obligation to avoid harm to future children. The significance of this new way of looking at the interests of future children is not that it requires intervention in every case, but that it requires justification in cases overlooked by more conventional notions of harm.

The strongest cases for state regulation are likely to involve dangerous reproductive conduct on the part of clinics, researchers, and other third parties. These regulations will least directly interfere with the procreative and privacy interests of would-be parents. Regulation of this kind might include rules governing the harvesting of eggs and the acquisition of sperm, prohibitions on use of stale gametes or embryos, and minimum accreditation requirements for fertility specialists. Other potential targets of regulation are the artificial reproductive practices that least directly implicate the traditional zone of procreative privacy. Cloning is an obvious example. So, too, are extra-corporeal techniques, like in vitro fertilization. Practices least likely to pass muster are interventions that directly interfere with a woman's bodily integrity, such as the mandatory genetic screening of a woman or her fetus.[51]

IV. DIFFERENT NUMBER CASES

The goal of respecting the interests of future children is easiest to operationalize when a choice must be made between two reproductive options that will each result in the birth of a single child. In these

---

In addition, we must avoid unsubstantiated assumptions about the burdens imposed by birth defects. Studies of persons with disabilities indicate that they view their quality of life more positively than others would expect.

50. *See, e.g.,* John Robertson, *Procreative Liberty and the Control of Conception, Pregnancy, and Childbirth,* 69 VA. L. REV. 405 (1983); John Robertson, *Surrogate Mothers: Not So Novel After All,* HASTINGS CENTER REP., Oct. 1983, at 28-29.

51. The extension of class-based interest analysis to genetic screening is discussed further in the text *infra* at notes 80-83.

390 *SOUTHERN CALIFORNIA INTERDISCIPLINARY LAW JOURNAL*

cases, the anticipated welfare of the child born using one method can be compared to the anticipated welfare of the child born using the other. Table 1, above, illustrates simple choices of this kind.

Maximizing the welfare of future children is a much more complex task when the choice among reproductive options will affect the number of children who are eventually born. Imagine, for example, that a fertility clinic is deciding whether to increase the number of embryos that it is willing to implant at one time. Assume further that using additional embryos will increase the risks of multiple pregnancy, premature birth, and serious medical problems.[52] Would it be better to aim for single pregnancies? Table 2 depicts a simplified version of this choice.[53]

---

52. *See supra* notes 9-12.

53. A more complex model would take into account the uncertainties in both the chance of injury and the odds of a live birth using each procedure. My own preliminary assessment is that the probability of injury can be taken into account in a relatively straightforward way by discounting the harm to reflect the odds. Taking the odds of live birth into account is likely to be more complex. Policy A, for example, may be to implant 3 embryos. It may pose a 40% chance of no births at all, a 50% chance of one child, and a 10% chance of multiple births. Policy B, by contrast, may be to implant 6 embryos. It could have a 20% chance of failure, a 50% chance of single birth, and a 30% chance of multiple birth. Any comparison between these policies must compare the sum of these probabilities. Interestingly, a recent British study found that transferring three embryos, rather than two, increases the chance of multiple births, but not the rate of pregnancy. Temple A. Morris, *Reducing the risk of Multiple Births by Transfer of Two Embryos After In Vitro Fertilization*, 339 N. ENG. J. MED. 573 (1998).

Although this complication certainly makes ethical analysis of the choice more complex, it raises only one new logical problem. That is how to take into account the chance that the procreative effort will fail altogether. It is easy to see how this prospect is contrary to the interests of the parents and, therefore, will need to be taken into account before final decisions about ethical and legal propriety are made. However, it is less clear how this possibility affects the interests of the future children. My tentative conclusion is that the case against a particular procreative choice will weaken in direct proportion to the odds that the safer course of action will fail to result in a live birth. A prima facie obligation to do the best you can assumes that an alternative, safer way of having a child is available. If not, then the avoidance of unnecessary suffering analysis is inapplicable and the wrongful life analysis should be used to evaluate the harmfulness of the reproductive choice.

This limitation on avoidability by substitution analysis is easiest to appreciate when a couple has absolutely no possibility of conceiving naturally and is unable to adopt. Under these circumstances, the choice to use assisted reproduction cannot be compared against natural conception. If the chosen method of assisted reproduction is the safest one available, then its use is only harmful to future children if their lives are worse than never existing at all.

The analysis is more complicated when the safer procreative strategies reduces, but does not eliminate, the risk of failure. The larger the chance of success using the safer procedure, the larger the cohort of future children whose lives could have been improved. The smaller the chance of success using the safer procedure, the smaller the opportunity for welfare gains and thus the weaker the case for intervention in the name of future children.

Table 2

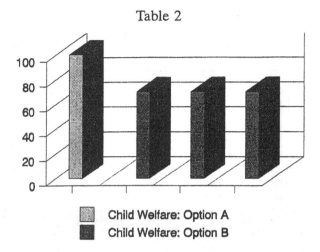

□ Child Welfare: Option A
■ Child Welfare: Option B

Option A will produce a single child with an anticipated welfare of 90. Option B will produce three children, each with an anticipated welfare of 70. Which choice optimizes the welfare of future children? The answer turns on the measure of utility used to compare the two outcomes. Option A will maximixe *average* utility, while Option B will maximize *total* utility.

A. Conflicting Paradoxes

Both average utility and total utility can lead to unappealing preferences under some circumstances. A preference for *total utility*, for example, seems to force us "to prefer a huge, wretched population to a smaller, happy one, as long as the quantity of the huge population allows its total utility to exceed the total utility of the smaller population."[54] Parfit called this "the Repugnant Conclusion."[55] Applied in the context of reproductive decisionmaking, a total utility approach would often prefer multiple pregnancies over single ones, even if multiple pregnancies were strongly associated with serious physical or emotional injuries. Table 3 illustrates the Repugnant Conclusion.[56]

---

54. Michael B. Laudor, *In Defense of Wrongful Life: Bringing Political Theory to the Defense of a Tort*, 62 Fordham L. Rev. 1675, 1679 (1994).

55. Parfit, *supra* note 31, at 388.

56. In addition, reliance on total utility measures arguably implies a duty to procreate as long as the utility generated by the additional lives outweighs the burden imposed on other persons. *See* Parfit, *supra* note 31, at 381-90. Summers argues, however, that we are already past the point where more population is the best means of promoting human welfare. L.W. Summers, *Classical Utilitarianism and the Population Optimum*, *in* Obligations to Future

392 *SOUTHERN CALIFORNIA INTERDISCIPLINARY LAW JOURNAL*

Table 3

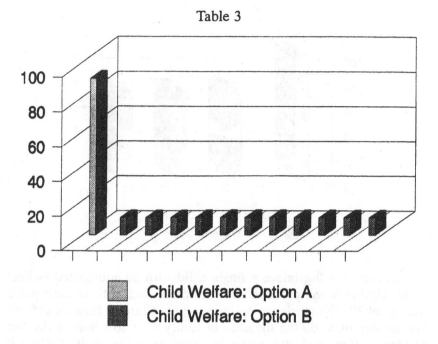

The Repugnant Conclusion can be avoided by relying on *average utility*.[57] Average utility favors choices that produce the greatest average welfare. In Table 3, that would be the single child option (Option A) because it produces an average welfare of 90, rather than 10.

Regrettably, average utility also has shortcomings. Average utility, for example, seems to favor a population policy that will result in 10 exquisitely happy people over a policy resulting in ten million very happy people. Average utility also seems to condemn the addition of one more happy person to a happy community if that person's well-

GENERATIONS 91 (R.I Sikora & Brian Barry eds., 1978). Furthermore, James Woodward argues that the repugnant conclusion is artificial because rights violations would occur well before the population is stretched to this point. Woodward, *supra* note 31, at 828.

At any rate, the duty proposed in this essay is narrower. It would require only that parents and providers who do decide to have children do a decent job of it.

57. *See* PARFIT, *supra* note 31, at 401.

[Vol. 8:375 1999]   *HARMING FUTURE PERSONS*   393

being is slightly lower than the others.[58] That is the Mere Addition Paradox.[59]

Parfit was unwilling to choose between these two measures of utility. He was, therefore, unable to extend his preference for having the happier child in same number cases (his "Q") into a broader principle (which he called "X") that would provide guidance for choices between courses of conduct that result in a different number of lives.[60] Nevertheless, he remained convinced that some such principle must exist.[61]

B.   Solving the Different Number Cases

The underlying difficulty with the choice between average and total utility is that each illuminates a morally relevant factor. Average utility emphasizes quality of life while total utility emphasizes quantity.[62] Because both indicia can be relevant in some circumstances, an acceptable theory of moral obligations must be able to take both into consideration.[63]

The possibility of combining the two considerations in a single formula has been most elegantly explored by Thomas Hurka.[64] Writing in the context of population ethics, Hurka persuasively argues that

---

58. *See* Laudor, *supra* note 54, at 1684. This is a standard characteristic associated with average utility. However, average utility considerations, properly interpreted, would not necessarily condemn every birth of a "below average" child. Michael Bayles wisely observes that:

> A rule utilitarian would adopt a rule concerning having children such that general conformity to that rule would not lead to a lower average happiness. Such a rule might permit having children whose happiness would be below average so long as there would be enough children above the average that it would not decrease."

Michael D. Bayles, *Introduction* to Ethics and Population ix, xx (Michael D. Bayles ed. 1976). By contrast, conduct, like cloning, that threatens to lower the overall average would be objectionable.

59. *See* Laudor, *supra* note 54, at 1678-79; Parfit, *supra* note 31, at 419-20.

60. Same number cases do not require a similar choice because having the happier child, as illustrated in Table 1, advances *both* average and total utility. For this reason, Parfit's "Q" principle is explicitly limited to "same number" cases.

61. *See* Parfit, *supra* note 31, at 380-441.

62. *See id.* at 401.

63. *See id.* at 405. Parfit considered combining the two. He hypothesized a combination of the two factors in which quality of life would count down to a threshold amount and then be discounted entirely. Because this threshold approach was quite blunt, it produced results that are vulnerable to criticism. However, the use of a sliding scale or weighted formula should eliminate the counterintuitive implications of more blunt combinations.

64. Thomas Hurka, *Value and Population Size*, 93 Ethics 496 (1983).

394 *SOUTHERN CALIFORNIA INTERDISCIPLINARY LAW JOURNAL*

total utility declines in importance relative to average utility as populations increase. Thus, the value that an additional individual contributes to the world is not constant, but varies with the number of other
humans alive. While the value of additional people would be enormous following a crisis that shrank the population dramatically, as
occurred in the biblical story of Noah or might occur following a
nuclear holocaust, its value diminishes greatly when the human population reaches its current size.[65]

A formula which captures this variability avoids many of the
unattractive aspects of both the average and total utility principles.
By giving more weight to average utility when population levels are
high, this approach avoids the Repugnant Conclusion except in the
rare circumstances when increased numbers are genuinely more
important than quality of life. By giving extra weight to increases in
population size when total population is low, this compromise reflects
how many of us already feel about population policy. This hybrid also
avoids the Mere Addition Paradox in the most objectionable cases; it
concedes that population increases are desirable despite a negative
impact on quality of life when human survival is least secure. Hurka's
hybrid, variable approach has the advantage of escaping the principal
problems of both average and total utility in those situations where
the shortcomings seem least tolerable. As a result, it constitutes a
genuine improvement over exclusive reliance on either total or average utility alone.[66]

A strong argument can be made that average utility should
receive greater weight than total utility in this hybrid formula. As Jan
Narveson notes, "we are in favor of making people happy, but neutral
about making happy people . . . it seems repulsive to think that the
goodness of a community is a function of its size."[67] And John Rawls

---

65. *See id.* at 497. A similar adjustment could be made to reduce the importance of marginal increases in average utility as the average gets higher.

66. Not everyone feels so favorably towards Hurka's work. James Hudson points out some
potential shortcomings of this compromise. James L. Hudson, *The Diminishing Marginal Value
of Happy People*, 51 PHILOSOPHICAL STUDIES 125 (1987). Hudson is a totalist who appears to
object to any compromise with averagism. Hudson concedes that a hybrid offers advantages
with respect to the Repugnant Conclusion. However, because he does not find the Repugnant
Conclusion to be repugnant, he feels that this advantage is not sufficient to justify accepting the
problems that he sees with average utilitarianism. *See id.* at 132, 134-35. He does not address
the advantages that a hybrid offers in connection with the Mere Addition Paradox.

67. Narveson, *supra* note 45, at 73.

has concluded that average utility is the only version of utility obtainable using his theory of justice.[68] Maintaining and improving the quality of life of people who actually exist seems more crucial than maximizing the number of persons who live, at least under current social and population conditions. As a result, average utility should be weighted more heavily in a hybrid formula that takes into account the impact of reproductive behavior on both average and total utility.

This solution of the dilemma posed by "different number" cases has direct implications for public health regulation. It instructs lawmakers who are considering restrictions on a particular reproductive technology to evaluate the likely impact of that technology on the average and total utility of the resulting children. Because the impact on average utility should be given greater weight, relatively small decreases in average utility could only be offset by relatively large increases in total utility. Promising candidates for such regulatory scrutiny would include fertility clinics that regularly transplant an extremely high number of embryos and fertility drugs strongly associated with multiple pregnancies.

V. CRITICISMS

Critics are likely to raise three key objections to the methodology proposed here. The first is that it identifies a phantom category of "harm" that has no victims and, therefore, has little, if any, moral significance. The second is that the utilitarian methodology underlying this notion of harmfulness has undesirable consequences. And the third is that an obligation to minimize future suffering could have unwanted implications for other reproductive conduct such as genetic screening.

A. VICTIMLESS HARM?

The conception of harmful conduct proposed here postulates that conduct can be harmful even though it makes no specific child worse off than he or she otherwise would have been.[69] It is harmful because

---

68. RAWLS, *supra* note 43, at 166; Narveson, *supra* note 45, at 77-78. However, Rawls ultimately rejects average utility as a general moral theory.

69. As a result, an action for conventional compensatory damages on behalf of the children actually born would be inappropriate except in those rare cases where life itself is harmful. However, a claim for child support might be defensible under some circumstances. *See* Philip G. Peters, Jr., *Rethinking Wrongful Life: Bridging the Boundary Between Tort and Family Law*, 67

396 *SOUTHERN CALIFORNIA INTERDISCIPLINARY LAW JOURNAL*

it causes unnecessary human suffering. Although there are no individual victims, future children suffer as a class if the technologies used do not maximize the well-being of the resulting children.[70] As they suffer, the community suffers. Dan Brock correctly observes that these reproductive choices are "person-affecting" in the sense that they inflict unnecessary human suffering.[71]

This way of conceptualizing harmful conduct explains better than any alternative model why we have such a strong negative reaction to the conduct of the Italian sperm bank and the impatient mother.[72] John Robertson has trivialized this insight by describing it as a "norm against offending persons who are troubled by gratuitous suffering."[73] It is not simply a norm about offending sensibilities. It is a norm against inflicting gratuitous suffering.[74]

B. UTILITARIAN VULNERABILITIES?

Many of those who feel uncomfortable with parental failure to use the safer alternative may, nonetheless, have misgivings about the utilitarian underpinnings of a class-based interest analysis. In particular, they may fear the trade-offs commonly associated with unrestrained utility analysis.[75] The typical illustration of these trade-offs involves the sacrifice of one person so that his organs can be used to save the lives of several other people.[76]

TULANE L. REV. 397 (1992). Those circumstances are much less likely to occur in the circumstances discussed in this Article than they are in a wrongful life case, where parents are trying to avoid conception or birth. However, unexpected multiple births might be a candidate.

70. *See* Brock, *supra* note 32, at 275.

71. *See id.* at 273.

72. Because this class interest approach compares the health or happiness of the two groups of possible children, it arguably assumes that causing a person to exist can benefit him. Parfit states that both views on this issue are defensible. PARFIT, *supra* note 31, at 490. But that controversial assumption is not essential to the conception of harm proposed here. Even if we cannot directly prove that causing someone to exist is a benefit, we can coherently ask whether a person's life is or would be good. *See id.* at 487-89. *See* Singer, *A Utilitarian Population Principle, in* ETHICS AND POPULATION 81 (1976). This question permits comparisons of *how good* life is or would be for different children. *See* PARFIT, *supra* note 31, at 489. As a result, the likely happiness of the two groups of possible children can be compared.

73. Robertson, *supra* note 13, at 76.

74. *See* Dan W. Brock, *Procreative Liberty*, 74 TEX. L. REV. 187, 203-04 (1995) (reviewing JOHN A. ROBERTSON, CHILDREN OF CHOICE: FREEDOM AND THE NEW REPRODUCTIVE TECHNOLOGIES (1994)).

75. *See, e.g.*, Laudor, *supra* note 54, at 1685-86.

76. *See* JOEL FEINBERG, OFFENSE TO OTHERS 80 (1985). Both the average utility approach and the total utility approach have sacrifice implications if accepted in their entirety. *See* MICHAEL D. BAYLES, MORALITY AND POPULATION POLICY 103-12 (1981).

Fortunately, it is not necessary to endorse utilitarianism so whole-heartedly in order to favor the analysis proposed here. Utilitarian tools are used here solely to solve a problem posed by the shortcomings of more traditional, rights-based analysis in the unique circumstances associated with existence-inducing acts. The analysis proposed here uses utilitarian calculus to give content to the idea of *beneficence* in the context of *future* people.[77] Most rights-based theories make beneficence an important moral consideration. Furthermore, no actual child is asked to suffer for the sake of the greater happiness of someone else.[78] As a result, one can reasonably endorse this limited use of utility analysis while insisting that the goal of beneficence be subject to other moral norms, such as equal justice or a Kantian reluctance to use people as means to an end.[79]

C. EXTENSION OF THE ANALYSIS TO GENETIC SCREENING

The normative implications of a class-based analysis of harm are not limited to the avoidance of dangerous reproductive technologies. The same logic could potentially impose affirmative obligations on parents in other settings as well. John Robertson, for example, assumes that a class-based analysis of harm would mandate "a moral duty to undergo carrier or prenatal diagnosis and abort if tests are positive."[80] In his view, "such a counterintuitive result suggests a flaw in the argument."[81]

In reaching this conclusion, Robertson mistakenly assumes that regulatory decision-making would turn exclusively on this class-based interest assessment. He overlooks the larger analysis of which class-based interest analysis is just one part. Class-based analysis only identifies the interests of future children in reproductive decisions. Determining whether a specific action is morally or legally obligatory also requires an analysis of the rights and interests of parents and providers who will be affected by a prohibition or restriction. As explained

---

77. *See* Derek Parfit, *Future Generations: Further Problems*, 11 PHIL. & PUB. AFFAIRS 113, 129 (1982).

78. *See* Feldman, *supra* note 31, at 202 n.22 (noting that this approach would not permit the killing of someone already in the world); Fishkin, *supra* note 25, at 30 (noting that these utility calculations apply only to future people, and not to actual people).

79. *See* PARFIT. *supra* note 31, at 366, 394. As James Woodward notes, we need a theory than combines both consequential and nonconsequential components. Woodward. *supra* note 31, at 83.

80. Robertson, *supra* note 50, at 448.

81. *Id.* However, Parfit specifically declined to require genetic enhancement. Parfit, *supra* note 77, at 126-27. *Accord* Kavka, *supra* note 47, at 99-104.

398 *SOUTHERN CALIFORNIA INTERDISCIPLINARY LAW JOURNAL*

above, regulation will be most defensible where the threat to the welfare of future children is serious and the conflicting interests are least powerful.[82]

Context will be crucial. Mandating an abortion after a positive test for genetic abnormality is qualitatively different from asking Parfit's mother to wait a few months before conceiving. Each proposed intervention must be analyzed on its own terms, exploring both the benefits likely to be conferred on future children and the degree of likely interference with the recognized rights and interests of the parents, providers, and, in the case of mandatory abortions, the fetus. Mandatory abortion would sacrifice a living fetus on behalf of future class welfare and would do so by forcibly invading the bodily integrity of the mother. That is radically different from, for example, placing a limit on the number of embryos implanted at one time. Just as American courts do not require individuals to donate organs to dying relatives,[83] they will not require women to undergo the coerced abortion of genetically impaired fetuses in order to protect the average well-being of future children. Mandatory abortions will remain unthinkable even if the analysis proposed here is adopted.

The virtue of this expanded conception of harm is that it forces us to address these contextual differences and account for them, rather than dismissing the welfare of future generations as morally irrelevant. The moral dimension of genetic screening, for example, is familiar to any woman who knows that she carries a dangerous gene or who conceives in her late forties. Under these circumstances, many women agonize over their choices. The wrongful life approach cannot account for this agony. A class-based analysis helps to fill that moral vacuum. By doing so, it enriches our understanding of the moral conflicts posed by the capacity to do genetic screening. Its ability to detect these moral dilemmas and bring them to the surface is a strength, rather than a weakness.

VI. CONCLUSIONS AND FUTURE QUESTIONS

The conventional model of harming overlooks an important category of harmful conduct. Because it focuses exclusively on the presence or absence of harm to individuals who are actually born, this model ignores the ability of actors, like the Italian sperm bank, to

---

82. *See supra* text accompanying notes 50-51.
83. *See* McFall v. Shimp, 10 Pa. D. & C.3d 90 (1978). *See also* Head v. Colloton, 331 N.W.2d 870 (Iowa 1983).

reduce human suffering by engaging in more responsible conduct. When a reproductive choice results in the birth of a child who will suffer more, rather than one who will suffer less, that choice causes unnecessary harm. Although no individual child can claim to have been personally harmed, the class of children conceived as a result of these choices will suffer more than they need to have suffered.

The narrow focus of the traditional model of harm is well-suited for use in tort litigation. In an action for compensatory damages, proof of harm to the claimant is essential. However, this narrow notion of harm is not appropriate for public health regulation. Because public health regulation is concerned with community welfare, it can and should take into account the unnecessary harm that reproductive choices can inflict on future children as a class.

Lawmakers who contemplate the regulation of existence-inducing behavior, such as cloning and surrogacy, should consider not only whether the children who owe their lives to that technology have lives worth living, but also whether happier, healthier children would be born if these technologies were used differently or not at all.

Treating the failure to maximize child welfare as harmful conduct is consistent with our moral barometers. It provides us with a more robust conception of the interests of future children. Consequently, it offers an important additional perspective for evaluating not only new reproductive technologies like cloning and genetic manipulation, but also older ones, like surrogacy, in vitro fertilization, and fertility drugs. In the current debate over cloning, furthermore, it provides a coherent basis for the NBAC's consideration of potential harms to cloned children.

At the same time, this model requires close attention to the reproductive options that are actually available to specific individuals. Only after those alternatives are compared can conclusions be reached about the harmfulness of the chosen course of action. In this respect, the NBAC's call for a blanket moratorium is too blunt and non-contextual. The propriety of running the risks associated with cloning will turn on the circumstances.

This unconventional approach does not dictate or even support state intervention every time that a harmful choice is made. Before a decision about regulation can be reached, lawmakers must also consider the interests of parents, providers, and others who may be affected by the regulation. The significance of this new methodology

400 *SOUTHERN CALIFORNIA INTERDISCIPLINARY LAW JOURNAL*

is not that it requires intervention, but that it requires justification in cases overlooked by more conventional notions of harm.[84]

---

84. This approach also raises some intriguing second-generation questions, such as whether adoption should sometimes count as an available option and how uncertainty about risks and about the odds of a live birth should factor into this analysis. For a preliminary assessment of the role of uncertainty, see *supra* note 53. On the relevance of adoption, see PETER SINGER & DEANE WELLS, MAKING BABIES: THE NEW SCIENCE AND ETHICS OF CONCEPTION 44-46 (1985) (forcing adoption not likely to be successful; but no right to genetic offspring); Jan Narveson, *Future People and Us*, *in* OBLIGATIONS TO FUTURE GENERATIONS 49 (1978). The adoption option is not strictly analogous to the conception choices previously examined because it does not offer the parents the option of bringing into the world a genetically related child. However, similarities between the two choices exist. In adoption, as with other cases of substitution, needless suffering can be avoided by not conceiving the would-be affected child and by rearing another available child. In fact, the case for intervention is arguably stronger here because the children who will benefit are actually living, unlike Parfit's unconceived healthy child.

[14]

In the Name of the Father? *Ex parte Blood*: Dealing with Novelty and Anomaly

Derek Morgan and Robert G. Lee*

The case of Diane Blood is likely to become a staple in discussions of English medical law and ethics.[1] It has the necessary ingredients to mark it out as a stigmata case; it is ethically controversial and raises legal questions which appear to be essentially contested.[2] One striking feature is its relative novelty.[3] Although parallels do exist in the United States and France,[4] *Blood* is the first litigated case

* Cardiff Law School.

Many friends and colleagues have read or listened to versions of this note, or provided briefs on specific points. Ideas which it contains were aired at seminars at the University of Wales Law Faculties' Meeting, Gregynog in March 1997 and at the University of Liverpool in May 1997. We owe a particular debt to Tony Downes, Gillian Douglas, Nigel Lowe, Paolo Nebbia, Tamara Hervey, Iain Macdonald, Akas Manolkidis and Celia Wells. The usual caveat applies.

1 *R v Human Fertilisation & Embryology Authority, ex parte Blood* [1997] 2 All ER 687 (Court of Appeal), (1997) 35 BMLR 1 (High Court and Court of Appeal); the judgment of the Court of Appeal (Lord Woolf MR, Waite and Henry LJJ) was given by Lord Woolf.

2 In the sense used by W. Gallie, 'Essentially Contested Concepts,' *Proceedings of the Aristotelian Society*, N.S. vol. LVI (March, 1956) 180.

3 Mrs Blood's is not the first attempt to make post mortem use of a partner's sperm which has given rise to public difficulties. In 1985, Sonia Palmer's desire to use the frozen sperm of her deceased husband was referred to the Infertility Services Ethical Committee of Central Manchester District Health Authority. The Committee refused her request to use the sperm at the hospital which had previously been treating her in an infertility programme, but said that she should be allowed to take the frozen sperm elsewhere if she could find a clinic which would treat her; see *The Guardian*, 25 September, 1985, 19. Nor is this the first time in which clinicians have knowingly agreed to assist in the posthumous use of sperm; for an example pre dating the 1990 Act of the use of the procedure in England & Wales see the affidavit of Professor Lord Winston, Professor of Fertility Studies at the Royal Post Graduate Medical School, Hammersmith Hospital, referred to by Sir Stephen Brown in the High Court in *Blood* ((1997) 35 BMLR 1, 14), which averred that to withhold the sperm here would be 'cruel and unnatural.' Shortly before the Court of Appeal's judgment in *Blood*, *The Guardian* (25 February 1997, at 4) reported that a woman whose husband had died three years previously was soon expecting to give birth to twins. Described as the first case of its kind, the woman had been inseminated with sperm stored with her husband's 'effective consent' under the Human Fertilisation & Embryology Act 1990.

4 *Hecht v Superior Court of the State of California for the County of Los Angeles (W E Kane. real Party in Interest)* (1993) 20 Cal Rptr 2d 275 (California Court of Appeals); (Supreme Court of California; petition for review denied and Court of Appeal judgment de-authorised for use as a precedent, 15 January, 1997, Case No S057498); *Pires v Centre Hospitalier Régional de la Grave* (Tribunal de Grande Instance de Toulouse, 11 May 1993 Cour de Cassation, 9 January 1996, Dict. Perm. Bioethic. bull. no. 30; JCP 1996, edition G. II 22666); *Parpalaix v CECOS* (Centre d'Etudes et de Conservation de Sperme), (Gazette du Palais, September 15, 1984); (see Garay, 'Recent aspects concerning medically assisted procreation in France,' Council of Europe, Third Symposium on Bioethics, 'Medically Assisted Procreation and the Protection of the Human Embryo', Strasbourg, 15–18 December 1996, and Mémetan, 'Post mortem assisted Procreation according to French Law' (1997) 4 EJ Health Law 199). For other examples of attempted post mortem recovery of sperm see *The Guardian* (21 October 1995, 7) — 'Dead Men Can Still Have Children', *The Independent* (26 October, 1995, 10), and of eggs see *The Guardian*, 12 January 1995, 11. For a brief consideration of other jurisdictional approaches see Law Reform Commission of Canada, Working Paper 65, *Medically Assisted Procreation* (Ottawa: Minister of Supply and Services, 1992) at 186–87.

which tests the application of domestic legislation to post mortem insemination where there is no written consent to the taking of the sperm.[5] Additionally, it exposes the Human Fertilisation and Embryology Authority to a particularly harsh glare of judicial review.[6]

Diane Blood wanted to become pregnant; hardly remarkable in itself — plans for pregnancy are often celebrated. She wanted to be able to use the process of artificial insemination to achieve this; in the late twentieth century, this is hardly unusual either.[7] Biologically speaking, she had all the necessary ingredients, and, as far as we presently know of her, there is no physical impediment to her plans. All that stood in her way was the Human Fertilisation & Embryology Act 1990 and the Authority charged with its enforcement, caricatured during litigation as inhuman, anti-fertilisation and authoritarian. Stephen Blood's *intent* to share children with his wife appears to have been clearly established,[8] what was missing was his *consent*; specifically, and crucially, his written consent.[9]

There was an additional hitch; Stephen Blood had been pronounced clinically dead on 2 March 1995, four days after contracting bacterial meningitis. Shortly before, Mrs Blood had raised with doctors the question of taking 'a sample of sperm by electro ejaculation from her husband who by that time was in a coma.'[10] Two samples were recovered and entrusted to the Infertility Research Trust at a second hospital for storage. The second sample was taken 'shortly before' Stephen

---

5 Tamara Hervey claims that *Blood* and the Irish abortion injunction case *Attorney General* v *X and Others* [1992] ILRM 401 taken together '... show that the provisions of European law may be capable of undermining national legal provisions ... concerning the regulation of human reproduction.' 'Buy Baby: The European Union and Regulation of Human Reproduction' (1998) 18 OJLS (forthcoming); we are grateful to Dr Hervey for an opportunity to cite from this draft). Given that the Irish Supreme Court discharged the injunction on its own preferred interpretation of the Irish constitution, *Blood* is really the first case effectively to underwrite Hervey's own conclusion. For discussion of some of the issues raised by posthumous use of gametes and embryos see John Robertson, 'Posthumous Reproduction' (1994) *69 Indiana Law Journal* 1027–1066 and Douglas Cuisine, 'Artificial Insemination with the Husband's Sperm after the Husband's Death' (1977) 3 J Med Ethics 163.

6 For the present we put the issue no higher than this. It was always clear that HFEA could be and one day would be subject to judicial review, but the nature and force of the Court of Appeal's judgment in *Blood* may yet complicate the working of the Authority.

7 Artificial insemination hardly qualifies to be regarded as a 'new' reproductive technology. One of the best brief introductions to the history of assisted conception is Edward Yoxen, *Unnatural Selection? Coming to Terms with the New Genetics* (London: Heinemann, 1986) esp 1–63. There is a characteristically comprehensive consideration of the social and particularly gendered aspects of fertility in Germaine Greer's compendious *Sex and Destiny: The Politics of Human Fertility*, (London: Martin Secker & Warburg, 1984) *passim*, and an early consideration of some of the legal and social issues in the context of contemporary medical practices and etiquette in, predictably, Glanville Williams's *Sanctity of Life and the Criminal Law* (London: Faber & Faber, 1958) at 110–138.

8 This much, at least, was accepted by Sir Stephen Brown: (1997) 35 BMLR 1 at 8, '[Mrs Blood] submits that although her husband died before insemination could take place nevertheless there was a common joint enterprise having regard to the fact that the sperm was taken from the body of her husband although unconscious in her presence and in the context of the fact that they had discussed their intention to have a child and had specifically addressed the possibility of posthumous artificial insemination.'

9 The significance of the requirement for there to be a written consent is examined by Sarah Franklin, 'Please Sign Here: Written Consent, Generative Capacitation and Gamete Storage as Kinship Technologies', paper presented at the Storage of Human Gametes and Embryos Workshop, Departments of Law and Philosophy, Keele University, 5 February 1997; we are grateful to Sarah Franklin for an early opportunity to see this paper.

10 Lord Woolf [1997] 2 All ER 687, 690. One wonders why the Trust or its advisers did not at this stage take advantage of the recently fashioned declaratory jurisdiction of the Family Division to address questions of the legality of such a procedure in respect of one who, like F in *Re F* [1990] 2 AC 1 and Tony Bland in *Bland*, n 13 below, was incapable of giving the necessary consents.

The Modern Law Review [Vol. 60

Blood was certified clinically dead.[11] Mrs Blood wanted to use the samples of the semen to have her husband's child.

The need for anomaly

It may be trite to say, but every legal system needs its Diane Blood, in the same way that it needs its Tony Bland. The long dying of a young man in a persistent vegetative state, trapped in the erosion of death,[12] provoked a re-examination of the essence of death and demise in western societies at the end of the twentieth century. Thus, when we read the speeches of the House of Lords,[13] there is a terrible sense in which we know that Tony Bland is already dead. Not in the dualistic (non) sense introduced by Sir Stephen Brown P in his judgment in the High Court,[14] but in the broader sense that we have already killed him. Bland may have been very far from the madding crowd, but he was certainly still much engaged in its ignoble strife. Tony Bland died because he no longer had interests which a family could care for, he had no continuing family interests. Diane Blood fought to continue the interests which she and her husband had in forming a family; the desire to prolong family interests. Stephen Blood is very much present throughout the legal argument. His widow (as she markedly styles herself) Diane Blood, comes to represent something enigmatic and anomalous as far as reproduction and sexuality is concerned. What she does, she does, patently, in the name of the father; what she does, she does rationally.[15] From the very outset of the unfolding drama, not for Diane Blood the prospect of new relationships, new horizons, new families, but the assumption of a role re-enforced by her attempts to have Stephen's child.[16]

Blood like *Bland* offers an opportunity to take stock, to re-examine the existing boundaries between the anomalous and the routine; between the normal and the pathological; to reflect upon the paradox which Ulrich Beck and Elizabeth Gernsheim-Beck observe, that while pregnancy may be a natural event, '... in the waning years of the twentieth century nature no longer exists in the sense we mean it; nature is usually in the hands of the experts.'[17] *Blood* and *Bland* help to render visible latent issues and tensions which, 'far from being aberrations or exceptions

---

11 *ibid.*
12 Naturally, the phrase is taken from Gabriel García Márquez, 'Death Constant Beyond Love' in *Innocent Eréndira and other Stories* (London: Picador, trans Gregory Rabassa, 1981) 62.
13 *Airedale NHS Trust* v *Bland* [1993] AC 789.
14 *Airedale NHS Trust* v *Bland* [1993] 1 All ER 821, 832: the withdrawal of artificial hydration and nutrition '... does not in my judgment alter the reality that the true cause of death will be the massive injuries which he sustained in what has been described as the Hillsborough disaster.'
15 For an important clarification of the nature of rationality in the case of reproductive technologies see Lene Koch, 'IVF — An Irrational Choice?' (1990) 3 *Issues in Reproductive and Genetic Engineering* 235–242.
16 Gillian Douglas remarked to us how clearly Diane Blood *ironically* represents both the 'archetypal wife' and would-be-mother and the singular woman determined to assert her 'right' to a child of her chosen genetic heritage. One of Diane Blood's metaphorical cousins is Sarah Woodruff, 'The French Lieutenant's Woman,' the eponymous heroine of John Fowles' classic novel of Victorian sensibilities and sexualities. Like the Lieutenant, Stephen Blood is present throughout the unfolding drama, made more so by his absence; see John Fowles, *The French Lieutenant's Woman* (London: Jonathan Cape, 1969). 'Lieu-tenant'; one who takes the place of another: *Shorter Oxford English Dictionary* (Oxford: Oxford University Press, 3rd ed, 1973) 1208.
17 Ulrich Beck and Elizabeth Gernsheim Beck, *The Normal Chaos of Love* (Cambridge: Polity Press, 1995) 116.

Legal and Ethical Issues in Human Reproduction

in [their practices], ... are its constituent elements.'[18] *Blood* helps to put reproductive medicine back into a context from which it has started to become separate; reproductive technologies are worthy of study because they remain controversial, and controversial because 'they crystallise issues at the heart of contemporary social and political struggles over sexuality, reproduction, gender relations and the family'.[19] As such, *Blood's case* raises the alchemy of marriage, family, fertility, rationality and rights, and — as it transpires — the nature of the European stamp on the envelope of reproductive technologies.[20]

Bland and *Blood* also raise the balance of personal interests and public interest. Both are also of interest to the public; in a very real sense there is an inquiry which asks, perhaps with some presumption, who *are* these people? They are subjects *of* the law's regulation and of the public gaze in the theatre of identity; it is important to know who they are and what kind of interests they have. Both are provocative in upsetting previously understood practices of law; in resistance to societal expectations of her new found role as widow, Diane Blood is the subject of *resistance* to law; she is a paradigm of the generation and reproduction of structures of meaning within the law, of what Clifford Geertz has called 'webs of signification.'[21]

'Till death do us part'; the case of Diane and Stephen Blood

Mr and Mrs Blood had been married for four years before his death in 1995; they had had a long courtship of nine years before they had married 'according to the rights of the Anglican church using the traditional service contained in the 1662 Book of Common Prayer.'[22] Beginning at the end of 1994 they 'actively

---

18 Simone Noaves and Tania Saleem, 'Embedding the Embryo' at 3; paper presented to a Workshop of the European Commission Biomed I Project, 'Fertility, Infertility & the Embryo', Barcelona, November 1994. Thus, in *Blood* and *Bland*, we see the emergence of a regulated, legalised, and in *Blood* constitutionalised practice of the art of medicine. In that both raise conflicts of interest, both cases are resolved for the benefit and protection of doctors rather than for others, who become the passive (and in *Blood* of course the grateful) recipients of the law for the profession.

19 Michelle Stanworth, *Reproductive Technologies: Gender, Motherhood and Medicine* (Cambridge: Polity Press, 1987) 4.

20 It is a remarkable example, almost a paradigmatic case, of the recommendation of the 'Glover Report' that the future shape of the family should evolve 'experimentally' with individuals taking control of their own reproductive processes. (Jonathan Glover and others, *Fertility and the Family* (London: Fourth Estate, 1989) 35). One difficulty with this, as Marilyn Strathern has intimated, is that it is an '... extraordinarily impoverished view of culture to imagine that how we conceive of parents and children only affects parents and children.' *Reproducing the Future: Anthropology, Kinship and the New Reproductive Technologies* (Manchester: Manchester University Press, 1993) 33.

21 Quoted in Austin Sarat and William Felstiner, *Divorce Lawyers and their Clients: Power and Meaning in the Legal Process* (New York and Oxford: Oxford University Press, 1995) 10. *Blood* is also a good example of the observation that *power* in lawyer-client interactions is part of the '... dynamic process [that] characterise the interaction of law with the culture of common sense, and the fluidity, negotiability and ever changing qualities of both law and everyday life.' (Engel, 'Law in the Domains of Everyday Life: The Construction of Community and Difference' in Austin Sarat and T. Kearns (eds), *Law in Everyday Life* (Ann Arbor: University of Michigan Press, 1993) 126, quoted in Sarat and Felstiner at 21–22.

22 Lord Woolf, note 1 above, 690, points to this version's emphasis on the importance of procreation of children within marriage; it is also the form of service which carries the words 'till death do us part'. There is a pertinent reflection on the nature of the marriage bond (compared with other forms of biological and social relationship) in Brenda Almond's 'Human Bonds' (1988) 5 *Journal of Applied Philosophy* 3–16, reprinted in Brenda Almond and Donald Hill (eds), *Applied Philosophy: Morals and Metaphysics in Contemporary Debate* (London: Routledge, 1991) 59–72 and her 'Parenthood — Social Construct or Fact of Nature' in Derek Morgan and Gillian Douglas (eds), *Constituting Families: A Study in Governance* (Stuttgart: Franz Steiner Verlag, 1994) 98–107.

The Modern Law Review [Vol. 60

decided to try for a family'[23] and, according to Mrs Blood's evidence, had discussed what Stephen Blood would want to happen should he die before they could complete their plans. Three months later he was dead. In these 'sad circumstances' the propriety of the doctors' response to Mrs Blood's request to recover sperm from her dying husband was, for Lord Woolf, clear; 'humanity dictated that the sperm was taken and preserved first, and the legal argument followed.'[24] The Human Fertilisation & Embryology Authority when contacted by the Infertility Trust advised that the recovery, storage and use of the sperm was unlawful. It was this advice and later decisions of the Authority which 'frustrated ... this desire' of Diane Blood 'to have her husband's child',[25] and led to her challenge.[26]

The Human Fertilisation & Embryology Act 1990 was introduced following the Warnock Committee's *Report of the Inquiry into Human Fertilisation & Embryology*.[27] The Act, while not a comprehensive code, is a major and complex piece of legislation, seeking to tackle sensitive and difficult ethical, legal, personal and social problems which surround and attend infertility. The major vehicle to effect supervision of clinical practice and research is the Human Fertilisation and Embryology Authority (HFEA).[28] The 1990 Act was one of the first effective European legislative schemes to respond to what has been called the 'reproduction revolution.'[29] A cornerstone provision of the legislation is the principle of 'effective consent' which had itself been emerging through the 1970s and 1980s as a benchmark for the negotiation of the proper relationship between health care professionals and people who became their patients. But assisted conception, rightly or wrongly, was felt to give rise to special and sensitive questions such that certain absolute prohibitions or restrictions were written into the Act, and the HFEA was given further regulatory powers.

---

23 Lord Woolf, n 1 above, 690.
24 *ibid*; this, of course, *produced* the 'agonising situation of Mrs Blood' and presented this 'anxious and moving' case which 'stirs the emotions and evokes what I believe to be universal sympathy' as Sir Stephen Brown was to put it in the High Court (1997) 35 BMLR 1 17.
25 n 1 above, 690.
26 Lord Woolf related that the facts disclosed an 'unexplored legal situation.' n 1 above, 695.
27 Cm 9314, 1984. The problems for Mrs Blood were the provisions of s 12 and paragraphs 1 and 3 of Schedule 3 of the 1990 Act; the 'consents' section s 4(1), the 'storage' section s 14, and ss 23 and 24, the 'directions' sections.
28 For commentary see Derek Morgan and Robert Lee, *Blackstone's Guide to the Human Fertilisation & Embryology Act 1990: Abortion and Embryo Research: The New Law* (London: Blackstone Press, 1991) 89–151; Jonathan Montgomery, *Health Care Law* (Oxford: Oxford University Press, 1997) 382–393 and his 'Rights, Restraints and Pragmatism' (1991) 54 MLR 524–534; and Joe Jacob, 'Human Fertilisation & Embryology Act 1990' [1990] 37 *Current Law Statutes Annotated*.
29 Peter Singer and Deane Wells, *The Reproduction Revolution: New Ways of Making Babies* (Oxford: Oxford University Press, 1984). In the sense that a revolution is usually understood to be something driven from below, the phrase is something of a misnomer; change in assisted conception practices is decidedly a top down driven exercise. In this sense, the enigmatic Diane Blood may properly be seen as a subversive element in the reproduction revolution. For legislation which addresses aspects of reproductive medicine see Jan Stephan (ed), *International Survey of Laws on Assisted Procreation*, (Zurich: Schilthess Polygraphischer Verlag, 1990) and the periodic *International Digest of Health Legislation*. A commentary on some of the international provisions is contained in Jennifer Gunning and Veronica English, *Human In Vitro Fertilization: A Case Study in the Regulation of Medical Innovation* (Aldershot: Dartmouth, 1993). There is an elegant review of the continuing issues of reproductive technologies in The Danish Council of Ethics, *Assisted Conception — A Report* (Copenhagen: The Danish Council of Ethics, trans Tim Davies, 1995). For a consideration of some of the reasons why reproductive technologies remain important and troubling aspects of the study of modern medical practice see Derek Morgan, 'Frameworks of Analysis for Feminisms' Accounts of Reproductive Technology' in Sally Sheldon and Michael Thompson (eds), *Feminist Perspectives on Health Care Law* (London: Cavendish Publishing, 1998, forthcoming).

It sometimes happens that gametes, or embryos derived from gametes, remain in storage at the death of one or rarely both[30] of the genitors. The surviving party might then nonetheless seek to make use of the stored gametes or embryos. The Warnock Committee wished to see the posthumous use of gametes 'actively discouraged.'[31] The Committee believed that birth in such circumstances might give rise to profound psychological problems for child and mother, and were worried about the lack of finality in the administration of estates which would be engendered by the possibility of such births.[32] It would have been open to the legislature to provide that no such use could be contemplated, but it did not. Instead, the Act provided that if posthumous use of gametes is to be made, the provider has to have given clear *written* indication that that conformed with, and certainly did not go against any specific wishes or views that they held;[33] not surprisingly the mechanism used to ensure this outcome was consent.[34]

One exception to the requirement of formal written consent is where sperm is being used in a treatment service for the benefit of the woman and the sperm provider *together*.[35] Use of gametes in contravention of the consents provisions carries a number of consequences; it may breach the licence issued by the HFEA to

30 The most publicised example of the death of husband and wife who had had embryos stored is that of the 'Rios' embryos', discussed briefly in John Robertson, *Children of Choice: Freedom and the New Reproductive Technologies* (Princeton, NJ: Princeton University Press, 1996 ed) 111–112, and more extensively in his 'Posthumous Reproduction', n 5 above, and G P Smith, 'Australia's Frozen "Orphan" Embryos: A Medical, Legal and Ethical Dilemma' (1985–86) 24 J Fam Law 27.

31 Cm 9314, para 4.4; it is in light of this that the evidence of (the now) Baroness Warnock comes to be considered. Warnock gave an affidavit, later admitted in evidence, that the Committee had given no consideration to the facts of a case such as that now before the court. In that sense, her affidavit was introduced to seek to persuade the court that *Blood* was such an unusual set of facts that the Committee had not even been thinking about the desirability or undesirability of what was being proposed at all.

32 *ibid*, paras, 10.9 and 10.15. For resolution of precisely this point under the Tasmanian Administration and Probate Act 1936 s 46(1) see *In the Matter of the Estate of the Late K and in the Matter of the Administration and Probate Act 1936, ex parte The Public Trustee* (22 April, 1996) [1996] Tas L R 211, and Derek Morgan, 'Rights and Legal Status of Embryos' (1996) 4 (7) *Australian Health Law Bulletin*, 61–67.

33 Somewhat cavalierly, Lord Woolf, n 1 above, 703 remarks that the legislative provision for written consent '... is not obvious in this situation.'

34 HFE Act, Sch 3: para 1: 'A consent under this Schedule must be given in writing and, in this Schedule, "effective consent" means a consent under this Schedule which has not been withdrawn'; para 2(2): 'A consent to the storage of any gametes or an embryo must (a) specify the maximum period of storage (if less than the statutory storage period), and (b) state what is to be done with the gametes or embryo if the person who gave the consent dies ...'; para 5(1): 'A person's gametes must not be used for the purposes of treatment services unless there is an effective consent by that person to their being so used and they are used in accordance with the terms of that consent; ... (3) This paragraph does not apply to the use of a person's gametes for the purpose of that person, or that person and another together, receiving treatment services.'

35 HFE Act s 4(1)(b). Both the High Court and the Court of Appeal dismissed argument that although Stephen Blood was dead, he and Diane Blood could nonetheless benefit from the saving in this provision. The HFEA countered that as between Mrs Blood and the stored sperm of Stephen Blood, after his death the sperm fell to be treated as if it were the sperm of a donor, and hence within the licensing regime so as to require the necessary consent. It is arguable (but still not free of doubt) that if it had been the Clinic's intention to provide Mrs Blood with the treatment services as her husband lay dying, immediately before the determination of his death, the marriage would still have subsisted and written consent would not have been required (see n 39 below). To the general principles established in English law might now be added the provisions of the Council of Europe, *Convention on Human Rights and Biomedicine (Convention for the Protection of Human Rights and Dignity of the Human Being with regard to the Application of Biology and Medicine)* (Strasbourg: Directorate of Legal Affairs, 1996) DIR/JUR (96)14, Articles 5 and 6 (1) '... an intervention may only be carried out on a person who does not have the capacity to consent, for his or her *direct* benefit' (emphasis added; and see *Explanatory Report to the Convention* ... (Strasbourg: Directorate of Legal Affairs, 1997) DIR/JUR (97) 1, but carrying no explanation of the notion of 'directness').

the 'person responsible' for the clinic where the treatment services are offered, it may amount to a criminal offence and it may affect the status of any child born of those treatment services.[36]

What also fell to be considered in *Blood* are the HFEA's powers to make what are called in sections 23 and 24 'Directions' to clinics about specific matters. Section 24(4) of the Act deals with what was to become one of the major vessels of Blood's argument in the Court of Appeal, the import and export of gametes and embryos. Section 24(4) gives to the HFEA a broad discretion to give directions on the export of gametes and general directions under that section were made in 1991.[37]

Mrs Blood, however, sought judicial review of the HFEA's decision not to make *specific* directions under section 24(4) of the Act in order to allow her access to and use of the sperm. For the application to proceed, it was necessary for the court to put aside what would seem to be the unlawful recovery and storage of the sperm. Storage of the sperm without consent, Lord Woolf admits, means that 'technically an offence was committed' but that 'there is no question of any prosecution being brought in the circumstances ...'.[38] In addition '... the question of the lawfulness of the storage is quite separate from the lawfulness of taking the sperm from Mr Blood as he lay unconscious.' However the Court did not hear argument on the propriety of these actions and 'it is therefore not necessary to make any comment about this.'[39]

Mrs Blood's desire to use the sperm of her dead husband collected from him specifically for this purpose appeared to have fallen irredeemably against the barrier of the express intentions of Parliament. The Court of Appeal, however, was ready to assist Mrs Blood in her 'agonising situation',[40] which it did in accepting

---

36 HFE Act ss 11–14, 17, 18, 41(2)(b) and 27–30 respectively. The 'status provisions' contained in ss 27–30 are examined in more detail in Derek Morgan and Robert Lee, *Blackstone's Guide to the Human Fertilisation & Embryology Act 1990: Abortion and Embryo Research: The New Law* (London: Blackstone Press, 1991) 152–169; the immediate provision of relevance, s 28(6)(b) is discussed there at 156–160 and in Ian Kennedy and Andrew Grubb, *Medical Law: Text with Materials* (London: Butterworths, 2nd ed, 1994) 819.
37 *Export of Gametes*: Directions made under the Human Fertilisation & Embryology Act 1990 s 24(4): D1991/8 (London: HFEA, 1991). Again these require that the donor consent in writing to the export of gametes, having been warned — in writing — that relevant legal provisions, as to parentage or anonymity, for example, may vary from jurisdiction to jurisdiction.
38 Lord Woolf, n 1 above, 695 and 697; the offence is one created under HFE Act s 41(2)(b).
39 *ibid*; the question of the lawfulness of the initial recovery of the sperm would, as Stephen Blood lay unconscious, fall to be considered under the common law provisions elaborated in *Re F* [1990] 2 AC 1 and *Airedale NHS Trust v Bland* (above). It would be necessary to show that the recovery of the sperm was in the 'best interests' of Stephen Blood. We do not have the space here fully to argue that point but it is clear that an argument might be made for it to be so considered; suppose that Stephen Blood had recovered from the meningitis but had been rendered sterile by the illness or, alternatively, that the notion of 'best interests' — clearly extending beyond *medical* interests alone, is taken to mean some interest in having his genetic line consensually continued after his death. For one of the earliest expressions of the notion that the dead can be harmed and ex hypothesi have interests see Aristotle, *The Nichomachean Ethics*, Book I, chap xi (trans J A K Thompson, London: Allen & Unwin, 1953) discussed in George Pitcher, 'The Misfortunes of The Dead' (1984) 21 Am Phil Q 183. The classic illustration of interests surviving beyond death is found in Homer's *Iliad*, Book xxii, and the treatment of Hector at the hands of the victorious Achilles (*Iliad*, trans Martin Hammond, Harmondsworth: Penguin, 1987 at 351–364, esp 361); even in this modern rendition, there is never mention of Hector's *body* being the object of the poem's lamentation, always that of Hector. There is a good exchange on harming the dead in (1984) *Ethics* 407 (Levenbook), (1985) *Ethics* 159 (Marquis) and (1987) *Ethics* 341 (Callahan); one of the strongest contemporary defences of the thesis that the dead can be harmed is in Joel Feinberg, *The Moral Limits of the Criminal Law: Harm to Others* (Oxford: Oxford University Press, 1984) chap 2.
40 Lord Woolf, n 1 above, 700.

argument that the HFEA's decision refusing to make specific directions allowing access to the sperm for export was an interference with her rights under Articles 59 and 60 of the Treaty of Rome.[41] These Articles provide that restrictions on one of the Union's four freedoms — here the right to receive services (as a concomitant of the guarantee of freedom of movement) — have at least to be justified by some imperative public interest requirement. Since the HFEA had not given an adequate account of such considerations, they were required to re-consider their decision, taking into consideration principles of EU law and, in the light of the Court's judgment on the legality of preserving sperm without consent, the unlikely possibility of such a case recurring. While stressing the HFEA's dominion of the substantive issue, the Court opined that Mrs Blood's position was 'much stronger' than when the Authority last considered the matter 'the legal position having received further clarification.' Moreover, although not ruling on whether the reasons presently given by the HFEA could pass European scrutiny, Lord Woolf thought this 'unlikely.'[42] So, not only does the Court use the trump of EU law to sweep aside the hand dealt by the UK Parliament, it deals the cards with which the HFEA must now play, and apparently leaves the applicant holding all the aces.

The potential consequences and significance of *Blood* go much further than the Court of Appeal's apparently deceptively simple finding that the provision of infertility treatment services is an economic activity provided for remuneration, and hence a 'service', within the terms of Article 59 of the Treaty of Rome, and we need to address this interplay of services and rights; this is the first matter for comment. *Blood* also provides an illustration of the way in which the implication of the courts in these medical and technical processes requires that they develop a social, even a moral, vision of family relationships and articulate appropriate responses to the public and moral dilemmas created by the social and cultural revolution of contemporary medicine.[43] This is the burden of our second comment.

Services and rights: desires and morality

It is difficult to overestimate the importance of the jurisprudence which is emerging under Articles 59 and 60. In that jurisprudence, four points are critical:

(i) Article 60 provides that the provisions on free movement of services will only apply where a particular restriction is not covered by the provisions on free movement of goods, persons, or capital;[44]

(ii) there must be an inter-state element to the provision;

(iii) the services provided must be economic in nature, in that they are provided for remuneration — whether the remuneration comes from one party to the transaction or from a party other than the intended service recipient;[45] and

(iv) the burden is on the member state to show legitimate public policy

---

41 See also *U* v *W (Attorney General intervening)* [1997] 2 FLR 282.

42 Lord Woolf, n 1 above, 700.

43 For the identification of these themes see Janet Dolgin, 'The "Intent" of Reproduction: Reproductive Technologies and the Parent-Child Bond' (1994) 26 *Connecticut Law Review* 1261, 1262.

44 Paul Craig and Gráinne de Búrca, *EC Law: Text, Cases & Materials* (Oxford: Clarendon Press 1995) 752 and generally their excellent discussion of Free Movement of Services at 750–776.

45 Although if the service is provided by the state, and hence is free at the point of consumption, the position is quite different: see Case 293/83, *Gravier* v *City of Liège* [1985] ECR 593, opinion of Advocate General Slynn at 603, and Case 263/86, *Belgium* v *Humbel* [1988] ECR 5365, discussed by Craig and de Búrca at 759 *et seq.*

requirements — 'the imperative requirements of public interest' — which justify a restriction on the freedom to provide or to receive services involving a 'fundamental ethical judgment.'[46] Such considerations of public interest are, of course, particularly relevant here.

In *Customs and Excise Commissioners* v *Schindler*,[47] the European Court of Justice held that Member States were entitled in deciding whether and how to regulate the provision of lotteries, to have regard to 'the moral, religious or cultural aspects' of gambling. Thus, it might be regulated in such a way that it does not become the source of generation of private profit, or so as to restrict the extent of criminal activity (including fraud) and to restrict the damaging individual and social consequences of this form of incitement to spend. Again this emphasis on wider social consequences beyond the interests of the consumers of the services is of note in the context of the *Blood* case.[48] Moreover, the ECJ in *Schindler* indicated that restrictions on import may be necessary to achieve the protection which the Member State seeks to secure.

If one asks where it is in *Blood* that any expression of or judgment on the public morality of Mrs Blood's intended course of conduct is to be found, then this can only be within the Warnock Report and its expression in the legislative form of the 1990 Act. Whatever is said of the merits of the choices made there in relation to post mortem usage of sperm in the absence of consent, it is difficult to find *alternative* expressions of public policy and morality. Even if one accepts the necessity for the HFEA to re-consider its position on freedom to benefit from services, it is hard to take the strong steer from the Court of Appeal to the effect that the Authority should consider the 'much stronger' position of Mrs Blood. Whether or not her position is stronger necessarily involves the very 'fundamental ethical value judgment' which is said to be part of the 'process in the application of Community Law.' And it is here that the Court of Appeal attempts to perform what turns out to be its most obvious sleight of hand; in treating rights to access services as though they are unrestricted, pretending that it raises no issues of morality or public policy, the Court effectively constructs a European by pass round the route which the Member State has signposted as carrying its fundamental ethical judgments; the vehicle which transports its national determination of the public policy issues is blocked.

In deciding that infertility treatment services unequivocally fall within the scope of Articles 59 and 60, the Court of Appeal has opened a number of other important lines of enquiry. For example, is the United Kingdom's strict licensing scheme for

46 Advocate General Van Gerven, C-159/90 *Society for the Protection of the Unborn Child* v *Grogan* Case [1991] ECR I-4685 at 4715 (the Irish 'abortion information' case). Such judgments must be defined by each individual state within its own scale of values and have to be justified by overriding public interest considerations; see also the judgment of the ECJ in *Customs & Excise Commissioners* v *Schindler & Anor* [1994] QB 610, [1994] 2 All ER 193 recognising 'a sufficient degree of latitude' to determine the moral or religious or ethical values which it regards as appropriate (at 667–669), including, in *Schindler* itself, consumer protection, protection of public morality, including (as in that case lotteries) where the effects would be damaging social *consequences*.
47 [1994] QB 610, [1994] 2 All ER 193.
48 *Schindler* [1994] 2 All ER 193, 229–230: the considerations of public policy advanced by the Member State when, as they must be, taken together, '... concern the recipients of the service and, more generally, of consumers as well as the maintenance of order in society. The court has already held that those objectives figure *among those* which can justify restrictions on freedom to provide services (see judgments in *Ministère Public* v *Van Wesemael* joined cases 110 and 111/78 [1979] ECR 35 at 52, *EC Commission* v *France* Case 220/83 [1986] ECR 3663 at 3709 and *Société Général Alsacienne de Banque SA* v *Koestler* Case 15/78 [1978] ECR 1981)' (emphasis added) [1994] 2 All ER 193, 229–230.

clinicians who wish to offer regulated infertility treatment services, established by the 1990 Act, fundamentally in contravention of Article 30 (free movement of goods) and Articles 59 and 60 (free movement of services)?[49]

In *Grogan*,[50] an Irish university's Students' Union was distributing information about the availability of abortion services in Member States which — unlike its own — did not make termination of pregnancy unlawful. This it was doing without direct payment from any student seeking a termination. The opponents of the Students' Union were therefore unable to establish an economic aspect to the provision of the information sufficient to be able to come within Article 59. This 'fortuitous element in the fact pattern'[51] undid the necessity of requiring the restriction placed on market access to be supported by objective justification. However, *Blood* indicates the potential of EU trade law as a mechanism for review of national laws not seen as immediately connected with trade,[52] which might, of course, include the entire licensing regime of the 1990 Act.[53] Whilst considerations of public morality might be weighed in the defence of such legislative provisions, there is something troubling about the very requirement to justify rules framed to protect social and moral values in order to satisfy an economic imperative.

> The application of the deregulatory Single European Market rules to issues of human reproduction, in particular the freedom to receive services, may tend to undermine regimes which have chosen a more regulatory approach.[54]

The import of this argument in respect of the European Court's decisions in *Koestler*[55] and *Gebhard*[56] and the principles there established we think is

49 The jurisprudence of the ECJ on these questions appears quite unequivocal: 'Where rules impede market access by suppliers based in other Member States they must be objectively justified. That the court has not been deterred from developing this principle despite Article 60(3) [permitting the supply of services to be regulated by the host state on 'the same conditions as are imposed by the state on its own nationals'] testifies to its determination to construct a core set of principles of Community trade law, drawing together the separate Treaty provisions, most of all Articles 30 and 59': Weatherill, *Law and Integration in the European Union* (Oxford: Clarendon Press, 1995) 253. For a compelling argument that the freedom to provide services provisions could, in so far as reproductive medicine is concerned, be 'ring-fenced' from the effect of Union law altogether, in a way analogous to the Court's exclusion of the free movement of goods provisions (Art 30) in certain circumstances (for example, Case C-145/88, *Torfaen Borough Council v B & Q* [1989] ECR 385 — the 'Sunday trading' case) see Hervey, n 5 above. We have benefited particularly from the advice of Paolo Nebbia and Akas Manolikidis on this point, although we have not fully adopted their caution.
50 *Society for the Protection of the Unborn Child v Grogan* (Case C-159/90) [1991] ECR I-4685.
51 Weatherill, n 49 above, 259.
52 *ibid*, '... the European Court has acquired a wide ranging power to review national laws against the standards of Community trade law. That requires the Court *to develop its own conception* of the importance of trade liberalisation judged against the relative weight of competing interests such as consumer protection, environmental standards, and maintenance of public morality that are expressed through national laws' (at 261, emphasis added).
53 HFE Act, especially ss 4, 11–22. It is clear from cases such as *Van Binsbergen v Bestuur van de Bedrijfsvereniging voor de Metaalnijverheid* (Case C-33/74) [1974] ECR 1299 that while the public good ground will normally be sufficient to support licensing or registration requirements imposed on a profession, those which inhibit the provision of services will only be permissible if they are: (a) non-discriminatory, (b) objectively justified and (c) proportionate.
54 Hervey, n 5 above. Boaventura de Sousa Santos's comment is particularly apposite here: 'The Treaty of Rome is based on the seemingly clear cut distinction between the economic, on the one hand, and the social and political, on the other. The economic, that is, the creation of the internal market, will be a matter for Community decision making, while the social and the political will be left to the sovereignty of the member states. This distinction, which is probably to be blamed for the relative poverty of the political debate about the EC integration, has been shown to be increasingly artificial, if not outright false': *Toward a New Common Sense: Law, Science and Politics in the Paradigmatic Transition* (London, Routledge, 1995) 284.
55 Case 58/78 [1978] ECR 1971.
56 Case C-55/94 [1995] ECR I-4165.

fundamental. For Articles 59 and 60 to apply there must be an inter-state element to the activity in question; the crucial requirement is that the person receiving services and the persons providing services are *established* in different Member States. The effect of the Court's recent jurisprudence in *Gebhard* is that if a service provider can show that they are established in, and that the main centre of their economic activity is in, Member State A, they could establish a temporary or 'irregular' site of service provision in Member State B, 'regardless of whether the service may lawfully be provided in that manner in Member State B's regulatory regime.'[57] The effect of this in *Blood's case* — which according to Lord Woolf will be a one-off[58] — is that a provider of reproductive services established and mainly active in another Member State may establish a temporary clinic in the UK, without burden of the HFEA's licensing scheme, and provide Mrs Blood with the fertility treatment services to which the Court of Appeal has said that she is entitled.

However, if anything, *Blood* goes further than this in two particular respects. Lord Lester, counsel for Mrs Blood submitted in the High Court that Articles 59 and 60 entailed that an individual's freedom from restriction to *receive* services (itself a right derivative from the freedom to provide services) implied freedom from restriction on the export of resources necessary to secure those services. In this he relied upon *Grogan* and *Luisi and Carbone* v *Ministero del Tesoro*.[59] This latter case had been brought by two Italian nationals who claimed that restrictions placed on the export of Italian currency infringed their rights to receive services (tourism) in another Member State. The European Court of Justice wrote that

> ... the freedom to provide services includes the freedom, for the recipients of services, to go to another Member State in order to receive a service there, without being obstructed by restrictions, even in relation to payments, and that tourists, persons receiving medical treatment and persons travelling for the purposes of education or business, are to be regarded as recipients of services.[60]

Of this argument, Sir Stephen Brown P commented in the High Court that the complaint, if correct would lead to the 'very surprising' conclusion that EU law would require the United Kingdom to permit the export of gametes even where this would conflict with the protective measures which Parliament has thought necessary, '... merely because these sensitive issues are less extensively regulated in Greece and Belgium.'[61] However, Lord Woolf suggested that whether the rule of the Member State of origin constitutes a restriction on the freedom to provide services was to be determined by a functional criterion. Of this he wrote, apparently without irony, that in a case where a woman wished to receive artificial insemination using sperm of her late husband, '... it is artificial to treat the refusal of permission to export the sperm as not withholding the provision of fertilisation treatment in another Member State ...', and concluded that from a functional point

---

57 Hervey, n 5 above.
58 Although as *U* v *W* (n 41 above) illustrates, the issues in Blood's case are unlikely to arise in isolation.
59 [1984] ECR 377.
60 At 399.
61 (1997) 35 BMLR 1, 16; this is precisely the burden of the point made by de Sousa Santos: 'Since the states can impose their own regulations on in-state products but have to accept out-of-state products in accordance with other, eventually lower regulations, the pressure will be toward deregulation at the national level, that is, toward a race-to-the-bottom rather than a race-to-the-top. In a seemingly total subversion of the distinction between market and regulation, the market will be allowed to choose the best regulation to which it wants to be submitted, which means that the legislative competition will result in the best legislation not in regulatory, but in market terms' (n 54 above, 285).

of view the ability to provide those services '... is not only substantially impeded but made impossible.' The HFEA's original refusal to permit the export of Mr Blood's sperm '... prevents Mrs Blood having the only treatment which she wants.'[62]

There are a number of problems with this formulation. Mrs Blood's desire to gain access to the gametes for export in order to seek treatment services tells us nothing about her enforceable Community rights. The HFEA decision prevented Blood from taking the means by which she might do something unlawful in the UK to another Member State; but did it thereby restrict the freedom to provide or hers to receive services? Lord Lester may indeed be correct that Member States cannot imperil the right of access to services by making its exercise impossible; in many cases a right to export the necessary resources must be appended to the right to receive services. But that does not mean that in a particular case the export of those resources must be allowed. This is where a reference back to the lawfulness of the initial recovery of the sperm could have been crucial. However far the 'right' to receive services is to be made to extend, surely it cannot be made to encompass access to services with the export of the necessary resources where the latter may have been unlawfully obtained, and certainly it should not be allowed to do so without discussion. And this is the second fashion in which *Blood* might be thought to exceed earlier decisions.

Suppose that the Court of Appeal had concluded that the sperm had been lawfully obtained. In contrast with *Grogan*, if you prohibit the provision of information about abortion you prevent women from that state travelling to others where the services to terminate pregnancy are lawfully provided. In that sense there is a restriction on the freedom to provide services, in that a market share will be reduced in a market *which has no substitutes*; all that a woman in that position wants is the termination of the pregnancy. In contrast, the applicant in *Blood* wants access to services for which there are a number of market alternatives, of which she chooses not to avail herself. The restriction on the export of the gametes does not make it impossible or excessively difficult in practice to receive the reproductive medical services in question, just one particular aspect of those services.

We can test the strength of this argument by taking three cases. First *Grogan*, and the freedom to receive services in the form of termination of pregnancy. By the very nature of the service which is sought, it would be quite untenable to draw any distinction between the freedom of the woman to receive the service and the need for the fact that the fetus 'accompanies' her. To that extent, Lord Lester's argument itself is not supported by reliance on *Grogan*; a fetus is not a 'resource necessary to secure the services' of the termination of the pregnancy, the fetus is the *reason* for seeking the service. It is difficult, in fact, to think of a descriptive form which would make legal let alone moral sense of what was an integral part of the service.

Second, consider what may in fact be a closer (but not exact) analogy of what Lord Woolf here proposes. Sections 2 and 3 of the Human Organ Transplants Act 1989 and the Human Organ Transplants (Unrelated Persons) Regulations 1989[63] create an offence of removing from a living person an organ, or transplanting an organ so removed into another person, unless the donor and recipient are 'genetically related' within the terms of the Act or unless the transplant has been approved by a regulatory body, the Unrelated Live Transplant Regulatory

---

62   [1997] 2 All ER 687, 700 and 698.
63   SI No 2480/1989.

Authority (ULTRA). Suppose that a person dying from kidney failure discovers a potential donor in respect of whom ULTRA will not or cannot give its imprimatur; suppose a potential donor who is incapable of understanding the nature of the procedures involved, or indeed any procedure at all. Is it seriously proposed that, *prima facie*, the person requiring the donation could, by invoking the right to receive medical treatment services in a Member State without such requirements, 'export' the donor, because refusal of permission to transplant the organ is tantamount to withholding the provision of transplant services in another Member State?

Third, recall that in *Luisi and Carbone* the European Court was concerned with the export of the wherewithal to access services which the Italian currency regulations otherwise would have precluded. Any relevant analogy between *Luisi and Carbone* and *Blood* would have been strengthened if the Italian nationals had been seeking to export currency presses or plates with which to utter the lira in question. But they were not, and the analogy with the export of the gametes is consequently the more tenuous for that. Perhaps the key objection to these arguments is disclosed in Lord Woolf's judgment itself. He relies on the opinion of Advocate General Jacobs in *Alpine Investments BV v Minister Van Financien*;[64] rather than the criterion of discrimination between nationals of individual Member States, what is more important in the notion of an internal market is what the Advocate General calls the functional criterion; from the point of view of the realisation of the internal market '... what matters is not whether the rules of a Member State are discriminatory but whether they have an adverse effect on its establishment or functioning.'

Some would say that hopefully some of them would. If freedom of trade in services is *all* that Articles 59 and 60 address, then it gives, albeit unintentionally a stronger, perhaps the strongest, argument to those who oppose the establishment or further integration of a single market. That is a ground which is no longer (just) an economic or financial or constitutional one — strong though those might be — but a *moral* ground. If the single European union is really about the freedom of provision of services — whether of abortion or in vitro fertilisation clinics or financial intermediaries — then it tends towards (not yet more) the argument that the European union is about the commodification of things which *by definition* ought *morally speaking* to be dissociated from commerce.[65] This is an area in which Craig and de Búrca have observed that the '... pattern of [ECJ] case law is more complex and less strategic.'[66] *Blood* is an unfortunate contribution to that

---

64 [1995] ECR 1141, considered at [1997] 2 All ER 687, 699–700.
65 For the classic exposition of this view (in relation to blood donation) see Richard Titmus, *The Gift Relationship — From Human Blood to Social Policy* (London: Allen & Unwin, 1971). A formulation of these arguments in one form of assisted conception (surrogacy) is Robert Pritchard, 'A Market for Babies' (1984) 21 Univ Toronto LJ 341. One irony of this, of course, is that as in nineteenth century England, it is likely that the state will have to '... intervene in order not to intervene': de Sousa Santos, n 54 above, 412. There will thus grow up rules, codes and regulations about what, previously, was taken (morally) for granted. On the growth of this phenomenon in medical practice see Bruce Jennings, 'Possibilities of Consensus: Toward Democratic Moral Discourse' (1991) 16 *The Journal of Medicine and Philosophy* 447, esp at 450: '... ethical choice and agency are now embedded as never before in a network of explicit rules and formal procedures and processes for making decisions.' This shifting ground of responsibility is part of what de Sousa Santos identifies as 'The Paradigmatic Transition' and is similar to what Ulrich Beck has called the *process* of 'reflexive modernization': see Ulrich Beck, Anthony Giddens and Scott Lash, *Reflexive Modernization: Politics, Tradition and Aesthetics in the Modern Social Order* (Cambridge: Polity Press, 1994). We return to one aspect of Beck's thesis, below.
66 n 44 above, 329.

jurisprudence.[67] In *Bulmer* v *Bollinger SA & Anor* Lord Denning likened European law to 'an incoming tide. It flows into the estuaries and up the rivers.'[68] And now, it seems, up the vas deferens of our adult populations.

Cultural change: changing cultures

Ulrich Beck has reminded us that reproductive medicine is one of the most visible demonstrations of the extent to which a '... noiseless social and cultural revolution ...' has been wrought in contemporary life.[69] While new and developing technologies may come with instructions, usually they do not say whether to use them or not. The exponential development of science and technology, while supposedly serving health, has in fact '... created entirely new situations, has changed the relationship of humankind to itself, to disease, illness and death, indeed, it has changed the world.'[70] This has at least two consequences.

First, whereas infertility used to be considered to be a matter of fate, it is nowadays turning into a deliberate decision; those who '... give up without having tried the very latest methods (an endless series) have to take the blame. After all, they could have kept trying ...,'[71] While it remains the case that for most women infertility is a life sentence,[72] (new technologies are characterised by their exclusivity, for the relatively more wealthy, 'suitable couple', who are eternal optimists, 'new rationalists' as we might call them), the social role of fertility will always in some sense be seen as chosen.[73] Secondly, the deep issue, as in *Blood* is not so much an individual one as a social one. The dimensions of this are identified by Marilyn Strathern, who has suggested that reproductive technologies and the legislative and other actions to which they have given rise seek to assist natural processes on the one hand and the social definition of kinship on the other. But

> ... this double assistance creates new uncertainties. For the present cultural explicitness is revolutionising former combinations of ideas and concepts. The more we give legal certainty to social parenthood, the more we cut from under our feet assumptions about the intrinsic nature of relationships themselves. The more facilitation is given to the biological reproduction of human persons, the harder it is to think of a domain of natural facts independent of social intervention. Whether or not all this is a good thing is uncertain. What is certain is that it will not be without consequence for the way people think about one another.[74]

---

67 Could this result have been avoided? In the *Bosman case, Union Royale Belge des Societies de Football Association ASBL* v *Bosman* (Case C-415/93) [1996] EC 97 (the 'overseas' footballers restriction challenge) the German government advanced a submission based on what it called 'subsidiarity taken as a general principle.' The ECJ rejected this argument, but only after considering its merits; it did not say that there was no such concept. The determination of the appropriateness of a particular form of medical treatment — which is no doubt the provision of a service — may yet fall to be a matter best left for individual Member States' determination. We are grateful to Tony Downes for suggesting this line of argument.
68 [1974] 3 WLR 202.
69 Ulrich Beck, *Risk Society: Towards a New Modernity* (London: Sage, trans Mark Ritter, 1992) 204.
70 *ibid.*
71 *ibid* 126, and see esp 102–139.
72 See Lesley Doyal, *What Makes Women Sick: Gender and the Political Economy of Health* (New Brunswick, NJ: Rutgers University Press, 1995) 145–149 for this argument.
73 Barbara Katz Rothman, *The Tentative Pregnancy: Prenatal Diagnosis and the Future of Motherhood* (London: Pandora, 1988) 29.
74 Marilyn Srathern, 'The Meaning of Assisted Kinship' in Meg Stacey (ed), *Changing Human Reproduction* (London: Sage Publications, 1992) 148, 167–168. This essay is a succinct introduction to cultural and linguistic concepts deployed in arguments about the family, demonstrating in her use of examples, the way in which what are taken as natural facts are themselves social and cultural constructs.

The deployment of reproductive technologies is affecting assumptions which we bring to understandings not only of family life but to the very understanding of family itself and cultural practice. That is, '... the way in which the choices that assisted conception affords are formulated, will affect thinking about kinship. And the way people think about kinship will affect other ideas about relatedness between human beings.'[75] The depth and range of this noiseless revolution (wrongly so called as we have said) can be gauged quite simply; recall that Diane Blood is not infertile.

It is already possible to identify four models of response which courts have adopted to deal with cases of posthumous use of reproductive technologies; we might call them the absolute rights and autonomy model, the 'intention' model, the 'best interests of the child' approach and the 'cultural change' model.[76] In the absence of specific legislative direction, it is becoming apparent that, at least in cases of posthumous conception, the rights or intentions of the parties take precedence over any consideration of the welfare or interests of the child. Whether or not that is a good thing is something which we do not intend to weigh or discuss here; what we want to emphasise is that this will not be without consequences for the nature and shape of family and family relationships created with the assistance of reproductive medicine. Whether or not that is a good thing is, again, a different question. It is, rather, to a model which points to the social and cultural dimensions of these concerns that we turn.

There are, in posthumous use cases such as that of Diane and Stephen Blood, a range of complex issues which need to be addressed, and a consequent necessity to take care in identifying which issue is being addressed at what point and by what arguments. Anne Maclean has suggested that the reason that surrogacy is a complex and difficult concept is because it raises not one issue

> ... but a cluster of issues, and issues of different sorts at that. It is easy to confuse considerations relevant to one of these issues with considerations relevant to another, or to misunderstand the character of a particular claim or a particular objection.[77]

There is no single moral issue called surrogacy, and in much the same way, this is true of reproductive technologies generally. People's (moral) worries about surrogacy arrangements will vary according to the type of surrogacy in question, the relationships of the parties involved to one another, whether it is a commercial transaction and in what circumstances and so on. And this moral concern will engage a variety of wider concerns too; not just about the family and parenthood but about, for instance, one's whole attitude to what life brings.[78] Mutatis mutandi reproductive technologies more generally.

---

75 Strathern, *Reproducing the Future: Anthropology, Kinship and the New Reproductive Technologies* (Manchester: Manchester University Press, 1993) 149.
76 Based upon an analysis of the cases cited at n 4 above. We develop and discuss the frameworks of these cases in a separate paper.
77 *The Elimination of Morality* (London: Routledge, 1993) 202.
78 Maclean, Correspondence. 'One's whole attitude to' infertility, for example, is not a static; being allowed access to infertility — being (finally) allowed to describe oneself as infertile, is something which 'advances' and oscillates with each new possible 'reproductive technology', as Lene Koch has so convincingly argued. Judged only against the likelihood of producing a baby a woman's initial introduction to and continued participation in an IVF programme might to outsiders lack rationality; it is transformed, however, when seen as 'a new element in the procedure by which the woman establishes her future identity.' The decision or the desire to try IVF becomes '... independent of the efficiency of the technology, because it is judged by the yardstick of another rationality', Koch, n 15 above 241.

And the sorts of worries, or objections, the 'issues of different sorts' as Maclean puts it, will carry different force in different circumstances depending on the nature of the concern and the nature of the circumstances. Thus, worries about resource implications (which can of course involve ethical concern), are very different sorts of worries from those deep, inarticulate (speech of the heart) worries about the basic legitimacy of an action or of a general attitude exemplified in an action. Concerns with surrogacy, like reproductive technologies more generally, cluster around commerce, commodity, consumerism and community. In the late twentieth century, the age when the belief is rife if not reasonable, and perhaps not novel, that anything can be bought, there is a concern with the notion that money can buy not only love (or at least its counterfeit) but also anything else (or at least its counterfeit). *Blood* begins to explore the fundamentals of a common social policy in the European union which has everything to do with economics, even the economics of reproductive life, which is beginning to emerge strongly as the binding parameter for a union which *can find no other guiding principle.*

The troubling aspect of this jurisprudence is that it emerges in parallel with another task which is being laid before the courts. This is to articulate and accentuate a vocabulary and then to calibrate and refine it to adjudicate upon disputes about the meaning and scope of family and family relationships. And all this, as *Blood* and *Bland* illustrate, within a model of response to changes in contemporary medical practice and possibilities.

Vorsprung durch Technik?

The remarkable thing about *Blood* is that it represents the transformation of the technology of assisted conception, in a way in which even the doctors involved in the sperm recovery had present doubts. Originally developed to address one specific cause of infertility in women, blocked fallopian tubes, IVF has moved rapidly from the experimental to the clinical and has come to occupy the domain of the usual, the commonplace, a routine ingredient on the reproductive menu.

Originally seen as a response to the emergent evidence that involuntary childlessness caused by reproductive inability might seriously harm or compromise a woman's physical and mental health, *Blood* illustrates how quickly we are moving along a direction which runs from desire and longing to demands and litigation. The careful, albeit controversial scheme put in place by the Human Fertilisation & Embryology Act less than a decade ago has been shaken to its foundations by someone who has only limited need of the techniques of reproductive medicine.

The underlying philosophy of that legislation was that subject to a system of regulated licences, the supervision of reproductive medicine could, by and large, be left in the charge of clinical specialists. The 'case' of Diane Blood only serves to illustrate not only how far we have moved in terms of human reproduction in the past 30 years, but also that the legislative assumptions of 1990 are being cross cut with the articulation of a fresh voice — that of the consumer who comes to the reproductive market with the usual range of assumptions about rights and guarantees. While Marilyn Strathern has reminded us that the more that facilitation is given to the biological reproduction of human persons, the harder it is to think of a domain of natural facts independent of social intervention, Diane Blood has shown us how far that process has already moved. Whether or not that is a good thing is uncertain. What is certain is that it will not be without consequences.

There is a sense in which advances in modern science have delivered Tony Bland and Stephen Blood not only to the ward of the hospital but also to the precincts of the court. In the face of novelty and uncertainty, the reason and the security in which medical practice was once practised have begun to evaporate.[79] One case raises questions where the capacity for meaningful life is said to be past, the other questions of what amounts to the meaningful capacity for life. In this, both cases challenge accepted notions and conceptions, in the one case of the limits and meaning of life and death, in the other on the limits and meaning of death and life. Both cases involve what would until recently have been thought to be unthinkable, the inconceivable.

Blood, like *Bland*, forces us to ask of the very basis of medical practice — not how but why; goals rather than methods are the primary concern, *Blood*, like *Bland*, is part of the meditation of a culture upon itself. New definitions of death and new conceptions of family formation challenge familiar assumptions about familial bonds, and the implication of the courts in these processes requires that they develop a social, even a moral, vision of families and family relationships so that they can determine the appropriate response to the social and moral dilemmas created by the social and cultural revolution of contemporary medicine.[80] In that, *Blood* is hopelessly lacking.

---

79 It is *only* thirty five years since Patrick Devlin offered his 'pleasant tribute to the medical profession' that '... by and large it has been able to manage its relations with its patients on the basis [that conduct be regulated by a general understanding of how decent people ought to behave] without the aid of lawyers and law makers': 'Medicine and Law' in his *Samples of Lawmaking* (Oxford: Clarendon Press, 1962) 83, 103.
80 For the identification of these themes see Janet Dolgin, n 43 above.

Name Index